THE EDUCATIONAL TECHNOLOGY HANDBOOK

A COMPREHENSIVE GUIDE

PROCESS AND PRODUCTS FOR LEARNING

THE
EDUCATIONAL
TECHNOLOGY
HANDBOOK

A
COMPREHENSIVE GUIDE

PROCESS AND PRODUCTS FOR LEARNING

STEVEN HACKBARTH

EDUCATIONAL TECHNOLOGY PUBLICATIONS
ENGLEWOOD CLIFFS, NEW JERSEY 07632

Library of Congress Cataloging-in-Publication Data

Hackbarth, Steven.
The educational technology handbook : a comprehensive guide :
process and products for learning / Steven Hackbarth.
  p.   cm.
Includes bibliographical references and index.
ISBN 0-87778-292-X
1. Educational technology—Handbooks, manuals, etc. 2. Computer
-assisted instruction—Handbooks, manuals, etc. 3. Interactive
multimedia—Handbooks, manuals, etc. I. Title.
LB1028.3.H33 1996
371.3'078—dc20   95-49722
                                                                          CIP

Printed in the United States of America.

Library of Congress Catalog Card Number:
95-49722.

International Standard Book Number:
0-87778-292-X.

First Printing: January, 1996.

Dedication

To my parents:
Viola M. (Geisinger) Hackbarth
Randall C. Hackbarth
who taught well by
being and doing

Table of Contents

Acknowledgments

Products of educational technology are responses to needs, tentative solutions to problems encountered by educators in the conduct of their enterprise. The impetus for this book, which is such a product, was an invitation from the American Psychological Association for George F. Kneller, then professor of education at UCLA, to present its membership with a critical response to the growing enthusiasm among them for mechanized means of instruction based on newly validated "laws of behavior."

After completing his presentation at the APA's annual meeting and publishing his views on the subject, Professor Kneller asked me, formerly with the Southwest Regional Laboratory for Educational Research and Development and at that time his doctoral student, to collaborate with him on a more thorough treatment. The result was our 1974 unpublished manuscript, "Technology in Education: A Friendly Analysis."

Comments by colleagues and reviewers resulted in production of several revised editions over the next decade. The 1984 edition was a product of my intense collaboration with George Kneller, John Harrison (then a doctoral candidate in the Department of English, University of California, Berkeley), and Lars Helgeson (then a school district administrator in Bakersfield, California). Words cannot fully express my debt.

While completing a postdoctoral master's program (instructional technology) at the University of Southern California, and while serving there as Director of Student Services, I communicated frequently with leaders in the field of educational technology, participated in product design and production, and class-tested the ever-evolving manuscript. Especially helpful were Professor George Booth and his students, faculty members Robert Casey, Richard Clark, Hillary Foliart, Jerrold Garlock, Frederick Knirk, and M. David Merrill, and Graduate Assistants Thomas Cresap and Nancy Daves. DeLayne Hudspeth gave valuable advice by letter. Executive Associate Dean Richard Clowes permitted use of facilities and equipment.

In 1986, Franklin Graham, a sponsoring editor, submitted the manuscript to four faculty who teach the subject: Gary Ferrington (University of Oregon), Doreen Keable (St. Cloud State University), Gary Morrison (Memphis State University), and Roger Volker (Iowa State University). Furthermore, Mr. Graham arranged for distribution of a needs analysis survey to scores of college instructors and met with me to discuss results. For his perceptive analyses of the market and his guidance in serving that market, I am grateful.

To Mr. Graham's team this book owes: (1) greater emphasis on educational technology as a process; (2) inclusion of specific guidelines permitting teachers themselves to engage in this process; (3) attention to how instructional messages may best be encoded in various formats and what skills students need to decode these messages; (4) inclusion of more examples of how teachers can better integrate existing instructional materials into district prescribed curricula; and (5) enhancement of sections on media selection, production, and utilization.

My correspondence with respondents to a later survey resulted in class testing and further recommendations from faculty as well as students for revisions in content and structure. To the following faculty, and to the students at Appalachian State University (critical essays were received from Angela Cone, Melinda Darnell, Allison Lynch, Lisa Miller, Sonya Taylor, Pam

Thornton, and Katrina Severt), I am especially grateful: Joe Brasher (Athens State College), Wenda Clement (Indiana Wesleyan University), Sheila Drake (Kansas Wesleyan University), Leticia Ekhaml (West Georgia College), Sam Evans (William Woods College), Jeffrey Fletcher (Appalachian State University), Barbara Grabowski (Pennsylvania State University), David Jenkins (North Carolina State University), Charles Kanyarusoke (Indiana University of Pennsylvania), Annette Lamb (University of Southern Indiana), Norman Licht (SUNY Potsdam), Carole McCollough (Wayne State University), Robert McFarland (Appalachian State University), Darlene Miller (HRS Professional Development Centres), Louis Polsgrove (Georgetown College), Val Sakovich (San Francisco State University), James Silliman Jr. (Alice Lloyd College), and Ellen Wagner (University of Northern Colorado).

A 1993 draft benefitted from another round of reviews by talented professionals to whom I am indebted. Lawrence Lipsitz (President, Educational Technology Publications) encouraged me in the process-oriented approach I had adopted and urged more coverage of cutting-edge technologies. LaVergne Rosow (Literacy Coordinator, Beaumont Library District, California) raised questions about the value of performance evaluation in teaching and its effects on students who have been burned out with failure to achieve goals they had no role in setting. Alice Scofield (Professor of Education, San Jose State University) provided insights into the felt needs and preferences of pre-service teachers. Rita Jones (Cordova Meadows Elementary School) shared her perspectives as mentor teacher and school district computer resource person.

At annual conventions in 1994 and 1995 of the Association for Educational Communications and Technology, I distributed diskette copies to interested colleagues. Subsequently, I received especially helpful comments from the legendary Walter Wittich, and insightful suggestions and careful editing from Jean Pratt (ID$_2$ Research Group, Utah State University). Lawrence Lipsitz continued to prod me to expand coverage of constructivism, situated learning, multimedia, virtual reality, and the Internet. To him I dedicate Chapters **12** and **13**. To Howard Lipsitz goes credit for the unpretentious title of this book. Cheryl and Pat Hufnagle at Sherman Typography and Jennifer Horowitz at ETP conscientiously made corrections on four rounds of updated page proofs.

During the academic years 1993–95, I completed a master's program in special education at New York University and qualified for certification in special and elementary education. NYU faculty shared with me their insights about current approaches to "constructivist" teaching and "authentic" assessment. Especially helpful were Howard Coron (social studies), Lisa Fleisher (special education), Alvin Hertzberg (science), Lenore Ringler (reading), Bernice Cullinan (reading), Lisa Simon (reading), Stephen Weiss (elementary education), Gloria Lodato Wilson (special education), Jerry Wishner (special education), and Christina Wright (mathematics). Judith Evans, my faculty supervisor, reinforced the theme of "reflective teaching," a practice that had been taught so consistently and ardently in courses, and one that epitomizes the essence of educational technology as site-based research. William Beck (computer literacy) provided knowledgeable suggestions for improvement of Chapters **11–13**. P.S. 6 (Manhattan) teacher Susan Renard gave much needed guidance and advocacy, and principal Carmen Fariña hired me as a computer consultant/teacher.

My Internet-mediated offer to send free pre-publication diskettes to educators willing to make suggestions resulted in flurries of constructive email exchanges. Thanks especially to Peter Cruikshank, Marie Karr, Rita Laws, Michelle Stanley, and Michael Pitsch.

My brother, Daryl Hackbarth, formerly a mentor teacher and now principal of Cordova Meadows Elementary School in Rancho Cordova, California, was helpful from the start, recruiting critical readers, and providing access to his classrooms for observations and photography. Fay Kerekes, principal of Rancho Cordova Elementary School, provided similar access. College classroom photography was taken with permission of USC School of Education faculty and students. The California Museum of Science and Industry (Los Angeles) graciously gave permission for me to freely photograph its wonderful exhibits. Abdul-Redha Kamal turned my sketches into publishable art. Finally, I am grateful to the Provider of good health, ability, inclination, and time.

Owing so much to so many, I nevertheless am solely responsible for deficiencies that remain in this evolving product. Further assistance from readers will be much appreciated and incorporated with acknowledgments in future editions.

Steven Hackbarth
Internet: hackbarths@aol.com

Preface

Technology has had a profound impact on our lives. Its procedures have revolutionized agriculture, industry, and government. Its products have saved lives and expanded horizons.

The creative use of technology to craft instructional programs has become commonplace. And as we approach the year 2000, educators increasingly are called on to make critical choices among advances in products and techniques. **Educational technology** is a response to these calls.

Educational technology is **a systematic process of developing solutions to problems of teaching and learning**. This entails analysis of educational aims followed by the design, production, field testing, evaluation, and revision of programs to achieve these aims. Each chapter in this book illustrates ways in which this process has taken place in the past and how teachers can do so now.

The purpose of this book is to enable teachers to make **cumulative progress** in the **quality** of their instruction as well as in **access** to it by rich and poor, gifted and disabled alike. **It is targeted specifically to assist both pre-service and in-service K–12 teachers in selecting instructional strategies and media that will ensure that their students achieve desired learning objectives.** Furthermore, it illustrates how teachers can develop **ever more effective, well-integrated curriculums by engaging in applied research**, research anchored directly to their own distinctive classroom practice over many years. As such, it serves to meet state-mandated teacher credential requirements for audiovisual methods, computer literacy, and educational technology.

I recommend that readers receive concurrent training in the assessment of learning needs and achievement appropriate for their particular subject fields and for the kinds of students they will encounter. Accurate assessments of gains in students' knowledge, attitudes, and skills are essential to the success of educational technology. Equally essential for the pre-service teacher is extensive practice in the selection, production, and utilization of mediated programs according to the principles and guidelines detailed in this book.

The 13 chapters that follow build upon one another, yet are sufficiently independent to be reordered or skipped to suit the interest and experience of faculty or students. Together, they provide:

- just enough **background** to foster appreciation of the decades of research that have brought practice to the present level;
- enough description and analysis of research to ground firmly **assessments** of each medium;
- plenty of explicit **guidelines** for selection, production, and utilization of instructional programs; and
- **study items** and **suggested activities** to ensure mastery of the information presented, integration with content from related courses, and transfer to "real" life.

Chapter **1** explores the **scope and promise** of educational technology—its roots in communications and engineering, its response to the challenge of constructivism, and its potential for the future. Chapter **2** provides explicit guidelines for the systematic **development** of instructional programs, and Chapter **3** for the systematic **conduct** of instruction. Chapter **4** presents models of **large-scale instructional program development.** In Chapter **5**, school-wide **integrated learning systems** are described and evaluated. These first five chapters comprise Part I, an overview of educational technology as a systematic process. During these first few weeks of the course, students should become acquainted with the instructor, requirements, the media lab, and each other. The first six units of Part II, Chapters **6** through **11**, survey and evaluate products of educational technology commonly used in schools. The chapters show how, and in what respects, educational technology has improved the **content** and **organization** of subject matter and its **delivery** via print, visuals, audio, film, television, and computers. Explicit guidelines are given for **selection, production,** and **utilization** of programs characteristically transmitted by each medium. Chapter **12** focuses upon **"interactive learning environments"**—student/teacher collaborations, computer-mediated simulations, and CD-ROM multimedia programs. Next, Chapter **13** describes journeys along the **"information superhighway."** Part III consists of some closing thoughts, a checklist, an assessment tool, a glossary, a list of computer acronyms, and selected sources. The focus of the course toward the end should be on collaborative crafting of systematically developed, multimedia instructional lessons and on the exploration of computer networks.

Educational technology has wide applications. It offers as much to the teacher of fine arts as it does to the industrial trainee. Its products enhance learning achievement, whether assessed in terms of performance objectives, general intellectual development, or emotional growth. Self-instructional packages provide drill in mathematics and foreign languages to ensure mastery; comprehensive curriculums incorporate electronic media as well as teachers to engage students' imaginations and stimulate their creativity. Initial investments typically are high, but they are justified in terms of progress toward the achievement of ambitious aims. Readers of this book will learn how technology:

- facilitates accumulation of the best insights of teachers, librarians, administrators, parents, and students alike;

- incorporates these insights creatively into programs targeted to meet identified learning needs of particular categories of students; and

- distributes the resulting programs widely, with provision for local adaptations to ensure successful integration into existing curriculums.

I hold no punches in assessing educational technology, and ceaselessly urge every teacher to exploit its merits while compensating for deficiencies. Long before today's "constructivists" advocated placing greater emphasis on students' making their **own** sense out of the world, and long before the current "authentic assessment" movement questioned the value of "objective" tests, my UCLA mentor, George Kneller, and I sought to present **a balanced view of educational technology that could be adapted to serve even within such open-ended environments.** My aim remains that readers will be challenged to make the **research and development process** of educational technology a **creative** part of their own teaching.

THE
EDUCATIONAL
TECHNOLOGY
HANDBOOK

A
COMPREHENSIVE GUIDE

PROCESS AND PRODUCTS FOR LEARNING

Educational Technology

Part I. A Systematic Process

Chapter 1

Scope and Promise

Chapter Content and Objectives

In this chapter, I describe the **background**, **achievements**, and **potential** of educational technology as a whole. After a careful reading of this chapter, you should be able to:

- Describe common media that are the building blocks of educational technology—print, still visuals, audiotapes, videos, computers.

- Discuss such influences as communications theory, learning theory, systems engineering, and constructivism.

- Define "educational technology" in terms of its four key dimensions—process, products, profession, and academic discipline.

- Specify ways in which technology can help you make instruction more individualized, valid, accessible, and economical.

- Cite some print references that pertain to mediated and systematic approaches to improving quality of instructional content and efficiency of its delivery.

The Technological "Revolution" in Education

A technological revolution in education surely is upon us. It is affecting what we know and believe as well as how we live and love. It is shaping the ways in which we teach and learn.

Television is revolutionizing education. Children wake up to the clamor of puppets chanting **"A, B, C; 1, 2, 3."**

As girls and boys eagerly mimic these sounds, parents learn to relinquish their roles in providing instructive verbal interaction and moral guidance. The pervasive message of fast-paced, visually rich children's programming is **"Watch Me!"**

Just about the time when adolescents used to break away from the comforts of home to explore the world first hand, they now are captured by an already too familiar cadence—**"Music Video TV!"** Youths today uncritically absorb erotic fantasies and antisocial rage. Meanwhile, working parents generally are relieved to no longer be bothered with questions about the "new math."

Microcomputers are revolutionizing education. Manufacturers provide them at substantial discounts to schools. Students entering college receive them during orientation week along with identification cards and tuition fee bills. School teacher candidates must complete courses in "computer literacy" to qualify for their credentials.

Schools soon find that microcomputers require various gadgets ("peripherals") and programs ("software") to function and then that all too often they do not behave as expected. Parents conduct bake sales to keep the machines operating, but usually fail to ask what they teach or what classroom activities have been displaced. At home, game playing is the most common use. Destroying something or somebody is the dominant theme. (See **Figure 1.01.**)

Undoubtedly, a technological revolution in education is upon us. However, there are no simple answers to be found in the piecemeal use of technological devices like televisions and computers. The severe problems facing educational enterprises worldwide are complex, and the

Figure 1.01. A generation raised on TV and video games presents special challenges (and opportunities) for teachers. What of **value** can we offer in the classroom to exceed the appeal of the arcade?

challenges put forth in "goals for the year 2000" manifestos are ambitious. The revolution needed to solve these problems and meet these challenges must be in terms of **deep, reflective,** and surely **more systematic, yet creative, thinking** about educational aims, student characteristics, teaching strategies, communications media, and the nature of learning within various contexts, as well as about **interactions** among these elements. These are the primary concerns of educational technology. And, as teachers, you and I share these vital concerns.

Antecedents of Educational Technology

Sir Eric Ashby was among the first to identify the use of electronic media in education as a "fourth revolution."[1] It follows the invention of **printing**, the acceptance of **written materials as adjuncts to oral instruction**, and the establishment of **public schools**. Over two decades ago, the Carnegie Commission reported that education "now faces the first great technological revolution in five centuries in the potential impact of the new electronics."[2]

The promised revolution not only has arrived; it has exceeded expectations. **Satellites** beam instructional radio and TV to remote villages and urban classrooms alike. **Video recordings** put programs in the hands of viewers. The marriage of **compact disc** and **computer technologies** enables us to have entire libraries at our fingertips, and even to "walk" or "fly" in simulated "virtual reality" environments. The joining of **computer networks** worldwide via the **Internet** has permitted free access to vast stores of data and the formation of "virtual communities" where people with common interests share their ideas.

The "fourth revolution," with its focus on electronic wizardry linked by the "information superhighway," promises to bring knowledge in all its splendor within the reach of everyone. At the core of this revolution has been an ever evolving focus upon the creative **process** by which educational programs are crafted. How has this process been reflected in the design of mediated programs?

Print. Before invention of the printing press, teachers used manuscripts, most of which were privately owned. Teachers would read from the handwritten pages and students had to memorize much of what they heard. Later, however, with printed books, all students could have copies. Teachers could conduct group study of selected sections, and readings could be assigned as homework.

The use of illustrations in schoolbooks was promoted by John Amos Comenius (1592–1670). In his *Great Didactic* (1628), the Czech educator outlined a structure for teaching and learning in which books and classroom walls would be filled with pictures, maps, and charts. Comenius also designed one of the first illustrated textbooks for children, *The World in Pictures* (1657). Each page contains drawings accompanied by stories told in both Latin (the scholarly language of the time) and the vernacular.

Expensive at first, early textbooks became more affordable through mass production. By the mid-nineteenth century the teacher's central role was to explain what was in the text. Soon, however, other media were used—first chalkboards, then (late in the century) magic lanterns (to present slides) and stereoscopes. Influenced by the Industrial Revolution, some visionaries even predicted mechanized schools. One 19th century cartoonist, for example, drew a sketch of a teacher feeding textbooks into a grinder, while an aide cranked out knowledge to students plugged into overhead transmission lines![3] (See **Figure 1.02.**)

Figure 1.02. Will instruction in the year 2000 be mediated by chemical and electronic means as envisioned here by a French cartoonist a century ago? To what extent is the image of students as passive recipients of subject matter still popular? Source: *Esquire,* 51 (January 1959), p. 96. Reprinted courtesy of *Esquire.*

Audiovisual Media. The recording and broadcast of sights and sounds enriched not just schools, but life itself. **Phonograph records, radio broadcasts,** and **films** were used in schools in the 1930s, and during World War II they were widely used by the military. **Television,** appearing pervasively in the late 1940s, was greeted skeptically by most educators, largely because they found little of instructional value in the programs. It was not until the mid-fifties that instructional television came to prominence, when the schools of Hagerstown, Maryland were wired to receive closed-circuit TV. The 1950s also brought the **language laboratory,** where students learned grammar and pronunciation from audiotape.

The use of audiovisual media was heralded as an **economical substitute** for direct, firsthand experience. Educators, then as now, agreed that students learn best when actively exploring rich environments, especially those environments that are closely connected with their lived worlds and anchored to the shared world in which they must function. However, they surmised, learning may proceed more efficiently through **vicarious experience,** say by viewing pictures and films. Audio and visual media could bring the world into the classroom at low cost and when convenient, and they could do so selectively to ensure achievement of specified objectives and transfer to remote contexts. Furthermore, they could communicate their messages effectively to students **lacking familiarity with written language or**

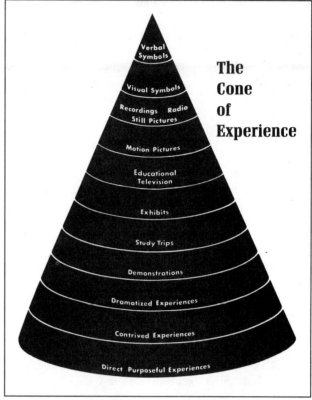

Figure 1.03. Edgar Dale's "Cone of Experience" portrays a progression of learning experiences from the concrete at the base to abstract at the top. Analysis of the cone raises interesting questions, such as: What sorts of "direct, purposeful experiences" are not mediated by language? Are these educationally significant? What sense (other than aesthetic) can we make of sounds (radio) and images (pictures) without words to describe them? Source: Edgar Dale, *Audiovisual Methods in Teaching,* 3rd ed. (New York: Holt, Rinehart, and Winston, 1969), p. 107. Copyright © 1969 by Holt, Rinehart, and Winston. Reprinted with permission of the publisher.

graphic symbols.[4] This special function of audiovisual media is portrayed in Edgar Dale's oft-cited "Cone of Experience." (See **Figure 1.03.**)

Dale's "Cone" had much appeal in the 50s and 60s during the gadget-oriented "audiovisual media" days of educational technology. And its apparent logic was buttressed by reference to psychologist Jerome Bruner's division of learning into three types: **"enactive"** (direct experience), **"iconic"** (pictorial experience), and **"symbolic"** (abstract experience).[5] It seemed natural enough to begin instruction with concrete experiences and then, by means of visual images, to progress to abstract symbols. However, the logic of such a progression broke down when it was realized that so-called "direct experience" and visual images **must be explained and interpreted by spoken and written words**. Indeed, rational thought is largely carried by abstract symbols, and these must be learned hand-in-hand with their concrete referents.

Teaching Machines and Programmed Instruction. Automated instruction was advanced in 1925 when Sidney Pressey discovered that his students were able to learn on their own by using a simple device he had invented to present and score tests. Then, in the early 1950s, psychologist Burrhus F. Skinner constructed a more complex apparatus, a **"teaching machine,"** which imparted subject matter in easy-to-learn, step-by-step sequences.[6] More important than teaching machines was the adoption of **"programmed instruction,"** a technique for writing lessons consistent with behavioral theories of learning. Subject matter was broken down into sequences of concise statements and short paragraphs, each followed by a question for the student to answer. Immediate feedback was provided by the appearance of the correct answer in the margin or on the next page. Programmed instruction was especially distinguished in that **before being marketed, lessons repeatedly were tested and revised until they imparted the desired information successfully**. Unfortunately, the appearance of clone programs, similar in format but lacking validation, dampened enthusiasm.[7]

Computers. Electronic computers appeared in the 1940s. With their capacity for **processing, storing,** and **communicating** masses of information, computers were first used by school administrators for budgeting and record keeping. In the early 1960s, programmers began adapting lessons for presentation by computer. Major projects at Stanford and the University of Illinois demonstrated that students could learn basic subject matter just as well from a computer as from books, films, or teachers.

Until the 1970s, computers remained too bulky and expensive for widespread use. The first microprocessor—a fingernail-sized chip of silicon containing the electronic circuitry of a computer's central processing unit—appeared in 1971. Microprocessor and memory chips (two types of miniature "integrated circuits") soon were incorporated into complete systems consisting also of

Figure 1.04. Important developments in computer technology are traced in this excerpt from an educational magazine. **"Integrated circuits"** like the one pictured here are used in microcomputers to process and store information. Source: "The Tandy Computer Whiz Kids: News by Computer Foils Kidnapper" (Fort Worth, TX: Tandy Corporation, 1986), p. 29. Reprinted with permission of Tandy Corporation.

input and output devices and, in 1976, sold as "Apple II," "TRS-80," and "Commodore PET" microcomputers. Of these, the greatest and most enduring success story is that of Apple Computer, Inc., the brainchild of two whiz-kids, Steven Jobs and Steven Wozniak. (See **Figure 1.04.**)

Competition in the microcomputer industry soon drove quality up and prices down. IBM's late entry into the personal computer market led to a clustering of clones and standards that, to this day, have been challenged only by Steve Jobs' Macintosh. Rapid development, led by another computer whiz-kid, Bill Gates (founder of Microsoft), of easy-to-use **software** (programs) for games, word processing, accounting, and instruction brought computer technology within reach of most middle class families. The impact has been so great as to raise valid concerns about the ever growing gap in computer access between rich and poor.[8]

More Recent Influences

During the past several decades, the way educational technology is conceived also has changed. Prior to the 1950s, most educators viewed it largely in terms of **hardware**. Film projectors, TV sets, and record players were valued for their capacity to present informative programs to wide audiences. Research studies concentrated on testing the relative effectiveness of "mediated" (especially television) and "traditional" (chalk and talk) instruction. The aim was to decide which was the **better** approach rather than to determine **how the distinctive features ("affordances") of each could best be exploited for particular purposes**.

Beginning in the 1950s and continuing through the 1990s, educators drew on emerging insights of **communications specialists**, **learning theorists**, and **systems engineers**. The 1990s have been marked by the challenge of **constructivism**.

Communications Theory. What is involved when people attempt to convey to others what is on their minds? What facilitates this process? What interferes with it? Such are the concerns of communications specialists.[9]

An early model of the communications process is presented in **Figure 1.05**. This model, designed by Claude Shannon, depicts the transmission of a message from an information **source** (e.g., a newscaster) to a **destination** (e.g., a home audience). The variety of forms in which messages may be transmitted includes written language, spoken language, graphic symbols, and representational images. The media of transmission include teachers, books, films, TV, and computers. Shannon's model illustrates the process by which communication takes place via electronic media. Messages are broadcast as **signals**, subjected to various sources of **"noise"** (e.g., static interference), picked up by suitable **receivers** (e.g., radio, TV), and thereby conveyed to the intended audience.

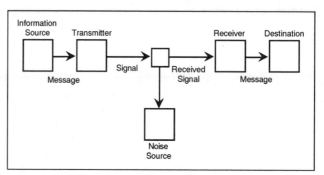

Figure 1.05. Claude Shannon's classic model of a **"general communication"** system portrays messages as the essential elements in communication, and media as mere vehicles for delivering messages. What conditions must prevail in order for a message sent to remain essentially the same as a message received? What are some non-electronic sources of "noise"? Source: Claude E. Shannon & Warren Weaver, *The Mathematical Theory of Communication* (Urbana: University of Illinois, 1949), p. 34. Copyright © 1949 by the Board of Trustees of the University of Illinois. Used with permission of the University of Illinois Press.

An impact of such models as Shannon's was to draw attention to the **message** rather than the medium. Media may permit **preservation**, **amplification**, and **distribution** of messages, but do not substantially affect the explicit **content** of messages they transmit. The realization that a televised lecture could convey essentially the same instructional message as one given in person, or a computer display the same verbal and graphic content as a textbook, dampened the earlier fascination of educational technologists with the particular means by which messages were presented. Research studies that had compared electronically mediated instruction with teacher-mediated instruction without taking into account such variables as instructional strategies incorporated in delivery of messages, teacher/student motivation, cultural diversity, and time-on-task were seen to be incomplete.

A further development in communications theory is illustrated in **Figure 1.06**. Here, Wilbur Schramm highlighted the significance of the **form** in which messages are encoded and the role that **life experience** plays in their communication. **Senders** (e.g., teachers) may encode messages about some topic in the form, say, of written words. **Receivers** (e.g., students) understand the message, provided they (a) can read at a sufficiently high level and (b) have some familiarity with the topic or closely related topics.

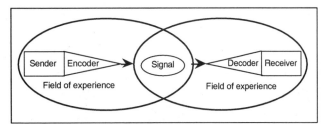

Figure 1.06. Wilbur Schramm's model of the communication process introduces the elements of codes and experience. What sorts of **codes** do **teachers** typically use to present subject matter? What sorts of skills and experience must students possess to decode each type? Source: Wilbur Schramm, "Procedures and Effects of Mass Communication," in Nelson B. Henry, *Mass Media and Education: The Fifty-Third Yearbook of the National Society for the Study of Education, Part II* (Chicago: The University of Chicago, 1954), p. 116. Reprinted with permission of the NSSE.

Conceptions of Learning. Improving the quality of programs required deeper insights into the nature of learning. The behavioral sciences had yielded many useful generalizations about how people learn, but these had not yet fully been incorporated **systematically** into program designs. The challenge was met by Robert Gagné and Leslie Briggs (among others). Drawing on the still popular **"information processing"** model of human cognition, Gagné and Briggs urged that instruction be designed to ensure that:

- subject matter is presented in a manner **consistent with the type of outcome sought** (e.g., application of a principle, change in attitude, performance of a skill);
- subject matter is in **accord with students' abilities** (e.g., level of intelligence, prior experience);
- students are **engaged actively** in the learning process, in part by providing them with opportunities to relate new knowledge to what they earlier had learned and with strategies for doing so;
- students are **called on to demonstrate progress** so their accomplishments can be analyzed and informational feedback given to confirm success, correct error, and guide subsequent effort; and
- students are given **ample practice** under a variety of conditions to ensure retention and transfer.[10]

For Gagné and Briggs, instruction was to provide the necessary **"conditions of learning"** for the target students. This was to be done by employing certain **"strategies"**:

- to direct students' **attention**;
- to help them **recall** previously acquired information;
- to facilitate their **mastery** of new material.

For example, strategies aimed at gaining **attention** are use of **bold** type (with printed text), color (with pictures and graphics), and **volume** (with teachers' voices and audio recordings). Strategies designed to facilitate the **integration** of new with previous knowledge include the use of **reviews, analogies, examples,** and **outlines.** Strategies to enhance **retention** and **transfer** (to "real-life" situations) include **summaries, follow-up discussions, projects,** and **practice.**[11]

Systems Engineering. Also contributing to the growth of educational technology has been "systems engineering." This approach entails **analysis** of problems and **synthesis** of solutions. In the **analysis** phase, a given situation is examined to identify the forces affecting it. The situation is viewed as a **system composed of interconnected parts and related to other systems.** For example, a classroom may be portrayed as a system in which teachers collaborate with students in the shared construction of meaning in the context of community expectations under the constraints of limited time and resources. **Analyses** are conducted to determine the sorts of knowledge and skills most useful to students and the order in which these should be learned. In the **synthesis** phase, modifications in the system (interventions) are designed to overcome forces that interfere with the achievement of the system's goals. In a classroom, such modifications generally take the form of instructional programs. These programs are **field tested** and the **results guide such further interventions as may be needed** to achieve the specified objectives.[12]

Communications theory, learning theory, and systems engineering together have contributed to the evolution of educational technology into a **systematic process of developing replicable solutions to problems entailed in imparting knowledge, values, and skills.** As such, educational technology **integrates** a vast array of communication resources—teachers, textbooks, audiovisual media, and computers—each **suitably programmed** (employing "proven" strategies), **appropriately mediated** (e.g., tutors for tots, satellite TV for rural adults), and **properly housed** (as in specially constructed classrooms).[13]

The Challenge of Constructivism. Rooted in the phenomenology of Martin Heidegger and the psychology of Jean Piaget, blossoming in the work of such "whole language" advocates as Kenneth Goodman, and embodied in the 1989 standards of the National Council of Teachers of Mathematics, constructivism has become a dominant force in education. The essential principle of this revolutionary theory is that each of us assembles the bits and pieces of our experience in ways that, in many respects, are unique. Drawing upon prior conceptions and feelings, we actively interact with our surroundings in an ongoing effort to make the diversity of our experiences all sensible and coherent.

The essential challenge of constructivism has been in its shifting the locus of control over learning from the teacher to the student. Educational technologists, with their roots in behavioral psychology, long have sought to design programs in such a way that students would be enticed to achieve prespecified objectives. Constructivists have claimed that this violates both what we now know about the nature of learning (situated, interactive) and about the nature of knowledge (perspectival, conventional, tentative, evolutionary). They have maintained that objectives should be negotiated with students based on their own felt needs, that planned activities should emerge from within the contexts of their lived worlds, that students should collaborate with peers in the social construction of personally significant meaning, and that evaluation should be a personalized, ongoing, shared analysis of progress.

The influences of constructivism on educational technology can be seen in many areas. Models of communication now portray the process as interactive, with the message as much determined by the selective perception of the recipient as by the style of the author. Mediated programs are seen now more in terms of providing students with opportunities to expand their horizons. "Microworlds," for example, permit them to manipulate variables and observe impacts on diverse simulated phenomena. Such interactive multimedia presentations are seen to provide students with insights into the thinking

of experts, and the "scaffolding" needed to enable their own uniquely colored construction of disciplined knowledge.

Instructional design models now are viewed more as heuristic devices than as recipes for success. Objectives are specified more tentatively, awaiting negotiation with students and confrontations with the vicissitudes of the classroom. Learning is seen to be situated within larger contexts that affect how students perceive and approach the tasks before them. Instructional activities are felt to be best if open-ended, yet linked ("anchored") to real-life situations that students typically will encounter outside the classroom. The emerging information superhighway, with its "World Wide Web" of hypermedia interlinking the world's computer networks, is being billed as a tool of student empowerment.

Electronic Performance Support Systems are being designed to provide information **as needed** by students, not just **if possibly needed** in a remote future. And while immersed in virtual reality environments, students are left to chart their own courses. Assessment in every case is individualized, collaborative, continuous, and multifaceted, with attention to both the process and products of learning.[14]

Definition of Educational Technology

Educational technology is a multidimensional concept:

- It is a **systematic process involving application of knowledge in the search for replicable solutions to problems inherent in teaching and learning.** For example, Norman Crowder identified targeted informative feedback as essential to efficient learning and invented the branching program and a multimedia teaching machine to provide it.

- It includes the **products of this process,** such as programmed texts, TV programs, computer software, and entire courses of instruction. Terms commonly associated with educational technology as a product include "audiovisual media," "interactive multimedia," "self-instructional programs," and "integrated learning systems."

- It is a **profession** composed of various job categories. Media technicians install, operate, and maintain equipment; media specialists advise teachers on the use of devices and programs; instructional developers systematically craft lesson units, courses, and entire curriculums.

- As a formal study of the above aspects, educational technology qualifies as an **academic specialty within the larger discipline of education.** Graduate degree programs, scholarly journals, and books (such as the one in your hands) are examples of such study.[15]

Within the context of doing wonderful things in service of humanity, a core aim of educational technology (ET) is **cost-effective achievement of measurable learning objectives,** or maximum bang for the buck. ET is especially important because we aspire to help our students achieve **high-level, worthwhile objectives,** but in the context of limited time and resources. It is our responsibility to compensate for ET's infatuations with the quick, easy, and cheap, as well as for technophiles' fascination with the glitzy. It is our active engagement in the process of ET that ensures proper attention to the ineffable and unpredictable, with the unique qualities and aspirations of each of our students, that make teaching such a daily challenge.[16]

Impacts of Technology on Instruction

As we have seen, systematically designed programs transmitted by books, radio, TV, and computers provide new and challenging learning experiences. Along with technology generally, these programs **enrich instruction** and make it more **individualized, valid, accessible,** and **economical.** How so?

Instruction is **enriched** through added dimensions, special effects, and unique programming. Time-lapse motion microphotography portrays actual chemical reactions and the life cycles of minute organisms. (See **Figure 1.07**.) Video technology allows us to observe the ongoing behavior of the heavens. Television provides documentaries, plays, and musicals. Computer simulations permit manipulating variables and observing consequences within manageable space and time frames. Virtual reality affords the sensation of acting within novel environments.

Instruction is **individualized** when we interact with students in the selection of objectives, content, and methods that match their abilities and interests. The

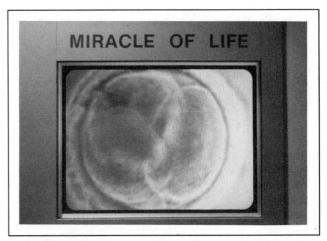

Figure 1.07. By pressing a button, viewers witness the wonders of the microscopic universe. What do such images add to written or spoken descriptions of the same events? Location: California Museum of Science and Industry.

computer not only diagnoses a student's difficulty in understanding a mathematical concept, for example, but also, it provides remedial instruction or recommends that the student view a film, read a section of text, or consult with the teacher. Interactive multimedia and tutoring systems and access to the Internet permit student-initiated explorations grounded in their lived worlds and guided by their felt needs to make sense of their experiences. (See **Figure 1.08**.)

Instructional programs are made more **valid** by field testing and revision. Script writers strive to make their material accurate and current. After careful editing and peer review, they detect further errors by testing programs with students similar to those for whom the programs are being designed. Students' comments and test performances serve to expose such deficiencies as inadequate content, poor organization, needless repetition, and ambiguity. Programs then are corrected and submitted to other groups of students for further testing and revision. (See **Figure 1.09**.)

Instruction is made more **accessible** by analyzing the learning needs of diverse students and creating programs to meet them. Radio and TV transmit valuable information via satellite to remote villages throughout the world and, by way of cable, to hospitals and homes. Special equipment ("assistive technology") helps to compensate for obstacles encountered by people with motor and sensory disabilities. Programs are sent via distance

Figure 1.08. A computerized "intelligent tutoring system" **diagnoses** the student's learning needs and either **prescribes** educational activities or **delivers** instruction itself. In what ways do these activities simulate those of a teacher? How can such a system be used to empower students rather than control them?

Figure 1.09. Programs are **field tested** and **revised** to make content more valid and to improve their effectiveness. What sorts of knowledge and skills are being used here? Which are equally of value in the crafting of computer-based learning software?

education systems to schools lacking enough teachers. Computer searches speedily locate material on library shelves and databases worldwide.

Instruction is made more **economical** by **increasing the ratio of learning** to its cost. Learning is ensured by designing programs in accord with tested experience. A high investment in quality may be offset by wide use, especially when programs are distributed to areas lacking sufficient numbers of qualified teachers. With routine instruction provided economically by various media, teachers may spend more time diagnosing the needs of individual students and tailoring instruction accordingly. Quicker and less expensive schooling means that students may leave school earlier or learn more while they remain.

What are the prospects for continued success? The promise of educational technology can be realized only through concerted effort. Producers, distributors, school personnel, and government together should engage in continuous **research and development. Producers** could help by concentrating on programs that meet specific needs and reduce drudgery, yet avoid duplicating

what the teacher can do better. **Distributors** could offer long-term loans of equipment and software. **Schools** could form networks to buy in quantity, thus reducing costs. **Administrators and teachers** could insist that innovations meet desirable objectives within the context of their curriculums. And they could engage much more actively in long-term, classroom-based research. **Governmental agencies** could support programs for special groups, such as the gifted and the disabled, who are not adequately served by standard curriculums.[17]

Ultimately, however, outcomes turn on the **attitudes and abilities of teachers**, for no educational program will succeed if teachers are uninterested or incapable. Some teachers resist setting explicit objectives and reject the notion of teaching their courses accordingly. Others are reluctant to use the newer media. They may have become frustrated by equipment that failed or turned out to be difficult to operate. They may have had problems locating appropriate books, films, or TV programs. Or they may have greater faith in traditional strategies and basic media that have served them well.

In any case, teachers should be provided with all necessary information on how best to **do** educational technology and to utilize its products. Such information is provided in the text and illustrations of succeeding chapters and in the source materials listed. (See **Figure 1.10.**)

Figure 1.10. Amidst the wasteland of failed hardware and inadequate programs and in the context of school bureaucracy and distracted students, we might feel like we have to reinvent the wheel each day. In many ways our feeling is justified. However, we can **rise to the challenge** of educational technology and may call upon others—parents, students, administrators, media specialists, librarians, instructional designers—who are capable of helping and eager to do so. Source: *Phi Delta Kappan,* 74 (May 1993), p. 684. Reprinted courtesy of James E. Hummel.

Summary and Prologue

Pundits celebrate advances in communications and computer technologies. Some call for wholesale adoption by schools to ensure the future competitiveness of our industries in world markets. Others see school bureaucracies as too restrictive and urge that students be liberated to seek knowledge through multimedia and computer networks.[18]

Critics warn that schools have caved in to the popular media, choosing to echo fleeting media messages rather than transmit our common cultural heritage and cherished values. Many object as well to the conception of subject matter as a commodity to be imparted whole-

sale rather than as tentative construction subject to interpretation.[19]

Pundits and critics alike face similar challenges. How can we harness the power of media to serve the most worthwhile aims of education? How can we design rich environments in which our students can discover connections between their lived worlds and the wonders of our shared universe?

As this chapter has shown, the essence of educational technology is revealed in its **advocacy of systematic, knowledge-based approaches to the improvement of lessons and courses.** Each of the following chapters illustrates how systematic approaches have been—and can best be—used creatively to improve programs presented by various media, from books to computers. Chapter **2** outlines steps that **we** can follow to plan and produce instruction systematically. Chapter **3** outlines steps that **we** can follow to conduct instruction more effectively. You may adapt these in collaboration with your students to suit your own situation and preferences.

Notes

[1]Ashby, Eric., "Machines, Understanding, and Learning: Reflections on Technology in Education," *The Graduate Journal,* 7 (1967), pp. 359–373.

[2]The Carnegie Commission on Higher Education, *The Fourth Revolution: Instructional Technology in Higher Education* (New York: McGraw-Hill, 1972), p. 1. See also Carnegie Task Force on Teaching as a Profession, *A Nation Prepared: Teachers for the 21st Century* (Washington, DC: Carnegie Forum on Education and the Economy, 1986); and Carey, James W., *Communication as Culture: Essays on Media and Society* (New York: Routledge, 1992), especially Chapter 5, "The Mythos of the Electronic Revolution."

[3]Marvin, Carolyn, *When Old Technologies Were New: Thinking About Electric Communication in the Late Nineteenth Century* (New York: Oxford University Press, 1988).

[4]Lewis, Thomas, *Empire of the Air: The Men Who Made Radio* (New York: HarperCollins, 1991); Barnouw, Erik, *Tube of Plenty: The Evolution of American Television*, 2nd rev. ed. (New York: Oxford University Press, 1990); Bianculli, David, *Teleliteracy: Taking Television Seriously* (New York: Continuum, 1992); McNeil, Alex, *Total Television: A Comprehensive Guide to Programming from 1948 to the Present*, 3rd ed. (New York: Penguin, 1991).

[5]Bruner, Jerome S., *Toward a Theory of Instruction* (Cambridge, MA: Harvard University, 1966), pp. 10–21, 49. See also his *In Search of Mind* (New York: Harper & Row, 1983).

⁶Skinner, Burrhus F., "The Science of Learning and the Art of Teaching," *Harvard Educational Review*, 24 (Spring 1954), pp. 86–97; "Teaching Machines," *Science*, 128 (October 24, 1958), pp. 969–977; "Why We Need Teaching Machines," *Harvard Educational Review*, 31 (Fall 1961), pp. 377–398.

⁷Kneller, George F., & Hackbarth, Steven L., "An Analysis of Programmed Instruction," *The Educational Forum*, 41 (January 1977), pp. 181–187.

⁸Bradbeer, Robin, De Bono, Peter, & Laurie, Peter, *The Beginner's Guide to Computers* (New York: Addison-Wesley, 1992); Blissmer, Robert H., *Introducing Computers: Concepts, Systems, and Applications* (New York: Wiley, 1992); Long, Larry, & Long, Nancy, *Microcomputers: Concepts*, 2nd ed. (Englewood Cliffs, NJ: Prentice-Hall, 1992); McClintock, Robert O., ed., *Computing and Education: The Second Frontier* (New York: Teachers College Press, 1988); Simpson, Alan, *Your First Computer* (San Francisco: SYBEX, 1992).

⁹Inglis, Fred, *Media Theory: An Introduction* (Cambridge, MA: Basil Blackwell, 1990).

¹⁰Gagné, Robert M., *The Conditions of Learning*, 4th ed. (New York: Holt, Rinehart, & Winston, 1985); Gagné, Robert M., ed., *Instructional Technology: Foundations* (Hillsdale, NJ: Lawrence Erlbaum Associates, 1987); Gagné, Robert M., & Briggs, Leslie J., *Principles of Instructional Design*, 2nd ed. (New York: Holt, Rinehart, & Winston, 1979); The "information-processing" model holds that the human brain operates much like an electronic computer. Data from the senses enter a short-term storage area where they are "processed" for long-term storage. Consistent with today's constructivist theory, this processing is seen to be much affected by a person's prior knowledge.

¹¹Briggs, Leslie J., Gustafson, Kent L., & Tillman, Murray H., eds., *Instructional Design: Principles and Applications*, 2nd rev. ed. (Englewood Cliffs, NJ: Educational Technology Publications, 1991); Aronson, Dennis T., & Briggs, Leslie J., "Contributions of Gagné and Briggs to a Prescriptive Model of Instruction," in Reigeluth, Charles M., ed., *Instructional-Design Theories and Models: An Overview of their Current Status* (Hillsdale, NJ: Lawrence Erlbaum Associates, 1983), pp. 75–100.

¹²van Gigch, J.P., *System Design Modeling and Metamodeling* (New York: Plenum, 1991).

¹³Saettler, Paul, *The Evolution of American Educational Technology* (Englewood, CO: Libraries Unlimited, 1990); Anglin, Gary, ed., *Instructional Technology: Past, Present, and Future*, 2nd ed. (Englewood, CO: Libraries Unlimited, 1995).

¹⁴Duffy, Thomas M., & Jonassen, David H., eds., *Constructivism and the Technology of Instruction: A Conversation* (Hillsdale, NJ: Lawrence Erlbaum Associates, 1992); Hannafin, Michael J., Hall, Craig, Land, Susan, & Hill, Janette, "Learning in Open-Ended Environments: Assumptions, Methods, and Implications," *Educational Technology*, 34 (October 1994), pp. 48–55: "The shift to open-ended learning systems, where indi-

viduals establish and mediate important issues such as what is to be learned, how learning will occur, which tools and resources will be used in what ways, and how (or if) ongoing learning will be assessed, marks a significant departure from traditional teaching and learning practices" (p. 48); Dunn, Thomas G., "If We Can't Contextualize It, Should We Teach It?" *Educational Technology Research and Development*, 42, 3(1994), pp. 83–92: "Those who work in ISD know that these procedures are more like heuristics that increase the likelihood of leading to success" (p. 85). See also Wilson, Brent G., ed., *Constructivist Learning Environments: Case Studies in Instructional Design* (Englewood Cliffs, NJ: Educational Technology Publications, 1996).

¹⁵For other definitions see Ellington, Henry, & Harris, Duncan, *Dictionary of Educational Technology* (New York: Nichols, 1986); Hansen, Douglas E., *Educational Technology Telecommunications Dictionary with Acronyms* (Englewood Cliffs, NJ: Educational Technology Publications, 1991); Rosenberg, Kenyon C., & Elsbree, John J., *Dictionary of Library and Educational Technology*, 3rd and enlarged edition (Englewood, CO: Libraries Unlimited, 1989); Seels, Barbara, & Richey, Rita, *Instructional Technology: The Definition and Domains of the Field* (Washington, DC: Association for Educational Communications and Technology, 1994): "Instructional technology is the theory and practice of design, development, utilization, management and evaluation [and **revision**, I would add] of processes and resources for learning" (p. 1).

¹⁶I believe that it was George Kneller's brother John, former President of Brooklyn College, who pointed out to us that "educational technology" (in the sense of a process) appears to be an **oxymoron**. "Educational" necessarily implies "worthwhile." These adjectives more properly qualify the noun "objectives." Technology seeks to make processes, such as instruction, more efficient largely without regard for merit of objectives. Nevertheless, the term "educational technology" is used extensively as a synonym for "instructional technology," perhaps to appear more inclusive (i.e., beyond schools, as in distance education) or to express rejection of its mechanistic roots ("instruction" tends to be identified with training in accord with behaviorist principles). As teachers, however, you and I should remain keenly aware of these roots so that we recognize more clearly **our crucial roles** within its machinations (a weakness for the quick, easy, and cheap with revisions "preferably" based on "objectively measured" outcomes on the one hand, and high-tech, costly, unproven innovation backed by whimsical testimonials on the other). My own motivation in using the popular oxymoron has been primarily to emphasize my **earnest desire** that technology be directed toward student/teacher negotiated high-level, worthwhile ends, including those difficult to anticipate or assess. Also, the term is not an oxymoron when used in reference to products, which clearly may or may not be worthwhile.

[17]Hackbarth, Steven L., "Contributions of Educational Technology to Persons with Special Gifts and Challenges," *Programmed Learning and Educational Technology*, 23 (May 1986), pp. 166–172; Thomas, R. Murray, & Kobayashi, V.N., eds., *Educational Technology: Its Creation, Development, and Cross-Cultural Transfer* (New York: Pergamon Press, 1987); Bailey, Gerald D., & Lumley, Dan, *Technology Staff Development Programs: A Leadership Sourcebook for School Administrators* (New York: Scholastic, 1994); Kearsley, Greg, & Lynch, William, eds., *Educational Technology: Leadership Perspectives* (Englewood Cliffs, NJ: Educational Technology Publications, 1994); Kemp, Jerrold E., *A School Changes* (Washington, DC: Association for Educational Communications and Technology, 1995); Means, Barbara, Blando, John, Middleton, Theresa, Morrocco, Catherine Cobb, Remz, Arlene R., & Zorfass, Judith, *Using Technology to Support Education Reform* (Washington, DC: Association for Educational Communications and Technology, 1993).

[18]The radical view is provocatively presented in Perelman, Lewis J., *School's Out: Hyperlearning, the New Technology, and the End of Education* (New York: William Morrow, 1992). Note that he argues for the end of formal **schooling**, not education, which he feels could better take place outside the confines of classrooms. For a critique see Luterbach, Kenneth J., & Reigeluth, Charles M., "School's Not Out, Yet," *Educational Technology*, 34 (April 1994), pp. 47–54.

[19]Bestor, Arthur, *Educational Wastelands: The Retreat from Learning in Our Public Schools*, 2nd ed. (Champaign, IL: University of Illinois Press, 1985); Postman, Neil, *Conscientious Objections: Stirring Up Trouble About Language, Technology, and Education* (New York: Vintage Books, 1988); *Technopoly: The Surrender of Culture to Technology* (New York: Knopf, 1992); Hlynka, Denis, & Belland, John C., eds., *Paradigms Regained: The Uses of Illuminative, Semiotic, and Postmodern Criticism as Modes of Inquiry in Educational Technology* (Englewood Cliffs, NJ: Educational Technology Publications, 1991); Yeaman, Andrew, "Deconstructing Modern Educational Technology," *Educational Technology*, 34 (February 1994), pp. 15–24: "There are severe problems with the univocal meaning of modern educational technology in a democratic society. It casts aside the epistemological dimensions of the social context as power relations; the cultural context of stereotypes; the varying interpretations of readers and viewers; the multiplicity of voices, messages and languages; and the choices of media as ways of representing and shaping thought. The accepted reality is that authors, teachers and instructional designers, and their technologies and devices, are the dispensers of unequivocable, objective truth. These blinders enable the field of educational technology to persist in maintaining the modern illusion of shared minds. By following and perpetuating the grand myth of technological and scientific progress, the modern profession of educational technology will neglect its ethical obligation to every human being" (p. 22).

Sources

Books related to this chapter include:

Anglin, Gary, ed., *Instructional Technology: Past, Present, and Future*, 2nd ed. (Englewood, CO: Libraries Unlimited, 1995).

Bailey, Gerald D., & Lumley, Dan, *Technology Staff Development Programs: A Leadership Sourcebook for School Administrators* (New York: Scholastic, 1994).

Barnouw, Erik, *Tube of Plenty: The Evolution of American Television*, 2nd rev. ed. (New York: Oxford University Press, 1990).

Bianculli, David, *Teleliteracy: Taking Television Seriously* (New York: Continuum, 1992).

Bozeman, Bill, & Baumbach, Donna, *Educational Technology: Best Practices from America's Schools* (Princeton, NJ: Eye on Education, 1995).

Briggs, Leslie J., Gustafson, Kent L., & Tillman, Murray H., eds., *Instructional Design: Principles and Applications*, 2nd rev. ed. (Englewood Cliffs, NJ: Educational Technology Publications, 1991).

Brock, Patricia Ann, *Educational Technology in the Classroom* (Englewood Cliffs, NJ: Educational Technology Publications, 1994).

Brody, Philip J., *Technology Planning and Management Handbook: A Guide for School District Educational Technology Leaders* (Englewood Cliffs, NJ: Educational Technology Publications, 1995).

Carey, James W., *Communication as Culture: Essays on Media and Society* (New York: Routledge, 1992).

Educational Media and Technology Yearbook (Littleton, CO: Libraries Unlimited, annual).

Ellington, Henry, & Harris, Duncan, *Dictionary of Instructional Technology* (New York: Nichols, 1986).

Ellington, Henry, Percival, Fred, & Race, Phil, *Handbook of Educational Technology*, 3rd ed. (London: Kogan Page, 1993).

Ely, Donald P., & Minor, Barbara B., eds., *Educational Media and Technology Yearbook, 1992* (Englewood, CO: Libraries Unlimited, 1992).

Gagné, Robert M., *The Conditions of Learning*, 4th ed. (New York: Holt, Rinehart, & Winston, 1985); *Instructional Technology: Foundations* (Hillsdale, NJ: Lawrence Erlbaum Associates, 1987).

Gayeski, Diane M., ed., *Designing Communication and Learning Environments* (Englewood Cliffs, NJ: Educational Technology Publications, 1995).

Hansen, Douglas E., *Educational Telecommunications and Technology Dictionary with Acronyms* (Englewood Cliffs, NJ: Educational Technology Publications, 1991).

Heinich, Robert, Molenda, Michael, & Russell, James D., *Instructional Media and the New Technologies of Instruction*, 4th ed. (New York: Macmillan, 1993).

Hlynka, Denis, & Belland, John C., eds., *Paradigms Regained: The Uses of Illuminative, Semiotic, and Postmodern Criticism* as *Modes of Inquiry in Educational Technology* (Englewood Cliffs, NJ: Educational Technology Publications, 1991).

Inglis, Fred, *Media Theory: An Introduction* (Cambridge, MA: Basil Blackwell, 1990).

Johnson, Jenny K., ed., *Degree Curricula in Educational Communications and Technology: A Descriptive Directory*, 5th ed. (Washington, DC: Association for Educational Communications and Technology, 1995).

Kearsley, Greg, & Lynch, William, eds., *Educational Technology: Leadership Perspectives* (Englewood Cliffs, NJ: Educational Technology Publications, 1994).

Kemp, Jerrold E., *A School Changes* (Washington, DC: Association for Educational Communications and Technology, 1995).

Leebaert, Derek, *Technology Two Thousand One: The Future of Computing and Communication* (Cambridge, MA: MIT Press, 1991).

Mackay, Hughie, Young, Michael, & Beynon, John, eds., *Understanding Technology in Education* (Bristol, PA: Falmer Press, 1991)

Means, Barbara, Blando, John, Middleton, Theresa, Morrocco, Catherine Cobb, Remz, Arlene R., & Zorfass, Judith, *Using Technology to Support Education Reform* (Washington, DC: Association for Educational Communications and Technology, 1993).

Nickerson, Raymond S., & Zodhiates, Philip P., eds., *Technology in Education: Looking Toward 2020* (Hillsdale, NJ: Lawrence Erlbaum Associates, 1988).

Postman, Neil, *Technopoly: The Surrender of Culture to Technology* (New York: Knopf, 1992).

Rosenberg, Kenyon C., & Elsbree, John J., *Dictionary of Library and Educational Technology*, 3rd and enlarged edition (Englewood, CO: Libraries Unlimited, 1989).

Ross, Steven M., & Morrison, Gary R., *Getting Started in Instructional Technology Research* (Washington, DC: Association for Educational Communications and Technology, 1995).

Saettler, Paul, *The Evolution of American Educational Technology* (Englewood, CO: Libraries Unlimited, 1990).

Salisbury, David F., *Five Technologies for Educational Change: Systems Thinking, Systems Design, Quality Science, Change Management, Instructional Technology* (Englewood Cliffs, NJ: Educational Technology Publications, 1996).

Seels, Barbara, & Richey, Rita, *Instructional Technology: The Definition and Domains of the Field* (Washington, DC: Association for Educational Communications and Technology, 1994).

Seels, Barbara B., ed., *Instructional Design Fundamentals: A Reconsideration* (Englewood Cliffs, NJ: Educational Technology Publications, 1995).

Wilson, Brent G., ed., *Constructivist Learning Environments: Case Studies in Instructional Design* (Englewood Cliffs, NJ: Educational Technology Publications, 1996).

Obtain current catalogs from the following publishers:

Allyn & Bacon: 1-800-852-8024; 1-617-455-1273

Association for the Advancement of Computing in Education: 1-804-973-3987

Association for Educational Communications and Technology: 1-202-347-7834

Educational Technology Publications: 1-800-952-BOOK; 1-201-871-4007

Heinemann: 1-603-431-7894

International Society for Technology in Education: 1-800-336-5191; 1-503-346-4414

Lawrence Erlbaum Associates: 1-201-666-4110

Libraries Unlimited: 1-800-237-6124; 1-303-770-1220

Mecklermedia Corp.: 1-800-573-3062; 1-203-226-6967

Nichols Publishing: 1-908-297-2862

Phi Delta Kappa: 1-800-766-1156; 1-812-339-1156. Note especially John Goodlad's staff development video program, *New Schools, New Teachers* (1994) that builds upon his books, *A Place Called School: Prospects for the Future* (New York: McGraw-Hill, 1984); *Teachers for Our Nation's Schools* (San Francisco: Jossey-Bass, 1990); *What Schools Are For*, 2nd ed. (Bloomington, IN: Phi Delta Kappa, 1994); *Educational Renewal: Better Teachers, Better Schools* (San Francisco: Jossey-Bass, 1994).

Waite Group Press: 1-800-368-9369; 1-415-924-2575

Ziff-Davis Publishing Co.: 1-800-688-0448; 1-510-601-2000

Keeping up with developments in the field of educational technology is greatly facilitated by joining professional organizations such as:

Association for Educational Communications and Technology
1025 Vermont Avenue, NW, Suite 820
Washington, DC 20005-3547
1-202-347-7834
Internet: aect@aect.org

Membership includes subscription to *TechTrends for Leaders in Education and Training* and, for an additional fee, to *Educational Technology Research and Development*. Call for a current free copy of the catalog *Resources for the Educational Media Professional* that lists books, audiotapes, and videos.

International Society for Technology in Education
1787 Agate Street
Eugene, OR 97403-1923
1-800-336-5191; 1-503-346-4414
Internet: iste@oregon.uoregon.edu

Membership includes subscription to *ISTE Update* and *Learning and Leading with Technology*. Call for catalog listing journals, videos, books, and courseware.

The Association for Educational and Training Technology
Centre for Continuing Education
The City University, Northhampton Square
London EC1V 0HB England
071-253-4399, ext. 3276

Publications include *Innovations in Education & Training International, Aspects of Educational & Training Technology,* and the *International Yearbook of Educational and Training Technology,* all by Kogan Page, Ltd., London.

Study Items

1. In what ways has technology "revolutionized" education? How has your schooling been affected for the better? For the worse?

2. What do illustrations add to the printed word? In your view, is a picture worth a thousand words or is it the other way around?

3. What are some insights you have gained from audiovisual media that you might not have otherwise acquired?

4. What special advantages might audiovisual media provide persons with perceptual or motor disabilities?

5. If "programmed" instructional materials are not subjected to field testing and revision before publication and general use, in what ways might they be less effective than if they had been so subjected?

6. In what ways have computers changed your schooling experiences? What was your first reaction? How have you coped since?

7. Draw a model of communications. How can you ensure that an intended message is received without distortion?

8. What is the role of the "receiver" in models of communication? In what senses might the receiver be considered an active component?

9. Describe some contributions of the "information-processing" model of human cognition to the practice of teaching. Do you find this model helpful? Do you perceive any limitations?

10. How might a teacher employ ideas from systems engineering to enable a group of students with little knowledge of the English language to make progress toward course objectives?

11. What distinguishes a product of educational technology from programs that have not undergone this systematic process of development? What are the extra costs entailed in ensuring quality and effectiveness of educational products?

12. If you were a teacher in a self-contained classroom faced with achieving specified district objectives, how would you integrate a newly released, exceptionally fine TV or computer program into your lesson plan for a given week?

13. Describe how educational technology has been affected by the challenge of constructivism.

14. Counter claims that educational technology necessarily presents a view of knowledge as fixed and of students as passive recipients.

15. In what ways has a textbook made the instruction in any one of your previous classes more enriched, individualized, valid, accessible, and economical?

16. Describe instances where electronically mediated presentations might enable students to gain insights that printed or spoken words alone might communicate less effectively, completely, or economically.

Suggested Activities

1. Make a list of instructional media used by your teachers while you were in grammar school, another for high school, and one for college. Rank each list in terms of how often each medium was used. Meet with classmates to compare and discuss results.

2. Obtain a self-instructional foreign language program presented by print, audiotape, videotape, or computer. Note which generalizations about learning the program incorporates.

3. Go to a college library and request recent periodicals about instructional or educational technology. Scan these and note references to products, processes, and professions.

4. Meet with experienced teachers and principals and ask them to tell you why they use instructional media. Also, ask them to share with you any reservations they may have about selected media. Categorize their positive responses into making instruction more "individualized," "valid" "accessible," or "economical." Compare responses made by teachers with those given by principals. Meet with classmates to discuss how the reservations expressed may be overcome.

5. Visit a computer software store and ask for demonstrations of "interactive multimedia." Design a lesson in which such programs could be brought to facilitate achievement of objectives in the subject you teach.

6. Check out any one of the references cited in the endnotes or sources and prepare a critical review.

7. Examine this chapter for inaccuracies and omissions and inform me at Internet: hackbarths@aol.com. Also, please send me your responses to the above study items so I can see if this textbook, with the help of your instructors in this class and others, is providing adequate information. This would make you an active participant in the process of educational technology (specifically, "learner verification") and would be of great assistance to me in the production of future editions.

Chapter 2

Development of Instructional Programs

Chapter Content and Objectives

This chapter builds upon ideas introduced in the first and serves as preface to those that follow. It presents **explicit step-by-step procedures** for the design and production of instructional programs. These procedures are consistent with the concept of educational technology as a systematic process. Nevertheless, **to be effective they must be adapted creatively by teachers**. After studying this chapter, you should be able to:

- List and describe the **five phases** of an instructional development model—**diagnose, design, procure, produce, refine**.
- Perform the **18 steps** recommended to design and produce an effective, efficient instructional program.
- Discuss several **virtues** and **limitations** of systematic instructional development.
- Speculate on how you would **adapt** an instructional development model **to suit your time and budget constraints**.

"Instructional Development" Defined

Communications media and computers are revolutionizing education, but their influences are not as beneficial as they could be. This is largely because of deficiencies both in program content and delivery. **What can be done in advance of full classroom implementation to ensure high quality of program content and effectiveness of delivery?**

We know well that dedicated teachers treasure their students, that they earnestly desire to enhance the quality of their students' lives, and that they strive daily to improve their own performance toward this end. Gifted teachers are especially sensitive to the intellectual and emotional strengths and needs of their students. They know their subjects well and accurately perceive how content and methods can be selected to meet those needs. Such teachers may rely heavily on their innate talents. However, their successes surely are affected greatly by their classroom experiences and the means they have devised to incorporate those experiences in the continuous process of improving their instructional materials and techniques.

Educational technologists, too, care deeply about students. They have studied what gifted teachers do and have witnessed creative advances in fields ranging from communications to engineering. Insights thus gained have contributed to their conception of **"instructional development."** This systematic, creative process may be defined as a **procedural identification and analysis of problems entailed in the transmission of knowledge, attitudes, and skills, and the crafting of replicable, cost-effective solutions.**[1]

Evidence for the value of instructional development (ID) comes from reviews of research on innovations in teaching. It has been found that the measured superiority of innovative techniques can be accounted for almost entirely by the enthusiasm aroused in trying something new and by differences in the amount of systematic program development. Indeed, the superiority of innovative approaches tends to diminish when the more conventional approaches with which they are compared undergo similar development efforts.[2]

It should not be surprising, therefore, that television and computers, while revolutionizing education, **have not yet greatly improved it**. These devices are delivery mechanisms, the former until recently almost exclusively a one-way mode of communication, the latter, only modestly interactive prior to the advent of multimedia and on-line databases and communications. Both have tended to be less cost-effective than print materials and radio.[3] The instructional programs presented by television, computers, and teachers alike can benefit from **systematic, reflective analyses of objectives, students, strategies, and media; testing of prototypes, and revisions based on periodic assessments of student learning**.

The purpose of this chapter is to present explicit guidelines for the systematic planning and production of instructional programs that you can follow **creatively** to make cumulative improvements in your performance and thereby ensure that your students achieve the objectives set for (and **in collaboration with**) them.[4] Chapter **4** presents instructional development models used by teams of specialists to plan and produce entire curriculums.

An Instructional Development Model

Figure 2.01 outlines a procedure that reflects a systematic approach to the development of instruction. The **18 steps** are divided into **five phases—diagnose, design, procure, produce**, and **refine**. Note that you need not proceed linearly from step 1 through 18. At any point you may need to review and revise the results of earlier steps. Indeed, you might well not begin to perceive clearly the particular learning needs and abilities of your students until you have begun to engage them collaboratively in your ever evolving lesson plan.

Phase I. DIAGNOSE

Step 1. Figure out what students need to know. The objectives of instruction generally are specified by school districts, derived from textbooks, and negotiated among teachers, students, and parents. Objectives in the knowledge (**cognitive**) domain include acquisition of facts, comprehension of principles, and application of

---

Phase I. DIAGNOSE
  Step   1. Figure out what students need to know.
  Step   2. Assess what students already know.

Phase II. DESIGN
  Step   3. Design tests of learning achievement.
  Step   4. Identify effective instructional strategies.
  Step   5. Select suitable media.
  Step   6. Sequence learning activities within program.
  Step   7. Plan introductory activities.
  Step   8. Plan follow-up activities.

Phase III. PROCURE
  Step   9. Secure materials at hand.
  Step 10. Obtain new materials.

Phase IV. PRODUCE
  Step 11. Modify existing materials.
  Step 12. Craft new materials.

Phase V. REFINE
  Step 13. Conduct small-scale test of program.
  Step 14. Evaluate procedures and achievements.
  Step 15. Revise program accordingly.
  Step 16. Conduct classroom test of program.
  Step 17. Evaluate procedures and achievements.
  Step 18. Revise in anticipation of next school term.

Figure 2.01. A systematic/creative approach to the development of instruction.

---

rules. Those in the feeling (**affective**) domain involve awareness and acceptance of values, preferences, and commitments. Those in the action (**psychomotor**) domain deal with skilled performances such as typing and ballet. If you can conceive of higher aspirations and other categories, do so. For example, give considerable thought to **process objectives** such as "paying attention," "staying on-task," "sharing ideas," "helping others,"

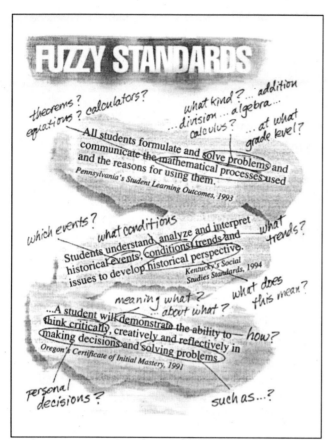

FUZZY STANDARDS

theorems? equations? calculators?

what kind?... addition division... algebra... calculus? ...at what grade level?

All students formulate and solve problems and communicate the mathematical processes used and the reasons for using them.
Pennsylvania's Student Learning Outcomes, 1993

which events? what conditions what trends?

Students understand, analyze and interpret historical events, conditions, trends and issues to develop historical perspective.
Kentucky's Social Studies Standards, 1994

meaning what? about what? what does this mean?

...A student will demonstrate the ability to— how? think critically, creatively and reflectively in making decisions and solving problems.
Oregon's Certificate of Initial Mastery, 1991

personal decisions?

such as...?

Figure 2.02. Educational aims tend to be stated in general terms. Communication about what is intended is facilitated when such aims are translated into more specific objectives. Ambiguities in typical statements of aims are identified above. Do you agree that even constructivist educators should be explicit about their objectives, however tentative these may be? Source: Mike Rose, "Standards: The Good, the Bad and the Fuzzy," *American Teacher,* 79 (March 1995), p. 7. Reprinted courtesy of The American Federation of Teachers.

"monitoring own progress," and "attributing success to effort rather than chance."

Instructional objectives specify desired learning achievements, usually in terms of observable behaviors. They ask the student to list, define, describe, compare, analyze, explain, demonstrate, etc. This is done both to facilitate communication about intended outcomes and to enable teachers to assess more precisely the extent to which their instruction has been successful. (See **Figure 2.02.**) Desired learning outcomes that cannot ade-

quately be expressed in terms of observable behavior may be expressed in more abstract terms, and the corresponding means of evaluation may require judgment by teachers and students. For example, interest in reading may be inferred by noting the amount of time voluntarily spent in the library and the number of books checked out, as well as by how productive the teachers and students judge the time spent and how good the books selected.

Objectives for particular units of instruction may be written in detail, possibly in the **"ABCD"** format. They state what students (the **"A**udience") are expected to do (the **"B**ehavior"), the **"C**onditions" under which they are to perform, and the expected level of proficiency (the **"D**egree"). Here is an example of an objective written in the ABCD format: "Given several columns of two-digit numerals [Condition], the second grade pupil [Audience] will write the correct totals [Behavior] for 90% of them [Degree]."

No need to be compulsive about this! Much of what we hope students will learn, and much of what they actually do learn, cannot so easily be anticipated. And don't let the existence of neatly written outcome objectives blind you to the importance of what students get out of the **process,** per se. Discovering the values of sharing and working collaboratively or experiencing the benefits of engaging in conflict resolution may well overshadow the significance of absorbing prescribed subject matter.

Step 2. Assess what students already know. Before starting any course, you inevitably will draw on your experience to anticipate what your students have learned in previous courses. However, you also should examine student files to ascertain academic performance, test results, interests, and special talents. During the first few class meetings, teacher-student conferences and subject matter pretests reveal the extent to which students may already have achieved instructional objectives. Also, students themselves may have urgent concerns rooted in their own experiences that provide opportune moments for grounding the curriculum in their lived worlds. At this point you might find it necessary to go back to step one and consider alternative objectives.

Phase II. DESIGN

Step 3. Design means of assessing learning achievement. Evaluation instruments and methods should be based on the content of specified instructional objectives. Questions should reflect the level of performance called for. For example, if the goal is simply to recall information, no cues should be given that enable students to recognize correct answers. Depth of comprehension may be assessed using instruments and methods (e.g., speak, draw, demonstrate) that allow for considerable latitude in responding.

Regarding format, true-false and multiple-choice tests can be written to assess a wide range of accomplishment. However, essay questions are more appropriate if, for example, you wish to assess how students answer questions that have no precisely "correct" answer. Changes in attitudes can be inferred from questionnaires, interviews, and observations of conduct. To assess the development of problem-solving skills, you might ask questions or pose problems requiring creative responses. These questions, or problems, have the form of "What would you do if . . . ?" or "Given such and such a situation, how would a scientist cope with it (or an economist, or you as a lay citizen)?"

Students also should be encouraged to select samples of their work for inclusion in portfolios. These should include both drafts and final products. For each piece, students should be asked to write why they selected it and how they feel about it. Your own criteria for assessing the quality of work should be made explicit in writing and in your conferences with students and their parents.

Step 4. Identify effective instructional strategies. For any given (reasonable) objectives, (willing) students, and (coherent) subject matter, the single most potent factor in teaching effectiveness is **combination of instructional strategies**. Given valid content (both accurate and appropriate), careful selection of instructional strategies ensures efficient learning, retention, and transfer.

Instructional strategies (methods) may be categorized according to function. Some capture students' attention and direct it to specific aspects of subject matter. Others arouse interest, stimulate curiosity, and encourage persistence. Still others serve to present content, guide students in learning it, ensure retention, and promote application. Combinations of strategies provide what has been called "scaffolding" needed to bridge the gap between the relatively immature thinking of students

and the insights of experts. As a teacher you should choose instructional strategies largely on the basis of:

- type and level of student performance expressed in your instructional objectives,
- subject matter area,
- student strengths and preferences,
- information derived from learning theory and research,
- insights from your experience,
- limitations of time and resources, and
- your talents and preferences. (See **Figure 2.03**.)

For example, if you expect average performing students to identify instances of a concept, you might first show them colorful slides or photos of objects that are clear cases of the concept. Distinguishing features could be identified with arrows and written on a chalkboard. Counterexamples then could be presented, taking care that the features that exclude them are clearly marked. Students could be asked to identify objects that exemplify the concept and those that do not. Students having difficulty might be given suggestions about how to remember the list of distinguishing features—by using a mnemonic, say, or thinking in terms of an analogy. If, on the other hand, an objective asks typically high independent functioning students merely to recall rules or facts, you might distribute a handout for them to take home and memorize in preparation for a quiz the next day.[5]

Step 5. Select suitable media. Base your selection of media on which ones can **best incorporate the instructional strategies most appropriate for your objectives**. Print, visual, and electronic media differ greatly in the range of strategies they can handle and in capacity to reach wide audiences at low cost. For example, audiotape can present information in a well-structured format and provide opportunities for practice. Computers can do the same but they also can adjust presentation and provide feedback in direct response to student input. Videotape affords immediate review of performance in such activities as sports, speech, and lab work. Second, consider distribution requirements. For small groups, filmstrips and computers generally serve well. But if you must reach a large, dispersed audience, radio

Learning Goals	Instructional Strategies	Learning Goals	Instructional Strategies
attention	size of print tone of voice volume of audio familiar music novelty use of color eye contact proximity		examples strategy suggestions collecting data analyses pacing modeling explanations questions responses

motivation	scheduling of presentation
	allusions to intrinsic value
	promises of extrinsic
	  rewards
	notices of examinations to
	  follow
	challenges
	competition
	appeals to pride
	encouragement
	relate to lived world
	peer grouping
			examinations
			informative feedback
			making connections with
			  prior knowledge

		mastery	repetition guided practice report writing take-home exams problem-solving activities fostering ownership of ideas making presentations

advance organization	pretests
	advance reading
	  assignments
	outlines
	overviews
	statements of objectives
	stimulate recall of what
	  already is known
	brainstorming
	semantic mapping
		transfer	generalizations
			applications
			field trips
			simulations
			"anchored" instruction
			  (tied to real life)
			solving "real" problems

comprehension	validity of content
	organization of content
	titles
	cues
	rules
		creativity	guided discovery
			independent projects
			interactive multimedia
			problem-solving
			  challenges
			interactive
			  communications
			cyberspace travels
			virtual reality explorations

	(continues top of next column)		

Figure 2.03. Factors to consider in selection of potent instructional strategies include student strengths, objectives, group size, and resources. Listed above are broad categories of learning goals and a sampling of strategies that might be used to achieve them. Can you think of additional goals and strategies?

Medium	Feature	Group Size	Distribution	Cost
book	typeface punctuation organization questions hyperbole rhyme metaphor drama comedy	small	local	low
picture	subjects composition perspective color contrast focus cues	small	local	low
audiotape	volume pitch rhythm inflection pacing	medium	local	low
slide/tape	all the above	medium	local	medium
film/videotape	all the above	medium	local	medium
radio	same as audio timeliness	large	distant	low
television	all the above	large	distant	medium
computer	all the above interactivity	small	local	high
network	all of the above	large	distant	low
tutor	most of the above flexibility empathy caring	small	local	medium
teacher	same as tutor authority wisdom	medium	local	high

Figure 2.04. Selection of appropriate media is guided by consideration of how the features of each permit use of potent instructional strategies previously identified, target group size, distribution requirements, cost per student, and availability. Examples are presented above. Can you think of others?

and TV may be called for. Third, consider the appeal of specific media to your students (and to yourself). Are they attractive and engaging? Finally, ascertain whether or not you have sufficient funds to obtain suitable programs and equipment.[6]

Source materials cited at the end of Chapter **3** abound with models that you can use to guide selection of media. All are based largely on refined common sense, a fairly accurate source. **Figure 2.04** can be used as a general guide. It is helpful in that it cues you to take into account instructional strategies previously identified, group size, distribution requirements, and costs.

Nevertheless, **no mere list or model obviates the need for using your common sense and good judgment.** Note especially that students with perceptual or motor deficits may require assistive technology and special arrangements (time, access). Hearing-impaired students benefit from amplification devices and audiotapes. Those with visual disabilities use video equipment to magnify text, or optical character recognition (OCR) technology to read it. Students with motor impairments operate computers using their voices and light-emitting eyeglasses. Students with learning disabilities and attention deficit disorders are reached using multiple sensory channel interactive instruction that capitalizes on their individually demonstrated strengths.

Again, once you arrive at what appears to be the best choice, considerations of availability and appeal come into play. Note also that while practical considerations in selection of media are based largely on common sense refined by tested experience, **program content, organization, and presentation** need be rooted in **expertise and research.**

Practical considerations for basic media are listed in **Figure 2.05**. Basic media are the prime alternatives to traditional "chalk and talk" instruction rooted in textbooks. To fully integrate into your classroom computer-based instruction, including multimedia CD-ROM and on-line communications, you may have to restructure facilities, time schedules, and activities. The ideal is a well-done, fully **"integrated learning system"** (ILS), as described in Chapter **5**.

Step 6. Sequence learning activities within program. Categorize planned lectures, brainstorming, semantic mapping, text readings, films, etc., according to function. Some will serve as previews, others, to help students re-

Material	Advantages	Limitations
Photographic print series	1. Permit close-up detailed study at individual's own pacing. 2. Are useful as simple self-study materials and for display. 3. Require no equipment for use.	1. Not adaptable for large groups. 2. Require photographic skills, equipment, and darkroom for preparation.
Slide series	1. Require only filming, with processing and mounting by film laboratory. 2. Result in colorful, realistic reproductions of original subjects. 3. Prepared with any 35mm camera for most uses. 4. Easily revised and updated. 5. Easily handled, stored, and rearranged for various uses. 6. Increased usefulness with tray storage and automatic projection. 7. Can be combined with taped narration for greater effectiveness. 8. May be adapted to group or to individual use.	1. Require some skill in photography. 2. Require special equipment for close-up photography and copying. 3. Can get out of sequence and be projected incorrectly if slides are handled individually.
Filmstrips	1. Are compact, easily handled, and always in proper sequence. 2. Can be supplemented with captions or recordings. 3. Are inexpensive when quantity reproduction is required. 4. Are useful for group or individual study at projection rate controlled by instructor or user. 5. Are projected with simple lightweight equipment.	1. Are relatively difficult to prepare locally. 2. Require film laboratory service to convert slides to filmstrip form. 3. Are in permanent sequence and cannot be rearranged or revised.
Recordings	1. Easy to prepare with regular tape recorders. 2. Can provide applications in most subject areas. 3. Equipment for use, compact, portable, easy to operate. 4. Flexible and adaptable at either individual elements of instruction or in correlation with programmed materials. 5. Duplication easy and economical.	1. Have a tendency for over-use, as lecture or oral textbook reading. 2. Fixed rate of information flow.
Overhead transparencies	1. Can present information in systematic, developmental sequences. 2. Use simple-to-operate projector with presentation rate controlled by instructor. 3. Require only limited planning. 4. Can be prepared by variety of simple, inexpensive methods. 5. Particularly useful with large groups.	1. Require special equipment, facilities and skills for preparation. 2. Are large and present storage problem.
Videotape/ videocassette	1. Permit selecting the best audiovisual media to serve program needs. 2. Permit normally unavailable resources to be presented. 3. Playback capability of video recording permits analysis of on-the-spot action.	1. Do not exist alone, but are part of total television production. 2. Must fit technical requirements of television.
Multi-media presentations (e.g., slide/ tape)	1. Combine presentation of slides with other media forms for presentations. 2. Use photographs, slides, filmstrips and recordings in combination for independent study. 3. Provide for more effective communications in certain situations than when only a single medium is used.	1. Require additional equipment and careful coordination during planning, preparation, and use.

Figure 2.05. While program content, organization, and presentation need be rooted in expertise and research, practical considerations in selection of media are based largely on common sense refined by tested experience. Above is a summary of practical considerations for basic media. These will be embellished in subsequent chapters and compared with other media including schoolbooks, computers, and teachers. Source: Alexander J. Romiszowski, *The Selection and Use of Instructional Media*, 2nd ed. (East Brunswick, NJ: Nichols, 1988), p. 98. Reprinted with permission of Nichols Publishing Company.

Figure 2.06. Following participation in an emotionally charged simulation game, these students share with their instructors feelings of frustration and accomplishment. Together they reinforce and expand on what was learned, thus ensuring retention and transfer. How much time would you allocate for discussion following a one-hour lecture? A 15-minute film? A 2-hour encounter with a CD-ROM multimedia encyclopedia or the World Wide Web?

call prerequisite information or skills, others still, to provide opportunities to integrate new learnings with prior ones and apply them to novel contexts. Organize the presentation to ensure smooth progress in learning from the simple to the complex, say, or from the concrete to the abstract. Leave space for the students' own perspectives and preferences to shine through.

Step 7. Plan introductory activities. Whether you are designing a single lesson or an entire course, you must relate it to what the students have done previously. Introductory activities include assigned readings, vocabulary lessons, preparatory remarks, and asking such questions "What do you know?" "What do you need or want to know?" and "How could you find out?" These refresh students' memories of previously learned material

and provide them with the background needed to grasp what is to come and how they might seek answers on their own.

Step 8. Plan follow-up activities. Make preparations to relate the planned lesson or course to what students will next encounter, be it another lesson, a more advanced course, or "real life." Typical follow-up activities include practicing and analyzing what was learned and applying it to the solution of problems and the creation of products. (See **Figure 2.06**.)

Phase III. PROCURE

Step 9. Secure materials at hand. Locate readily available notes, pictures, handouts, books, films, etc., that relate closely to the subject you intend to teach.

Step 10. Obtain new materials. Search commercial catalogs, periodicals, and on-line databases to find learning materials related to your subject and most appropriate for your students.

Phase IV. PRODUCE

Step 11. Modify existing materials. Add or delete sections, change vocabulary, and rearrange presentation to suit your students and the objectives set for (and with) them.

Step 12. Craft new materials. If suitable materials are not readily available at a reasonable price, you may want to produce your own. Production of simple media like lectures, printed handouts, overhead transparencies, slides, and audiotapes should be routine. More complex media require more time and expense to produce—investments that can be justified for special purposes and when they are to be used by many students over many years. In every case, students can assist with design, production, testing, and revision.

Phase V. REFINE

Step 13. Conduct small-scale test of program. Try out a prototype of your program with a sample of students or, if such a sample is not available, with colleagues or family.

Step 14. Evaluate procedures and achievements. Evaluation of progress during the small-scale test should focus on the quality of teaching and learning. Note that the quality of program delivery may be adversely affected by equipment breakdowns, scheduling problems, cost overruns, and other unexpected events. Evaluations of student progress may be based on test results, conferences, and systematic observations of behavior. Look for unanticipated outcomes as well as achievement of previously specified process and product objectives.

Step 15. Revise program accordingly. Draw on evaluation data to revise the course where appropriate. You may need to consider what instructional objectives merit higher priority, given limited time and resources. New techniques and materials may be called for in light of external pressures or unforeseen events. Evaluation instruments themselves may require revision as a result of item analyses and the addition of new objectives.

Step 16. Conduct classroom test of program. Present the revised program to your students within the context of the entire school curriculum. Teach with conviction. Capture and sustain attention by skilled use of voice and visuals, and by relating the subject at hand to what students already know and care about. Furnish instructional frameworks, such as previews, outlines, and summaries; and provide opportunities for student participation, exploration, and practice.

Step 17. Evaluate procedures and achievements. Employ instruments earlier developed to test for knowledge comprehension, skill performance, and attitude change. You also may assess the extent to which students can apply what they have learned to the solution of problems. More subtle techniques such as informal interviews and observations may be needed to ascertain the depth and breadth of comprehension, appropriation, and commitment. An evaluation may be "formative," in that it leads to further revision. An evaluation may be "summative," in that it serves as a basis for grading. Ask students what they think they have learned, how well they think they were taught, and what they would change.

Step 18. Revise in anticipation of next school term. Your course objectives and the characteristics of your students remain constant in some important respects from year to year. Without losing sight of the uniqueness of each student and the evolution of knowledge itself, you can use what you learn to make cumulative gains in the quality of your instruction.

Alternative Conceptions of Instructional Development

To encourage your creative approach to the systematic development of instruction, I will share here three additional models. The first, by Britain's Fred Percival and Henry Ellington, illustrates more clearly than my list of steps how the activities of formulating objectives, selecting methods, implementing the course, and conducting evaluations inform each other **and** provide insights into student characteristics. (See **Figure 2.07**.)

Jerrold Kemp's model goes even further in portraying the non-linearity of instructional design in practice. (See **Figure 2.08**.) Kemp's encircling of the intimately related design and development processes with revision guided

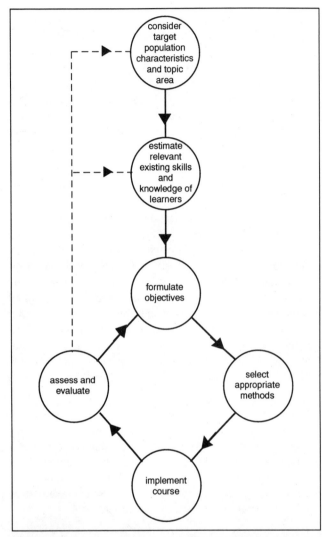

Figure 2.07. This model of instructional development illustrates how engagement in production and testing of prototypes often illuminates student characteristics and instructional objectives. Have you found this to be the case in your own observations of classroom practice? Source: Fred Percival & Henry Ellington, *A Handbook of Educational Technology,* 2nd ed. (East Brunswick, NJ: Nichols, 1988), p. 49. Reprinted with permission of Nichols Publishing Company.

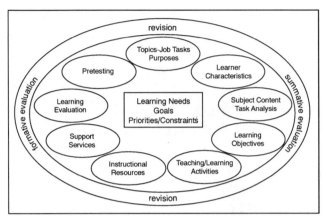

Figure 2.08. Jerrold Kemp's model of instructional development portrays the reality of having to consider all aspects simultaneously. The only constant is continuous testing and revision, in the spirit of John Dewey's conscientious, systematic "trying and undergoing" as the key to personally significant learning. Given limited time and resources, how will you prioritize the activities suggested in these instructional design models? Source: Jerrold E. Kemp, *The Instructional Design Process* (New York: Harper & Row, 1985), p. 11. Copyright © 1985 by Harper & Row, Publishers, Inc. Reprinted with permission of HarperCollins Publishers, Inc.

by both formative and summative evaluation expresses well the essence of educational technology as a creative enterprise.

Kent Gustafson, past President of the Association for Educational Communications and Technology, noted that although instructional design (ID) has served well in training contexts: "Clearly, what we need are alternative ID paradigms that more closely match the goals and purposes of K–12 education and the reality of how it is organized and functions."[7]

Barbara Martin and Rebecca Clemente examined reasons why instruction systems design (ISD) models have not yet found wide use in schools. They concluded that:

> An ISD model that has been adapted for school use taking into account present operating conditions and teachers' perceptions and beliefs about education and learning may be most appropriate. Such a model would be sensitive to the present structure of the school, how teachers plan, and how they implement instruction, and it would retain the best features of instructional systems design.[8]

Sharon Shrock and Norman Higgins have added to the call for seeing ID as a non-linear, creative process. Consistent with the views expressed throughout this book, they suggest that:

> Often an instructional developer can see an instructional problem only through a glass darkly. It is only in coming face to face with the reality of teaching something for the first time that objectives become clarified, instructional strategies are developed, and

modes of assessment are determined. Intelligent, sensitive, wondering people make these decisions, not impersonal instructional development models.[9]

Thus, we teachers are immersed in the dynamic context of our enterprise. As front-line ID practitioners, we can draw selectively upon models and resources to address with sensitivity the ever-evolving needs of our students.

Robert Branch's research has addressed some of the above concerns. He and his colleagues have identified over 20 essential components of instructional development and have provided "translations" of these from the jargon of specialists to the language commonly used by classroom teachers. This allowed him to identify areas where teachers appear to be guided by instructional development principles (setting course goals, aligning subgoals and activities, organizing content around themes, and fitting lessons within the larger curriculum), and areas where more training, encouragement, and time may be needed (collaboration with other teachers, establishing media selection criteria, drawing upon subject matter experts).[10]

Branch's model of instructional development reflects his desire to communicate ID principles in an easily comprehensible form (see **Figure 2.09**). His "situational assessment" corresponds with my Phase I, Diagnose, but much more elegantly. In the text of his paper, he translates "instructional analysis" to entail determining goals based on the larger curriculum and relating components of these goals to activities students may engage in to achieve them. The revision of objectives based on formative evaluation, and of goals based on a pilot study, are clearly illustrated, as is the distinction between formative and summative evaluation. Elements that might be added include early design of assessment instruments and procedures, collaboration with students and colleagues, production of materials, and feedback loops from the pilot study to other components.

Again, although I presented 18 steps in the design and development of instructional programs linearly **for ease of expression**, your task calls for a much more **tentative, holistic, and evolutionary approach**. You **can** do it! Indeed, research suggests that in spite of lack of consensus about models, materials revised

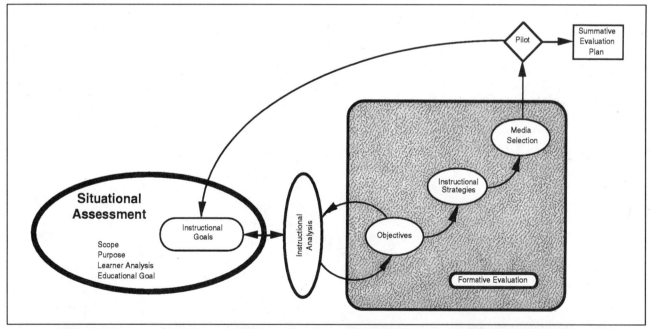

Figure 2.09. Robert Branch's model of the instructional design/development process is elegantly asymmetrical. It's simple and largely self-explanatory, yet includes the essential components. How might you revise this to include other elements covered in this chapter? Source: Robert C. Branch, "Common Instructional Design Practices Employed by Secondary School Teachers," *Educational Technology,* 34 (March 1994), p. 28. Reprinted courtesy of Educational Technology Publications.

by our fellow teachers have been found as effective as those revised by instructional design experts, and that both tended to be more effective than the original material.[11]

And, once again we should recognize that there is much more affecting learning than our instructional methods and media. David Jonassen, John Campbell, and Mark Davidson, among many others, remind us that:

> The environment in which learning occurs affects the experiences of the learner and therefore defines the content of the knowledge constructed. These environments may be enhanced by the inclusion of various kinds of media, but realistically the effect on knowledge construction is modified very little as the perceptual systems continue to take and use information from each and every sense in an effort to contextualize the input.[12]

Thus, educational technologists increasingly are taking into account the context in which instruction takes place, the fact that **learning is "situated."** Increasingly they are writing about "authentic tasks" anchored within "real world" settings in which strategies and media provide opportunities for the construction of shared meanings and transfer, rather than merely for achievement of narrowly preconceived outcomes. For example,

> When attempting to develop situated learning environments, designers use media to provide rich contexts that reflect their interpretation of the real world. Although exact replication of a particular real-world context is impossible, a designer seeks to provide a learning environment that resembles the real-world context so the learner can construct and transfer knowledge.[13]

Today's interactive multimedia, including virtual reality, go a long way toward recontextualizing knowledge that previously my have been presented mostly in textbooks and lectures. Yet context now is seen to encompass far more than stereo sound and 3-D images. The systematic development of instruction must take into account many and diverse influences upon the thinking and feeling both of students and teachers.

Summary and Conclusions

There are many critical challenges facing teachers today. Technological developments have had many beneficial as well as adverse effects on our well-being. The educational value of such technologies as television and computers rests largely upon the quality of programs they present. Systematic approaches to the design of instruction promise to ensure quality.

Advocates of a systems design approach to instruction view the orderly, pragmatic style of the engineer as one worthy of emulation by teachers. Like engineers faced with construction problems, teachers are portrayed as facing problems of getting students to learn prescribed subject matter. Such an approach might not appeal to those who see teaching as an art based largely on well-informed intuition or who prefer to emphasize students' capacity for constructing personally significant knowledge. In much the same way that mass communications media may impose the values explicitly and implicitly embedded in content, systematic approaches to instructional design might induce a mechanistic manner of teaching at odds not only with more dynamic, transactional conceptions of how learning best takes place but with cherished customs and accepted authorities as well.[14]

Nevertheless, systematic instructional development **can** be conducted creatively by teachers and communities to suit **their own purposes and those of students** within the limits of **their own** natural and human resources. Such an "appropriate technology" need not do violence to the values of students, parents, teachers, and community. Indeed, used with sensitivity and guided by the "ethic of care," it can foster constructive articulation and effective communication of these values.[15] The primary virtues of systematic instructional development approaches are that they:

- make explicit how we can identify problems (and challenges) students encounter in trying to make sense of the world; and

- detail how we may collaborate with students in rising to those challenges based on the best information and resources available.

Systematic approaches to instructional development are not recipes nor panaceas. Even at their best, such approaches do not substitute for our **judgment, compassion,** and **creativity,** nor for the active engagement of students in their dynamic construction of meaning and values. Rather, they **incorporate and encourage** these qualities of good teaching and learning in the systematic, reflective conduct of instruction, the focus of Chapter **3**.

Notes

[1]This definition is a synthesis of those found in published literature and the comments of critical readers. Richard E. Clark at the University of Southern California preferred inclusion of the strong term **"scientific"** over the objections of my mentor at UCLA, George F. Kneller. Clark's rationale rested largely on our ability to assess program effectiveness based on achievement of measurable objectives. Kneller held that **truly significant learning cannot be quantified and that classroom dynamics are too unpredictable to be generalized.** See his *Educationists and Their Vanities: One Hundred Missives to My Colleagues* (San Francisco: Caddo Press, 1994). My pragmatic adviser at UCLA, Gary D. Fenstermacher, then director of the Teacher Education Laboratory, advocated a compromise: **"If you cannot in some way assess achievement, you have no grounds on which to make claims of progress."** Kneller and I agreed that the term **"craft"** best expressed the nature of technology as something along a continuum between art and science. The uniqueness of each instructional situation, long a foundation of Kneller's position, also has more recently found expression in Clark's terms, for example, when he wrote: "The most efficient mode and medium used to express and deliver a method like feedback is likely to be specific to one set of learners in a particular context." In "Media and Method," *Educational Technology Research and Development*, 42, 3(1994), p. 8. Thus, the replicable solutions offered by educational technology may best be viewed as suggestive rather than definitive.

Note also that I prefer to use the term "development" as including, rather than following, "design." This use is consistent with current views (especially of M. David Merrill and the ID$_2$ Research Group at Utah State University) of the value, especially in school contexts, of tentative, "rapid prototyping" both to efficiently illuminate design and to speed production.

[2]Clark, Richard E., "Reconsidering Research on Learning from Media," *Review of Educational Research*, 53 (Winter 1983), pp. 445–459; Kulik, James A., Kulik, Chen-Lin C., & Cohen, Peter A., "Effectiveness of Computer-Based College Teaching: A Meta-Analysis of Findings," *Review of Educational Research*, 50 (Winter 1980), pp. 525–544. This topic was pursued in Clark, R.E., "Media Will Never Influence Learning," *Educational Technology Research and Development*, 42, 2(1994), pp. 21–29, with alternative views expressed in this special issue (based on a challenge to Clark's position by Robert B. Kozma) and in Tennyson, Robert D., "The Big Wrench vs. Integrated Approaches: The Great Media Debate," *Educational Technology Research and Development*, 42, 3(1994), pp. 15–28. Leading figures also presented their views at the 1995 meeting of the Association for Educational Communications and Technology. An audiotape of that session may be obtained from InfoMedix (1-714-530-3454). Most agreed that no medium has yet to be shown consistently superior when the variables of novelty, content, and strategies are taken into account. However, many argued that this does not preclude the possibility that interactive multimedia might be found uniquely capable of incorporating sophisticated combinations of strategies (e.g., learner control, simulation, time compression, graphic representation, animation, prediction/confirmation, immediate feedback) that enable students to gain insights characteristic of the thinking of experts more readily than by alternative media and methods.

[3]Schramm, Wilbur, *Big Media, Little Media: Tools and Technologies for Instruction* (Beverly Hills, CA: Sage, 1978).

[4]More detailed analyses and models are found in Briggs, Leslie J., *et al.*, *Instructional Design: Principles and Applications*, 2nd rev. ed. (Englewood Cliffs, NJ: Educational Technology Publications, 1991); Dick, Walter, & Carey, Lou, *The Systematic Design of Instruction*, 3rd ed. (Glenview, Illinois: Scott, Foresman, 1990); Gagné, Robert M., *Principles of Instructional Design* (New York: Holt, Rinehart, and Winston, 1985); Gagné, Robert M., ed., *Instructional Technology: Foundations* (Hillsdale, NJ: Lawrence Erlbaum Associates, 1987); Kemp, Jerrold E., *The Instructional Design Process* (New York: Harper & Row, 1985); Reigeluth, Charles M., ed., *Instructional Theories in Action: Lessons Illustrating Selected Theories and Models* (Hillsdale, NJ: Lawrence Erlbaum Associates, 1987); Romiszowski, Alexander J., *Producing Instructional Systems: Lesson Planning for Individualized and Group Learning Activities* (London: Kogan Page, 1984); Edmonds, Gerald S., Branch, Robert C., & Mukherjee, Prachee, "A Conceptual Framework for Comparing Instructional Design Models," *Educational Technology Research and Development*, 42, 4(1994), pp. 55–72.

[5]Jonasson, David, ed., *Instructional Designs for Microcomputer Courseware* (Hillsdale, NJ: Lawrence Erlbaum Associates, 1988); Merrill, M. David, "Component Display Theory," in Reigeluth, Charles M., ed., *Instructional-Design Theories and Models: An Overview of Their Current Status* (Hillsdale, NJ: Lawrence Erlbaum Associates, 1983).

[6]Knirk, Frederick G., & Gustafson, Kent L., *Instructional Technology: A Systematic Approach to Education* (New York: Holt, Rinehart, and Winston, 1986); Reiser, Robert A., & Gagné, Robert M., *Selecting Media for Instruction* (Englewood Cliffs, NJ: Educational Technology Publications, 1983).

[7]Gustafson, Kent L., "Instructional Design Fundamentals: Clouds on the Horizon," *Educational Technology*, 33 (February 1993), p. 29.

[8]Martin, Barbara L., & Clemente, Rebecca, "Instructional Systems Design and Public Schools," *Educational Technology Research and Development*, 38, 2(1990), p. 74.

[9]Shrock, Sharon, & Higgins, Norman, "Instructional Systems Development in the Schools," *Educational Technology Research and Development*, 38, 3(1990), p. 79.

[10]Branch, Robert C., "Common Instructional Design Practices Employed by Secondary School Teachers," *Educational Technology*, 34 (March 1994), p. 28.

[11]Davidove, Eric A., & Reiser, Robert A., "Comparative Acceptability and Effectiveness of Teacher-Revised and Designer-Revised Instruction," *Educational Technology Research and Development*, 39, 2(1991), pp. 29–38.

[12]Jonassen, David H., Campbell, John P., & Davidson Mark E., "Learning *with* Media: Restructuring the Debate," *Educational Technology Research and Development*, 42, 2(1994), p. 31.

[13]*Ibid.*, p. 36.

[14]Bowers, C.A., *The Cultural Dimensions of Educational Computing: Understanding the Non-Neutrality of Technology* (New York: Teachers College Press, 1988); Eisner, Elliot W., *Educational Imagination: On the Design and Evaluation of School Programs*, 2nd ed. (New York: Macmillan, 1985); Postman, Neil, *Technopoly: The Surrender of Culture to Technology* (New York: Knopf, 1992).

[15]Hackbarth, Steven, "Instructional Systems Design: An Appropriate Technology for Developing Nations," *Programmed Learning and Educational Technology*, 22 (February 1985), pp. 35–38. See also Rowland, Gordon, "Instructional Design and Creativity: A Response to the Criticized," *Educational Technology*, 35 (September/October 1995), pp. 17–22.

Sources

Systematic approaches to improving instruction are covered in:

Anglin, Gary J., ed., *Instructional Technology: Past, Present, and Future*, 2nd ed. (Englewood, CO: Libraries Unlimited, 1995).

Banathy, Bela H., *Systems Design of Education: A Journey to Create the Future* (Englewood Cliffs, NJ: Educational Technology Publications, 1991).

Banathy, Bela H., *A Systems View of Education: Concepts and Principles for Effective Practice* (Englewood Cliffs, NJ: Educational Technology Publications, 1992).

Borich, Gary D., *Effective Teaching Methods* (New York: Macmillan, 1992).

Briggs, Leslie J., Gustafson, Kent L., & Tillman, Murray H., eds., *Instructional Design: Principles and Applications*, 2nd rev. ed. (Englewood Cliffs, NJ: Educational Technology Publications, 1991).

Dick, Walter, & Carey, Lou, *The Systematic Design of Instruction*, 3rd ed. (Glenview, IL: Scott, Foresman & Co., 1990).

Dills, Charles, & Romiszowski, Alexander J., eds., *Instructional Development Paradigms* (Englewood Cliffs, NJ: Educational Technology Publications, 1996).

Earl, Tony, *The Art and Craft of Course Design* (New York: Nichols, 1987).

Eisele, James E., & Eisele, Mary E., *Educational Technology: A Planning and Resource Guide Supporting Curriculum* (Hamden, CT: Garland Publishing, 1990).

Ely, Donald P., & Minor, Barbara B., *Educational Media and Technology Yearbook* (Englewood, CO: Libraries Unlimited, yearly).

Fleming, Malcolm, & Levie, W. Howard, eds., *Instructional Message Design: Principles from the Behavioral and Cognitive Sciences*, 2nd ed. (Englewood Cliffs, NJ: Educational Technology Publications, 1993).

Gagné, Robert M., Briggs, Leslie J., & Wager, Walter W., *Principles of Instructional Design*, 4th ed. (Fort Worth, TX: Harcourt Brace Jovanovich College Publishers, 1992).

Gentry, Castelle G., *Introduction to Instructional Development: Process and Technique* (Belmont, CA: Wadsworth, 1994).

Hoey, Ross, ed., *Designing for Learning: Effectiveness with Efficiency* (London: Kogan Page, 1994).

Hudspeth, Delayne, & Brey, Ronald G., *Instructional Telecommunications: Principles and Applications* (New York: Praeger, 1986).

Kaufman, Roger, Rojas, Alicia M., & Mayer, Hanna, *Needs Assessment: A User's Guide* (Englewood Cliffs, NJ: Educational Technology Publications, 1993).

Kemp, Jerrold E., *The Instructional Design Process* (New York: Harper & Row, 1985).

Kemp, Jerrold E., Morrison, Gary R., & Ross, Steven M., *Designing Effective Instruction* (New York: Merrill, 1994).

Knirk, Frederick G., & Gustafson, Kent L., *Instructional Technology: A Systematic Approach to Education* (New York: Holt, Rinehart, and Winston, 1986).

Lamb, Annette, & Johnson, Larry, *Technology and Change Cowboy Style* (Evansville, IN: Vision to Action, 1994).

Leshin, Cynthia, Pollock, Joellyn, & Reigeluth, Charles M., *Instructional Design Strategies and Tactics* (Englewood Cliffs, NJ: Educational Technology Publications, 1992).

Lyons, Paul, *Thirty-Five Lesson Formats: A Sourcebook of Instructional Alternatives* (Englewood Cliffs, NJ: Educational Technology Publications, 1992).

Merrill, M. David, edited by Twitchell, David G., *Instructional Design Theory* (Englewood Cliffs, NJ: Educational Technology Publications, 1994).

Merrill, M. David, Tennyson, Robert D., & Posey, Larry O., *Teaching Concepts: An Instructional Design Guide*, 2nd ed. (Englewood Cliffs, NJ: Educational Technology Publications, 1992).

Percival, Fred, & Ellington, Henry, *A Handbook of Educational Technology*, 2nd ed. (East Brunswick, NJ: Nichols, 1988).

Reigeluth, Charles M., ed., *Instructional Theories in Action: Lessons Illustrating Selected Theories and Models* (Hillsdale, NJ: Lawrence Erlbaum Associates, 1987).

Reigeluth, Charles M., & Garfinkel, Robert J., eds., *Systemic Change in Education* (Englewood Cliffs, NJ: Educational Technology Publications, 1994).

Reiser, Robert A., & Dick, Walter, *Instructional Planning: A Guide for Teachers*, 2nd ed. (Boston: Allyn & Bacon, 1996).

Reynolds, Angus, & Anderson, Ronald H., *Selecting and Developing Media for Instruction*, 3rd ed. (New York: Van Nostrand Reinhold, 1991).

Romiszowski, Alexander J., *Developing Auto-Instructional Materials* (East Brunswick, NJ: Nichols, 1986).

Romiszowski, Alexander J., *Producing Instructional Systems* (East Brunswick, NJ: Nichols, 1986).

Romiszowski, Alexander J., *Selection and Use of Instructional Media*, 2nd ed. (East Brunswick, NJ: Nichols, 1988).

Romiszowski, Alexander J. *et al., Case Studies in Instructional Design & Development* (Woodstock, NY: Beekman, 1990).

Rothwell, William J., & Kazanas, H.C., *Mastering the Instructional Design Process: A Systematic Approach* (San Francisco, Jossey-Bass, 1992).

Seels, Barbara B., ed., *Instructional Design Fundamentals: A Reconsideration* (Englewood Cliffs, NJ: Educational Technology Publications, 1995).

Smith, Patricia L., & Ragan, Tillman J., *Instructional Design* (New York: Merrill, 1993).

West, Charles K., Farmer Jr., James A., & Wolff, Phillip M., *Instructional Design: Implications from Cognitive Science* (Boston: Allyn and Bacon, 1991).

Study Items

1. What are the five phases of the instructional development model presented in this chapter? Briefly describe each.

2. Describe the four main components of an instructional objective written in the ABCD format. What value do you see in using this format?

3. Characterize the relation between instructional objectives and measures of their achievement. Provide an example of an objective and of a measure that would serve as valid evidence of its achievement.

4. What role might students have in setting their own objectives?

5. Distinguish between instructional strategies and media of instruction.

6. What are some advantages and limitations of media selection models? (See **Figure 2.10.**)

7. Specify several ways in which the instructional development model presented in this chapter incorporates generalizations about learning presented in the previous chapter.

8. What sorts of programs are easiest to adapt to your own needs? What kinds require great effort and expense to modify?

9. What does it mean to "integrate" an existing program into the larger school curriculum? Give an example of how you might do this.

10. What sorts of things would you expect to discover about a draft program when subjected to field testing?

11. Specify advantages and limitations of designing and producing instructional programs according to the procedures described in this chapter.

"I need software for laying out the blueprints of a brick house, and could you hurry?"

Figure 2.10. When we root instruction in students' lived worlds, learning is energized. Students come to feel a greater sense of responsibility for their inquiries, and ownership of their discoveries. For us to be effective facilitators in this dynamic process, we need to have previously assimilated ID and media selection models and inventoried readily available resources. Reproduced with permission of Andrew Toos.

12. Describe some alternative conceptions of instructional development.

13. How might the larger context in which students are situated affect what they learn from given instructional methods and media?

14. How would you adapt for your own use any one of the models presented in this chapter?

Suggested Activities

1. Draw a poster-sized model of the systematic approach to the development of instruction presented in this chapter. Add color and illustrations.

2. Write an instructional objective in the ABCD format for each of the three domains—cognitive, affective, psychomotor.

3. For each objective in #2 above, select instructional strategies and media that you believe would best ensure achievement.

4. Prepare a grid with instructional strategies across the top and media of instruction listed down the side. Note within the grid how each strategy might be incorporated into programs presented by each medium.

5. Prepare a grid with group size (or subject area, or student ability) across the top and media of instruction (or strategies) listed down the side. Make comments within the grid about what you believe would best serve to achieve any objective you specify.

6. Make an inventory of instructional materials and devices readily available to you at your school.

7. Go to the reference section in your college library and ask to see any publication listing mediated programs. Decide upon a topic of interest and list programs that you believe to be most suitable. Write to publishers to find out if they will provide information concerning proven effectiveness.

8. Design a simple, one-hour lesson on a subject of your choosing according to the steps presented in this chapter. Take special note of what your field test reveals and revise accordingly.

9. Interview several experienced teachers to learn the extent to which they use any measure of student learning to make revisions in their lessons for subsequent terms.

10. Check out some references cited above and prepare a critical essay.

11. Send your comments and study item responses to me at Internet: hackbarths@aol.com.

Chapter 3

Conduct of Instruction

Chapter Content and Objectives

Teaching is a complex enterprise. It involves both development and conduct of instructional programs. Evaluation and revision are essential elements of planning as well as of implementation. The previous chapter provided guidelines for the systematic development of instruction; the present chapter provides guidelines for the systematic, yet creative, conduct of instruction. After studying this chapter you should be able to:

- List and define the **four phases** of a systematic approach to the conduct of instruction—**prepare, perform, follow up, evaluate.**

- Perform the **12 steps** recommended to conduct an effective, efficient instructional program.

- Distinguish between **systemic analysis** and **systematic procedures.**

- Describe several valid, potent **generalizations about learning.**

- Express what might be meant by the integration of **cognitive** and **affective dimensions** of situated learning.

- Discuss relations between **media and learning.**

- Cite a variety of **source materials** that pertain to the conduct of instruction.

Teachers as Conductors of Instruction

There is an intimate link between the development and conduct of instructional programs. An essential part of the development process entails **incorporating what experience has shown to be the most effective strategies given specified objectives, students, and resources**. Hence, what I present here as guidelines for the conduct of instruction already should have served to structure its development. Indeed, an ambition of educational technologists historically has been to craft programs in which every aspect is prescribed. Such an "ideal" may require that the teacher be an automaton, perhaps even a clever, perceptive, and responsive automaton, operating in accordance with a set of procedures. This is the sense in which technologists have sought to make instructional programs "teacher proof."

There are many reasons why instructional programs may never be made entirely teacher-proof. Most obvious are that:

- teachers are not automatons,

- students are unpredictable,

- interactions between teachers and students present precious opportunities for mutual growth,

- learning entails construction of personally significant meaning and value, not just absorption of information, and

- aims of education always are much broader than the objectives of any particular lesson.

Rodney Earle (Brigham Young University) has expressed similar views in more eloquent terms:

> The scientific application of instructional theories cannot guarantee successful teaching or learning because the dynamic, ever-changing interaction of

people, ideas, objects, and events involved in the teaching-learning process tends to be complex and often unpredictable. A teacher must be sensitive to the particular situation and to those involved. A teacher must creatively apply the scientific techniques and principles to the specific circumstances. The human factors are the major variables. The integration of various elements of an instructional environment is a very personal process. This integration is the artistic companion of the science of instructional theory. The personal artistic involvement of the teacher gives the process life.[1]

Perhaps less obvious is that for any program to be successful, teachers must not only behave in certain ways, but also **must believe in what they are doing**. One sure way to gain their confidence is to involve them in the design of the programs they are to conduct. Another is to involve them in the continuing evaluation and revision of these programs. Merit pay alone is not enough! And **what applies to teachers applies to students as well**. They must be given ample opportunities to participate in selecting books, projects, and evaluation criteria. Only with such empowerment will participants gain the sense of **ownership** that ensures sustained attention, diligent effort, and authentic appropriation.

The primary reason that you and I need to know how best to conduct instruction is that educational technologists remain far from their dream of teacher-proof programs. We may select fine, systematically developed textbooks or series of films and computer software for use in a particular class. But it is **you and I**, in collaboration with our students, who must **integrate** the chosen medium and the material it presents into the larger school curriculum. Even if we are given specific instructions on how to proceed, **it is you and I who must have the intelligence, sensitivity, and will to do so**. (See **Figure 3.01**.)

The following step-by-step procedures for the conduct of instruction presume ability as well as wit and will. They can serve to guide:

- initial **design** of instructional programs,
- **integration** of existing programs into the larger curriculum,
- **revision** of materials, and
- timely **adjustments** in presentation.

However, they are no substitutes for being sensitive to the unique needs and capabilities of individual stu-

Figure 3.01. Even "proven" instructional programs must be **integrated** into the curriculum under conditions that may be both fluid and raw. A **systemic** analysis of your classroom situation would reveal an interplay of powerful forces, some of which are suggested here, from a white male perspective. How might African-American, Asian, Hispanic, and female perspectives differ? Source: *Phi Delta Kappan,* 74 (February 1993), p. 492. Reprinted courtesy of Joe Lee.

dents, nor should they interfere with pursuing unanticipated opportunities as they might arise. Without laboring the metaphor of our roles as conductors of instruction, surely we must orchestrate strategies and media within classroom contexts according to scripts (and whims) that take into account the multifaceted talents (including those needed to compensate for disabilities) of our students and the contexts in which they learn.

A Model for the Conduct of Instruction

The presentation of an instructional program may be divided into **four phases—prepare, perform, followup,** and **evaluate**. These are diagrammed in **Figure 3.02** and described below.

Phase I.　PREPARE
Step　1.　Review course components.
Step　2.　Practice presentation.
Step　3.　Procure equipment and materials.
Step　4.　Prepare facilities and personnel.
Phase II.　PERFORM
Step　5.　Provide orientation.
Step　6.　Present lesson.
Step　7.　Elicit responses.
Step　8.　Provide feedback.
Phase III.　FOLLOW-UP
Step　9.　Review and refine.
Step 10.　Expand on achievement.
Phase IV.　EVALUATE
Step 11.　Assess achievements.
Step 12.　Assess program.

Figure 3.02. A systematic/creative approach to the conduct of instruction.

Phase I. PREPARE

Step 1. Review course components. Note student characteristics you previously have assessed. Determine if you can group certain students for some activities and what special provisions may have to be made for others. Identify students who may serve as tutors. Examine course and lesson objectives to help you focus the day's activities on achieving them. Review assigned readings, lectures, audiotapes, films, etc. Note sections needing emphasis or deletion. Check the day's time/event schedule and modify as needed.

Step 2. Practice presentation. Record your planned presentation on audio- or videotape. Review the tape and ask: Do I speak in a monotone? Too rapidly? Too hesitantly? Do I use filler words (uh, um, you know)? Display distracting mannerisms? Am I an engaging speaker or a mere information provider? Do I successfully convey the import of my subject? Preview programs to be presented electronically. Rehearse your introductory comments, questions you expect to ask, and conclusions you want to reach.

Step 3. Procure equipment and materials. Obtain needed books, visuals, projectors, computers, and so on. Make sure that you have extra batteries, bulbs, fuses, paper, chalk, film, blank recording tapes, and diskettes.

Step 4. Prepare facilities and personnel. Arrange furniture consistent with type of presentation planned. Adjust windows, shades, and room temperature as needed. Set up and test equipment. Inform teaching assistants and student tutors what they are expected to do and when they are to do it. (See **Figure 3.03**.)

Phase II. PERFORM

Step 5. Provide orientation. Gain student attention, make necessary announcements, and distribute materials. Prompt students to recall information and skills learned previously that are relevant to current lesson. Inform them of the immediate objectives and how they relate to those of the course. Arouse interest with personal comments and probing questions. Demonstrate use of equipment, explain rules of conduct, and tell students how to obtain assistance. Ask for questions and comments.

Step 6. Present lesson. Provide students with an overview of subject matter to be covered. Define unfamiliar terms and ask leading questions. Present your subject matter with enthusiasm and sustain student attention by gestures, eye contact, and appropriate movement (e.g., towards center stage or near distracted students). Remain present during mediated presentations to ensure smooth operation and proper conduct.

Step 7. Elicit responses. Encourage students to brainstorm, engage in discussion, take notes, write summaries, draw semantic maps, and make critiques. Permit slow learners to express confusion without embarrassment, and advanced ones to share their insights. Interview individuals and administer examinations.

Step 8. Provide feedback. Be sure to inform students when they have demonstrated comprehension and help them correct misunderstandings. Reward both effort and achievement in relation to each student's capacity. (See **Figure 3.04**.)

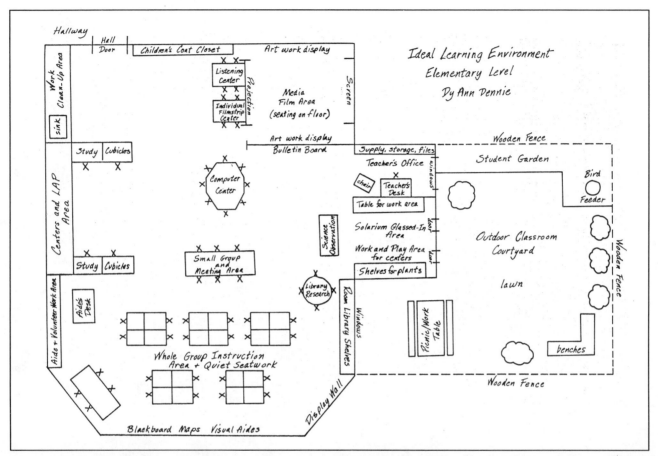

Figure 3.03. Effective conduct of instruction is facilitated by thoughtful arrangement of facilities, furniture, equipment, materials, and supplies. What aspects of this plan might you adapt for improvement of the classroom where you teach? Source: Arthur K. Ellis, *Teaching and Learning Elementary Social Studies,* 5th ed. (Boston: Allyn and Bacon, 1995), p. 351. Copyright © 1995 by Allyn and Bacon. Reprinted with permission.

Phase III. FOLLOW-UP

Step 9. Review and refine. Summarize the lesson and ask students for their reactions. Provide opportunities for applying new learnings to solve "real world" problems and for practicing newly acquired skills.

Step 10. Expand on achievement. Assign outside readings, projects, reports, and similar activities. Relate lesson to the larger curriculum, to the students' lives, and to the interests of the community.

Phase IV. EVALUATE

Step 11. Assess achievements. Administer tests to determine how well students achieved the lesson objectives. Where possible, draw on individual conferences and direct observations of behavior. Note if students learned something of value not covered in the objectives. Did they enjoy the experience? Were they bored? Challenged? Ask them to discuss with you or write in a journal about the quality of your teaching and the value of what they learned.

Step 12. Assess program. Note if the lesson went smoothly or if any parts were ineffective or tedious. Rate technical quality of materials used. Ask students what they found helpful and what they would change. Determine if the investments in time and resources resulted in sufficient gains in learning to justify continued refinement and use of the program.

Does following such a structured routine conflict with your preferred approach? Yes, I too have encountered the rhetoric that an effective teacher is a **"guide by the**

Figure 3.04. Once students complete an assignment, feedback and encouragement correct misunderstandings and energize continued effort. For these recent immigrants from Vietnam, much direct contact was essential. Other students may benefit nearly as well from written, audiotaped, or computer-mediated comments. Can you think of other ways to guide the learning of large groups of students with diverse backgrounds?

side," not a **"sage on the stage."** Like most either/or dichotomies, this one also is misleading. In my experiences and observations across grade levels, it has appeared to me that if we have not carefully prepared our instructional settings and lessons, if we do not assert our legitimate authority before the whole class, we will be granted by our students neither opportunities nor credibility to serve as their mentors. What has been your experience?

Generalizations About Learning

In the previously described **systematic** approaches to developing programs and conducting instruction, I referred to problems of learning. These problems arise for a variety of reasons that need to be identified and dealt with. The most obvious pertain to complexity of subject matter and the distractions of daily living. **Systemic** analyses of classroom situations and their contexts within society reveal related systems that interact to facilitate or interfere with productive learning.

Figure 3.05 is a rather cynical description of the context in which many students live today. Following are some generalizations about learning that can help us

Many American children wake up early and immediately turn on the TV. They go to school either hungry or filled with Sugar Smacks. For lunch it's Twinkies, chips, processed meat with butter and white bread. Be surprised they're not brain dead. Bart Simpson is a folk hero ("underachiever, and proud of it"), and going through the motions ("blowing it off") is the work ethic.

After school, kids pick up soda, chips, and candy and meet at the neighborhood latch key house where they can gorge and watch TV. Working parents bring home pizza and, following some accusations and denials, the family settles in before the TV.

"What did you learn in school today?" a few zealous parents may ask.

"Nuthin."

Adolescents have no interest in morning TV nor in breakfast. They are pushed out the door, arrive to school late, and sleep through their a.m. classes. Lunchtime permits off-campus rendezvous with fellow gang members for a smoke and a Coke. Conversations consist entirely of how to score (video game or date) and plans are made accordingly.

The afternoon for suburban youths is punctuated with gas-powered leaf blowers and motorcycle revs. Wired to their *Walkmans* or tuned to MTV, few read for pleasure, much less to enhance their school performance. For urban youths, auto alarms sound through the night as police sirens wail and helicopters hover. Fire trucks surround the complex putting out fires in trash chutes. Weekend days are passed at the beach or park soaking in ultraviolet rays. Nights are spent high and fast and too often ultra violent.

"Did you finish your homework?"

"Yeah, whatever."

According to the U.S. Department of Justice and the National Association of School Psychologists: *"Every day, 100,000 children [in the U.S.] take guns to school. Every day, 6,250 teachers are threatened and 260 are attacked. Every day, 14,000 young people are attacked on school property. Every day, 160,000 children miss school because of the fear of violence."* [Felicia R. Lee, "Disrespect Rules," *The New York Times* (4 April 1993), Section 4A: 16.]

Figure 3.05. A **systemic analysis** of the context in which your students are expected to learn may include some of the above in addition to the standard references to objectives, resources, and time constraints. How must we adapt our teaching strategies to be effective within such contexts?

capture our students' attention, sustain their interest, and ensure progress toward objectives, even under such difficult conditions.

a. **People learn best when they see value in what they study**. Successful teachers, textbook authors, and media script writers hold the key to revealing the value of subject matter. They do so by helping students to grasp knowledge both as an expression of human aspirations and as a means to achieving personally desired ends. Knowledge that makes sense out of experience and provides insights into natural phenomena and human relations is likely to be studied conscientiously, absorbed readily, and remembered long.

b. To a large extent, **students construct their own meanings** out of the subject matter to which we expose them. What they come to know depends as much on what they already believe to be true, as on what we present, how they have organized their beliefs ("schema"), and how they feel about themselves, us, other media, school, and life in general. These need be taken into account in the planning, implementation, and evaluation of instruction. (See **Figure 3.06**.)

c. **Individuals learn differently**. Some are slow to learn; others speed along. Students who have trouble following a lecture or are too shy to take part in discussions may excel when left alone with a workbook or computerized lesson. Those who lack self-discipline may need precise assignments and specific deadlines. Some thrive in collaborative learning environments, challenged to share what they know. Others take advantage of such situations, relying on others to complete assignments. Only monitoring and evaluation of **individuals** ensures that all stretch their capacities and thereby benefit "equally" from group activities.

d. **How students are taught influences what they learn**. If students are asked simply to memorize information, they may have difficulty applying it. Stressing phonics without reading for meaning may diminish interest in literature. Teaching to attain specified objectives from a single domain (e.g, cognitive) may impede achievement of objectives in other domains (e.g., affective). In fact, the domains of learning are intimately connected. The student learns, or should learn, content and techniques together with the attitudes and perspectives that go with them—physics and the experimental

Figure 3.06. Among the most fundamental concepts in philosophy is René Descartes' syllogism, *"Cogito ergo sum [thinking implies existence]."* Yet, as shown here, **students draw their own conclusions** based not simply on what and how we teach, but on what they already know and how they feel about themselves. How will you deal with the tension that exists between each student's unique perspective and the intersubjective validity of subject matter? Source: *Phi Delta Kappan,* 74 (May 1993), p. 673. Reprinted with permission of Luci Meighan.

method, for instance, together with greater respect for methodologies that minimize bias and the relatively "objective" knowledge thus derived. If students are given workbook and computerized instruction to do on their own, they might make tremendous progress, but at the expense of gaining social skills of cooperation and compromise so valuable in the home and workplace. (See **Figure 3.07**.)

e. **Participation is preferable to passive reception**. When students engage in class projects and discussion, they generally pay closer attention and are more ready to apply what they learn. Physical activities such as performing experiments and acting out roles may also improve learning. But the crucial element is **thinking**. Watching TV may seem more passive than producing TV programs, but **seeking** themes in TV presentations, **ana-**

Figure 3.07. Grouping of students to encourage **cooperative problem solving** (sometimes in **competition** with other groups—"**coopetition**") is a valuable and efficient technique. To ensure that students having diverse capabilities and interests contribute and benefit "equally," we may find it best to overtly monitor the performance and assess the products of each. Can you guess what sort of activity has these students so engaged?

lyzing character, **evaluating** style, and **anticipating** plot are more "active" in the ways that count than simply videotaping scripts.

f. **Information is learned best when well organized.** A story that proceeds chronologically is easier to absorb than one in which events are random. A textbook that first defines terms and possible outcomes usually makes a subject easier to master. A teacher who outlines material and asks pertinent questions before showing a film alerts students to what they are expected to learn and gives them a framework for doing so. Computer lessons that offer previews, permit fruitful exploration, and provide summaries and practice, capitalize on students' interest while keeping what they learn in the perspective of the course as a whole.

g. **"Time-on-task" is a crucial variable.** Along with effort expended, the amount of time spent actively engaged in study often determines how much a student learns. Hence, we (and mediated programs) should highlight important elements in a presentation and provide

explicit guidelines on how best to do assignments. Such guidelines should stress:

- what materials are needed,
- which sections are to be covered,
- what activities must be completed,
- what to do in case of difficulty, and
- when the assignment is due.

h. Learning is assisted by **"informative feedback."** Informative feedback is a response that you (or another medium) makes to student performance. It generally **reveals** to students whether they are making progress and **provides them with guidance** in doing so. It recognizes good performance, gives further suggestions, and corrects errors. Informative feedback not only affects what students learn but how they feel about that learning. (See **Figure 3.08**.)

i. **"Coopetition"** generally is superior to either competition among individuals or group collaboration alone. Cooperative problem solving and peer tutoring are powerful and efficient strategies in which gifted and slow alike benefit. Adding the element of friendly, **fair competition among teams** ignites motivation and enhances performance. Here we strive to ensure that our students' satisfaction comes from achieving excellence, not defeating others. And the means to that excellence serves as a model and inspiration for all.

j. **Extrinsic rewards often help**. A pat on the shoulder, an encouraging word, or even a gold star now and then may provide needed incentives when the value of subject matter is not readily apparent. Especially effective rewards are extra time to engage in favorite learning activities, like working on the computer, viewing a video, going to the library, or reading silently in the hallway. Prizes and certificates may be given to every student to acknowledge significant achievement, not just to the first and fastest. Purely token rewards, like points toward some goodies, should be used sparingly and for a short time to avoid drawing attention away from the true learning objectives. Token economies might be justified in some special education settings.

k. **Learning is "situated."** Students encounter challenges within the context of their lived worlds, yet which contain elements beyond their immediate grasp. Diverse

"You're getting warmer."

Figure 3.08. This drawing satirizes "informative feedback" provided by an uninspired teacher. To be effective, we must **diagnose errors, correct misunderstandings,** and **reward effort.** How would you handle this situation to ensure that the student adopts a more constructive strategy **and** preserves self esteem? Source: *Phi Delta Kappan,* 74 (January 1993), p. 385. Reprinted with permission of Martha Campbell.

contexts afford opportunities for making meaning out of experience, meaning that may be generalized to other contexts. To say that learning is "situated" is to acknowledge that what students learn is a product of complex and often unpredictable interactions between them and their environment as uniquely perceived, valued, and acted on. The environment extends far beyond the classroom walls, teachers, and peers to include also family, community resources, and constraints.

1. **"Anchored instruction" best ensures transfer.** Relating classroom activities to those that take place in the "real world" is a way to "recontextualize" subject matter that has been abstracted from the academic disciplines. This entails more than just having students wrestle with the big issues of our time and taking them on field trips to factories. It involves guiding them in the conduct of inquiry, what has been called "cognitive apprenticeship." Many and varied problem solving adventures closely connected with those that characterize productive activities in the world's workplaces vitalize learning and enhance competence.

Cognitive and Affective Integration Within Situated Learning

Children are actively engaged in exploration of the world long before they first enter the classroom. They continuously are seeking answers to their own questions in a quest to expand their own alternatives for action. Our first task as teachers is not so much to arouse this primordial curiosity (although at times this may be necessary) as it is to guide its probes of those aspects of the universe embodied in the curriculum.

A teacher who devotes much class time to informing students of the accepted facts and principles within each subject area might give them the stultifying impression that such knowledge is fixed and remote from their own experiences and from human concerns in general. If students are led to believe that all the truly significant knowledge can be found in textbooks, videos, and CD-ROM multimedia, and no longer is subject to modification based on further investigation or to interpretation from their own perspectives, they might not feel challenged to undertake explorations of their own. On the other hand, by collaborating with our students in discovery activities, we might successfully arouse them to investigate the world as embodied in the curriculum in the same high spirit of adventure with which they naturally seek answers to their own felt questions. The activities we prescribe will result in what is now commonly referred to as "authentic" learning to the extent that they are rooted in those questions that arise in students' quest to make sense of the context in which they perceive themselves to be situated.

Merely imitating the techniques of scholars and scientists is not enough. We must take special steps to ensure that our students grasp connections between their own experiences and the ways in which scholars and scientists eagerly approach their chosen endeavors. Questions of significance within a discipline must become connected with genuine questions in the mind of each student.

For some pupils, procedures of disciplined inquiry might come quite naturally. A minimum of explanation or demonstration might be sufficient to set them on productive paths. Others may benefit from "job aids" such as illustrations and checklists. For others, the most academically significant aspects of phenomena under study might currently exceed their grasp. While every student surely learns **something** as a consequence of active exploration, the dimension of importance within a given discipline might not be perceived by some. Academically pertinent aspects of a phenomenon might fail to stand out as "figures against a background" in the perceptual fields of those who lack adequate experiential and conceptual frameworks.

As teachers, we will be effective to the extent that we can draw upon our own past experience and current observations to accurately perceive what each student appears to be gaining from a lesson and then modify instruction accordingly. Only by observing individual students can we discover those patterns of behavior that signify either productive inquiry or frustration, aroused curiosity or apathy, and then make insightful, targeted interventions.

As students begin to display sufficient grasp of fruitful methods of inquiry and begin to draw seminal conclusions from their observations, they may be given ever more latitude in exploring on their own. Thus, they will experience how personal concerns may legitimately become subjects of disciplined inquiry. It is this experience of felt needs being satisfied through systematic inquiry that might be considered a "paradigm case" of the **"integration of cognitive and affective dimensions of situated learning."**[2]

Such immersion in discipline-based inquiry has become known in the field of educational technology as "cognitive apprenticeship," based on provocative articles by John Seely Brown, Allan Collins, and Paul Duguid and others. Drawing upon Alfred North Whitehead, John Dewey, and Lev Vygotsky, Brown *et al.* have suggested that: "To learn to use tools as practitioners use them, a student, like an apprentice, must enter that community and its culture."[3] Students, they added, "need to be exposed to the use of a domain's conceptual tools in authentic activity—to teachers acting as practitioners and using these tools in wrestling with problems of the world."[4]

The Cognition and Technology Group at Vanderbilt has related the concepts of situated learning and cognitive apprenticeship to its **"anchoring" of instruction** in videodisc-based, problem-solving environments (the *Jasper Woodbury Problem Solving Series, The Young Sherlock Program*) where:

> The major goal of anchored instruction is to overcome the inert knowledge problem [identified by Whitehead]. We attempt to do so by creating [rich, shared] environments that permit sustained exploration by students and teachers and enable them to understand the kinds of problems and opportunities that experts in various areas encounter and the knowledge that these experts use as tools. We also attempt to help students experience the value of exploring the same setting from multiple perspectives (e.g., as a scientist or historian).[5] (See **Figure 3.09**.)

Figure 3.09. This drawing illustrates well the long recognized tension that exists between abstracted subject matter and the contexts in which our students ultimately must function. By anchoring our instruction to real world tasks we can vitalize learning and better ensure transfer. How might you do so in your classroom right now? Source: *Teacher Magazine*, 6 (April 1995), p. 44. Reprinted with permission of Bob Dahm.

Nel Noddings (Stanford University) also has argued persuasively that traditional decontextualized, impersonal study of the liberal arts and sciences is based on "an outmoded and dangerous model. . . ." In addition to proposing alternative means of teaching, she has challenged our priorities. In her view, reflective of the emerging field of **feminist ethics**:

> Our society does not need to make its children first in the world in mathematics and science. It needs to care for its children—to reduce violence, to respect honest work of every kind, to reward excellence at every level, to ensure a place for every child and emerging adult in the economic and social world, to produce people who can care competently for their own families and contribute effectively to their communities.[6]

Noddings, writing in opposition to current emphases on national goals and assessments, proposed that "our main educational aim should be to encourage the growth of competent, caring, loving, and lovable people."[7] I can only agree, wholeheartedly. And, she added rightly, "Such an aim does not work against intellectual development or academic achievement. Rather, it supplies a firm foundation for both."[8]

What about **interdisciplinary learning**? Much has been made recently of making connections across the academic disciplines. After all, the world-as-experienced is not parsed into biology, history, mathematics, etc. In response to challenges from those who advocate doing away with specialized study in favor of a more holistic approach, Albert Shanker, President of the American Federation of Teachers, rightly noted that: "A discipline is not an arbitrary set of restrictions that keeps us from seeing the whole picture. It is an essential body of information, built up over the centuries, about how to explore a particular area of knowledge." He added that:

> Children are not born with disciplinary knowledge. They develop it as they learn what questions they can ask in history and math and science and literature, and how they can answer them. And the K–12 years are essential to this process. . . . It is then that teachers begin to help children learn that you don't look at the structure of a leaf using the same tools that you use to examine the structure of a poem about trees—even though both could be part of an interdisciplinary unit about nature.[9]

We shall return to this core theme when we explore interactive multimedia (Chapter **12**) and the information superhighway (Chapter **13**).

Media and Learning

Did you ever try to explain a complex process or concept to a passenger in your car? The tradeoff for having a captive audience is having to rely almost entirely on our voice to communicate. Here we have no paper and pencil handy to write related terms, outline steps, or draw diagrams. Our extemporaneous speech may be guided by conceptual schemes and mental images we have constructed over many years. However, our polite listeners must actively strive to interpret the flow of our words from their own perspectives, ones that differ in many respects from our own.

I recall attempting to explain (while driving) the conjugation of Spanish verbs. In my mind was the familiar two by three table (singular/plural; first person, second, third). However, with my hands on the steering wheel I was constrained to use only the medium of my voice. First I gave examples (*yo hablo, tu hablas*, etc.); then I described the endings common to regular verbs ending in *ar*. As I spoke, I visualized the two by three grid and, failing to communicate the concept of conjugation with mere examples, attempted to describe the grid itself. Still frustrated, I began finger painting the grid in the air. Like a construction engineer, I was attempting to provide a "scaffold" around my listener's present understanding of language that could be used to reshape that framework. Without visual representations, however, I found it difficult to communicate what I intended.

When my daughter began teaching me about declensions in the German language, she knew better than to rely upon her voice alone. Seated in a park near U.C. Irvine, following tennis, brunch, and an exchange of views on life, love, literature, and theology, Valerie proceeded to diagram cases (nominative, dative, etc.), person (first, second, third), singular/plural, and gender. She then provided examples with and without action verbs and had me recite those prepositions that take the accusative and those that take the dative. Perhaps I could have grasped the concepts without visual aids, but life is short.

Surely it is **possible** to communicate verbally the schemes by which we have organized bits and pieces of information that themselves have been embellished by our unique perspectives. Clerics, cocktail partygoers, and taxicab drivers do so routinely. However, generally speaking, it is more sure and efficient to employ textual symbols and graphic representations mediated by pencil and paper, if not by videos and computers.

Throughout this book are illustrations of how various media serve as vehicles for delivering the raw data out of which students construct personally significant meaning ("scaffolds" and "schema") within diverse, uniquely perceived and valued, contexts. As earlier noted, the instructional strategies long employed by teachers—providing structured content, asking and responding to questions, arousing curiosity, giving informative feedback—all have been incorporated into programs delivered by media ranging from books to computers.

As we enter the 21st century, opinion remains divided over the primary role of media in learning. One view, long ago introduced by Marshall McLuhan, is that the medium **is** the message. When we look at effects of media, per se, we may agree that specific content (comedy, news, weather, games, drama, terror) is less significant than changes in human relations brought about by reading, viewing, and playing. Yet the pervasive exploitation of sex and violence across media also surely has deleterious effects on society. Another view, expressed most cogently and persuasively by our colleague at the University of Southern California, Richard Clark, is that media are mere vehicles for delivering the goods of education. Thus, learning is affected by such variables as organization of content, match with student characteristics, and appropriate instructional strategies. Media only afford more or less expensive packaging. In Clark's words, "Media influence cost or speed (efficiency) of learning but methods are causal in learning."[10] Methods, claimed Clark, are what provide "cognitive processes . . . necessary for learning but which students can not or will not provide for themselves. [And] any necessary teaching method can be delivered to students by many media or a variety of mixtures of media attributes—with similar results."[11]

With the emergence of constructivist theory in education, rooted in Jean Piaget (and phenomenology in general), taken up by Seymour Papert (the inventor of *Logo* as a means of giving students control over computers rather than vice versa), and pursued actively in the context of videodisc and computer technologies by The Cognition and Technology Group at Vanderbilt University, discussion of the relationships between media and learning has been revived. All seem to agree that media are capable of presenting sounds and images in dramatic and moving ways. Beyond this, however, is the notion that computers in particular are uniquely capable of providing students with experiences instrumental in their grasping complex concepts and processes **in ways**

that characterize the mature, evolutionary thinking of experts. For example, the simultaneous display on a monitor of a beaker filled with water, a thermometer, and animated molecular activity as affected by students' manipulation of heat, pressure, and salinity, may present opportunities for students to make deeper sense of phenomena they previously had observed, but had not fully understood.[12]

Sharon Shrock (Southern Illinois University), among many others, made a strong case for the view that effects of media and methods are confounded. "If media attributes are uniquely capable of delivering a given effective instructional strategy," she claimed, "and no single strategy is required for learning, then media are as much an influence upon learning outcomes as the methods are. . . ."[13] Her case for the cost-effectiveness of high tech multimedia (e.g., *ThinkerTools*) is especially convincing.

> *ThinkerTools* may look similar to other treatments in terms of measurable outcomes, but expensive in terms of equipment and development costs. On the other hand, programs like *ThinkerTools* may result in more sophisticated and adequate schemata relevant to the solution of physics problems. And perhaps *ThinkerTools* is exceedingly cost-effective in creating cognitive schemata that resemble those of experts, when compared to whatever the experts had to endure to reach a similar understanding.[14]

Gary Morrison (Memphis State University), along with Clark and others, contested claims that research has conclusively supported the superiority of such programs as *ThinkerTools* and *The Jasper Woodbury Problem Solving Series* over alternative, equally creative methods. "One might ask," he wrote,

> what would have been the result if the instructor had taken the control [group] sixth-grade class to a billiard parlor and allowed them to conduct similar experiments [as those simulated in *ThinkerTools*]? Might the more concrete hands-on experience . . . produce the same effect? If similar results are obtained, are the results due to the medium or the strategy?[15]

Media differ in their capacities ("affordances") to incorporate the full range of instructional strategies. Books have cues and hooks and questions and answers. Computers adjust their presentations to student input, much like a human tutor. Beyond this, recording media preserve programs for editing, review, and widespread distribution. The emerging information superhighway is creating communities of like-minded cybersouls, and the technology of virtual reality is opening up new dimensions of experience. Clearly, media selection decisions will continue to rest both on efficiency in helping students achieve specified learning objectives as well as in providing opportunities for them to "go where no one has gone before" at any cost.

Summary and Conclusions

The essence of educational technology is revealed in its advocacy of **systematic, knowledge-based approaches to the improvement of programs whether they be presented by text or teacher, television or computer.** The guidelines I have provided for the development of programs and conduct of instruction are based on this conception of educational technology.

Admittedly, however, the improvement of instruction requires more than recipes. It requires teachers who are sensitive both to the needs and interests of students and to those of society. It requires parental as well as community support, human and material resources.

Systematic approaches to instruction are meant to assist teachers in **identifying student strengths and needs and in making the best use of available resources to draw upon those strengths to meet those needs.** They may be adapted for use in every subject and grade level and to achieve long-cherished objectives in every community. In the next chapter, I describe how this is done on a large scale.

Notes

[1]Earle, Rodney S., "Instructional Design and the Classroom Teacher: Looking Back and Moving Ahead, *Educational Technology*, 34 (March 1994), p. 7.

[2]Hackbarth, Steven L., "The Integration of Cognitive and Affective Dimensions of Learning from the Perspective of Merleau-Ponty's Philosophy," in Jelinek, James J., ed., *Philosophy of Education in Cultural Perspective* (Tempe, AZ: Far Western Philosophy of Education Society, 1977), pp. 481–496. This is a synopsis of my doctoral dissertation (UCLA, 1976) in which I drew upon the writings of the French phenomenologist Maurice Merleau-Ponty, in an effort to provide a coherent interpretation of what at the time was called "humanistic" or "confluent" education. It pertains directly to what today is called "situated learning," that each of us perceives and acts from the vantage points of our own unique perspectives within personally interpreted social contexts. See also Young, Michael F., "Instruc-

tional Design for Situated Learning," *Educational Technology Research and Development*, 41, 1(1994), pp. 43–58; and the March 1993 and the October 1994 issues of *Educational Technology* devoted to this topic.

[3]Brown, John Seely, Collins, Allan, & Duguid, Paul, "Situated Cognition and the Culture of Learning," *Educational Researcher*, 18 (January/February 1989), p. 33. See challenges and their reply in the May 1989 issue, and McLellan, Hilary, ed., *Situated Learning Perspectives* (Englewood Cliffs, NJ: Educational Technology Publications, 1996).

[4]*Ibid.*, p. 34.

[5]The Cognition and Technology Group at Vanderbilt, "Anchored Instruction and Its Relationship to Situated Cognition," *Educational Researcher*, 19 (August/September 1990), p. 3. See also their "Anchored Instruction and Situated Cognition Revisited," *Educational Technology*, 33 (March 1993), pp. 52–70; and Damarin, Suzanne K., "Schooling and Situated Learning: Travel or Tourism?" *Educational Technology*, 33 (March 1993), pp. 27–32.

[6]Noddings, Nel, "A Morally Defensible Mission for Schools in the 21st Century," *Phi Delta Kappan*, 76 (January 1995), p. 366.

[7]*Ibid.*

[8]*Ibid.*, p. 368. See also her *The Challenge to Care in Schools* (New York: Teachers College Press, 1992).

[9]Shanker, Albert, "The Power of Disciplinary Learning," *American Teacher*, 79 (April 1995), p. 5.

[10]Clark, Richard E., "Media Will Never Influence Learning," *Educational Technology Research and Development*, 42, 2(1994), p. 26.

[11]*Ibid.*, p. 27. Clark's responses to critics are in "Media and Method," *Educational Technology Research and Development*, 42, 3(1994), pp. 7–10.

[12]See the 1994 issues of *Educational Technology Research and Development* (volumes 2, 3, and 4) devoted to this topic. An audiotape of a special session at the 1995 meeting of the Association for Educational Communications and Technology in which Clark, Robert Kozma and others further clarified their views is available from InfoMedix (1-714-530-3454).

[13]Shrock, Sharon A., "The Media Influence Debate: Read the Fine Print, but Don't Lose Sight of the Big Picture," *Educational Technology Research and Development*, 42, 2(1994), p. 50.

[14]*Ibid.*

[15]Morrison, Gary R., "The Media Effects Question: 'Unresolvable' or Asking the Right Question," *Educational Technology Research and Development*, 42, 2(1994), p. 41.

Sources

Analyses of teaching and learning are found in:

Adams, Dennis M., Carlson, Helen, & Hamm, Mary E., *Cooperative Learning and Educational Media: Collaborating with Technology and Each Other* (Englewood Cliffs, NJ: Educational Technology Publications, 1990).

Adams, Dennis M., & Hamm, Mary E., *Cooperative Learning: Critical Thinking and Collaboration Across the Curriculum* (Springfield, IL: Charles C. Thomas, 1990).

Armstrong, Thomas, *Multiple Intelligences in the Classroom* (Alexandria, VA: Association for Supervision and Curriculum Development, 1994).

Bigelow, Bill, *et al., Rethinking Our Classrooms: Teaching for Equity and Justice* (Milwaukee: Rethinking Schools, 1994).

Bigge, Morris L., & Shermis, S. Samuel, *Learning Theories for Teachers,* 5th ed. (New York: HarperCollins, 1992).

Brien, Robert, & Eastmond, Nick, *Cognitive Science and Instruction* (Englewood Cliffs, NJ: Educational Technology Publications, 1994).

Chaiklin, Seth, & Lave, Jean, *Understanding Practice: Perspectives on Activity and Context* (Cambridge: Cambridge University Press, 1993).

Darling-Hammond, Linda, Wise, Arthur E., & Klein, Stephen P., *A License to Teach: Building a Profession for 21st Century Schools* (Boulder, CO: Westview Press, 1995).

Dewey, John, *Experience and Education* (New York: Collier Books, 1963, 1st published, 1938).

Dewey, John, *John Dewey on Education: Selected Writings* (Chicago: University of Chicago Press, 1964, 1974 printing).

Driscoll, Marcy Perkins, *Psychology of Learning for Instruction* (Boston: Allyn and Bacon, 1994).

Duffy, Thomas M., & Jonassen, David H., eds., *Constructivism and the Technology of Instruction: A Conversation* (Hillsdale, NJ: Lawrence Erlbaum Associates, 1992).

Duffy, Thomas, Lowyck, J., & Jonassen, David, eds., *Designing Environments for Constructivist Learning* (New York: Springer-Verlag, 1993).

Eisner, Elliot, *Cognition and Curriculum Reconsidered,* 2nd ed. (New York: Teachers College Press, Columbia University, 1994).

Freire, Paulo, *Pedagogy of the Oppressed* (New York: Continuum, 1985, ©1970).

Fry, Prem S., *Fostering Children's Cognitive Competence Through Mediated Learning Experiences: Frontiers and Futures* (Springfield, IL: Charles C. Thomas, 1992).

Gage, N.L., *Hard Gains in the Soft Sciences: The Case of Pedagogy* (Bloomington, IN: Phi Delta Kappa, 1986).

Gagné, Ellen D., Yekovich, Frank R., & Yekovich, Carol Walker, *The Cognitive Psychology of School Learning,* 2nd ed. (New York: HarperCollins, 1993).

Gagné, Robert M., *Studies of Learning: 50 Years of Research* (Tallahassee, FL: Florida State University, Learning Systems Institute, 1989).

Gagné, Robert M., & Driscoll, Marcy P., *Essentials of Learning for Instruction,* 2nd ed. (Boston: Allyn and Bacon, 1988).

Gardner, Howard, *Frames of Mind: The Theory of Multiple Intelligences* (New York: Basic Books, 1986).

Gardner, Howard, *The Unschooled Mind: How Children Think and How Schools Should Teach* (New York: Basic Books, 1991).

Gerstner, Louis V., Jr., *et al., Reinventing Education* (New York: Dutton Books, 1994).

Goodlad, John I., *A Place Called School: Prospects for the Future* (New York: McGraw-Hill, 1984).

Goodlad, John I., *Teachers for Our Nation's Schools* (San Francisco: Jossey-Bass, 1990).

Goodlad, John I., *What Schools Are For,* 2nd ed. (Bloomington, IN: Phi Delta Kappa, 1994).

Heidegger, Martin, edited by Krell, David Farrell, *Basic Writings* (New York: Harper & Row, 1977).

High Standards for All Students (Washington, DC: U.S. Department of Education, 1994).

Hirschfeld, Lawrence A., & Gelman, Susan A., eds., *Mapping the Mind: Domain Specificity in Cognition and Culture* (New York: Cambridge University Press, 1994).

Hohn, Robert L., *Classroom Learning and Teaching* (White Plains, NY: Longman, 1995).

Jagla, Virginia M., *Teachers' Everyday Use of Imagination and Intuition: In Pursuit of the Elusive Image* (Albany, NY: State University of New York Press, 1994).

James, William, *Talks to Teachers on Psychology: And to Students on Some of Life's Ideals* (New York: H. Holt and Company, 1906, new edition, 1938).

Johnson, David W., & Johnson, Roger T., *Learning Together and Alone: Cooperative, Competitive and Individualistic Learning,* 3rd ed. (Boston: Allyn and Bacon, 1991).

Jonassen, David H., *Mindtools for Schools* (New York: Macmillan, 1995).

Kauchak, Donald P., & Eggen, Paul D., *Learning and Teaching: Research-Based Methods,* 2nd ed. (Boston: Allyn and Bacon, 1993).

Kneller, George F., *Movements of Thought in Modern Education* (New York: Wiley, 1984).

Kneller, George F., *Educationists and Their Vanities* (San Francisco: Caddo Gap Press, 1994).

Kulman, Edward, *Agony in Education: The Importance of Struggle in the Process of Learning* (Westport, CT: Bergin & Garvey, 1994).

Lave, Jean, & Wenger, Etienne, *Situated Learning: Legitimate Peripheral Participation* (Cambridge: Cambridge University Press, 1991).

Mandinach, Ellen Beth, & Cline, Hugh F., *Classroom Dynamics: Implementing a Technology-Based Learning Environment* (Hillsdale, NJ: Lawrence Erlbaum Associates, 1993).

Martin, Barbara L., & Briggs, Leslie J., *Affective and Cognitive Domains: Integration for Instruction and Research* (Englewood Cliffs, NJ: Educational Technology Publications, 1986).

McLellan, H., ed., *Situated Learning Perspectives* (Englewood Cliffs, NJ: Educational Technology Publications, 1996).

Noddings, Nel, *The Challenge to Care in Schools* (New York: Teachers College Press, 1992).

Papert, Seymour, *Mindstorms* (New York: Basic Books, 1980).

Papert, Seymour, *The Children's Machine: Rethinking School in the Age of the Computer* (New York: Basic Books, 1993).

Papert, Seymour, & Harel, Idit, eds., *Constructionism* (Norwood, NJ: Ablex Publishing, 1991).

Pauly, Edward, *The Classroom Crucible: What Really Works, What Doesn't, and Why* (New York: Basic Books, 1991).

Phillips, Denis C., & Soltis, Jonas F., *Perspectives on Learning*, 2nd ed. (New York: Teachers College Press, 1991).

Piaget, Jean, *The Construction of Reality in the Child* (New York: Basic Books, 1954).

Piaget, Jean, *Genetic Epistemology* (New York: Columbia University Press, 1970).

Piaget, Jean, with Inhelder, Bärbel, *The Psychology of the Child* (New York: Basic Books, 1969).

Pressley, Michael, with McCormick, Christine, *Cognition, Teaching, and Assessment* (New York: HarperCollins, 1995).

Regian, J. Wesley, & Shute, Valerie J., eds., *Cognitive Approaches to Automated Instruction* (Hillsdale, NJ: Lawrence Erlbaum Associates, 1992).

Slavin, Robert E., *Cooperative Learning: Theory, Research, and Practice* (Boston: Allyn and Bacon, 1990).

Sleeter, Christine, & Grant, Carl, *Making Choices for Multicultural Education: Five Approaches to Race, Class, and Gender* (New York: Merrill, 1993).

Sizer, Theodore R., *Horace's School: Redesigning the American High School* (Boston: Houghton Mifflin, 1992).

Sotto, Eric, *When Teaching Becomes Learning: A Theory and Practice of Teaching* (London: Cassell, 1994).

Steffe, Leslie P., & Gale, Jerry, eds., *Constructivism in Education* (Hillsdale, NJ: Lawrence Erlbaum Associates, 1995).

Stevenson, Rosemary J., & Palmer, Joy, *Learning: Principles, Processes, and Practices* (London: Cassell, 1994).

Sugarman, Susan, *Piaget's Construction of the Child's Reality* (New York: Cambridge University Press, 1987).

Vygotsky, Lev S., *Mind in Society: The Development of Higher Psychological Processes* (Cambridge, MA: Harvard University Press, 1978)

Wade, Anne, Abrami, Philip C., Poulsen, Catherine, & Chambers, Bette, *Current Resources in Cooperative Learning* (Lanham, MD: University Press of America, 1995).

Wilhite, Stephen C., & Payne, David E., *Learning and Memory: The Basis of Behavior* (Boston: Allyn and Bacon, 1992).

Wilson, Brent G., ed., *Constructivist Learning Environments: Case Studies in Instructional Design* (Englewood Cliffs, NJ: Educational Technology Publications, 1996).

Study Items

1. Surely we are conductors of instruction. Are we also like conductors of trains and transformers of knowledge, conduits between the complex universe and the minds of our students?

2. In what sense does the model of instructional development presented in Chapter **2** presuppose the model of instructional conduct presented in this chapter?

3. Why is it unlikely that educational technologists ever will be able to design comprehensive curriculums that are entirely teacher-proof?

4. For what sorts of limited objectives might teacher-proof programs successfully be designed?

5. What are the four phases in the conduct of instruction model presented in this chapter? Briefly describe each.

6. What are some advantages and disadvantages of grouping students of similar ability? What are some advantages of mixed-ability groups?

7. What sorts of things would you expect to discover when viewing a videotape of a lesson you conducted without students present? What provisions would you have to make to record a lesson with students present? What would you expect to discover about your teaching given this added dimension?

8. List several ways of gaining students' attention. What techniques might you use to sustain that attention over the course of an hour just before lunch?

9. How would you handle a student who does not pay attention or one who is disruptive either by making distracting noises or by asking questions that do not pertain to the subject?

10. What would you ask your students to do while you are attempting to determine what has gone wrong with a piece of equipment? At what point would you abandon the planned lesson?

11. What are the benefits of eliciting student responses and providing timely feedback?

12. What is likely to occur if students practice a skill, but are not given both encouragement and corrective feedback?

13. What role does assignment of readings and projects beyond the classroom serve in efforts to integrate particular classroom lessons into the larger school curriculum?

14. In your view, how important is it that students enjoy the process of learning? Do you see this as an end in itself or as a means to ensure their cooperation?

15. State several techniques for keeping students actively engaged in, for example, an in-class report writing assignment.

16. How might adherence to the model of instructional conduct presented in this chapter improve your efforts to integrate a film or simulation game into a course you teach?

17. Would you characterize your approach to teaching as being a "guide by the side" or a "sage on the stage"? Critically evaluate my claim that we must be both.

18. List several of the generalizations about learning described in this chapter. Which three of these do you think most important? Why? Which three appear to you least pertinent to your teaching? Why?

19. In what senses might learning be considered "situated?"

20. Critique the conception of "integrated learning" presented in this chapter.

21. Propose your own conception of integrating cognitive and affective dimensions of learning.

22. Describe some probable relationships among media, methods, and learning.

Suggested Activities

1. Reread **Figure 3.05** and write a description from your own experience. Speculate how the situation may differ in other countries noted for high academic achievement.

2. Design a simple, one-hour lesson on a subject of your choosing based on the steps presented in this chapter.

3. Videotape your presentation of this or another short lesson and analyze your conduct in light of recommendations made in this chapter.

4. Visit several classroom sessions and note the extent to which the recommendations described in this chapter appear to be taken into account by the instructors.

5. A cost/benefit analysis entails assessment of what was learned and an estimate of per student cost. Assume that what a given group of students learned is represented by a score on a final exam. Estimate the per student cost of a given course (salary, materials, facilities) and calculate a ratio of benefit over cost for each student. Speculate on how you might rate different instructional strategies and media using this method, but note complexities and limitations.

6. Obtain some of the books cited above and make photocopies of their graphic models of learning for your own study. Obtain authors' and publishers' authorization for any other use of these copyrighted materials.

7. Contrast generalizations about learning made in any one of the above books with the ones presented in this chapter.

8. Write The Foundation Center, 79 Fifth Ave., New York, NY 10003 or telephone (1-800-424-9836; 1-212-620-4230) to obtain information about funding sources for your technology-based classroom projects. Also, check recent issues of *Classroom Connect, Instructor,* and *Multimedia Schools,* and obtain *How to Get Connected to the Internet: Facts and Funding* from Wentworth Worldwide Media (1-800-638-1639; 1-717-393-1000; Internet: connect@wentworth.com).

9. Contact local businesses to inquire about mutually beneficial funding assistance.

10. Explore other sources of funding on the education forums of commercial online services (e.g., America Online, CompuServe, eWorld, The Microsoft Network, Prodigy) and on the Internet.

11. Critically analyze this chapter and inform me at Internet: hackbarths@aol.com. Your suggestions will assist me in making revisions.

12. Send me your responses to the above study items. This will permit what educational technologists call **"learner verification,"** a key to progress.

Chapter 4

Large-Scale Instructional Development

Chapter Content and Objectives

In Chapter **2**, I defined instructional development (ID) as the procedural identification and analysis of problems entailed in the transmission of knowledge, attitudes, and skills, and the crafting of replicable, cost-effective solutions. I encouraged you creatively to apply ID in your own teaching and provided guidelines toward that end.

In this chapter, I describe how ID is conceived and, **to the extent feasible**, practiced by teams of specialists to develop individual courses as well as entire curriculums. Also, I suggest how we can, **and should**, participate from start to finish. Study of this chapter will enable you to:

- Outline the major steps entailed in the process of **systems engineering.**
- Sketch major components of exemplary ID models: **UCIDT, A. J. Romiszowski,** and **M. D. Merrill.**
- List **pros** and **cons** of ID.
- **Evaluate the potential** of ID to facilitate the development of comprehensive, integrated curricula.
- Describe **our role** in the ID process.
- Cite **source materials.**

Key Terms and Concepts

Instructional development (ID) is a **systematic process of identifying learning problems and crafting knowledge-based solutions.** It adapts methods of "**systems engineering**" to achieve these objectives. Systems engineering is the study of alternative solutions to specialized problems. A **problem** is defined as an unsatisfactory state of a system. A **system** consists of a network of interconnected parts functioning under various constraints to achieve specific ends.

Any aspect of reality, such as a school or a classroom, may be analyzed as a system. A typical classroom, for instance, consists of a teacher, students, subject matter, and instructional materials. The main purpose of such a system is to impart knowledge, skills, and values. Problems are analyzed within the context of the entire system and, very often, within related systems such as family, peers, and community. Solutions, in turn, affect the entire system, and their impact must be assessed to guide further intervention.

A model of systems engineering is given in **Figure 4.01**. The first step in the process is to define (or identify) an unsatisfactory state of affairs—in this case a river gorge is obstructing a projected travel route. In Step 2, engineers survey the terrain and otherwise "analyze the setting." Next (Step 3), a team of specialists is assigned duties and deadlines. One group of specialists identifies project objectives (Step 4); another determines the best means to achieve these objectives (Step 5). Small-scale prototypes are constructed (Step 6) and tested (Step 7). Results of the tests are analyzed (Step 8) and used to develop the final product (Step 9). The product, in turn, is evaluated to determine how well it has solved the original problem and, where necessary, refinements are made until a satisfactory level of performance is attained.

The engineering model of instruction first gained popularity in the late 1960s, and since then many types have emerged. However, all contain the same essential

Figure 4.01. The orderly manner in which engineers are said to work is reflected in models like the one shown here. What of value can teachers learn from such models? Reproduced courtesy of the University Consortium for Instructional Development and Technology (Kent L. Gustafson).

elements. They **identify a problem, develop a tentative solution, test it, evaluate results, make revisions, and try again.**[1] Noting that ID is a subset of design, Gordon Rowland (Ithaca College) described the process in these terms:

> Design is a disciplined inquiry engaged in for the purpose of creating some new thing of practical utility. It involves exploring an ill-defined situation, finding—as well as solving—a problem(s), and specifying ways to effect change. Design is carried out in numerous fields and will vary depending on the designer and on the type of thing that is designed. Designing requires a balance of reason and intuition, an impetus to act, and an ability to reflect on actions taken.[2]

Advocates of a systems development approach to instruction view the orderly, pragmatic style of the engineer as worthy of emulation by teachers. Like engineers faced with construction problems, teachers are portrayed as being confronted with problems of getting students to learn prescribed subject matter. Obviously, teachers today generally reject production line models of schooling and are placing ever greater emphasis on negotiating with students about what and how they learn. Thus, as

we examine models of ID, we need to think in terms of how we can draw upon their strengths while compensating for their shortcomings.

Toward this end of analyzing ID in its diverse contexts, Robert Branch (Syracuse University) provided us with a list of practices commonly associated with ID, and approximate translations in terms more familiar to teachers. In his chart (see **Figure 4.02**), what his team found to be characteristic of "teacher language" is in the left column. In the right column are corresponding activities expressed in what Branch called the "jargon of instructional design." As noted in Chapter **2**, use of terms more familiar to teachers in an inventory permitted more accurate assessment of the extent to which a sample of teachers incorporated ID practices into their own teaching.

Drawing upon such translations **may** enable us to interpret better the work of ID specialists. However, we must keep in mind that similarities in terminology may mask significant differences in meaning. Superficial correspondences found between teacher talk and ID jargon very well might not reflect contrasting views of knowledge, students, and teaching. For example, over a decade ago I presented a paper at a joint meeting of the Far

Teacher Language	ID Jargon
1. Determine goals based on the curriculum.	Conduct an instructional analysis.
2. Break down curriculum goals into learning tasks.	Conduct an instructional analysis.
3. Find out the backgrounds, abilities, needs and attitudes of your students.	Identify the characteristics of the intended audience.
4. Map out a guide for yourself which serves as a plan throughout the entire school term.	Generate a blueprint for each planned instructional episode.
5. Determine the characteristics of the content for the purpose of organizing the entire curriculum.	Present the content information as a knowledge structure.
6. Determine minimum skills that are required of the students in order to complete the lesson.	Specify requisite entry behaviors of the intended audience.
7. Discuss lesson objectives with department leaders.	Obtain the endorsement of the appropriate managers and administrators.
8. Discuss lesson plans with resource center personnel.	Confer with other instructional designers, instructional developers, and media specialists.
9. Discuss lesson objectives with other teachers.	Confer with other instructional designers, instructional developers, and media specialists.
10. Ensure the planned lesson will be appealing from the students' perspective.	Consider the overall appeal of any planned instructional episode.
11. Specify for myself what the students should be able to do at the end of each lesson.	Generate objectives that match each performance required of the learner.
12. Based on the lesson objectives, match teaching methods to those lesson objectives.	Employ instructional strategies based on pre-determined learning outcome.
13. Use teaching methods that are based on learning theory.	Plan information presentation methods based on predetermined learning outcome.
14. Select and sequence objectives that would be taught during a single lesson.	Sequence performance objectives.
15. Organize the content of each lesson around related themes of knowledge and skills.	Define instructional episodes by grouping related skills, subskills, and critical knowledge.
16. Make a checklist for selecting appropriate materials for each lesson.	Outline evaluation criteria for selecting instructional materials.

(continued on next page)

Figure 4.02. Robert Branch's chart (above) was derived by taking samples of teacher talk and then matching these with terms more commonly used by ID specialists. To what extent might the different contexts in which each professional operates affect the validity of translations? Source: Robert C. Branch, "Common Instructional Design Practices Employed by Secondary School Teachers," *Educational Technology,* 34 (March 1994), pp. 30–31. Reprinted courtesy of Educational Technology Publications.

Teacher Language	**ID Jargon**
17. Make sure lessons relate to each other.	Show the relationships between each instructional episode and the entire curriculum.
18. Make sure that lessons fit the entire curriculum.	Show the relationships between each instructional episode and the entire curriculum.
19. Make assessments during your lesson as a way to check your teaching strategies.	Determine formative evaluation activities and criteria for the entire instructional development process.
20. Make sure your teaching accommodates the range of abilities of each student.	Accommodate individual differences.
21. Contact resource persons who are experts on the subject matter of the lesson.	Initiate working relationships with content specialists.
22. Include motivating activities to grab attention.	Identify motivational information as an introduction to the instructional episode.
23. Organize efforts with other teachers in planning lessons.	Coordinate cooperative efforts during the design of instructional episodes.
24. Write test items to measure students' performance against a standard for each lesson objective.	Generate criterion-referenced test items to match each performance objective.

Western Philosophy of Education Society and the Comparative and International Education Society about how ID could be implemented as an appropriate technology for developing nations. I placed emphasis on local control and collaboration among all concerned. I was stung by the challenge from Evelina Orteza y Miranda (University of Calgary) that imposition of such a mechanistic model in itself might conflict with alternative, more vital perspectives of reality characteristic of non-Western societies. As we examine deceptively over-simplified models of ID, we need be aware of their underlying assumptions and how these might surface in value-laden, inter-human, culturally diverse contexts.

ID Models

Armed with the conceptual framework of ID and with the above list of typical components, it should be fairly easy now to interpret and evaluate some exemplary models. Presented below are three I found most appealing, a classic by the University Consortium for Instructional Development and Technology, a more context sensitive, dynamic one by Alexander Romiszowski, and another by M. David Merrill and associates that is billed as "second generation" (ID_2).

The UCIDT Model. The University Consortium for Instructional Development and Technology (UCIDT) was formed to advance the study and application of educational technology.[3] During the early 1970s, the Consortium drew upon teachers, administrators, and systems experts to produce the ID model depicted by the legendary Walter Wittich and Charles Schuller in **Figure 4.03**. This model consists of three stages: **definition**, **development**, and **evaluation**, divided into nine interrelated steps as follows.

Step 1. Identify Problem. The **"definition"** stage of ID involves identifying a problem, here defined as a gap between what is and what should be the case. More specifically, an instructional setting is examined to determine what students know and what they should know. If learning deficiencies are discovered, causes are identified and means of removing the deficiencies are

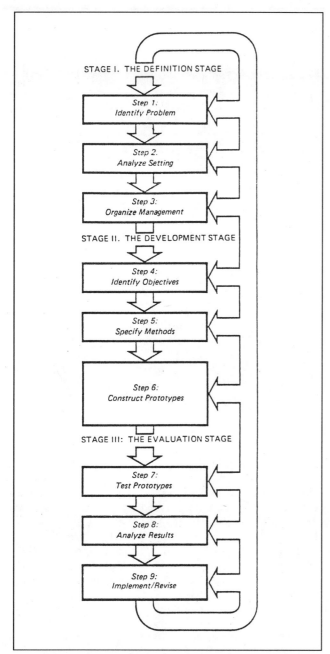

Figure 4.03. The UCIDT model of instructional development illustrates a time when school reform was seen to be much more straightforward than it is commonly perceived to be today. What has changed? Source: Walter A. Wittich & Charles F. Schuller, *Instructional Technology: Its Nature and Use*, 6th ed. (New York: Harper & Row, 1979), p. 310. Copyright © 1979 by Walter A. Wittich and Charles F. Schuller. Reprinted with permission of HarperCollins Publishers, Inc.

proposed. If it appears that the problem can be solved simply and economically, say by purchasing new textbooks or removing environmental distractions, such action might be taken. Otherwise, we proceed to Step 2.

Step 2. Analyze Setting. The instructional environment typically includes students, teachers, administrators, and material resources. Since students are the "target audience" of any proposed instructional program, their abilities and interests are taken into account. Also, because teachers and administrators are called on to implement any new program, their competencies and attitudes are assessed as well. And since any instructional program proposed must conform to limitations of time and resources, an accounting is made of available facilities, personnel, and funds.

Step 3. Organize Management. Next, project leaders specify areas of responsibility and establish lines of authority and communication. They also may detail timeliness and draft budgets for completing each phase of the project.

Step 4. Identify Objectives. The **"development"** stage of ID begins by identifying specific learning objectives that, if achieved, will solve the problem of deficiencies identified in Step 1. As you may recall from Chapter **2**, objectives state (a) what students (**audience),** (b) should be able to do (**behavior)** after completing the program, (c) under what **conditions** they will be expected to perform, and (d) the "passing" level (**degree)** of proficiency.

Step 5. Specify Methods. In general, the constraints of a given setting analyzed in Step 2 and the objectives identified in Step 4 dictate which methods and media should be employed. All options are considered: group activities and individual tutoring, live presentation and mediated, textbooks and tours, etc. In making selections, designers take into account elements such as proven effectiveness in similar circumstances, availability of equipment and programs, and costs.

Step 6. Construct Prototypes. Next, program components are obtained; lectures are drafted, film scripts written, examinations constructed, and specific guidelines are produced for conducting and evaluating the program.

Step 7. Test Prototypes. The **"evaluation"** stage begins by trying out each component of the program. A small sample of students is enlisted to read printed materials and observe mediated presentations. Student comments are solicited and assessments made of what they have learned.

Step 8. Analyze Results. Data collected in Step 7 determine which components of the program contributed significantly to the achievement of desired outcomes and which did not. Unexpected outcomes are categorized as either beneficial or not.

Step 9. Implement/Revise. Program adjustments might range from simply substituting a lecture for a film to reassessing the priority of certain instructional objectives. This return to earlier stages is represented in **Figure 4.03** by the "feedback loop."

The Romiszowski Model. A similar approach to the creation of instructional programs has been elaborated and advocated by Alexander J. Romiszowski, now at Syracuse University. The main stages of his model are **design**, **development**, and **dissemination**. The key objective is to determine how best to bridge the gap between "what is" and "what ought to be." (See **Figure 4.04.**)

In the **design** stage, as in the UCIDT "definition" stage, problems are identified and tentative solutions proposed. If a suggested program looks promising, a prototype is **developed**. (This corresponds with the "development" and "evaluation" stages of the UCIDT model up to the point of "implementation.") The program is produced for general **dissemination** ("implemented") only after repeated testing and revising leads to demonstrated effectiveness. Each stage within the model includes evaluation and revision, indicated by feedback loops, while the broken lines (in the Figure) represent less traveled paths to earlier stages.

Romiszowski's model has two distinguishing features. **First**, it provides guidelines for analyzing problems within the broadest context possible. For example, in the design stage Romiszowski asks such questions as: Why and how is the problem so perceived? Who perceives it differently? What other problems have been identified? Does a proposed solution have undesirable side effects? If so, is it worth pursuing? What about costs and outcomes? Who will pay? Who benefits? Romiszowski urges that these questions be answered early in the game in order to avoid waste and to set a project on its most promising path.[4]

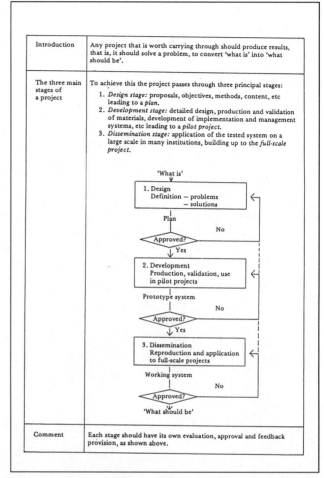

Figure 4.04. A. J. Romiszowski's ID model. Source: Alexander J. Romiszowski, "Troubleshooting in Educational Technology or, Why Projects Fail," *Programmed Learning and Educational Technology*, 18 (August 1981), p. 174. Also in his *Producing Instructional Systems: Lesson Planning for Individualized and Group Learning Activities* (East Brunswick, NJ: Nichols, 1984), p. 270. Reprinted with permission of Nichols Publishing Company.

A **second** distinguishing feature is Romiszowski's explicit portrayal of ID as a **heuristic technique**, not a recipe. "Step-by-step procedures," he maintains,

exist for certain activities (e.g., for task analysis) but these are only at the level of collecting or organizing information. What to do with the information is not governed by an immutable algorithm. Creative solutions pop up as sudden flashes of insight (and one then backtracks to check them out for viability) rather than as a result of plodding carefully and completely through each step in sequence.[5]

Others have expressed similar views. According to John Feldhusen, ". . . each new project is unique . . . . Thus, we must be prepared to use informal experience and intuition in solving design problems."[6] Even in the most rigid of training contexts, wrote Brian Atkins, the effectiveness of instructional development models "depends largely on the skill, intuition and experience of the trainer in operationalizing the models and his [or her] recognition of relevant problematic issues in any particular circumstance."[7]

Second Generation ID. Calls for flexibility, speed, and economy have stimulated interest in new breeds of ID. Noted ISD [instructional systems design] pioneer Walter Dick rightly claimed that:

> Perhaps the single most frequent criticism of ISD is that it simply takes too long to implement it. Cycle time—the time that elapses from identification of a need until the solution is implemented—may kill ISD unless it can be significantly reduced.[8]

The response of the typical practitioner has been to curtail or eliminate steps, especially field testing. More constructive responses have been made by Dave Merrill and his associates, Mark Jones and Zhongmin Li.

One innovation in Jones/Li/Merrill's "second generation instructional development" (ID₂) model is "to provide a more integrated approach . . . with greater interaction and more sharing of data [among] the steps."[9] A second feature is "rapid prototyping," the tentative production and testing of program components. A third is use of an "electronic performance support system" (EPSS) to automate some elements of the ID process.[10] The Jones/Li/Merrill ID₂ model is diagrammed and described in **Figure 4.05**.

The first four components of ID₂ entail a variety of interrelated design activities. "Knowledge analysis" involves collecting and refining subject matter content. "Audience/environment analysis" identifies student and context characteristics. "Strategy analysis" selects and sequences instructional transactions (e.g., exposition, examples, questioning, feedback). "Transaction configuration" involves "setting parameters for transactions to customize their behavior." To comprehend fully the detail and expertise represented in these four components would require extensive study of Merrill's work and involvement in a courseware project. My own study and appreciation of this work has made me hopeful of **genuine advances** in professionally produced instructional

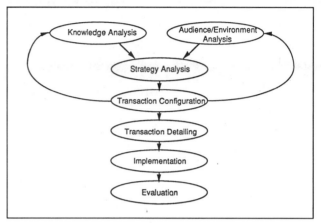

Figure 4.05. This "ID₂" model is distinctive in its portrayal of the first four (design) steps as highly interactive and of the fifth step, which entails "rapid prototyping" of program segments. Lacking is an explicit feedback loop from "evaluation" to revision of earlier stages, perhaps because this function is considered to be inherent from start to finish. Source: Mark K. Jones, Zhongmin Li, & M. David Merrill, "Rapid Prototyping in Automated Instructional Design," *Educational Technology Research and Development,* 40, 4(1992), p. 99. Copyright © 1992 AECT.

programs. Also, advances in development of EPSSs put this expertise into our hands.

"Transaction detailing" is the refinement of units of instruction—graphics, video footage, text, voice as required by content, strategies, and distribution requirements. Use of mockups, drafts, existing visuals during this phase is called "rapid prototyping." "Implementation" and "evaluation" refer to "delivery" and "assessment" of the program. Continuous feedback and revision are implied from start to finish.

Although the steps of ID₂ generally parallel those of traditional ISD models, the authors claim substantial differences in products and in interaction among steps as follows:

> The products developed in the early phases (domain knowledge base, transaction instances) are precisely those products that will be carried all the way through the development cycle, including the delivery of instruction if it is computer-based. This is in sharp contrast to the progression of abstract intermediate products, translated one into the other, that is seen in ISD. These products, and the concrete feedback they provide early in the development process as a result of the rapid prototyping approach they support, are the key differences between ID₂ and ISD.[11]

Evaluation of ID

Instructional development long ago was credited with serving as the "intellectual underpinning" of many success stories worldwide.[12] However, subsequent research has found that even among ID specialists:

> The notion of gaining "complete" problem understanding before trying to solve [it]—something implied in most ID models—was contradicted by the almost immediate consideration of solutions . . . . Use of instructional-design principles was not evident, and adherence to a formal plan (e.g., a sequence of steps to be taken) was not observed.[13]

According to Kent Gustafson, past President of the Association for Educational Communications and Technology:

> The combination of knowledge and tools, derived from both theory and practice, has served the field well in those settings in which it has been most extensively applied: business and industry training and proprietary vocational skills training. However, ID has not met with any significant degree of success in K–12 education, and only modest applications have been made in higher education in the United States.[14]

What **can we claim** with assurance about the value of ID? Used as a **heuristic technique**, we know that ID serves to remind and encourage teachers to:

- state their objectives clearly,
- break content into manageable units,
- account for student abilities and interests,
- choose methods and media according to their demonstrated merit,
- assess student achievement, and
- make revisions in light of results.

Large-scale ID brings together teams of specialists to examine educational needs and to produce instructional programs of considerable magnitude and precision.

Are systematically developed programs more effective than their conventional counterparts? Evidence **suggests** that they may be. They tend to produce more learning in less time and are better liked by most students. Furthermore, the success of development projects in diverse settings has been found to correlate positively with the extent to which ID models have guided planning and implementation.[15]

However, these findings need interpretation. We know that comparisons between conventional and innovative teaching are strongly influenced by at least two factors—program **preparation** and **novelty**. As a rule, innovations generate enthusiasm among teachers and students alike. However, long-term studies reveal that once the novelty has worn off, teachers and administrators themselves become disenchanted. Their disenchantment is reflected in the test scores of students new to the program—**those for whom novelty tends to enhance motivation**—that tend to be lower than those of students who participated when the innovation was first introduced.[16]

Then, too, we should be aware that innovations usually are designed to compete with whatever occurs in conventional classrooms, whether this is an uninspired lecture or an obsolete text. Research suggests that **when conventional and innovative lessons are given the same attention and presented with the same enthusiasm, they are equally effective**. Also, differences tend to disappear when teachers who assisted in developing ID courses employ similar techniques to revamp the conventional classes with which they were compared.[17]

Research has not yet consistently supported selection of one ID model over the other. Nor have specific key elements been identified. To ensure that future research is more fruitful, Richard Clark urges that it: (a) involve much deeper levels of conceptualization, (b) draw more thoroughly upon current findings and insights from related disciplines, and (c) consider separately the stages of design and implementation.[18] As discussed in Chapter **2**, Kent Gustafson and others call for entirely new models more suited to the realities of teaching in public schools.[19]

The greatest challenges to systematic instructional development are rooted in the debates held long ago between B. F. Skinner (*Walden Two*) and Carl Rogers (*Freedom to Learn*). During the past few decades, while behaviorism and cognitive psychology held sway over teacher training institutions and state legislatures, such leaders as George Kneller (*Movements of Thought in Modern Education*), Maxine Greene (*Teacher as Stranger*) and Elliot Eisner (*Educational Imagination: On the Design and Evaluation of School Programs*) held out for students' need and right to appropriate knowledge in their own ways. A new breed of "constructivist" thinkers has taken up this call. Their admonition to instructional designers is to:

turn from structuring instruction to designing environments which are characterized by rich contexts, authentic tasks, collaboration for the development and evaluation of multiple perspectives, an abundance of tools to enhance communication and access to real-world examples and problems, reflective thinking, modeling of problem solving by experts in the content domain, and apprenticeship mentoring relationships to guide learning.[20]

Seymour Papert coined the term "constructionism" to refer to his application of a constructivist view of learning as a result of making of what he calls "sharable" objects. He contrasts this with "instructionism," a view of learning as the relatively passive acquisition of prescribed subject matter. Consistent with his *Logo* philosophy, Papert argues for empowering students to **create meaning** rather than merely receive it.[21]

In response to challenges from constructivists, David Merrill countered that there is **no inherent contradiction** between their view of learning and systematic instructional development based largely on prespecified objectives. It is only if one takes the extreme position that no objectives can or should be prespecified and that all learning outcomes are distinct for each student and unpredictable that ID could be seen as an entirely futile, anti-human enterprise.[22] Such conditions, I believe, may hold in the context of nondirective psychotherapy, but much less so in public schooling with its vested interest in a common, multi-ethnic culture.

Thomas Dunn further advanced the cause of reconciliation between ISD specialists and constructivists. He urged that "We need to find ways to live with the unavoidable tension that exists between those who advocate and respect the individual construction of knowledge and those who see that some preplanning [and] standard setting [are] necessary. While it may be true that students construct meaning, this does not make it illogical to expect that in many instructional situations there [is] a considerable amount of shared understanding. . . . [Thus,] Good constructivist teaching and good ISD may not be that far apart."[23]

Resolution of these issues will not come easy, and challenges continue to mount. The work of Nel Noddings earlier described (Chapter **3**) has been taken up by such thoughtful critics as Suzanne Damarin (The Ohio State University), who wrote that:

At its most extreme, instructional design is clearly anti-ethical in that it denies the voice of "the learner" in the determination of the learner's need. Analyzing the learner through abstract systems whose relation to the needs of the learner are theoretical rather than experientially concrete, "ideal systems" proscribe treatments which work by colonizing the minds of learners. Even the positioning of the real live student as the "learner" denies the autonomy and intentionality of the person, and imposes upon him or her the needs of the designer. . . . Within the context of an ethic of care, we ask, then, whether ISD . . . can escape this anti-ethical position. It seems to me that the answer is "Maybe, and only with great effort." [24]

For Damarin, that great effort entails "the design of methods, models, and materials which can serve as resources for teacher and student as each pursues the continuation of the caring relation with each other and the student's caring relation with the subject matter of instruction."[25] The message for today's large-scale instructional designers—**don't even think about teacher-proofing it!**

Surely, we all wish the best for our students and have some notions of what that might be for each. Many of these notions are derived from our interactions with students themselves, not just curriculum guides. Furthermore, we all have insights into what sorts of activities foster child development, we know how to assess their effectiveness, and we are prepared to make adjustments in response to students' performances and preferences. We know the differences between being ready and being rigid. In the context of schooling especially, contrasted with training, we have long thought in terms of what is best for each student, not in terms of getting all to learn the same sets of prescribed subject matter.

Summary and Conclusions

Instructional development models serve to remind us to continue doing what experience has shown to be good pedagogy—setting explicit objectives, carefully observing progress, providing corrective feedback, encouraging students to stretch their powers, and making adjustments in presentation as needed. ID challenges us to do all this in more structured fashion.

Unfortunately, too few teachers have either the time or resources needed for the sorts of systematic instructional development described in this chapter, much less that outlined in Chapter **2**. We are constrained by excessive enrollments, administrative paperwork, and shortages of many kinds. We rightly are being encouraged to pay ever greater attention to providing rich environments in which students may construct personally significant interpretations of subject matter. We are expected to engage in more one-on-one "authentic" assessment of each student's unique development.

Moreover, few of us receive adequate training and practice in applying ID principles. State-mandated courses in media applications and computer literacy are dominated by guidelines for selection, production, and utilization to the neglect of **processes by which mediated programs may be integrated into existing curriculums and by which entire curriculums can be systematically improved**. This textbook has evolved in response to demands within the profession of educational technology for greater emphasis on such processes.

Like any new, promising technique, ID must become an essential element in the preparation of both teachers and administrators before it can take its proper place in the classroom. And **incentives** need be offered to ensure the high level of out-of-classroom work and long term commitment required for success.

In Chapter **5** we will explore the marriage of ID and computer technology, a union that has produced "integrated learning systems."

Notes

[1]Logan, Robert S., *Instructional Systems Development: An International View of Theory and Practice* (New York: Academic, 1982), pp. 3–5; Gustafson, Kent L., *Survey of Instructional Development Models*, 2nd ed. (Syracuse, NY: ERIC Clearinghouse on Information Resources, Syracuse University, 1991); Reigeluth, Charles M., ed., *Instructional-Design Theories and Models: An Overview of Their Current Status* (Hillsdale, NJ: Lawrence Erlbaum Associates, 1983); Branch, Robert C., "Common Instructional Design Practices Employed by Secondary School Teachers," *Educational Technology*, 34 (March 1994), pp. 25–34.

[2]Rowland, Gordon, "Designing and Instructional Design," *Educational Technology Research and Development*, 41, 1(1993), p. 80.

[3]At its inception in 1965, the Consortium consisted of Michigan State University, Syracuse University, the United States International University, and the University of Southern California. It later was joined by Indiana University (1971), Florida State University (1978), Arizona State University (1982), and the University of Georgia (1984).

[4]Romiszowski, Alexander J., "Troubleshooting in Educational Technology or, Why Projects Fail," *Programmed Learning and Educational Technology*, 18 (August 1981), pp. 168–189; *Designing Instructional Systems: Decision Making in Course Planning and Curriculum Design* (London: Kogan Page, 1981); *New Technologies in Education and Training* (East Brunswick, NJ: Nichols, 1993).

[5]"Troubleshooting in Educational Technology," p. 171.

[6]Feldhusen, John F., "Instructional Technology and Innovation in Higher Education," *Educational Technology*, 20 (February 1980), p. 57.

[7]Atkins, Brian, "To What Extent Is a Systems Model Appropriate to the Diagnosis of Training Needs and the Conduct of Training in Organizations?" *Programmed Learning and Educational Technology*, 20 (November 1983), p. 250.

[8]Dick, Walter, "Enhanced ISD: A Response to Changing Environments for Learning and Performance," *Educational Technology*, 33 (February 1993), p. 14.

[9]Jones, Mark K., Li, Zhongmin, & Merrill, M. David, "Rapid Prototyping in Automated Instructional Design," *Educational Technology Research and Development*, 40, 4(1992), p. 100.

[10]Li, Zhongmin, & Merrill, M. David, "ID Expert 2.0: Design Theory and Process," *Educational Technology Research and Development*, 39, 2(1991), pp. 53–69.

[11]Jones, Li, Merrill, pp. 99–100.

[12]Block, Clifford, "Matching Educational Needs with Available Technology: What Is Happening in the Rest of the World?" in *Technology and Education: Policy, Implementation, Evaluation, Proceedings of the National Conference on Technology and Education, January 26–28, 1981* (Washington, DC: Institute for Educational Leadership, 1981), p. 72.

[13]Rowland, Gordon, "Designing and Instructional Design," *Educational Technology Research and Development*, 41, 1(1993), p. 90. See also Wedman, John, & Tessmer, Martin, "Instructional Designers' Decisions and Priorities: A Survey of Design Practice," *Performance Improvement Quarterly*, 6, 2(1993), pp. 43–57. Less than one-third of those surveyed had conducted tryouts of the programs they otherwise had developed systematically. **I believe that teachers may have an advantage here over relatively transient training consultants. They have long-term, vested interests in making cumulative improvements in their instruction.**

[14]Gustafson, Kent L., "Instructional Design Fundamentals: Clouds on the Horizon," *Educational Technology*, 33 (February 1993), p. 28.

[15]Kulik, James A., Kulik, Chen-Lin C., & Cohen, Peter A., "Effectiveness of Computer-based College Teaching: A Meta-analysis of Findings," *Review of Educational Research*, 50 (Winter 1980), pp. 525–544; Dijkstra, S., *et al.*, *Research on Instruction: Design and Effects* (Englewood Cliffs, NJ: Educational Technology Publications, 1990).

[16]Romiszowski, Alexander J., "What's Happening to Individualized Mathematics?" *Programmed Learning and Educational Technology*, 16 (May 1979), pp. 148–149; Clark, Richard E., "Reconsidering Research on Learning from Media," *Review of Educational Research*, 53 (Winter 1983), pp. 445–459.

[17]Kulik, *et al.,* p. 539: "Outlining objectives, constructing lessons, and preparing evaluation materials (requirements in both computer-based and personalized instruction) may help teachers do a good job on their conventional teaching assignments."

[18]Clark, Richard E., "Current Progress and Future Directions for Research in Instructional Technology," *Educational Technology Research and Development,* 37, 1(1989), pp. 57–66.

[19]Martin, Barbara L., & Clemente, Rebecca, "Instructional Systems Design and Public Schools," *Educational Technology Research and Development,* 38, 2(1990), pp. 61–75; Shrock, Sharon, & Higgins, Norman, "Instructional Systems Development in the Schools," *Educational Technology Research and Development,* 38, 3(1990), pp. 77–80.

[20]Duffy, Thomas M., & Bednar, Anne K., "Attempting to Come to Grips with Alternative Perspectives," in Duffy, Thomas M., & Jonassen, David H., eds., *Constructivism and the Technology of Instruction: A Conversation* (Hillsdale, NJ: Lawrence Erlbaum Associates, 1992), p. 132. See also, Hlynka, Denis, & Belland, John C., eds., *Paradigms Regained: The Uses of Illuminative, Semiotic and Postmodern Criticism as Modes of Inquiry in Educational Technology* (Englewood Cliffs, NJ: Educational Technology Publications, 1991); Hannafin, Michael J., "Emerging Technologies, ISD, and Learning Environments: Critical Perspectives," *Educational Technology Research and Development,* 40, 1(1992), pp. 49–63; Richey, Rita C., "Instructional Design Theory and a Changing Field," *Educational Technology,* 33 (February 1993), pp. 16–21; Tripp, Steven D., "Theories, Traditions, and Situated Learning," *Educational Technology,* 33 (March 1993), pp. 71–77; Wager, Walter W., "Instructional Systems Fundamentals: Pressures to Change," *Educational Technology,* 33 (February 1993), pp. 8–12; Winn, William, "Instructional Design and Situated Learning: Paradox or Partnership?" *Educational Technology,* 33 (March 1993), pp. 16–21.

[21]Harel, Idit, & Papert, Seymour, eds., *Constructionism* (Norwood, NJ: Ablex Publishing, 1991).

[22]Merrill, M. David, "Constructivism and Instructional Design," in Duffy & Jonassen, eds., *Constructivism,* pp. 99–114.

[23]Dunn, Thomas G., "If We Can't Contextualize It, Should We Teach It?" *Educational Technology Research and Development,* 42, 3(1994), p. 91.

[24]Damarin, Suzanne K., "Equity, Caring, and Beyond: Can Feminist Ethics Inform Educational Technology? *Educational Technology,* 34 (February 1994), p. 37.

[25]*Ibid.,* p. 38.

Sources

Guidelines for systemic and systematic changes in schooling are found in:

Banathy, Bela H., *Systems Design of Education: A Journey to Create the Future* (Englewood Cliffs, NJ: Educational Technology Publications, 1991).

Banathy, Bela H., A *Systems View of Education: Concepts and Principles for Effective Practice* (Englewood Cliffs, NJ: Educational Technology Publications, 1992).

Briggs, Leslie J., Gustafson, Kent L., & Tillman, Murray H., eds., *Instructional Design: Principles and Applications,* 2nd rev. ed. (Englewood Cliffs, NJ: Educational Technology Publications, 1991).

Brody, Philip J., *Technology Planning and Management Handbook: A Guide for School District Educational Technology Leaders* (Englewood Cliffs, NJ: Educational Technology Publications, 1995).

Byrum, David C., *Instructional Technology Laboratory Manual: An Introduction to the Technologies of Instruction* (Dubuque, IA: Kendall/Hunt, 1991).

Castaldi, Basil, *Educational Facilities: Planning, Modernization, and Management,* 3rd ed. (Newton, MA: Longwood Division, Allyn & Bacon, 1987).

Eisele, James E., & Eisele, Mary E., *Educational Technology: A Planning and Resource Guide Supporting Curriculum* (Hamden, CT: Garland Publishing, 1990).

Eisner, Elliot W., *Educational Imagination: On the Design and Evaluation of School Programs,* 2nd ed. (New York: Macmillan, 1985).

Fleming, Malcolm, & Levie, W. Howard, eds., *Instructional Message Design: Principles from the Behavioral and Cognitive Sciences,* 2nd. ed. (Englewood Cliffs, NJ: Educational Technology Publications, 1993).

Gallini, Joan K., & Gredler, Margaret E., *Instructional Design for Computers: Cognitive Applications in BASIC and Logo* (Glenview, IL: Scott, Foresman, 1989).

Gagné, Robert M., Briggs, Leslie J., & Wager, Walter W., *Principles of Instructional Design,* 4th ed. (Fort Worth, TX: Harcourt Brace Jovanovich College Publishers, 1992).

Goodlad, John I., *What Schools Are For,* 2nd ed. (Bloomington, IN: Phi Delta Kappa, 1994).

Greer, Michael, *ID Project Management: Tools and Techniques for Instructional Designers and Developers* (Englewood Cliffs, NJ: Educational Technology Publications, 1992).

Hannum, Wallace J., & Hansen, Carol, *Instructional Systems Development in Large Organizations* (Englewood Cliffs, NJ: Educational Technology Publications, 1989).

Havelock, Ronald G., with Zlotolow, Steve, *The Change Agent's Guide,* 2nd ed. (Englewood Cliffs, NJ: Educational Technology Publications, 1995).

Hennesey, David E., & Hennesey, Mildred J., *Instructional Systems Development* (Frederiksted, VI: Harris & Connor, 1989).

Johnson, Kerry A., & Foa, Lin J., *Instructional Design: New Alternatives for Effective Education and Training* (Washington, DC: American Council on Education, 1989).

Kearsley, Greg, & Lynch, William, eds., *Educational Technology: Leadership Perspectives* (Englewood Cliffs, NJ: Educational Technology Publications, 1994).

Kemp, Jerrold E., *A School Changes* (Washington, DC: Association for Educational Communications and Technology, 1995).

Knirk, Frederick G., *Instructional Facilities for the Information Age* (Syracuse, NY: ERIC Clearinghouse, 1987).

Knirk, Frederick G., & Gustafson, Kent L., *Instructional Technology: A Systematic Approach to Education* (New York: Holt, Rinehart, and Winston, 1986).

Leshin, Cynthia, Pollock, Joellyn, & Reigeluth, Charles M., *Instructional Design Strategies and Tactics* (Englewood Cliffs, NJ: Educational Technology Publications, 1992).

Lyons, Paul, *Thirty-Five Lesson Formats: A Sourcebook of Instructional Alternatives* (Englewood Cliffs, NJ: Educational Technology Publications, 1992).

Merrill, M. David, edited by Twitchell, David G., *Instructional Design Theory* (Englewood Cliffs, NJ: Educational Technology Publications, 1994).

Merrill, M. David, Tennyson, Robert D., & Posey, Larry O., *Teaching Concepts: An Instructional Design Guide*, 2nd ed. (Englewood Cliffs, NJ: Educational Technology Publications, 1992).

Reigeluth, Charles M., ed., *Instructional Theories in Action: Lessons Illustrating Selected Theories and Models* (Hillsdale, NJ: Lawrence Erlbaum Associates, 1987).

Reigeluth, Charles M., & Garfinkle, Robert J., eds., *Systemic Change in Education* (Englewood Cliffs, NJ: Educational Technology Publications, 1994).

Romiszowski, Alexander J., *Producing Instructional Systems: Lesson Planning for Individualized and Group Learning Activities* (London: Kogan Page, 1984).

Romiszowski, Alexander J., *Case Studies in Instructional Design and Development* (Woodstock, NY: Beekman, 1990).

Romiszowski, Alexander J., *New Technologies in Education and Training* (East Brunswick, NJ: Nichols, 1993).

Seels, Barbara B., ed., *Instructional Design Fundamentals: A Reconsideration* (Englewood Cliffs, NJ: Educational Technology Publications, 1995).

Smith, Patricia L., & Ragan, Tillman J., *Instructional Design* (New York: Merrill, 1993).

Spector, J. Michael, Polson, Martha C., & Muraida, Daniel J., eds. *Automating Instructional Design: Concepts and Issues* (Englewood Cliffs, NJ: Educational Technology Publications, 1993).

Tessmer, Martin, & Harris, Duncan, *Analysing the Instructional Setting: Environmental Analysis* (London: Kogan Page, 1992).

Vickers, Joan N., *Instructional Design for Teaching Physical Activities: A Knowledge Structures Approach* (Champaign, IL: Human Kinetics, 1990).

West, Charles K., Farmer Jr., James A., & Wolff, Phillip M., *Instructional Design: Implications from Cognitive Science* (Boston: Allyn and Bacon, 1991).

Study Items

1. Define "instructional development" and describe its features.

2. What are the key elements of a "system" as conceived by systems engineers? Provide an example within a schooling context.

3. Distinguish among thinking in terms of "systems," "systemic thinking," and "proceeding systematically." What does each contribute to the process of developing instructional programs?

4. To what extent do you think it appropriate to apply engineering techniques in educational contexts? Consider a variety of contexts (school, business, military) and student age groups.

5. Compare and contrast the "products" of engineering with those of education.

6. List and describe the nine steps of the UCIDT model of instructional development. What role does the engineering concept of "feedback loop" play in this model?

7. What elements are included in the UCIDT model that do not appear in the model of instructional development prescribed for individual teachers in Chapter 2? What does each of these new elements add to the prospect of realizing the promise of educational technology described in Chapter 1, to make instruction more enriched, individualized, valid, accessible, and economical?

8. Describe the three principal stages in Romiszowski's model of instructional development? What is the role of feedback in this model? Who feeds what to whom?

9. What does Romiszowski mean by his reference to converting "what is" into "what should be"? Give an example of how you might assess "what is" and "what should be."

10. What does Romiszowski mean when he refers to his model as a "heuristic technique?" Do you agree with this portrayal?

11. Compare and contrast the UCIDT, Romiszowski, and Merrill models of instructional development. Which do you find most appealing? Why? What are the roles of teachers and students in each?

12. What value do you see in attempts to develop instructional programs according to models like those presented in this chapter? What are some limitations? How would you attempt to overcome these limitations?

13. In what ways might any of these models of ID serve to ensure that resulting programs are readily integrated into existing school systems and curriculums? What role ought the ultimate users (teachers and students) play in the development process to ensure such integration?

14. What are two factors that appear to account for many of the differences found thus far between conventional and innovative approaches to instruction? Why do you think these

factors have been found potent? Can you think of any other possibly potent factors?

15. State objections that constructivists make to the practice of instructional development. What is your position?

Suggested Activities

1. Draw an example of systems engineering like that illustrated in **Figure 4.01**, but in an educational context.

2. Modify the UCIDT, Romiszowski, or Jones/Li/Merrill model so that it makes more sense to you. Prepare a transparency or slide of your model and present it to the class.

3. Divide your class into three groups. Have one group simulate an instructional development project according to the UCIDT model, another according to Romiszowski's, and a third according to Merrill's.. Rejoin the groups to discuss the ease with each was able to proceed and what suggestions participants gave to improve the process.

4. Visit a corporate training enterprise. Meet with the range of specialists called for in large-scale ID and discuss with them their roles. Obtain a copy of their ID model and contrast it with those presented in this chapter.

5. Follow any model of ID to develop a program in collaboration with classmates or colleagues.

6. Check the original sources of the models presented in this chapter and compare my summary of them with that provided by the authors who designed them.

7. Look up references in the **Notes** that pertain to the measured effects of innovation. Locate some additional research articles and write a summary.

8. Send your comments and study item responses to me at Internet: hackbarths@aol.com.

Chapter 5

Integrated Learning Systems

Chapter Content and Objectives

The most ambitious efforts to achieve effective, well-integrated curriculums entail exploiting both instructional development (ID) and advances in computer technology. In this chapter, I describe and evaluate integrated learning systems (ILSs) and suggest how, with **our** help, they can help fulfill the promises of educational technology. Study of this chapter will enable you to:

- Define and diagram an **integrated learning system.**
- Describe interrelations between **ID** and **ILS.**
- List **pros and cons** of ILSs.
- **Evaluate the potential** of ILSs to facilitate the development of comprehensive, well-integrated curriculums.
- Describe **our roles** within an ILS.

Concepts and Exemplars

The products of instructional development (ID) may be as simple as booklets, filmstrips, and audiotapes. Or they might consist of detailed sets of guidelines for conducting entire courses or workshops. More ambitious, however, is the embodiment in computer programs of entire curriculums. Such programs fall under the general rubric of **"computer-managed instruction"** (CMI) or **"integrated learning system"** (ILS).

An ILS uses all the objectives, methods, media, and evaluation instruments identified during the process of ID. The computer first administers and scores tests earlier designed to diagnose students' abilities and levels of achievement. It then recommends instructional options that prior research has suggested will best achieve learning objectives. It may recommend films, textbooks, teacher-led discussions, and field trips. Or it might provide a tutorial lesson or simulation game of its own. The computer monitors the student's performance through tests and teacher evaluations and uses the results to guide further instruction. (See **Figure 5.01.**)

One of the best known of early CMI systems is the **Program for Learning in Accordance with Needs** (PLAN). Designed by the American Institutes for Research and managed by the Westinghouse Learning Corporation, PLAN carries students through much of their primary and secondary education in mathematics, science, social studies, and language arts. Curricular materials are assembled in "Teaching-Learning Units" that periodically are updated and revised.

Equally notable is the **Individually Prescribed Instruction/Management Information System** (IPI/MIS), created by the University of Pittsburgh's Learning Research and Development Center in collaboration with the Research for Better Schools organization. Using its own curricular materials, IPI/MIS guides elementary school learning in reading, mathematics, and science. One version—the Expanded Individualized Prescriptive Instruction System—seeks to treat students "holistically"; that is, it accounts for a wide range of factors affecting their education, not just those limited to classroom activities. Students take pretests to assess their cognitive skills, learning styles, and personality traits. Advisers then help tailor a program accordingly.

Since the early 1970s, Miami-Dade Community College has been using a CMI system engagingly called **Response System with Variable Prescriptions** (RSVP). Benefits claimed include:

- significant gains in student motivation and learning,
- increased faculty participation in developing courses,
- greater accuracy in record keeping, and
- easier reporting.

Students are said to "cherish . . . the personalized feedback for correcting their errors, appreciate the 'caring' shown by their faculty, and like the provision for self-paced learning."[1]

Two prominent British systems are **Computer-Assisted Management of Learning** (CAMOL) and **CICERO** (not an acronym). Designed for educational, industrial, and military uses, CAMOL assesses student progress, keeps records, and routes students through courses in math, physics, business, humanities, and communications.

The Open University's CICERO system is geared for home study in cases where there are shortages of teachers and resources. Students complete their assignments and then work at a computer terminal in a community study center. The computer assesses their progress, supplies information as needed, and makes recommendations for further study. Some of that study takes place on the computer itself where students receive instruction, immediate feedback, and further guidance.

Microcomputer technology has brought ILSs within the reach of nearly every teacher. Today, ILS software effectively collects data about students, sets learning objectives based on demonstrated need, prescribes activities to achieve specified objectives, monitors progress, and generates reports. IBM's **Classroom LAN Administration System** tracks students working on a local area network. It facilitates loading of software onto the network and generating reports of student progress. **SuccessMaker** is a multimedia, K–12 ILS by Computer Curriculum Corporation that has undergone over 25 years of schoolroom testing and development. Jostens Learning Corporation's **Instructional Management System** includes installation, training, and on-going support. Other sources are listed at the end of this chapter.

Though essential features of ILSs remain intact, today's versions are ever more responsive to advances in computer technology, and to calls for ever higher, more open-ended educational aims. Thus, Steven Mills (Direc-

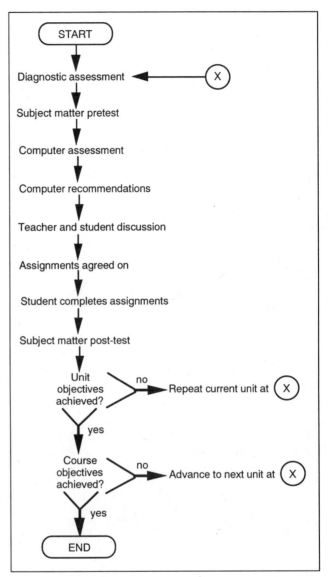

Figure 5.01. This flow diagram depicts a course managed by computer with the collaboration of a teacher.

tor of Adult Education, Southern Oklahoma Area Vocational Technical Center) rightly observed that:

Multimedia is impacting the ILS world with more and more systems offering high-quality sound effects, digitized human speech and music, still photos, animation, and video. . . . While many segments of ILS courseware consist of drill and practice and tutorials, some courseware offers more open-ended activities that combine academic skills development with an emphasis on problem solving and higher-order thinking skills. Many systems are incorporating tools for research and exploration by including word processors and reference tools such as electronic encyclopedias, atlases, and dictionaries.[2]

In the United States and Great Britain, the national governments long ago mandated that each and every student with a disability receive an "Individualized Education Program" (IEP). Recent advances in ILS software enable every student, disabled or not, to have an "IEP."[3] Some special advantages for students who have had difficulty with the traditional school curriculum were identified by Judy Jones, a teacher in the Performance-Based Diploma Program at the Florida high school where she also serves as Assistant Principal:

- Since the computer is the instructor, the adversarial relationship which often exists between at-risk students and teachers is replaced with a mentoring, facilitator relationship [between the teacher and each student].

- Students are held responsible for their own learning but may choose the pace at which they work.

- Feedback on work is immediate and positive; students do not have to wait for a teacher to grade their work.

- Students' self-esteem is enhanced as they can see their progress and know that they did it themselves.[4]

Jones added that within their ILS, teachers remained the key players in assisting students. The main difference, she claimed, was that the role of the teacher was transformed from one of being a conduit for the transfer of information to being more of a coach and counselor. Teachers individualized lessons to meet students' needs and carefully monitored progress. When students received their high school diplomas after passing the required examinations, they were able to take pride in knowing that they had truly earned them. (See **Figure 5.02.**)

The Promise of ILSs

As we have seen, ILSs that are products of systematic instructional development promise to provide effective programs across entire contexts ranging from village schools to urban industrial plants. They account for wide variations in student abilities, subject matter types, and budgetary constraints. Large-scale ID brings into

Figure 5.02. Within an integrated learning system, the computer takes over many routine instructional functions. What opportunities does this open up for teachers? Source: *Phi Delta Kappan,* 76 (March 1995), p. 561. Reprinted courtesy of Jem Sullivan.

being computer-managed school districts, where students are guided not only through classes, but into productive employment as well.[5] What are the conditions for further success?

The success of ILSs in orchestrating comprehensive curriculums depends on satisfying at least **four conditions:**

- Educators and public must **agree on the objectives** to be achieved.

- Systems workers must **simulate the educational process** accurately.

- Researchers must **specify optimum instructional inputs.**

- **Resistance to innovation must be addressed** with sensitivity.

To meet the **first condition,** broad educational goals will have to be successfully translated into more concrete and detailed instructional objectives. Most ID specialists generally insist that goals be specified in terms of observable changes not only in what students are expected to know, but also in how they are to act and feel as a result of instruction.[6]

However, many educators reject this view. General agreement, they say, is difficult to achieve even on the broad goals of education let alone specific objectives. Others maintain that precise objectives can be specified only for highly regulated contexts, as in the armed forces and industry. They cannot be specified for schools, because higher level outcomes such as appropriation, appreciation, interpersonal sensitivity, and creativity do not lend themselves to precise measurement.[7] Still others question **who** should set the objectives. "Educational technologists," according to Derek Rowntree, "are no more unanimous than other educators as to how far . . . they should be helping the student reach the system's objectives and how far . . . they should help the system meet those of the student."[8]

In reply to these critics, if total agreement was a prerequisite to success, few educational schemes of any kind would be adopted. Action often is taken on issues where both educators and public are divided. Either a compromise is reached or the majority prevails. For a start, take Article 29 of the United Nations *Convention on the Rights of the Child*, which asserts that education shall be directed to:

> (a) The development of the child's personality, talents and mental and physical abilities to their fullest potential;
> (b) The development of respect for human rights and fundamental freedoms, and for the principles enshrined in the Charter of the United Nations;
> (c) The development of respect for the child's parents, his or her own cultural identity, language and values, for the national values of the country in which the child is living, the country from which he or she may originate and for civilizations different from his or her own;
> (d) The preparation of the child for responsible life in a free society, in the spirit of understanding, peace, tolerance, equality of sexes, and friendship among all peoples, ethnic, national and religious groups and persons of indigenous origin;
> (e) The development of respect for the natural environment.[9]

To ensure that the higher aspirations of education fit within the empirical framework of educational technol-

ogy, less stringent forms of evaluation could be used than those limited to documenting the achievement of highly specific behavioral objectives. Changes in attitudes and types of achievement require subtle, intersubjective judgments by people who are both informed and aware. One persistent advocate of such an approach is Elliot Eisner: ". . . our preoccupation with measured behavior distracts us from appreciating and understanding what students experience in school and what they genuinely learn after all the test taking has been completed."[10]

Regarding the **second condition**, critics maintain that no complex social system can be simulated accurately, and therefore an entire school operation cannot be planned in detail. Any model of the educational process, they say, must rest on agreed assumptions about the nature of teaching, learning, knowledge, and value, and about the interplay among these and other variables (family, peers, religion, work, mass communications)—assumptions that now are in conflict. Take just one example. Though learning has been studied intensively, there still is no generally accepted learning theory. Behaviorists have developed techniques for achieving precisely specified objectives. Cognitive psychologists have found that students learn (and recall) more when they use mnemonics, mental imagery, and conceptual schemes. "Humanistic" theorists value attitude formation above all and therefore advocate sensitivity training, group therapy, and meditation. Constructivists view knowledge acquisition as a personal, creative process. How can such diverse approaches possibly support a single instructional system?[11]

Fortunately, instructional planning need not be based on a completely predetermined system. Do we, for want of certainty, refuse to plan such systems as business enterprises and governmental agencies? No, we plan them so that they can be modified as needed. When our knowledge is incomplete, we plan incompletely. When we can predict only more or less probably, we plan accordingly. Thus, when we design a model school, we proceed tentatively, testing parts, modifying and replacing them, always adjusting to a changing, often unexpected, reality. Alexander Romiszowski has consistently and forcefully maintained that: "Right from the start of a project, plan and insist on the maximum possible levels of administrative and decision-making flexibility, in order to adapt the project to unexpected developments as they occur."[12] Such thinking should be carried over to project **implementation** as well—freeing teachers and students **not only to take advantage of unforeseen and unforeseeable opportunities, but to engage in diverse, exploratory activities that serve to trigger such opportunities**.

Designers, furthermore, need not be delayed by disagreements among theorists; they can build the findings of different theorists into alternative methods and courses of instruction. Let some students follow prescribed linear programs and let others direct their own learning. Let temperament and preferred learning style decide. Granted, the learner's psyche holds much that the system may never be able to handle; but this only means that teachers should not completely surrender to systems designers. Teaching, after all, has both artistic and technical dimensions. In the words of Elliot Eisner, "To say that excellence in teaching requires artistry implies that the teacher is able to exploit opportunities as they occur. It implies that goals and intentions are fluid."[13] In the application of instructional technology, Denis Hlynka and Barbara Nelson early reported having found that: "Art, craft, science, and technology are all present in a synergistic combination. All domains provide input and relevance."[14] Charles Reigeluth urges educational technologists to "be more pragmatic and eclectic, drawing from diverse theoretical perspectives as each proves useful in facilitating different kinds of learning."[15]

The **third condition** involves selection of instructional inputs. As we have seen, decades of research comparing the effects of diverse media have yielded only the broadest of guidelines. The situation was summarized by Richard Clark as follows:

> . . . all current reviews of media comparison studies suggest that we will not find learning differences that can be unambiguously attributed to any medium of instruction. It seems that existing research is vulnerable to rival hypotheses concerning the uncontrolled effects of instructional method and novelty.[16]

The clear implication is that choice of medium should follow, not precede, the initial stages of program planning. As maintained throughout this book, we should first identify collaboratively the nature and substance of what our students need and want to learn and then identify potent strategies and media that will ensure this learning. Each medium has distinctive attributes that make it a good choice under certain conditions. This

view has been echoed by many. For example, David Jonassen, John Campbell, and Mark Davidson have suggested that:

> we should examine the process of learning first, then the role of context and the kinds of environments and cognitive tools needed to support that learning. Only then should we consider the affordances of media for creating those environments or providing those tools.[17]

Satisfying the **fourth condition** requires balanced analyses of vested interests and competing values followed by close communication, cooperation, and compromise. **Figure 5.03** illustrates views of many innovators as to why educators tend to resist change. Looking in from the outside, it appears to would-be innovators that teachers tend to reject technological intervention as both inappropriate in their domain and as a threat to their job. Performance-oriented technologists long have measured teacher resistance in terms of objections to a factory model of schooling. The new breed of constructivist technologists fathom teacher resistance in terms of loss of control.[18]

More trenchant objections to the invasion of schools by technology are raised by Neil Postman and Michael Apple. Postman rightfully raises "conscientious objections" to the "surrender of culture" to the emerging "technopoly." Apple denounces manipulation of fertile minds in the interests of mercenary enterprises. Others join with Marshall McLuhan in warning that, in some respects, "The medium is the message." To all that is valid in these deeply felt, forcefully expressed caveats, teachers and educational technologists alike must respond conscientiously and cooperatively.[19]

The impression of teachers as highly resistant to change for reasons of naivety or insecurity alone is not accurate. Most welcome advances in technology, especially those that clearly enrich their curriculums while preserving their roles as diagnosticians, communicators, authorities, and models. Their confidence will further be rightly won to the extent that they and their students are **involved in the processes** of design, production, implementation, evaluation, and revision of instructional innovations and if they **receive just compensation** for doing so.

For the most part, instructional programs will successfully enhance that most ambitious inter-human enterprise we call "education" to the extent that they:

Figure 5.03. Frustrated technologists hypothesize why teachers resist their innovations. They suggest that teachers view their mission narrowly or are threatened professionally. They suggest that schools are accustomed to passively receiving clients who are compelled to attend. Schools, they say, cannot easily adjust to outreach and competition. **What steps need be taken to ensure that mutual prejudices are broken down, and meaningful discussion fostered?** Source: Dean W. Hutton, "Video Technology in Higher Education: State of the Art?" in Ortrun Zuber-Skerritt, ed., *Video in Higher Education* (East Brunswick, NJ: Nichols, 1984), p. 19. Reprinted with permission of Nichols Publishing Company.

- **attract** and maintain student attention,

- **induce** students to study subject matter,

- **connect** new information with what has been learned previously,

- **relate** subject matter to students' life experiences,

- **provide** opportunities for student responses, informative feedback, guided practice, problem solving, and creative expression.

- **engage** teachers and students in drawing upon their own insights,

- **respond** to the pressing needs of society.

Furthermore, the effectiveness of any instructional program is influenced by student perceptions of the demands of the medium and the learning tasks set by the teacher. Because students **perceive** that some types of learning from textbooks and computers may be more demanding than learning from the relatively passive viewing of TV or film, they may tend to invest more intellectual energy in textbook and computer lessons.[20] And the energy invested in reading **and** viewing is further increased if they expect the teacher to assess them **fairly and personally** on what they have learned. (See **Figure 5.04.**)

In a computer-managed school, the electronic wizard would indeed prescribe and evaluate as well as provide instruction. But we would be expected to challenge our students to seek deeper levels of comprehension, to solve intriguing problems, and to test novel hypotheses. If, for example, the computer tests for knowledge of certain historical facts and events, we could test one-on-one for an understanding of the concept of historical

Figure 5.04. Within an ILS, teachers share in development and are key players in implementation. Students are motivated to measure up to **teachers' high expectations**, especially if their own are low (as in viewing a film or listening to an audiotape), and are shown how to do so by the tasks set and the guidance provided. Would the students pictured here be as fully engaged if their assignment had been dictated by a computer, but not endorsed by their teacher, Joan Bain?

inevitability or its opposite. The depth of our personal involvement is expressed well by Gary Fenstermacher and Jonas Soltis. Writing of what they call the "therapist" approach to teaching, they suggested that:

> one's aim is far more than getting learners to acquire knowledge and skill. It is also enabling and empowering them to use, interpret, and extend what is learned in ways that advance their own sense of identity and meaningfulness. For the therapist, the wisdom of humanity cannot become wisdom for learners unless they make it their own, working it through by and for themselves.[21]

However, according to Fenstermacher and Soltis, it is not sufficient for us rigidly to follow the script of a "therapist" approach nor of what they call "executive" or "liberationist" approaches. Our greater challenge is to:

> dig deeply into what humankind thinks it knows and into yourself to learn what the known means to you and how you will live. And you must do this *for* your learners, *before* your learners, where they can see the manner of an educated person and choose to model themselves after you. Then you truly will have become a teacher.[22]

A properly designed ILS encourages and guides us in doing so.[23]

Modeling exemplary behavior, **exerting legitimate authority**, and **inspiring students** both to master the prescribed curriculum and to reach beyond it remain for us, and teachers like us, among our highest responsibilities and greatest challenges. These we cannot delegate to even the most ambitious of computer-managed curriculums. For them, you and I always will remain fully accountable.

Summary and Conclusions

As this chapter has shown, developing comprehensive, integrated learning systems is a formidable challenge. Whatever is offered will be hotly debated. Yet the possibilities for compromise are greater than most critics have allowed.

Success is best ensured for programs that **include alternatives** and **are flexible** enough to adjust to unexpected events. And these programs must **merit and win the endorsements** of those who ultimately will administer them. If such programs incorporate the **tested experience** of our finest educators, and if they reflect sensitivity to concerns of students, teachers, and community alike, they will do much to fulfill the promise of educational technology.

In the chapters that follow, I survey and evaluate media commonly used for instruction—print, visuals, audiotapes, radio, film, television, computers, and teachers themselves. I illustrate how programs have been systematically planned and produced to ensure the most and best student learning at a reasonable cost. I then provide explicit guidelines for the selection, production, and utilization of programs typically designed for each medium.

Notes

[1] Anandam, Kamala, & Kelly, J. Terence, "Evaluating the Use of Technology in Education," in *Technology and Education: Policy, Implementation, Evaluation: Proceedings of the National Conference on Technology and Education, January 26–28, 1981* (Washington, DC: Institute for Educational Leadership, 1981), p. 134.

[2] Mills, Steven C., "Integrated Learning Systems: New Technology for Classrooms of the Future," *Tech Trends*, 39 (January/February 1994), p. 28.

[3]Budoff, Milton, Thorman, Joan, & Gras, Ann, *Microcomputers in Special Education: An Introduction to Instructional Applications*, 2nd ed. (Cambridge, MA: Brookline Books, 1985), pp. 167–177; Hackbarth, Steven, "Contributions of Educational Technology to Persons with Special Gifts and Challenges," *Programmed Learning and Educational Technology*, 23 (May 1986), pp. 166–172.

[4]Jones, Judy A., "Integrated Learning Systems for Diverse Learners," *Media & Methods*, 31 (September/October 1994), p. 16.

[5]Szabo, M., & Montgomerie, T.C., "Two Decades of Research on Computer-Managed Instruction," *Journal of Research on Computing in Education*, 25 (Fall 1992), pp. 113–133: "CMI has been shown to be efficient, effective, and relatively easy to develop . . ." (p. 130). See also, Megarry, Jacquetta, "Educational Technology: Promise and Performance," *Programmed Learning and Educational Technology*, 20 (May 1983), pp. 134–135; Martin, Barbara L., "Internalizing Instructional Design," *Educational Technology*, 24 (May 1984), pp. 13–19; Hackbarth, Steven, "Instructional Systems Design: An Appropriate Technology for Developing Nations," *Programmed Learning and Educational Technology*, 22 (February 1985), pp. 35–38.

[6]Gagné, Robert M., & Merrill, M. David, "Integrative Goals for Instructional Design," *Educational Technology Research and Development*, 38 1(1990), pp. 23–30.

[7]See "A Dialogue with Ralph W. Tyler," *Journal of Thought*, 21 (Spring 1986), pp. 110–111: "I manufactured the term [behavioral objectives] originally, but not with the intent that it was going to be taken as little bits of things. But what happened was, of course, that Robert Mager, who was director of training for Litton Industries, working with girls who in a few hours learned to wind coils and so on, thought that these training objectives had something to do with educational objectives. Our role in education isn't to teach girls to wind little coils. It is helping persons to understand, or at least to decide for themselves, how to wind coils if they have to deal with that sort of thing."

[8]Rowntree, Derek, *Educational Technology in Curriculum Development*, 2nd ed. (London: Harper & Row, 1982), p. 29.

[9]*Human Rights Fact Sheet No. 10: The Rights of the Child* (Geneva: United Nations, 1990), p. 23.

[10]Eisner, Elliot W., *The Educational Imagination: On the Design and Evaluation of School Programs*, 2nd. ed. (New York: Macmillan, 1985), p. 362.

[11]Phillips, Denis C., & Soltis, Jonas F., *Perspectives on Learning*, 2nd ed. (New York: Teachers College Press, 1991), p. 3: "Theorists do not all agree about what learning is and how it happens. Psychologists, anthropologists, linguists, neurophysiologists, philosophers, and others are still trying to understand how the mind works and how people learn." Briggs, Leslie J., "Instructional Design: Present Strengths and Limitations, and a View of the Future," *Educational Technology*, 22 (October 1982), p. 21: "Instructional Design began with models growing out of behaviorism; we are now moving more to an information processing model; and I expect that the future models will draw upon humanistic models." Merrill, M. David, "Constructivism and Instructional Design," in Duffy, Thomas M., & Jonassen, David H., eds., *Constructivism and the Technology of Instruction: A Conversation* (Hillsdale, NJ: Lawrence Erlbaum Associates, 1992), p. 111: "In the eternal scheme of things, none of us understands very much about how humans learn, how the mind functions . . . . We take the pragmatic stand that there may be competing systems of instruction based on different assumptions about learners and learning." Seels, Barbara, "The View Looking Back: Curriculum Theory and Instructional Technology Programs," *Educational Technology*, 33 (February 1993), p. 24: "One of the problems that may arise in any attempt to define the structure of the discipline of instructional technology is the need for pluralism in philosophy, method, and application."; Gibbons, Andrew S., Fairweather, Peter G., & O'Neal, A.F., "The Future of Computer-Managed Instruction (CMI)," *Educational Technology*, 33 (May 1993), p. 10: "Predicting the future of CMI is not so much gazing at a horizon as it is looking over a precipice. Advances in the psychology of learning have debased the currency of the psychology of instruction by challenging the status of what it is instructors think their students learn. Some notions with which they have grown comfortable abandon them in the light [of] contemporary analyses of learning." For a brief history, see Cooper, Peter A., "Paradigm Shifts in Designed Instruction: From Behaviorism to Cognitivism to Constructivism," *Educational Technology*, 33 (May 1993), pp. 12–19.

[12]Romiszowski, Alexander J., "Troubleshooting in Educational Technology or, Why Projects Fail," *Programmed Learning and Educational Technology*, 18 (August 1981), p. 185.

[13]Eisner, p. 184.

[14]Hlynka, Denis, & Nelson, Barbara, "Educational Technology as Metaphor," *Programmed Learning and Educational Technology*, 22 (February 1985), p. 14. See also Davies, Ivor K., "Instructional Development as an Art: One of the Three Faces of ID," in Hlynka, Denis, & Belland, John C., eds., *Paradigms Regained: The Uses of Illuminative, Semiotic and Post-Modern Criticism as Modes of Inquiry in Educational Technology* (Englewood Cliffs, NJ: Educational Technology Publications, 1991), pp. 93–106.

[15]Reigeluth, Charles M., "Reflections on the Implications of Constructivism for Educational Technology," in Duffy and Jonassen, *Constructivism*, p. 150.

[16]Clark, Richard E., "Reconsidering Research on Learning from Media," *Review of Educational Research*, 53 (Winter 1983), p. 457. Similar views are expressed in Unwin, Derick, "The Cyclical Nature of Educational Technology," *Programmed Learning and Educational Technology*, 22 (February 1985), p. 66: "No magic combination of the letters C, A, I, M, and L [acronyms for computer-based learning] is going to do much for us that could not have been done, albeit less excitingly for the

innovator, by visual aids, programmed learning . . . etc." See also Winn, William, "Why Media?" *Instructional Innovator*, 29 (February 1984), pp. 31–32. Winn states (p. 31) that we "need to make clear distinctions among media, messages, and methods. A medium . . . is nothing more than a device for getting information from one point to another." See the 1994 issues 2, 3, and 4 of *Educational Technology Research and Development* for alternative perspectives on this issue. The upshot is that if certain media are uniquely capable of incorporating instructional strategies that provide those combinations of experiences that help students arrive at understandings characteristic of the thinking of experts, then methods are confounded with media (i.e., it is problematic to isolate the influence of one apart from the other).

[17]Jonassen, David H., Campbell, John P., & Davidson, Mark E., "Learning *with* Media: Restructuring the Debate," *Educational Technology Research and Development*, 42, 2(1994), p. 38.

[18]Hannafin, Robert D., & Savenye, Wilhelmina, "Technology in the Classroom: The Teacher's New Role and Resistance to It," *Educational Technology*, 33 (June 1993), pp. 26–31.

[19]Postman, Neil, *Conscientious Objections: Stirring Up Trouble About Language, Technology, and Education* (New York: Vintage Books, 1988); *Technopoly: The Surrender of Culture to Technology* (New York: Knopf, 1992); Apple, Michael, "Is the New Technology Part of the Solution or Part of the Problem in Education?" in Beynon, John, & MacKay, Hughie, eds., *Technological Literacy and Curriculum* (Bristol, PA: The Falmer Press, 1992), p. 120: "Our task as educators is to make sure that when [technology] enters the classroom it is there for politically, economically, and educationally wise reasons, not because powerful groups may be redefining our major educational goals in their own image." Kneller, George F., *Movements of Thought in Modern Education* (New York: Wiley, 1984), Chapter 6, "Marxism"; McLuhan, Marshall, & Powers, Bruce R., *The Global Village: Transformations in World Life and Media in the 21st Century* (New York: Oxford University Press, 1989); Newcomb, Horace, ed., *Television: The Critical View*, 4th ed. (New York: Oxford University Press, 1987).

[20]Cennamo, Katherine S., "Students' Perceptions of the Ease of Learning from Computers and Interactive Video: An Exploratory Study," *Journal of Educational Technology Systems*, 21, 3(1992–93), pp. 251–263. TV generally is perceived as best (easiest) for learning attitudes and psychomotor skills; books and computers are seen as best for gaining intellectual skills and verbal information. Jonassen, Campbell, and Davidson ("Learning *with* Media") added: "When we consider the role of media, we should realize that . . . . [t]hey are complex entities with multiple sets of affordances that are predicated on the perceptions of users and the context in which they are used" (p. 38).

[21]Fenstermacher, Gary D., & Soltis, Jonas F., *Approaches to Teaching*, 2nd ed. (New York: Teachers College Press, 1992), p. 61.

[22]*Ibid.*

[23]Johnson, Michael, "The Mindful Uses of Integrated Learning Systems," *Media & Methods*, 29 (May/June 1993), p. 52; Chrisman, Gerald J., "7 Steps to ILS Procurement," *Media & Methods*, 28 (March/April 1992), pp. 14–15; Wiberg, Ewald, "Purchasing and Managing an ILS," *Media & Methods*, 29 (January/February 1993), pp. 12–13.

Sources

Books pertaining to broad uses of technology in education include:

Anglin, Gary J., ed., *Instructional Technology: Past, Present, and Future*, 2nd ed. (Englewood, CO: Libraries Unlimited, 1995).

Bailey, Gerald D., ed., *Computer-Based Integrated Learning Systems* (Englewood Cliffs, NJ: Educational Technology Publications, 1993).

Bailey, Gerald D., & Bailey, Gwen L., *101 Activities for Creating Effective Technology Staff Development Programs: A Sourcebook for Games, Stories, Role Playing, and Learning Exercises for Administrators* (Washington, DC: Association for Educational Communications and Technology, 1994).

Bailey, Gerald D., & Lumley, Dan, *Technology Staff Development Program: A Leadership Sourcebook for School Administrators* (New York: Scholastic, 1994).

Baker, Eva L., & O'Neil Jr., Harold F., eds., *Technology Assessment in Education and Training* (Hillsdale, NJ: Lawrence Erlbaum Associates, 1994).

Baker, Frank B., *Computer Managed Instruction: Theory and Practice* (Englewood Cliffs, NJ: Educational Technology Publications, 1978).

Brody, Philip J., *Technology Planning and Management Handbook: A Guide for School District Educational Technology Leaders* (Englewood Cliffs, NJ: Educational Technology Publications, 1995).

Duffy, Thomas M., & Jonassen, David H., eds., *Constructivism and the Technology of Instruction: A Conversation* (Hillsdale, NJ: Lawrence Erlbaum Associates, 1992).

Gibbons, Andrew, & Fairweather, Peter, *Designing Computer-Based Instruction* (Englewood Cliffs, NJ: Educational Technology Publications, 1996).

Hlynka, Denis, & Belland, John C., eds., *Paradigms Regained: The Uses of Illuminative, Semiotic and Post-Modern Criticism as Modes of Inquiry in Educational Technology* (Englewood Cliffs, NJ: Educational Technology Publications, 1991)

Komoski, P. Kenneth, *Educational Technology: The Closing-In Or the Opening-Out of Curriculum and Instruction* (Syracuse, NY: ERIC Clearinghouse, 1987).

Leebaert, Derek, *Technology Two Thousand One: The Future of Computing and Communication* (Cambridge, MA: MIT Press, 1991).

Lumley, Dan, & Bailey, Gerald D., *Planning for Technology: A Guidebook for School Administrators* (New York: Scholastic, 1993).

Mackay, Hughie, Young, Michael, & Beynon, John, eds., *Understanding Technology in Education* (Bristol, PA: The Falmer Press, 1991).

Means, Barbara, Blando, John, Middleton, Theresa, Morrocco, Catherine Cobb, Remz, Arlene R., & Zorfass, Judith, *Using Technology to Support Education Reform* (Washington, DC: U.S. Department of Education, Office of Education Research and Improvement, 1993).

Morton, Chris, & Beverly, Don, *School District Instructional Computer-Use Evaluation Manual* (Englewood Cliffs, NJ: Educational Technology Publications, 1989).

Nickerson, Raymond S., & Zodhiates, Philip P., eds., *Technology in Education: Looking Toward 2020* (Hillsdale, NJ: Lawrence Erlbaum Associates, 1988).

Ormrod, Jeanne E., *Using Your Head: An Owner's Manual* (Englewood Cliffs, NJ: Educational Technology Publications, 1989).

Ritchie, Mark L., *Quality Management for Educational Technology Services* (Washington, DC: Association for Educational Communications and Technology, 1994).

Twitchell, David, ed., *Robert M. Gagné and M. David Merrill: In Conversation* (Englewood Cliffs, NJ: Educational Technology Publications, 1991).

More current publications are listed and described on the AECT gopher. Use the command: gopher sunbird.usd.edu 72, or the URL: gopher://sunbird.usd.edu:72/1.

Also request current catalogs from: aect.aect.org, aace@virginia.edu, and iste@oregon.uoregon.edu.

More information about ILS software may be obtained by calling:

Chancery Software: 1-800-999-9931
Computer Curriculum Corporation: 1-800-227-8324
Curriculum Networking Specialists: 1-800-372-3277
Educational Resources: 1-800-624-2926
Eduquest/IBM: 1-800-IBM-4EDU
Glencoe/McGraw-Hill: 1-800-848-1567
Ideal Learning: 1-800-999-3234
Jostens Learning Corporation: 1-800-422-4339
National Computer Systems: 1-800-447-3269
New Century Education Corporation: 1-800-833-NCEC

TRO Learning/PLATO: 1-800-44-PLATO
University Communications, Inc.: 1-800-876-8257
Wasatch Education Systems: 1-800-877-2848

Study Items

1. Describe the steps entailed in computer-managed instruction (CMI or ILS).

2. In what ways can ID contribute to development of ILSs?

3. Spell out the following acronyms and describe any one of them: PLAN, IPI/MIS, RSVP, CAMOL.

4. What four conditions must be satisfied to ensure development of effective, computer-managed school districts? To what extent must each be satisfied? Can you list any others?

5. What reservations might you have if confronted with an ILS in your school district? What suggestions would you make to ensure that you could remain an effective teacher within an ILS context?

6. Instructional programs that are attractive, age appropriate, and have valid content are likely to be effective. What are several other features that ensure subject matter mastery?

7. What essential roles must teachers play within the context of an ILS to ensure achievement of the highest aims of education, especially problem solving ability, initiative, creativity, and good character?

Suggested Activities

1. Locate a school district that uses an ILS and note the degree to which the system does, in fact, manage instruction. Obtain evaluations from users.

2. Construct a questionnaire or guided interview based on sources of resistance to innovation alleged in **Figure 5.03**. Obtain and analyze responses from teachers, principals, school district personnel, college of education faculty, and instructional development specialists.

3. Look up references in the **Notes** that pertain to the supposed effects of innovation. Locate some pertinent research articles and write a summary.

4. Request information about *SuccessMaker*, the *Classroom LAN Administration System*, etc., from the sources listed above. Share what you find with classmates.

5. Critically analyze this chapter and share with me your findings and suggestions at Internet: hackbarths@aol.com.

6. Send me your responses to the above study items and expect some feedback. I am grateful for your participation in testing this textbook.

7. Reinforce your instructor with a hug (or lunch).

Educational Technology

Part II. A Survey of Products

Chapter 6

Printed Words

Chapter Content and Objectives

This chapter deals with the medium most familiar to educators. Until quite recently, the printed word was the dominant vehicle for preserving and transmitting information. It **remains**, apart from teacher talk, the primary means of communicating subject matter to students and serves as a "hard copy" basis for crafting programs presented by electronic media.

Technology improves the **quality** of print materials and makes them more widely **accessible**. After studying this chapter you should be able to:

- Discuss how **quality** of and **access** to print materials have been affected by advances in technology.

- Describe the nature and use of **schoolbooks, periodicals,** and **imaginative literature.**

- Give several examples of **how other media compensate** for the limitations of print (and vice versa).

- Specify ways in which print materials **can be used effectively in teaching.**

- **Select, produce,** and **use** print materials that best facilitate achievement of objectives you have set in collaboration with your students.

- Cite **source materials.**

Print and Related Technologies

Throughout history, knowledge has been spread mostly by voice and inscriptions. Over five thousand years ago the Sumerians wrote on clay tablets. Some of these have lasted to the present day. Until 3000 B.C. the Egyptians carved messages on stone, a durable medium but, like clay tablets, difficult to handle. Hence, the switch to papyrus. (See **Figure 6.01.**) The Hellenistic Greeks preferred parchment and vellum. They glued pages end to end to form rolls or else fastened them together as in modern books.

Although written works took a long time to produce, some large collections were assembled. The Sumerian library at Telloh held over 30,000 tablets, and the Museum at Alexandria, when the Romans sacked it,

Heavy reading

Figure 6.01. Stone remains a durable medium ideal for messages meant to last. What materials are better suited to carry timely messages meant for wide distribution? Source: R. Armour, *The Happy Bookers: A Playful History of Librarians and Their World from the Stone Age to the Distant Future* (New York: McGraw-Hill, 1979), p. 23. Reprinted courtesy of McGraw-Hill, Inc.

housed over 700,000 rolls. Fourth century Rome boasted some 30 public libraries. However, no holdings could be checked out; they were chained to desks to prevent theft!

The early Renaissance witnessed demand for written works so insatiable that craft technologies had to be combined to meet the challenge. Ink that clung to metal type came from artists' oil paints; paper, from linen rags. Manuscripts were bound on screw presses, originally designed for olives and grapes. Putting these technologies together, Johann Gutenberg in the 1450s built the first printing press with movable type. Printed first were the Scriptures and ancient classics, then works of science and fiction.

By the late 19th century, type was set mechanically and roll-type presses ran at high speeds. Wood pulp was used for paper; cloth-covered hardboard replaced leather binding. Better library techniques made books more accessible, and the addition of tables of contents, indexes, and headings made information easier to find.

Today, the entire enterprise of writing has been transformed. Authors now type (**"word process"**) their manuscripts at a computer, which displays the text on a screen. They distribute drafts via **e-mail** (aka "email") and **fax** to be checked by colleagues for content, organization, and style. They then make revisions easily by striking over errors, inserting new sections, rearranging paragraph order. The computer checks spelling, punctuation, and even grammar; it makes corrections automatically or suggests alternatives.

"Desktop publishing" technology employs microcomputers and laser printers to permit selection of typeface, arrangement of text and graphics, color, and production of finished documents. Large quantities may be reproduced in color on photocopy machines. Or, since page content is encoded electronically, the work can be transmitted worldwide via telephone or satellite to printing facilities, where receiving computers start the presses rolling. In this way text and photos are relayed by such newspapers as *USA Today* and *The Wall Street Journal* and such magazines as *Time* and *Newsweek*.

These transformations of text production by computer technology pervade today's elementary school classrooms. *The Bank Street Writer* has made word processing a snap for children. *The Children's Writing and Publishing Center* and *Kid Works 2* have enabled them to integrate text and graphic images. And the *Children's Newspaper Maker* has put them in competition with *The New York Times*.

Advances in print technology have spearheaded the information explosion that today characterizes all branches of knowledge. They have provided new ways of organizing, preserving, and disseminating information both ancient and modern. By keeping details of their holdings in computers, automated libraries speed access to specific print sources. Instead of using card catalogs, people now find what they want at a computer terminal. (See **Figure 6.02**.) Once found, the material may easily and cheaply be duplicated, subject to copyright restrictions, for personal use or for presentation to colleagues or students.

Microforms, too, simplify the storage and distribution of printed matter. Microforms are miniature photographic copies of printed pages on transparent rolls (microfilm) or flat sheets (microfiche) of plastic. They are read by placing them in specially designed projectors that magnify the images and produce paper copies as needed.

Microforms are used for such print materials as conference reports, research studies, and dissertations, and for old, rare, and out-of-print documents. For educators, a familiar reference system is the Educational Resources Information Center (ERIC), formed in the 1960s to ensure wide distribution of research materials. ERIC has offices across the United States, each with its special focus,

Figure 6.02. Computer technology makes library holdings more easily accessible. This terminal enables students to make searches of holdings across all campuses of the University of California system. What other uses would you make of such technology? How about a database of student-generated critiques of books, films, and computer software?

such as early childhood education, community college education, and the education of slow learners, the disadvantaged, and the gifted. These centers, or "clearinghouses," catalog documents and journal articles, and list them in *Resources in Education* and the *Current Index to Journals in Education.* Each clearinghouse also publishes bibliographies and fact sheets, and reviews articles on important topics within its specialty.

Access to print materials has been further enhanced by computer technology. Abstracts of ERIC documents, professional journal articles, and the like are listed in computer files by author, subject, and date of publication. To find information about a particular topic, students input key terms ("descriptors") on a computer terminal. If the search proves successful, a printout of the desired materials may be obtained. Documents also may be accessed via the Internet (see Chapter **13**) and questions about educational issues may be sent via electronic mail (email) to AskERIC. Teachers can locate suitable instructional programs by using their microcomputers and a telephone line link to the National Information Center for Educational Materials (NICEM). Scholars subscribe to services that provide periodic printouts of article abstracts in their fields of specialization. UNESCO distributes information worldwide through its Computerized Documentation System/Integrated Set of Information Systems (CDS/ISIS).

Carefully selected articles from newspapers, magazines, government publications, and journals now are preserved on CD-ROM by Social Issues Resource Series, Inc., Newsbank, Inc., and others. Searches for desired information can be made by topic or keyword combinations. At UNICEF I have assisted in the development of an Evaluation Database on CD-ROM, conceived as an "institutional memory." This system permits field officers around the world to readily access pertinent findings, recommendations, and "lessons learned" from child survival and education program reports to guide their own efforts.

The first **"hypertext"** software permitting non-programmers to sequence ("stack") pages of related screen output was OWL International's "Guide," offered in 1986. Apple Computer followed in 1987 with its *Hyper-Card,* created by Bill Atkinson and packaged with every new Macintosh. It wasn't long before the visual and audio capabilities of CDs were exploited to produce **"multimedia,"** covered in Chapter **12.** Britain's Jacquetta Megarry lauds these developments for giving us "interactive control over not only text, but also sounds, pho-

tographs, moving pictures and computer software, weaving them into a seamless carpet of knowledge."[1]

Thus, in ever more exciting ways, technology multiplies the **amount of information** contained in text and makes that information **more readily accessible.** The greater availability of knowledge stimulates discovery to the extent that this knowledge is communicated effectively. It follows that one of the main tasks of today's teachers is to introduce students to the many and diverse types of printed matter, especially **schoolbooks, periodicals,** and **imaginative literature,** which contribute to and complement the electronically saturated environments in which we live.

Print Materials in Education

Schoolbooks. Among the earliest schoolbooks was the *New England Primer,* first published in England around 1680 and later, with modifications, by American printers unrestrained by copyright laws. It contained the alphabet set in verse ("In Adam's fall, We sinned all; Thy life to mend, This Book attend. . . .") along with biblical information, prayers, spelling words, and a "catechism" of 100 or so questions and answers. Two early (1780s) spelling books were Thomas Dilworth's *A New Guide to the English Tongue* and William Perry's *The Only Sure Guide to the English Tongue, or New Pronouncing Spelling Book.*

One of the most prolific of early schoolbook writers was Noah Webster (1754–1843). In the 1780s he published *The Grammatical Institute of the English Language,* issued in three parts. Though patterned on earlier British spellers, Part I reflected the spirit of American independence. Place names were Americanized and religious homilies gave way to non-sectarian lessons on such qualities as humility, mercy, purity of heart, justice, and truth. In 1787 Webster retitled Part I *The American Spelling Book,* and in 1829 it appeared as *The Elementary Spelling Book; Being an Improvement on the American Spelling Book.* Having earned enough in royalties, he then devoted himself to the more enduring task of writing dictionaries. His spellers remained popular till the end of the 19th century, selling over 100 million copies.

Just as remarkable was the success of reading books written by William Holmes McGuffey (1800–1873), sales of which reached 120 million copies by 1920. The McGuffey readers were successful because they more adequately **met the increasingly varied needs of teachers and students** and were more **effectively marketed** than their predecessors.

Most nineteenth century schoolbooks sought to develop character as well as intellect. They summoned the young to industry, thrift, perseverance, and self-denial. They showed that virtue would be rewarded and vice punished as surely as night follows day. Success in business was attributed primarily to virtue; skill came second. Realistically enough, most nineteenth century schoolbooks did not portray a genial world beyond school gates. Life was rewarding, but it also was hard and perilous.

Modern schoolbooks focus more on subject matter than character. Information is presented in textbooks and supplemented by **teacher's guides, workbooks,** and **tests**. To these, teachers add classroom **handouts** that provide summaries, vocabulary lists, assignments, study questions, and graphic illustrations. Reference works such as dictionaries and encyclopedias also are available, specifically for use in schools. (See **Figure 6.03.**)

Textbooks introduce students to a structured body of knowledge and acquaint them with the terms and principles needed to acquire it. Study questions and sug-

gested activities—often found in accompanying workbooks—enable students to test and increase their knowledge. Tables of contents, indexes, and bibliographies allow them to pursue topics on their own.

Textbooks remain the principal aid to teaching and learning, especially in higher grade levels. Based on her review of pertinent studies, noted reading expert, Jeanne Chall, estimated that:

> By the time most students complete high school, they will have been exposed to over 32,000 pages in textbooks. Almost all of their time in reading instruction and at least three-fourths of their time in content classes will be spent with a textbook.[2]

Over 90 percent of the typical American school district's instructional materials budget goes for schoolbooks. These drive the curriculum. Frustrated media specialists long have lusted for a piece of this multi-billion dollar pie. Only recent advances in CD-ROM multimedia and telecommunications technologies have led to a growing consensus on the need to "restructure" schools in such a way that the grip of schoolbooks (and the lock-step, vanilla approach critics say such tomes tend to induce) can be broken. For electronic media to fit effectively within schools, flexibility is needed in terms of movement of students, scheduling of classes, student advancement through grade levels, and teacher access to funds and facilities. (See **Figure 6.04.**)

Programmed instruction is distinctive in that it laces text with questions. Students are asked to write their answers and then to check these against those provided in the text.. This "**immediate feedback**" keeps them on the right track. Programmed instructional workbooks today are used in schools primarily to enable students to learn new terms and to practice skills on their own. For example, my daughter progressed through a mathematics series in grammar school, and I used a programmed workbook on neuroanatomy terms to supplement textbook and dissection in graduate school. (See **Figure 6.05.**)

Periodical Literature. Teachers use **newspapers** and **magazines** to broaden their students' reading and to improve their critical skills. They select "news and views" types to give practice in data collection and analysis. Such periodical literature, carefully chosen, provides news, data, commentary, humor, and advice suitable for class discussion. It describes scientific discoveries, dis-

Figure 6.03. Dictionaries designed for young people are written in simple terms and abundantly illustrated. They enable students to look up the meanings and spellings of unfamiliar words. In what ways can dictionaries facilitate individualization of instruction?

Figure 6.04. Phonographs, radios, televisions, and now computers all have been perceived by advocates as the "wave of the future" for education. Yet, as shown here, sales of schoolbooks continue to soar. Do you believe that recent advances in CD-ROM multimedia and telecommunications technologies justify a reversal of this trend? Source: *Phi Delta Kappan,* 74 (May 1993), p. 727. Reprinted courtesy of James E. Hummel.

Figure 6.05. Programmed instruction individualizes learning, in part, by enabling students to work on their own. This, in turn, frees the teacher to assist those in need.

cusses court cases, and treats moral controversies in terms the average reader can readily understand.

Primary schools distribute copies of *Children's Digest,* a magazine featuring mathematical games, crossword puzzles, short stories, and articles of many kinds. It is designed to impart basic subject matter, build vocabulary, improve reading and writing skills, and stimulate interest in a variety of fields. *Junior Scholastic* uses short stories to lead older students to think about current events and moral issues. It asks such questions as, "Who do you think was right?" and "What would you have done if you were there?" *The Scholastic,* first published in 1922, is designed to arouse the interest of high school students in such subjects as literature, history, the arts, and current events. *Creative Kids* provides youths 8–14 with fiction, puzzles, brain teasers, book reviews, art, and pen pal addresses. *Brakes: The Interactive Newsletter for Kids with ADHD* addresses the special needs of children ages 7–14 diagnosed as having attention deficit hyperactivity disorder. *Radio AAHS! Kid's Magazine* includes games, stories, product reviews, an entertainment guide, and a CD with up to 10 new songs each month.

Newsweek magazine offers teachers complete programs in social studies and language arts. The main objectives of the social studies program are to: (a) familiarize students with major world events, (b) describe methods used by social scientists to gather information, (c) promote critical thinking (e.g., by evaluating information sources), (d) give practice in the use of charts, tables, and cartoons, and (e) relate what students have learned to their own concerns. The primary objectives of the language arts program are to (a) increase reading comprehension, (b) expand vocabulary, and (c) improve writing style. *Newsweek* provides a teacher's guide, filmstrips, transparencies, posters, and examinations. Similar programs are offered by other news magazines, such as *Time* and *U.S. News & World Report,* and by such outstanding newspapers as *The New York Times.*

Imaginative Literature. A great way to teach about how people think and feel is through a good story or poem. Most teachers today, "whole language" and "phonics" advocates alike, would echo the sentiments of the editor of *The Child's Own Book*, published two centuries ago:

> It must be evident to all who reflect much upon the subject of early education that many little books have been written which contain stories, anecdotes, legends, etc., well calculated to engage the infant mind; and to lead it gradually, by the flowery paths of amusement and pleasing moral instruction, toward those higher branches of literature which must at a later period occupy the attention of the well-educated.[3]

Early in this century two multi-volume sets were published: *Young Folk's Library* (1902) and *Journeys Through Bookland* (1909). Thomas Bailey Aldrich, Editor-in-Chief of the 20-volume *Library*, dilated on the contents:

> Each volume deals with a distinct department of letters, and has an especial character of its own. There is a book for almost every mood and hour—narratives of adventure and exploration by land and sea; episodes of boy and girl life at home and at school; poetry, biography, history, science, etc., etc.[4]

More so than in the past, much contemporary fiction confronts the young with the harsh realities of life—personal and interpersonal conflict, fear, anxiety, punishment, death. Judy Blume, for instance, describes pre-adolescents at grips with peers, teachers, and parents. The classmates in her *Blubber* are cruel (as they often are). Maurice Sendak's *We Are All in the Dumps with Jack and Guy* explores the tragedy of children living in urban shantytowns. Other works depict life in the round, "life with its joys and sorrows." Children, after all, feel as passionately as adults. They experience love and hate, acceptance and rejection, satisfaction and disappointment. Literature helps young people to understand these feelings in non-threatening contexts and provides them with models of successful coping.

Evaluation of Print Materials

Print materials have many advantages. A book needs neither equipment nor electrical power; it is **convenient** to use and requires very **little maintenance**. It is **self-paced**; students can skim through it, reread at will, and read ahead. By making notes in their own copies, by grappling with the text, students may appropriate both content and book. A book can become a highly personal document preserving private notations for a long time to come.

For centuries, scientists have relied on the printed word to communicate their findings and poets to embody their visions. True, **"email"** and **"electronic publication"** (the transfer of information via **computer networks**) now are serving to reduce such reliance. However, deep study of a book or article often calls for jumping from one section to another, comparing widely separated statements, analyzing graphics in context, and making notations. Such tasks are made easier by holding an entire work in one's hands.

As with other media, market forces tend (*caveat emptor*) to ensure that print materials are of good quality. Authors often devote many years to the preparation of personally satisfying, professionally acceptable manuscripts. Careful and cautious in selecting from the best of these manuscripts, publishers submit their choices to experts for evaluation. Manuscripts then are accepted as they stand (rarely), returned for revision, or rejected entirely (mostly). Schoolbook manuscripts most likely to succeed are those that have been tried out in classes for which they are intended and revised according to student performance and teacher comment.

But printed works have limitations. They **lack the pizazz** of electronic media, are out of reach of students with impaired vision who lack "assistive technology" to compensate, and do not permit "real time" interactivity. And when it comes to reaching widely dispersed audiences with timely messages, they fall flat. The capacities of electronic media to compensate are covered in subsequent chapters.

Text itself, even when "hyper" (highlighted keywords linked to pertinent information by computer), requires considerable **reading skill** and **intellectual effort**. (See **Figure 6.06**.) The letters and words that comprise text are abstract symbols. Their meaning can be discerned only by those who already have learned their relation to language as spoken and thought. To persons unable to read, the written word means little. To those with a limited vocabulary or familiarity with grammatical structure, text communicates imperfectly. Even people who read well may not benefit unless they **attend carefully to word meanings and context**. Multimedia help by complementing text with audio and visual tracks. For example, the *Macmillan Dictionary for Children* not only

Figure 6.06. Reading requires considerable skill and concentration. Teachers must provide materials within their students' grasp and conditions conducive to study. What steps do you take toward these ends?

displays words, it illustrates and pronounces them!

Nevertheless, although films, computers, and other media commonly are used in classrooms, print materials still dominate the curriculum. Indeed, one of the most powerful forces in schooling today, the "whole language approach" rooted in constructivist philosophy, seeks to replace basal readers and textbooks with "quality literature" across the curriculum, not with computers. (See **Figure 6.07.**) And even in **distance education**, which broadcasts radio and TV lessons to students' homes, print materials typically are used to help students correspond with their school, review content, prepare assignments, and take examinations.

How may other media compensate for the limitations of print? **Pictures** and **graphics** may convey some kinds of information more effectively. A picture of an Egyptian pyramid registers more vividly than a verbal description, though not necessarily more completely. The picture focuses the student's attention on a concrete object, while the text or teacher describes the object's cultural and religious attributes. **Charts** and **diagrams** may communicate statistical data readily. Most schoolbooks cope with this duality by complementing the written word with attractive visuals.

Films may convey certain experiences more powerfully than either print or still visuals. Films depicting war, soil erosion, or the growth of a fetus tend to have

more impact than descriptions in print or even pictures. The words of media pioneer Wilbur Schramm ring true today: Electronic and photographic media, he wrote,

> have always held out, in their different ways, the bright hope of delivering educational information and experiences widely, quickly, vividly, with a realism and immediacy that print could hardly match. They can bring experience without clothing it in the abstractions of printed language . . . .[5]

Within a multimedia environment, students have instant access to vast libraries of informative and affecting CD-ROM (compact disc, read-only memory) "books" that supplement text with sensational sights and stereo sound. *Compton's Interactive Encyclopedia* is illustrated, animated, and enhanced with sound, video, and over 15,000 pictures. *Microsoft Encarta* combines 26 volumes of text with over an hour of video clips, and thousands of graphic images.

Despite such advances in technologies, most media productions still are based on printed scripts that relate narration to visuals. (See **Figure 6.08.**) For all their advantages of motion, color, and sound, feature movies often fail to capture fully the multiple dimensions of the works on which they are based. Even in this fast paced

Figure 6.07. Even in classrooms with ready access to a variety of media, print materials dominate. Here students are playing a simulation game involving the proper arrangement of cards with printed messages. What characteristics of print materials make them particularly well suited to such an exercise?

Figure 6.08. Most media productions are based on print sources. And, as shown here, detailed operation manuals continue to be printed even for computer programs in which supposedly ample help is provided on-line. Where do **you** turn when drafting a script or seeking a remedy? Reproduced with permission of Andrew Toos.

electronic information age, the printed word remains a viable medium for expressing thoughts with precision and emotions with depth. In the academic context of grappling with subject matter and critically analyzing fiction, curling up in a quiet corner and penciling in marginal notes may remain for many a preferred approach. For most of the world's population, **print materials**—complemented with instructional **radio and television**—are the best hope for reaching the 1990 World Conference goal of "Education for All" by the year 2000.

Practical Guidelines

Selection. In **Figure 6.09**, I have divided selection criteria for print materials into seven categories: (1) Content, (2) Presentation, (3) Illustrations, (4) Supplementary Materials, (5) Technical Features, (6) Effectiveness, and (7) Overall Impression. Specific questions relating to each subcategory also are listed. Rate material on each

Title _____ Author _____

Publisher _____ Date _____ Price _____

Subject _____ Grade Level_____

Objectives _____

Prerequisites _____

Selection Criteria	Rating (1 = low; 10 = high)	Comments
1. Content of Text		
a. match with objectives	____	_____
b. accuracy	____	_____
c. currency	____	_____
d. scope	____	_____
e. stereotyping	____	_____
f. reference sections	____	_____
2. Presentation		
a. appeal	____	_____
b. organization	____	_____
c. teaching strategies	____	_____
d. integration	____	_____
e. interactivity	____	_____
f. motivation	____	_____
g. use of cues	____	_____
h. difficulty	____	_____
3. Illustrations		
a. accuracy	____	_____
b. relation to text	____	_____
c. placement	____	_____
d. captioning	____	_____
e. technical quality	____	_____
f. aesthetic quality	____	_____
4. Supplementary Materials		
a. teacher's guide	____	_____
b. examinations	____	_____
c. audiovisuals	____	_____
5. Technical Features		
a. print clarity	____	_____
b. paper quality	____	_____
c. binding	____	_____
6. Effectiveness		
a. student interest	____	_____
b. student achievement	____	_____
c. student evaluation	____	_____
7. Overall Impression	____	_____

Figure 6.09. Print materials evaluation form.

from **1** (low, unsatisfactory) to **10** (high, excellent) and select those with the highest average scores that also are **available** and **affordable**. Modify the form to suit your circumstances.

1. Content. Before selecting any printed material, note how well it responds to the following questions:

    a. Does it relate clearly to your instructional **objectives**?

    b. Is the content **accurate**?

    c. Is the content **up to date**?

    d. Is the coverage sufficiently **comprehensive**?

    e. Are people treated **equally** regardless of sex, race, or religion?

    f. Does it have **references**, **appendices**, and an **index**—all complete and easy to use?

2. Presentation. Concerning the manner in which information is presented:

    a. Does the book attract and hold **attention**? Does the cover invite readers to pick it up and do headings and illustrations keep them interested?

    b. Is the text **organized systematically**? Does it proceed from the simple to the complex or in accord with some other logical, spatial, geographical, or chronological order?

    c. Does it provide such **keys to comprehension** as objectives, examples, illustrations, headings, and footnotes?

    d. Are **references** made to relevant visual materials and/or audio recordings?

    e. Are readers **invited** to respond to questions, look up answers, or to pursue related activities? Are they **directed** to other sections in the text based on their performance or interest?

    f. Are readers **encouraged** to concentrate and persevere?

    g. Does the use of **space**, **typeface** style and size, **color**, **lines**, and **arrows** focus attention and ease comprehension?

    h. Do **vocabulary**, **grammatical structure**, and **writing style** accord with the preparation and competence of your students? (See **Figure 6.10**.)

3. Illustrations. Regarding maps, graphs, pictures, and drawings, you should ask:

    a. Are they **accurate** portrayals of their subjects?

    b. How well do they **clarify** or **enhance** text content?

Making Estimates of Text Reading Grade Level (with caveats)

$$rgl = 0.4 \, (wps + \%hw).$$

"**rgl**" is the grade level of students who, on the average, should have no difficulty reading and understanding the text.

"**wps**" is the total number of words in a selected passage (at least 100 words in length) divided by the number of sentences in that passage.

"**%hw**" is 100 times the number of "hard words" divided by the total number of words in the selected passage. "Hard words" are defined as those having three or more syllables excluding: (a) proper nouns; (b) combinations of short, easy words like "forevermore"; and (c) verbs made into three syllables by the addition of a suffix (e.g., "studying").

By adding **5** to the result, you will obtain the reading age level (i.e., first graders are about six years old, and so on).

Note that reading level is affected by criteria other than the two (word and sentence length) computed in the formula. To get a more accurate estimate you must examine text content and style. Watch for profound thoughts expressed in simple terms (e.g., "To be or not to be . . . ."), ambiguities, figures of speech, and complex grammatical constructions. See if there are illustrations included that might serve to clarify the meaning of unfamiliar terms.

Grammatik, *Readability Plus*, *Right Writer*, and *The Writer's Toolkit* are computer software that scan your word processed documents in seconds to provide a variety of readability statistics.

Figure 6.10. An estimate of reading grade level **(rgl)** for text may be obtained using the above formula. Note, however, that "readability" depends as much on what our students bring to the task (e.g., prior knowledge, attitudes) as on what is printed on the page. Source: Adapted from Henry Ellington, *Producing Teaching Materials: A Handbook for Teachers* (New York: Nichols, 1985), p. 40. Reprinted with permission of Nichols Publishing.

    c. Are they **identified** in the text and placed near associated sections?

    d. How well do **captions** reflect intended messages?

    e. Are they sufficiently **large, detailed, well focused**?

f. Are they visually **appealing**, employing a balance of line, color, and proportion as appropriate?

4. Supplementary Materials. Along with teachers' guides, many publishers provide examination questions and audiovisual aids. These, too, should be examined as follows:

   a. Does the teachers' guide prescribe **sound pedagogy**?
   b. Do examination questions properly reflect the **depth and breadth** of the coverage?
   c. To what extent do the audiovisual aids **reinforce** the learning of textual material?

5. Technical Features. A good text includes certain desirable technical and physical features.

   a. Do **size and style of print** ease reading?
   b. Is the paper sufficiently **strong and smooth**?
   c. Is the binding **sewed rather than glued**?

6. Effectiveness. Since many schoolbooks have been reviewed in professional journals or have been classroom tested, you should examine the results.

   a. To what extent has the text **aroused students' interest** in the subjects covered?
   b. How well have students **learned what they "should"** from reading the text?
   c. Do students find it **responsive to their desires to make sense** out of the world?

7. Overall Impression. In selecting materials, personal preferences and impressions are important. For example, an otherwise solid text might not be particularly challenging. Works of fiction may be judged more subjectively than textbooks; teachers generally choose novels and poems they personally have enjoyed. And we always should be sensitive to the opinions of parents and community members—opinions expressed, surprisingly enough, as early as 1902.

> If there is wholesome and stimulating nourishment for young minds, there is also, unhappily, a vast quantity of tempting and poisonous food within easy reach. Into this category come the lurid juvenile dramas in which a glamour of romance is thrown over the adventures of personages who in real life generally find their apotheosis in the prisoner's dock. Books of this kind are widely circulated and work incalculable harm. Their power of demoralization is by no means indirect or disputable.[6]

Controversy continues over which books are "wholesome." Books deemed sexually explicit are special targets, but those dealing with romance, drug addiction, minority struggles, and evolution have not escaped attack. Even classic literature frequently appears on censors' lists. Noted titles include the *Bible* (for obscenity), J.D. Salinger's *The Catcher in the Rye*, Steinbeck's *The Grapes of Wrath*, Orwell's *Nineteen Eighty-Four*, Harper Lee's *To Kill a Mockingbird*, Hawthorne's *The Scarlet Letter*. Jane Smiley's Pulitzer Prize winner, *A Thousand Acres*, was banned in a Washington state high school for having "no literary value in our community right now." Teachers in Pennsylvania blacked out passages in Dian Fossey's *Gorillas in the Mist* that described mating and masturbation. (Can you think of a more sure way to draw attention? Perhaps we should black out the most educationally significant portions.) The most challenged book in 1994 was Michael Willhoite's *Daddy's Roommate*, reflecting the heated controversy over whether "alternative lifestyles" may openly be depicted to children as within the range of normalcy.[7]

To most such concerns I reply that students should be encouraged to analyze controversial literature rather than avoid it. They should be taught that literature is an art form in which authors openly reveal their impressions of the human condition. By its very nature, literature is not always a model on which students should pattern their behavior. Instead, different kinds of literature, for or against certain views, can become objects for lively discussion, critical analysis, even rejection. Even books that advocate lawlessness can profitably be examined to ascertain the authors' motivations and rationales. (See **Figure 6.11**.) Article 13 of the United Nations *Convention on the Rights of the Child* may serve as a guide:

1. The child shall have the right to freedom of expression; this right shall include freedom to seek, receive and impart information and ideas of all kinds, regardless of frontiers, either orally, in writing or in print, in the form of art, or through any other media of the child's choice.

2. The exercise of this right may be subject to certain restrictions, but these shall only be such as are provided by law and are necessary:

   (a) For respect of the rights or reputations of others; or
   (b) For the protection of national security or of public order (*ordre public*), or of public health or morals.[8]

*"Now that we know how to read,
they're banning all the good stuff."*

Figure 6.11. Strong forces remain at work today as they did in the 70s and 80s to restrict the contents of school libraries. Who decides what is the "good stuff" at the school where you teach? What are **your** limits? Source: *Phi Delta Kappan,* 64 (October 1982), p. 89. Reprinted with permission of Ed Lepper.

While serving as a volunteer classroom assistant at NYC P.S. 151 (1993–94), I encountered a humorous compromise one teacher made with her students' "thirst for knowledge." Imagine 10 upper elementary age boys, all diagnosed as learning disabled, some with attention deficits, hyperactivity, and impulsiveness. Each morning the teacher, Rachael Miliken-Weitzman, struggled to keep order while going through the routines of a highly structured, yet creative curriculum. By the end of the day, when both teacher and students were nearing exhaustion, Ms. Miliken-Weitzman would say, "Okay, you may all now go to the Reading Center. Read whatever you like, but you may not look at the Waldo book" (*Where's Waldo?*). I had noticed the frenzy with which the boys consumed this book at every opportunity and, wanting to channel this fascination, I occasionally would sit with a group and read to them the postcards describing Waldo's travels. But it wasn't until much later that they let me in on the nature of the appeal. Sure, they loved scanning every page to locate Waldo among hordes of other tourists engaged in all sorts of mischief. But the really big attraction was that topless sunbather. "Rachael," I whispered later, "Do you know what those boys have found of such great interest in that Waldo

book?" (Silly, you say, but you would have to know what a proper and stern teacher she appeared to be.) Much to my surprise, she knew very well. Indeed, the book was her own! Her very clever ploy was engaging these preliterate ("emergent") boys into the world of print. They were handling the book, turning the pages, and seeking the meaning it offered, often much beyond the silliness. I was reminded of the techniques my brother Daryl had used years ago in teaching illiterate Army recruits— "You mean those printed letters say THAT?!!"

Production. Use pertinent criteria listed above to guide production of such classroom handouts as course summaries, checklists, assignments, and examinations. The criteria also apply to your production of text to be presented on transparencies, slides, films, TV, and computers. Regardless of medium, always strive to relate content directly to **course objectives** and ensure that information presented is **accurate**. Make your presentation **well organized** and **engaging.** See to it that the **technical qualities** of text and the medium on which it is to be displayed are suitable for the intended purpose. And consider availability and cost.

Writing so that subject matter is **effectively communicated** to students is equally important. At the end of this chapter, I list several books that provide explicit suggestions for improving one's writing skill. A sample of Robert Horn's fine work is presented in **Figure 6.12**. Additional hints are given below.

Write at a level your students readily can understand. When introducing new terms and concepts, use vocabulary with which they are familiar. Less able students learn best when grammar is kept simple and paragraphs short. Advanced students can handle more complex constructions. Metaphors may serve both groups, but allusions tend to serve only the well informed.

Write in an engaging style. You can present even the most technical, complex information in a way that attracts and sustains student attention. One technique is to address the reader in a conversational manner, using the subjects "you" and "I" rather than "one" or "the student." Another is to use the active voice (e.g., "The scientist discovered it" rather than "It was discovered by the scientist.") Other techniques include the use of action verbs, rhetorical questions, and illustrations (verbal

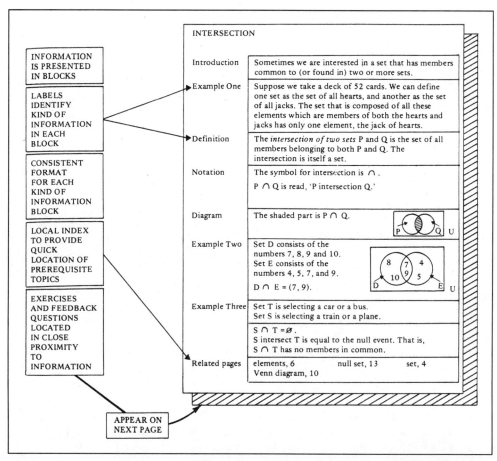

Figure 6.12. Scores of techniques are available to draw readers' attention to the printed word and to assist their comprehension. These include use of bold, underline, arrows, color, marginal notes, subtitles, diagrams, questions, and feedback. The sample of "Information Mapping" presented above integrates a variety of such techniques. Source: Original material by Robert Horn, Information Mapping, Inc., who included it in a chapter written collaboratively with Alexander J. Romiszowski, *Developing Auto-Instructional Materials: From Programmed Texts to CAL and Interactive Video* (New York: Nichols, 1986), p. 215. Reprinted with permission of Nichols Publishing.

and pictorial). Things to avoid are negative statements, ambiguities, clichés, and undefined technical or foreign terms.

Write several drafts. There is a vast gulf between the mind and the blank page. It takes much self-discipline simply to gather the necessary materials, settle down at a desk, and commit the first few sentences to paper. The result nearly always is a rough approximation of what you originally had in mind. And the act of writing often affects those original thoughts, exposing their ambiguities and forcing you to fill in gaps. Therefore, you should plan to give your first draft a critical reading

and revise accordingly. In anticipation of such revision, you should write just one paragraph on each sheet of paper (or index card), a firm rule of my UCLA mentor, George Kneller. You then will have adequate space for corrections, can add or delete paragraphs as needed, and move paragraphs into a more coherent sequence.

Did I say **"write on paper?"** Yes, I insist that my students write their first draft the old fashioned way. In my experience, first drafts done on a word processor appear to lack coherence, more like collages than mosaics. And once the text has been input, it is difficult to unscramble, viewing just one screen at a time.[9] Furthermore, something magical happens in the transition of the second or third draft from paper to computer. Relieved of the need to fill pages, recall facts, provide structure, and select words, the mind is free to consider logic and style. And **fingers have the minds of an editor**, catching errors the eyes have overlooked countless times. Use of a word processor, with or without prewriting, has been shown to result in documents that are longer and have fewer "typos" than those produced by pen alone.[10] **With** guided prewriting using pen and paper, and attention directed to **thoughtful revision** of several drafts, word processing results will be superior.

Arrange text, headings, and graphic illustrations in a way that enhances communication of essential ideas. This has been done in the figures described here. The first, **Figure 6.13**, is a page from a science textbook. It contains background information and an illustrated procedure. The second, **Figure 6.14**, is a revision of this page made to help the student in grasping the information and in performing the procedure. Specific improvements include: placing answers directly below questions, spelling out "15 lbs.," deleting one unneeded question, separating disconnected sentences that had been in an artificial paragraph form, setting off the list of things needed to perform the demonstration, isolating the "method" section, placing illustrations directly above associated text, and listing procedural steps one-by-one rather than in paragraph form. Try to make such improvements as these in the print materials you develop.

Test and revise. Once you are satisfied with the quality of your work, it is time to test it. Colleagues may be asked to comment on the validity of content and the quality of style. Students may identify unfamiliar terms and gaps in presentation. You then may assess the extent to which they learned from it what you intended they should. Revise text, illustrations, and layout accordingly. Computer technology can be of much help in preparing series of drafts, but heed these caveats:

> Style checkers offer judgment without understanding, based on whatever guidelines about style could be easily codified as rules with no regard to meaning. They are crude parodies of bad teachers, a mockery of any serious reflection on style, and a discouragement of the development of individual styles.[11]

Nevertheless, spelling and grammar checkers have spared **me** considerable embarrassment by catching careless errors and and (it catches these) have improved

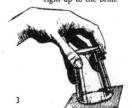

AIR PRESSURE

How do you know that air is all around you?

Can you see it?	No.
Can you smell it?	No, only when it carries some substance which has a smell.
Can you feel it?	Yes, when the wind blows.
Has air any weight?	Yes. The weight of air, or "air pressure", is approximately 15 lb. per square inch on *every* surface in *every* direction.
Does air push upwards as well as downwards?	Yes.

EXPERIMENT TO SHOW THAT AIR CAN SUPPORT A COLUMN OF WATER

1 Air can support things. You can carry out an experiment to show that air can support a column of water. You will need a tumbler, a piece of cardboard and water.

Method

1. Fill a glass tumbler with water right up to the brim.

2. Slide a piece of cardboard over the top of the glass so that it touches the water. Do not allow any bubbles of air to creep in.

3. Turn the tumbler upside down holding the card against the glass. Take your hand away from the card. If you do this carefully, the water will remain in the tumbler. It will not fall out because it is supported by the air pressure below.

Figure 6.13. This page from a science book does not communicate its instructional messages as effectively as it might. Can you suggest five ways to improve it? Source: James Hartley, *Designing Instructional Text,* 2nd ed. (East Brunswick, NJ: Nichols, 1985), p. 37. Reprinted with permission of Nichols Publishing.

my writtings (and these) buy alerting me too (but not those two) worthy alternative words and phrases. Yet careful proofreading remains necessary to check not only for such word slips as "on" for "in" and "then" for "than," but for lapses in logic, inadequate transitions, excessive alliteration, and sheer nonsense. Insertions are especially dangerous, leading to errors ranging from subject/verb mismatch to redundancy.

A systematic process by which you may approach production of print materials is presented in **Figure 6.15**. This adaptation of Patricia Callender's diagram appeared in the 1974 early draft of this textbook and I haven't found one more elegant since. As with all linear appearing models in this book, we have to **adapt this one creatively** to suit our purposes. Also, we may benefit from the advice Steven Tripp, Barbara Bichelmeyer,

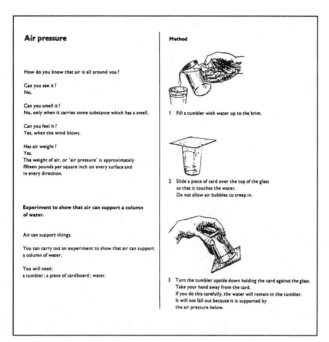

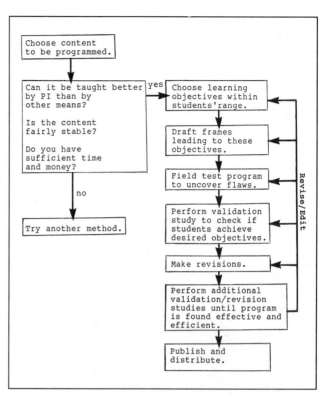

Figure 6.14. This is a revision of the page shown in Figure 6.13. What improvements can you detect? Can you think of any others (e.g., font size)? Source: James Hartley, *Designing Instructional Text,* 2nd ed. (East Brunswick, NJ: Nichols, 1985), p. 38. Reprinted with permission of Nichols Publishing.

Figure 6.15. The main steps in the preparation of programmed instructional materials (PI) are diagrammed above. These apply as well to production of handouts, textbooks, audiovisual programs, and computer-based instruction. Extensive experience in the use of such models has led experts to suggest that early, tentative prototypes be produced to gain the immersion and feedback needed to illuminate and reassess design decisions. Source: Adapted from Patricia Callender, *Programmed Learning: Its Development and Structure* (London: Longmans, Green, 1969), p. 73. Copyright © 1969 Patricia Callender.

David Merrill, *et al.* who advocate **early, tentative production of prototypes.**[12] This permits the kind of immersion needed to really get a feel for student needs and abilities and how best to proceed. In my own experience, I have found that I really don't know what I don't know until I try to write it down. Only after the struggle to express do I find myself having to go back to the library. Instructional **design** is a process that **takes place concurrently** with instructional **development.**

Teaching with Print Materials. Dictionaries, atlases, textbooks, basal readers, periodicals, poems, and novels all present us with different sorts of opportunities. Following are a few hints.

Reference books are best used while pursuing some related activity. Students following the *Where in the World Is Carmen Sandiego?* television series (also available as computer software) may be challenged to locate in the classroom atlas those places mentioned on the

program. Or they may trace the geographic origins of their ancestors and those of their peers. Use of printed sources may be supplemented with such computer software as *U.S. Atlas, World Atlas,* and *Microsoft Bookshelf.*

Dictionary study is encouraged by having students create a *Personal Glossary.* This evolving document, preserved and updated on a word processor, would contain words they encountered in their study and everyday activities. With *The Writer's Toolkit,* they could check spelling and import pronunciation, definitions, synonyms, antonyms, and even pertinent famous quotations. Here's a sample of what the *Toolkit* did for my *Personal Glossary:*

abrogate (ab-ruh-gAYt): to put an end to formally and with authority; annul (to nullify or cancel, as a marriage or a law); void; vitiate (to make ineffective or worthless). "Divorce is probably of nearly the same date as marriage. I believe, however, that marriage is some weeks the more ancient." Voltaire (1694–1778), French philosopher, author. "A Roman divorced from his wife, being highly blamed by his friends, who demanded, 'Was she not chaste? Was she not fair? Was she not fruitful?' holding out his shoe, asked them whether it was not new and well made. 'Yet,' added he, 'none of you can tell where it pinches me.'" Plutarch (46–120), Greek essayist, biographer.

adroit (UH-droit): skillful and adept under pressing conditions; dexterous; apt; facile; nimble. "Art is skill, that is the first meaning of the word." Eric Gill (1882–1940), British sculptor. "It needs more skill than I can tell To play the second fiddle well." C. H. Spurgeon (1834–1892), English preacher.

ague (AYgy): a fever accompanied by chills or shivering, esp. malarial; anguish; Italian mal'aria, foul air. "If prolonged it cannot be severe, and if severe, it cannot be prolonged." Seneca (c. 5–65), Roman writer, philosopher, statesman, writing of illness.

Other computerized reference works include *The American Heritage Dictionary*, *The Merriam-Webster On-Line Dictionary*, and the *Random House Webster's Electronic Dictionary and Thesaurus: College Edition*. Youngsters and the learning disabled are best served by the *Macmillan Dictionary for Children*. It not only illustrates words, it pronounces them!

Textbooks typically permit a variety of approaches. As a rule, you may assign chapters in order of their appearance. Sometimes, however, you may omit parts or alter the sequence to accord with your own course objectives. In any case, readings always should be discussed in class, supplemented by lectures, films, and other print materials, and followed by evaluations of student learning. Learning from all forms of printed matter—textbooks, periodicals, handouts, etc.—is greatly enhanced when you explain unfamiliar content, engage students in varied learning activities, and teach study skills such as outlining and note-taking.

In teaching **literature**, encourage your students to do literary analysis. They should decide whether characters are well developed and whether conflict is credibly re-solved. They should do detective work, seeking the origins of stories and the backgrounds of authors. Thus, they may discover that Lewis Carroll was really Charles Lutwidge Dodgson, a shy, learned mathematician, who wrote not only the charming *Alice's Adventures in Wonderland* (based on the fanciful tales he made up to please a neighborhood girl) but heavy treatises like the *Syllabus of Plane Algebraical Geometry*. They may learn, too, that Kenneth Grahame wrote *The Wind in the Willows* in a series of letters to his son, who was spending the summer in the country and missed his father's bedtime stories. The lives of authors abound in such fascinating details. Such reference works as *The Young Reader's Companion* provide information not only about authors, but characters, plots, and allusions as well.

By studying the lives of authors and discovering the sources of their material, students gain the confidence needed to describe their own experiences. They learn how to express their turbulent feelings by analyzing similar feelings in the lives and works of great writers. Reading good literature improves the skills of those who want to write well.

Having your students read carefully selected literature also serves the ends of moral education and cultural literacy. Novels that present moral dilemmas involving such themes as responsibility, fairness, and charity demonstrate moral reasoning, and reveal the consequences of acting rightly or wrongly, providing opportunities to challenge students to reflect upon their own attitudes and behavior. Readings about influential people and significant events may entertain, inform, and inspire. A prime example is Alex Haley's *Autobiography of Malcolm X*. From such reading, your students would, in the words of Diane Ravitch, "learn not only the lives and struggles of real people, but would also absorb significant social and political history that would strengthen their knowledge of the world and how it came to be as it is."[13]

Nel Noddings (Stanford University) has written eloquently about the "challenge to care in schools." She has identified core aims of education as encouraging both intellectual and social competence. Toward the end of fostering the capacity for friendship among students, she suggested that:

> They should hear about Damon and Pythias, of course. But they should also examine some incongruous friendships: Huck and Jim in Mark Twain's The *Adventures of Huckleberry Finn*; Miss Celie and Shug in Alice Walker's *The Color Purple*; Lenny and George in John Steinbeck's *Of Mice and Men*; Jane and Maudie in Doris Lessing's *Diaries of Jane Somers*.[14]

"I'm taking an innovative approach to teaching this semester. I'm using BOOKS!"

Figure 6.16. The virtues of schoolbooks constantly are being rediscovered. What are some of their advantages over other media? What can other media contribute to instruction beyond what print materials have to offer? Source: *Phi Delta Kappan,* 59 (February 1978), p. 416. Reprinted with permission of Randy Glasbergen.

Each of these friendships, wrote Noddings, might be analyzed in relation to the classification scheme provided by Aristotle's *Nicomachean Ethics.* The aim here is not merely to have students critically evaluate great literature, which surely they should be encouraged to do. More importantly, it is to help them develop greater awareness of the precious roles of loving relations in their own lives.

Summary and Conclusions

Though challenged by rapidly emerging technologies that I explore in later chapters, print remains the foremost source of structured knowledge for students. Schoolbooks are designed to communicate this knowledge clearly and effectively. (See **Figure 6.16.**) Periodicals keep us up to date; reference works help to ensure accuracy. Good literature challenges readers to bring their own imagination into play in a manner generally unrivaled by films and television.

What do pictures and graphics contribute to the printed word and to communication generally? These are the concerns of Chapter **7.** Later chapters pursue the transformation of the printed page along with sights and sounds into impulses of light beamed across continents, displayed on computer terminals, and stored on compact discs.

Notes

[1]Megarry, Jaquetta, "Hypertext and Compact Discs: The Challenge of Multimedia Learning," in Bell, Chris, Davies, Jim, & Winders, Ray, eds., *Aspects of Educational and Training Technology, Vol. XXII: Promoting Learning* (New York: Nichols, 1989), p. 52.

[2]Chall, Jeanne S., & Conard, Sue S., with Harris-Sharples, Susan, *Should Textbooks Challenge Students? The Case for Easier or Harder Books* (New York: Teachers College Press, 1991), p. 1.

[3]Quoted in Norton, Charles E., ed., *The Story Teller,* vol. 1 (Boston: Hall and Locke, 1902), pp. xxi–xxii.

[4]Quoted in Norton, p. xvii.

[5]Schramm, Wilbur, *Big Media, Little Media: Tools and Technologies for Instruction* (Beverly Hills, CA: Sage, 1977), p. 13.

[6]Aldrich, Thomas B., ed., *Young Folk's Library* (Boston: Hall and Locke, 1902), p. xv.

[7]Hardigg, Viva, "Free Speech: Censors at Work," *U.S. News & World Report,* 117 (September 26, 1994), p. 29; *The Schoolbook Protest Movement: Forty Questions and Answers* (Bloomington, IN: Phi Delta Kappa Educational Foundation, 1986); Altbach, Philip G., Kelly, Gail P., Petrie, Hugh G., & Weis, Lois, eds., *Textbooks in American Society: Politics, Policy, and Pedagogy* (Albany, NY: State University of New York Press, 1991). For an analysis of the debate concerning "great books" versus "relevant books," see Atlas, James, *Battle of the Books: The Curriculum Debate in America* (New York: W.W. Norton, 1992).

[8]*Human Rights Fact Sheet No. 10: The Rights of the Child* (Geneva: United Nations, 1990), p. 17.

[9]Eklundh, Kerstin S., "Problems in Achieving a Global Perspective of the Text in Computer-Based Writing," *Instructional Science,* 21 1/3(1992), pp. 73–84; Erickson, Barbara J., "A Synthesis of Studies on Computer-Supported Composition, Revision, and Quality," *Journal of Research on Computing in Education,* 25 (Winter 1992), pp. 172–183. These researchers both found that writers tend to muck things up when they compose first drafts on the screen. An initial phase of brainstorming on paper, especially for students having less than one year of word processing experience, was highly recommended. (See **Figure 6.17.**)

[10]Bangert-Drowns, Robert L., "The Word Processor as an Instructional Tool: A Meta-Analysis of Word Processing in Writing Instruction," *Review of Educational Research,* 63 (1993), pp. 69–93; Snyder, Ilana, "Writing with Word Processors: A Research Overview," *Educational Research,* 35 (Spring 1993), pp. 49–68. Note, however, that in many of the classroom-based

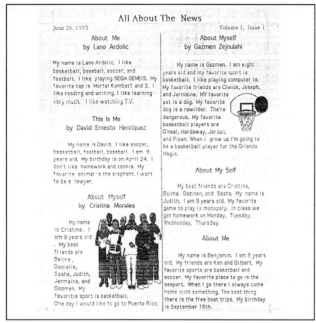

Figure 6.17. Alice Hom (P.S. 6, Manhattan) and I engaged third graders in process writing—brainstorming, drafting, editing, sharing, rereading, revising—before they diligently began keyboarding their contributions into a team newsletter. Reproduced with permission of Ms. Hom, her students, and the principal, Ms. Carmen Fariña.

studies reviewed by Snyder, "change or lack of change in writers' composing processes and/or texts cannot be attributed to computers alone; the writing pedagogy is also important in shaping the influence of computers" (p. 63).

[11]Chandler, Daniel, "The Purpose of the Computer in the Classroom," in Beynon, John, & Mackay, Hughie, eds., *Technological Literacy and the Curriculum* (Bristol, PA: The Falmer Press, 1992), p. 182.

[12]Tripp, Steven D., & Bichelmeyer, Barbara, "Rapid Prototyping: An Alternative Instructional Design Theory," *Educational Technology Research and Development*, 38, 2(1990), pp. 31–44; Jones, Mark K., Li, Zhongmin, & Merrill, M. David, "Rapid Prototyping in Automated Instructional Design," *Educational Technology Research and Development*, 40, 4(1992), pp. 95–100. Their work is cutting edge computer-based instruction, but their insights apply as well to production in all media.

[13]Ravitch, Diane, "Cultural Literacy: We Must Sustain Our Heritage," *Instructor*, 96 (January 1987), p. 16.

[14]Noddings, Nel, "A Morally Defensible Mission for Schools in the 21st Century," *Phi Delta Kappan*, 76 (January 1995), p. 367. See her *The Challenge to Care in Schools* (New York: Teachers College Press, 1992).

Sources

Whether we intend to produce classroom handouts, guide our students in process writing, or draft multimedia scripts with them, **we need to be able to write clearly.** I have included here many suggestive titles primarily to guide your search in finding those most related to your needs that might be readily available, perhaps in updated editions. As with all the media sources listed at the end of each chapter of this book, you may easily find related and more current works by accessing college library online catalogs via the Internet.

Aaron, Jane E., *The Essential Handbook for Writers* (New York: HarperCollins, 1994).

Aldrich-Ruenzel, Nancy, ed., *Designer's Guide to Print Production* (New York: Watson-Guptill Publications, 1990).

Atwell, Nancie, *Workshop I: Writing and Literature* (Portsmouth, NH: Heinemann, 1989).

Atwell, Nancie, ed., *Coming to Know: Writing to Learn in the Intermediate Grades* (Portsmouth, NH: Heinemann, 1990).

Atwell, Nancie, *Side by Side: Essays on Teaching to Learn* (Portsmouth, NH: Heinemann, 1991).

Au, Kathryn Hu-Pei, *Literacy Instruction in Multicultural Settings* (Fort Worth: Harcourt Brace College Publishers, 1993).

Bender, Hy, *Essential Software for Writers: A Complete Guide for Everyone Who Writes with a PC* (Cincinnati, OH: Writer's Digest Books, 1994).

Bogen, Nancy, *How to Write Poetry,* 2nd ed. (New York: Macmillan, 1994).

Bohle, Robert, *From News to Newsprint: Producing a Student Newspaper,* 2nd ed. (Englewood Cliffs, NJ: Prentice-Hall, 1992).

Brandt, Deborah, *Literacy as Involvement: The Acts of Writers, Readers, and Texts* (Carbondale, IL: Southern Illinois University Press, 1990).

Brigham, Nancy, with Catalfio, Maria, & Cluster, Dick, *How to Do Leaflets, Newsletters & Newspapers* (Detroit, MI: PEP Publishers, 1991).

Britton, Bruce K., Woodward, Arthur, & Binkley, Marilyn, eds., *Learning from Textbooks: Theory and Practice* (Hillsdale, NJ: Lawrence Erlbaum Associates, 1993).

Calkins, Lucy McCormick, *The Art of Teaching Writing,* new edition (Portsmouth, NH: Heinemann, 1994).

Clark, Margaret, *Writing for Children* (London: A & C Black, 1993).

Duffy, Thomas, & Waller, Robert, eds., *Designing Usable Texts* (Orlando, FL: Academic, 1985).

Ellington, Henry, *Producing Teaching Materials: A Handbook for Teachers and Trainers,* 2nd ed. (East Brunswick, NJ: Nichols, 1993).

Fishman, Stephen, *The Copyright Handbook: How to Protect and Use Written Works* (Berkeley, CA: Nolo Press, 1992).

Fitzgerald, Sallyanne H., *Essay Writing Simplified* (New York: HarperCollins, 1993).

Gordon, Emily R., & Troyka, Lynn Quitman, *Simon & Schuster Workbook for Writers*, 3rd ed. (Englewood Cliffs, NJ: Prentice-Hall, 1993).

Gropper, George L., *Text Displays: Analysis and Systematic Design* (Englewood Cliffs, NJ: Educational Technology Publications, 1991).

Hartley, James, *Designing Instructional Text*, 2nd ed. (London: Kogan Page, 1985).

Heller, Mary F., *Reading-Writing Connections: From Theory to Practice* (New York: Longman, 1991).

Hillocks Jr., George, *Teaching Writing as Reflective Practice* (New York: Teachers College Press, 1995).

Hopper, Vincent F., & Gale, Cedric, revised by Griffith Jr., Benjamin W., *Essentials of Writing: A Practical Workbook of Effective Techniques in English Composition* (Hauppauge, NY: Barron's Educational Series, 1991).

Jonassen, David H., ed., *The Technology of Text: Principles for Structuring, Designing, and Displaying Text*, Vol. 2 (Englewood Cliffs, NJ: Educational Technology Publications, 1985).

Karl, Jean E., *How to Write and Sell Children's Picture Books* (Cincinnati, OH: Writer's Digest Books, 1994).

Leggett, Glenn, Mead, C. David, Kramer, Melinda G., *Prentice Hall Handbook for Writers*, 11th ed. (Englewood Cliffs, NJ: Prentice-Hall, 1991).

Lies, Betty B., *The Poet's Pen: Writing Poetry with Middle and High School Students* (Englewood, CO: Libraries Unlimited, 1993).

Lindemann, Erika, *A Rhetoric for Writing Teachers*, 3rd ed. (New York: Oxford University Press, 1995).

Litowinsky, Olga, *Writing and Publishing Books for Children in the 1990s: The Inside Story from the Editor's Desk* (New York: Walker and Co., 1992).

Lockwood, Fred, *Activities in Self Instructional Texts* (East Brunswick, NJ: Nichols, 1993).

Marzano, Robert J., & Paynter, Diane E., *New Approaches to Literacy: Helping Students Develop Reading and Writing Skills* (Washington, DC: American Psychological Association, 1994).

Misanchuk, Earl R., *Preparing Instructional Text: Document Design Using Desktop Publishing* (Englewood Cliffs, NJ: Educational Technology Publications, 1992).

Mizokawa, Donald T., *Everyday Computing in Academe: A Guide for Scholars, Researchers, Students, and Other Academic Users of Personal Computers* (Englewood Cliffs, NJ: Educational Technology Publications, 1994).

Mogilner, Alijandra, *Children's Writer's Word Book* (Cincinnati, OH: Writer's Digest Books, 1992).

Olson, David R., *The World on Paper: The Conceptual and Cognitive Implications of Writing and Reading* (Cambridge: Cambridge University Press, 1994).

Packard, William, *The Art of Poetry Writing: A Guide for Poets, Students, and Readers* (New York: St. Martin's Press, 1992).

Smith, Brigid, *Through Writing to Reading: Classroom Strategies for Supporting Literacy* (New York: Routledge, 1994).

Stillman, Peter R., *Write Away: A Friendly Guide for Teenage Writers* (Portsmouth, NH: Heinemann, 1995).

Strunk Jr., William & White, E. B., *Elements of Style: With Index*, 3rd ed. (New York: Macmillan, 1979).

Styles, Morag, Bearne, Eve, & Watson, Victor, eds., *The Prose and the Passion: Children and Their Reading* (London: Cassell, 1994).

Talab, Rosemary S., *Copyright and Instructional Technologies: A Guide to Fair Use and Permission Procedures*, 2nd ed. (Washington, DC: Association for Educational Communications and Technology, 1989).

Temple, Charles A., *et al.*, *The Beginnings of Writing* (Boston: Allyn and Bacon, 1993).

Vlcek, Charles W., *Adoptable Copyright Policy: Copyright Policy and Manuals for Adoption by Schools, Colleges & Universities* (Washington, DC: Association for Educational Communications and Technology, 1992).

Wyndham, Lee, revised by Madison, Arnold, *Writing for Children & Teenagers*, 3rd ed. (Cincinnati, OH: Writer's Digest Books, 1992).

Zinsser, William, *On Writing Well: An Informal Guide to Writing Nonfiction*, 5th ed. (New York: HarperCollins, 1994).

Reading different sorts of material for different purposes, whether presented in print or on a computer screen, entails a host of skills that comprise functional literacy today. Approaches to the **teaching of reading** and related topics, especially the **analysis and appreciation of literature** may be found in:

Adams, Marilyn Jager, *Beginning to Read: Thinking and Learning About Print* (Cambridge, MA: The MIT Press, 1990).

Adler Jr., Bill, *Tell Me a Fairy Tale: A Parent's Guide to Telling Magical and Mythical Stories* (New York: Penguin, 1995).

Atwell, Nancie, *In the Middle: Writing, Reading, and Learning with Adolescents* (Montclair, NJ: Boynton Cook, 1987).

Balajthy, Ernest, *Computers and Reading: Lessons from the Past and the Technologies of the Future* (Boston: Allyn and Bacon, 1989).

Barchers, Suzanne I., *Creating and Managing the Literate Classroom: Making the Whole Language Transition* (Englewood, CO: Libraries Unlimited, 1990).

Barr, Rebecca, & Johnson, Barbara, *Teaching Reading in Elementary Classrooms: Developing Independent Readers* (New York: Longman, 1991).

Borders, Sarah G., & Naylor, Alice Phoebe, *Children Talking About Books* (Phoenix, AZ: Oryx Press, 1993).

Braddon, Kathryn L., Hall, Nancy J., & Taylor, Dale, *Math Through Children's Literature: Making the NCTM Standards Come Alive* (Englewood, CO: Teachers Idea Press, 1993).

Butzow, Carol M., & Butzow, John W., *Science Through Children's Literature: An Integrated Approach* (Englewood, CO: Libraries Unlimited, 1989).

Carruth, Gorton, *The Young Reader's Companion* (New Providence, NJ: Bowker, 1993).

Chall, Jeanne S., Conard, Sue S., with Harris-Sharples, Susan, *Should Textbooks Challenge Students? The Case for Easier or Harder Textbooks* (New York: Teachers College Press, 1991).

Chall, Jeanne S., & Jacobs, Vicki A., with Baldwin, Luke E., *The Reading Crisis: Why Poor Children Fall Behind* (Cambridge, MA: Harvard University Press, 1990).

Chamot, Anna Uhl, & O'Malley, J. Michael, *The CALLA Handbook: Implementing the Cognitive Academic Language Learning Approach* (Reading: MA: Addison-Wesley, 1994).

Ciborowski, Jean, *Textbooks and the Students who Can't Read Them: A Guide to Teaching Content* (Cambridge, MA: Brookline Books, 1992).

Cooper, J. David, *Literacy: Helping Children Construct Meaning*, 2nd ed. (Boston, MA: Houghton Mifflin, 1993).

Cox, Carole, & Zarrillo, James, *Teaching Reading with Children's Literature* (New York: Merrill, 1993).

Cramer, Eugene H., & Castle, Marietta, eds., *Fostering the Love of Reading: The Affective Domain in Reading Education* (Newark, DE: International Reading Association, 1994).

Cullinan, Bernice E., & Galda, Lee, *Literature and the Child*, 3rd ed. (Fort Worth, TX: Harcourt Brace College Publishers, 1994).

Cunningham, Patricia M., Moore, Sharon Arthur, Cunningham, James W., & Moore, David W., *Reading and Writing in Elementary Classrooms: Strategies and Observations*, 3rd ed. (White Plains, NY: Longman, 1995).

Danielson, Kathy Everts, & LaBonty, Jan, *Integrating Reading and Writing Through Children's Literature* (Boston: Allyn and Bacon, 1994).

Dechant, Emerald, *Whole-Language Reading: A Comprehensive Teaching Guide* (Lancaster, PA: Technomic, 1993).

DelFattore, Joan, *What Johnny Shouldn't Read: Textbook Censorship in America* (New Haven, CT: Yale University Press, 1992).

Doll, Carol A., *Nonfiction Books for Children: Activities for Thinking, Learning, and Doing* (Englewood, CO: Libraries Unlimited, 1990).

Durkin, Dolores, *Teaching Them to Read*, 6th ed. (Boston: Allyn and Bacon, 1993).

Farr, Roger, & Tone, Bruce, *Portfolio and Performance Assessment: Helping Students Evaluate Their Progress as Readers and Writers* (Fort Worth, TX: Harcourt Brace College Publishers, 1994).

Fredericks, Anthony D., *Involving Parents Through Children's Literature* (Englewood, CO: Libraries Unlimited, 1993).

Fusco, Esther, Quinn, Mary C., & Hauck, Marjorie, *The Portfolio Assessment Handbook Reading: A Practical Guide for Implementing and Organizing Portfolio Evaluation* (Roslyn, NY: Berrent Publications, 1993).

Gillespie, John T., & Naden, Corinne J., *Juniorplots: A Book Talk Guide for Use with Readers Ages 12-16* (New York: Bowker, 1993).

Glazer, Susan, & Brown, Carol, *Portfolios and Beyond: Collaborative Assessment in Reading and Writing* (Norwood, MA: Christopher Gordon Publishers, 1993).

Gough, Philip B., Ehri, Linnea C., & Treiman, Rebecca, eds., *Reading Acquisition* (Hillsdale, NJ: Lawrence Erlbaum Associates, 1992).

Graves, Donald H., & Sunstein, Bonnie S., eds., *Portfolios Portraits* (Portsmouth, NH: Heinemann, Reed Publishing, 1992).

Hayes, David A., *A Sourcebook of Interactive Methods for Teaching with Texts* (Boston: Allyn and Bacon, 1992).

Heilman, Arthur W., Blair, Timothy R., Rupley, William H., *Principles and Practices of Teaching Reading*, 8th ed. (New York: Merrill, 1994).

Hill, Mary W., *Home: Where Reading and Writing Begin* (Portsmouth, NH: Heinemann, 1995).

Howie, Sherry H., *Reading, Writing and Computers: Planning for Integration* (Boston: Allyn and Bacon, 1989).

Irving, Jan, & Currie, Robin, *From the Heart: Books and Activities About Friends* (Englewood, CO: Libraries Unlimited, 1992).

Jensen, Janice, illustrated by Jerde, Susan, *Literature-Based Learning Activities Kit: Ready-to-Use Whole Language Lessons & Worksheets for Grades 2-6* (West Nyack, NY: Center for Applied Research in Education, 1991).

Krashen, Stephen D., *The Power of Reading: Insights from the Research* (Englewood, CO: Libraries Unlimited, 1992).

Kruise, Carol S., *Learning Through Literature: Activities to Enhance Reading, Writing, and Thinking Skills* (Englewood, CO: Libraries Unlimited, 1990).

Laughlin, Mildred K., & Watt, Letty S., *Developing Learning Skills through Children's Literature: An Idea Book for K-5 Classrooms and Libraries* (Phoenix, AZ: Oryx, 1986).

Leonhardt, Mary, *Parents Who Love Reading, Kids Who Don't: How It Happens and What You Can Do About It* (New York: Crown Trade Paperbacks, 1995).

Leu, Donald J., & Kinzer, Charles K., *Effective Reading Instruction*, 3rd ed. (New York: Merrill, 1995).

Linksman, Ricki, *Solving Your Child's Reading Problems* (New York: Citadel Press, 1995).

Lukens, Rebecca J., *A Critical Handbook of Children's Literature*, 5th ed. (New York: HarperCollins, 1995).

Lynch-Brown, Carol, & Tomlinson, Carl M., *Essentials of Children's Literature* (Boston: Allyn and Bacon, 1993).

Lyons, Carol A., Pinnell, Gay Su, & Deford, Diane E., *Partners in Learning: Teachers and Children in Reading Recovery* (New York: Teachers College Press, 1993).

Marriott, Stuart, *Picture Books in the Primary Classroom* (London: Paul Chapman, 1991).

May, Frank B., *Reading as Communication*, 4th ed. (New York: Merrill, 1994).

McCarthy, Mary-Jane, Rasool, Joan, & Banks, Caroline, *Reading and Learning Across the Disciplines* (Belmont, CA: Wadsworth, 1993).

McElmeel, Sharron L., *McElmeel Booknotes: Literature Across the Curriculum* (Englewood, CO: Libraries Unlimited, 1993).

Miller, Wilma H., *Complete Reading Disabilities Handbook: Ready-to-Use Techniques for Teaching Reading Disabled Students* (West Nyack, NY: Center for Applied Research in Education, 1993).

Mohr, Carolyn, Nixon, Dorothy, & Vickers, Shirley, *Books that Heal: A Whole Language Approach* (Englewood, CO: Libraries Unlimited, 1991).

Montgomery, Paula Kay, *Approaches to Literature Through Theme* (Phoenix, AZ: Oryx Press, 1992).

Moore, David W., Moore, Sharon Arthur, Cunningham, Patricia M., & Cunningham, James W., *Developing Readers & Writers in the Content Areas K–12*, 2nd ed. (White Plains, NY: Longman, 1994).

Moore, Terry Jeffers, & Hampton, Anita Brent, illustrated by Kropa, Susan, *Book Bridges: Story-Inspired Activities for Children, Three Through Eight* (Englewood, CO: Teachers Ideas Press, 1991).

Neamen, Mimi, & Strong, Mary, illustrated by Servatt, Karen, *Literature Circles: Cooperative Learning for Grades 3–8* (Englewood, CO: Teachers Ideas Press, 1992).

Nodelman, Perry, *The Pleasures of Children's Literature* (New York, Longman, 1991).

Olsen, Mary Lou, *More Creative Connections: Literature and the Reading Program, Grades 4–6* (Englewood, CO: Teachers Ideas Press, 1993).

Paulin, Mary Ann, *More Creative Uses of Children's Literature* (Hamden, CT: Library Professional Publications, 1992).

Raines, Shirley, & Isbell, Rebecca, *Stories: Children's Literature in Early Education* (New York: Delmar Publishers, 1994).

Rhodes, Lynn K., ed., *Literacy Assessment: A Handbook of Instruments* (Portsmouth, NH: Heinemann, 1993).

Richardson, Judy S., & Morgan, Raymond F., *Reading to Learn in the Content Areas*, 2nd ed. (Belmont, CA: Wadsworth, 1994).

Robertson, Debbie, & Barry, Patricia, *Super Kids Publishing Company* (Englewood, CO: Libraries Unlimited, 1990).

Roser, Nancy L., Martinez, Miriam G., eds., *Book Talk and Beyond: Children and Teachers Respond to Literature* (Newark, DE: International Reading Association, 1995).

Rubin, Dorothy, *A Practical Approach to Teaching Reading*, 2nd ed. (Boston: Allyn and Bacon, 1993).

Russell, David L., *Literature for Children: A Short Introduction*, 2nd ed. (New York: Longman, 1994).

Ryder, Randall J., *Reading and Learning in the Content Areas* (New York: Merrill, 1994).

Sampson, Michael R., Allen, Roach Van, & Sampson, Mary Beth, *Pathways to Literacy: A Meaning-Centered Perspective* (Fort Worth, TX: Holt, Rinehart and Winston, 1991).

Sitarz, Paula Gaj, *More Picture Book Story Hours: From Parties to Pets* (Englewood, CO: Libraries Unlimited, 1990).

Slaughter, Judith Pollard, *Beyond Storybooks: Young Children and the Shared Book Experience* (Newark, DE: International Reading Association, 1993).

Smith, Frank, *Understanding Reading: A Psycholinguistic Analysis of Reading and Learning to Read*, 5th ed. (Hillsdale, NJ: Lawrence Erlbaum Associates, 1994).

Stewig, John Warren, & Buege, Carol, *Dramatizing Literature in Whole Language Classrooms*, 2nd ed. (New York: Teachers College Press, 1994).

Strong, Mary, & Neamen, Mimi, *Writing Through Children's Literature, Grades 3–8: From Authors to Authorship* (Englewood, CO: Libraries Unlimited, 1993).

Sullivan, Emilie P., *Starting with Books: An Activities Approach to Children's Literature* (Englewood, CO: Libraries Unlimited, 1990).

Sutherland, Zena, & Arbuthnot, May Hill, *Children and Books*, 8th ed. (New York: HarperCollins, 1991).

Tierney, Robert J., Readence, John E., & Dishner, Ernest K., *Reading Strategies and Practices: A Compendium*, 4th ed. (Boston: Allyn and Bacon, 1995).

Vacca, Jo Anne L., Vacca, Richard T., & Gove, Mary K., *Reading and Learning to Read*, 3rd ed. (New York: HarperCollins, 1995).

Valencia, Sheila W., Hiebert, Elfrieda H., & Afflerbach, Peter P., eds., *Authentic Reading Assessment: Practices and Possibilities* (Newark, DE: International Reading Association, 1994).

Vandergrift, Kay E., *Children's Literature: Theory, Research, and Teaching* (Englewood, CO: Libraries Unlimited, 1990).

Van Vliet, Lucille W., *Approaches to Literature Through Genre* (Phoenix, AZ: Oryx Press, 1992).

Vine Jr., Harold A., & Faust, Mark A., *Situating Readers: Students Making Meaning of Literature* (Urbana, IL: National Council of Teachers of English, 1993).

Watt, Letty S., & Street, Terri Parker, *Developing Learning Skills Through Children's Literature: An Idea Book for K–5 Classrooms and Libraries*, vol. 2 (Phoenix, AZ: Oryx Press, 1994).

Weaver, Constance, *Reading Process and Practice: From Socio-Psycholinguistics to Whole Language*, 2nd ed. (Portsmouth, NH: Heinemann, 1994).

Wepner, Shelley B., & Feeley, Joan T., *Moving Forward with Literature: Basals, Books, and Beyond* (New York: Merrill, 1993).

Wildberger, Mary Elizabeth, *Approaches to Literature Through Authors* (Phoenix, AZ: Oryx Press, 1993).

Wiseman, Donna L., *Learning to Read with Literature* (Boston: Allyn and Bacon, 1992).

Wood, Karen D., & Algozzine, Bob, eds., *Teaching Reading to High Risk Learners: A Unified Perspective* (Boston: Allyn and Bacon, 1994).

Wood, Karen D., ed., with Moss, Anita, *Exploring Literature in the Classroom: Content and Methods* (Norwood, MA: Christopher-Gordon, 1992).

Yopp, Ruth H., & Yopp, Hallie K., *Literature-Based Reading Activities* (Boston: Allyn and Bacon, 1992).

Computer programs designed to teach **reading skills to children** include *Reader Rabbit's Ready for Letters, Reader Rabbit 1*, and *Reader Rabbit 2*, all from The Learning Company (1-800-852-2255). See also Chapter **12** and the Sources section at the end of this book.

Computer programs designed to teach reading and writing to **students with disabilities** (using computer generated speech and touch sensitive screen) include *Breakthrough To Language, Volume I* and *Volume II*, and *Breakthrough to Writing, Volume III*, all from Creative Learning, Inc. (1-800-842-5360).

Additional information about teaching children to read may be obtained from:

International Reading Association
1-800-336-READ; 1-302-731-1600

Reading Is Fundamental, Inc.
1-202-287-3220

Educational technology guides us in designing enriched classroom environments that foster achievement of the highest of educational aims, academic and moral. Good quality schoolbooks and imaginative, wholesome literature are core elements in these environments. **Lists, reviews, and selection guidelines** are found in:

Bailey, William G., *Guide to Popular U.S. Government Publications*, 2nd ed. (Englewood, CO: Libraries Unlimited, 1990).

Barchers, Suzanne I., *Wise Women: Folk and Fairy Tales from Around the World* (Englewood, CO: Libraries Unlimited, 1990).

Benedict, Susan, & Carlisle, Lenore, eds., *Beyond Words: Picture Books for Older Readers and Writers* (Portsmouth, NH: Heinemann, 1992).

Book Review Index (bimonthly).

Buck, Claire, ed., *The Bloomsbury Guide to Women's Literature* (Englewood Cliffs, NJ: Prentice-Hall, 1992).

Carlin, Margaret F., Laughlin, Jeannine L., & Saniga, Richard D., *Understanding Abilities, Disabilities, and Capabilities: A Guide to Children's Literature* (Englewood, CO: Libraries Unlimited, 1991).

Children's Book Council, *More Kids' Favorite Books: A Compilation of Children's Choices, 1992–1994* (Newark, DE: International Reading Association, 1995).

Children's Book Review Index (Detroit, MI: Gale Research, annual).

Children's Books in Print (New York: Bowker, annual).

Donavin, Denise P., ed., *American Library Association Best of the Best for Children* (New York: Random House, 1992).

El-Hi Textbooks and Serials in Print (New York: Bowker, annual).

Estell, Doug, Satchwell, Michele L., & Wright, Patricia S., *ARCO Reading Lists for College-Bound Students*, 2nd ed. (New York: Prentice-Hall, 1993).

Fakih, Kimberly Olson, *The Literature of Delight: A Critical Guide to Humorous Books for Children* (New Providence, NJ: R.R. Bowker, 1993).

Fredericks, Anthony D., *The Integrated Curriculum: Books for Reluctant Readers, Grades 2–5* (Englewood, CO: Libraries Unlimited, 1992).

Gillespie, John T., ed., *Best Books for Junior High Readers* (New York: Bowker, 1991)

Gillespie, John T., ed., *Best Books for Senior High Readers* (New York: Bowker, 1991)

Gillespie, John T., & Gilbert, Christine B., *Best Books for Children: Preschool Through the Middle Grades*, 3rd ed. (New York: Bowker, 1985).

Gillespie, John T., & Naden, Corinne J., eds., *Best Books for Children: Preschool Through Grade 6*, 4th ed. (New York: Bowker, 1990).

Hearne, Betsy, *Choosing Books for Children: A Commonsense Guide* (New York: Delacorte Press, 1990).

Hobson, Margaret, Madden, Jennifer, & Prytherch, Raymond John, *Children's Fiction Sourcebook: A Survey of Children's Books for 6–13 Year-Olds* (Brookfield, VT: Gower, 1992).

Immell, Myra, ed., *The Young Adult Reader's Adviser, Volume 1: The Best in Literature and Language Arts, Mathematics and Computer Science* (New Providence: NJ: Bowker, 1992).

Immell, Myra, ed., *The Young Adult Reader's Adviser, Volume 2: The Best in Social Sciences and History, Science and Health* (New Providence: NJ: Bowker, 1992).

Kuipers, Barbara J., *American Indian Reference Books for Children and Young Adults* (Englewood, CO: Libraries Unlimited, 1991).

Landsberg, Michele, *Reading for the Love of It: Best Books for Young Readers* (New York: Prentice-Hall, 1987).

Lee, Sul H., ed., *Access to Scholarly Information: Issues & Strategies* (Ann Arbor, MI: Pierian, 1985).

Liggett, Twila C., & Benfield, Cynthia Mayer, *Reading Rainbow Guide to Children's Books: The 101 Best Titles* (New York: Citadel Press, 1994).

Lima, Carolyn W., & Lima, John A., *A to Zoo: Subject Access to Children's Picture Books*, 4th ed. (New York: Bowker, 1993).

Lipson, Eden Ross, *The New York Times Parent's Guide to the Best Books for Children*, revised and updated (New York: Times Books, 1991).

March, Andrew L., *Recommended Reference Books in Paperback*, 2nd ed. (Englewood, CO: Libraries Unlimited, 1992).

McGovern, Edythe M., & Muller, Helen D., *They're Never Too Young for Books: A Guide to Children's Books for Ages 1 to 8* (Buffalo, NY: Prometheus Books, 1994).

Moir, Hughes, ed., with Cain, Melissa, & Prosak-Beres, Leslie, *Collected Perspectives: Choosing and Using Books for the Classroom*, 2nd ed. (Boston: Christopher-Gordon, 1992).

Moss, Anita, & Stott, Jon C., *The Family of Stories: An Anthology of Children's Literature* (New York: Holt, Rinehart and Winston, 1986).

National Council of Teachers of English, *High Interest–Easy Reading: For Junior and Senior High School Students*, 5th ed. (Urbana, IL: National Council of Teachers of English, 1988).

Nichols, Margaret I., *Guide to Reference Books for School Media Centers*, 4th ed. (Englewood, CO: Libraries Unlimited, 1992).

Oppenheim, Joanne, Brenner, Barbara, & Boegehold, Betty D., *Choosing Books for Kids: Choosing the Right Book for the Right Child at the Right Time* (New York: Ballantine Books, 1986).

Pearlman, Mickey, *What to Read: The Essential Guide for Reading Group Members and Other Book Lovers* (New York: HarperCollins, 1994).

Pilla, Marianne L., *The Best: High/Low Books for Reluctant Readers* (Englewood, CO: Libraries Unlimited, 1990).

Puckett, Katharyn E., *My Name in Books: An Annotated Guide to Children's Literature* (Englewood, CO: Libraries Unlimited, 1993).

Ramirez Jr., Gonzalo, & Ramirez, Jan L., *Multiethnic Children's Literature in Early Education* (New York: Delmar Publishers, 1994).

Rasinski, Timothy V., & Gillespie, Cindy S., *Sensitive Issues: An Annotated Guide to Children's Literature, K–6* (Phoenix, AZ: Oryx Press, 1992).

Reed, Arthea J. S., *Comics to Classics: A Guide to Books for Teens and Preteens* (New York: Penguin, 1994).

Rosenberg, Betty, & Herald, Diana T., *Genreflecting: A Guide to Reading Interests in Genre Fiction*, 3rd ed. (Englewood, CO: Libraries Unlimited, 1991).

Sarkissian, Adele, *High Interest Books for Teens: A Guide to Book Reviews & Bibliographic Sources* (Detroit, MI: Gale Research, 1981).

Smith, Laura J., *Children's Book Awards International: A Directory of Awards and Winners, from Inception Through 1990* (Jefferson, NC: McFarland & Co., 1992).

Spencer, Michael, *Free Publications from U.S. Government Agencies: A Guide* (Englewood, CO: Libraries Unlimited, 1989).

Thomas, James L., *Play, Learn, and Grow: An Annotated Guide to the Best Books and Materials for Very Young Children* (New Providence, NJ: Bowker, 1992).

Trelease, Jim, ed., *Hey! Listen to This: Stories to Read Aloud* (New York: Penguin, 1992).

The California Department of Education has prepared lists of recommended books for grades K–12. Included are books that have "compelling intellectual, social, and moral content," those that have "emotional, intellectual, and aesthetic substance," and "recreational/motivational literature." Request the *Educational Resources Catalog* from:

California Department of Education
Bureau of Publications, Sales Unit
P.O. Box 271
Sacramento, CA 95812-0271
1-800-995-4099; 1-916-445-1260

Guidelines for selecting children's books may be obtained from:

Children's Book Council
568 Broadway, Suite 404
New York, NY 10012

"High interest-easy reading" materials are available for students lacking either skill or interest in reading literature in its original form. They include "High Noon Books" from Academic Therapy Publications with their novels for teens and adults, the "Hi-Lo" Dell paperbacks with their sporting, romance, and science fiction stories, "High Interest Materials" from Troll Books with their humorous stories and books about sports, "The Reading Scene" and "Talewind Hoops" from Continental Press with their adventure stories and sports biographies, and the "Now Age Illustrated Series" of Pendulum Press (now handled by Desert Sky Publications) with their simplified renditions of great literature. (See **Figure 6.18**.)

Richly illustrated subject matter may be found in "Beginners Documentary Comic Books" (Writers and Readers Publishing), *Introducing . . .* (Totem Books), and Larry Gonick's *Cartoon Guide to . . .* (HarperCollins Publishers).

Free materials are listed in the following regularly updated Educators Progress Service publications:

Educators Grade Guide to Free Teaching Aids
Educators Index to Free Materials
Elementary Teachers Guide to Free Curriculum Materials

A catalog listing **informative booklets** may be obtained from:

Consumer Information Center
U.S. General Services Administration
Consumer Information Catalog
Pueblo, CO 81009
1-719-948-4000

Figure 6.18. Mature subject matter is brought within reach of poor readers when written in elementary terms and amply illustrated. What are the advantages and disadvantages of students reading literature in this form? Source: Charles Dickens, *A Tale of Two Cities* (West Haven, CT: Pendulum Press, 1974), p. 61. Copyright © 1974 Pendulum Press. Reprinted courtesy of Desert Sky Publications.

Magazine and newspaper publishers provide timely information of value to teachers and students. In addition to news weeklies and daily newspapers, we **teachers** can benefit from reading issues of the following:

Instructor
Journal of Learning Disabilities
Journal of Reading
Journal of Reading Behavior
Language Arts
Media & Methods

Research in the Teaching of English
Reading Research Quarterly
The Reading Teacher
Teacher Reports
Teaching K–8

For students try:

The Barney Family Magazine
Barney Magazine
Brakes: The Interactive Newsletter for Kids with ADHD
Children's Digest
Creative Classroom
Creative Kids
Humpty Dumpty's Magazine
Jack & Jill
Junior Scholastic
Kid City
Kids Discover
Kidstuff
The MAILBOX Magazine
Mickey Mouse Magazine
NewsCurrents
Nickelodeon Magazine
Radio AAHS! Kid's Magazine
Sesame Street
The Scholastic
3-2-1 Contact
Weekly Reader

The comprehensive **index** to periodical articles is:

Reader's Guide to Periodical Literature (New York: H. W. Wilson, monthly).

Some major periodical publishers (e.g., *U.S. News & World Report, Time, Newsweek, The Los Angeles Times, The New York Times*) offer teachers comprehensive study guides along with paid class subscriptions. These serve to integrate their products into school curriculums in ways that should serve as **models for classroom use of interactive multimedia and the Internet.** Suggestions for productive **classroom use of periodical literature,** whether in print or electronic form, may be found in:

Anderson, Frances J., *Classroom Newspaper Activities: A Resource for Teachers, Grades K–8* (Springfield, IL: Charles C. Thomas, 1985).
Barnhurst, Kevin G., *Seeing the Newspaper* (New York: St. Martin's Press, 1994).
Carroll, Deborah Drezon, *Good News: How Sharing the Newspaper with your Children Can Enhance Their Performance in School* (New York: Penguin, 1993).

Cheyney, Arnold B., *Teaching Reading Skills Through the Newspaper*, 3rd ed. (Newark, DE: International Reading Association, 1992).

DeRoche, Edward F., *The Newspaper: A Reference Book for Teachers and Librarians* (Santa Barbara, CA: ADC-CLIO, 1991).

Granfield, Linda, *Extra! Extra! The Who, What, Where, When and Why of Newspapers* (New York: Orchard Books, 1993).

Heitzmann, William R., *The Newspaper in the Classroom*, 2nd ed. (Washington, DC: National Education Association, 1986).

Olivares, Rafael A., *Using the Newspaper to Teach ESL Learners* (Newark: DE: International Reading Association, 1993).

Information about **Newspapers in Education** programs is available from:

American Newspaper Publishers Association Foundation
The Newspaper Center
11600 Sunrise Valley Dr.
Reston, VA 22091
1-703-648-1000

Also call the **Educational Resources Information Center** (1-800-LET-ERIC) to locate additional sources, or pose questions via the Internet (askeric@ericir.syr.edu).

Indexed **print** and searchable CD-ROM **reprints of articles** from newspapers, magazines, government publications, and journals are available from Social Issues Resources Series, Inc. (1-800-232-SIRS) and Newsbank, Inc. (1-800-762-8182).

Information about **microforms** may be found in:

Guide to Microforms in Print (Westport, CT: Meckler, published annually)
Microform Review

A sample request to use **copyrighted materials** is provided in **Figure 6.19**. I found that book authors must include expected date of publication, number of copies to be printed, whether the book is to be hard or soft bound, and market for book (USA or world), along with photocopies of the title and copyright pages of the source. If you receive no reply, a follow-up handwritten plea of "please help" written in green ink on a copy of the original request might work as well for you as it did for me.

SAMPLE REQUEST FOR PERMISSION

April 2, 1976

Permissions Department
XYZ Company
111 Main St.
Anytown, U.S.A. 11111

Dear Sir or Madam:

I would like permission to use five frames from one of your filmstrips. These frames, showing the ring-formation of a young tree, will be combined for presentation with frames from filmstrips from two other companies showing the development of the tree through the years.

Title: <u>Trees and Their Importance</u>
      Collaborator: William M. Harlow
      Color Film Number 2392

Material to Be Duplicated: Frames 245, 246, 247, 248, and 249

Type of Reproduction: Color slides will be made of each frame.

Number of Copies: Only one copy will be made of each frame.

Use to Be Made of Copies: The five slides will be shown in sequence with three slides each copied from two other filmstrips.

Distribution of Copies: The slide presentation will be shown via carousel projector to three classes of sixth-grade science students. Average class size is 35.

A self-addressed envelope and a copy of this letter for your files are enclosed for your convenience.

Please let us know what conditions, if any, apply to this use.

Sincerely,

John Smith
Media Director

JS:cml.

Permission granted: _____ _____
                  Signature   Date

Conditions, if any: _____ _____
                  Signature   Date

Figure 6.19. Some liberties that we have under the "fair use" doctrine of copyright law include "one time only," "spontaneous use," of "short segments." For any material that we wish to reuse or incorporate into our lessons we must both obtain permission in writing from the publisher **and** acknowledge the source. Here is a form to guide our requests. Source: Rosemary S. Talab, *Copyright and Instructional Technologies: A Guide to Fair Use and Permissions Procedures,* 2nd ed. (Washington, DC: Association for Educational Communications and Technology, 1989), p. 24. Reprinted with permission of AECT. Copyright © 1989.

Study Items

1. Compare and contrast the processes of inscribing clay tablets, handwriting with pencil and paper, and word processing.

2. In what ways have printed documents provided windows on history? Speculate on how your life might have been different if these works had not endured.

3. List some distinctive qualities and educational uses of microform technology.

4. In what ways do textbooks make instruction more individualized, accessible, valid, and economical?

5. How would you use periodical literature to supplement textbook materials?

6. State three ways in which works of fiction might contribute to achievement of instructional objectives in a subject you teach.

7. What are some advantages of printed materials over text presented on a computer screen?

8. Describe special skills needed to decipher text? What characteristics of text make this task easier?

9. Compare use of a printed dictionary with an electronic one like that found in *The Writer's Toolkit* (now *The Author's Toolkit*, available from Sunburst Communications) or your word processor.

10. What do pictures and graphics contribute to communication of ideas expressed in words?

11. Provide several examples of contributions that electronic media have made to the storage, distribution, and classroom presentation of printed text.

12. To what extent can electronic media effectively and economically end reliance on printed letters, forms, contracts, scripts, and lesson plans?

13. List six categories of criteria for selection of print materials. Describe any one of them in depth, adding to those described in this chapter elements that you believe pertinent.

Suggested Activities

1. Visit a museum to view samples of Sumerian clay tablets and Egyptian papyrus. Write a report on what the translations reveal about life and values during those times. (See **Figure 6.20.**)

2. Examine exhibits on the development of print technology, from hand-written manuscripts to automated typesetting. Note what is claimed about the future of the printed word.

3. Check one of your classroom handouts with *Grammatik* (Novell/WordPerfect) or *Right Writer*. List suggestions made that you find to be entirely in error as well as those that are helpful. Share findings with class members.

4. Word process a few pages from a textbook assignment you have given your students. Have your grammar checker provide readability scores. Do the scores reveal that the material assigned was perhaps too difficult or too easy for your students?

5. Use *Grammatik* to identify difficult words in material you intend to assign and prepare a glossary to accompany the assignment.

6. Use *The Author's Toolkit* to determine if the text you have used in a handout is suitable for your students. Do the same for a notice to parents.

Figure 6.20. The Egyptian papyrus *Book of the Dead* (350-250 B.C.), amply illustrated, provides a glimpse into that mysterious era. Location: The Metropolitan Museum of Art (New York City).

7. Using *Adobe Illustrator, Aldus PageMaker, Microsoft Works, Microsoft Publisher, Harvard Graphics, Freelance Graphics, Express Publisher, Ami Pro, Publish It!, Ventura Publisher* (with their CD-ROM libraries of clip-art), or other such software (e.g., *ClarisWorks* or *The Writing Center*), to produce a class newsletter. Have each student contribute text and graphics, and collaborate on page layout.

8. Visit a computer exhibition, retailer, or media library and examine *The Bank Street Writer, Children's Newspaper Maker, The Children's Writing and Publishing Center*, and *Kid Works Deluxe*. Note adaptations for children and prepare a report to share with your classmates.

9. Examine the microform collection in your college library. Ask a staff person to show you how to find a microform on a topic of interest to you and produce a paper copy of any frame.

10. Investigate the process by which textbooks are selected in your school district. Does this process ensure selection of the best available?

11. List unfamiliar words you encounter in your readings. Input the list on your word processor and provide simple definitions. Carry a pocket notebook with you to note words for input when convenient to keep your *Personal Glossary* current.

12. Visit a media production facility. Note the extent to which printed documents dominate. Ask why printed text is used rather than electronic text.

13. Use **Figure 6.09** to evaluate a textbook you use.

14. Use **Figure 6.09** to craft a handout for presentation to your class. Ask students to grade the handout based on the criteria listed.

15. Revise **Figure 6.09** to relate more directly to your concerns and prepare a transparency or poster of your version to share with classmates.

16. Examine such computer software as *U.S. Atlas, World Atlas,* the *Random House Dictionary,* the *American Heritage Dictionary,* and the *Macmillan Dictionary for Children.* Report on ease of use in comparison with corresponding print sources.

17. Examine CD-ROM versions of the *Oxford English Dictionary,* the *Funk & Wagnalls New Encyclopedia (Microsoft Encarta), The Concise Columbia Encyclopedia* and *The Hammond Atlas (Microsoft Bookshelf),* and *Front Page News.* Demonstrate one to your classmates and, with their help, list advantages of interactive multimedia presentations over print alone.

18. View CD-ROM versions of *Great Literature* and *Greatest Books Collection* and compare with your own experience in reading the printed sources. Consider possible physiological effects on the eyes of children.

19. It is my belief that reading and writing require undivided attention. "Background music" or TV, in my view, diminish the concentration needed to grasp or express difficult concepts. Some would call this a good strategy for coping with attention deficient disorder (ADD). Meet with your fellow students and share your views on the best conditions for reading and writing.

20. After a period of study, I believe that it is best to sit in silence, have a meal, or go to sleep. In my view, turning on the radio or TV "erases" what was learned ("retroactive inhibition") and prevents creative interpretation and appropriation. Reflect on this and then share your views with your classmates.

21. Examine some source materials listed in this chapter and report to your class any that you find especially helpful.

22. Participate in **"learner verification"** by sharing with me your responses to the above study items. This will enable me to determine if this text, with the help of your instructors in this and other classes, is providing adequate information.

23. Let me know about any errors you find in this chapter or about information that should be added or deleted (Internet: hackbarths@aol.com).

Chapter 7

Still Pictures and Graphics

Chapter Content and Objectives

Like the printed word, pictures and graphics are means of expressing ideas. Each employs lines and patterns, colors and shades, to convey information. In this chapter, I assess the use of pictures and graphics in education and expect that, after careful reading, you will be able to:

- Define **essential characteristics** of still pictures and graphics ("still visuals").
- Describe means of **displaying** and **projecting** still visuals.
- **Summarize effects** of still visuals on learning.
- **Evaluate use** of still visuals in children's literature and schoolbooks.
- Specify criteria for **selecting** and **producing** still visuals.
- State **guidelines** to ensure that students capture intended messages from still visuals.
- Define **"visual literacy"** in terms of skill in evaluating and creating images.

Still Pictures

Throughout history, people everywhere have invented ways of depicting what they see. Prehistoric tribes sketched beasts of prey. Early civilizations carved objects in metal and stone. Sculpture in classical Greece and painting in the Renaissance achieved new heights of realism.

Long before the invention of writing, people used drawings to depict folklore and ways of survival. The earliest handwritten manuscripts were illustrated with woodcut figures, more for purposes of adornment, however, than to enhance understanding of the text.

In 1816 Nicéphore Niepce, a French scientist and lithographer, used metal plates to produce rather fuzzy and temporary images, which he called "heliographs." In 1839, Louis Daguerre made clear, permanent images on silvered copperplate. These early "daguerreotypes," now found in museum collections, took 15 minutes' exposure time. Samuel Morse, in France to patent his telegraph, was so impressed that he introduced the process to America.

The problem with daguerreotypes was that the images adhered directly to the plates, hence, they could not be reproduced. The process of producing positive images on paper from photographic "negatives" was invented across the English Channel by William Henry Fox Talbot, also in 1839. His *The Pencil of Nature* (1844–46) was the first commercially published book illustrated with photos. In 1888, Kodak brought photography to the masses with its hand-held, roll film camera.

The immediate impact of photography has been poetically expressed as follows:

> The magical quality of the momentous event is today almost impossible to grasp; it was as if one of the thousands of images that flicker across the eye had alighted like a butterfly on a sheet of paper.[1]

The first "butterflies" were portraits. Then, photographers set out to record the wonders of the world—the Sphinx, the Acropolis, the Colosseum. But the enduring power of photography was not realized until it was used to document the tragedies of war and social injustice—bodies at Gettysburg, child laborers in Northern factories, "liberated" slaves being lynched in the South.

Pictures generally fall under the rubric "graphic arts," in contrast to "literary arts." Webster defined pictures as **visual representations** (as of persons, landscapes, buildings) on canvas, paper, or other surfaces, produced by painting, drawing, engraving, or photography. They may be distinguished from other graphic forms (e.g., maps and diagrams) in that they usually portray objects as they appear to the eye rather than as abstract symbols.

The mental images evoked by pictures are, in many respects, similar to those we experience when viewing objects directly. Admittedly, such images ordinarily lack depth perspective and multi-sensory context, and they typically occupy just a small, centralized portion of the visual field. Nevertheless, pictures serve as **efficient substitutes** for firsthand experience, especially when such experience is costly and/or time-consuming. They enable students to experience vicariously what otherwise might not be readily available.

Pictures made for instructional purposes are called **"study prints."** They range from textbook illustrations to photographs framed on cardboard, complete with commentary and study suggestions. Their content can be as varied as reality itself—finger positions on a keyboard or musical instrument, stages in the manufacture of a product, structural features of a building, and customs of people in distant times and places. (See **Figure 7.01.**)

Pictures help instruction in many ways:

- They **attract attention;** most people like to look at them.
- They provide **realistic images** of objects, some of which might not be observable by other means.
- They document events that may be **unique,** thus permitting "first hand" analysis.
- They give **precise expression** to abstract, verbal descriptions.
- Shown as a series, they may **illustrate a process** or a motor skill in a way that can be readily duplicated.
- Pictures **speak to the deaf** and to those unable to read.

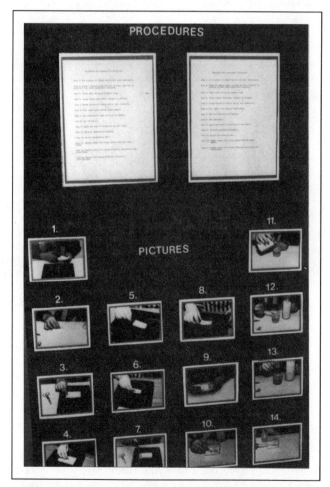

Figure 7.02. The steps in a procedure are best illustrated with a series of still photographs. What sorts of procedures might you profitably illustrate in this way? Location: California Museum of Science and Industry.

Figure 7.01. Study prints cover many subjects and come in sizes large enough for group viewing. How could such prints enhance your teaching?

Figure 7.03. The accelerating pace of growth in knowledge is dramatically illustrated in this "history wall" time-line. The entries on this timeline relate primarily to developments in mathematics. Sketch a timeline that relates to a subject you teach. Location: California Museum of Science and Industry.

- By **depicting desirable models,** they help foster more positive attitudes toward learning and interpersonal relations.
- They help **promote transfer** of learning to contexts beyond the confines of the classroom.

Still visuals have certain advantages over motion pictures. The latter effectively display a process that must be grasped as a whole, whereas a photograph enables students to analyze a single entity in depth. Athletes and actors wishing to study their performance will turn to a videotape rather than a series of stills. But students examining a machine, an architectural style, or a geological terrain will get more information from a still picture, which they can view as long as they like. This holds especially well with line drawings that label components. Still photos also are ideal for illustrating a sequence of actions, as in an experimental procedure. (See **Figure 7.02.**)

Nevertheless, pictures serve education only as far as viewing them promotes desirable learning. And their power to attract is most beneficial when attention is drawn to aspects related to subject matter at hand. Otherwise, pictures may distract students from what the teacher is explaining, or from accompanying written text. Worse, they may confuse students about what they are expected to learn.

Graphics

Unlike pictures, graphics present the world in shorthand. They contain pictures and words, but are distinguished by their **use of symbols** representing the phenomena they portray. They come in many forms: **maps, diagrams, charts, tables, graphs, posters, cartoons.** They may be readily interpreted, like stop signs, or abstract, like time lines (see **Figure 7.03**) and construction blueprints.

Graphics serve to **condense data** for ease of understanding. A terrain can be described in words, but a relief map makes it more vivid. Statistics can be read from tables, but graphs and diagrams illuminate their meaning. As the lines, shapes, and symbols of graphics become familiar, their messages grip us more forcibly than words or numbers. (See **Figure 7.04**.) On the other hand, if we are unfamiliar with the cultural or symbolic significance of particular graphics, we may need help in interpreting them.

Words commonly associated with graphics are **simplicity**, **impact**, and **aesthetic appeal**. Graphics are designed to communicate messages clearly, precisely, and efficiently. In advertising, they are exploited to arouse subconscious yearnings for sex and status. Like pictures, graphics can be worth more than a thousand words.

Maps have an illustrious history. Around 150 A.D., Ptolemy invented the technique of projection—the representation of a "round" earth on a flat surface. His maps were used for almost fifteen hundred years, though none was accurate by today's standards. In the 16th century, Edinburgh became the "Metropolis of Mapmaking." Here in the late 18th century George Bartholomew practiced cartography, and in 1870 the firm of Bartholomew & Son published an atlas for students, followed by classroom wall maps and maps for the *Encyclopaedia Britannica*.

Today, many kinds of maps are available. **Physical maps** show geographical characteristics such as land masses and lakes. **Relief maps** use raised surfaces to represent mountains. (See **Figure 7.05**.) **Political maps** use lines, symbols, and colors to identify cities, states, and nations. **Historical maps**, often in series, trace the rise and fall of empires and the spread of religions. Most maps are printed on paper for display in textbooks and on classroom walls. Others require more complex technologies, like those that appear in three dimensions when viewed through special lenses and those produced electronically by computers.

Map-reading is a critical skill in occupations ranging from trucking to space flight. Tourists need maps to travel, sailors to find a port, engineers to plan a city. Maps help explain history as well as nature. National boundaries change as wars are won or lost. Oceans and mountain ranges affect trade and migration. Especially in today's shrinking world, students should be exposed to a variety of maps and shown how to interpret them.

From subway walls to highway billboards, **posters** are one of the most ubiquitous of media. With their large,

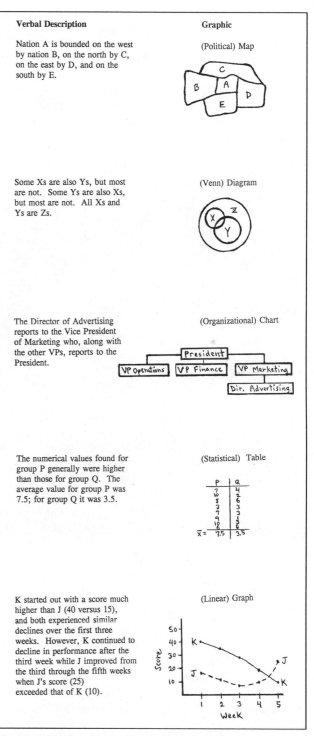

Figure 7.04. Graphics embody the meanings of words and the magnitudes of numbers, making both more readily understood. Compare the verbal descriptions above with their corresponding graphic representations.

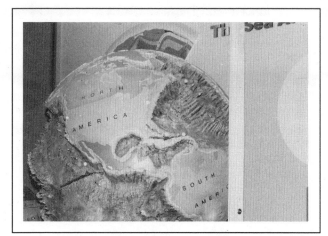

Figure 7.05. Most relief maps show mountain ranges found on land surfaces. This globe is distinctive in that it outlines the rugged surfaces beneath the oceans. What things of value might students learn by constructing relief maps of their neighborhoods based on their direct observations or of entire regions based on elevation figures printed on flat maps? Location: California Museum of Science and Industry.

clear letters, bold colors, simple line drawings, and popular symbols, posters announce coming events, promote ideas, and advertise products. Their primary function always has been to **influence behavior**—increase sales, win votes, and, especially in education, stimulate learning.

Many posters seen in classrooms today promote good health practices (see **Figure 7.06**), portray the benefits of travel, illustrate scientific concepts, and explain the rules of mathematics, spelling, and grammar. Most feature attractive photographs, brightly colored cartoon characters, and instructive messages.

Visual Display Devices

Chalkboards long have been used to display abbreviated text and graphics. The American educator Horace Mann saw them in Europe and recommended their use back home. "Indeed," he said, "in no state or country have I ever seen a good school without a blackboard or a successful teacher who did not use it frequently."[2]

Wherever instruction takes place—schools, factories, business offices—chalkboards abound. Even in outdoor

Figure 7.06. This collage of posters illustrates the theme of dental health. All sorts of travel, safety, and health posters are available commercially. However, you can produce some that relate more directly to the subjects you teach, and students may be challenged to do likewise.

classrooms, as in tribal schools, they are one of the most valuable aids to teaching and learning.

What makes chalkboards so popular? For one, they provide a large, prominent space for lecture notes, vocabulary lists, and homework assignments, all of which may be written just before class meetings. For another, they are a "live" medium. They permit ready expression and revision and focus attention where the speaker wants it. Students use chalkboards to share their ideas with the whole class. Together with the teacher, they record terms during brainstorming sessions and then draw semantic maps connecting the terms. Chalkboards

Figure 7.07. The chalkboard is used for "live" presentations by teachers and students alike. Here students show their work and are encouraged to correct errors both for their own benefit and that of the class. What other uses can you think of for chalkboards?

are inexpensive, simple to use, and durable. (See **Figure 7.07.**)

Markerboards have certain advantages over chalkboards. They have white, non-glare surfaces that contrast sharply with the markings of multi-colored, water-soluble ink felt pens. Although the pens cost more than chalk, the enhanced visibility and absence of dust more than compensate. (See **Figure 7.08.**)

Figure 7.08. Markerboards were designed to enhance visibility and eliminate the nuisance of chalk dust. What other advantages do they have over chalkboards?

Also popular with teachers are a variety of portable display boards. **Felt boards** are made easily by stretching felt fabric over plywood. Objects to be displayed, such as letters of the alphabet and geometric shapes, may be cut out of fabric or other rough-surfaced, light-weight material. **Hook-and-loop boards** are made out of the popular plastic fastener "Velcro." A board is covered with the loop material and various objects are backed with patches of the hook material. This makes for a firmer hold than that possible with felt boards. **Magnetic boards** rely on ferromagnetic material for backing and magnets attached to objects to achieve the same effect. With children now walking around class with computer diskettes in hand, I wouldn't want such a board around.

All the above sticking types of display boards enable teachers to manipulate previously prepared letters, numbers, and objects, thus helping students visualize sequences of ideas, events, and operations. Students, in turn, may do the manipulations, rearranging letters within words until they get the correct spellings, grouping like items, adding and subtracting fractions, and so on. Thus, these boards may be used for teaching, practice, or testing in many subject areas.

Flipcharts consist of large sheets of paper attached at the top to a solid backing and placed on an easel. The sheets typically are turned from page to page during a lecture to reveal text and drawings earlier prepared. Drawings may be modified during a lecture or blank pages may be used to create new ones. A quick review of the presentation may be made by flipping through the sheets from the first to the last.

Bulletin boards, in contrast, are static displays used extensively to present items of general and current interest—announcements, news articles, cartoons. What bulletin boards lack in live action they compensate for in attractiveness and location. Kept current and informative, the board draws the attention of students otherwise distracted by peers, fashion, and status.

Projection Devices

Projectors for still visuals descend from the **"magic lantern,"** a 17th century invention for projecting images, drawn on glass, through a condensing lens onto a screen. The light source was usually an open flame, often a candle. (See **Figure 7.09.**) The first lantern slides—

easily screened, and take less space to store. Today, both come in learning packages complete with captions and accompanying print matter and audiotapes.

Opaque projectors, too, have found use in classrooms. These enable teachers to display flat visuals (e.g., the pages of magazines) and small specimens (e.g., stamps and coins). The images produced are satisfactory, especially when viewed in a darkened room, but lack the clarity attainable by passing light through film.

Figure 7.09. Early projectors like these used candles or kerosene lanterns, and though they were thought of as "magic," the danger of fire limited their use in schools. Do you convey to your students a sense of magic when projecting visuals? Location: California Museum of Science and Industry.

Figure 7.10. The overhead projector is one of the most versatile devices for displaying still visuals. You can project commercially prepared drawings or those you make yourself. You can write on them as they are being projected on a screen, and you can reproduce the images by tracing them as they are projected on a chalkboard. A special attachment (e.g., the Kodak *DataShow*) allows projection of whatever appears on your computer screen.

photographic positives on glass—appeared in the mid-nineteenth century.

Slide and **filmstrip projectors** soon became commonplace in schools, enabling teachers to screen images of anything that could be photographed. A major advantage of **slides** is that they can be arranged in any order and new ones added any time. This permits easy updating of instructional slide sets. **Filmstrips** come in a fixed sequence and must be discarded entirely when found invalid. The advantages of filmstrips are that they are less expensive to mass produce than slides, are more

Perhaps the most successful of all has been the **overhead projector,** an ideal medium for displaying line drawings. **Transparencies** (sheets of clear plastic) are available commercially on many subjects, but they also can be hand-drawn or produced directly from print or pictures by using a standard photocopy machine. During projection, transparencies may be written on or overlaid if information needs to be changed. Even in a lighted room the images of this "electric chalkboard" are bright and clear. Moreover, teachers can address their classes, even as they work the projector or write on a transparency. With the Kodak *DataShow* placed on the overhead projector platform, all the action generated by your computer may be projected for class viewing. (See **Figure 7.10.**)

Series of slides and transparencies can be prepared using such computer software as *Astound, Delta Graph* and *Microsoft PowerPoint.* These include integrated word processing, graphing, and drawing features. They transform numerical data into diagrams and processes into flow charts. You may chose from a variety of color schemes, fonts, and editable clip-art images. Such programs permit previewing your planned presentation and making needed revisions prior to actually screening your production. Speaker notes and audience handouts are generated automatically once initial testing and revision are complete. After collecting data on student achievement of lesson objectives, the program permits insertion of additional text and graphics or deletion of errors as needed prior to engaging in another round of production.

Evaluation of Visuals

Visual Representations. Visual materials may be evaluated on at least two levels. The first relates to **how faithful** they are to the objects they are intended to represent, the second to **how effectively they express** desired information.

Objects, or **"realia,"** as they exist in context, obviously are good sources of information about themselves, at least as pertains to physical properties. From them come the stimuli that affect our senses and recording devices directly. Realia may be brought into laboratories and classrooms for study, but much of their context is left behind. We build **terrariums** and **dioramas** to restore some of this context. History and significance of objects generally must be gleaned from books and videos.

Figure 7.11. The enormous size of this locomotive is revealed by comparison with me. Viewing angle enhances perception of size, but a wall prevented Dad from backing up further to capture the imposing front. How well could you express the size of this behemoth [the train!] in words?

Models are constructed when realia are unavailable or their use impractical. Granted, the substitution of models for realia results in great loss of fidelity, but this loss may be compensated for when models are used that allow students to focus on elements closely related to course objectives. For example, students can more easily identify parts, connections, and functions of a model human eye than a real one.

Photographic prints generally provide realistic visual representations of objects and their surroundings. However, fidelity is affected by a photographer's selection of subjects, surroundings, camera angles, and exposure settings. (See **Figure 7.11.**) And since prints occupy just two dimensions (height and width), they cannot be manipulated like models.

Photographic transparencies retain the advantages (and limitations) of prints and offer in addition the options of viewing by large groups (when projected on a reflecting screen) and providing automated synchronization with recorded sound (e.g., slide/tape, filmstrip/tape). However, to gain these advantages, we need expensive equipment and the means of maintaining it.

Drawings may be likenesses of real things (e.g., people, places) or symbolic representations (e.g., maps, charts, graphs, cartoons). Small versions may be displayed on bulletin boards, included in textbooks, or enlarged for group viewing with an opaque projector.

Larger versions may be drawn on chalkboards and flipcharts or printed on wallcharts. There are at least two advantages of drawings over models and pictures. They focus attention on essential aspects of complex objects and are easy and inexpensive to produce. The main disadvantage is that they may be so far removed in form, color, and context from the objects they represent that students have difficulty interpreting them correctly.

Illustrations with Text. When pictures and graphics provide essentially the same information as that contained in associated text, learning is increased. The extent of this increase is approximated in **Figure 7.12**. (I present this more as an opportunity to compare textual and graphic representations of data than to deify dated research.)

The first (left side) set of three rectangular bars in the figure reveals that in 46 experiments, groups receiving a combination of text and illustrations excelled over groups exposed to text alone. The average improvement in learning with illustrations was about 36 percent.

The right-hand set of three bars in the figure reveals that in 20 experimental comparisons of learning text information that was not contained in illustrations, the percentage of cases in which groups exposed to text having unrelated illustrations learned more was about 55 percent—chance level. Such "decorative" illustrations neither helped nor hindered learning of unrelated textual material.

The middle set of bars represents studies in which groups were tested on a mixture of illustrated and non-illustrated text information. As expected, the performance of groups exposed to illustrated text tended to be better than that of those given non-illustrated text.

However, the results were not as one-sided as those found when tests measured learning of illustrated text information alone (as shown in the left-hand set).

Examining these findings, one might be tempted to conclude simply that illustrations improve the learning (and recall) of related text. Just as likely, however, is the conclusion that students learn (and recall) the content of illustrations quite apart from what they decipher from text. The reported benefit of illustrations may be explained largely by the fact that in many studies, students in the combination "text/picture" groups are given not only two different sources of information, words and images, but also are allowed more time to study them than that allowed "text only" groups. Studies that control for

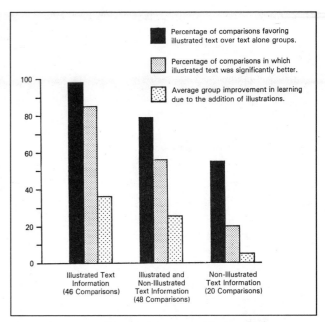

Figure 7.12. This bar graph illustrates the results of many experiments comparing groups of students exposed to illustrated text with those exposed to text alone. Do you find these results surprising? Source: W. Howard Levie & Richard Lentz, "Effects of Text Illustrations: A Review of Research," *Educational Communication and Technology Journal,* **30** (Winter 1982), p. 214. Copyright © 1982 AECT.

such extra "time on task" by allowing a second reading of text material (for the "text only" groups) show a narrowing of differences between groups.[3]

Maps have been found to help students remember related text material. However, this facilitative relationship obtains only when students are aware of the connection. Research has suggested that:

> Students need to be told that learning the map will help them remember information in related text. In fact, . . . the content of such instructions directly influences what kind of information is learned. . . . instructions to encode the map as an intact unit are prerequisite to the text retrieval advantage.[4]

The above findings justify the inclusion of illustrations that essentially duplicate information contained in text (as done in this book), but only when constraints on study time are few and mastery of content is the goal. The best textbooks contain the same information in both forms, thus enabling them to reach students of widely different abilities. Students can study these textbooks at their leisure, skipping sections they find redundant. Decorative illustrations and white space may enhance aesthetic appeal.

Researchers at the University of California, Santa Barbara, suggested that annotated illustrations can serve effectively as:

- signals that help readers select relevant words and images,
- structural summarizers that help readers to organize the material into a cause-and-effect system, and
- elaborative cues that help readers connect visual and verbal representations of the same systems.[5]

A sample of their effort to integrate textual and visual information is presented in **Figure 7.13.** It can serve as a model for all of us.

The use of more than one source to communicate essentially the same information might be inappropriate (i.e., might add to instructional time without adding significantly to instructional effectiveness) in cases where:

- the objective is simply one of learning a procedure or understanding a spatial relation (a single diagram or map should suffice);
- students are capable of fully and correctly interpreting material in one form without having to rely on supplementary material in different forms (e.g., textual descriptions of historic events may accompany drawings of famous persons, but drawings depicting events already described verbally, or text describing what the persons already pictured looked like, might be superfluous);
- highly capable students have no control over program content or rate of presentation (as in group viewing of film and TV) and, therefore, cannot skip material they find repetitious rather than illuminating.

Again, we see that choices of instructional strategies and media are best guided by considerations of objectives and student characteristics.

Research on grasping information contained exclusively in illustrations suggests that students tend to learn primarily what teachers, text, and captions draw their attention to. Tests of recall reveal little benefit from non-directed gazing. Maps are more effective than verbal descriptions alone in communicating spatial relations,

The Process of Lightning

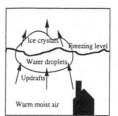

1. Warm moist air rises, water vapor condenses and forms cloud.

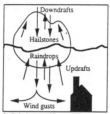

2. Raindrops and ice crystals drag air downward.

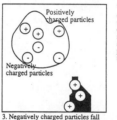

3. Negatively charged particles fall to bottom of cloud.

Figure 7.13. Illustrations that are carefully integrated with corresponding text are especially helpful. Here we see effective use of proximity, cues, and captions to integrate textual and visual messages. Reprinted from Richard E. Mayer, Kathryn Steinhoff, Gregory Bower, & Rebecca Mars, "A Generative Theory of Textbook Design," *Educational Technology Research and Development,* 43, 1(1995), p. 42. Copyright © 1995 AECT.

and diagrams more effective in communicating conceptual relations. However, these results obtain only when students are shown how to interpret abstract graphics.[6]

Teaching Children to Read. Children's books abound in colorful line drawings. Children, like all of us, are attracted to color, and line drawings usually provide sufficient detail to convey essential information. Although children may learn more from a combination of pictures and related text than from text alone, inclusion of pictures may interfere with learning to recognize written or printed words. That is, when pictures carry a story, children are less inclined to read and study the associated text. Without guidance, they often fail to learn what they should from pictures—even from the ones they like.

The implications are clear. If you want your students to absorb meaning, select books that are well illustrated. If you want to develop reading skills, ask students to read sections of these books aloud. To achieve both objectives simultaneously, tell them that they will be asked for their interpretations of **both** text and illustrations.[7]

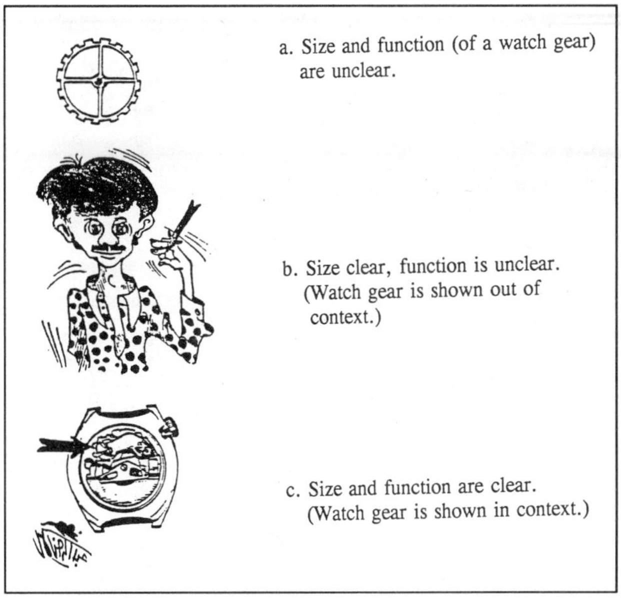

Practical Guidelines

Selection. As a teacher, you should select pictures and graphics based on your **instructional objectives**. If you wish to attract attention to a particular book or display, colorful drawings will help. To affect emotions and attitudes, use photographs. To ensure breadth of knowledge, combine lectures, textual materials, and closely related visuals. This combination would be especially appropriate if your objective is to have students reproduce images (e.g., draw a butterfly), identify structures (e.g., point to parts of a flower), assemble a complex device (follow diagrams), or get from one place to another (use a street map).

However, illustrations are far less important, and may be distracting, if your objective is, for example, to have students define terms and concepts or list causes and effects. Here, the use of similes, metaphors, and mnemonics may be more effective.

Selection of visuals also should be based **how you intend to use them**. If students are to be given ample time to examine illustrations under close guidance, intricate details may be included, and guidance generally should precede independent study. On the other hand, if the visuals are to be studied largely as homework assignments, they should be closely adapted to fit the abilities and experiences of your students. For most instructional purposes, simple diagrams, charts, and drawings will suffice. With slide and transparency presentations, you may adjust the time of exposure needed for students to make well-grounded interpretations.

Other important criteria you should use to select illustrations include **aesthetic appeal** and **quality of reproduction**. In photography, for example, both criteria depend on proper perspective, lighting, focus, and expo-

Figure 7.14. Contextual clues usually are needed to figure out the size and function of unfamiliar objects, in this case a watch gear. If illustrations lack sufficient clues to proper interpretation, we should provide them.

sure. Next come realism and composition. Is the illustration true to the reality of what it is supposed to represent? Are objects taken out of context? Are they familiar to most students? Students need both realistic detail and contextual cues if they are to interpret visual images removed from their ordinary experience. (See **Figure 7.14**.) However, as detail increases, you will need to provide more guidance in "reading" visuals and more time to do so.[8]

Color may serve to highlight objects that otherwise may blend with their surroundings. It also emphasizes related elements, identifies objects in context, and points up differences between otherwise similar objects. Used carelessly, however, color may distract or draw attention to irrelevant features.

As for maps, you can choose from a wide variety, again based on your objectives and the abilities of your students. Some maps are too detailed; some are of interest only to specialists. Here are several questions you might ask:

- Is the map large enough for group viewing?
- How well will it survive normal handling?
- Is the print legible?

		Rating (1 = low; 10 = high)	
Selection Criteria			**Comments**
1.	Content of Visual		
	a. match with objectives	_____	_____
	b. accuracy	_____	_____
	c. currency	_____	_____
	d. scope	_____	_____
	e. stereotyping	_____	_____
2.	Presentation	_____	_____
	a. impact	_____	_____
	b. aesthetic appeal	_____	_____
	c. use of cues	_____	_____
	d. use of color	_____	_____
	e. simplicity	_____	_____
3.	Associated Text	_____	_____
	a. spatial relations	_____	_____
	b. text references	_____	_____
	c. text descriptions	_____	_____
	d. captions	_____	_____
	e. labels	_____	_____
4.	Technical Quality	_____	_____
	a. visual clarity	_____	_____
	b. paper quality	_____	_____
5.	Effectiveness	_____	_____
	a. student interest	_____	_____
	b. student achievement	_____	_____
	c. student evaluation	_____	_____
6.	Overall Impression	_____	_____

Title _____ Artist _____

Publisher _____ Date _____ Price _____

Subject _____ Grade Level _____

Objectives _____

Prerequisites _____

Figure 7.15. Visual materials evaluation form.

- Are the labels and symbols easily interpreted, with their meanings stated in a legend?
- Is a wall map needed, or one that rolls up like a projection screen?

Charts, diagrams, and statistical tables should be kept simple. This is done, in part, by limiting the number of elements (i.e., objects, variables, relations) they contain and, if necessary, by producing a series. Technical questions you might ask include:

- Are general categories in a prominent position, usually at the top or top-left?
- Are related categories placed near each other?
- Are the main features highlighted by position, size, and/or color?
- Do labels accurately represent the ideas and variables portrayed by the graphic?
- Are variables arranged according to size, quantity, age, or according to another useful scheme?
- Are numerical quantities reduced to a few figures by rounding decimals (3.8 for 3.76) or counting whole numbers in multiples of 100 or 1000 (e.g., 2 for 2000, 3 for 3000)?
- Are drawings kept simple to ease interpretation?
- Are labels and legends repeated on each graph or map in a series?
- How well do captions or associated text clarify the nature and significance of the graphic illustration?

Figure 7.15 is an evaluation form that can be used to select a broad range of pictures and graphics. With the above considerations in mind, you may rate each visual from **1** (unsatisfactory) to **10** (excellent) and select those with the highest average scores. Give considerable weight to student interest and achievement as well as to how much of value they claim to have learned.

Production. At the heart of visual production for instructional purposes is a sense of what images will best communicate essential information. Both instructional objectives and student capabilities must be considered. The criteria outlined for the selection of visual materials apply as well to their production.

Once suitable images have been conceived, they must be found, drawn, or photographed. Finding takes perseverance, drawing requires talent (even with the help of such computer software as *Aldus Freehand, CorelDRAW!, DrawPerfect, ClarisWorks,* and *PC Paintbrush*), and photographing requires special skills (even with fully "automatic" cameras). Producing charts and diagrams is made simple using such software as *Harvard Graphics, Visio,* and *Microsoft PowerPoint,* but selecting among options for the best means of communicating statistical comparisons is entirely in our hands.

Whether you draw graphics freehand or use computer software, keep the following guidelines in mind:

- Present just **one idea per graph.**
- **Keep content simple** (just a few words, lines, drawings).
- Organize content to have both **impact** and **aesthetic appeal.**
- Make **text legible** and **images clear.**
- Use the format that best **embodies the data.**

Figure 7.16 illustrates four common graph formats from which you may choose, depending on your objectives. **Bar graphs** permit ready comparisons of several different things or of the same thing at different times. **Pictorial graphs** employ likenesses of the things represented to effect greater impact. **Circle graphs** display the relative quantities of parts that constitute a whole. The example shows the relative portions of each type of shape (triangle, square, circle) in a set of nine shapes. **Line graphs** permit comparisons of changes in quantities of two or more things over time. They also permit comparisons of two of more things on two dimensions (e.g., the relation of height and weight for apes compared with that for monkeys).

When diagramming relationships among concepts, particularly those unfamiliar to students, research of media pioneer William Winn and associates confirms a common sense approach. They suggest that designers should be particularly careful to:

(1) place causes to the left of or above effects;

(2) include [sub]ordinate categories within superordinate ones rather than express category membership by horizontal and vertical arrangements;

(3) place attributes to the right of, below, or inside the objects that possess them; and

(4) in general, follow a left-to-right, top-to-bottom sequence that corresponds to English word order.[9]

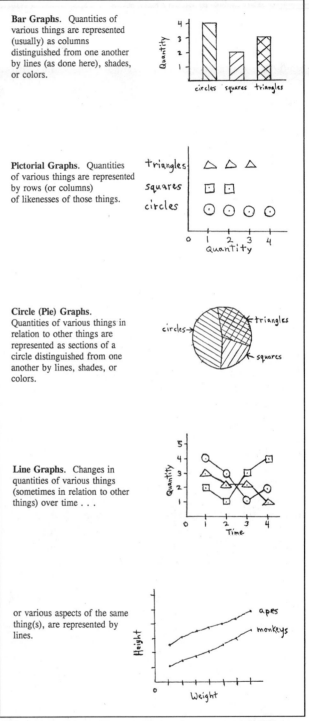

Figure 7.16. Graphs permit a variety of ways to express statistical data. Here, the first three present the same information. The fourth adds the dimension of time. Which of these do you find most expressive?

Photography long has served to democratize artistic expression. Anyone can "point-and-shoot." However, if the resulting photos are going to educate rather than distract, a modicum of expertise is needed. This chapter already has described criteria that pertain to composition, lighting, viewing angle, and focus. Setting lens opening (aperture) and shutter speed to obtain "correct" exposure requires hands-on experience, best provided by your instructor or camera dealer. I will share with you here just a few hints.

The biggest joke on the market today is the "focus free" camera. This corporate trick is meant to play on consumers' failure to distinguish between "focus free" and "automatic focus." My grandmother had a focus free, point-and-shoot camera before I was born. It did well on everything over six feet away in good light. Recently, a sales clerk tried to switch me from an on-sale automatic focus camera he said was unavailable to a focus free one at the same price. Outrageous!

Fully automatic cameras are ideal for family photography. They wind the film, adjust for film type, set aperture and shutter speed, and advise on use of flash. About the only trouble one can get into is aiming at something other than your subjects, such as the space between them or an object in front of them. Some cameras let you lock in the focus by aiming at one subject and pushing the shutter release button down half way. You then aim at the space between your subjects and press the rest of the way. Automatic cameras generally require a slow squeeze on the trigger because they do not begin adjusting settings until the press is begun. This is a good practice with all cameras to prevent blurred images from camera shake. Some cameras allow disabling the automatic focus for shooting through the glass windows of your fast-moving tourist bus. You might find this feature useful in taking photos of dioramas in a natural history museum. Don't even think about using the flash through glass. A nice feature is the "fill-in flash" setting that permits brightening backlighted subjects, especially dark faces. Another is the "red-eye reduction" feature that contracts your subjects' pupils by emitting a series of flashes prior to opening the shutter.

To really have fun, you need a single-lens-reflex (SLR) camera where you set speed, aperture, and focus yourself. Apart from the satisfaction that comes from "making it from scratch," you are empowered to make adjustments needed to get the results you want. One good practice is to set aperture one stop above, and then

one below the presumed "correct" setting. This will give you three photos from which to select the best. Another is to increase aperture one notch for backlighted subjects so their features will appear and not just a dark outline. Daylight flash helps here too, especially when the subjects are dark skinned. According to my daughter, the real fun of photography begins when you get into telephoto lenses. Here one must seriously consider resorting to a tripod, since camera shake is magnified with image.

The only complex idea I have encountered in photography has been "depth of field." It happens, God knows why, that as you reduce the aperture size, say from a gaping f/8 to a squinting f/16 (yes, one-**fourth** as much light!), and make a corresponding adjustment in shutter speed, that is, from a quick 250 (1/250th second) to a leisurely 60 (1/60th second), giving you about the "same" exposure, more of the background comes into focus. That's nice. Put another way, if you ever get an urge to obliterate the background (and stop action), use a lightning quick shutter speed (1/1000 second) and a wide enough aperture (low number) to compensate.

The secret of flash photography? Well, if you are at the Hollywood Bowl listening to a concert or at a Yankee Stadium night game, and you want to see some bald crowns shine, use your flash. However if you want to record what is on stage, line the players up within 10 feet or so and, with shutter speed at 60 (1/60th second for most cameras), set aperture according to distance as shown on the chart provided with your flash equipment.

Selection of film depends entirely on what you want to do. If you want to stop fast-moving action or take indoor photos without flash (unobtrusive and the resulting colors are mellow), use a "fast" film (400 to 1000 ISO/ ASA). Fast film also serves those who cannot be bothered with tripods or never learned to **squeeze** the shutter release rather than punch it. I used 100 ISO for most purposes until 200 ISO film came out with "equally" good color and detail. For photos at the lake, beach, or in snow, I still use 100.

Think about these things. Take a class. Read a book. Draw on your own experience. Then **make a habit of writing down the settings for each shot and analyzing results**. If you don't understand why something came out the way it did, ask your local photo dealer or write Kodak at the address provided at the end of this chapter.[10]

After you find or produce a visual that meets the criteria of relevance and quality, you may wish to:

- frame or laminate it for viewing by individual students,

- photocopy it onto acetate sheets for use with an overhead projector,

- transfer the image to a photographic slide for projection, or

- import it with a scanner into *Aldus PhotoStyler, Kodak PhotoEdge, Gallery Effects,* or *Adobe PhotoShop* for revision and inclusion in a handout, newsletter, or multimedia program.

Text, drawings, cartoons, maps, etc., are most suitable for use with an overhead projector. Finer reproductions, especially of flat pictures, are better transferred to slides. This commonly is done using the easily constructed equipment shown in **Figure 7.17**. You need only:

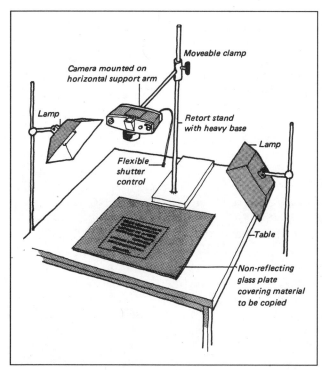

Figure 7.17. Copy stands permit photography of small pictures and graphics for enlargement or projection. Constructing such a stand and using it are worthwhile class projects. Source: Henry Ellington, *Producing Teaching Materials: A Handbook for Teachers and Trainers* (East Brunswick, NJ: Nichols, 1985), p. 111. Reprinted with permission of Nichols Publishing.

1. Set the visual in place below the camera.
2. Turn on the lights.
3. Frame the shot, leaving adequate borders (by moving the camera up or down or by changing lenses).
4. Focus the camera.
5. Set the exposure time and aperture.
6. Release the shutter with a remote switch.

As with all photography, you need to experiment with different lighting and camera settings and compare the results. This entails **keeping records as you shoot**.

So what about **digital photography**? This is a great way to go if you and your students plan to use still images in computer-based projects. For about the price of a camcorder, digital cameras (e.g., the Apple QuickTake 100, Electronic Still Camera [Chinon], Photo Video Imager FV-7 [Digital Vision], FotoMan Pixtura [Logitech]) have all the features of the best fully automatic film cameras. Kodak's The Digital Camera 40 has four megabytes of memory and file compression software that permits storage of up to 48 high resolution images. Download these into your computer and you're ready for another 400+ shots before changing batteries. Note, however, that each high resolution image may take up over one megabyte of memory. Fortunately, special drives and storage tapes are available to handle the load.

Teaching Visual Literacy. Students everywhere are immersed in seas of visual information. Pictures in commercial media solicit their attention every waking hour. Women, especially, are targets of ads that attempt to brainwash them into the consciousness of seduction, and African Americans are targets of ads that equate status with smoking and drinking. Adolescent-appearing models appear half nude in suggestive poses, and the cigarette, long taboo, has reappeared as a fashion piece. A year after the Berlin Wall came down I found the only color across the bleak East German landscape to be "Marlboro Man" posters. **More talent and money are being invested by advertisers in the seduction of our children than in their education**. The consequences of such pervasive, persuasive advertising are demoralizing and deadly.

To combat these influences, students need to be guided in developing their "**visual literacy**." Such literacy entails skills not only in analyzing illustrations but also in creating them.[11]

What sort of guidance should you provide to enable students to interpret pictures critically? You should explain that artists represent aspects of a three-dimensional reality in two dimensions. The aspects they choose to portray and the ways in which they do so (film type, angle, background, exposure) reflect their understanding of and attitudes toward these aspects. Choices of images are affected by the messages artists want to convey. Colors, shapes, and positions are meant to arouse basic instincts for food, sex, and status, and often sell cars, clothing, and liquor.

To encourage analysis of study prints, you could ask your students such questions as: How many objects can you name in this picture? Where do you think the picture was taken or drawn? What has just happened to the people pictured? Would you like to have lived at this time in history? You also could encourage students to look for clues to the ways people live, work, and play. In the life sciences, students could learn to read photographs for information about climate, soil, and animal life. In the physical sciences, they could seek cues indicating the presence of chemical compounds or the effects of stress on equipment. In the social sciences, students should be taught to detect the motives of artists. What message is conveyed, and how well is it expressed? Why is a scene or person presented in a certain way? Through analysis students learn how artists handle media for particular purposes, such as to sell, ridicule, caricature, propagandize, or educate. (See **Figure 7.18**.)

Media & Methods

Illustration by Scott Harris

Figure 7.18. Students should analyze visual images in all media. They should be able to distinguish those that serve to inform from those slanted merely to persuade. In what ways does the illustration above (by Scott Harris) attempt to do both? Source: *Media & Methods,* 16 (January 1980), p. 47. Copyright © 1980. All rights reserved. Reprinted courtesy of the publisher.

You can further develop visual literacy by encouraging students to produce a **"photo essay"**—a series of captioned illustrations related to a single theme. Students choose a subject of personal interest (such as playing a game, going on a vacation, or caring for a pet), describe it in several scenes, and draw each scene on a separate card, so that the set may be arranged on a desk top or tacked to a board. They then select or produce illustrations to replace the sketches. Finally, they organize the illustrations and compose a caption for each.

Photo essays appeal to students of all ages and abilities. They often are used in primary schools to teach language skills. Here youngsters learn to create a simple paragraph consisting of a title, a series of sentences describing the photos, and a concluding statement. Young children especially, and those with learning disabilities, benefit from arranging and captioning photos chosen by the teacher. They learn not only to write but to speak and listen better as they discuss their projects with teachers and classmates. Taking photos, especially those that make instant prints, gives immediate satisfaction. It is an ideal means of self-expression and creativity.

With a few modifications, photo essays may be turned into **"storyboards"** for use in producing audiovisual programs. The sketches trace the content of the visual portion of the planned slide set, film, or videotape; the captions may serve as the basis for narration. (See **Figure 7.19**.) If text, audio, and visuals are transferred to computer storage, **object linking and embedding** (OLE) technology permits them to be integrated, reviewed, and revised electronically. *Astound, Q/Media, Compel, Action, Charisma, Freelance Graphics, Delta Graph, WordPerfect Presentations, Harvard Graphics Presentation Pak,* and *Microsoft PowerPoint* all permit transformation of storyboards into integrated presentations. Following pretesting and revision of prototypes, the resulting program can be shown as is, projected, or transfered to videotape.[12]

The **"collage"** also may be used to teach paragraph writing. Here, too, students choose a topic and create a collage to illustrate it. They write a paragraph describing the theme, bring both collage and paragraph to class, and there write a second paragraph on the challenges encountered in expressing the same idea visually and verbally. Both collage and paragraph must have a unifying idea and coherent structure. Making a collage not only reinforces many principles of prose writing, it also gives students confidence in their power to create.

Visual compositions of all kinds can be used to enhance learning in almost any field. Students can arrange visuals to depict historic events, illustrate scientific ideas,

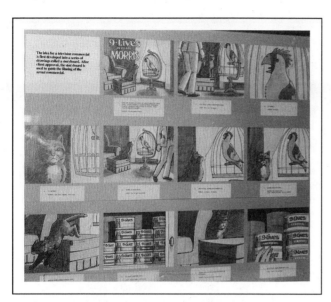

Figure 7.19. In a storyboard, illustrations outline the visual part of a planned program and the written text outlines the audio. Here is part of a storyboard used in the production of a TV commercial. (Perhaps your instructor remembers "Morris the [fussy] cat.") Location: California Museum of Science and Industry.

and document social issues. Their products can be displayed with pride on classroom walls for all to see and appreciate.

Visual literacy also involves being able to grasp the intended messages embodied in graphics. So much of what we see on TV and in printed media is in the form of charts, diagrams, and maps. Students should be made familiar with the major formats and symbols so they can better understand the messages such graphics were designed to express. One method is to project graphic images from the pages of popular news periodicals onto a screen and then explain their significance. Another is to have students classify and count objects and then represent the results in various graphic forms. Also, students could be asked to express their interpretations of graphics they have come across in their own readings, class members could contribute their insights, and you could suggest alternative views.

To aid their understanding of time lines, students could obtain names and dates pertaining to their ancestors and produce a time line tracing their family history. Historical events then could be added as points of reference. These may serve to explain why their ancestors moved from place to place. Using *TimeLiner* and *Chronos*

they could instantly import events relating to politics, innovation, literature, the arts, and popular culture.

Map reading is another aspect of visual literacy. Children can begin by locating places that interest them, such as their homes, the city where Grandpa lives, or the locations of Disneyland and Disney World. Older students could be encouraged to look up places they have read about (Huck's Mississippi, or the Atlanta adored by Scarlet, ravaged by Sherman, and transformed by Martin Luther King Jr.) or nations in the TV news (Somalia, Bosnia, and the South Africa of Desmond Tutu and Nelson Mandela). Many games can be played with maps, such as schoolyard treasure hunts and route tracing to community attractions. In choosing a vacation spot, students can list the various ways to get there, the most important sites to visit, and the right clothes to wear, depending on climate and terrain. Printed map reading can be reinforced with exploration of computerized versions—*AUTOMAP, Global Explorer, Expert Maps, Global Express Atlas.*

Geographic facts can be taught imaginatively. For example, topographic symbols can be learned by constructing a relief map from a simplified one drawn on the chalkboard. Concepts of longitude and latitude can be acquired from games like *Battleship,* in which players attempt to locate (and thereby "sink") each other's naval vessels. Learning is reinforced by pre- and post-game discussions about the relations between the gameboards and maps representing actual terrain. A computerized simulation game called *Geography Search* pits competing teams on a voyage of exploration. Like Columbus and the Vikings before him, they must find their way across the ocean, calculating their changing positions, and accounting for winds and currents. Versions of *Where in the World Is Carmen Sandiego?* appear as computer software and TV programs and engage youths in tracking elusive villains across the earth.

Summary and Conclusions

Visual representations have many virtues. Photos take viewers inside living cells, to foreign countries, and into space. Photography enables students to portray the world as they see it; instant prints provide opportunities for self-expression. Drawings facilitate identification of objects and comprehension of abstract ideas. Graphics condense information for ease of understanding. Diagrams give point to numerical data. Cartoons offer in-

Figure 7.20. Long after these plants perished, the written word documents and the graph dramatizes the results of this science project. Location: California Museum of Science and Industry.

sights into current events. Maps improve our understanding of geography and its role in history. All these visuals can be projected for group viewing or beamed via satellite to classrooms throughout the world.

Print and visual media together present content in breadth and depth. (See **Figure 7.20.**) They arouse interest, stimulate learning, and allow for creative expression. They also are economical.

Electronic technologies have given voice to print and motion to visuals. They have permitted quicker production and wider distribution. Contributions of these technologies comprise the following chapters.

Notes

[1]Hambourg, Maria M., Apraxine, Pierre, Daniel, Malcolm, Rosenheim, Jeff L., & Heckert, Virginia, *The Waking Dream: Photography's First Century. Selections from the Gilman Paper Company Collection* (New York: The Metropolitan Museum of Art, 1993), p. 3.

[2]Quoted in Dale, Edgar, *Audio-Visual Methods in Teaching,* 3rd ed. (New York: Holt, Rinehart, and Winston, 1969), p. 146.

[3]Pettersson, Rune, *Visual Information* (Englewood Cliffs, NJ: Educational Technology Publications, 1993); Winn, William, Li, Tian-Zhu, & Schill, Donna, "Diagrams as Aids to Problem Solving: Their Role in Facilitating Search and Computation," *Educational Technology Research and Development,* 39, 1(1991), pp. 17–29.

[4]Kulhavy, Raymond W., Stock, William A., & Kealy, William A., "How Geographic Maps Increase Recall of Instructional

Text," *Educational Technology Research and Development,* 41, 4(1993), p. 59.

[5]Mayer, Richard E., Steinhoff, Kathryn, Bower, Gregory, & Mars, Rebecca, "A Generative Theory of Textbook Design," *Educational Technology Research and Development,* 43, 1(1995), p. 40.

[6]Kulhavy, Raymond W., Lee, J. Brandon, & Caterino, Linda C., "Conjoint Retention of Maps and Related Discourse," *Contemporary Educational Psychology,* 10 (January 1985), pp. 28–37.

[7]My literacy expert friend, La Vergne Rosow, cautions against reliance on tests to intimidate students to learn. Her points are especially applicable in cases where students have endured so much failure that they no longer will put forth the needed effort under threatening conditions. My view is that in a world of many distractions and with much good, hard work to be done, a bit of coaxing is justified. Rewards, however, should be based largely on effort and improvement. Promotion and graduation should be based on fair standards of achievement (criterion-referenced tests, products, performances, portfolios) rather than on the basis of comparisons with peers (norm-referenced).

[8]Brody, Philip J., "A Research-Based Guide to Using Pictures Effectively," *Instructional Innovator,* 29 (February 1984), pp. 21–22; "In Search of Instructional Utility: A Function-Based Approach to Pictorial Research," *Instructional Science,* 13 (May 1984), pp. 47–61; Hittleman, Daniel R., "A Picture Is Worth a Thousand Words . . . If You Know the Words," *Childhood Education,* 62 (September/October 1985), pp. 32–36; Wileman, Ralph E., *Visual Communicating* (Englewood Cliffs, NJ: Educational Technology Publications, 1993).

[9]Winn, William, & Solomon, Cliff, "The Effect of the Spatial Arrangement of Simple Diagrams on the Interpretation of English and Nonsense Sentences," *Educational Technology Research and Development,* 41, 1(1993), pp. 29–41.

[10]Comprehensive coverage and explicit guidelines are provided in Busselle, Michael, *The Complete 35mm Sourcebook* (New York: Watson-Guptill, 1992); and *How to Take Good Pictures: A Photo Guide by Kodak,* 36th ed. (New York: Random House, 1990).

[11]Clemente, Rebecca, & Bohlin, Roy M., *Visual Literacy: A Selected Bibliography* (Englewood Cliffs, NJ: Educational Technology Publications, 1990).

[12]McCracken, Harry, "Presentation Powerhouses Review," *Multimedia World* 1 (June 1994), pp. 63–74. Taking into account ease of learning and features, including incorporation of audio and video clips, top programs were judged to be *Astound, Charisma, Action, Compel,* and *Q/Media.*

Sources

Annotated lists of **visual materials** may be found in the following publications (updated regularly until recently) of the National Information Center for Educational Materials (NICEM, Albuquerque, NM):

Index to Educational Overhead Transparencies
Index to Educational Slides
Index to 35mm Educational Filmstrips

The latter two now appear as: *Filmstrip & Slide Set Finder*, available from Plexus Publishing (1-609-654-6500).

Sources of **free materials** are found in the annual publications of Educators Progress Service (Randolph, WI: 1-414-326-3126):

Educators Index to Free Materials [the 100th edition appeared in 1991]
Educators Guide to Free Films, Filmstrips and Slides
Educators Guide to Free Health, Physical Education and Recreation Materials
Educators Guide to Free Home Economics and Consumer Education Materials
Educators Guide to Free Science Materials
Educators Guide to Free Social Science Materials
Elementary Teachers Guide to Free Curriculum Materials

Commercial suppliers of **manipulatives and richly illustrated materials** across all subjects and grade levels include:

Academic Therapy Publications: 1-800-422-7249
Attainment Company, Inc.: 1-800-327-4269
Childswork/Childsplay: 1-800-962-1141
Continental Press: 1-800-233-0759
Cuisenaire Co. of America, Inc.: 1-800-237-3142
Curriculum Associates: 1-800-225-0248
Dale Seymour Publications: 1-800-827-1100
Educators Publishing Service, Inc.: 1-800-225-5750
Lakeshore Learning Materials: 1-800-421-5354
Modern Curriculum Press: 1-800-321-3106
Therapy Skill Builders: 1-602-323-7500

Reviews of visual materials may be found in current issues of:

Instructor
Learning: The Magazine for Creative Teaching
Media & Methods

Acquiring skills in the crafting of pictures enhances our ability to interpret those we encounter. Essentials of **photography** are covered in:

Alesse, Craig, *Basic 35mm Photo Guide for Beginning Photographers* (Amherst, NY: Amherst Media, 1994).

Busselle, Michael, *The Complete 35mm Sourcebook* (New York: Watson-Guptill Publications, 1992).
Freeman, Michael, *Guide to Photography* (New York: Watson-Guptill, 1993).
Freeman, Michael, *The New 35mm Handbook* (Philadelphia: Running Press, 1993).
Frost, Lee, *Photography* (Lincolnwood, IL: NTC Publishing Group, 1993).
Hedgecoe, John, *John Hedgecoe's Complete Guide to Photography* (New York: Sterling Publishing, 1990).
Hedgecoe, John, *John Hedgecoe's Photography Basics* (New York: Sterling Publishing, 1993).
Hedgecoe, John, *The Photographer's Handbook*, 3rd ed., revised (New York: Knopf, 1995).
How to Take Good Pictures: A Photo Guide by Kodak, 36th ed. (New York: Random House, 1990).
Joseph, Michael, & Saunders, Dave, *The Complete Photography Course* (New York: Penguin, 1994).
Langford, Michael, *Michael Langford's 35mm Handbook*, 3rd ed. (New York: Knopf, 1993).
Lovell, Ronald P., Zwahlen Jr., Fred C., Folts, James A., *Handbook of Photography*, 3rd ed. (Albany, NY: Delman Publishers, 1993).
Schaub, George, *Using Your Camera: A Basic Guide to 35mm Photography* (New York: Watson-Guptill Publications, 1990).
Spillman, Ron, *The Complete Photographer* (Surrey, England: Fountain Press, 1994).
Stone, Amy, *How to Take Great Photos with 35mm Autofocus Point & Shoot Cameras* (Los Angeles: HPBooks, 1990).

The Eastman Kodak Company provides inexpensive **pamphlets and books** on all aspects of photography. Samples include:

Audiovisual Projection: Motion Pictures, Slides, Filmstrips.
Composition.
Effective Lecture Slides.
How to Set Your Adjustable Camera.
KODAK Guide to 35 mm Photography.
KODAK Pocket Guide to Great Picture Taking.
Kodak Tips for Better Pictures.
Making Effective Slides for Lectures and Teaching.
Picture-Taking–A Self-Teaching Guide.
Picture-Taking in 5 Minutes.
Simple Copying Techniques with a Kodak Ektagraphic Visualmaker.

For a list of available **publications** request the *Index to KODAK Information* from:

Eastman Kodak Company
Photographic Products Group
Rochester, NY 14650

May 7, 1993

Steven Hackbarth Ph.D.
PO Box 650
New York, NY 10156

Dear Dr. Hackbarth:

Thanks for writing about the differences between SLR and "fully automatic" cameras.

Eastman Kodak Company does not sell SLR cameras at this time, and I must be somewhat general in my comments. However, you've hit the nail on the head with your question -- an SLR camera will allow you to adjust the shutter speed and lens opening, whereas most automatic cameras make those decisions for you. SLR (single lens reflex) cameras also allow you to view the scene directly through the picture-taking lens (thus the name "single lens"), whereas many automatic cameras use viewfinders separate from the actual lens. Because of the quality of today's cameras, this is usually not a major consideration, but it is something to remember.

There are no Kodak cameras which allow for adjustment, and I cannot comment on other manufacturers' products. The best I could recommend is that you visit a reputable camera dealer, describe your needs, and ask for a demonstration. You might want to prepare for your visit by reading a few photographic magazines to give you a general awareness of what's on the market today.

One possibility might be an SLR camera which can be set to function automatically. That type of camera would allow you to grow a bit as you acquire more photographic knowledge and decide just how creative you'd like to be. Another possibility is what is referred to as a "bridge" camera -- one which combines some features of both SLR and automatic models. Some examples would be the Chinon Genesis product line or the Canon Photura camera. Local camera stores can provide further information.

Enclosed is a brochure on existing light photography which may illustrate the advantages of an SLR camera. As you can see, these examples require adjustment of the camera, which will not be possible with most automatic models.

I hope this information will be of help. If you have any further questions about Kodak products and services, please write again or call us at the toll-free number below.

Sincerely,

Dale C. Pittenger

Dale C. Pittenger
Consumer Affairs Advisor
Kodak Information Center

DCP:dcp/5230
Tel. (800) 242-2424
Enc.
AC-61

EASTMAN KODAK COMPANY · 343 STATE STREET · ROCHESTER, NEW YORK 14650

Figure 7.21. I was so impressed with the above response to my inquiry, I obtained permission to share it with you here. How might you and your students best draw upon this resource? Reproduced courtesy of Eastman Kodak Company.

Specific **questions** may be addressed to:

Eastman Kodak Company
Kodak Information Center
343 State St.
Rochester, NY 14650
1-800-242-2424
(See **Figure 7.21**.)

For information about Kodak's **photo CD presentation software** call 1-800-454-9449.

The Polaroid Corporation distributes a guide to **instant photography** and offers teachers free cameras (subject to pre-purchase of film) as part of its "Polaroid Education Program." For details write:

Polaroid Corporation
549 Technology Square, 3rd Floor
Cambridge, MA 02139
1-800-343-5000

A complete **home study course** (audiotapes and booklets) may be purchased from:

The Seattle FilmWorks Photography School
1260 16th Avenue West
P.O. Box 34062
Seattle, WA 98124-1062
1-800-445-3348

Note also that Seattle FilmWorks does low-cost developing, enlarging, cropping, and transfer of images to diskette (just $3.95 extra per 24 exposure roll). Their free *PhotoWorks* software permits viewing of the images on your computer monitor, importing them into your documents, and sending them via your modem.

Guidelines for the **interpretation, production, and use** of visuals may be found in:

Aldrich-Ruenzel, Nancy, ed., *Designer's Guide to Print Production* (New York: Watson-Guptill, 1990).

Arnold, Carolyn, *Maps and Globes: Fun, Facts, and Activities* (Danbury, CT: Watts, 1984).

Barnhurst, Kevin G., *Seeing the Newspaper* (New York: St. Martin's Press, 1994).

Berger, Arthur Asa, *Seeing Is Believing: An Introduction to Visual Communication* (Mountain View, CA: Mayfield, 1989).

Bohle, Robert H., *From News to Newsprint: Producing a Student Newspaper*, 2nd ed. (Englewood Cliffs, NJ: Prentice-Hall, 1992).

Brigham, Nancy, with Raszmann, Ann, & Cluster, Dick, *How to Do Leaflets, Newsletters & Newspapers* (Detroit, MI: PEP Publishers, 1991).

Brookes, Mona, *Drawing with Children: A Creative Teaching and Learning Method that Works for Adults, Too* (New York: G.P. Putnam's Sons, 1986).

Carey, Helen, *How to Use Maps and Globes* (Danbury, CT: Watts, 1983).

Carroll, Joyce A., *Picture Books: Integrated Teaching of Reading, Writing, Listening, Speaking, Viewing, and Thinking* (Englewood, CO: Libraries Unlimited, 1991).

Casciero, Albert J., & Roney, Raymond G., *Audiovisual Technology Primer* (Englewood, CO: Libraries Unlimited, 1988).

Cravotta, Mary E., & Wilson, Savan, *Media Cookbook for Kids* (Englewood, CO: Libraries Unlimited, 1989).

Ellington, Henry, *Producing Teaching Materials: A Handbook for Teachers and Trainers*, 2nd ed. (East Brunswick, NJ: Nichols, 1993).

Gill, Bob, *Forget All the Rules about Graphic Design: Including the Ones in this Book* (New York: Watson-Guptill, 1985).

Green, Lee, *501 Ways to Use the Overhead Projector* (Englewood, CO: Libraries Unlimited, 1982).

Green, Lee, *Creative Slide-Tape Programs* (Englewood, CO: Libraries Unlimited, 1986).

Lowe, Ric, *Successful Instructional Diagrams* (London: Kogan Page, 1993).

Moore, David M. (Mike), & Dwyer, Francis M., eds., *Visual Literacy: A Spectrum of Visual Learning* (Englewood Cliffs, NJ: Educational Technology Publications, 1994).

Pettersson, Rune, *Visual Information* (Englewood Cliffs, NJ: Educational Technology Publications, 1993).

Rabb, Margaret Y., *The Presentation Design Book*, 2nd ed. (Chapel Hill, NC: Ventura Press, 1993).

Richey, Virginia H., & Puckett, Katharyn, *Wordless/Almost Wordless Picture Books: A Guide* (Englewood, CO: Libraries Unlimited, 1992).

Richey, Virginia H., & Puckett, Katharyn E., *Using Wordless Picture Books: Authors and Activities* (Englewood, CO: Libraries Unlimited, 1993).

Robertson, Bruce, *How to Draw Charts & Diagrams* (Cincinnati, OH: North Light Books, 1988).

Satterthwaite, Les L., *Instructional Media: Materials, Production, and Utilization*, 2nd ed. (Englewood, CO: Libraries Unlimited, 1991).

Shulevitz, Uri, *Writing with Pictures: How to Write and Illustrate Children's Books* (New York: Watson-Guptill, 1985).

Smith, Robert C., *Basic Graphic Design* (Englewood Cliffs, NJ: Prentice-Hall, 1985).

Thomas, James L., *Nonprint Production for Students, Teachers, and Media Specialists: A Step-by-Step Guide*, 2nd ed. (Englewood, CO: Libraries Unlimited, 1988).

Volker, Roger, & Simonson, Michael, *Media for Teachers: An Introductory Course in Media for Students in Teacher Education*, 5th ed. (Dubuque, IA: Kendall/Hunt, 1989).

Wileman, Ralph E., *Visual Communicating* (Englewood Cliffs, NJ: Educational Technology Publications, 1993).

Willows, Dale M., & Houghton, Harvey A., eds., *The Psychology of Illustration* (New York: Springer-Verlag, 1987).

Many commercial suppliers have programs designed to teach students how to **interpret and craft their own graphics.** Continental Press (1-800-233-0759) offers a

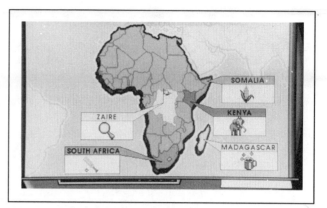

Figure 7.22. In addition to constructing all sorts of maps and using them to solve problems, students also benefit from playing computer games that introduce them to the locations of nations. Screen from *Carmen World Jr.* is reproduced here courtesy of Brøderbund Software, Inc.

Map Skills Series (grades 2–9), a programmed instruction booklet, *Map Skills* (grades 5–7), and problem-solving lessons, *Tables & Graphs: Topical Tasks* (grades 3–6, remedial 7–9). Curriculum Associates (1-800-225-0248) also has geography series, *The World We Share* (grades 3–5) and *Global Views* (grade 5–adult education). The *Macmillan Instant Activities Program* (A Newbridge Educational Program, P.O. Box 938, Hicksville, NY 11802) includes a *Map Skills* unit. See the Sources at the end of this book for additional titles in print, video, and computer formats (e.g., National Geographic's *Zip Zap Map! World,* and Brøderbund's *Where in the World Is Carmen Sandiego? Junior Detective Edition* [see **Figure 7.22**]).

Study Items

1. Describe cases where line drawings may be superior to photographs in instruction.

2. Give examples of when it would be advantageous to use still pictures rather than motion visuals in a subject you teach.

3. What can color contribute to learning from textbook print and illustrations?

4. What are some disadvantages of "focus-free" cameras? What are disadvantages of "automatic-focus" cameras compared with those for which you must set speed and aperture yourself? (Note that top-of-the-line automatic cameras permit manual operation.)

5. Represent the same numerical data on three different types of graphs.

6. Illustrate changes over time in the above data using a line graph.

7. Name three different types of maps. How might you use any one of them to achieve an instructional objective in a subject you teach?

8. Describe three means of displaying visuals without electricity. What are some advantages and limitations of each?

9. Compare and contrast use of a chalkboard with use of an overhead transparency projector. Give an example of good use of each in a subject you teach.

10. What sorts of illustrations contribute most to learning of subject matter in textbooks?

11. In what ways might illustrations affect learning to read?

12. Describe several criteria by which to evaluate schoolbook illustrations.

13. What elements have you seen in graphic advertising that you could incorporate in your class handouts or bulletin board?

14. Define "visual literacy." Give an example of how you could contribute to the visual literacy of your students.

15. Distinguish between a "photo essay" and a "collage." Give an example of how you would use either to achieve a specific objective in your class.

Suggested Activities

1. Visit a curriculum materials center and locate collections of study prints, transparencies, and filmstrips.

2. Examine a dictionary designed for students in the grade level you teach. List words typically illustrated and divide into such categories as concrete and abstract, noun and verb.

3. Collect several samples of graphs from *USA Today*. Categorize them by type and analyze the kinds of data characteristically embodied in each type.

4. Watch the TV program *Where in the World Is Carmen Sandiego?* Assess its use of graphic images. Does it teach map reading skills or merely the location of cities? What else does it teach? Integrate the program into a lesson plan.

5. Craft a poster to express a core concept in a subject you teach.

6. Prepare a series of transparencies that can be overlaid to illustrate an idea or process in a subject you teach.

7. Obtain some books listed above that pertain to photography topics about which you remain unfamiliar. Practice the skills learned, and share results with classmates.

8. Evaluate the illustrations in this chapter according to the criteria listed in **Figure 7.15**.

9. Prepare a transparency of **Figure 7.15** and present it to one of your teacher education classes. Seek students' responses and revise accordingly.

10. Visit a computer exhibition and ask to see demonstrations of drawing (e.g., *DrawPerfect, Kid Pix*) and graphics (e.g., *Harvard Graphics, Visio*) software.

11. Ask to see a demonstration of computer software, such as *Adobe Illustrator, Microsoft Works, Microsoft Publisher,* or *Ventura Publisher* that facilitate integration of text, drawings, and graphics.

12. Devote a summer to mastering an integrated software package such as *Microsoft Works* or *ClarisWorks*, including their spreadsheet and database features. Keep your skills current by using the one you select to produce and **revise** reports, class handouts, and examinations.

13. Produce a "photo essay" or "collage" to illustrate a concept in a subject you teach. Integrate it into a lesson plan, try it out, test for intended outcomes, look for unintended outcomes, and revise accordingly.

14. View a demonstration of *Gallery Effects, PhotoStyler, Kodak PhotoEdge,* or *PhotoShop* and report on features you could use to adapt your photos for inclusion in handouts and newsletters.

15. Visit an elementary school classroom and identify ways in which the teacher integrates visual materials into lesson units (See **Figure 7.23**).

16. View a demonstration of such geography software as *Street Atlas USA, U.S. Atlas, Global Explorer, 3D Atlas, Zip Zap Map! World,* and *World Atlas*. Compare ease of integrating these into a geography curriculum with printed handouts, wall maps, and globes.

17. View such CD-ROM encyclopedias as *Microsoft Encarta* and *Compton's Interactive Encyclopedia*. List instructional objectives that might be more easily achieved using these than the printed works. Compare ease of accessing information and cost.

Figure 7.23. Visuals are most valuable when directly related to subject matter and explained by text or teacher. Here David Sato employs a cross-section illustration of a flower (one that each student is constructing) to help him in explaining the 'facts of life' to first graders.

18. Purchase *Aldus PageMaker, WordPerfect, Microsoft Word, ClarisWorks, FreeHand, PhotoStyler,* or other such software to bring your handouts, exams, and newsletters up to professional quality.

19. Plan a slide or transparency based lesson using a program like *Astound, Charisma, Compel, Action, Q/Media, Freelance Graphics, Delta Graph, Harvard Graphics, WordPerfect Presentations,* or *Microsoft PowerPoint.*

20. Draft an outline of steps you might take in the conduct of a lesson. Use *ABC FlowCharter* or *Visio* to produce a diagram illustrating these steps.

21. Examine source materials listed above and report to your class any that you find especially helpful.

22. Inform me of errors or omissions in this chapter so I can revise accordingly (Internet: hackbarths@aol.com).

23. Send me your responses to the above study items to help me decide if I need to provide more explicit information.

Chapter 8

Sound Recordings and Radio

Chapter Content and Objectives

The unaided voice has long been used to enlighten and entertain. Today electronic equipment makes it possible to **amplify, record,** and **broadcast** sounds of every kind. This chapter covers how sound recordings and radio have been used to improve education. Reading it should enable you to:

- List **instructional uses** of sound recordings.
- Describe how audiotape is used to **individualize learning.**
- Specify ways in which **radio** contributes to education.
- List some **strengths** and **limitations** of audio media.
- Indicate what audio media **contribute to visuals** and vice versa.
- State **guidelines** to consider in selecting, producing, and using audio media.
- Cite **source materials.**

Antecedents and Overview

Audio media hold a special fascination for me. Although I was early diagnosed as hard-of-hearing, the doctor advised against prescribing correction. He convinced my parents that my reduced sensitivity would help me concentrate on my studies.

My dear sister, Valerie, had a toy phonograph record player, and I recall the magic it did in extracting voice and melody from brightly colored discs. It did so with a steel needle attached to a black head containing a sheet of metal foil. The head was attached to a short yellow horn and produced a scratchy sound. I didn't understand why at the time, but I spent considerable time attempting various means to make that horn produce more volume.

About the same time, I obtained a simple crystal radio kit—a coil of copper wire, a shiny little rock set in lead, a stylus, and one earphone. To my amazement, when the stylus was sunk into a particular spot on that rock, I heard the voice of a newscaster. Hoping to bring in more variety, I stretched one wire to a water pipe (ground) and another to the top of the pear tree across the yard (antennae). Still, just one audible voice and a few faint melodies.

It wasn't until I was a graduate student in psychology (Sacramento State) that I heard a stereo recording. After donning the headphones and adjusting volume and balance, I entered the realm of normal hearing for the first time. It was a magical experience, similar in effect to viewing images through a stereoscope.

Children today are born with CD (compact disc) players wired to their ears. Armed with *Genesis* and *Super Nintendo*, they engage in death defying battles of wit and skill. CD-ROM multimedia software and *Sound Blaster* circuit boards have rendered drug induced trips obsolete. The emerging technology of "virtual reality" enables them to pass through Alice's looking glass to interact with environments of their choosing.

Young and old alike now take audio technologies for granted. We all record phone messages, lectures, and "notes." Joggers are wired to popular music, and commuters are absorbed in recorded novels. Inspirational, self-help, and instructional tapes abound. Business executives routinely hold teleconferences with representatives from around the world. Radio programming provides news, talk, and music. And it does so without imprisoning our eyes so we can listen as we run, shop, work, and play. The impact of talk radio was evidenced in the 1994 U.S. national elections that witnessed a popular uprising against "liberal" Democrats. A causal relation? The Democrats surely must have thought so as they scrambled to fill the airways with more sympathetic voices.

One of the most pervasive influences on youth today is popular music, available on tape and CD. Lyrics commonly glorify escapism and the consumption of drugs. Some preach a mindless, hedonistic existence. Others advocate violence. Even seemingly benign ballads commonly are steeped in what Scott Peck (*The Road Less Traveled*) has called "The Myth of Romantic Love," really a war of opposites rather than a meeting of equals.

On the other hand, performers have dedicated songs and profits to charitable causes. The *We Are the World* album and the "Live Aid" concert raised millions of dollars for famine-ravaged Africa. In 1992, over one hundred musicians took part in "A Concert for Life" to benefit AIDS organizations around the world. Michael Jackson's "Heal the World Foundation" contributed over two million dollars to refugees in Yugoslavia. The impacts of such events go far beyond funds collected. They have served admirably to awaken youths to the plight of others less fortunate.

Also keeping youths awake—and parents too—are advances in computer generated speech and sound effects. *Sound Blaster Pro* comes with "built-in CD-ROM interface, power amplifier, digital and analog mixer with programmable individual and master volume control, and more." *Fusion CD* allows recording, audio manipulation, and stereo playback. *Microsoft SoundBits* and *Windows AudioClips* provide lines and music from movies, computer dictionaries (the *Macmillan Dictionary for Children*) pronounce words, and encyclopedias (*Compton's Interactive Encyclopedia*) provide sound bites from history. MIDI (Musical Instrument Digital Interface) technology permits composition and performance of original scores as well as note-by-note revision of classics.[1]

So, are simple audio technologies long passé? I don't believe so.

In the spring of 1995, I encountered two dramatic examples of how powerful even the simplest of audio technologies can be. The morning after completing a revision of this chapter I brought a portable audiotape recorder to the elementary school (P.S. 151, Manhattan) where I was completing requirements for a credential in special education. My plan was to record reading assessment sessions with some of my students with learning disabilities. One student who previously required extensive support during reading struggled through largely on her own in anticipation of hearing her recorded voice. Another zipped through the test passages and then became animated and began singing. Later, as I sat in the classroom quietly reviewing the tape, the students returned from a break and crowded around begging to hear. Those who had "performed" proudly gave permission. Visions of writing projects that students would be motivated to complete in anticipation of recording began dancing in my head.

That same afternoon I went to P.S. 6, where I was a computer specialist teacher for the (gifted) third grade classes. After my planned lesson, students could explore whatever they liked on their new multimedia Macs. On this day I showed them the feature that permits recording of a 10-second sound clip. For the next half hour beyond my scheduled time, the students were so joyfully engaged that they forgot about their yard time. Their classroom teacher, Merle Egers, expressed utter amazement: "Look how enthralled they are!"

In the sections that follow, I share with you some significant developments in audio technologies and their uses in promoting learning. I then describe how they effectively combine with other media and suggest how we can integrate them into our own teaching.

Sound Recordings

Phonograph Records. In 1887 Thomas Edison recorded his voice on a cylinder wrapped in tinfoil. Edison's cylinders remained popular until the early 1900s, when Emile Berliner introduced phonodiscs. These sounded better, lasted longer, and could be reproduced from a master.

The phonograph was used for educational purposes soon after it was invented. In 1904 a French language course was recorded in Britain on an Edison cylinder and adopted almost immediately by Yale University and other American institutions. RCA (the Radio Corporation of America) began recording marches and folk songs in 1911 for use in schools. By 1920, self-instructional courses were available in many subjects. Dramatizations brought history to life and readings by poets illuminated their work.

Figure 8.01. Most children enjoy and learn from soundbooks. Here my godchild, Jennifer, delights in reading along with the recording. What are advantages and disadvantages of learning in this way?

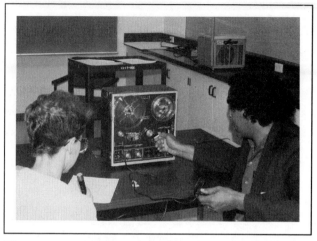

Figure 8.02. Reel-to-reel tape recorders, like the one pictured here, have long served as the standard for professional-quality production. The portability of cassette recorders has driven reel-to-reelers off the consumer market.

Children, especially, were thrilled by recordings of familiar tales skillfully narrated and enhanced by sound effects. Accompanying "soundbooks" provided illustrations and text, thereby providing a multimedia introduction to reading. (See **Figure 8.01.**)

Popular music recordings also have enlivened classroom experience. In social studies classes, they have offered diverse views on issues such as crass materialism, militarism, and human relations generally. In English classes, their lyrics have been analyzed to disclose meanings couched in poetic language. In the humanities, hit records have been used to stimulate discussion about growing up, using drugs, being alone, and facing death.[2]

Phonograph records held out against the onslaught of the more convenient and versatile audiotapes until the 1980s. But their fate was sealed when dual cassette recorders overcame legal barriers and thus made possible the widespread piracy of tapes.

Audiotapes. Magnetic recording of sound was invented in 1898 by a Danish engineer, Valdemar Poulson, who stored electrical impulses on a steel wire. But the wire often broke, and a reliable tape recorder was not made till 1935. The growth of wartime electronics and the invention of strong, plastic tape hastened development, so that by 1949 the major American recording studios were using tape to produce masters for transfer to phonograph records. Audiotape technology then evolved quickly. Transistors made recorders portable, reliable, and affordable. The cassette format simplified handling, operation, and storage. The move from analog recording to digital improved fidelity. (See **Figure 8.02.**)

Another advance was **"variable speech control"** or "rate-controlled audio playback." First to compress taped speech without raising the pitch was W. D. Garvey, who cut out segments of tape and spliced the remainders together. Today, using electronics, machines can vary the playback speed of any standard cassette from 40 to 300 percent without distorting the pitch. This is done by randomly skipping small segments of tape when speed is increased and by adding sound bits when it is decreased.

Rate-controlled audio playback offers something to all learners. The gifted can absorb more information than is conveyed at the normal speaking rate of 150-175 words per minute. (For most students the optimum rate is 275–300 wpm.) Visually impaired or otherwise "print handicapped" students with normal ability in other respects also may benefit from the playback of tapes at high speed. Reduced speed helps students of lower ability and those insufficiently fluent in English. Since students may adjust the rate to suit their capacity, they can learn without becoming bored.

The tape recorder is a highly versatile medium. Lectures, radio broadcasts, and musical performances can be recorded for later study and enjoyment. Several audio inputs can be recorded simultaneously and special

Figure 8.03. Clarity and durability make audiotape ideal for commentaries on educational exhibits. Telephone handsets can withstand years of use. Here both are employed, along with posters and photos, to persuade visitors at a UCLA health fair to donate blood. (Something my eldest brother, Vaughn, has been doing every month for decades!)

sounds or comments added any time. Tapes can be edited either by cutting out pieces and splicing the remaining sections or by using a second recorder. The listener can adjust playback speed, skip ahead, or review with ease. Tapes can be reused, stored, and played hundreds of times without deteriorating. (See **Figure 8.03**.) Photographic slides or filmstrips can be added to provide information in pictorial and graphic forms. These can be advanced automatically through a series of frames by electronic cues encoded on the tape.

Audio recordings are especially useful in teaching language, speech, drama, and music, where students need to hear their own performances. Awkward constructions, missing transitions, and grammatical errors may be more obvious to the ear than the eye. Also, teachers may tape their evaluations of student work, and these evaluations often are more personal and informative than written ones.

Today audiotape increasingly is used for self-instruction. In many schools, students can go to a media center, duplicate the tapes they want, and study them at their convenience. Students also may check out a recorder to tape a lecture or concert.

An example of more formal instruction by tape is the language laboratory. In 1924, at the Ohio State University, the first language lab was set up by two professors of speech, Ralph Waltz and G. Oscar Russell. The idea

was slow to catch on, and it wasn't until 1947 that a fully equipped facility appeared, this one at the Louisiana State University under the direction of Alfred Hayes. A few years later, at LSU and other universities, record players were replaced by tape recorders.

Then in 1958, the National Defense Education Act provided funds to buy equipment and train teachers to use labs. Although millions of dollars were spent on thousands of language labs and tens of thousands of teachers received training, the project failed, and for many reasons. Most programs were adapted uncritically from textbooks; content was chosen for universities rather than schools; lab sessions were handled mostly by inexperienced teaching assistants; tapes were amateurish; and funding was erratic. Fortunately, the equipment proved reliable and by the mid-1960s book-and-tape combinations designed for youths hit the market and were widely adopted. The labs have been popular ever since.

Language programs generally consist of two main exercises—pronunciation and structured drill. To learn pronunciation, students listen to a word or phrase, repeat it, compare their version with the master recording, and try again. Since the beginning student has an unpracticed ear, the teacher must monitor pronunciation. Structured drill relies on audiotape with two separate tracks—one to present the lesson, the other to record student responses. Only the latter of these "dual tracks" can be erased after each use. A typical lesson begins with a question or statement on the master track. Students answer the question or translate the statement aloud on a second track. They then listen to the correct response on the master and compare this with their own. Since students themselves can tell whether their responses agree with the master, structured drill exercises need little monitoring.

The **independent learning laboratory** was based on the audio-tutorial system developed in the 1960s by Samuel Postlethwait to teach botany to Purdue University undergrads. Here learning was guided by the teacher's taped instructions. Students spent most of their time at a carrel equipped with an audio player, an 8mm movie projector or videotape player, books, and other materials. Still today, in an audio-tutorial session in biology, for example, students pick up the tape and other materials in the laboratory, take them to a carrel, and switch on the tape. After providing some background, the tape may tell them to place a particular slide under the microscope. The tape is stopped, the instruction obeyed, and the tape turned on again. Students then are told to observe a specimen or read a handout. They stop the recorder, make the observation or do the reading, take notes, and return to the tape. They then attend discussion and quiz sessions, and complete their research projects.

Compact Discs. For prerecorded material, compact discs (CDs) are superior to phonograph records and audiotapes. These 4.75 inch diameter flat discs are made with tiny indentations on their surface that can be "read" by laser beams. Since no stylus or magnetic recording head ever touches them, CDs are not prone to wear. The laser beam, being very selective in what it detects, overlooks dust and small scratches.

A single CD can hold over an hour of audio material that can be accessed in any order. (See **Figure 8.04**.) Furthermore, all CD player models now on the market are compatible with standard audio systems. This permits any CD player to serve as an alternative to other audio inputs (e.g., mikes, turntables, tape players) already connected to an amplifier and speakers. Computer drives have been designed to read not only audio data, but also text and other visual data from CDs. These developments have made possible the crafting of multi-

Figure 8.04. The American Museum of Natural History (New York) enhances access to its treasures with CD technology. As Mitch Tracy and I entered each area, we were greeted with a recorded overview. When we wanted information on one of the special exhibits, we entered a code number. The CD players also feature illuminated display of the audio script.

media, interactive computer games and instruction that are covered in subsequent chapters.

Like phonodiscs, most CDs are designed to be played. Their "read-only memory" (ROM) is imprinted to last without alteration. CDs that allow for recording of new material are based on use of laser beams to induce changes in magnetic fields on the surface of the disc. At least two factors have slowed the diffusion of this complex technology. First, digital recording of audiotape results in sound reproduction comparable in quality and durability to that obtained with CDs. Second, the recording industry long fought marketing of CD recorders as they did dual cassette recorders. Piracy is common and it undermines profits rightly needed to satisfy stockholders and sponsor new talent.

Radio

Early News and Drama. Commercial radio began November 2, 1920, when the Westinghouse Corporation broadcast the Harding/Cox presidential election returns. Within a year, over 500 stations went on the air, largely to boost the sale of radio receivers. By 1923, over a million people were listening. In 1925, as amateur operators flooded the airways, the stations appealed to the federal government to license frequencies. When the government refused, the stations formed networks to protect themselves. To meet costs, they accepted advertising. In 1927, with the stations at loggerheads, Congress passed the Federal Radio Act, and the Federal Radio Commission (FRC) was created to license stations and assign frequencies.

In 1934 the Radio Act was replaced by the Federal Communications Act and the FRC by the Federal Communications Commission (FCC). The latter was authorized to regulate interstate and foreign commerce by wire and radio consistent with the public "interest, convenience, and necessity."

Ironically, the Depression was radio's golden age. As people stayed home for entertainment, series such as *The Lone Ranger*, *Gang Busters*, and *The Shadow* drew ever larger audiences. Advertising revenues soared. In 1938 on *Mercury Theater*, Orson Welles convinced millions of people that invaders had landed from Mars. The simulated news flashes, sound effects, and eerie silences aroused near hysteria. (See **Figure 8.05**.)

Such programming opened radio to blame for interfering with meals, household chores, and sleep. Children

Figure 8.05. The power of radio was dramatically revealed with the airing of *War of the Worlds*. Is the TV viewing audience of today any less gullible? Location: California Museum of Science and Industry.

went to bed late, some claimed, only to wake screaming from nightmares brought on by programs they had heard. Like comic books, said the critics, radio competed with natural play, gave a distorted view of the world, and vulgarized speech. Supporters countered that radio educated the electorate, raised morale, launched community service projects, and warned of natural dangers like floods and hurricanes. Thus, in times of triumph and tragedy, radio served as a global meeting place.

Television broke radio's grip. It captured the home audience. Smaller radio audiences shrank advertising dollars, so that by 1960 the once-powerful networks no longer could finance costly dramas. People now used the radio mostly while on the go—driving, working, playing. Transistor models, like the ones Mom got for us kids in 1959 from Macy's, were a hit at school and on the beach. At home the radio welcomed us to a new day, accompanied our household routines, and lulled us to sleep. With our attention divided and listening time short, we sought less complex programs, such as popular music, news summaries ("You give us 22 minutes; we'll give **you** the world!"), and weather reports. Today, stations target their audiences ever more precisely, some by age, others by ethnicity. "Talk radio," on which listeners call in to air their views, has become immensely popular.

Noncommercial radio began inauspiciously. In the early 1920s, many universities went on the air, though more as an experiment in electronics than as a public service. Operating on shoestring budgets, noncommercial radio stations could not compete with the networks, but excelled in providing information of local interest.

In 1965, the 11-station Wisconsin State Broadcasting Service created a telephone network (ETN) linking various university extension locations and enabling radio listeners to call in questions and make comments. Later, programs were transmitted via SCA (Subsidiary Communications Authorization) signals, which rode piggyback on FM signals through what is called "multiplexing," and were picked up by special receivers (like those playing continuous music in department stores). The ETN-SCA system originally was created to offer continuing education to medical doctors throughout the state. However, it soon expanded to provide a variety of programs to professionals living in remote areas.

For noncommercial radio, the tide turned in 1967, when Congress created the Corporation for Public Broadcasting (CPB). With the passage of the Public Broadcasting Financing Act (1975) and the Public Telecommunications Financing Act (1978), the number of licensed, noncommercial radio stations jumped from 455 in 1970 to nearly eleven hundred in 1980.

National Public Radio (NPR), a nonprofit organization (established in 1971), today sets the pace for public radio stations. Its prime offerings have included *All Things Considered*, an in-depth news program; a Shakespeare festival; live coverage of concerts; original radio plays; *A Question of Place*, a 12-part series portraying artists and thinkers, past and present; and airing of George Lucas's *Star Wars*. Like other public stations, NPR is striving to increase minority coverage through such offerings as *Enfoque Nacional*, a Spanish-language news program, and *Crossroads*, which interviews minority leaders and artists.

Instructional Radio. Schools across the United States began receiving instructional radio programs as early as 1923. Benjamin Darrow, founder of the *Ohio School of the Air*, held that:

> The central and dominant aim of education by radio is to bring the world to the classroom, to make universally available the services of the finest teachers, the inspiration of the greatest leaders . . . and [the] unfolding [of] world events.[3]

For Darrow and his contemporaries, radio was destined to become the "textbook of the air."

There were several notable accomplishments in the early days of school radio. The weekly program *Little Red Schoolhouse* informed Chicago's children about such topics as farming, transportation, and science. NBC's weekly *Music Appreciation Hour* lasted from 1928 to 1942. CBS's biweekly *American School of the Air* began in 1930. Its programs reached nearly a million students and included biographies, civics lessons, literature reviews, and dramas. A leader in school radio was the Cleveland Board of Education station, WBOE, which, during the 1930s and 40s, broadcast programs covering nearly every subject in the curriculum.[4]

The spread of school radio in the United States was not without setbacks. Before 1945 receivers were expensive and reception was poor by today's standards, thus reinforcing the resistance of teachers unwilling to adapt their course content and methods of instruction. Just as these problems were being resolved, the attention of educators shifted to television, where there was no "visual gap" to be bridged.

Nevertheless, educational radio programming for children has survived by combining elements of music, humor, story telling, and news into what might be called audio **"edutainment."** For example, *We Like Kids* has used this format to engage children and their parents in thinking about language arts, African-American history, and getting along with others. *Pickleberry Pie* features characters who investigate topics of interest to children and explore their concerns. Both of these programs are carried by NPR. The offerings of local radio stations and such other producers as Disney and Sesame Street are carried over Digital Cable Radio and broadcast throughout the day and night via the Children's Satellite Network. The CSN day begins with *The All American Alarm Clock* (contests, music, quizzes, weather) and then moves to storytelling and music (e.g., *Great Music for Great Kids*). *Kinetic City Super Crew* is a series of half-hour programs targeted at youths. Each presents a science mystery story, interesting findings, and a suggested home project. Workshops that engage children in radio production include *Inside Radio, Sound and Imagination,* and *The Sound Experience.*[5]

School radio has also been used successfully in the United Kingdom. BBC (British Broadcasting Corporation) School Radio, begun in the mid-1920s, now reaches over 90 percent of the nation's schools. Preschoolers are treated to stories, songs, and rhymes in the daily broadcast of *Listening Corner*. Primary school children currently learn math, history, and health. Older students hear experts discuss their work in science, industry, and literature. The British *Radio Shop* provides lists of recommended readings, filmstrips, computer software (for follow-up exercises), and teachers' guidebooks.[6]

BBC School Radio program producers ensure that students pay attention in several ways. Content is made lively and engaging and is accented with sound effects and music. Readings and filmstrips reinforce program content and all clearly relate to explicit instructional objectives. Finally, vocabulary, grammar, and pacing are closely matched to the abilities of intended audiences.

Radio thrives abroad as "extended schooling," where students at remote locations are instructed by radio under the direction of a parent or tutor. Since 1970, for instance, Mexico's *Radioprimaria* has provided 4th, 5th, and 6th grade education in several rural communities. This is accomplished at a fraction of the cost of training and paying teachers to take on such assignments.

Equally successful is the use of radio in broadcasting to students in their homes. Called "distance learning," it is a modification of the correspondence school, in that broadcasting has added "live" teaching and more disciplined study schedules. Programs usually are complemented by print materials. Students mail assignments to their teachers and occasionally meet with them. Distance learning is practiced worldwide: in the United States (e.g., Coastline Community College, California; Miami-Dade Community College), Great Britain (The Open University), China (China Radio and Television University), France, Germany, Japan, and elsewhere.

In the Third World, radio provides social, political, and economic education. Called "development communication," one of its purposes is to spread religious teachings. In Latin American, for example, church-supported radio stations preach to the rural poor. Another purpose is to give information on services, for example, when and where to have children vaccinated. A third purpose is to teach certain skills: cognitive (such as numeracy and literacy), information-seeking (like using a dictionary or phone book), work (such as planting and harvesting), and health (oral rehydration therapy and first aid). Finally, radio is used to affect behavior, advocating prenatal care, breastfeeding, delayed marriage, and "safe" sex.[7]

Evaluation of Audio Media

Audio media reproduce only one aspect of events, their physical vibration, which may be heard or felt. How much does this matter? If we are interested mainly in sounds, as in musical performance (^{ta ta ta} TA!) and the audio identification of distinctive events (see **Figure 8.06**), it does not matter much. Yet engaging in face-to-face dialogue and attending concerts obviously are richer experiences. Even lectures lose much of their effect when presented on tape, for lecturers often rely on gestures to enhance their message. Pronunciation of new words is helped by seeing them formed on the lips of speakers.[8]

Audio programs allow listeners to concentrate on program content and to create their own corresponding images. Indeed, radio commonly is called the "theater of the mind," as illustrated by adaptation for radio of the highly visual movie *Star Wars* with little loss of dramatic impact. Narrative and sound effects bring images to mind often more awesome than those provided for us by film and TV producers. Gary Ferrington, Administrative Director of the Center for Advanced Technology in Education (University of Oregon), suggested that good radio programming might "facilitate a child's integration of life-based experiences into a 'movie.'" "Each child," he wrote,

> becomes his or her own director with no two children having the same imaginary experience. A dinosaur that a child creates while listening to a science fiction drama, for example, is not the same as one manufactured by Hollywood. It is a very personal dinosaur which comes from that child's own needs, perceptions, joys, fears, and emotionally enriched experiences.[9]

Each type of audio medium has distinctive strengths and weaknesses. **Phonograph records**, for instance, cover many subjects and are easy to play. However, they are prone to wear and are easily scratched or broken. **Compact discs** overcome these limitations and make possible quick access to desired sections, but the selection of **educational** programs remains relatively limited. In the domain of music, critics have objected to the artificially clean sound. **Audiotape** is versatile. Even preschoolers can make their own tapes, and they can start, stop, and replay them at will. However, instructional audiotape sometimes lacks sufficient appeal to hold student interest for long. One clear advantage of the **audio-tutorial method** is that it enables students to work at their own pace with teacher guidance only when needed. It is especially well suited to classes requiring laboratory work.

The **learning laboratory** also meets individual needs for self-pacing and is a boon to students having perceptual impairments. To those of us who are hard-of-hearing, a tape played at the right volume for an entire class conveys little. We fare better in a carrel where we can adjust volume and tone controls. For those with visual handicaps, video magnifiers and computerized scanners (optical character recognition and speech synthesis) are more beneficial. (See **Figure 8.07**.)

Radio is cheap and timely; it presents experts "in person," and can be used both for basic instruction and enrichment in understaffed schools. On the other hand, radio rarely allows more that a few of the listeners to talk back. Students may question radio teachers by telephone, but only a few calls can be handled without disrupting a presentation. Nevertheless, research suggest that students enjoy the programs and learn from them. For example, a study evaluating effects of *Kinetic City Super Crew* (exposure to just one to four half hour programs over a period of two weeks) found that:

Figure 8.06. In this exhibit, attention is focused on the acoustic dimension of distinctive phenomena. In what professions is it important to be able to interpret sounds correctly? Location: California Museum of Science and Industry.

Figure 8.07. Special equipment has been designed to compensate for sensory and speech handicaps. Can you identify the compensatory devices pictured? Can you think of others? Location: California Museum of Science and Industry.

Figure 8.08. Commercially produced audiotapes promise health, wealth, and happiness. Those with valid content and convincing narration, and supplemented with illuminating textual materials, might well help listeners achieve these objectives.

. . . the series appears moderately successful at communicating its information to listeners in the home setting. Significant recall of information for the TIME program occurred at least three weeks after broadcast, indicating the potential of an informal medium like radio to have long-term effects on children's knowledge. . . . Listeners reported doing significantly more science activities at home . . . .[10]

Nevertheless, instructional audiotape and radio programs are best when complemented with printed text, pictures, and graphics. These permit listeners to follow along with the narrative and to make marginal notes for later study. Compressed tapes associated with text tend to speed reading with no loss in comprehension. Addition of graphic illustrations enables students to capture ideas visually that might escape them aurally and vice versa.[11] (See **Figure 8.08**.)

Practical Guidelines

Selection. Your choice of audio materials may be guided by **Figure 8.09**. Rate materials on each criterion from **1** (unsatisfactory) to **10** (excellent) and select the ones that are available, affordable, compatible with your equipment, and score highest overall. First, consider **subject matter content**:

a. How well does it match **instructional objectives**?
b. Is it **accurate**?
c. Is it **current**?
d. Is the coverage sufficiently **comprehensive**?
e. Are people **treated equally** whatever gender, race, or religion?

Next, assess the **pedagogical quality** of the presentation:

Title _____ Artist _____

Publisher _____ Date _____ Price _____

Subject _____ Grade Level _____

Objectives _____

Prerequisites _____

Hardware Requirements _____

Selection Criteria	Rating (1 = low; 10 = high)	Comments
1. Content of Audio	____	_____
a. match with objectives	____	_____
b. accuracy	____	_____
c. currency	____	_____
d. scope	____	_____
e. stereotyping	____	_____
2. Presentation	____	_____
a. impact	____	_____
b. organization	____	_____
c. teaching strategies	____	_____
d. integration	____	_____
e. interactivity	____	_____
f. motivation	____	_____
g. use of sound	____	_____
h. difficulty	____	_____
3. Associated Text	____	_____
a. relation to audio	____	_____
b. match with objectives	____	_____
c. overall quality	____	_____
4. Associated Visuals	____	_____
a. relation to audio	____	_____
b. match with objectives	____	_____
c. overall quality	____	_____
5. Technical Quality	____	_____
a. audio clarity	____	_____
b. audio volume	____	_____
c. tape quality	____	_____
6. Effectiveness	____	_____
a. student interest	____	_____
b. student achievement	____	_____
c. student evaluation	____	_____
7. Overall Impression	____	_____

_____
_____
_____
_____
_____
_____
_____
_____
_____

Figure 8.09. Audio materials evaluation form.

a. Does the narration **attract and hold attention**?

b. Are ideas presented in chronological, logical, or otherwise **meaningful order**?

c. Does the narration provide a **preview** followed by **definitions**, **elaborations**, **examples**, **problems**, and **practice**?

d. Are **references** made to relevant textual and visual materials?

e. Are listeners invited to **interrupt** the program to engage in related activities? (See **Figure 8.10.**)

Figure 8.10. When we speak of audio media as being "interactive," we usually mean that the listener can start and stop a program at will and can access desired sections with ease. This was the case with the program featured here. Beyond this, listeners might be directed to interrupt the program, as with the audio-tutorial method. What deeper senses of interactivity might you expect with computer support? Location: American Museum of Natural History (New York).

f. Are they encouraged to **concentrate** and **persevere**?

g. Are **sound effects** and **music** used effectively to focus attention and/or generate mood?

h. Does the **level of difficulty** suit the intended listeners?

Concerning **associated text and visuals**:

a. Are they **clearly related** to the narration, music, and sound effects?

b. How well do they **contribute** to the achievement of instructional objectives?

c. To what extent do they meet the standards of **quality** set forth in Chapters **6** and **7** of this book?

When judging program *effectiveness,* consider how interested students appear to be and how well they perform. Also, ask them how much they enjoyed it and how much of value they think they learned.

Let's examine an exemplary program. **Figure 8.11** shows the introductory page from a booklet accompanying the BBC School Radio course, *Human Biology.* **Figure 8.12** consists of a sample narrative script and an associated diagram. Notice how it directs student attention, explains the nature of representation (enlarged, simplified), and describes the processes portrayed. The language is clear and the style engaging. The narrator adds a friendly, conversational touch.

```
SELF-HELP - YOUR WAY THROUGH TAPE AND BOOKLET

Using the BBC tape and this booklet you can work your way through
material which will extend your knowledge of biology and will be
helpful for your examinations. Work through at your own pace and
do not feel under pressure to complete a topic in one single
session.

EXPLANATION OF THE SYMBOLS

(p)   PREPARATION - to read this section

(t)   TAPE - now press the 'play' button

(r)   REVISION   - go back over this part of the tape or booklet

(e)   EXERCISE - try something out for yourself
```

Figure 8.11. Booklet from the BBC School Radio course *Human Biology* provides explicit instructions enabling students to work on their own. Source: Peter Ward, "The BBC Help-Yourself Approach to Learning," *Media in Education and Development,* 18 (December 1985), p. 164. Reprinted courtesy of Taylor & Francis Group Ltd.

Figure 8.13 shows a pair of graphs based on information earlier presented to students in the course *Human Biology.* Students are asked to make simple observations about each graph and then to draw a conclusion based on the relation between them.

Production. Ken Loge, a University of Oregon professor who teaches a summer enrichment course in sound design for middle school students, was credited as having observed that:

> when children work with video, they do so with preconceived ideas of what a finished product should look like, given their extensive experience with commercial television. Children often feel disappointed when their own videos do not hold up to the standards of the viewing experiences. Audio. . . is a new medium for most kids and they are enthralled with the illusions and imagery they can create through sound.[12]

You and your students may experience such highs by creatively following these steps:

Step 1. Select recorder and tape capable of producing the desired level of sound quality. For most purposes, a cassette recorder or one built into your computer will do. However, if very high fidelity is desired, as in the recording of classical music, use an open-reel recorder. Whereas cassette recorders advance the tape at just $1^7/8$ inches per second (ips), open-reelers can be adjusted to higher speeds (e.g., $3^3/4$ or $7^1/2$ ips). Greater speed permits greater fidelity, especially in the recording of material having high-pitched sounds.

A good recorder will have jacks that allow connection of two microphones, two speakers, and two auxiliary sources (e.g., a phonograph record turntable, an AM/FM stereo radio, another tape or CD player). Also, it will have dials that show the levels of input from auxiliary sources and that permit adjustment of this level.

Most tapes have particles of ferrous oxide as the recording medium. Higher fidelity can be achieved by using tapes coated with chromium dioxide. For master recordings, use the best. Copies may be made using the economy lines of brand name tapes. Long playing, thin tapes tend to break or get caught up in the machinery.

Step 2. Select a suitable microphone ("mike"). The human mind cleverly ignores most background noise and focuses on sounds of interest. Listeners may move

VISUAL   AUDIO

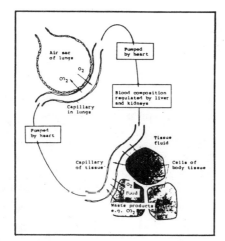

Presenter: Now I'd like you to look at the drawing on page five. It's a bit of a cheat really . . . what I mean is we've emphasized the microscopic parts and pushed the big bits, the heart and kidneys and things, rather into the shade. Make a start at the top left which represents a microscopic section of the lungs. There's an air sac . . . you'll see its single lining of cells. And what I want you to appreciate is that it lies very close to the blood capillary. You'll see the bend of the capillary. Notice that gas molecules, oxygen and carbon dioxide, are being exchanged. D'you see the arrows? Oxygen . . . *from* the air in the lungs *to* the blood in the capillary. And carbon dioxide, which is an unwanted waste product, *from* the blood capillary *to* the lungs. And that's the point! Putting it a little simply . . . the capillaries leak! Gas molecules diffuse across the cell membranes of the capillaries, but it's all very much under control.

Figure 8.12. This section of script reveals the intimate relation between audio and visual elements in an exemplary instructional program. Source: Peter Ward, "The BBC Help-Yourself Approach to Learning," *Media in Education and Development,* 18 (December 1985), pp. 164–165. Reprinted courtesy of Taylor & Francis Group Ltd.

closer to the source, turn their heads, or cup their ears. Since tape recorders cannot distinguish sounds of interest from noise, it is necessary to use microphones that best detect those coming from the direction of the former and shut out much of the rest. **Figure 8.14** illustrates the directional sensitivity of the four most common types of mikes.

Omni-directional mikes permit recording of sounds coming from all directions. They are most suitable for group discussions. **Bidirectional** mikes are sensitive to sounds coming from just two opposite directions, but not to the directions at right angles to these. This makes them a good choice for recording class sessions in which speaker and audience both participate. They are okay

for interviews, but two separate mikes serve better. **Cardioid** mikes are most sensitive to sounds emanating from one direction and, to a lesser extent, to sounds from the immediate left and right of this direction. They are good for recording stage performances; but, again, multiple mikes work even better. **Gun** mikes pick up sounds coming from just one direction. Since they eliminate most peripheral noise, they allow recording of sounds too distant or subtle to be heard with the unaided ear.

Step 3. Prepare the material to be recorded. A script should be written which includes all narration and references to music and sound effects. This should meet

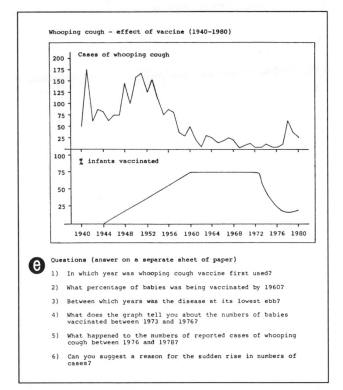

Whooping cough - effect of vaccine (1940-1980)

Cases of whooping cough

% infants vaccinated

1940 1944 1948 1952 1956 1960 1964 1968 1972 1976 1980

e Questions (answer on a separate sheet of paper)

1) In which year was whooping cough vaccine first used?

2) What percentage of babies was being vaccinated by 1960?

3) Between which years was the disease at its lowest ebb?

4) What does the graph tell you about the numbers of babies vaccinated between 1973 and 1976?

5) What happened to the numbers of reported cases of whooping cough between 1976 and 1978?

6) Can you suggest a reason for the sudden rise in numbers of cases?

Figure 8.13. Learning from radio and audiotape is best ensured when adjunct textual and visual materials provide examples, review, and practice as illustrated in this excerpt from *Human Biology.* Source: Peter Ward, "The BBC Help-Yourself Approach to Learning," *Media in Education and Development,* 18 (December 1985), p. 165. Reprinted courtesy of Taylor & Francis Group Ltd.

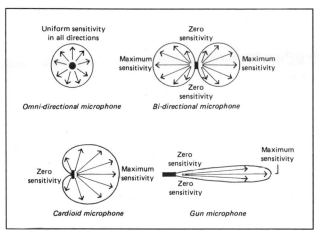

Figure 8.14. Different types of microphones allow selective detection of sounds. Which mike should you use to record (1) remote conversations? (2) stage performances? (3) two sources in opposite directions? (4) open discussions? Source: Henry Ellington & Phil Race, *Producing Teaching Materials: A Handbook for Teachers and Trainers,* 2nd ed. (East Brunswick, NJ: Nichols, 1993), p. 155. Reprinted with permission of Nichols Publishing.

the relevant criteria among those for selection of print materials discussed in Chapter **6.** The draft script should be subjected to review by colleagues and students and then revised accordingly. The final version should be rehearsed using the best talent available.

Step 4. Prepare the setting. Find a quiet location where you can record without being interrupted. Carpeting and drapes help reduce unwanted noise. Post signs outside each door.

Step 5. Adjust recording level. During a rehearsal, set the recording level such that the indicator moves frequently into the high range, but rarely into the red. Do not rely on automatic adjustment because the recorder will increase its sensitivity to unwanted sounds during pauses in your program.

Step 6. Use the "pause" control to begin and end recording segments. This minimizes the noise and distortion that tend to occur between segments, especially those recorded using "record" and "stop" switches only.

Step 7. Edit the recording to eliminate segments or to rearrange their order. Open-reel tapes may be cut and spliced with special tape. Recordings on cassette tape may be transferred segment by segment by using a "patch cord" to a second recorder. Such computer software as *Sound Blaster Pro, Fusion CD,* and *AddImpact* ease both editing and addition of sound effects and music.[13]

Recordings of special events require more than careful preparation. I recently attended a lecture at Teachers College, Columbia University. The distinguished speaker had seen to the set-up of equipment to record his timely remarks on "peace education." After a glowing introduction from the dean, the speaker made gracious remarks to his hosts and launched into his theme. Sitting in the front row, I happened to notice that the cassette tape on the speaker's platform was not advancing. Sensing that an historic moment was about to pass unrecorded, I interrupted. "Excuse me. Did you intend to record this talk?" While the audience of education faculty and students waited for the audio technician to be retrieved, the person next to me walked bravely up to the tangle of wires and machines and after a moment's survey of the situation, she pressed the pause control to set the tape in motion.

Production of **slide/tape** programs is facilitated by using one of two basic **storyboard** techniques. The first employs 4 x 6 inch cards like that diagrammed in **Figure 8.15**. Each card contains a sketch or description of the slide and accompanying narration. The cards may be tacked to a board to give a global perspective and to ease rearranging order.

The second storyboard technique, **scripting**, is illustrated in **Figure 8.16**. Here media expert Lee Green provided a clear format and explicit instructions. Note that it often is helpful to add sketches of visual content, especially if the slides have not yet been selected or shot.

Once the slides and audiotapes have been prepared, it is a relatively simple matter to load the carousel trays and to program automatic advancing on the tape. Alternatively, images and sound can be transferred to computer and then, using such software as *Astound, Persuasion, Cricket Presents, Symantec MORE!, Presentations, Delta Graph,* and *PowerPoint,* can be sequenced for presentation to class. Ease of editing by computer greatly facilitates creative, timely, efficient revision based on field test data. Such is the essence of educational technology as conceived from cover to cover in this book.

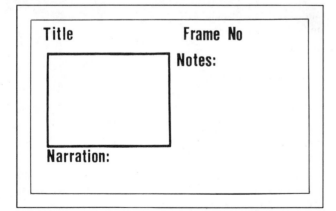

Figure 8.15. All forms of audiovisual production, including CD-ROM multimedia, typically start with preparing a series of storycards like the one shown here or a script like that illustrated in Figure 8.16. Source: Lee Green, *Creative Slide/Tape Programs* (Littleton, CO: Libraries Unlimited, 1986), p. 7. Reprinted courtesy of Libraries Unlimited.

VISUAL INSTRUCTIONS	SLIDE #	AUDIO
VISUAL INSTRUCTIONS GO DIRECTLY OPPOSITE AUDIO INSTRUCTIONS AT THE PRECISE POINT AT WHICH SOMETHING SHOULD OCCUR.	1	SPECIFIC AUDIO INSTRUCTIONS SUCH AS FADE IN MUSIC . . . FADE UNDER NARRATION ARE WRITTEN IN CAPITALS AND UNDERLINED. When writing scripts, put all visual descriptions on the left and all audio on the right. Double space all audio copy. Keep even margins on the left. Never break a word at the end of a line, nor a sentence at the end of a page.
VISUAL INSTRUCTIONS GO ON THE LEFT IN CAPS AND ARE SINGLE-SPACED IF MORE THAN ONE LINE IS REQUIRED FOR ONE SET OF INSTRUCTIONS.	2	To indicate emphasis in a script, underline words to be stressed. Also, underline all information that refers to music or sound other than the actual words to be read. THESE DIRECTIONS ARE UNDERLINED AND ARE IN ALL CAPITALS.
FOR SLIDE SCRIPTS, PUT THE NUMBER OF THE SLIDE IN THE MIDDLE BETWEEN THE AUDIO AND THE VISUAL COLUMNS AND AT THE EXACT POINT YOU WANT TO SEE THAT SLIDE.	3	Write out the words the way you want them to be expressed (for example, "three dollars and eighty cents" vs. "three-eighty").
DESCRIPTIONS OF SLIDES SHOULD BE CONCISE BUT EXACT. THEY SHOULD INCLUDE TYPE OF SHOT (CU, ECU, MS, LA, ETC.).	4	Each page of a multiple-page script, except for the first one, should be numbered at the top. Write "MORE" at the bottom center of each page except the last one.
SLIDE DESCRIPTIONS CAN ALSO BE SIMPLE DRAWINGS. THESE ARE GOOD FOR GRAPHICS, CHARTS, PICTOGRAMS, OR SPECIAL EFFECTS.	5	If the script is a partial script, be sure to include the outcue. For example, a script may have long stretches without narration. An outcue will cue slide changes.
SLIDE DESCRIPTIONS CAN ALSO BE SIMPLE DRAWINGS SUCH AS STICK FIGURES.	6	Make sure all of the above instructions are adhered to on the script. Remember, others working with you will be counting on it.

Special Tips for Scripting

1. Choose words carefully. Don't use more than you need. Think of words costing 25 cents each, as in a telegram.

2. Write in a conversational tone. Read the script out loud to confirm that it reads well, or have someone read it to you.

3. Vary your shots. Use high- and low-angle shots rather than having them all eye level. Photograph pets and children from their eye level.

4. Use medium and close-up shots to tell the story. Too often slides become a series of snapshots and lack visual impact.

5. Remember you are developing an *audiovisual* program. Try to visualize the situations you are describing. Reorient yourself to think in pictures. The visuals will carry at least 80 percent of the message.

6. The narration is important not only for the part it plays in explaining details as the *audio* of "audiovisual"; it also may call attention to relationships and indicate emphasis that should be given in some pictures. Avoid describing what the audience sees on the screen.

Figure 8.16. Basic reading script form with instructions. Source: Lee Green, *Creative Slide/Tape Programs* (Littleton, CO: Libraries Unlimited, 1986), pp. 124–25. Reprinted courtesy of Libraries Unlimited.

Figure 8.17. Audiotapes are priced so low that every school can afford them. Collections can be filed in compact cabinets and used for many years. Here my brother, then a third grade teacher, is pretending to scrutinize a tape.

Utilization. Authors of the BBC course *Human Biology* worked on the premise that reliance on the spoken word alone is not enough; students must be actively engaged in the study of audiotape programs. In their words, the student "has to prepare, listen to short sections of tape, revise [review] material and carry out exercises. It is by no means a merely passive experience but makes a considerable demand."[14]

If the audiotape recording you select is not part of a comprehensive course, you may have to prepare your own supplementary materials: introductory remarks, vocabulary lists, discussion questions, and follow-up activities. Be sure to adapt your programs in view of what students already know, assign readings in advance, and supply program outlines.

Stage management also enhances the learning experience. Before students arrive, make sure that the equipment is working, that there is comfortable seating and adequate ventilation, and that all required materials are nearby. During presentation, listen to the program yourself and watch student reactions. Be ready to adjust volume or tuning and supplement the presentation with personal commentary.

Tape collections should be stored in cabinets with easy access and so designed as to protect against potential hazards (e.g., heat, magnets, liquids, fire, and theft). (See **Figure 8.17.**) Duplicates of the most valuable tapes should be stored elsewhere and used only for producing fresh copies as needed.

Students enjoy crafting their own audiotape programs. Singly or in groups, they can interview local celebrities, assemble sound portraits of friends, and record episodes from their own lives. They can record the **"soundscape"** of their school playground or cafeteria, edit and enhance the results using *Sound Blaster Pro*, and recreate the scenes for the class. Among several intriguing suggestions made by Gary Ferrington for productive explorations (and modifications) of soundscapes was to have students:

> generate a multi-column form. In column one is listed the sounds which are a part of their immediate environment. Sounds are classified in column two as being informational (like an alarm clock. . .), pleasurable (a wind chime. . .), or distracting (a noisy leaf blower). Students then identify, in column three, an emotional response each sound creates when it is heard. Column four is used to note possible options for modification or elimination of a sound. The student also notes how these changes might alter the emotional factors listed in column three.[15]

Ferrington suggested that: "The understandings students develop about the nature of the soundscape will facilitate decisions later in life related to their creating a community in which it is more acoustically pleasant to live."[16] I can only add that, if such an exercise discourages one future boomboxer, motorcycle pipe rapper, or misguided leaf blower, it has served a function vital to our survival as a species!

Good results using a variety of audio technologies have been obtained in special education classes. One

Figure 8.18. Audiotape recorders meet the needs of both teachers (who may present lectures *in absentia*) and students (who may record classroom sessions for later study). However, education is best served when both are present to listen and respond.

high school teacher, for example, who had a class of students with learning disabilities, sought to improve their oral and written expression, enhance their self-esteem, and increase their acceptance by other students. To arouse interest, she played some tapes of old-time radio variety shows. She then proposed that the students prepare their own program and broadcast it during lunch period over the school's public address system. The students were enthusiastic. They collected material and recorded and edited it. The final product was a hit.

For teachers tempted to let media take over while they escape to the lounge, here is a cautionary tale. A certain professor, who had to be out of town, taped his lecture and asked the class to listen to it as scheduled. Unexpectedly, he returned to give the lecture in person. There, as arranged, was his tape recorder, but there were no students. On the seats a hundred (voice activated) portable recorders were waiting for the lecture to begin.[17] (See **Figure 8.18**.)

Summary and Conclusions

Sometimes dubbed "the little media," books, photos, filmstrips, audiotapes, and radios tend to score highly on:

- technical **quality** and **reliability**;
- depth, breadth, and **validity of content**;
- **convenience** and **flexibility**;
- **power** to promote learning;
- **economy**.

The conclusion of pioneer Wilbur Schramm that basic media give us more "bang for the buck" rings true today.[18]

Audio technologies continue to contribute to education worldwide. Audio recordings permit selection of diverse content and opportunity for boundless creation. Radio allows timely distribution of life saving information to remote populations. Supplemented with print materials and instructors, tape and radio bring the world closer to the ambitious, United Nations sponsored, 1990 World Conference goal of "Education for All" by the year 2000.

Nevertheless, movies and television—the media that intimately link visual and auditory messages—have certain advantages over media that appeal to a single sense or must rely on adjunct materials. The marriage of sight and sound approximates human presence—the facial expressions of the lecturer, the lip positions of the speaker of a foreign language, the baton of the conductor. When coupled with CD-ROM, cable networks, and interactive computer technologies, audiovisual media provide students with ever greater control over access to information meeting **their own** needs and interests.

Thus, the wave of the future is multimedia/hypertext open learning environments in which subject matter abstractions are **"recontextualized,"** that is, placed back in the times and surroundings from which they were derived. It is these developments that are pursued in succeeding chapters.

Notes

[1]Sirota, Warren, "MIDI Sequencer Buyers' Guide," *Multimedia World*, 1 (April 1994), pp. 71–76.

[2]Seidman, Steven A., "Music Video Grows Up," *Media & Methods*, 22 (May/June 1986), pp. 8–9.

[3]Darrow, Benjamin, *Radio: The Assistant Teacher* (Columbus, OH: R.G. Adams, 1932), p. 79.

[4]Cuban, Larry, *Teachers and Machines: The Classroom Use of Technology Since 1920* (New York: Teachers College Press, 1986), pp. 19–24.

[5]Ferrington, Gary, "Kids Radio Is on the Air!" *Tech Trends*, 39 (January/February 1994), pp. 38–40.

[6]Chatterley, Albert, "The Radio Shop," *Media in Education and Development*, 18 (December 1985), pp. 166–167.

[7]Thomas, R. Murray, & Kobayashi, V.N., eds., *Educational Technology: Its Creation, Development, and Cross-Cultural Transfer* (New York: Pergamon Press, 1987); Pease, Edward C., & Dennis, Everette E., eds., *Radio: The Forgotten Medium* (New Brunswick, NJ: Transaction Publishers, 1995).

[8]Beagles-Roos, Jessica, & Gat, Isabelle, "Specific Impact of Radio and Television on Children's Story Comprehension," *Journal of Educational Psychology*, 75 (February 1983), p. 128: "Recognition of expressive [and figurative] language was facilitated by a radio [audiotaped] story, whereas picture sequencing [and recall of story details were] augmented by a television story. [However,] . . . recall of the explicit story content was equivalent across media."

[9]Ferrington, Gary, "Kids Radio Is on the Air!", p. 39.

[10]Flagg, Barbara N., "Learning Science From Children's Radio: Summative Evaluation of *Kinetic City Super Crew*," *Educational Technology Research and Development*, 42, 3(1994), p. 41.

[11]Fulford, Catherine P., "Can Learning Be More Efficient? Using Compressed Speech Audio Tapes to Enhance Systematically Designed Text," *Educational Technology*, 33 (February 1993), pp. 51–59. Note that "systematic" paring down of the text to essential information worked just as well. McKenna, Linda M., "The Relationship Between Attributes of a Children's Radio Program and its Appeal to Listeners," *Educational Technology Research and Development*, 41, 1(1993), pp. 17–28. McKenna found that to attract and maintain interest of children, radio programming needed to minimize talk, jokes, and instruction while maximizing use of popular music. (See **Figure 8.19.**)

[12]Ferrington, Gary, "Kids Radio Is on the Air!", p. 40.

[13]Ellington, Henry, *Producing Teaching Materials: A Handbook for Teachers and Trainers*, 2nd ed. (East Brunswick, NJ: Nichols, 1993).

[14]Ward, Peter, "The BBC Help-Yourself Approach to Learning," *Media in Education and Development*, 18 (December 1985), p. 164.

[15]Ferrington, Gary, "Kids, Noise and Orchestrating the Soundscape," *Tech Trends*, 39 (January/February 1994), pp. 41–43.

[16]*Ibid.*, p. 43. See also Berendt, Joachim-Ernst, *The Third Ear: On Listening to the World* (New York: Holt, Rinehart, & Winston, 1992).

[17]Ashby, Eric, *Adapting Universities to a Technological Society* (San Francisco: Jossey-Bass, 1974), p. 36.

"*Ms. Pine said beginning next Monday we'll be studying classical music. Does she mean like Chuck Berry and The Beatles?*"

Figure 8.19. Music may be studied as an art form (as planned by this student's teacher), or used to spice up instructional programs. How might you incorporate music into your teaching? Source: *Phi Delta Kappan,* 76 (January 1995), p. 398. Reprinted with permission of John R. Shanks.

[18]Schramm, Wilbur, *Big Media, Little Media: Tools and Technologies for Instruction* (Beverly Hills, CA: Sage, 1978), p. 137: "Between Big and Little Media (television versus radio, film versus filmstrip, computer-assisted instruction versus programmed instruction), the cost ratio for comparable scale of use (except for very large or very small audiences) and comparable quality of production is usually 5:1 or more. The question that must necessarily be asked, therefore, is whether ITV [instructional television] will accomplish enough more than radio to justify paying five times as much, and so on with other such comparisons."

Sources

The premiere source of **educational audio recordings** long has been the **National Information Center for Educational Media** (NICEM, 1-800-926-8328; 1-505-265-3591). Their *Audiocassette & Compact Disc Finder* has been updated regularly since the 1993 1st edition and may be obtained from Plexus Publishing (1-609-654-6500). Audiophiles also might want to check their local libraries for NICEM's earlier editions of *Index to Educational Records* and *Index to Educational Audio Tapes*.

Additional information about **audio products and programs** may be found in:

Alten, Stanley R., *Audio in Media*, 4th ed. (Belmont, CA: Wadsworth, 1994).

Audio Video Market Place: A Multimedia Guide (New York: Bowker, updated annually, 1984–1988).

Baert, Luc, Theunissen, Luc, Vergult, Guido, Maes, Jan, & Arts, Jan, *Digital Audio and Compact Disc Technology,* 3rd ed. (Boston: Focal, 1995).

Broch, Patricia A., *Educational Technology in the Classroom* (Englewood Cliffs, NJ: Educational Technology Publications, 1994).

Collins, Mary, *National Public Radio: The Cast of Characters* (Washington, DC: Seven Locks Press, 1993).

Ditingo, Vincent M., *The Remaking of Radio* (Boston: Focal, 1995).

Donavin, Denise P., ed., *American Library Association Best of the Best for Children* (New York: Random House, 1992).

Educators Guide to Free Audio and Video Materials (Randolph, WI: Educators Progress Service, annual).

Erlewine, Michael, & Bultman, Scott, eds., *All Music Guide: The Best CDs, Albums & Tapes* (San Francisco: Miller Freeman, 1992).

Harley, Robert, *The Complete Guide to High-End Audio* (Albuquerque, NM: Acapella Publishing, 1994).

Heintze, James R., *Scholar's Guide to Washington, D.C., for Audio Resources: Sound Recordings in the Arts, Humanities, and Social, Physical, and Life Sciences* (Washington, DC: Smithsonian, 1985).

Heller, Craig A., *From Metal to Mozart: The Rock and Roll Guide to Classical Music* (San Francisco: Chronicle Books, 1994).

March, Ivan, Greenfield, Edward, & Layton, Robert, *The Penguin Guide to Compact Discs and Cassettes: New Edition* (New York: Penguin, 1994).

McKee, Gerald, *Directory of Spoken-Word Audio Cassettes,* 3rd ed. (Guilford, CT: J. Norton, 1983).

Pease, Edward C., & Dennis, Everette E., eds., *Radio: The Forgotten Medium* (New Brunswick, NJ: Transaction Publishers, 1995).

Pemberton, J. Michael, *Policies of Audio Visual Producers and Distributors: A Handbook for Acquisition Personnel,* 2nd ed. (Metuchen, NJ: Scarecrow, 1989).

Smulyan, Susan, *Selling Radio: The Commercialization of American Broadcasting 1920–1934* (Washington, DC: Smithsonian, 1994).

Watkinson, John, *An Introduction to Digital Audio* (Oxford: Focal, 1994).

Wilby, Pete, & Conroy, Andy, *The Radio Handbook* (New York: Routledge, 1994).

Words on Cassette: An International Guide (Westport, CT: Meckler, updated annually until 1991).

The "world's largest selection of **unabridged audio books**" is available from Books on Tape (1-800-626-3333). Also contact The Audio Store (1-800-972-8346), Recorded Books, Inc. (1-800-638-1304), and InteliQuest Learning Systems (1-800-275-6940). The following titles are part of ***The Audio Classics Series*** from Knowledge Products (1-800-876-4332).

The Giants of Political Thought
The United States Constitution
The Great Economic Thinkers
The United States at War
The Giants of Philosophy
Science & Discovery
The World's Political Hot Spots

Periodicals devoted to CD titles and hardware include:

Digital Audio and Compact Disk Review
Green Compact Disc Catalog
International CD Exchange
Schwann Compact Disc Catalog

Audio recordings produced by radio stations, government agencies, and industry may be obtained from:

National Center for Audio Tapes
Educational Media Center, Stadium Bldg.
University of Colorado
Campus Box 379
Boulder, CO 80309

For **radio** program information and recordings contact:

KidsNet (1-202-291-1400), also accessible via America Online (kidsnet@aol.com).
National Public Radio (1-202-414-3232).

Or write to some of the **sources** identified by Gary Ferrington:

Children's Radio Productions
Jamie T. Deming, Producer
North Boulevard East
Norwich, NY 11732

Imagination Parade
Paul Butler, Producer
WFDU Radio
Fairleigh Dickinson University
Teaneck, NJ 07666

KBPS-AM
Jacqueline Loucks, Producer
Portland Public Schools
515 N.E. 15th Avenue
Portland, OR 97232

Knock on Wood
Steve Charney, Producer
WAMC Public Radio
318 Central Avenue
Albany, NY 12206-2522

New Generation Radio
Tina Hubbs, Producer
KOPN-/New Wave Corporation
915 East Broadway
Columbia, MO 65201

Pickleberry Pie
P.J. Swift, Producer
305 Dickens Way
Santa Cruz, CA 95064

We Like Kids
Jeff Brown, Producer
KTOO-FM
224 4th Street
Juneau, AK 99801

Shortwave radio broadcasts from many nations range in programming from news and weather to music and talk. The following sources may serve to enliven your curriculum with this fascinating medium.

Bennett, Hank, Hardy, David T., & Yoder, Andrew, *The Complete Shortwave Listener's Handbook*, 4th ed. (Blue Ridge Summit, PA: TAB Books, 1994).

McCormick, Anita Louise, *Shortwave Radio Listening for Beginners* (Blue Ridge Summit, PA: TAB Books, 1993).

McCormick, Anita Louise, *The Shortwave Listener's Q and A Book: Everything You Need to Know to Enjoy Shortwave Listening* (Blue Ridge Summit, PA: TAB Books, 1994).

Pickard, Captain James D., *North American Shortwave Frequency Guide* (Burbank, CA: Artsci, 1994).

World Radio TV Handbook, 1995 Edition (Amsterdam, The Netherlands: Billboard Books, 1995).

For **audio production** guidelines, see:

Aldridge, Henry B., & Liggett, Lucy A., *Audio-Video Production: Theory and Practice* (Englewood Cliffs, NJ: Prentice-Hall, 1990).

Alkin, Glyn, *Sound Recording and Reproduction*, 2nd ed. (Boston: Focal, 1991).

Baragary, Ray, *The Billboard Guide to Home Recording* (New York: Watson-Guptill, 1990).

Bartlett, Bruce, *Stereo Microphone Techniques* (Boston: Focal: 1991).

Cascierto, Albert J., & Roney, Raymond G., *Audiovisual Technology Primer* (Englewood, CO: Libraries Unlimited, 1988).

Cravotta, Mary E., & Wilson, Savan, *Media Cookbook for Kids* (Englewood, CO: Libraries Unlimited, 1989).

Green, Lee, *Creative Slide-Tape Programs* (Englewood, CO: Libraries Unlimited, 1986).

Gross, Lynne S., & Reese, David E., *Radio Production Worktext: Studio and Equipment*, 2nd ed. (Boston: Focal, 1993).

Huber, David M., & Runstein, Robert E., *Modern Recording Techniques*, 4th ed. (Indianapolis, IN: Sams, 1995).

Linderman, Hank, *Hot Tips for the Home Recording Studio* (Cincinnati, OH: Writer's Digest Books, 1994).

McLeish, Robert, *Radio Production: A Manual for Broadcasters*, 3rd ed. (Boston: Focal, 1994).

Nelson, Mico, *The Cutting Edge of Audio Production & Audio Post Production: Theory, Equipment and Techniques* (White Plains, NY: Knowledge Industry, 1995).

Nisbett, Alec, *The Use of Microphones*, 4th ed. (Boston: Focal, 1993).

Nisbett, Alec, *The Sound Studio*, 6th ed. (Boston: Focal, 1995).

Reynolds, Angus, & Anderson, Ronald H., *Selecting and Developing Media for Instruction*, 3rd ed. (New York: Van Nostrand Reinhold, 1991).

Rumsey, Francis, & McCormick, Tim, *Sound & Recording: An Introduction*, 2nd ed. (Boston: Focal, 1994).

Satterthwaite, Les L., *Instructional Media: Materials, Production, and Utilization*, 2nd ed. (Dubuque, IA: Kendall/Hunt, 1991).

Slawson, Ron, *Multi-Image Slide/Tape Programs* (Englewood, CO: Libraries Unlimited, 1988).

Volker, Roger, & Simonson, Michael, *Media for Teachers: An Introductory Course in Media for Students in Teacher Education*, 5th ed. (Dubuque, IA: Kendall/Hunt, 1989).

Willis, Edgar E., & D'Arienzo, Camille, *Writing Scripts for Television, Radio, and Film*, 3rd ed. (Fort Worth, TX: Harcourt Brace Jovanovich College Publishers, 1992).

Musical composition software may be obtained from:

Midisoft Corporation
P.O. Box 1000
Bellevue, WA 98009-9864
1-800-776-6434; 1-206-391-3610, ext. 247

Study Items

1. Compare and contrast characteristics of prerecorded CDs with other prerecorded media.

2. What advantages might audiotape hold over recordable CDs in producing instructional programs and doing class projects?

3. Describe some instructional uses for "variable speech control."

VISUAL	AUDIO
(An earlier part of the slide set, showing the role of communication to instruction.)	(An earlier section of script, about as long as the part reproduced here.)
	Now, how about the SENSORY CHANNELS used for communicating our messages? Our message may use any one, or a combination of the senses, to reach its destination. For example, the girl here is receiving the boy's message by the AUDIO channel.
	But what about the girl's message to the boy? (pause — 4 seconds) The hankie she has dropped is a VISUAL 'come on' message to the boy . . . and a pretty old fashioned one at that!
	The boy however is a bit more up to date. He knows not only WHAT message content will be effective but also that sending it by both AUDIO and VISUAL channels, simultaneously, will be more efficient! (pause — 4 seconds)
	As our tale unfolds, the other sensory channels come into play . . . taste, smell and the tactile, or touch senses . . . . . . How many sensory channels do we use in communication anyway? (pause — 4 seconds)

Figure 8.20. This script is written clearly, but could be made more explicit by employing conventions illustrated in Figure 8.16. Revise accordingly. Also, you are invited by Professor Romiszowski to remove the elements of sexual harassment and stereotyping that, he informed me graciously, "were quite common and acceptable in media scripting practice of the 1960s/70s." Source: Alexander J. Romiszowski, *The Selection and Use of Instructional Media,* 2nd ed. (East Brunswick, NJ: Nichols, 1988), p. 12. Reprinted with permission of Nichols Publishing.

4. In what ways can audiotape individualize instruction?

5. What do audio technologies contribute to students who are hard-of-hearing, homebound, or learning disabled?

6. Characterize the variety of informative radio programming currently available worldwide. What form do you find most valuable?

7. What characteristics of radio make it more popular abroad than in America?

8. Identify what sorts of materials, personnel, and activities typically are needed to supplement educational radio.

9. List instructional objectives that would best be achieved with lessons mediated **primarily** with recordings of sounds or voice.

10. Describe criteria for selection and production of audio programs.

11. Specify ways in which visual and audio media can work in harmony to simplify teaching of a concept you choose.

12. Compare what might be learned reading a novel versus hearing it on tape.

13. Describe how language learning labs use audio playback and recording to ease acquisition of vocabulary, pronunciation, and grammar.

14. List steps in the production of an audiotaped script covering a short lesson in your subject. Justify selection of recorder, microphone, and tape.

15. Evaluate benefits and costs of having students produce a "radio" variety show.

16. Summarize advantages of "little media" (print, visuals, audiotape) over "big media" (film, TV, computers) given local distribution requirements only.

17. Speculate on how advantages of "big media" might be enhanced by mass production and wide distribution.

Suggested Activities

1. Visit your district media center and ask to see lists of available audio hardware and programs. Figure out what is in good working order. Plan future needs and use accordingly.

2. Collaborate with classmates in producing a "radio" news program. Have teams prepare separate segments on world news, business, sports, and weather. Edit results and combine them on one tape.

3. Obtain one of the above listed books about shortwave radio and a suitable receiver. Audiotape portions of what you discover and share this with your classmates.

4. Select a short story to record. Prepare a script that includes notes about pacing and sound effects. Produce the program and observe reactions when played to your target audience. Compare this approach with simply reading the story or with having students do so.

5. Organize a set of slides to teach a lesson in your subject area. Prepare and record taped commentary. Synchronize the audio track with the visuals. Try the program out on classmates, test for learning, solicit comments, and revise accordingly.

6. Visit a computer software exhibition and listen to demonstrations of *AddImpact*, *Fusion CD*, and *Sound Blaster*. Prepare a report on what their capabilities could add to a computer-mediated lesson you might design.

7. Examine the *Macmillan Dictionary for Children*. What do the recorded pronunciations add to those given in print?

8. *Microsoft Encarta* interactive encyclopedia on CD-ROM provides text, visuals, and sound (samples of 45 languages and 350 musical segments). Evaluate the quality and integration of audio according to criteria listed in **Figure 8.09**. Compare it with other software such as *Compton's Interactive Encyclopedia*.

9. The partial script illustrated in **Figure 8.20** (on the preceding page) employs quite different conventions than those described in **Figure 8.16**. Revise this one paying attention to Lee Green's suggestions about slide number placement, type of shot ("close up," "medium shot," "long shot," etc.), use of capital letters, underlining, and outcue.

10. *Multimedia Beethoven: The Ninth Symphony* provides the musical score and measure-by-measure commentary. Evaluate text, visuals, and audio according to criteria listed in this and preceding chapters.

11. Search *The Grammy Awards: A 34-Year Retrospective* and *Jazz: A Multimedia History*, for titles, themes, artists, and other background data you could use in a class you teach.

12. The *Miracle* software program boasts of an innovative, individualized approach to teaching piano. Evaluate the approach and describe to your classmates what it does that some teachers might not do as well.

13. Use *Astound*, *WordPerfect Presentations*, *Delta Graph,*, or *Microsoft PowerPoint* or similar software to craft a simple lesson based on a storyboard linking audio and visual input.

14. Share with me your responses to the above study items and experiences in pursuing the suggested activities.

15. Critically evaluate this chapter and inform me of results (Internet: hackbarths@aol.com).

Chapter 9

Film and Television

Chapter Content and Objectives

Film and television are among the most compelling media of our time. A film recreates a part of the world to express what is essentially the maker's vision. Movie theaters enfold their audiences, seal them from the outside world, and deliver them to the universe of the screen. Television, broadcasting 'round the clock, pervades the private lives of its viewers. Intimate and insistent, it brings the turbulent world to their homes. This chapter covers how these media serve educational ends. After reading it, you should be able to:

- Trace the **evolution** of film and TV.
- Describe **educational uses** of film and TV.
- Assess **merits** of using film and TV for educational purposes.
- Specify criteria for **selecting** film and TV programs to achieve educational aims.
- State **guidelines** for using film and TV in the classroom.
- Locate **sources**.

Film

George Eastman invented celluloid roll film in 1888, and a few years later Thomas Edison's assistant, William Dickson, used it to produce continuous action motion pictures up to 30 seconds in length. By the mid-1890s, Edison's peephole viewers, called **Kinetoscopes**, were installed in viewing parlors across the nation. Edison's high-speed camera was studied by the Lumiere brothers of France, who developed a portable model that both exposed film and projected it. On December 28, 1895, they opened the world's first commercial movie theater (in Paris).

Silent films thrilled audiences. Chaplain, Gish, and Garbo became stars and Hollywood the center of the burgeoning industry. With the addition of sound in the late 1920s, "movies" became "talkies."

Nineteen thirty-nine was a landmark year with stunning renditions of popular literature. *The Wizard of Oz* immortalized L. Frank Baum's vision of life over the rainbow (and spooked my brother so much he hid under his seat). *Gone with the Wind* brought to life Margaret Mitchell's impressions of the glamorous/racist Old South, the siege of Atlanta, and post-war Reconstruction (and enchanted my daughter decades later). In the 1950s, *The Thing* and *Invasion of the Body Snatchers* reflected growing paranoia about space invaders, and it wasn't until the 1980s that Steven Spielberg turned fear into love with his *E.T.* Meanwhile, George Lucas stretched the limits of special effects cinematography with his *Star Wars* trilogy.

Thus, today, feature films run the gamut of human experience and imagination. One year, Disney's animated *Beauty and the Beast* won the Oscar for best picture. In the next, *The Silence of the Lambs*, the chilling entrapment of a vicious serial killer, took top prize. And just when we thought it was safe to walk the streets of Carmel, Clint Eastwood won best director and best picture with his *Unforgiven*. ("I've been lucky when it comes tuh killin' folks.") Deeper reflections on meanings of life (efficacy, chance, fate) were taken up in *Forrest Gump*. New perspectives have been contributed by women and

Figure 9.01. Early attempts to add recorded sound to motion pictures relied on phonodisc players, some of which were built into the projector. Reliable synchronization was achieved only when the soundtrack was recorded on the film itself. Location: California Museum of Science and Industry.

minorities (e.g., Barbara Streisand's *Yentl*, Jodie Foster's *Home for the Holidays*, Spike Lee's *Malcolm X*), and historical events have been recreated with precision (e.g., Ron Howard's *Apollo 13*).

The educative potential of motion pictures was recognized soon after their invention. The *Catalogue of Educational Motion Pictures* (1910) listed over a thousand titles available for rent. From 1916 on, the Ford Motor Company produced a succession of films (*Ford Educational Weekly*, *Ford Educational Library*) on such subjects as agriculture, history, geography, and civics. In 1923 the Yale University Press made several silent films on episodes in American history called *The Chronicles of America Photoplays*. Costumes were recreated, historic

sites rebuilt, and teachers solicited to provide information. In 1926, as an experiment, several geography and general science films by the Eastman Kodak Company were shown to over ten thousand school children in a dozen cities. The results so impressed Kodak that over the next 20 years the company made some 300 films expressly for school use.

These early films were awkward to screen. The first projectors weighed up to 2,500 pounds, and truly portable ones did not arrive till the mid-1930s. Film was made of highly flammable nitrocellulose; it varied in width from 9-1/2mm to 35mm, each size requiring a different model of projector. Sound, on phonodiscs, had to be synchronized with projection. (See **Figure 9.01**.)

Nevertheless, during the 1920s **"film education"** caught on as more regional schools acquired projectors and films and shared them among several schools. Teacher training colleges accelerated the movement by offering courses in "audiovisual methods" of instruction. Surveys revealed that by 1933 half the nation's elementary school teachers were using films, growing to about three-fourths by 1954. By the early 1950s, about half the secondary school teachers surveyed reported using films. However, most teachers screened only one or two a month.[1]

Rapid growth of film education may be attributed in part to extensive use by the military during World War II. Thousands of 16mm documentary and training films were made, as were those to rouse public support. Filmmakers advanced their craft and introduced such special effects as slow motion and time-lapse photography. Postwar incentives brought these experts into education to serve the "baby boom" generation.

Today there are tens of thousands of films available for classroom use. They run the gamut of traditional studies to drug abuse, sexual reproduction, and suicide. There are films on the energy crisis, the solar system, AIDS, automotive safety, and self-esteem. Many include statements of instructional objectives, teachers' guides, and examination forms. Most school districts maintain extensive collections. (See **Figure 9.02**.)

Classroom film viewing has given way to use of videos. However, quality of the projected image remains unmatched by conventional TV, and it will be a long time before high definition TV (HDTV) finds its way into schools. In a darkened room, film viewers are shielded from their surroundings and become absorbed in a separate reality as it unfolds before them. Thus, for example, in viewing *Schindler's List*, students are trans-

Figure 9.02. 16mm film long was the standard for classroom use, but has been largely supplanted by video. Here preservice teachers at USC get hands-on practice. How might competence in operating projectors, VCRs, and computers favorably affect our credibility with students in other areas?

ported to wartime Eastern Europe and witness reenactments of concentration camp atrocities primarily against Jewish people. Given proper introduction to such a powerfully moving film, and ample follow-up discussion, it is unlikely that students will miss the messages of recalling history so as not to repeat it and of our responsibility to reach out to persecuted people regardless of ethnicity.

Television

Although the first TV license was issued as early as 1928, commercial broadcasting did not begin until July 1941, only to be stopped short by World War II. Nevertheless, the big radio companies began pouring money and know-how into their TV subsidiaries, so that soon after the war, television's growth was spectacular. As early as 1952, despite a Federal Communications Commission (FCC) freeze on new station allocations, one family in three owned a television set. Most programs were based on radio shows (*Amos and Andy, Break the Bank*) and most stars were radio personalities (Red Skelton, Jack Benny). Children were entertained by *Howdy Doody, Kukla, Fran, and Ollie, Bozo the Clown,* and *Captain Kangaroo.* Roy Rogers, Gene Autry, and Hopalong Cassidy became legends. The Lone Ranger gave us silver

bullets, and when the *Mickey Mouse Club* came on at 5:00 p.m., my grammar school playground was deserted.

By 1960, 90 percent of American homes had TVs. New programs were invented, such as the adult western (*Gunsmoke*) and the (rigged) big-prize quiz show (*The $64,000 Question*). Saturday mornings became a wasteland of cartoons geared to attract children to commercials for sugary breakfast cereals and for toys that didn't live up to their TV images.

During the 1960s, history was made on TV. As the nation watched, President Kennedy ushered in the "New Frontier," Martin Luther King Jr. spoke eloquently of his dream, and Neil Armstrong took "one small step for [a] man." As society became more outspoken, television courted controversy. Dramas and documentaries took on racism, drug abuse, venereal disease, and abortion. During peak evening viewing hours, producers like Norman Lear (*All in the Family*) mocked bigotry, politics, and television itself.

As screen violence and sex increased, so did opposition. In response, the networks introduced a family hour of "chaste" programming (in "prime time" from 8–9 p.m.). Filling this slot were new genres of programming that appealed to the intellect as well as to the heart. Docudramas (*Roots, Holocaust*) sought to portray significant events in history and reached record numbers of viewers. The popular, long-running series, *M*A*S*H*, brought to life a wartime field hospital with its blend of tragedy, compassion, friendship, devotion to duty, integrity, and humor. Later, as the economy sagged, and the nation became more somber, television responded by producing escapist programs. The late 1970s witnessed a rash of crime and high adventure stories, while top escapist shows of the 1980s (*Dallas, Dynasty,* and the daytime serials) glamorized greed and corruption.

The 90s have witnessed ever greater "realism" on TV. **Daytime serials** have explored new frontiers of televised sexual intimacy, but have largely ignored sexual responsibility. Abstinence and condoms are unknown, as are work and reading. To be fair, serials have become increasingly multiethnic and have openly addressed interracial relations as well as physical disability, child abuse, homosexuality, infidelity, and rape. **Prime time** also has become increasingly frank about sexuality and social issues with such offerings as *Beverly Hills 90210, Mad About You, Melrose Place,* and *My So-Called Life.* Growing concerns about real-life violence seem to have contributed to the popularity of such voyeuristic shows as *Rescue 911* and *Trauma Center.*

Talk shows have engaged experts, criminals, victims, and a diverse representation of troubled people in lively discussion. Studio audiences respond and home viewers call in with questions and comments. Prejudices are exposed, stereotypes are challenged, valuable insights are shared, rage is vented, and compromises are proposed. Hosts now better represent the audiences they serve—Oprah, Sally, Vicki, Jane, Jenny, Montel, Geraldo, Maury, Les, Phil, David, Jay, Arsenio. Nevertheless, news and scholarly analyses—*60 Minutes, MacNeil/Lehrer Newshour, Larry King Live, Nightline, Charlie Rose*, and Bill Moyers' specials—remain largely dominated by white males.

Prime time has seen Bill Cosby restore dignity to the image of parents, and Diane English to the image of women. Fed up with family situation comedies in which moms and dads appeared both incompetent and impotent, Cosby modeled a family much like his own (*The Cosby Show*) in which parents successfully managed careers, children, and love. Diane English's *Murphy Brown* highlights female career leadership, collaboration among men and women coworkers, unplanned pregnancy, and single parenthood. Murphy's stands against misguided government policies in the real world gained worldwide attention. Live coverage of Anita Hill's testimony brought sexual harassment out of the closet. Repeated airing of Rodney King being beaten by police officers exposed racial injustice already well known to African-Americans, but less well comprehended by whites. Televised revelations of direct involvement in "Irangate" and pre-war support of Iraq might well have affected the 1992 presidential elections.

With television serving so well to inform and entertain, it is not surprising that nearly everyone tunes in. In the average home the set is on seven hours a day, and children watch it over 25 hours per week. Much of this is Public Broadcasting Service (PBS) programming, like *Sesame Street* and *Barney & Friends*. Yet persistent and growing concern about commercialism and cartoon violence in broadcast shows targeted at children led the FCC to pass the **Children's Television Act of 1990** to ensure more emphasis on education. To the networks, this translated to *Winnie the Pooh* and *The Smurfs*, lovable characters that model friendship and sharing—but also model for toys and clothing. And the popular cartoon version of *Where on Earth Is Carmen Sandiego?* glosses over geography while glamorizing crime. Worse, since passage of the Act we have witnessed the emergence of *Mighty Morphin Power Rangers, SuperHuman*

Samurai SyberSquad, VR Troopers, and *Tattooed Teenage Alien Fighters from Beverly Hills*—all portraying violence as the primary means of resolving conflict.

By the time of graduation from high school, youth typically will have viewed 20,000 hours, more time than spent in school. (See **Figure 9.03**.) In spite of *Music Videos, MTV Jams, Rap City, Video Soul*, and *Video LP* without end, viewing drops off during the active teen years (when youths are on the move and tuned to their portable radios and CD players), but soon returns to 25 hours per week. The elderly watch more than any other age group, largely due to limited mobility, greater leisure, and social isolation.

Considering the advent of cable and the richness of programming available today, it is perhaps surprising that studies have not shown **increases** in viewing across all age levels. If viewing recorded shows, playing *Nintendo* and *Genesis*, and sitting in front of a computer screen were taken into account, little time would be left for sleep, and none for conversation.

Perhaps the most significant "TV culture" development of the 90s is the growing gap between the viewing habits of African-Americans and whites. Indeed, the top 10 choices of blacks for 1993 do not appear among the

"Says here the average child watches four to five hours of TV a day. Somewhere out there are two kids who don't watch any."

Figure 9.03. As this cartoon suggests, averages can be misleading. In many homes, the TV is on the entire day; it is a companion to preschoolers and housekeepers. In others, programs are watched selectively. How many hours of sheer escape TV do you watch each week? How many hours that are personally or professionally enriching? How many hours in front of any sort of CRT (cathode ray tube)? Are you aware of potential damage to eyes and genomes? Source: *Phi Delta Kappan*, 61 (November 1979), p. 165. Reprinted with permission of Glen Bernhardt.

top 10 shows for the total audience. Of these 10 shows, eight had predominantly black casts (e.g., *In Living Color, Martin, Hangin' with Mr. Cooper, Where I Live*). Add to this the fact that viewing in black households reportedly is 50 percent higher than in nonblack households and you have not just a reflection, but the **making of a cultural divide**. This divide, evidenced once again in public reactions to the O. J. Simpson verdict, finally has prompted President Clinton to call for resolution.[2]

Television programming targeted at blacks (including *Black Entertainment Network*) undoubtedly contributes to black identity and pride. And such shows as *In Living Color* serve to vent anger (in a humorous context) against the "dominant" culture. Meanwhile, white parents relate (perhaps too) comfortably to *Roseanne*, but also to Ted Koppel, Barbara Walters, Ron Wood, Ken Burns, Russell Baker, Bill Moyers, David Frost, Dick Cavett, Michael Wood, Tom Snyder, William Buckley Jr., John McLaughlin, Leslie Stahl, scholars, doctors, attorneys, and a host of other brilliant commentators, including Les Brown and Charlayne Hunter-Gault. Thus catered to by the networks, it is possible that many white parents are given an unfair advantage when it comes to helping their children succeed in school. PBS has taken a "positive" step to redress the imbalance with its *Positively Black*. And its offerings for children, with their multiracial casts, appeal equally to all. The networks have a long way to go.

Hispanic parents, in contrast, have been relatively well served by *Spanish International Network* and *Telemundo*, with news and views programming to match the English language networks. In addition, PBS offers targeted (e.g., *Visiones*) and Spanish language (e.g., *GED en Español*) programming. First generation Hispanic immigrants may have difficulty with language acquisition, but they retain their cultural identity **and** are well informed about subjects and issues their children encounter in the classroom. Nevertheless, the fact that nearly three times as many Hispanic students as either white or black drop out of school before graduation remains an issue of critical concern.

The interests of **indigenous peoples** (e.g., Native Americans), are largely ignored by all but recipients of Oscars and Emmies. Professional sports teams like the "Braves" and the "Redskins" still flaunt the most demeaning of stereotypes. Images of feathered chiefs crying over polluted streams do little to enlighten us about the diversity of indigenous peoples and their unique concerns and do nothing to address those concerns.

The problems of unemployment, substance abuse, and school dropout remain severe. Specialized cable services hold the most promise for ameliorating these problems while respecting local customs and languages. Public television shows (e.g., *Native Americans*) contribute much to awareness of the special gifts and challenges of indigenous peoples worldwide.

Among the best commercial TV programs for children are those produced by Nickelodeon (*All That, Legends of the Hidden Temple, Rugrats, AAAHH!!! Real Monsters, Allegra's Window, The Secret World of Alex Mack, Are You Afraid of the Dark?*), The Learning Channel (*Ready, Set, Learn!, Beakman's World*), Fox Children's Network (*Steven Spielberg Presents Animaniacs, The Tick*), HBO (*Happily Ever After: Fairy Tales for Every Child*), and Showtime (*Shelley Duvall's Bedtime Stories*). Winners from the major broadcast networks include *Bump in the Night, The Bugs Bunny & Tweety Show, Disney's Aladdin, Fudge, Gargoyles, Name Your Adventure*).[3] Popular shows that may stimulate family discussions about everything from relationships to world events include *Coach, Home Improvement, Jeopardy!, Nature, Rescue 911, Roseanne, 60 Minutes, Star Trek: Voyager, Star Trek: Deep Space Nine*, and *Today*.[4]

Public television, like public radio, was created by Congress to provide quality programs of educational value. At the hub of public TV are the Corporation for Public Broadcasting (CPB) and the Public Broadcasting System (PBS). CPB helps produce and obtain programs; PBS distributes programs and funds to member stations. PBS stations, now nearly 350 strong and reaching 98 percent of the U.S. population, vary greatly in management, size, and sophistication. Many are run by universities and local governments; others by "community corporations" consisting of large firms and foundations (e.g., WTTW, Chicago; KCET, Los Angeles; WGBH, Boston; WNET, New York; KQED, San Francisco).

The most outstanding PBS program for children is ***Sesame Street***, created in 1969 by the Children's Television Workshop (CTW). Taking into account children's limited attention spans and appealing to their interest in animals, cartoons, music, and monsters, *Sesame Street* has fascinated youngsters of all backgrounds, while teaching them symbolic representations (letters, numbers, geometric forms) and cognitive processes (perception, classification, reasoning, problem solving). The series has attracted more viewers than any other educational program. Although each episode costs tens of thousands of dollars to produce, this breaks down to only a fraction of a cent per viewer. (See **Figure 9.04**.)

"In my dream, my students won't pay attention to me. I make a wish upon a star. The next morning I go to class, and I look just like Big Bird. I live happily ever after."

Figure 9.04. No one disputes that Sesame Street captures the attention of children. To what extent might such programming condition them for later acceptance of MTV and other forms of passive entertainment? Source: *Phi Delta Kappan*, 62 (February 1981), p. 455. Reprinted with permission of Randy Glasbergen.

For a while, *Sesame Street* could do no wrong; it captivated children and critics alike. Then doubts set in. Some researchers, not impressed with documented gains in cognitive learning alone, maintained that the show's frantic pace created shortened attention spans, sensory overload, and expectation of rapid change in the real world. Children could reel off letters and numbers but could not properly use or reflect on them. In response, the pace was slowed and the engaging characters began talking about real life, values, and feelings. When Mr. Hooper died, the writers chose to let the characters deal with it. After a period of grieving and coming to terms, Big Bird said to the drawing he had earlier made, "I'll miss you, Mr. Hooper."

Mister Rogers' Neighborhood is the creation of Fred Rogers, who originally produced each weekly show over 25 years ago on a budget of $30. Rogers, who also serves as host, aims to reassure preschoolers of their uniqueness, guide their social and emotional growth, and give them a feeling of personal worth. Gentle and sensitive, he speaks to children as if they were present in the studio. Parents may find his presentation tedious, but he is not talking to them. He is relating to children, for whom the world often is confusing and to whom kindness and patience are crucial.

Mister Rogers' Neighborhood centers on such themes as self-regulation (following rules, waiting one's turn, controlling aggression), recognizing and expressing feelings, and helping, sharing, and cooperating. These worthy themes are expressed first in a fictional story set in the

"Neighborhood of Make-Believe," a place of conflict and strong emotion. Feelings are examined and conflict resolved through discussion, cooperation, and thoughtful effort. Rogers then talks to viewers directly, explaining the themes and telling them how valuable each person is. Rogers expressed the special, *in loco parentis*, responsibilities of PBS as follows:

> In a young child's mind, parents probably condone what's on the television set, just like they choose what's in the refrigerator or on the stove! That's why we who make television for children must be especially careful with what we produce, with the people we present, and with the attitudes we show in television relationships—attitudes of respect, kindness, healthy curiosity, determination, and love . . . just as parents would want for their children.[5]

Another fine series, **Inside/Out**, made by the Agency for Instructional Technology (AIT), seeks to foster the emotional growth of youths. Its themes include learning that people express their feelings in many ways, dealing with the relation of freedom to responsibility, understanding that teasing may lower another's self-esteem, and coping with traumatic events. These themes are dramatized in 15-minute episodes set in home or school and seen through a child's eyes. The episodes include sibling competition and peer conflict, as well as deeper experiences such as divorce, child abuse, and death in the family. The episodes are open-ended to encourage interpretation and discussion.

Ghostwriter, from CTW, is part of an ambitious effort to promote reading and writing among children seven to ten years of age. It's an adventure series that features a group of youths who solve mysteries using their literary skills. Complementing the series are a magazine, a newspaper feature, and paperback books. CTW staff establish and maintain contact with a variety of youth organizations that provide after school care.

To these fine programs add *Reading Rainbow*, *Long Ago & Far Away*, *WonderWorks*, *Shining Time Station*, *Barney & Friends*, *Slim Goodbody*, *The Adventures of Dudley the Dragon*, *Bill Nye, the Science Guy*, *The Magic School Bus*, and *Lamb Chop's Play-Along*. All have contributed to children's cognitive and affective development and have provided them with alternatives to mindless cartoons, situation comedies, and commercials. Indeed, Lamb Chop (the gifted Shari Lewis) has testified before Congress in support of TV programming suitable for children.

The list of outstanding PBS programs suitable for adults and youths alike is virtually endless. For weekday news coverage, nothing beats *The MacNeil/Lehrer News Hour*. Tragic human rights violations around the world have been documented by *Rights & Wrongs*. *Masterpiece Theatre*, *American Playhouse*, and *Mystery!* have indulged literary minds while *Great Performances*, *Live from Lincoln Center*, and *The Metropolitan Opera Presents* have brought us the best in music. Nature and wildlife lovers have been treated to *Eyewitness*, *David Attenborough's Natural World*, *The Living Planet*, *Wild America*, *Wild Kingdom*, *The Wide World of Animals*, *The Dinosaurs!* and, of course, *Nature*. Those fascinated by life in distant lands have enjoyed *National Geographic*, *Explore*, *The Africans*, and *Travels*. Different perspectives on history have appeared in *Connections*, *The Real Thing*, *The Day the Universe Changed*, *Shoah*, *The Story of English*, *The Civil War*, and *Clive James' Fame in the 20th Century*. The methods and findings of science and technology have been taken up in *Nova*, *Mechanical Universe*, *The Creation of the Universe*, *The Nature of Things*, *The Human Quest*, *The Nobel Legacy*, *Cosmos*, *Newton's Apple*, *Scientific American Frontiers*, *3-2-1 Contact*, *Discover*, *The Machine that Changed the World*, *The Nature of Sex*, and *The Secret of Life*. Cultural contributions of diverse peoples have been illustrated in *Cantos Latinos*, *Eyes on the Prize: America's Civil Rights Years*, and *Native Americans*. Women scientists were featured in *Discovering Women*.

Figure 9.05. Production of good quality educational TV requires considerable investment in equipment and time. Here USC students are videotaping a three-minute program that took them several weeks to prepare.

Accomplishments of people with disabilities were highlighted in *People in Motion: An Innovation Miniseries*. Each of these programs took years to produce and drew upon talents of countless scholars and artists. Many challenge conventional views and special interests. (See **Figure 9.05.**)

Docudramas especially have been both informative and thought provoking. Programs on McCarthyism, the Cuban missile crisis, the Vietnam War, and Watergate have made viewers think about recent history. Some programs have met conventional views head on. *Kill Me if You Can*, on Caryl Chessman, attacked the death penalty. *I Will Fight No More Forever* and *Farewell to Manzanar* gave harrowing accounts of the suppression of Native Americans that continues to this day and the detention of Japanese-Americans during World War II. *Last Stand at Little Big Horn* analyzed this infamous battle from the eyes of the Sioux, Cheyenne, and Crow peoples and the settlers who wanted their lands. *Stand and Deliver* highlighted gifted teaching in the Hispanic community and attracted record numbers of viewers and funding pledges.

Granted, some docudramas have been cavalier with history, distorting facts and indulging in stereotypes. Yet if docudramas have bent the facts, they have done so generally to highlight the clash of principles, the struggle between right and wrong. A more serious fault is the docudrama's frequent claim to be both literally true and true to the moral conflict within the developments it probes.

What makes PBS programs a success in class? For one thing, they are available on **videocassette** (and earlier ones on **16mm film**), so they can be viewed when convenient and interrupted for commentary as needed. For another, **study guides** summarize content, provide questions, make suggestions for preparatory and follow-up activities, and list supplementary readings.

The programs described above are valuable because they inform and enlighten rather than merely entertain. Programs designed specifically for presenting subject matter are referred to as **"instructional television"** (ITV). ITV began in the mid-1950s when many school districts bought television equipment and produced their own programs. One such project was the Midwest Program on Airborne Television Instruction (MPATI), in which a DC6 flew daily over Montpelier, Indiana, beaming programs to schools in six states. The project cost the Ford Foundation $18 million, but teachers were not receptive enough to justify continuation. On the other hand, in Hagerstown, Maryland, again with aid from the Ford Foundation, a station was built to transmit six programs simultaneously to schools in Washington County. The project was so successful that both school board and teachers voted approval.[6]

Today, local public stations air many programs designed for elementary and secondary schools. Most of these programs come from national distributors like the Agency for Instructional Technology, the Corporation for Public Broadcasting, the Great Plains National Instructional Television Library, and the National Geographic Society. Programs are divided fairly evenly among the humanities, natural sciences, social sciences, and the arts. The toll-free numbers of several major providers of instructional videos are presented at the end of this chapter and, along with illustrative titles, in the **Sources** section at the end of this book.[7]

Offering televised courses for college credit began in the early 1950s at such institutions as the University of Houston and Iowa State. By 1980 about two-thirds of all U.S. postsecondary institutions were providing televised instruction and over half a million students were enrolled in one or more of some seven thousand courses aired. These **"telecourses"** expand educational opportunities to people who are unable to attend regular classes on campus. They also attract students who, for lack of time or money, otherwise would not continue formal study. Students taking telecourses are likely to be older than on-campus students and usually work full time.[8]

Among the best known of the ITV producers is the **British Open University**. It was established in 1971 to provide opportunities to all those who have been unable to achieve their educational aims through existing institutions. Even today there are no formal entrance requirements, but students must pass examinations to get course credit and earn degrees. The curriculum is designed and periodically updated by committees made up of regular faculty and BBC personnel. Print materials are the basis of instruction, supplemented by BBC radio and TV programs. The Open University's academic degrees are widely recognized and its programs are solicited by educational agencies across the world.

Evaluation of Film and Television

Many researchers have studied the impact on youth of film and television, but the results are inconclusive, largely because there are too many conflicting variables.

Figure 9.06. Does TV induce viewers to imitate aggressive behavior, or does it serve as a cathartic release? My daughter Valerie illustrated a dialectical perspective above. What do you think? What might be the effects of modeling socially constructive behaviors?

These media rank among many forces that influence the young, such as parents, peers, the school, the neighborhood, and the economy. Since we do not know precisely how all these forces interact, we cannot accurately assess their roles. Many observers have sought to pinpoint the effects of TV violence, for instance, but their conclusions vary widely. Some say it arouses violent urges in most children, others, that it arouses only the violence-prone, others still, that it serves as a catharsis.[9] (See **Figure 9.06.**)

In early 1995, as part of the National Campaign to Reduce Youth Violence, a PBS *Frontline* program posed the question bluntly—*Does TV Kill?* George Gerbner (University of Pennsylvania) suggested that "What television seems to cultivate is a sense of meanness. If you're growing up in a heavy viewing home, for all practical purposes you live in a meaner world and you act it." According to Barry Sanders (Claremont College), "We may be inadvertently through television creating a new kind of human being. We are producing generations of kids without imaginations, with an inability to conjure up their own images." *Frontline* correspondent Al Austin concluded that the most stunning revelations of recent research on TV viewing are "the stupefying amount of it that people watch, and the power of the hold the appliance has on its owners."[10] I agree. Though parents may prefer to have their children sitting before the tube to being hustled on the street, unrestricted viewing may be having deleterious effects on their children's intellectual, social, and moral development.

Why do media executives continue their assaults on society? The *Frontline* writers compared them to counterparts in the tobacco industry who continue to explain away research results as inconclusive. The motive in both cases is clear. In a 1995 news conference, Bill Moyers summed up the obvious: "It is the bottom line that is driving the violence in television, videos, and other forms of the media. The message of violence in the media is if you want juice, money, power, ratings, respect, use violence because violence sells."[11] In my view, if research were left to media moguls, it would focus on finding the optimal mix of sex, profanity, and violence needed to attract each of its target audiences.

As for the favorable impacts of these media, clearly today's children know more about the world than they would otherwise. They have seen all kinds of behavior among all sorts of people, and have come to see their town as a mere dot on the earth's surface and the earth a speck in space. One could just as readily attribute wider vision and greater creativity rather than hyperactivity and impatience to film and television.

As seen throughout this book, I have many concerns about commercial media. I believe that they not only **manipulate public opinion** in the cause of corporate profit, but also give **explicit instruction in violence and promiscuity** and implicitly **promote substance abuse**. Much of children's programming **advocates consumerism** while **conditioning children to stay tuned**. Even watching Fred Rogers replaces human interaction and physical activity. Yet I have learned a great deal from these media and, like you, have been moved to cheers and tears. Do Madonna's music video celebrations of sensuality help to distract anguished adolescents from drugs and suicide? I don't know. Might Ice T's vented anger toward white society serve to demonstrate that oppressed peoples retain freedom of expression short of actually engaging in violence? Ask your students.

Our compromises must be to set limits on viewing at home and to be very selective in the classroom use of film, TV, **and** computer-mediated programs. Setting limits on time alone does not ensure selection of good programming, but at least it opens doors for other opportunities. When I restricted my daughter to just two shows during school weekdays she selected the mind-numbing *Roger Ramjet* and *The Brady Bunch*. Why? She **needed a break** between schoolwork and homework.

Unable to watch beyond these two half hours, she taught herself to play the piano, took up portrait drawing, practiced flute, absorbed literature, and talked with friends. (See **Figure 9.07**.)

What about **educational** uses of films and TV? Do students learn more from them than from other media? The answer is that they are superior only when they show what cannot be shown otherwise. Can films and TV change attitudes? They certainly can, so care should be taken not to change them for the worse. Do the expressed learning objectives match their effects? Not always. A foreign language series, for instance, may improve proficiency while simultaneously raising students' anxiety about the difficulties of communication abroad. Can they increase interest in a topic? Yes, depending on how well the topic is treated rather than on the medium as such.[12]

Most students thrive on curricula rich in media. The gifted especially profit from fast-paced presentations via film and TV. They readily absorb the text, pictures, graphics, and narrative combined in these media. Other students benefit more from slides, photos, and filmstrips that they can examine at length and audiotapes they can review at their own pace. On the other hand, audiovisual media may inspire students with disabilities to learn be-

"Why don't you read a book until the vertical roll is fixed?"

Figure 9.07. Parents should be encouraged not merely to set limits on TV viewing, but to provide their children with constructive options as shown here. Better still, invite parents to model the options. How might you do so tactfully? Source: *Phi Delta Kappan,* 76 (October 1994), p. 117. Reprinted with permission of Scott Arthur Masear.

| Title _____ Producer _____ |
| Publisher _____ Date _____ Price ___ |
| Subject _____ Grade Level _____ |
| Objectives _____ |
| Prerequisites _____ |
| Hardware Requirements _____ |

Selection Criteria	Rating (1 = low; 10 = high)	Comments
1. Content of Audio	___	___
a. match with objectives	___	___
b. accuracy	___	___
c. currency	___	___
d. scope	___	___
e. stereotyping	___	___
2. Content of Visual	___	___
a. match with objectives	___	___
b. accuracy	___	___
c. currency	___	___
d. scope	___	___
e. stereotyping	___	___
f. match with audio	___	___
3. Presentation	___	___
a. impact	___	___
b. organization	___	___
c. teaching strategies	___	___
d. interactivity	___	___
e. motivation	___	___
f. use of cues	___	___
g. use of color	___	___
h. use of motion	___	___
i. difficulty	___	___
4. Supplementary Materials	___	___
a. teacher's guide	___	___
b. examinations	___	___
c. student's text	___	___
5. Technical Quality	___	___
a. audio clarity	___	___
b. visual clarity	___	___
6. Effectiveness	___	___
a. student interest	___	___
b. student achievement	___	___
c. student evaluation	___	___
7. Overall Impression	___	___

Figure 9.08. Film and TV program evaluation form.

fore they can read the printed word. For the homebound student, instructional radio and TV may serve as economical substitutes for private tutors. To the extent that minorities are well represented in positive roles, minority viewers gain pride and confidence.

Practical Guidelines

Selection. Specific criteria for use in selecting instructional films and videos are listed in **Figure 9.08**. Rate each program from **1** (unsatisfactory) to **10** (excellent) and select those with the highest average scores that are available and affordable. The meanings of terms are given in Chapters **6, 7,** and **8**.

Production. Video production is covered in Chapter **10** as are issues pertaining to copyright. In **Figure 9.09**, Kenneth Murray (professor of school law, University of Central Florida) has done us a great service by summarizing "fair use" guidelines across several media. Note that interpretations of "fair use" continue to evolve in response to court decisions.

Teaching with Film and TV. How can you best use films and TV in your classroom? Since some students perceive these media as primarily entertainment, they might not take them as seriously as they do textbooks and computers. You may counter this perception by taking the following steps:

- **Study programs** in advance.
- **Obtain supplementary materials** such as printed transcripts of the narrative and study guides.
- Provide your students with **background information**, explain unfamiliar concepts, and anticipate outcomes. (See **Figure 9.10**.)
- Assign **outside readings**.
- Ask **"cuing" questions** (i.e., those that direct students' attention to selected aspects of the program).
- **Watch along with the students**, serving as a model student yourself.
- **Observe students' reactions**.
- **Follow up** viewing with discussions and related activities.

- **Involve parents** in discussing with their children issues raised.
- **Test students** on program content and significance, leaving ample room for creative interpretation.

Above all, students should be taught to **watch critically**. They should be encouraged to find examples of integrity, justice, and courage on the one hand and, on the other, hypocrisy, prejudice, and oppression. How often, you might ask, are problems solved by reasoning and compromise rather than by violence? What reasons are given for purchasing this or that product? What sorts of behaviors are shown to be most worthwhile? How is success portrayed?

Some programs are so persuasive that we teachers ourselves can be seduced. We should remain aware that the reality that producers portray invariably contains some artifice. Even so-called "spontaneous" interviews are edited and retaped until they come out "right." Network news shows have gone as far as to "recreate" scenes without explicitly informing viewers. The 1994 case of adding explosives to dramatize a truck crash test went

---

TABLE 1.
Fair Use Guidelines for Educational Use of Designated Materials

Material	Copy for Teacher Use	Copies for Class	Number of Uses Per Term*
Books (fiction and nonfiction)	1 chapter	1,000 words or 10%	2
Encyclopedias, anthologies, storybooks	1 story	2,500 words or 1 story	3
Poems	1 poem	250 words or 1 poem	2
Periodicals	1 article	2,500 words or 1 article	3
Charts, cartoons, pictures	1 per book	1 per book	3
Lectures, sermons, speeches	1 per book	1 per book	3
Computer programs	Not applicable because of the need to copy the entire program		
Videotapes of TV broadcasts (non-educational TV)	May be shown twice to students within 10 days of broadcast and retained for a maximum of 45 days for evaluation by educators; daily newscasts may be recorded by qualified libraries for research use only		
Videotapes of TV broadcasts (educational TV)	May be recorded and used for educational purposes for a maximum of seven days		
Lawfully made videotapes	May be used for educational purposes in face-to-face classroom teaching.		

*Total use of reproductions should not exceed nine times per class term.

Figure 9.09. Classroom use of copyrighted materials may be guided by the Table above. Source: Kenneth T. Murray, "Copyright and the Educator," *Phi Delta Kappan,* 75 (March 1994), p. 555. Reprinted courtesy of Kenneth Murray.

Figure 9.10. Teachers should make sure that students get the most out of viewing television and other electronically mediated programs. Here my brother is providing a preview to a video about the human costs of war and famine. What might he do for an effective "postview"?

far beyond the bonds of integrity. Since watching films and TV is one of the least supervised of all children's activities, parents and teachers should help young people both to appreciate and challenge program content, thereby increasing their **"media literacy."**[13]

Dramas and situation comedies help students understand problems they face in their own lives. They might compare several TV families on such factors as honesty, independence, exercise of authority, and search for identity. They might ask: How should a family solve problems? Are the problems internal or caused by outside events? How should we deal with sibling rivalry? Contrasting *I Love Lucy* with *The Bill Cosby Show*, for example, would reveal vast progress in the depiction of family conflict resolution. *Full House* and *Home Improvement* may be compared with *Hangin' with Mr. Cooper, Me and the Boys, The Fresh Prince of Bel-Air, The Parent 'Hood,* and *Sister, Sister* with respect to portrayals of family roles and relations in Anglo and African-American households. Comparison of *The Mary Tyler Moore Show* with *Murphy Brown* would reveal contrasting styles women have used, from charming competence to assertive leadership, to cope in male-dominated workplaces. The misogyny and hostility of *In Living Color* ("What are you doing here [to black woman], I thought I flushed the toilet?" A white male judo instructor is stabbed and beaten nearly to death by minority students. A white woman is

called a "bitch.") and of *Martin* (Man to couple, "Is that your wife, or is your dog walking backwards?" Woman, "Get your hand off my thigh." Man, "Sorry, I thought it was on your butt.") may give clues either to what some African-Americans feel or to what the establishment media find profitable to misrepresent. *Married . . . With Children, Roseanne, Unhappily Ever After,* and a host of similar *Life with Riley, Jackie Gleason* shows (yes, even *Dinosaurs*) attempt to portray how common white folks "really" live. These views may be contrasted with students' own experiences and those expressed in literature.

Unfortunately, many students have become so accustomed to factual learning in school that they screen out some of the **emotional content** of films and television. Teachers encourage this habit when they place too much emphasis on "correct" interpretations. Film and TV have much to offer students who are open to seeing, hearing, and feeling the unexpected. To stimulate a fuller response, you might try waiving the silence rule during a showing. Students are used to laughing, crying, and passing remarks on programs while viewing them at home or in the theater; they may gain more from such expression if allowed to do so in class.

Some commercial feature films can be used to study topics of intellectual as well as emotional appeal. Such films both mirror and criticize contemporary culture. More viscerally than the novel and more radically than television, a film expresses its maker's response to the moods and beliefs of the era it portrays. Students will find those moods and beliefs expressed in characters, settings, and plots; and they could appraise them in light of a filmmaker's expression of them. Students could say how **they** would have filmed a given subject and what values **they** would have portrayed. Viewing the documentary, *Visions of Light: The Art of Cinematography,* students could witness first-hand accounts of the creative process from giants in the field throughout the history of filmmaking.

Like novels, films and TV show us how people think and act in a range of situations. Therefore, a class might compare films with literary classics. *The Childhood of Maxim Gorky,* for instance, gives a child's view of some grotesque adults that are akin to Pip's view in Dickens' *Great Expectations.* In *Citizen Kane,* Orson Wells displays the hubris of the entrepreneur, as Theodore Dreiser does in *The Titan.* Akira Kurosawa's *Ran* plays out themes also found in Shakespeare's *King Lear.* Like Nathaniel Hawthorne, film director Ingmar Bergman probes the anguish of moral and religious doubt. The class also might analyze how the literary classics have been transformed into feature films and TV series (e.g., *Gone with the Wind, A Farewell to Arms, Autobiography of Malcolm X, Roots, Little Women*). In evaluating the viewing experience, we might ask:

- Was content **clearly expressed**?
- Did it **relate directly** to instructional objectives?
- Did the program use **models, interviews, color, music, slow motion, time lapse**, and other techniques **when appropriate**?
- Did students **attend closely, ask relevant questions, make insightful comments, express feelings**?
- Did they **learn things of value** from viewing and discussing?
- Did they **ask for more information** about the topics covered?
- Did they **mention the program** later in the year?

In the spirit of **"authentic assessment"** (which, at its best, can only mean **"valid"**), you might ask students to demonstrate what they learned by crafting products and engaging in performances. Pay attention to the process of learning—on-task effort, sharing, questioning, persistence, originality—as well as to products.

Finally, never overestimate how much your students gain from films and TV. The younger they are and the less familiar with North American culture and media, the more likely much will go way over their heads or be wrongly interpreted. For example, one Thanksgiving Day I was standing next to a family watching "The Parade." As the towering yellow figure approached, their four-year-old exclaimed in bewilderment, **"Big Boid's uhbuh LOON???"**

Summary and Conclusions

Films and television enrich our lives and enliven the classroom. They heighten everyday experience and thrust the student into new environments. Films present ordinary subject matter as well as exotic phenomena, from ocean depths to outer space, from prehistoric times to time travels. Television transports viewers to remote villages across the globe and into the halls of Congress. Both are used most effectively when students receive, interpret, and analyze their messages under the guid-

Figure 9.11. Viewing documentaries about world hunger, students not only learn about life in distant lands, they are moved to take part in campaigns to raise emergency relief funds. In what other ways might you "recontextualize" subject matter?

ance of skilled teachers. Both provide opportunities for creative expression. (See **Figure 9.11**.)

This chapter focused on **viewing** of film and TV programs. Chapter **10** explores means by which video signals are **recorded** and **distributed**. These technologies put programming in the hands of teachers and students, allow for instruction more precisely tailored to specific groups and individuals, and enhance access.

Notes

[1]Mast, Gerald, *A Short History of the Movies*, 4th ed. (New York: Macmillan, 1986).

[2]Kolbert, Elizabeth, "TV Viewing and Selling, by Race," *The New York Times* (April 5, 1993), p. D7. Evidence of a growing "cultural divide" was found in a 1993 Gallup Poll—a majority of blacks reportedly think that racial problems cannot be resolved (up from 26% three decades ago) whereas the majority of whites "now think that racial discrimination does not exist." **As teachers we should take active roles in "The Great Dialogue" among racial groups that might serve to "expose the yawning gap between black and white perceptions, suggest where common ground exists and build upon it."** Ruby, Michael, "Time to Listen Up, Citizens!" *U.S. News & World Report*, 116 (June 13, 1994), p. 124. Continued negative stereotyping of African Americans on TV moved **Bill Cosby** to chastise his colleagues when he was inducted into the Television Hall of Fame (1992). **"I'm begging to you all,"** he said, **"stop this horrible massacre of images that are being put**

on this screen now. It isn't fair. It isn't fair to your children watching, because that isn't us. It isn't us. It isn't us." Quoted in Wilkerson, Isabel, "Black Life on TV: Realism or Stereotypes?" *The New York Times* (August 15, 1993), Section 2, p. 28.

[3]Mitchard, Jacquelyn, "The Best Shows for Kids," *TV Guide*, 43 (March 4, 1995), pp. 12–22.

[4]Overbeck, Joy, "Ten to Watch Together, *TV Guide*, 43 (March 4, 1995), pp. 33–35.

[5]Quoted in Guthrie, Fred, "Growing Up with Public Television," *The New Yorker* (30 November 1992), p. 89.

[6]Platte, Mary K., *The Beginning of Satellite Communication: Airborne ITV, MPATI, and the Ohio Story* (Dubuque, IA: Kendall/Hunt, 1982). Cuban, Larry, *Teachers and Machines: The Classroom Use of Technology Since 1920* (New York: Teachers College Press, 1986).

[7]Falten, Diane, "Curriculum Related ITV Programs: What's New, What's Hot," *Media & Methods*, 31 (November/December 1994), pp. 12–13.

[8]Brock, Dee, "PBS Tunes in to Adult Learning," in Miller, Elwood E., & Mosley, Mary L., eds., *Educational Media and Technology Yearbook, 1985* (Littleton, CO: Libraries Unlimited, 1985), pp. 49–53.

[9]Gunter, Barrie, *Dimensions of Television Violence* (New York: St. Martin's, 1985); Gunter, Barrie, & McAleer, Jill, *Children and Television: The One-Eyed Monster?* (New York: Routledge, 1990); Huesmann, L. Rowel, & Eron, Leonard D., eds., *Television and the Aggressive Child: A Cross-National Comparison* (Hillsdale, NJ: Lawrence Erlbaum Associates, 1986); Meyrowitz, Joshua, *No Sense of Place: The Impact of Electronic Media on Social Behavior* (New York: Oxford University Press, 1986); Kaplan, James, "Why Kids Need Heroes," *TV Guide*, 43 (March 4, 1995), p. 31: "Yes, it may be catharsis, or the triumph of good over evil, or getting swept away, but it's also something else. . . . Action shows may lack the story-telling worth of fairy tales, yet they do something similar: They help kids feel less alone about their own fears and aggressions."

[10]Kushman, Rick, "'Frontline' Looks at Link Between TV and Violence," *The Sacramento Bee* (January 9, 1995), p. C5.

[11]*Ibid.*, p. C1.

[12]Cohen, Peter A., Ebeling, Barbara J., & Kulik, James A., "A Meta-Analysis of Outcome Studies of Visual-Based Instruction," *Educational Communication and Technology Journal*, 29 (Spring 1981), pp. 26–36; Salomon, Gavriel, & Gardner, Howard, "The Computer as Educator: Lessons from Television Research," *Educational Researcher*, 15 (January 1986), pp. 13–19; Sammur, Gloria B., "Selected Bibliography of Research on Programming at the Children's Television Workshop," *Educational Technology Research and Development*, 38, 4(1990), pp. 81–92; Thompson, Ann, Simonson, Michael, & Hargrave, Constance, *Educational Technology: A Review of the Research* (Washington, DC: Association for Educational Communications and Technology, 1992); Barnard, John, "Video-Based Instruction: Issues of Effectiveness, Interaction, and Learner Control," *Journal of Educational Technology Systems*, 21, 1(1992–93), pp. 45–50.

[13]Joffe, Bruce H., "Television: Prime Time for Learning?" *The American School Board Journal*, 173 (May 1986), pp. 38–39; "Television: America's Neglected Teacher," *Education* (Fall/Winter 1987), pp. 15–18; Brown, James A., *Television "Critical Viewing Skills" Education: Major Media Literacy Projects in the United States and Selected Countries* (Hillsdale, NJ: Lawrence Erlbaum Associates, 1991).

Sources

The National Information Center for Educational Media (NICEM, owned by Access Innovations, Inc.) is one of the **premiere sources for locating educational programs in a variety of formats.** Regularly updated print indexes (by Plexus Publishing, 1-609-654-6500) include:

Film & Video Finder
Index to AV Producers & Distributors

Online searches of NICEM files (*A-V Online, File 46,* updated quarterly) are available ($30/hr. + $.20/unit) through Knight Ridder Information (formerly Dialog, 1-800-334-2564; 1-415-858-7869). The CD-ROM version of NICEM's *A-V Online* is available (for about $800) from SilverPlatter Information (1-800-343-0064; 1-617-769-2599). NICEM's database of nearly a half million titles, growing at a rate of about 20,000 per year, also is available on computer tape ($5,000 up). For more information call NICEM's Marketing Department (1-800-926-8328; 1-505-265-3591), or email them at tnaccess@technet.nm.org.

A less expensive alternative to NICEM is **Precision One MediaSource** (1-800-233-8467, ext. 522), a joint venture of the Consortium of College & University Media Centers and Brodart Co. Their site license goes for just $395. Also consider the many and varied services (e.g., *Curriculum Analysis Services for Educators, Integrated Instructional Information Resource, Textbook PRO/FILES, Microcomputer PRO/FILES, EPIEgram: The Newsletter About Educational Materials and Technology*) of the long respected, "not-for-profit" **Educational Products Information Exchange (EPIE) Institute** (1-516-728-9100; the distinguished P. Kenneth Komoski, President). Ambitious individuals on tight budgets are well served by the non-profit American Society of Educators' bimonthly *Media & Methods: Educational*

Products, Technologies & Programs for Schools & Universities ($29 per annum subscription, 1-800-523-4540; 1-215-563-3501) with its regularly updated *Buyers' Guides (Pull-Out Resource Directory of the Leading Producers and Distributors of Educational Technologies), Videodisc and CD-ROM Supplements, Media Reviews,* right-to-the-point one-page articles, and postage-paid *Reader Action Cards.* **KidsNet: A Computerized Clearinghouse for Children's Television and Radio** can be reached at 1-202-291-1400, or via the Internet at kidsnet@aol.com. Also see Chapter **13** for subject/title/author searchable Internet sites.

Do you like **free stuff?** After you have made appeals to local businesses, charitable foundations, and the big name corporate enterprises, take a look in your local library at **Educators Progress Service's** (1-414-326-3126) regularly updated guides such as *Educators Guide to Free Videotapes* and *Educators Guide to Free Films, Filmstrips and Slides.*

Films, videos, and **TV programs** are listed in the following publications, many of which are regularly updated. Also, note that searches may be made using CD-ROM reference software (see Chapter **12**) and the Internet (see Chapter **13**). My primary sources for checking references in all chapters have been the user-friendly online catalogs of New York University and Columbia University, Barnes & Noble bookstores, and publishers' catalogs. Note that my bibliographic style follows closely that found in the *Phi Delta Kappan.* Though I taught APA style while serving as Writing Lab Instructor at the California School of Professional Psychology, I prefer using authors' first names, capital letters, and quotation marks with article titles, and months of the year instead of index numbers (whether or not pagination is continuous throughout the volume).

Altschuler, Glenn C., & Grossvogel, David I., *Changing Channels: America in TV Guide* (Urbana: University of Illinois Press, 1992).

Atkinson, Doug, & Zippan, Fiona, *Videos for Kids: The Essential, Indispensable Parent's Guide to Children's Movies on Video* (Rocklin, CA: Prima Publishing, 1995).

Audio Video Market Place: A Multimedia Guide (New York: Bowker, updated annually, 1984–1988).

Bowker's Complete Video Directory (New York: Bowker, updated regularly).

British National Film & Video Catalogue (London: British Film Institute, updated quarterly).

Catchpole, Terry, & Catchpole, Catherine, *The Family Video Guide* (Charlotte, VT: Williamson Publishing, 1992).

Cella, Catherine, *Great Videos for Kids: A Parent's Guide to Choosing the Best* (New York: Citadel, 1992).

Cowie, Peter, ed., *Variety International Film Guide 1995* (Hollywood, CA: Samuel French Trade, 1995).

Davis, Jeffrey, *Children's Television, 1947–1990: Over 200 Series, Game and Variety Shows, Cartoons, Educational Programs, and Specials* (Jefferson, NC: McFarland, 1995).

Ebert, Roger, *Roger Ebert's Video Companion 1995 Edition* (Kansas City, MO: Andrews and McMeel, 1994).

Educational Film/Video Locator (New York: Bowker).

The Entertainment Weekly Guide to the Greatest Movies Ever Made (New York: Warner Books, 1994).

Givanni, June I., *Black [and Asian] Film and Video List* (London: BFI Education, 1992).

Katz, Ephraim, *The Film Encyclopedia*, 2nd ed. (New York: HarperCollins, 1994).

Lankford, Mary D., *Films for Learning, Thinking, and Doing* (Englewood, CO: Libraries Unlimited, 1992).

Maltin, Leonard, ed., *Leonard Maltin's 1996 Movie and Video Guide* (New York: Penguin, 1995).

Martin, Mick, & Porter, Marsha, *Video Movie Guide for Family Viewing* (New York: Ballantine, 1993).

McNeil, Alex, *Total Television, Including Cable: A Comprehensive Guide to Programming from 1948 to the Present*, 3rd ed. (New York: Penguin, 1991).

Microsoft Cinemania [computer-based, multimedia guide to feature films].

Milne, Tom, *Time Out Film Guide: The Definitive A–Z Directory of Over 10,000 Films*, 3rd ed. (New York: Penguin, 1993).

Office of Special Education and Rehabilitative Services, U.S. Department of Education, *Catalog of General Interest Films/Videos* [microform list of captioned titles] (Washington, DC: author, serial).

Ogle, Patrick, *Facets' African-American Video Guide* (Chicago: Facets Multimedia, 1994).

Pallot, James, and the editors of CineBooks, *The Movie Guide*, 2nd ed. (New York: Berkeley Publishing Group, 1995).

Satern, Mark A., *Mark Satern's Illustrated Guide to Video's Best* (Phoenix, AZ: Satern Press, 1994).

Spencer, James R., *The Complete Guide to Special Interest Videos, 1995–1996 Edition*, 3rd ed. (Scottsdale, AZ: James-Robert Publishing, 1995).

Terrace, Vincent, *Television Specials: 3201 Entertainment Spectaculars, 1939–1993* (Jefferson, NC: McFarland, 1995).

VideoHound's Family Video Retriever (Detroit: Visible Ink Press, 1995).

Video Rating Guide for Libraries (Santa Barbara, CA: ABC-CLIO, semi-annual).

Walker, John, ed., *Halliwell's Filmgoer's & Video Viewer's Companion*, 11th ed. (New York: HarperCollins, 1995).

Walker, John, ed., *Halliwell's Film Guide 1995*, 10th ed. (New York: HarperCollins, 1994).

Weiner, Ed, and the editors of TV guide, *The TV Guide TV Book: 40 Years of the All-Time Greatest: Television Facts, Fads, Hits, and History* (New York: HarperPerennial, 1992).

Educational film and video catalogs may be obtained *gratis* from:

Agency for Instructional Technology: 1-800-457-4509
AIMS Media: 1-800-367-2467
Allyn and Bacon: 1-800-852-8024
Ambrose Video Publishing: 1-800-526-4663
Arthur Mokin Productions: 1-800-238-4868
Baker and Taylor Video & Audio: 1-800-775-2800
Barnes & Noble: 1-800-242-6657
Barr Films: 1-800-234-7878
Bennu Productions: 1-212-213-8511
Bergwall Productions, Inc.: 1-800-645-3565
Bullfrog Films: 1-800-543-FROG
Centre Communications, Inc.: 1-800-886-1166
Children's Television Workshop: 1-800-678-0613
Chip Taylor Communications: 1-800-876-2447
Churchill Media: 1-800-334-7830
Coronet/MTI Film & Video: 1-800-621-2131
Corporation for Public Broadcasting, The Annenberg/ CPB Collection: 1-800-LEARNER
Direct Cinema Limited: 1-800-525-0000
Encyclopaedia Britannica: 1-800-554-9862
Films for the Humanities & Sciences: 1-800-257-5126
Great Plains National: 1-800-228-4630
Human Relations Media: 1-800-431-2050
International Historic Films: 1-312-927-2900
International Video Network: 1-800-767-4486; 0181-742-2002 (London)
Kentucky Educational TV: 1-800-354-9067
KidsNet: 1-202-291-1400 (also via America Online)
Library Video Co.: 1-800-843-3620
Lucerne Media: 1-800-341-2293
The Media Guild: 1-800-886-9191
Media Projects, Inc.: 1-800-826-3863
Menninger Video Productions: 1-800-345-6036
Meridian Education Corporation: 1-800-727-5507
Modern Talking Picture Service: 1-800-446-6337
National Film Board of Canada: 1-800-542-2164
National Geographic Society: 1-800-368-2728; 1-800-548-9797 TDD
New Dimension Media: 1-800-288-4456
Newsbank, Inc.: 1-800-762-8182
Nystrom New Media: 1-800-621-8086
Pacific Mountain Network: 1-303-837-8000
PBS K-12 Learning Services: 1-703-739-5402
PBS Video: 1-800-344-3337

Perennial Education, Inc.: 1-800-323-9084
Public Media Incorporated: 1-800-343-4312
Pyramid Film & Video: 1-800-421-2304
Rainbow Educational Media: 1-800-331-4047
RMI Media Productions: 1-800-745-5480
SONY Wonder: 1-800-765-2500
Stanton Films: 1-310-542-6573
TV Ontario: 1-800-331-9566
United Nations Publications: 1-800-253-9646
Western Instructional Television: 1-213-466-8601
Zenger Media: 1-800-421-4246

For **additional information** about film and TV, including **selection and utilization guidelines** see:

Alvarado, Manuel, & Boyd-Barrett, Oliver, eds., *Media Education: An Introduction* (London: British Film Institute, 1992).

Alvarado, Manuel, Buscombe, Edward, & Collins, Richard, eds., *The Screen Education Reader: Cinema, Television, Culture* (New York: Columbia University Press, 1993).

Bianculli, David, *Teleliteracy: Taking Television Seriously* (New York: Continuum, 1992).

Blakey, Scott, *Kid Vid: How to Select Kid's Videos for Your Family* (New York: HarperCollins, 1995).

Bogle, Donald, *Toms . . .: An Interpretive History of Blacks in American Films,* new 3rd ed. (New York: Continuum, 1994).

Brown, James A., *Television "Critical Viewing Skills" Education: Major Media Literacy Projects in the United States and Selected Countries* (Hillsdale, NJ: Lawrence Erlbaum Associates, 1991).

Buckingham, David, *Children Talking Television: The Making of Television Literacy* (London: Falmer Press, 1993).

Buckingham, David, ed., *Watching Media Learning: Making Sense of Media Education* (London: Falmer, 1990).

Clifford, Brian R., Gunter, Barrie, & McAleer, Jill, *Television and Children: Program Evaluation, Comprehension, and Impact* (Hillsdale, NJ: Lawrence Erlbaum Associates, 1995).

Davis, Douglas, *The Five Myths of Television Power, or, Why the Medium is not the Message* (New York: Simon & Schuster, 1993).

Directory of Video, Multimedia, and Audio-Visual Products (Fairfax, VA: The International Communications Industries Association, annual).

Fuller, Linda K., *Community Television in the United States: A Sourcebook on Public, Educational, and Governmental Access* (Westport, CT: Greenwood Press, 1994).

Gianetti, Louis D., *Understanding Movies*, 6th ed. (Englewood Cliffs, NJ: Prentice-Hall, 1993).

Gilder, George, *Life After Television: The Coming Transformation of Media and American Life,* revised ed. (New York: W.W. Norton & Company, 1994).

Hartwig, Robert L., *Basic TV Technology,* 2nd ed. (Boston: Focal, 1995).

Hicks-Harper, Patricia Thandi, *Black Educators, Black Elementary School Students, and Black Rap Music Artists on Educational Entertainment Rap Music Video for Pedagogy: A Cultural and Critical Analysis* (Ann Arbor, MI: UMI Dissertation Services, 1994).

Hodge, Winston William, *Interactive Television: A Comprehensive Guide for Multimedia Technologists* (New York: McGraw-Hill, 1995).

Hoynes, William, *Public Television for Sale: Media, the Market, and the Public Sphere* (Boulder, CO: Westview Press, 1994).

Inglis, Andrew F., *Behind the Tube: A History of Broadcasting Technology and Business* (Boston: Focal, 1990).

Jacobson, Ronald L., *Television Research: A Directory of Conceptual Categories, Topic Suggestions, and Selected Sources* (Jefferson, NC: McFarland, 1995).

Jankowski, Gene F., & Fuchs, David C., *Television Today and Tomorrow: It Won't Be What You Think* (New York: Oxford University Press, 1995).

Jensen, Carl, & Project Censored, *Censored: The News that Didn't Make the News—and Why: The 1995 Project Censored Yearbook* (New York: Four Walls Eight Windows, 1995).

Jhally, Sut, & Lewis, Justin, *Enlightened Racism: The Cosby Show, Audiences, and the Myth of the American Dream* (Boulder, CO: Westview Press, 1992).

Kamenshine, Lesley, *A-V Troubleshooter: Audio-Visual Equipment Operation, Maintenance and Repair* (Englewood Cliffs, NJ: Prentice-Hall, 1985).

Kaplan, Don, *Teaching with Video: Strategies for Creative Television* (White Plains, NY: Knowledge Industry, 1985).

Kaplan, Don, *Television and the Classroom* (White Plains, NY: Knowledge Industry, 1986).

Livingstone, Sonia M., & Lunt, Peter K., *Talk on Television: Audience Participation and Public Debate* (London: Routledge, 1994).

Kinder, Marsha, *Playing with Power in Movies, Television, and Video Games: From Muppet Babies to Teenage Mutant Ninja Turtles* (Berkeley: University of California Press, 1991).

King, John, Lopez, Ana M., & Alvarado, Manuel, eds., *Mediating Two Worlds: Cinematic Encounters in the Americas* (London: British Film Institute, 1993).

Lloyd-Kolkin, Donna, & Tyner, Kathleen, R., *Media and You: An Elementary Media Literacy Curriculum* (Englewood Cliffs, NJ: Educational Technology Publications, 1991).

Masterman, Len, *Teaching the Media* (New York: Routledge, 1990).

Meyer, Manfred, ed., *Aspects of School Television in Europe: A Documentation* (Munich: K. G. Saur, 1992).

Minoli, Daniel, *Video Dialtone Technology: Digital Video Over ADSL, HFC, FTTC, and ATM* (New York: McGraw-Hill, 1995).

Monaco, James, and the editors of Baseline, *The Encyclopedia of Film* (New York, NY: Perigee Books, 1991).

Moore, David M. (Mike), & Dwyer, Francis M., *Visual Literacy: A Spectrum of Visual Learning* (Englewood Cliffs, NJ: Educational Technology Publications, 1994).

Newcomb, Horace, *Television: The Critical View*, 5th ed. (New York: Oxford University Press, 1994).

Office of Educational Research and Improvement, U.S. Department of Education, *TV Viewing and Parental Guidance: Education Research Consumer Guide, No. 10* (Washington, DC: author, 1994).

Postman, Neil, with Powers, Steve, *How to Watch TV News* (New York: Penguin, 1992).

Prentiss, Stan, *HDTV: High Definition Television*, 2nd ed. (Blue Ridge Summit, PA: Tab Books, 1994).

Reynolds, Angus, & Anderson, Ronald H., *Selecting and Developing Media for Instruction*, 3rd ed. (New York: Van Nostrand Reinhold, 1991).

Roberts, Nancy, Blakeslee, George, Brown, Maureen, & Lenk, Cecilia, *Integrating Telecommunications into Education* (Englewood, CO: Libraries Unlimited, 1990).

Salomon, Gavriel, *Interaction of Media, Cognition, and Learning* (Hillsdale, NJ: Lawrence Erlbaum Associates, 1994).

Satterthwaite, Les L., *Instructional Media: Materials, Production, and Utilization*, 2nd ed. (Dubuque, IA: Kendall-Hunt, 1991).

Simatos, Anastasios, & Spencer, Ken, *Children and Media: Learning from Television* (Liverpool: Manutius Press, 1992).

Simpson, Robert S., *Effective Audio-Visual: A User's Handbook*, 2nd ed. (Boston: Focal, 1992).

Staiger, Janet, *Interpreting Films: Studies in the Historic Reception of American Cinema* (Princeton, NJ: Princeton University Press, 1992).

Staiger, Janet, ed., *The Studio System* (New Brunswick, NJ: Rutgers University Press, 1994).

Stevens, Matthew, ed., *International Film, Television, and Video Acronyms* (Westport, CT: Greenwood Press, 1993).

Thomas, Erwin K., & Carpenter, Brown H., eds., *Handbook on Mass Media in the United States: The Industry and Its Audience* (Westport, CT: Greenwood Press, 1994).

Toulet, Emmanuel, *Birth of the Motion Picture* (New York: Harry N. Abrams, 1995).

Wetzel, C. Douglas, Radtke, Paul H., & Stern, Hervey W., *Instructional Effectiveness of Video Media* (Hillsdale, NJ: Lawrence Erlbaum Associates, 1994).

Williams, Linda, *Viewing Positions: Ways of Seeing Film* (New Brunswick, NJ: Rutgers University Press, 1995).

Willis, Edgar, & Aldridge, Henry B., *Television, Cable, and Radio: A Communications Approach* (Englewood Cliffs, NJ: Prentice-Hall, 1991).

North American and British **Periodicals** include:

Bacon's TV/Cable Directory

Digital Video Magazine

E-ITV

Entertainment Weekly

Film Quarterly

GMV: The Government Video Magazine

The Home Video & Cable Yearbook

The International Journal of Micrographics and Video Technology
International Motion Picture Almanac
International Television & Cable Almanac
International TV & Video Guide
Journal of Educational Television
Journal of Film and Video
The Journal of Popular Film and Television
The Listener
Media & Methods
Media Review Digest
Millimeter
Movie: The Video Magazine
Quarterly Review of Film and Video
Screen: The Journal of the Society for Education in Film and Television
Spectator
Television & Cable Factbook
Television Magazine
Television Quarterly
TV Guide
Video Annual
Video Collection
Videodisc and Optical Disk Update
Videodisc, Videotex
Video Manager
Videotex World

Also see: Loughney, Katharine, *Film, Television, and Video Periodicals: A Comprehensive Annotated List* (New York: Garland, 1991); and the *International Index to Television Periodicals* (London: International Federation of Film Archives, serial).

Study Items

1. Describe distinctive features of film that have made it an asset to teaching.

2. Contrast classroom viewing of film with that of television.

3. Provide examples of when film might serve better than TV in achieving specific instructional objectives.

4. Indicate how you would integrate viewing of a feature film into a lesson plan.

5. Distinguish among entertainment, educational, and instructional TV.

6. What impact do you believe children's viewing of television four or more hours a day has on their intellectual and emotional development? Consider unrestricted versus guided viewing.

7. How would you go about involving parents in efforts to make home viewing of TV more beneficial?

8. How might you tactfully encourage parents to watch more "news and views" programming so that they might serve as better sources for their children?

9. How would you integrate a PBS series into your curriculum?

10. Assess merits and limitations of instructional TV.

11. Contrast objectives and style of *Sesame Street* and *Mister Rogers' Neighborhood*.

12. Speculate on what role after school dramatic specials and such popular shows as *In Living Color* and *Beverly Hills, 90210* might play in giving teenagers the self esteem and courage needed to take precautions against pregnancy and AIDS.

13. Alex Haley's book on which the docudrama *Roots* was based has been criticized for its contrived documentary and investigative research. Describe how you would justify and handle its inclusion in your school's curriculum.

14. List criteria for selection of audiovisual programs.

15. In what ways might minority representation affect your choice of program?

16. Describe how you would prepare your students for viewing a short film or TV program.

17. Suggest activities to follow up classroom viewing of film or TV.

18. How would you evaluate what was learned from viewing a program designed to discourage substance abuse?

19. List techniques to encourage critical viewing of film and TV.

20. It is likely that students learn more subject matter from one hour of reading or lecture and notetaking than from one hour of viewing film or TV. Presuming this is so, justify classroom use of film and TV.

Suggested Activities

1. Meet with a group of classmates to brainstorm about possible uses of commercial films and TV in the classroom. List examples by grade level and subject area.

2. View *Visions of Light: The Art of Cinematography* and make a chronological list of developments in the craft of filmmaking. Prepare a handout to share and refine with your classmates or students.

3. Visit your school district media center and your local college library to locate film and video indexes listed above. Locate programs in your subject area and make a note of procedures for obtaining them and costs.

4. Obtain *Microsoft Cinemania* and use it to locate feature films (among its nearly 20,000 reviews) for use in your teaching.

5. Draft a week-long lesson plan that integrates viewing of a feature film.

6. Draft a semester-long lesson plan that incorporates viewing a TV series.

7. View *Destinos* or *French in Action* and phone the Annenberg/CPB Collection (1-800-Learner) to obtain descriptions of texts, workbooks, audiocassettes, and videotapes. Note especially diversity of methods and integration of media.

A bit on the dim side, Josh thought it was some kind of low-impact aerobics.

Figure 9.12. Though subject to misinterpretation, as shown above, television programming at its best serves as an authoritative source of information, a competent instructor, and an engaging companion. Reproduced with permission of Scott Arthur Masear.

8. Make a month-long log of television programs you watch. Categorize each according to specific personal and professional goals you may have, including escape. (See **Figure 9.12.**)

9. Ask your students to keep a log of TV programs watched and how they spend their after-school and weekend hours otherwise. Then have them watch no TV for one week, still logging their other activities. Have them share their experiences with classmates, and encourage them to discuss and write about achieving balance among TV viewing, reading, studying, socializing, and playing.

10. Many music videos present collages of stirring images of people, places, and events. Select some for analysis of content and issues.

11. Once you begin teaching, keep in touch with issues on the minds of your students by watching music videos popular among each racial and ethnic group. Engage students in discussions about technique, art, craft, science, talent, hard work, collaboration, drugs, violence, sex, AIDS, life, beauty, death.

12. View the PBS program *Learning to Read,* and compare the suggestions made with those presented in Chapter **6**.

13. View the PBS program *Cover to Cover,* and analyze use of visuals in relation to narration according to hints given in Chapter **6**. Is the focus of the show to impart reading skills or is it rather to stimulate interest in reading?

14. Examine suggestions for use of instructional films and TV programs provided by manufacturers. Compare them with those described in this chapter and note deficiencies in either.

15. Explore reference materials from your other classes and speak with your instructors to find suggestions for conducting "authentic" evaluation of cognitive and affective effects of viewing films and TV programs.

16. Examine this chapter for deficiencies and inform me (Internet: hackbarths@aol.com).

17. Share with me your responses to the above study items and your experiences in pursuing the above activities.

Chapter 10

Video Recording and Distribution

Chapter Content and Objectives

Video recording and telecommunications technologies have brought about efficient delivery of TV programming to homes and schools. **Videotapes** permit more convenient production and scheduling. **Laser videodiscs** make possible instant access to desired sections of prerecorded programs. **Coaxial cables** multiply channels, make local programming feasible, and enable viewers to talk back to the tube. **Videotext** links viewers with computer networks through which they can bank, shop, obtain information, and leave messages. **Satellites** relay signals round the globe, bringing **distance education** to remote locations. After reading this chapter, you should be able to:

- Describe how videotape makes production more **feasible** and viewing more **convenient**.

- List features of videodisc and barcode technologies that **enhance instruction**.

- Discuss how cable television has increased **quantity** of and **access** to educational programming.

- Give examples of **commercial** and **educational** uses of videotext and other on-line database systems.

- Describe contexts in which satellites serve **educational ends**.

- Provide a **critical assessment** of video technologies.

- List **criteria** that can serve to guide selection and production of audiovisual programs.

- Specify considerations in the **effective design** of distance education programs.

Video Recordings

Videotape recorders appeared in 1956, and by 1970 one public school in four had one. Home equipment (recorders and cameras) went on the market in 1975, and within a few years more than a million units had been sold. Today nearly every school and library has at least one VCR (video **cassette** recorder) and most families have purchased their own.

What has made video recording technology so popular? First, the VCR can be used to record broadcast and cable TV programs for viewing at any convenient time. It can be set to record automatically even when the owner is away or watching another channel. Second, videotape cassettes, for rent or purchase, carry a wide range of material: feature-length movies, "adult" entertainment, commercial TV shows, lessons in sports and cookery, and most of the educational films and PBS programs listed in Chapter **9**. Third, video "camcorders" enable teachers and students alike to make their own programs. Finally, playback equipment lets the viewer skip forward, or back, or stop at any point. (See **Figure 10.01**.)

To what extent is it legal to use these video technologies? It is legal to tape television programs "off-the-air" for personal use. Taping for educational purposes, under specific circumstances, is sanctioned by **"fair use"** legislation.

The fair use of a copyrighted work, including such use by reproduction in copies or phonorecords . . . for purposes such as criticism, comment, news reporting, teaching . . . scholarship or research, is not an infringement of copyrights.[1]

Figure 10.01. Videotaped programs may be played anywhere, any time (with permission of the copyright holder). Here a program is part of a portable exhibit (at UCLA) about earthquake preparedness. What sorts of educational messages might you want to take to selected audiences?

It is illegal to replay the programs outside the home or for commercial gain. Neither broadcast nor cable programs may be used for **repeated** viewing without permission from the copyright holder. This applies to everyone—the public, teachers, and school libraries. Teachers, however, may capture a program *on the spur of the moment* (in other words, without preplanning, so time does not permit contacting the producers for permission) and screen it shortly thereafter. They must then either erase it or obtain permission to keep it.[2]

The cost of producing quality shows naturally must be borne by the consumer. The legal and moral obligations of educators to pay licensing fees force educators to be more selective in choosing programs and more creative in their use of video technology.

Viewing films and videotapes serves as a springboard for **creating** them. Film has long served to record student performance in skill subjects such as athletics, dance, drama, and speech. Videotaping now is the preferred medium, since feedback is instantaneous. Such **"video feedback"** has become a standard technique in training counselors and teachers. Following a period of instruction, students perform before the camera. The entire class may then view the videotape and make suggestions for improvement. Guidance and encouragement by supportive peers and teachers ensure that students' initial embarrassment—or smugness—is turned to efforts to improve subsequent performance.

Even more creative is the production by teachers and students of **their own** TV programs. Teachers may record their lectures for later viewing, or produce entire video lessons for students to complete on their own. Students can participate in the production of documentaries, dramas, and variety shows. For example, at UCLA's University Elementary School (UES), youngsters assumed roles of cub reporters and newscasters. They were taught videotaping techniques and, equipped with camcorders, went out to look for stories. They covered the launches of the UES rocketry club, did a documentary on a local storm drain, and interviewed strikers picketing a supermarket. Every child rotated through the positions of director, camera operator, and reporter. The youngsters wrote stories and soon distinguished between those that were merely entertaining and those that were newsworthy. Some even complained that too much of the news they viewed on TV was devoted to sensationalism rather than straight reporting. Having worked as a team, every member of the class shared in the glory when their tape was shown to other classes and parents.

The **laser videodisc**, introduced in the late 1970s, has encoded on its surface video images and stereo sound. Players spin the 12-inch plastic disc at 1,800 rpm and a laser beam "reads" the encoded signals. The impressions on each revolution are converted into electronic impulses for display on a standard television set.

On each side of a videodisc are enough individual frames to encode all 30,000 plus pages of the *Encyclopaedia Britannica* with space for duplicate copies. For motion visuals, these frames are sequenced like movie film and may be played at normal speed, accelerated, decelerated, reversed, or stopped. Since only a light beam scans the disc, program quality does not deteriorate. (See **Figure 10.02.**)

With the aid of a barcode reader, individual frames of a videodisc can be accessed (i.e., located and displayed), thus enabling viewers to select desired pages in a recorded book or choose scenes from a simulated tour. Computers make possible the presentation of programmed instructional lessons—carefully sequenced written passages, still pictures, diagrams, historic film footage, interviews with experts, and laboratory demonstrations. Called **"computer-based interactive video"** (CBIV), it permits the routing of students through material in accordance with their responses to questions displayed under the control of a computer. **Generic discs** covering a variety of subjects and lesson-oriented software have been developed to enable teachers to craft their own barcoded displays and CBIV programs.

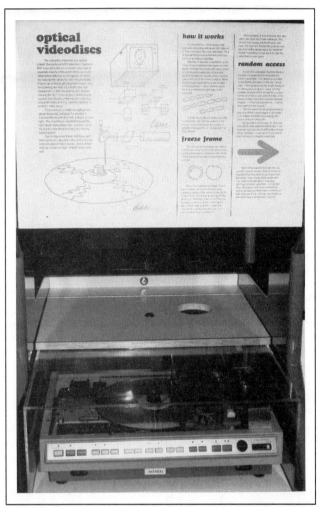

Figure 10.02. This display reveals how a laser beam is used to "read" the images and sound encoded on a videodisc. The principle is identical for audio CD and multimedia CD-ROM. Location: California Museum of Science and Industry.

Leticia Ekhaml (West Georgia College) described the varieties of videodisc access in terms of three levels of control.

> In Level I, the videodisc player is controlled through either the control panel on the videodisc player, the videodisc player's remote control unit or the barcode reader. In Level II, the player has a built-in programmable memory. The videodisc has a short computer program encoded into the videodisc which, in turn,

controls the player. The program on the videodisc allows the user, for instance, to make several choices from a menu of chapter and frame numbers. The user can then make the selection on a keypad or a touch screen and the microprocessor locates the appropriate frame. In Level III, the videodisc player is controlled by an external computer. . . . Authoring or interactive software is used to develop an instructional program to control the videodisc player.[3]

Great ideas for using barcodes to access videodisc segments were provided by Sally Bower, Donna Baumbach, and Mary Bird (University of Central Florida).

> Take barcodes which are correlated to an anatomy disc and attach them to an inexpensive cardboard Halloween skeleton. Want to add another dimension to that three dimensional globe? Add barcodes so students can listen to the music or languages of other lands, or video images of the people of the world. Add life to a timeline by adding barcodes which relate to particular video clips, graphics, or sounds of the time. Generate barcodes which are tied to images and sounds that can motivate students' writing or stir their curiosity. Students can generate their own barcodes to enhance a research report or story with videodisc images or sounds. . . . Use barcodes everywhere. They can truly transform a classroom into something special.[4]

CBIV instruction and simulation (to be covered more fully in the next two chapters) were early adopted by agencies ranging from the American Heart Association to the U.S. Army. The former used it to teach cardiopulmonary resuscitation; the latter, to train personnel in the operation and maintenance of electronic communications systems. At the Massachusetts Institute of Technology, an interactive video program was developed to enable students to explore motion picture and map representations of unfamiliar terrains. Students control direction of travel, speed, and even season of the year. They also can obtain detailed information about each location. Though such **"surrogate travel"** through **"virtual reality"** is used primarily to train aircraft pilots, it also teaches children how to read maps and become familiar with diverse regions of the earth. Thus, computer technology has transformed the videodisc player from an electronic page turner into a magic carpet.[5] The premiere source of educational applications long has been *Media & Methods*. Producers of videodiscs for school use are listed at the end of this chapter.

Cable Television

Cable TV, which sends signals by wire, started in the 1940s. Due to poor reception in many valleys of rural Pennsylvania, TV sales were weak. So one day an enterprising salesperson hoisted an antenna on the highest hill and hooked homes to it for the price of a receiver. Thus, **"Community Antenna Television"** (CATV) was born. Since cable did not use the airwaves (already apportioned by the FCC), it could carry a range of channels. These could be used by many suppliers who could divide the audience into smaller groups seeking more specialized programs. Cable was dubbed a "television of abundance," and the FCC endorsed it as a local resource.

In 1972, however, the FCC, fearing that cable might endanger broadcast networks, directed cable companies to provide public access for "much-needed community expression." It also limited the number of distant signals (mostly network programming picked up from nearby large cities) that could be cablecast. This inevitably reduced the audience for cable stations, and so, contrary to the FCC's intention to increase public access, diminished it. Since then the FCC has removed most of its restrictions on cablecasting and empowered local governments to regulate rates and negotiate services directly with the cable companies.

Cable now carries programs paid for by viewers. These programs come not only by cable ("pay cable") but also by air in scrambled form to sets equipped with decoders ("paid subscription TV"). Cable programming, and especially that on pay cable, is boosted by communications satellites, which relay signals across the world. Satellite TV gives rise to such pay TV services as *Home Box Office*.

Cable confined to a single location, such as a college campus, is called **"closed-circuit television"** (CCTV). It is used mostly in cases where direct contact with instructors is not considered essential. With CCTV, a single lecturer can reach hundreds of students simultaneously in many different classrooms. Strategically placed cameras make chalkboard writing, pictures, and laboratory demonstrations visible to all. A two-way intercom allows for teacher-student discussion.[6]

Figure 10.03 shows a classroom equipped with a CCTV system. An aide located in a control booth adjusts cameras to show both instructor and demonstration materials. The presentation is relayed via cable to several classrooms and to nearby subscribing industries. On-campus students flip a switch to indicate when they

Figure 10.03. Closed-circuit TV (at USC) distributes class presentations to all parts of a room, across campus, and to community learning centers. What possibilities does this offer for local programming, interaction, and individualization?

have a question or comment. Off-campus students use a telephone answered by the aide. The instructor acknowledges the calls, and the voices of both are piped through the intercom for all to hear.

Another development in cable TV is **"videotext,"** a viewer-controlled information retrieval service (aka "interactive television") for use in the home, school, and business. The British Post Office was the first to offer such access to computer memory banks. Its Prestel system, started in 1979, was followed by *Antiope* in France, *Telidon* in Canada, *Bildschirmtext* in West Germany, CAPTAIN in Japan, and in the U.S., Viewtron, Viewdata, and Main Street. France's *Minitel* system, begun in 1980, connects home computers with databases via telephone lines.

Videotext subscribers select the information they need by using a keypad. They may request encyclopedic facts, updates on news events, travel information, weather reports, the balance of their checking account, or an instructional lesson. They also may purchase airline and concert tickets, transfer funds from their savings to checking accounts, buy merchandise, pay bills, or leave messages for other subscribers **("email").** Users must pay for the special equipment, the cost of the cable (or telephone) transmission, and from $1 to $250 per hour to access databases. The first successful systems, like those in England and France, were boosted by generous government subsidies. (See **Figure 10.04.**)

Figure 10.04. Videotext systems connect viewers to a computer network, enabling them to select reading material, view movies, shop, bank, and play games. As these catch on in the U.S., video movie rental stores will have to find new lines of business. What might some consequences be for education? Location: California Museum of Science and Industry.

In the United States, widespread computer networking got a jump on TV-mediated videotext before it could catch on. Such commercial online services as CompuServe, America Online, and Prodigy are accessed by microcomputers connected to the telephone with modems ("modulator/demodulator" electronic transmission devices). These online services, the Internet, and the rest of the rapidly evolving "information superhighway" are described more fully in Chapter **13**.

The cable TV industry has been fighting back with promises of 500 channels of programming, access to libraries of videos, and other such "interactive" features. Their special advantage in the education market is that they have been wiring classrooms at no cost for years, while telephone companies have been charging commercial rates to wire and service only the administrative offices. Another advantage is that fiber optic cables have much more capacity than conventional home phone (copper) wiring.[7]

Cable TV connections to the "information superhighway" began in 1994 when Continental Cablevision began offering its Cambridge, Massachusetts, subscribers the option of Internet access, made possible by Zenith, for about $100 per month. Later that same year, Digital Equipment (DEC) offered to cable companies the *ChannelWorks Internet Brouter* (it **br**idges communications systems and **route**s data) for about $7,000 each.

Communications Satellites

Artificial earth **satellites** have been aloft since 1957, when the Soviets orbited Sputnik I ("fellow traveler"), a 184-pound ball that triggered the space race that my generation remembers well. The USA launched Vanguard in 1958 and I recall my mother and me watching it traverse the night sky. Four years later the first commercial satellite, TELSTAR I, was launched by the United States, and in 1965 the **International Telecommunications Satellite Consortium** (INTELSAT) orbited "Early Bird," first in a series of highly successful communications satellites. During the 1970s, commercial satellites carried broadcasts of the Olympic Games and the Apollo moon landings, while America's National Aeronautics and Space Administration (NASA) satellites relayed **"distance education"** programs across India, Canada, Brazil, the South Pacific, and parts of the United States. INTELSAT now has over 100 nation members and is providing many of them with domestic TV service.

During the late 1970s, commercial firms such as Western Union, AT&T, and RCA built satellites as a prelude to leasing communications channels. By 1980 a score of "superstations" such as WTBS (Ted Turner's pioneer Atlanta, Georgia, station that began in 1976); *Home Box Office, Showtime,* and the 24-hour-a-day *Cable News Network* were beaming programs by satellite to a quarter of the nation's broadcast stations (including all PBS outlets) and half its cable stations. In response to the boom in sales of "dish" antennae that could receive signals directly from satellites, superstations began scrambling their signals. The 1990s have been marked by the emergence of Digital Satellite System (DSS) services. Backed by RCA, Sony, and Hughes Electronics (General Motors), DSS services provide clear reception of 175 channels using an 18-inch diameter dish.[8]

Early research into the educational potential of satellites relied heavily on NASA's six **Applications Technology Satellites** (ATS). ATS-1, launched in 1966 with an expected life of 18 months, continued to function for many years. In 1969 NASA offered corporations, universities, and other organizations free use of the satellites for communications experiments lasting up to one year.

The first experiment, conducted by the University of Hawaii, involved a satellite-based, two-way radio network linking the nations of the Pacific basin. By 1971, the University was operating a pilot project, **Pan-Pacific Education and Communication Experiments**

by Satellite (PEACESAT), with stations on the Honolulu campus and at Hilo College on the island of Hawaii. Wellington Polytechnic, New Zealand, and the University of the South Pacific in Fiji soon joined the project. PEACESAT was the first to offer a course for credit by satellite and the first use of a satellite to connect libraries.

In 1975 the Indian government used ATS-F (the sixth and final one in a series) for its **Satellite/Instructional Television Experiment** (SITE). The project employed the satellite's powerful UHF television transmitter to bounce signals to earth stations with three-meter diameter antennas. The satellite relayed programs to 3½ million people in over two thousand remote villages. Programs were telecast for children a half hour in the morning and for adults a half hour in the evening. The former covered mainly science, the latter, agriculture, health, and family planning. Listeners turned a dial to hear the audio portion in their own language. At the conclusion of the experiment, limited broadcasting continued via terrestrial stations until 1982, when the Indian government launched a satellite of its own.

Although entertainment and information services continue to dominate North American satellite TV programming, several networks now are providing **"distance education"** to schools in the United States and Canada. The *Appalachian Community Service Network* offers telecourses along with programs on such general education topics as the arts, aging, energy, and travel. The *Pacific Mountain Network*, based in Denver, provides programs to western states, including Hawaii and Alaska. Other valuable sources are *The Learning Channel* and *The Discovery Channel* which broadcast educational TV courses. *The Education Network* offers programming ranging from elementary school level Spanish to high school level art history through its *Mind Extension University*. Subscribing schools take turns calling in and, using speaker phones, entire classes of students interact with the TV instructors. Classroom materials are provided and local "facilitators" receive televised training. The Cable News Network's *CNN Classroom* and C-SPAN's *In the Classroom* help keep students well-informed.[9]

The Channel One Communications Network, an ambitious enterprise set in motion about five years ago by the founders of the schooling-for-profit Edison Project, Whittle Communications, was designed to enhance students' knowledge of current events. However, the impact of providing over forty percent of the nation's secondary schools with complete TV satellite/cable systems has been much more dramatic. According to researchers Drew Tiene and Evonne Whitmore (both at Kent State University):

> Survey results indicate that most schools subscribing to the Channel One newscast also use the television equipment provided [at no cost] for a variety of other purposes, including showing instructional television programs, school announcements, special events, and student productions. Eighty-three percent indicated increased use of educational television in their building since subscribing . . . .[10]

Thus, though we may find it a challenge to integrate the contract-mandated 10-minute school-wide viewing of news (with commercials), having the top-notch equipment permits taking full advantage of the resources described in this and the previous chapter. (See **Figure 10.05**.)

Merger of regional satellite networks promises to link the nation's schools to each other, and to the international computer "network of networks," the "Internet" (see Chapter **13**). The ambitious **Interactive Distance Education Alliance** (IDEANET) combines resources of several agencies to reach all 50 states. The alliance, forged in 1994, includes the Missouri School Boards

Figure 10.05. A trade-off for accepting Whittle Communications' free video and satellite down-link equipment is agreeing to subject your students to advertisements. As illustrated here, it may be difficult enough to integrate the news content into the curriculum, much less the commercials, but substantial advantages might well offset any drawbacks. Source: *Phi Delta Kappan,* 76 (February 1995), p. 431. Reprinted with permission of Joel Pett.

Association (Education Satellite Network serving 300 schools in seven states, publisher of *SATLINE* magazine), Oklahoma State University (ASTS distance learning network, 300 schools in 21 states), Northern Arizona University (Educational Systems Programming, 100 schools in seven states), the Educational Service District 101, Spokane, Washington (Satellite Telecommunications Education Programming/Pacific Northwest Star Schools Partnership, "STEP/Star," network, 700 schools in 18 states), RXL Pulitzer (a private distance education program producer/distributor), and the Network for Instructional TV, Inc. (a national not-for-profit corporation serving 825 schools in 12 states). In addition to classroom instructional programming, IDEANET provides for professional staff development and access to Satlink On-Line, Post Link (daily newspapers), and the Internet.[11]

Thus, we see that video recording and distribution technologies are intimately linked. Telephonic, video, and computer signals are transformed into pulses of light and travel along strands of glass or are relayed by satellites. Worldwide telecommunications have made visions of a **"global village"** a reality. Governments, corporations, and educational institutions now routinely conduct **"teleconferences"** among staff working around the world. Participants can both hear and see each other. Exchanges are instantaneous. Sales figures, budgets, and clips from earlier meetings can be accessed and displayed. Proceedings can be taped and edited for posterity. School children in the States regularly "visit" their video pals in Europe and Asia to discuss common concerns. (See **Figure 10.06.**) As we shall see in Chapter **13**, the "marriage" of video, computer, and telecommunications technologies, along with widespread "adoption" of open-ended, "constructivist" approaches to teaching, are expanding our conception of **distance learning** ". . . from a vision of students remotely participating in a class to one of **distance acquisition of knowledge from remote databases, peer support, and collaboration.**"[12]

Evaluation of Video Technologies

Video recording and distribution technologies provide wide access to everything television has to offer. They capture and preserve images and sounds of both entertainment and educational value, and they deliver programs to homes and classrooms across the world. For the

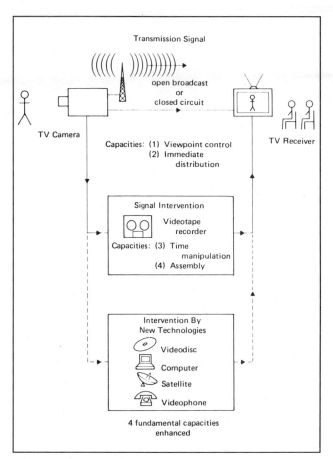

Figure 10.06. Interrelations of video technologies are diagramed here. Between the initial "witnessing" of events by a camera and ultimate display by a TV receiver, electronic devices permit recording, editing, and immediate or delayed distribution. Source: Dean W. Hutton, "Video Technology in Higher Education: State of the Art?" in Ortrun Zuber-Skerritt, ed., *Video in Higher Education* (East Brunswick, NJ: Nichols, 1984), p. 13. Reprinted with permission of Nichols Publishing.

homebound student, broadcast and cable TV supplement printed materials and tutors. (See **Figure 10.07.**)

Compared with motion picture film, **videotape** has the following advantages:

- It is relatively **inexpensive** to buy, edit, duplicate, and store.
- Programs may be **viewed during** and **immediately after** shooting.
- Videotape can by **reused** many times without noticeable loss of image or sound quality.

Figure 10.07. Video distribution technologies bring rich programming to those unable to attend classes. Cable systems permit viewing of class presentations "live." Questions may be directed to instructors via telephone.

- Loading and rewinding are much **simpler** than with a film projector.

- VCRs permit comparatively **rapid access** to any desired section of a program along with repeated viewing in a way that would devastate film.

- As VCRs become commonplace in the home, more students may check out instructional tapes for **viewing at their leisure**.

- Live or recorded video programs can be **distributed via cable** to countless classrooms and, via satellite, simultaneously to the entire world.

- Video segments can be **loaded directly into computer memory** for timely, efficient editing, mixing, and presenting.[13]

The primary disadvantage of videotape is that image quality is inferior to that obtained with film—prints, slides, and motion pictures. And if one has to study an image carefully, perhaps measuring distances or making notations, flat pictures and drawings are best.

The distinctive qualities of film and video dictate use. Clearly, when instructional objectives call for fine visual discriminations, photographic representations are needed. When an event is to be recorded for immediate distribution to wide audiences, video technologies are essential. Whereas film and projector must be delivered to each remote location, reception of broadcast video programs requires only a TV set—a common possession across most of the earth.

When an immediate analysis and correction of students' performance is desired, teachers can tape, observe, and advise. Such **"video feedback"** can be quite effective when used within the context of a systematic training program. True, many students are at first intimidated by the camera and may experience considerable anxiety and embarrassment when viewing an unfavorable image of themselves. No one likes to be confronted with his or her inadequacies. However, the initial uneasiness can be turned to good use by skilled teachers who are quick to provide guidance and encouragement. Teachers who employ video feedback are especially effective when they also serve as exemplary models of the performance students are attempting to master.[14]

Class filmmaking and videotaping involve many operations: cooperative planning, budgeting, research, creative writing, and technical production. Every student may participate and results generally bring considerable satisfaction. The positive attitudes experienced may well transfer to other activities, such as more willingly engaging in discussions about subject matter and collaborating with peers to achieve common ends.[15]

For prerecorded material, the laser videodisc is superior to tape. It has the following advantages:

- Disc-generated **images and sound are superior** to those obtained from most videotapes available today. Digital recording serves to eliminate these differences in quality.

- Videodiscs are **slow to deteriorate**; unlike tapes, they are unaffected by moisture and magnetism, and are highly resistant to breakage. (Just don't place one under your car's back seat window.)

- Individual frames encoded on videodiscs can be **indexed and displayed instantaneously**, and they can be presented systematically under control of a computer.

Videodiscs have the following disadvantages:

- Like phonodiscs, they **can't be edited or erased** for reuse on equipment commonly available to the public.

- The **cost** of producing even one disc is too great for an individual teacher or student. Savings come only with mass production.

- Videodisc players are **single purpose machines** with relatively limited utility in schools compared to microcomputers with CD-ROM drives and modems.

Video technologies make it possible to open schools where there is a shortage of teachers. Lessons may be presented to one group while the teacher works with another. At the high school and especially the college levels, entire courses may be presented by tape or disc. However, such practices are restricted in most states by the requirement that a credentialed teacher always be present (in person!) in the classroom.

Such restrictions may be appropriate for elementary schools, but not necessarily at the secondary level. Fully "accredited" TV courses might well benefit certain students in such subjects as calculus, organic chemistry, or elementary German for which no local teachers are available. Students could put questions to the program producers or other experts by email or telephone. Discussions and exams could be handled by tutors, themselves trained by TV. Even at high schools having comprehensive curricula, TV courses would enable some students to add electives by viewing lessons over the weekend. Other students could make up for courses missed or failed, while still others could graduate early by completing required courses during summer breaks. (See **Figure 10.08**.)

Commercial cable TV affords a wide range of programming. People living in areas not served by the networks may receive both network and PBS offerings. For those served by cable TV, a host of special interest programs may be seen—movies, news in depth, sports, dramatic and musical performances (often "live"), instructional courses, and so-called "adult entertainment." Unlike broadcast TV, the number of cable channels is not limited by available frequencies.

One danger of commercial cable is that it brings into the home programming that may be banned from public airwaves. When parents are out for the evening, youngsters may be exposed to unsavory programs. Another danger is that the best programming may find a more rewarding home in cable, thereby adversely affecting broadcast television. To cope with the problem, the FCC will have to continue monitoring trends in programming and regulating joint ownership of networks and cable companies.

The quality of cable TV should be constantly examined and its services put to constructive use. Religious

"*This never would've been possible, of course, before we got the VCR.*"

Figure 10.08. Especially in subjects where there is a shortage of teachers, entire lessons can be presented using videotape or interactive videodisc. What might be some limitations in doing so at the elementary school level? How might these be managed? Source: *Phi Delta Kappan,* 68 (September 1986), p. 84. Reprinted with permission of Martha Campbell.

and charitable organizations, municipal governments, and school districts could have their messages cablecast or may contract with a cable company to program a channel of their own. Educators could obtain a channel to provide regular instruction to homebound students, rally public support against gang violence and drug abuse, or take a stand on pending legislation. Such a channel would provide a forum where teachers, parents, students, and others could express their views.

Closed circuit TV permits even more extensive local control of programming. Teachers may lecture or perform demonstrations "live" before several groups of students in different classrooms. Also, taped presentations can be shown when teachers are unavailable. With CCTV there need be no concern to satisfy the commercial interest of a cable operator or the broadcast licensing requirements of government. To reach an adjoining campus not wired directly, short-range microwave transmissions can be arranged.

Along with cable, satellite technology makes the long-anticipated "television of abundance" more of a reality. The major networks long have dominated programming because in most American communities only three or four channels were available. In contrast, a communications satellite offers a wealth of programs to many different audiences. With satellite relay, a school may use the district station or a local cable station to broadcast its own programs across the country or even across the world. Students in San Francisco can exchange programs with their peers in Boston or Moscow.

In developing nations especially, satellites make possible the realization of instant communications networks. Contrast this with a nationwide terrestrial TV system with its infrastructure of roads and power stations—a system that would have taken India, for example, over a decade to build. Yet when NASA placed a satellite in orbit over Lake Victoria, East Africa, its TV broadcast signals could be picked up by any suitably equipped receiver on the subcontinent.

No doubt many developing nations similarly will continue to leapfrog the long, costly process of ground network-building to bring the advances in health and education needed to achieve sustained economic growth and full realization of their peoples' human potential. Communications satellites will help them move faster toward their most urgent goals—to reduce infant mortality, grow more food, cut birth rates, arrest the spread of AIDS, promote literacy, develop industrial skills, improve health services, and contribute to a sense of national identity **within the context of our common humanity**. Obstacles that need to be overcome are as follows.

First, there are **technical limitations** on space and broadcast frequencies. Communications satellites line up in geosynchronous orbits along the same equatorial ribbon. Those parked too close together may interfere with each other's signals. Obviously, advances in technology may reduce these and other technical problems, but nations still must cooperate if satellite broadcasting capability is to be distributed fairly. (See **Figure 10.09.**)

The second obstacle is **economic**. NASA's ATS-F showed that TV programs could be beamed to remote areas without expensive facilities—roads, buildings, power stations, personnel—ordinarily needed by a regional transmitting station. Nevertheless, making and launching satellites is costly, and community receiving stations, special home antennas, and TV sets may remain beyond the budgets of many developing nations for some time to come.

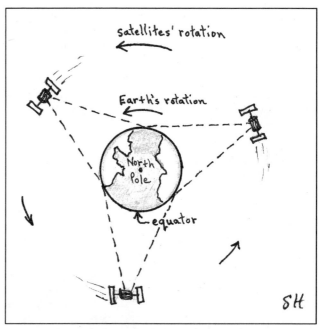

Figure 10.09. Communications satellites are "parked" in orbits about 22,300 miles directly above the equator. At this altitude, their speed of travel is such that they remain fixed above the same point on the earth below. As few as three such satellites are needed to provide telecommunications services across the globe. Nevertheless, the need to transmit vast quantities of electronic data of every sort—telephone, radio, TV, computer—has created a ring of satellites to match Saturn's.

A third obstacle is **political**. Many governments oppose uninvited direct broadcasting of television programs by foreign agencies. Others cite Article 19 of the *Universal Declaration of Human Rights* in support of the practice:

> Everyone has the right to freedom of opinion and expression; this right includes freedom to hold opinions without interference and to seek, receive, and impart information and ideas through any media and regardless of frontiers.

Why do so many nations object to direct broadcast satellite (DBS) television? There are many reasons. For example:

- Totalitarian regimes do not want their people to hear external criticism.

- Nations with deep religious and cultural traditions wish to insulate their people from secular thinking.

- Economically poor nations worry lest foreign TV unduly raise the material expectations of their people.

Nevertheless, nations have successfully shared satellite communications in pursuit of such common ends as vocational and language training and the containment of epidemics. In short, technology has provided essential tools for meeting human needs. It is up to people everywhere to learn how best to use them for the benefit of all. (See **Figure 10.10.**)

Benefits of film and TV, as with other media of mass communication and instruction, will be enhanced both by more selective viewing and by greater efforts to ensure wholesome programming. Responsibilities of governments are outlined in Article 17 of the United Nations *Convention of the Rights of the Child* as follows:

(a) Encourage the mass media to disseminate information and material of social and cultural benefit to the child and in accordance with the spirit of Article 29 [development of child's potential and of respect for human rights and cultural identity];

(b) Encourage international co-operation in the production, exchange and dissemination of such information and material from a diversity of cultural, national and international sources;

(c) Encourage the production and dissemination of children's books;

(d) Encourage the mass media to have particular regard to the linguistic needs of the child who belongs to a minority group or who is indigenous;

(e) Encourage the development of appropriate guidelines for the protection of the child from information and material injurious to his or her well-being, bearing in mind the provisions of Articles 13 [freedom to seek, receive, and impart information] and 18 [parents have primary responsibility for the upbringing of their children].[16]

Practical Guidelines

Production. If you can't find a suitable instructional film or TV program, why not produce, along with your students, a work of your own? The following guidelines, elaborations of those given in Chapter **9**, apply to the production of all types of programs having both audio and visual components. Most of the selection criteria for print, audio, pictures and graphics, and motion pictures described in previous chapters apply here as well.

Figure 10.10. Communications satellites provide instant radio and TV programming to areas lacking infrastructure ordinarily required for ground station transmission. In remote villages across the globe, people share in the benefits (as illustrated here). Local production of print materials and training of local "facilitators" ensure successful adaptation of programs made for mass audiences.

Step 1. Select a suitable topic. Consider your instructional objectives, the abilities of your students, and the availability of alternative instructional resources. Select a topic that matches objectives and abilities, yet is not adequately covered in readily available materials. Do not include subject matter that can be taught just as effectively by lecture and printed handouts. Include content that is stable, basic, and best expressed both visually and aurally. Also excellent as candidates for mediated presentation are complex, expensive, and possibly dangerous procedures in the sciences, and techniques in music and art.

Select a topic that can be covered in a program 10–30 minutes in length, allowing time for introduction and follow-up. Consider time and money needed for such tasks as production, testing, revision, duplication, and distribution. Allow for equipment, materials, facilities, travel, and talent. Involve students in all stages of planning, production, evaluation, and revision. (See **Figure 10.11.**)

"Higher."

Figure 10.11. Students are of great help in crafting video programs. Here they are setting up a "candid" shot that just might result in their experiencing some "real world" consequences. Reproduced with permission of William Canty.

Step 2. Write the specific objectives of the planned program. These should include the following elements:

Audience. Identify characteristics of the students for whom the program is being designed (e.g., age, abilities, interests, achievements).

Behavior. State what you expect your students to do after viewing and hearing the program. Reference might be made to tests involving factual recall, or to observations of performance (e.g., drawing, dancing), specific behaviors (e.g., sharing, studying), or crafting of a product (e.g., essay, poem, computer program, sculpture).

Conditions. Describe conditions under which your students are to show what they have learned. Such conditions include location, materials, and time constraints.

Degree. Specify the level of performance you deem to be acceptable. This might be given as a score on a test, or a degree of precision, quality of a product, or another observable standard of achievement.

Step 3. Select and organize program content. List facts, concepts, and other subject matter your students need to learn. Add connections to what they already know, to other parts of the curriculum, and to the ultimate objectives of the course. Decide which elements are best presented visually and which aurally. Think of strategies to gain students' attention, arouse their interest, and promote comprehension.

Write essential content on 4 by 6 inch index cards, one paragraph per card. Using a large cork display board or similar device, tack closely related cards under appropriate headings and then in proper order under subheadings. Eliminate redundant cards and fill gaps with new ones. Add introductory cards and those that provide examples, questions, and reviews.

Step 4. Make a storyboard. Based on the planning cards produced in step 3, draft a series of storycards like the one illustrated in **Figure 8.15**. The main features of these cartoon-like cards are sketches of planned visual images and written descriptions of planned narration, music, and sound effects. Also included are: (a) comments about how these two elements are to be produced, (b) a program title, and (c) a number (in pencil to allow for revisions) representing the card's place in the program sequence.

Tack the completed storycards to a large display board in proper sequence from left to right beginning at the top to produce what is called a "storyboard." Examine each card and consider how well the planned visual image complements the planned narration, sound effect, or music. Then assess how well each card relates to those preceding and following it. Revise and reorder cards as needed.

Step 5. Ask colleagues and students to examine your storyboard. Ask them to study it from beginning to end and then evaluate the extent to which they learned what you intended. If learning is found to be adequate at this stage, reexamine your objectives, instruments, and motives. Why incur additional expense if you can reliably achieve objectives by mass producing and distributing your storycards and call it a book? Will the film of TV version teach things not adequately covered in your stated objectives or measured by your tests? Well, do the best you can in revising your objectives and tests. Will the planned program take significantly less time to complete than paging through storycards? If so, proceed. Is electronic distribution to remote locations planned? That is a good justification for TV production, but books can be delivered almost as cheaply as film. Weigh carefully the distinctive qualities of each medium and the benefits of novelty. Reexamine any blind attachment you may have for one medium over the other.

Step 6. Make revisions based on comments and test results. Technical errors are easily corrected. Learner comments concerning the validity of content must be checked against authoritative sources. Poor test performance requires even more extensive analyses of content, pedagogy, and of the tests themselves. Once revisions have been made, try out the modified version with a new group of students. Repeat this test/revise procedure until the program is found effective near the levels specified in your objectives. I say "near" because, again, if your draft program meets the criteria of effectiveness and efficiency, why proceed any further? Bind it and move on to the next project. If some objectives remain unmet and electronic distribution is required to reach the target audience, advance to Step 7.

Step 7. Write a detailed script based on the completed storyboard. Divide a standard-sized piece of typing paper into three columns—"Notes," "Visual," and "Audio." Under "Notes" indicate number in sequence, type of shot ("close up," etc.), camera angle, camera motion, special effects, time (duration of shot), and transition technique ("fade out," "dissolve," etc.). Under "Visual" describe in words or sketch what is to appear on the screen, usually beginning with the program title and proceeding through each planned scene to the end of the program. Under "Audio" write everything the narrator is to say and specify what music and other sounds are to be included. (See **Figure 10.12.**)

Step 8. Test and revise your script as you did your storycards. If you have endured to this point, I'll share with you that fact that no one has ever found the time or money to do as much testing and revising as I suggest here would be beneficial. I believe that it was Jacquetta Megarry who decades ago, writing of programmed instruction, suggested that we make "successive approximations" to the ideal. Feature filmmakers routinely screen early cuts, and make changes based on audience reactions. The concept is valid; your budget and patience are limited. So "think globally; act locally." Perhaps you could profitably use the script in the target class for several semesters before committing it to film or tape.

Step 9. Prepare for production. Obtain equipment and materials. Select suitable locations and talent. Make sure that technicians and performers are familiar with the script. Conduct rehearsals until all goes smoothly.

Step 10. Record performances in easily-managed segments. This permits performers and technicians to review their parts carefully right before the "shoot" and to maintain a high level of attention throughout. It also permits retaking of difficult scenes more times at less cost than if they are shot as part of longer segments.

Step 11. Edit the best "takes" and piece them together as dictated by the script. This procedure is most commonly done with two recorders and special effects equipment for fading in and out and for generating titles, etc. *Microsoft Video for Windows*, *Pro Movie Spectrum*, *Premiere*, *Media Merge*, *Splice*, and *Video Blaster* enable you to cut, copy, and paste digital video and audio data from a variety of sources to produce products adequate (jumpy video and poor audio/video synchronization remained problems in mid-1990s) for most educational purposes. Besides the video clips that come with these programs and those you shoot yourself, you might add familiar voices, lines, and tunes to spice up the presentation (e.g., *Microsoft SoundBits*, *Windows AudioClips*).[17]

Utilization. Linda Wolcott (Utah State University) has called attention to limitations inherent in providing live video-based instruction at a distance. To compensate for diminished contextual cues, immediate feedback, and peer interactions she recommended that teachers reflect on distinctive attributes of their **context, learners,** and **strategies.**[18]

With respect to **context** Wolcott suggested that teachers ask themselves:

- What are my expectations of this delivery medium?
- What can I count on to be the same and what will be different about teaching and learning in this environment?
- Can the objectives I have for this course be adequately met in this context?

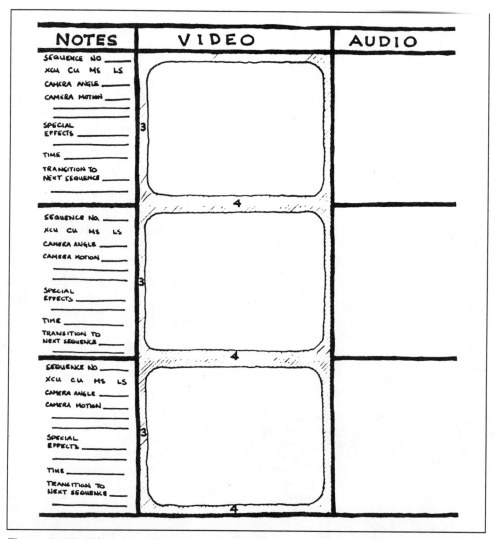

Figure 10.12. Although audiovisual programs may be produced directly from storycards, a script like the one shown here eases photoduplication and adds visual coherence for use by crew and talent. I suggest that you enlarge the "Notes" and "Audio" sections of your adaptation of this form to fill standard-sized sheets of paper and thereby permit entry of all required information. Source: John LeBaron, *Making Television: A Video Production Guide for Teachers* (New York: Teachers College Press, 1981), p. 196. Reprinted courtesy of Teachers College Press.

- What are the influences, both positive and negative, on learning in this setting?

- How do I make maximum use of this medium while minimizing its limitations?

To guide reflecting on **learners** she suggested asking:

- What are students' needs and what do they expect from this course?

- What do I know (and how can I find out) about the students' entry skills, cognitive styles and background?

- What do students find motivating about instruction?

- How can I build on students' experiences and provide instruction that is relevant and applicable?
- How can I guide and support students in their learning?
- How do I assure the students a quality learning experience?

In relation to **instructional strategies** she suggested that teachers ask:

- Am I considering methods because they are familiar and comfortable?
- Are the methods under consideration those which utilize the medium to its best advantage, or are they attempts to reproduce face-to-face instruction?
- What strategies would optimally achieve expectations in light of the variables of students, content, and context?
- What adjustments are required to accommodate instructional activities and visuals to distance delivery?
- Are the methods and techniques likely to encourage participation and interaction?

Such careful reflection, rightly claimed Wolcott, would best contribute to design of distance education programs that would reduce interpersonal distance, nurture interaction, increase feedback, and enhance learning.

Summary and Conclusions

In this chapter we have looked at ways in which video technologies are being used to create a "television of abundance." Videotape and disc preserve TV shows made to entertain or enlighten. Cables and satellites carry these images and sounds across the globe. Problems of technical quality have largely been solved by advances in electronics. Camcorders enable everyone to produce videos and computer technology eases editing. (See **Figure 10.13**.)

Nevertheless, educators still must strive to ensure that the dazzling programs they craft clearly reflect **worthwhile objectives, subject matter expertise**, and **sound pedagogy**. In Chapters **2–5** we saw how systematic procedures and computer technologies contribute to

"It's the annual elementary school play."

Figure 10.13. With so many families now owning camcorders, parents have become a great resource to help our students collaborate in the production of videos. How might we best enlist their services? Source: *Phi Delta Kappan,* 75 (April 1994), p. 583. Reprinted with permission of William Canty.

this endeavor. In the next chapter we explore in more detail diverse and exciting uses of computers to facilitate learning.

Notes

[1]17 U.S.C., Section 107 of PL#94-553, the *1976 Copyright Act.* **Note that these guidelines apply also to print, visual, audio, and computer technologies.** Rosemary Talab, in her "Copyright, Legal, and Ethical Issues in the Internet Environment," *Tech Trends,* 39 (March 1994), p. 12, identified sections of law pertaining to classroom use of all such copyrighted materials, noting that such use must:
- be part of "systematic instructional activities". . . ,
- be "directly related . . . to teaching" . . . ,
- be "in classrooms or similar places" . . . ,
- be "without any purpose of direct or indirect commercial advantage" . . . , and
- be "without payment of any fee or other compensation" . . . .

[2]Sinofsky, Esther R., *A Copyright Primer for Educational and Industrial Media Producers,* 2nd ed. (Washington, DC: Association for Educational Communications and Technology, 1993); *Off-Air Videotaping in Education: Copyright Issues, Decisions, Implications* (New York: Bowker, 1984); Miller, Jerome K., *Using Copyrighted Videocassettes in Classrooms, Libraries, and Training Centers,* 2nd ed. (Friday Harbor, WA: Copyright Information Services, 1988).

[3]Ekhaml, Leticia, "10 Most Common Questions About Videodiscs," *Media & Methods,* 30 (November/December 1993), p. 31.

[4]Bower, Sally, Baumbach, Donna, & Bird, Mary, "Barcode Bonanza," *Media & Methods,* 29 (January/February 1993), p. 73. See also "Creating and Using Barcodes for Laser Videodiscs," *Media & Methods,* 30 (March/April 1994), p. 12; Smith, Mac, & Gustafson, Kent, "Using a Barcode Reader with Interactive Videodiscs," *Tech Trends,* 40 (January/February 1995), pp. 29–32.

[5]*The Educational Technology Anthology Series, Volume One: Interactive Video* (Englewood Cliffs, NJ: Educational Technology Publications, 1990); Graeber, Janet, & Sullivan, Jamie, "Update on Videodiscs Across All Subjects," *Media & Methods,* 31 (September/October 1994), pp. 27–28.

[6]Lochte, Robert H., *Interactive Television and Instruction: A Guide to Technology, Technique, Facilities Design, and Classroom Management* (Englewood Cliffs, NJ: Educational Technology Publications, 1993).

[7]Boroughs, Don L., "Battle of the Boxes: Interactive Television Fights the PC for the Consumer's Time and Money," *U.S. News & World Report,* 117 (September 12, 1994), pp. 70–72.

[8]Wiener, Leonard, "A Little Dish that Does a Big Job," *U.S. News & World Report,* 117 (November 28, 1994), p. 125.

[9]Gilbert, John K., Temple, Annette, & Underwood, Craig, *Satellite Technology in Education* (New York: Routledge, 1991); Hudspeth, DeLayne R., & Brey, Ronald G., *Instructional Telecommunications: Principles and Applications* (New York: Praeger, 1986); *Educational Technology Anthology Series, Volume Three: Telecommunications for Learning* (Englewood Cliffs, NJ: Educational Technology Publications, 1991); Willis, Barry, *Distance Education: A Practical Guide* (Englewood Cliffs, NJ: Educational Technology Publications, 1993); Wagner, Ellen D., "Variables Affecting Distance Educational Program Success," *Educational Technology,* 33 (April 1993), pp. 28–32.

[10]Tiene, Drew, & Whitmore, Evonne, "Beyond 'Channel One': How Schools Are Using Their Schoolwide Television Networks," *Educational Technology,* 35 (May/June 1995), p. 38.

[11]"IDEANET to Connect U.S. Schools," *Tech Trends,* 39 (April/May 1994), pp. 3–4.

[12]Stout, Connie, "Issues Facing the National Information Infrastructure," *ISTE Update,* 6 (April/May 1994), p. 5.

[13]Gilkey, Richard W., "16mm Film, Videotape, Videodisc—Weighing the Differences," *Media & Methods,* 22 (March/April 1986), pp. 8–9; Davis, Bernard, *et al.,* "A Comparison of the Effects of Film and Videotape Presentation on Student Recall," *Programmed Learning and Educational Technology,* 20 (May 1983), pp. 115–116; Barnard, John, "Video-Based Instruction: Issues of Effectiveness, Interaction, and Learner Control," *Journal of Educational Technology Systems,* 21, 1(1992–93), pp. 45–50; Thompson, Ann, Simonson, Michael, & Hargrave, Constance, *Educational Technology: A Review of the Research* (Washington, DC: Association for Educational Communications and Technology, 1992).

[14]Zuber-Skerritt, Ortrun, ed., *Video in Higher Education* (East Brunswick, NJ: Nichols, 1984).

[15]Berg, Bryan, & Turner, Dianne, "MTV Unleashed: Sixth Graders Create Music Videos Based on Works of Art,"

EDUCOM Review, 27 (January/February 1992), pp. 39–43; Brown, Kenneth, "Video Production in the Classroom: Creating Successes for Students and Schools," *Tech Trends,* 38 (April/May 1993), pp. 32–35; Barron, Ann, & Fisher, Hugh, "Affordable Videodisc Production: A Model for Success," *Tech Trends,* 38 (March 1993), pp. 15–21; Sorge, Dennis H., Campbell, John P., & Russell, James D., "Evaluating Interactive Video: Software and Hardware," *Tech Trends,* 38 (April/May 1993), pp. 19–26.

[16]*Human Rights Fact Sheet No. 10: The Rights of the Child* (Geneva: United Nations, 1990), p. 18.

[17]Benton, Jeffrey E., "Focus on Video Production," *Media & Methods,* 29 (May/June 1993), pp. 28, 30; Brown, Kenneth, "Video Production in the Classroom: Creating Successes for Students and Schools," *Tech Trends,* 38 (April/May 1993), pp. 32–35.

[18]Wolcott, Linda L., "The Distance Teacher as Reflective Practitioner," *Educational Technology,* 35 (January/February 1995), pp. 39–43.

Sources

Video recording and filmmaking are covered in:

Aldridge, Henry B., & Liggett, Lucy A., *Audio-Video Production* (Englewood Cliffs, NJ: Prentice-Hall, 1990).

Bermingham, Alan, Talbot-Smith, Michael, Angold-Stephens, Ken, & Boyce, Ed, *The Video Studio,* 3rd ed. (Boston: Focal, 1994).

Bryant, Steve, *Basic Camcorder Guide* (Amherst, NY: Amherst Media, 1994).

Caruso, James R., & Arthur, Mavis E., *A Beginner's Guide to Producing TV: Complete Planning Techniques and Scripts to Shoot* (Englewood Cliffs, NJ: Prentice-Hall, 1990).

Caruso, James R., & Arthur, Mavis E., *Video Editing and Post Production* (Englewood Cliffs, NJ: Prentice-Hall, 1992).

Cooper, Dona, *Writing Great Screenplays for Film and TV* (New York: Prentice-Hall, 1994).

The Educational Technology Anthology Series, Volume One: Interactive Video (Englewood Cliffs, NJ: Educational Technology Publications, 1990).

The Educational Technology Anthology Series, Volume Three: Telecommunications for Learning (Englewood Cliffs, NJ: Educational Technology Publications, 1991).

Ellington, Henry, *Producing Teaching Materials: A Handbook for Teachers and Trainers,* 2nd ed. (East Brunswick, NJ: Nichols, 1993).

Fielding, Ken, *Introduction to Television Production* (White Plains, NY: Longman, 1990).

Fleming, Malcolm, & Levie, W. Howard, eds., *Instructional Message Design: Principles from the Behavioral and Cognitive Sciences,* 2nd ed. (Englewood Cliffs, NJ: Educational Technology Publications, 1993).

Hausman, Carl, with Palombo, Philip J., *Modern Video Production: Tools, Techniques, Applications* (New York: HarperCollins, 1993).

Hitchcock, Peter, *Videography: The Successful Home Video Series* [8 videocassettes] (Toronto: Peter Hitchcock Productions and TV Ontario, 1992).

Huber, Michael, *A–Z of Camcorders and Video* (Hove, Sussex: Hove Foto Books, 1991).

Imke, Steven, *Interactive Video Management and Production* (Englewood Cliffs, NJ: Educational Technology Publications, 1991).

Kallenberger, Richard N., & Cvjetnicanin, George D., *Film into Video: A Guide to Merging the Technologies* (Boston: Focal, 1994).

Kardas, Pat, *Cheap Shots: Video Production for Nonprofits* (Metuchen, NJ: Scarecrow Press, 1993).

Lewis, Roland, *Learn to Make Videos in a Weekend* (New York: Knopf, 1993).

Lochte, Robert H., *Interactive Television and Instruction: A Guide to Technology, Technique, Facilities Design, and Classroom Management* (Englewood Cliffs, NJ: Educational Technology Publications, 1993).

Mason, David, & Enzmann, Alexander, *Making Movies on Your PC: Dream Up, Design, and Direct 3-D Movies* (Corte Madera, CA: Waite Group Press, 1993).

Matza, Aleks, *The Video Production Organizer: A Guide for Businesses, Schools, Government Agencies, and Professional Associations* (Boston: Focal, 1995).

McComb, Gordon, & Rathbone, Andy, *VCRs & Camcorders for Dummies* (Foster City, CA: IDG Books Worldwide, 1994).

Miller, Jerome K., *Using Copyrighted Videocassettes in Classrooms, Libraries, and Training Centers*, 2nd ed. (Friday Harbor, WA: Copyright Information Services, 1988).

Miller, Jerome K., ed., *Video Copyright Permissions: A Guide to Securing Permission to Retain, Perform, and Transmit Television Programs Videotaped Off the Air* (Friday Harbor, WA: Copyright Information Services, 1989).

Millerson, Gerald, *Video Production Handbook*, 2nd ed. (Boston: Focal, 1992).

Musburger, Robert B., *Single-Camera Video Production* (Boston: Focal, 1993).

Rabb, Margaret Y., *The Presentation Design Book*, 2nd ed. (Chapel Hill, NC: Ventura Press, 1993).

Reynolds, Angus, & Anderson, Ronald H., *Selecting and Developing Media for Instruction*, 3rd ed. (New York: Van Nostrand Reinhold, 1991).

Rosenthal, Alan, *Writing Docudrama: Dramatizing Reality for Film and TV* (Boston: Focal, 1995).

Rowlands, Avril, illustrated by Cant, Colin, *The Continuity Handbook: A Guide for Single-Camera Shooting*, 3rd ed. (Boston: Focal, 1994).

Satterthwaite, Les L., *Instructional Media: Materials, Production, and Utilization*, 2nd ed. (Dubuque, IA: Kendall-Hunt, 1991).

Sherman, Mendel, *Videotaping the Pictorial Sequence* (Washington, DC: Association for Educational Communications and Technology, 1991).

Sinofsky, Esther R., *A Copyright Primer for Educational and Industrial Media Producers* (Washington, DC: Association for Educational Communications and Technology, 1988).

Squires, Malcolm, *Video Camcorder School: A Practical Guide to Making Great Home Videos* (Pleasantville, NY: The Reader's Digest Association, 1992).

Swain, Dwight V., & Swain, Joye R., *Scripting for the New AV Technologies*, 2nd ed. (Boston: Focal, 1991).

Talab, Rosemary S., *Copyright and Instructional Technologies: A Guide to Fair Use and Permissions Procedures*, 2nd ed. (Washington, DC: Association for Educational Communications and Technology, 1989).

Thomas, Erwin K., *Make Better Videos with Your Camcorder* (Blue Ridge Summit, PA: Tab Books, 1991).

Thomas, James L., *Nonprint Production for Students, Teachers, and Media Specialists: A Step-by-Step Guide*, 2nd ed. (Englewood, CO: Libraries Unlimited, 1988).

Utz, Peter, *Video User's Handbook*, 3rd ed. (Englewood Cliffs, NJ: Prentice-Hall, 1989).

Utz, Peter, *Create Excellent Video* (Englewood Cliffs, NJ: Prentice-Hall, 1990).

Utz, Peter, *Today's Video Equipment, Set Up, and Production*, 2nd ed. (White Plains, NY: Knowledge Industry, 1992).

Van Nostran, William, *The Scriptwriter's Handbook: New Techniques for Media Writers* (White Plains, NY: Knowledge Industry, 1989).

Valmont, William J., *Creating Videos for School Use* (Boston: Allyn and Bacon, 1995).

Verna, Tony, edited by Bode, William T., *Global Television: How to Create Effective Television for the Future* (Boston: Focal, 1993).

Vleck, Charles W., *Adoptable Copyright Policy: A Board Policy and Faculty Copyright Manual for Use by School Districts, Colleges & Universities* (Washington, DC: Association for Educational Communications and Technology, 1992).

Watkinson, John, *The Art of Digital Video*, 2nd ed. (Boston: Focal, 1994).

Watkinson, John, *Compression in Video & Audio* (Boston: Focal, 1995).

Whitver, Kathryn Shaw, *The Digital Videomaker's Guide* (Studio City, CA: Michael Wiese Productions, 1995).

Wiegand, Ingrid, *Professional Video Production*, 2nd ed. (White Plains, NY: 1992).

Williams, Gene B., *Guide to VCRs, Camcorders & Home Video* (Radnor, PA: Chilton Book Co., 1990).

Willis, Edgar E., & Aldridge, Henry B., *Television, Cable, and Radio: A Communications Approach* (Englewood Cliffs, NJ: Prentice-Hall, 1991).

Willis, Edgar E., & D'Arienzo, Camille, *Writing Scripts for Television, Radio, and Film*, 3rd ed. (Fort Worth, TX: Harcourt Brace Jovanovich College Publishers, 1992).

Wolenik, Robert I., *Camcorder Survival Guide* (Carmel, IN: Sams, 1990).

Wurtzel, Alan, & Rosenbaum, John, *Television Production,* 4th ed. (New York: McGraw-Hill, 1995).

Zettl, Herbert, *Television Production Handbook,* 5th ed. (White Plains, NY: Knowledge Industry, 1992).

Zettl, Herbert, *Television Production Workbook,* 5th ed. (Belmont, CA: Wadsworth, 1992).

Video distribution is covered in:

Arwady, Joseph W., & Gayeski, Diane M., *Using Video: Interactive and Linear Designs* (Englewood Cliffs, NJ: Educational Technology Publications, 1989).

Barron, Ann E., & Orwig, Gary W., *New Technologies in Education: A Beginner's Guide* (Englewood, CO: Libraries Unlimited, 1993).

Bosworth, David P., *Open Learning* (London: Cassell, 1991).

Calder, Judith, *Programme Evaluation and Quality: A Comprehensive Guide to Setting Up an Evaluation System* (London: Kogan Page, 1994).

De Vaney, Ann, ed., *Watching Channel One: The Convergence of Students, Technology, and Private Business* (Albany, NY: State University of New York Press, 1994).

Duning, Becky S., Van Kekerix, Marvin J., & Zaborowski, Leon M., *Reaching Learners Through Telecommunications* (San Francisco, CA: Jossey-Bass, 1993).

Gayeski, Diane M., *Corporate and Instructional Video* (Englewood Cliffs, NJ: Prentice-Hall, 1991).

Gilbert, John K., Temple, Annette, & Underwood, Craig, *Satellite Technology in Education* (New York: Routledge, 1991).

Grant, August E., ed., *Communication Technology Update,* 3rd ed. (Boston: Focal, 1994).

Hansen, Douglas E., *Educational Technology Telecommunications Dictionary with Acronyms* (Englewood Cliffs, NJ: Educational Technology Publications, 1991).

Harry, Keith, Magnus, John, & Keegan, Desmond, eds., *Distance Education: New Perspectives* (London: Routledge, 1993).

Henry, Jane, *Teaching Through Projects* (London: Kogan Page in association with the Institute of Educational Technology, Open University, 1994).

Hodge, Winston William, *Interactive Television: A Comprehensive Guide for Multimedia Technologists* (New York: McGraw-Hill, 1995).

Holmberg, Borje, *Theory and Practice of Distance Education,* 2nd ed. (London: Routledge, 1995).

Hudspeth, DeLayne R., & Brey, Ronald G., *Instructional Telecommunications: Principles and Applications* (New York: Praeger, 1986).

Inglis, Andrew F., *Satellite Technology: An Introduction* (Boston: Focal, 1991).

Keegan, Desmond, ed., *Theoretical Principles of Distance Education* (London: Routledge, 1993).

Kember, David, *Open Learning Courses for Adults: A Model of Student Progress* (Englewood Cliffs, NJ: Educational Technology Publications, 1995).

Milheim, William D., ed., *Distance Education: A Selected Bibliography* (Englewood Cliffs, NJ: Educational Technology Publications, 1992).

Mirabito, Michael M. A., *The New Communications Technologies,* 2nd ed. (Boston: Focal, 1994).

Peters, Otto, edited by Keegan, Desmond, *Otto Peters on Distance Education: The Industrialization of Teaching and Learning* (London: Routledge, 1994).

Platte, Mary K., *The Beginning of Satellite Communication: Airborne ITV, MPATI, and the Ohio Story* (Dubuque, IA: Kendall/Hunt, 1982).

Race, Philip, *The Open Learning Handbook: Promoting Quality in Designing and Delivering Flexible Learning,* 2nd ed. (London: Kogan Page, 1994).

Roberts, Nancy, Blakeslee, George, Brown, Maureen, & Lenk, Cecilia, *Integrating Telecommunications into Education* (Boston: Allyn and Bacon, 1990).

Rowntree, Derek, *Exploring Open and Distance Learning* (East Brunswick, NJ: Nichols, 1992).

Schlosser, Charles A., & Anderson, Mary L., *Distance Education: Review of the Literature* (Washington, DC: Association for Educational Communications and Technology, 1994).

Schwartz, Ed, *The Educator's Handbook to Interactive Videodisc,* 2nd ed. (Washington, DC: Association for Educational Communications and Technology, 1987).

Van den Brande, Lieve, *Flexible and Distance Learning* (Chichester, England: Wiley, 1993).

Verduin Jr., John R., & Clark, Thomas A., *Distance Education: The Foundations of Effective Practice* (San Francisco: Jossey-Bass, 1991).

Watkins, Barbara L., & Wright, Stephen J., eds., *The Foundations of American Distance Education: A Century of Collegiate Correspondence Study* (Dubuque, IA: Kendall/Hunt, 1991).

Willis, Barry, *Distance Education: A Practical Guide* (Englewood Cliffs, NJ: Educational Technology Publications, 1993).

Willis, Barry, ed., *Distance Education: Strategies and Tools* (Englewood Cliffs, NJ: Educational Technology Publications, 1994).

Providers of instructional videodiscs include:

AIMS Multimedia: 1-800-367-2467
BFA Educational Media: 1-800-221-1274
CEL Educational Resources: 1-800-235-3339
Churchill Media: 1-800-334-7830
Coronet/MTI: 1-800-777-8100
Davidson & Associates: 1-800-545-7677
D.C. Heath: 1-800-235-3565
Decision Development Corp.: 1-800-835-4332
Emerging Technology Consultants: 1-612-639-3973
Encyclopaedia Britannica: 1-800-554-9862
Films for the Humanities & Sciences: 1-800-257-5126
Fred Lasswell, Inc.: 1-813-289-4486
Glencoe/McGraw-Hill: 1-800-848-1567

Great Plains National: 1-800-228-4630
Harcourt Brace Publishing: 1-800-782-4479
Houghton Mifflin: 1-800-758-6762
Laser Learning: 1-800-70-LASER
Laser Learning Technologies: 1-800-722-3505
McDougal Littel: 1-800-323-5435
National Geographic Society: 1-800-368-2728
Nystrom New Media: 1-800-621-8086
Optical Data Corporation: 1-800-248-8478
Optilearn: 1-800-850-9480
PBS Video: 1-800-344-3337
Rainbow Educational Media: 1-800-331-4047
Scholastic: 1-800-541-5513
Scott Resources: 1-800-289-9299
Silver Burdett Ginn: 1-800-848-9500
Sunburst/Wings for Learning: 1-800-321-7511
Tom Snyder Productions: 1-800-342-0236
Videodiscovery: 1-800-548-3472
The Voyager Co.: 1-800-446-2001
VTAE: 1-800-821-6313
Ztek: 1-800-247-1603

Providers of satellite/cable/ITV programming include:

Agency for Instructional Technology: 1-800-457-4509
Arts & Entertainment Network: 1-212-661-4500
Arts and Sciences Teleconferencing Service, Oklahoma State University: 1-800-452-2787
Cable in the Classroom: 1-703-845-1400
Cable News Network: 1-800-344-6219
C-SPAN: 1-800-523-7586
The Discovery Channel: 1-301-986-1999
Great Plains National: 1-800-228-4630
The Kentucky Network: 1-800-354-9067
The Learning Channel: 1-800-346-0032
Pacific Mountain Network: 1-303-837-8000
PBS K–12 Learning Services: 1-703-739-5402
Public Media Incorporated: 1-800-343-4312
Mind Extension University: 1-800-777-MIND
TI-IN Network: 1-800-624-2272
TV Ontario: 1-800-331-9566
Western Instructional Television: 1-213-466-860

Journals of interest to distance educators worldwide include:

The American Journal of Distance Education (USA)
Distance Education (Australia)
The Distance Educator (USA)
India Journal of Open Learning
Journal of Distance Education (Canada)
Open Learning (United Kingdom)

Figure 10.14. Equipment and supplies long have been provided *gratis* to schools in exchange for a bit of favorable corporate name exposure. Do you think that airing a few commercials during class time is a reasonable price to pay? Source: *Phi Delta Kappan,* 73 (December 1992), p. 339. Reprinted with permission of Andrew Toos.

Study Items

1. List features and primary uses of videotape. Identify those of most value to you as a teacher.

2. Summarize copyright regulations concerning conditions under which teachers may use taped TV programs in their classes.

3. Give three examples of school use of "video feedback." Identify any reservations you might have about any one of these uses.

4. What advantages do videodiscs have over videotape in the production of instructional programs?

5. Assess the relative merits of "in-person" instruction versus "live" instruction carried to remote locations by cable.

6. How much do you think is added to the value of a televised lesson for the student who can ask questions of the instructor by telephone?

7. How would you integrate videotext or another form of on-line database retrieval system into a class you might teach?

8. In what senses is computer-based interactive video "interactive?" Identify other senses of interaction that might be lacking.

9. Describe some specific examples of using communications satellites to provide instruction.

10. The thousands of school districts who accepted *Channel One* initially were required to air two minutes of commercials with each ten minutes of programming. Would you accept this condition to obtain free video or computer equipment? Justify your answer. (See **Figure 10.14**.)

11. Diagram technologies that might intervene between the shooting of a scene and viewing of that scene.

12. What advantages does the process of videotaping have over filming? Consider shooting, editing, and special effects.

13. What special advantages do communications satellites offer schools in rural areas?

14. Identify obstacles to realizing the educational potential of satellite broadcasting. How might these be overcome?

15. Rank video recording and distribution technologies in accord with how much you anticipate each will enhance your teaching. Justify your ranking in terms of student characteristics, instructional objectives, and resources.

16. Identify keys to the success of distance education ("telecourses") apart from video content and quality.

17. How would you integrate teleconferencing into your teaching?

Suggested Activities

1. Obtain a source book listed above about audiovisual production. Write a short script designed to illustrate a concept. Transfer the script to storycards and order these on a storyboard.

2. Visit a bookstore and ask to see selections on amateur video recording. Purchase one that best meets your needs and summarize the main points for your classmates.

3. Attend a computer software exhibition to see a demonstration of *Microsoft Video for Windows, Pro Movie Spectrum, Premiere, Media Merge, Splice,* and *Video Blaster.*

4. See demonstrations of interactive video at your local shopping mall. Many stores now use it to help you select, order, and use the merchandise they sell.

5. Prepare a short speech and record your presentation of it. Describe how it feels to see your performance. List changes you might make as a result of viewing the tape. Make the changes and try again.

6. Write to the addresses given above to obtain lists of programs currently available via satellite. Also request procedures and fees.

7. Visit an elementary school for one day and note use of video recording and distribution technologies. Note instances where they appear helpful and others where they appear obtrusive. Identify areas where you think such technologies might contribute.

8. Inform me of errors in this chapter and let me know of important material I have omitted at Internet: hackbarths@ aol.com.

9. Share with me your responses to the above study items and your experiences in completing suggested activities.

Chapter 11

Computer-Based Learning

Chapter Content and Objectives

Computers have revolutionized industry and communications, managing our finances, and prolonging our lives. They have become indispensable to science and engineering and are transforming education. Computer-based learning has been mainstreamed into classrooms. After reading this chapter, you should be able to:

- Define **basic terms**—"bit," "byte," "RAM," "ROM."
- Describe **pioneering projects** in the use of computers to provide instruction.
- Distinguish among several kinds of **computer-based learning** (CBL).
- List characteristics of **programming languages**.
- Assess **uses** of CBL in education.
- Specify **criteria** for selecting and designing CBL materials.
- Describe aspects of **"computer literacy"** and how to teach them.

How Computers Work

A computer not only receives information, it manipulates, communicates, and stores it. It breaks these processes down into logical operations that can be carried out using **"binary"** numbers—0001 for the number "one," 0010 for a "two," 0011 for "three," etc., and such strings as 11000001 ("A") and 11000010 ("B") to represent letters of the alphabet, and it can perform millions of operations a second.

Each digit in the string of zeros and ones is called a **"bit."** The group of digits making up a single number or character is called a **"byte."** Most early microcomputers encoded each character with a set of eight digits. Today's micros are being fitted with 16- and 32-bit chips to expand vastly the magnitude of data they can handle.

The core of a computer is the **"central processing unit."** This unit interprets instructions, operates on data, and coordinates activities of the entire system. In a personal computer, this unit is a small silicon chip, called a **"microprocessor,"** having up to one million electronic components. Other chips form the two main types of "memory"—"random-access memory" (**RAM**), for receiving instructions and data that can be modified, and "read-only memory" (**ROM**) for holding instructions that are permanent (like how to control the flow of data among a computer's components).

Information (test scores, statistics, student responses, etc.) is **"input"** to the computer through a keyboard, mouse, magnetic tape, diskette, CD-ROM, light pen, touch-sensitive screen, barcode reader, or microphone The computer's **"output"** usually is displayed on a **"monitor"**—either a cathode-ray tube (CRT) or liquid crystal display (LCD)—and may be printed on paper. A device called a **"modem"** (for modulator-demodulator) converts the digital output into analog signals for transmission by telephone lines to other computers anywhere in the world. (See **Figure 11.01**.)

A personal computer may be connected to just one set of input and output units (**"peripherals"**) for exclusive use by a single operator. Alternatively, several computers can be linked to form a **"local area network"** (**LAN**) for the purpose of sharing information. The "host" computer appraises the input from each "node" so quickly that it can serve many users concurrently, a process called **"timesharing."**

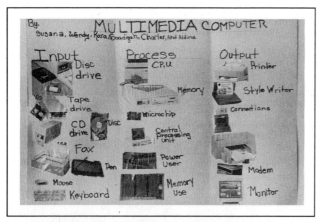

Figure 11.01. Following a lesson in which I engage students in distinguishing among categories of computer hardware, I ask them to construct a collage like the one shown here by Lorna Davis's (P.S. 6, Manhattan) fourth graders. Can you identify components that are under the wrong category or that could have been placed under two categories? Reproduced with permission of Carmen Fariña.

Computer hardware can do little by itself. To operate, it needs programs, or sets of instructions, known as **"software."** Software for today's microcomputers comes ready to use in the form of small (3½ inch) plastic diskettes, circuit boards, and CDs. When loaded (**"booted up"**) into the computer's RAM, the software enables one to write letters (**"word processing,"** e.g., *WordPerfect, WordStar, Microsoft Word*), organize information (**"database management,"** e.g., *dBASE IV, Paradox, Microsoft Access*), draft a budget (on a **"spreadsheet,"** e.g., *Lotus 1-2-3, Excel, Quattro Pro*), receive instruction, obtain information, or play games. The first three functions, indispensable to business, commonly are integrated in packages that allow moving information from one application to the other (e.g., *Claris Works, Enable, Microsoft Works*). Instructional programs, ranging from *Reader Rabbit* to *Math Blaster*, cover most subjects and all grade levels. CBL software that integrates text, audio, and video to provide information as requested by the user is called **"interactive multimedia,"** covered more thoroughly in Chapter **12.**

Advances in software design have made computers more **"user friendly"** (or "discoverable") so that many functions can now be done by people with no technical background. Little drawings (**"icons"**) represent programs and files, and by moving a hand-held device

(**"mouse"**) across a desk top and pushing a button (**"clicking"**), the operation is carried out. In effect, icons provide "windows" (**graphical user interface** or GUI, "gooey") to the operations without having to use complex commands of the **"operating system."** (See **Figure 11.02.**)

The terminology of computer failure is steeped in metaphor. A **"bug"** in a program's list of instructions to the computer prevents proper operation. The term reportedly arose from discovery of an insect caught in a switch of an early computer. Such a defect may cause the program to fail (**"crash"**) at an inopportune moment. Hard disk (an enclosed stack of disks that are **"read"** from and **"written"** to by multiple magnetic heads) failure sometimes occurs from electric power

"Here—take this course in domestic tranquility and solve your own problems."

Figure 11.02. As illustrated here, from the dawn of the microcomputer age a major goal has been to enable ordinary people to run programs with ease. Early software required typing code words, and mistakes were met with the unhelpful message "syntax error." Today, graphical user interfaces ("gooeys") make computer operation "user-friendly." Source: *Educational Technology,* 19 (October 1979), p. 27. Reprinted courtesy of Educational Technology Publications.

surges and movement when a head isn't properly **"parked."** **"Viruses"** are miniprograms, maliciously written to **"infect"** computers through shared software and networks. These may scramble data or fill disk space.

As you can see, learning about computers has much to do with gaining a new vocabulary. This can best be done by living within a variety of computer environments. Only by using a computer regularly to **satisfy your needs** or to **solve problems you may have** will you become **"computer literate."** Points of easy entry like games, word processing, and multimedia are immediately rewarding and lay the groundwork for ever more efficient production and creative expression. Also invaluable are PBS series (*The New Literacy: An Introduction to Computers; The Machine that Changed the World*) and regularly scheduled TV programs (*The Computer Chronicles, PC-TV, The CNN Computer Connection*).

CBL Then and Now

Conceived in 1959 by **Donald Bitzer** at the University of Illinois, **PLATO** (Programmed Logic for Automatic Teaching Operations) evolved into an international network with over a thousand terminals linked by satellite and telephone to central computers located in the United States and Europe. Each terminal gave access to thousands of hours of instructional material. Lessons were displayed on a "plasma panel" that was touch-sensitive, enabling children and students with disabilities to respond by using their fingers or a pointer. Audio capabilities included random access to prerecorded material and a voice synthesizer. Visuals included microfiche, slides, film, and computer-generated graphics. PLATO continued to operate for many years under the ownership of Control Data Corporation and its courseware was adapted to run on microcomputers.

Another early project, launched in 1963 by **Richard Atkinson** and **Patrick Suppes**, began as a computer-equipped learning laboratory at Stanford's Institute for Mathematical Studies in the Social Sciences (IMSSS). The project studied the learning process and used its findings to develop courseware. Then, in 1965–66, the Institute offered computerized mathematics drill to high school students. Next came arithmetic and reading instruction to over a hundred elementary school children, followed by college-level CBL with courses in axiomatic set theory and introductory logic. Twelve terminals,

available 24 hours a day, six days a week, served a hundred students each term.

Established in 1973 by the state legislature, the Minnesota Educational Computing Consortium (**MECC**) first provided computing services on a timesharing basis using a mainframe computer and remote terminals. When microcomputers appeared, MECC purchased them *en masse*, distributed them throughout the state, and provided teachers with training in their use. The teachers, in turn, themselves have contributed to a growing library of courseware, much of which now is being marketed internationally (e.g., *The Oregon Trail*)

In Great Britain, several CBL projects were started during the late 1960s—at Leeds University, in the London Borough of Havering, and at Cambridge University's Department of Applied Mathematics and Theoretical Physics. The chief stimulus was a recommendation of the (British) National Council for Educational Technology that the government fund a five-year "National Development Programme in Computer-Assisted Learning" (**NDPCAL**) During the mid-seventies, dozens of projects were sponsored in schools, universities, industry, and the armed forces. By 1980, a quarter of Britain's six thousand secondary schools and nearly all its universities had adopted computerized instruction. Since then, the national Microelectronics Education Programme (**MEP**) increasingly has focused on the purchase of computer equipment and courseware and the training of teachers in their use. The Open University also has adapted the Post Office's videotext system, "Prestel," for CBL.

Dramatic advances in computer hardware and software since 1980 have shifted CBL from being university-based demonstration projects to residing comfortably in classrooms and homes. The Apple II series of computers, introduced widely in the late 1970s, made the technology affordable, and the Macintosh, which appeared in 1984 with its graphical user interface and mouse input, made it easily accessible to children and adults alike. IBM's early 1980s entries into the microcomputer market were made similarly accessible by Bill Gates's successive versions of Microsoft *Windows,* the first of which appeared in 1985, through the one billed to make PCs "really" operate as nicely as Macs, *Windows 95.* Ever faster, more powerful (do more stuff) microprocessors (e.g., Intel's *Pentium,* Motorola's *PowerPC*) made possible interactive multimedia CBL (see Chapter **12**). Explorations of the Internet, a network of computer networks, has been facilitated by *Gopher* software and its successors, and the World Wide Web of hypermedia links across the Internet has been opened up by *Mosaic* and the now market leading *Netscape Navigator* (see Chapter **13**).[1]

Computers are rapidly expanding their role in education across the globe. Much of the impetus for their current attraction comes from young people. Accustomed by television to watching a screen and familiar with video games down at the arcade, youngsters deal confidently and enthusiastically with computer technologies. Many get their own at an early age and attend workshops to learn how to use them. (See **Figure 11.03**.)

Varieties of CBL

There are at least eight major categories of CBL: **drill-and-practice, tutorial, problem solving, simulation, inquiry, electronic performance support system, testing**, and **programming**.

Drill-and-Practice. At this level the teacher introduces new concepts and skills, and the computer gives practice in using them. A teacher of Spanish, for example, may spend one lesson explaining the use of the imperfect tense, and for the next lesson may assign computerized practice in handling this tense. As a drill medium, the computer has some advantages over the ordinary teacher. It submits questions and appraises answers quickly and tirelessly, while allowing students to pace themselves.

Tutorial. Here the computer introduces and explains concepts and skills in which it gives practice. Like programmed instructional texts and teaching machines, tutorial CBL presents informational frames and asks questions about them. The Stanford project, for example, included a course in elementary Russian. The computer handled everything except pronunciation (practiced in the language laboratory) and the teaching of Cyrillic script. At this level the computer offers explanations when needed, asks appropriate questions, and takes account of possible difficulties when providing further material, much like a human tutor. (See **Figure 11.04**.)

An alternative conception of an "intelligent tutoring system," is presented in **Figure 11.05**. The "User interface" is the means by which the student acts and the system responds. The "Expert Model" is a database representation of knowledge within a subject matter do-

Figure 11.03. Children and adults alike are fascinated with computing and they flock to commercial exhibits to test the latest products. What might you and your students gain from such an adventure?

main. The "Learner Model" is a database of common misconceptions as well as those manifested by students using the system. On the basis of an ongoing diagnosis of discrepancies between a learner's performance and that of an expert, and application of "Pedagogic Knowledge," the system continuously adjusts its presentation.

Michael Orey and Wayne Nelson elaborated on their conception of an intelligent tutoring system as follows:

> . . . the various components . . . work together to produce an instructional system that can recognize patterns of learner behavior and respond with instruction appropriate to those patterns. This process is driven by a representation of an expert's reasoning in the domain (the expert model), but the other components must also be designed to facilitate the learning process. The interface is important as a communication medium, as a problem-solving environment that supports the student in the task, and as an external representation of the system's internal model of expertise. The use of a cognitive model for making diagnoses of learner errors or misconceptions has the potential not only to present knowledge to the learner, as does traditional CBI [Instruction], but to communicate knowledge in actual use during the solution of relevant problems rather than abstract knowledge that must be applied in subsequent situations. The possibilities of communicating knowledge situated in actual practice also provide opportunities to implement pedagogical strategies that provide a scaffold for the learner during early phases of learning and then gradually fade as the learner develops expertise.[2]

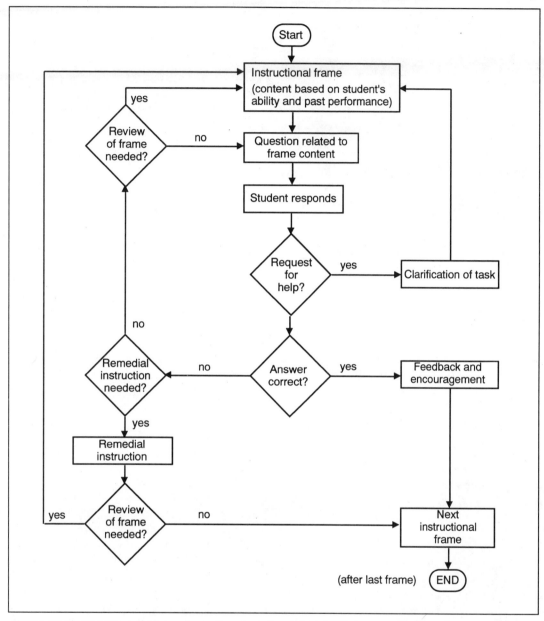

Figure 11.04. This flow diagram shows the steps in a tutorial CBL lesson. Students first are presented with an instructional frame and questioned; they then proceed either to a review or to the next frame.

For several reasons it is harder to prepare tutorial than drill CBL. Good (human) tutors present subjects in personally chosen detail, give examples from their own lives, and ask challenging questions. They respond sensitively to students as persons, adapt their instructional techniques to students' abilities, and can switch their approach on the spot. These tasks are demanding enough for a human tutor, let alone an electronic one.

Nevertheless, the computer-tutor can simulate sensitivity. It is equipped to change its instructional strategies in response to student performance. For instance, it can record how long the student takes to read certain passages displayed on the monitor and then use this performance as a standard of comparison with performance on a later passage. It can ask, is the student taking too little time (and perhaps not reading carefully enough)?

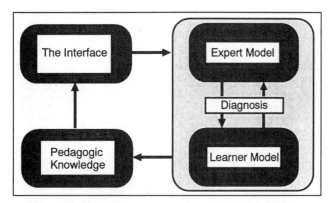

Figure 11.05. Diagrammed here is a dynamic model of an "intelligent tutoring system." In what ways might such a system excel even over one-on-one teaching? Source: Michael A. Orey & Wayne A. Nelson, "Development Principles for Intelligent Tutoring Systems: Integrating Cognitive Theory into the Development of Computer-Based Instruction," *Educational Technology Research and Development*, 41, 1(1993), p. 61. Copyright © 1993 Association for Educational Communications and Technology.

Or too much time (and perhaps having difficulty)? It then adjusts its presentation accordingly. The good computer-tutor also can converse with the student using suitable terms and correct grammatical usage. To do so, it must be programmed to "understand" what students write or say, and respond accordingly. For this it needs a modicum of "common sense" and the capacity to size up the learner. The more the computer can do these things, the more it may favorably compare with human tutors.

Problem Solving. Once students have achieved a basic grasp of subject matter, whether by conventional teaching or CBL, they are ready to tackle problems posed by the computer. These may require recall of information, application of rules, or calculation.

Problem solving CBL currently is used not only in basic school subjects but also in professional studies of teaching, counseling, medicine, and engineering. The aim of problem solving at such high levels of instruction goes beyond leading students to reasonable solutions by merely changing their behavior with strategically scheduled rewards (the aim of much drill and tutorial CBL). Constructive changes in behavior surely are desirable, but of more interest are changes in ways of thinking about and attacking problems.

Simulation. Here students confront an environment that operates under a set of rules. Their role is to act within this environment and then observe results. For example, in *Geography Search*, students relive the voyages of early explorers making their way across the Atlantic. They plot their course and make adjustments along the way, accounting for changes in winds and currents. *SimEarth* provides them with opportunities to redesign our planet and its inhabitants and then witness the consequences over eons. Other simulations permit laboratory-style dissection and experimentation.

Inquiry. Students also may use computers to retrieve information from diskettes, CDs, and remote data sources (e.g., via the Internet). At a basic level, such inquiry CBL involves merely gaining access to pages of text taken from books (e.g., *The Great Books*) and periodicals (e.g., the quarterly CD-ROM *Newsweek*) or to the products of "electronic publication" that appear in no other form. At its finest, multimedia inquiry CBL entails selective and systematic explorations of sources ranging from the contents of encyclopedias (e.g., *Microsoft Encarta*) to the holdings of the Library of Congress and World Wide Web home pages for such purposes as solving problems and producing reports. (See Chapter **13**.)

Electronic Performance Support System. The essential function of an EPSS is to make information available as it is needed to solve immediate problems. It has been described by Betty Collis and Carla Verwijs as an electronic environment in which "the user can interact . . . to obtain various types of local or distributed help and resources for individual or group-oriented activities related to learning, problem-oriented thinking, and collaboration."[3] For example, the *Teacher Tool Kit* consists of databases to identify resources and expert systems to facilitate decision making. *The Study Planner* provides course information and guidelines for use by students distributed in remote locations. The *Alternative Assessment Resource Center for Teachers* provides guidance in conducting performance assessment. Wanting to focus on the learners' role rather than merely the electronics, Collis and Verwijs proposed distinguishing functions in terms of activities that users typically engage in when confronted with challenging tasks—"browsing and getting information," "focusing and coming to a tentative solution," and "getting feedback on the tentative solution and on its revisions." Thus conceived, the relation of EPSS technology to automated instructional development (ID) is clear.

Testing. Computers are ideal for presenting and scoring tests. And in providing feedback, they "teach" what may be considered good answers. **Figure 11.06** illustrates a testing device commonly found in exhibits. People **line up** to see how they **measure up**, something they would rarely do if the examiner were human. In schools, computer-based testing is similarly non-threatening and individualized. Students may be given items based on their responses, thus saving time and permitting precise diagnosis of difficulties.

Programming. Computers are made to do specific tasks by "programs." These are sets of instructions written in one of several codes called **"programming languages,"** a few of which are described below. Although students need not know how to program to benefit from computer technology, gaining such a skill gives them greater control of the medium and opens opportunities for later employment.

Even children can learn to write computer programs. For example, many are being introduced to ***"Logo,"*** an easily learned, logically structured language developed by Seymour Papert. Here they define a term such as "square" as a sequence of actions. The command "go forward 10 units and turn left 90 degrees" is repeated four times and is coded simply as: REPEAT 4 [FORWARD 10 LEFT 90]. Students then see the results as drawings on the monitor or as the motions of a **"turtle"** robot. If the turtle doesn't behave as expected, children learn to seek out and correct errors (**"debug"** the program), perhaps walking through the desired motions themselves to get a feel for what needs to be done.

Papert, a pioneer in **placing children in control of computers rather than the other way around**, early proclaimed that "computers can be carriers of powerful ideas and the seeds of cultural change . . . . they can help people form new relationships with knowledge that cut across the traditional lines separating humanities from science and knowledge of self from both of these."[4] By using his *Logo* language to move a "turtle" across the screen or floor, Papert claimed that "a child can learn some specific mathematical ideas, some important programming ideas, some 'thinking skills' and a lot of self-

Figure 11.06. Educational exhibits like this one illustrate Sidney Pressey's principle of "teaching by testing." People of all ages enjoy showing off what they know and being informed about what they don't know, especially by a non-threatening examiner. Location: California Museum of Science and Industry.

confidence."[5] By writing *Logo* programs to modify the *LogoWriter* word processing package, children "gain the sense of control over the computer that lies at the heart of the *Logo* philosophy."[6]

In a broad sense, we may think of programming to include the use of computers to craft all sorts of products. Thus, when students input data to produce colorful graphs, when they incorporate downloaded videos into their multimedia reports, and when they design classroom World Wide Web home pages (using HTML, hypertext markup language) they surely are changing the dynamics of computer/human interaction in ways consistent with high aims of education, especially those pertaining to efficacy and creative expression.

Programming Languages

Microcomputer **"courseware"** is coded in such programming languages as: updated versions of *BASIC* (Beginner's All-Purpose Symbolic Instruction Code), *Pascal* (in honor of the 17th Century French mathematician/philosopher, Blaise Pascal), or *C* (a public domain product of AT&T's Bell Laboratories). These languages allow the greatest flexibility, but also require considerable study to exploit fully. More immediately accessible to teachers are *PILOT* (Programmed Inquiry Learning Or

Teaching [for Apple computers]), *HyperCard* (for Macintosh computers), *LinkWay Live!* (for *DOS/Windows* IBM compatibles), and other such **"authoring tools"** as *Authorware Professional, Digital Chisel, Icon Author,* and *Asymetrix Multimedia Toolbook*. These were designed to simplify crafting of **"computer-based training"** (CBT) instructional lessons, most in a multimedia format, in which subject matter is presented, questions are asked, students respond, and feedback is given.[7]

Each language has distinctive characteristics. Early versions of **BASIC** were used for reasons more of convenience than merit. Many microcomputers used to come with *BASIC* built in, and it is easy to learn. As shown below, such *BASIC* programs are marked both by lines numbered consecutively and by explicit one-word command statements. Writing the command "PRINT" on line 10, for example, instructs the computer to print out whatever follows on line 10 that is enclosed in quotation marks. The "LIST" command prints out a previously entered program for analysis and revision. A "REM" (remark) in the program is for explanation only; it is not acted on by the computer, but programmers find it useful as a reference point when making revisions. The "RUN" command signals the computer to execute the previously encoded instructions in numerical order. When run, the following program segment would display a question for students, wait for their answer, and provide appropriate feedback.

```
10 PRINT "What is the sum of 2 plus 2?"
12 REM Computer displays question on the
   monitor.
20 INPUT A
22 REM Computer waits for the student's answer.
30 IF A = 4 THEN GOTO 70
32 REM If answer is correct, the computer skips
   ahead to line 70.
40 IF A < 4 THEN PRINT "Too low. Please try
   again."
50 IF A > 4 THEN PRINT "Too high. Please try
   again."
60 GOTO 10
62 REM If answer is incorrect, the computer
   repeats question.
70 PRINT "Good, you are correct."
```

Pascal has distinct advantages over early versions of *BASIC*. Whereas *BASIC* forced programmers to write in the linear fashion of computer logic, *Pascal* lets them write in a more natural style, defining sets of instructions in ordinary English and marking off discrete program sections in outline form. Since these sections may be called up at any point in the program, or even employed in an entirely different program, they save considerable programmer time and computer memory space. Also, speed of execution is quicker with *Pascal*. Whereas in *BASIC* the computer reads a program line by line, translates it into a form it can act upon, and then executes the instructions, in *Pascal* it electronically "compiles" programs so they can be executed without having to interpret (using a lower level "interpreter" language built into the system) the English language commands. Whereas *BASIC* has to "draw" a picture line by line, *Pascal* can flash it on the screen instantaneously. Furthermore, in early *BASIC,* the program commands needed to produce such a picture could consume a large portion of available space on a diskette, leaving little room for the lesson itself. More recent versions of *BASIC* have resolved these problems (e.g., Microsoft's *Quick-BASIC* and *Visual BASIC*).

Following is a program written in *Pascal* that has the same screen appearance as the previous one written in *BASIC*. The commands used are largely self-explanatory; remarks appear in brackets.

```
var [alerts computer that variable is going to
     be defined]
   A: integer;
Begin [marks beginning of program]
 Write ('What is the sum of 2 plus 2?')
 [Computer displays question on the monitor.]
 Read (A); [Computer waits for the student's
            answer.]
If A = 4 then
    begin [marks beginning of subroutine]
      Write ('Good, you are correct!');
    end [marks end of subroutine]
    else [that is, if the answer given is not
          "4"]
      If A < 4 then
    begin
      Write ('Too low. Please try again.');
    end
    else
      If A > 4 then
    begin
      Write ('Too high. Please try again.');
    end;
End. [marks end of program]
```

PILOT is a specialized "authoring" language early developed explicitly for "interactive" (question and answer) CBL (aka CBT) on Apple computers. Its command statements are abbreviations for sets of instructions written in a "host" language. For example, "T" (type) corresponds to *BASIC*'s PRINT command, "A" (answer) to INPUT, and "R" (remark) to REM. *PILOT*'s highly versatile "M" (match) command is used in CBL to compare student input with answers the programmer deems acceptable. Incorrect spellings and variations in tense may be recognized as essentially correct answers by inserting the "wild card" apostrophe ("f**r" accepts "fuor"; "play*" accepts "playing"). Apostrophes also mark the beginnings of sections to which students may be sent based on their responses to questions. When students answer correctly, a "TY" (type if yes on match) statement provides appropriate feedback. When they answer incorrectly, a "TN" statement so indicates. The "J" (jump) command functions like GOTO in *BASIC*. A simple program segment might read:

```
*FIRST
T: What is the sum of 2 plus 2?
R: Computer displays question.
A:
R: Computer waits for the student's answer.
M: 4, four, IV, for
R: The correct answer and acceptable variants
   are listed.
TY: Good, you are correct!
JY: SECOND
R: If answer is correct, computer proceeds to
   next section.
TN: Your answer is not correct. Please try
   again.
JN: FIRST
R: If answer is incorrect, computer repeats the
   question.
*SECOND
```

Whatever programming language is used, it remains essentially a tool for getting computers to perform desired tasks. Knowledge of a programming language enables teachers to modify existing CBL courseware and create their own. For students, it means making the computer do their bidding, whether to draw pictures or craft multimedia reports. In every case, **quality of the finished product rests more on the accuracy and organization of content than on the particular language in which it is coded**.

Evaluation of CBL

Assessing computer-based learning activities is made wonderfully complex by the versatility of the medium, and by the talents of those who use it. Chapter **5** covers its virtues as a curriculum manager, and Chapter **6** comments about its use as a word processor and database system. Subsequent chapters cover its graphing, drawing, and multimedia editing features. Chapter **12** explores the nature of computer/user interactivity, and Chapter **13** assesses the merits of computer networks. Thus, I have narrowed the scope of the present evaluation to use of computers in the presentation of instructional lessons.

Drawing upon a long history of research, we can reasonably conclude that when used as a **supplement** to classroom instruction at the elementary level, CBL produces substantial increases in academic achievement. At the secondary and college levels, CBL may serve as an effective **replacement** of classroom instruction, often taking less time to complete and enhancing student attitudes toward subject matter.[8]

A four-year Educational Testing Service study conducted in Los Angeles city schools found that 10 minutes a day of math and 10 of reading drill-and-practice CBL over the course of a school year resulted in gains of 12 and 23 percent, respectively, above the level expected. A review of earlier studies suggested that only "cross-age" (older peers and adults) tutoring worked better, while increasing time devoted to conventional classroom instruction by one-half hour a day was not nearly as effective. Reducing class size from 35 to 20 students resulted in achievement gains of 22 percent in math and 11 percent in reading. Lesser reductions in class size had negligible impact. When the measured effectiveness of each type of innovation was divided by an estimate of cost, **only peer tutoring was found more cost-effective than CBL**.[9]

However, examination of a broader range of research revealed that the above estimate of peer-tutoring effectiveness was overstated and that of CBL understated, leading to the conclusion that compared to peer tutoring, adult tutoring, increasing the length of school day, and decreasing class size, "an average CAI program produces the greatest gains per $100 of instructional expenditure."[10] (See **Figure 11.07**.)

In interpreting research on CBL, we should be aware of several factors contributing to its success. These include:

Figure 11.07. CBL is especially effective when **combined with peer tutoring**. Such **collaborative learning** schemes enable students to share what they know and to engage in cooperative problem solving. What might students gain from these experiences that they miss when working in isolation? What are special advantages for students with disabilities? Reproduced with permission from P.S. 116 (Manhattan), principal Anna Marie Carrillo.

- **differences in content and presentation** between CBL and conventional lessons,
- **special attention** given teachers and students participating in CBL research studies,
- **novelty** of the medium, and
- **high expectations**.

Let us examine each factor in turn.

Content and presentation. CBL courseware used in experimental studies often has been designed by teams of experts. Achievement of students using this courseware sometimes is compared with that of students receiving instruction conceived and taught by ordinary teachers working in isolation. We know that computers can simulate the instructional strategies employed by good teachers (i.e., gaining attention, delivering content systematically, asking questions, providing immediate feedback). In fact, computers might be more thorough, consistent, and "attentive" than some teachers, especially those faced with over 30 students. However, research suggests that CBL's advantage over conventional instruction diminishes when equal effort is made to develop each. And CBL's advantage also diminishes in cases where teachers, aware that they are in a contest, make special efforts to excel—a phenomenon called **"compensatory rivalry."** So, although CBL can be designed to raise the quality of instruction, good teachers can do likewise. Differences in the performance of computers and teachers in achieving many clearly defined objectives have more to do with quality of content and presentation than with anything inherent in being a machine or a human being.[11]

Attention. The introduction of computers into the classroom often attracts the attention of administrators, school boards, and parents. Thus, teachers find themselves pressured to either use the technology or prove that their own approaches are more effective. They may come to class better prepared than usual, show greater interest in rousing student enthusiasm, and more actively engage them in discussions about their CBL experiences. Students, too, may come to feel a deeper sense of involvement when principals begin to make unannounced visits and parents ask "What did you learn online today?"

Novelty. Compared with teachers and books, computers remain a relatively novel medium of instruction. Even if program content was essentially the same as that of a textbook, the new packaging would arouse curiosity. The monitor looks like a TV screen, and the presentation is as lively as an arcade game. Push a few buttons and the computer talks to you like a pal. However, the novelty effect is short-lived. The advantage of CBL over conventional instruction has been shown to diminish as experience with computers increases.[12] (See **Figure 11.08.**)

Expectations. Each medium brings with it expectations about its value. For most people, computers retain a certain mystique—they are perceived to be powerful, dependable, and demanding. Students quickly learn that they must pay attention and act appropriately, for computers are not as indulgent as commercial TV. High expectations, real or imagined, very often translate into high effort with consequent high performance.[13]

Although CBL has many obvious virtues, some excitement it generates may be unrelated to education. Some students enjoy simply manipulating the machine and getting it to do things not intended by programmers.

Figure 11.08. Here a video projector connected to the teacher's computer keyboard makes for an "electronic chalkboard." Students pay close attention in part because the technique is novel. What are some enduring merits of this display technology?

One infamous CBL vocabulary program displayed a sinking battleship whenever students made an error. Teachers discovered that many students became more interested in sinking the ship than in learning the desired vocabulary. Some students even told their peers which wrong answers sank the ship most rapidly. Other program features like animation, flashing lights, sound effects, and humorous quips may attract attention, but sometimes at the expense of grasping content and taking longer to complete.

CBL that strikes a balance between multimedia appeal and efficient, interactive instruction remains expensive to produce. This is due primarily to the cost of labor involved in writing effective lesson materials, programming them for presentation by computer, field testing, evaluation, and revision. And the quality of courseware will not improve significantly until we know more about the problems different students have with different kinds of subject matter. Program authors must pay more attention to research on learning from text and visuals under a variety of conditions. Like their counterparts in all areas of instructional development, they must expand their use of **student response data** to guide the process of revision.

Meanwhile, specialists have developed a range of programming languages to help teachers prepare their own courseware. Especially with *HyperCard* installed in every Macintosh, teachers now routinely produce CBL lessons. Much successful commercial courseware has been adapted from programs first designed and tested by teachers. An ideal arrangement is one in which teachers and publishers cooperate from the start of a project to its completion. More commonly, teachers are being employed full time by software companies and some teachers have gone into business for themselves.

Instruction mediated by machine may never escape the criticism that **information it presents appears fixed rather than fluid**, that there are **right answers to every question**, and **what an individual may think and feel are of secondary import**. Today, we are becoming increasingly aware that the most significant forms of learning take place while **working collaboratively in search of solutions to pressing environmental and social problems**, not exclusively sitting in isolation reading a book or screen.[14] The words of an educational philosopher, C.A. Bowers, about the collaborative role of teachers in an age of CBL hold true today:

> . . . if we take seriously a twentieth-century view of knowledge—that facts represent the objectification of somebody's interpretation, that interpretations are influenced by the conceptual guidance system of a culture, that objective knowledge is about a world of events and objects that become more fully understood as we trace their historical development, that language and thought are metaphorical in nature, that explicit-calculating forms of knowledge are quite different from the tacit-heuristic forms of understanding and problem solving, and that the structure of knowledge and individual understanding is shared

and filtered by what individuals take for granted—then it becomes possible to recognize the unique contribution that only the teacher can make to the educational process.[15]

In spite of these reservations, the clear advantages of CBL properly integrated within the larger curriculum by knowledgeable teachers justify wide use. Teachers possibly could outperform CBL in presenting vast quantities of detailed, current subject matter in a multimedia format, but few have the time or inclination to do so. Their larger roles within the CBL context are both to **manage these resources** and to **intervene with elaborations and challenges.** Students may be able to dance all over the surface of *Microsoft Encarta* and to pursue Carmen Sandiego to the ends of the earth, but they need guidance in the systematic acquisition of reliable, structured knowledge. CBL programs may describe to them how historians, scientists, artists, and philosophers go about their work, cooperatively and interdisciplinarily, but **personalizing** the pursuit of knowledge and **inspiring** students to do so remain for teachers their special gifts. Writing of "intelligent tutoring systems" (ITSs), Michael Orey and Wayne Nelson similarly concluded that they "cannot replace teachers, nor should they, but these systems can augment . . . the capabilities of good teachers by personalizing [i.e., **individualizing**] instruction and motivating students through enriching learning situations that recreate real-world environments."[16]

Practical Guidelines

Selection. CBL programs typically consist of text, graphics, audio, and video presented on a monitor. Criteria for judging the instructional qualities of these formats have been outlined in previous chapters. Again, here are important questions pertaining to selection.

- Does it run on your **equipment**?
- Do program **objectives match** those you have set for your students?
- Is program **content accurate**?
- Is the program as a whole **effective**?
- Do students **enjoy it**?
- Is it readily **available**?
- Can you **afford** it?

As with other media, selection of CBL programs begins with consulting reviews and seeking comments from users. Once you have a promising copy in hand, compare the content with that implied in your instructional objectives. Next, consider the abilities of your students. Programs will be effective only insofar as they are readily understood by your students and if they permit proceeding at an appropriate pace.

To ease selection, you may refer to **Figure 11.09.** Rate CBL programs on each criterion from **1** (unsatisfactory) to **10** (excellent) and select the ones that are **available, affordable, compatible** with your equipment, and **rate highest** overall.

Since CBL programs can simulate the behavior of tutors, some criteria listed in **Figure 11.09,** such as **"interactivity"** and **"learner control,"** take on special meanings.

When I earlier wrote of **interactivity** in relation to print, audio, and visual media, I had in mind the extent to which these **engage students** in such activities as **attending, listening, exploring,** and **reflecting.** Questions, underlines, arrows, sound effects, color, motion, etc., serve these functions in the media of print, audio, and video, as well as in computer-generated text and images. With CBL, however, a higher level of interactivity is possible. A good instructional program **adjusts presentation** to student performance, always **striving to enhance that performance while reducing time to do so.** Each screen consists of a unit of information that students must grasp before proceeding. Their understanding is tested at the end of one or more screens, often by a question to which they must provide their own answer rather than one selected from given alternatives. If they take too long, the computer may give a hint. If they err, the computer diagnoses their error and responds appropriately (e.g., provides more time, information, or examples). A cumulative score informs them of their progress.

"Learner control" refers to the power given students to change pace and content. Good CBL programs allow students to adjust level of difficulty, density of cues, number of practice exercises, and amount of material covered in one sitting. They also allow them to skip previously mastered sections by calling for and passing tests and to obtain assistance by typing "help." Such features generally reduce student frustration and time needed to complete a program. However, learner control should be assessed in relation to instructional objectives and students' capabilities. You may find, for example, that your

Title _____ Author _____

Publisher _____ Date _____ Price _____

Subject _____ Grade Level _____

Objectives _____

Prerequisites _____

Hardware Requirements _____

Selection Criteria	Rating (1 = low; 10 = high)	Comments
1. Content of Program	____	_____
a. match with objectives	____	_____
b. accuracy	____	_____
c. currency	____	_____
d. scope	____	_____
e. stereotyping	____	_____
2. Presentation	____	_____
a. impact	____	_____
b. organization	____	_____
c. teaching strategies	____	_____
d. interactivity	____	_____
e. motivation	____	_____
f. use of sound	____	_____
g. learner control	____	_____
h. difficulty	____	_____
3. Supplementary Materials	____	_____
a. print	____	_____
b. visual	____	_____
c. audio	____	_____
d. video	____	_____
e. teacher's guide	____	_____
f. examinations	____	_____
4. Technical Quality	____	_____
a. visual clarity	____	_____
b. screen layout	____	_____
c. response speed	____	_____
d. ease of use	____	_____
e. automatic scoring	____	_____
5. Effectiveness	____	_____
a. student interest	____	_____
b. student achievement	____	_____
c. student evaluation	____	_____
6. Overall Impression	____	_____

_____
_____
_____
_____
_____
_____

Figure 11.09. CBL materials evaluation form.

best students tend to select strategies rich in examples and practice, while your lower ability students select discovery approaches that do not demand mastery of basics. Perhaps the gifted would benefit more from discovery and the less gifted from drill. In any case, learner control should be balanced with teacher guidance.

Other things to look for in CBL are **visual clarity**, good **screen layout**, **quick response** to input, **ease of use**, and **automatic scoring**. **Visual clarity** is affected by information density in relation to monitor capabilities. That is, given the limitations of monitors, visual clarity declines as information density increases. These limitations are overcome, in part, by enlarging text characters and using simplified graphics. A clear, crisp writing style ensures that sufficient information fits in each screen. Use of "super video graphics displays" allows presentation of more information in each screen while maintaining high visual clarity. Select courseware that best exploits the capabilities of your equipment.

Good **screen layout** is achieved by placing text and graphics in the order in which they are to be read and in positions consistent with their significance. Look for essential information in the upper middle portion of the screen, perhaps set off in an attention-getting box. Page and section numbers generally should appear on the left, instructions as how to proceed, at bottom, right.

Rapid computer **response time** is important in filling the screen on command and providing feedback to students. Look for instantaneous appearance of text and graphics on a blank screen (rather than scrolled) unless progressive, timed exposure is being employed as an instructional strategy. Courseware should respond to student input within a few seconds, at most. Obviously, response time largely is a function of your computer's microprocessor speed, but it is affected by programming as well.

CBL courseware should be **easy to use**. It should be designed so that students can proceed without getting stuck. As you test the program, assume the perspective of your students. Do not rely too much on your experience to help you find desired sections, make responses, or seek help. Rather, look for cues in the program on which your students will have to rely. Also, make several consecutive errors to see if the program traps you in failure or if it automatically comes to your aid. Then punch a few odd keys like "control c" and "escape" to see if the program ends prematurely (**"crashes"**). In the jargon of the profession, CBL programs should be **"user friendly,"** making the computer equipment itself **"transparent,"** that is, unobtrusive.

Look for "interactive" multimedia courseware that presents lessons like teachers who effectively use chalkboards, overhead projectors, and VCRs. Computers, like teachers, can time disclosure of information, present images and sound effects, highlight key words and phrases with various cues, insert humorous and imaginative examples, isolate information with boxes and blank space, and call students by name. However, such **"enhancements"** should be evaluated based on quality rather than quantity. Some may distract or merely delay or obstruct progress, while some may be beneficial only during early phases of instruction or for computer novices. Good courseware permits teachers and students to eliminate enhancements once they are found not to be making the intended contributions to learning, often with the bonus effect of reducing completion time.[17]

Robert Reiser (Florida State University) and Harald Kegelmann (Santa Fe Community College) have reminded us of the central role that students should take in evaluating software. In their view, widely shared,

> . . . students should be observed as they use a software program, and conclusions about the quality of that program should be based, in part, upon what the evaluators observe. Evaluators should also ask students to share their opinions of each of the software programs they work through.
>
> Most importantly, evaluators should assess how much students have learned as a result of using a particular program.[18]

This holds equally true for programs mediated by print, video, teachers, etc.

Teaching Computer Literacy. What need our students know, beyond the vocabulary presented in this chapter, to be considered computer literate? (See **Figure 11.10**.)

First, they should know how to **operate the hardware**. This means knowing how to turn on the power, insert a diskette, and press the keys. They then should learn how to set up the equipment—connecting monitor, keyboard, and peripherals to the computer, and perhaps inserting expansion cards as needed. Proper care and feeding of diskettes are essential skills. Students should learn to keep magnets, paper clips, food, drink, and heat at a distance. They should learn to grasp a diskette only by its label and slide it smoothly into the drive.

Next, our students should be able to **run programs**. Once they have placed a diskette in a drive and have directed the computer to "read" it, they should study instructions on how to proceed, to obtain assistance, or to

Figure 11.10. The teaching of every subject involves communicating the meanings of special terms. Teaching computer literacy entails introducing students to a field where familiar terms are used in peculiar ways, and where new terms have been invented to express emerging concepts. How would you proceed, considering what you learned from previous chapters in this book? Source: *Phi Delta Kappan,* 74 (January 1993), p. 365. Reprinted with permission of Kyle Kaser.

end the session. They should look for **"menus"** (tables of contents) from which to select desired sections, and seek **"documentation"** that covers details not included in the program. Game and instructional programs should be easy to handle, because they are especially "user friendly"; that is, directions are simple and explicit, while help and encouragement are generously given. However, **"applications"** programs such as word processing, database managing, accounting (with "spreadsheets"), and network communicating (e.g., email, *Kermit, Gopher,* FTP [see Chapter **13**]) require more skill. In all cases, the greatest challenges are those of deciding precisely what to write and what form data should take. Inputting text and data is easy, but it must be done with precision and according to prescribed form.

Students need not know how to run every type of application program, but they should know the general characteristics of some and be able to operate at least one for word processing. They should know how to **"format"** (prepare diskette for use by erasing old material and coding its magnetic surface to accept new), **"edit"** (make corrections in text and move sections around), **"save"** (transfer text from the computer's RAM to a diskette), and **print**. They should know how to avoid losing work by preserving input every 10–20 minutes, and they should get in the habit of making **duplicate diskettes** for storage in a separate location. Diskettes are cheap, but their contents may be priceless. Clever users never forget to remove them from the disk drives at the lab because they keep the empty plastic dust covers in plain view. **"Backing up"** hard disks is another essential habit. It should be done immediately after setting up a file structure **("directory tree")** and regularly after that. Having your computer stolen without having backed up the hard disk is a bit like being carjacked with your infant in the back seat.

Although graphical user interfaces (GUIs, e.g., *Macintosh System 7, Microsoft Windows 95, Windows NT, OS/2*) have made knowing more fundamental operating system commands obsolete, a computer literate person knows how to cope when the window closes. For IBM-compatible users, this means knowing how to move from one drive to another (e.g., from "a" to "c"), how to change directories (e.g., from *DOS* to *WordPerfect*), and how to list files (using a DIRectory command at the *DOS* "prompt" (>). Also essential for *DOS* and even *DOS*-based *Windows* users is knowing that to boot a program, shall we say, "manually," one typically must type the name of a file having an "exe" ("execute") extension (e.g., "install.exe" or "tutorial.exe") or a "com" or "bat" extension. Going beyond being a WIMP (Window/ Icon/Mouse/Pull-down) aficionado remains helpful when one enters the world of minicomputer operating systems (e.g., *UNIX, Virtual Memory System*) that provide access to the Internet (see Chapter **13**). But here again, development of reliable GUIs (e.g., *Mosaic*) renders this suggestion ever less relevant.

Students need not know how to program computers to use them effectively. In fact, most of the jobs in our Information Age are in applications, not programming. However, computer literate students know what programming is and how it connects keyboards with magnetic patterns. At the very least they have copied a program in a language such as *BASIC, LOGO, C,* or *Pascal*. They not only have run it; they have experimented to make it run differently.

One need not become a **"hacker"** (a positive term, maligned by the press) to be considered computer literate. At the precollege level especially, the aim is not to produce expert programmers. Rather, it is to provide skills needed to **use computers in everyday life.** An applications-based curriculum focuses on skills that are applicable in a variety of real-life situations, thereby serving as an appropriate introduction to computers for many kinds of students.

Another aspect of computer literacy is knowing **how to select** appropriate hardware and software. (See **Figure 11.11.**) First, students should **list** all the things they want to do—play games, write, access databases. Second, they should consult magazines like *Popular Computing, PC World, Macworld, Multimedia World,* and *Home PC* to find out what programs are available. Third, they should go to a reputable computer store and ask a competent consultant to **identify the equipment** needed to run programs that perform the desired functions. Fourth, they should **test** both programs and equipment. Finally, their purchases should include those that have received favorable reviews in such magazines as *Consumer Reports, PCWorld,* or *MacWorld* (for hardware) and *Electronic Learning* or *MultiMedia Schools* (for educational software).

What about **social aspects** of computer technology? Computers have evolved from mechanical calculating machines into devices that can mimic complex human behaviors (e.g., speech recognition, object discrimination, algorithmic "reasoning"). Along the way they have altered human existence in countless respects, many of which are controversial. For example, they have accelerated the pace of scientific discovery and technological development, yet perhaps brought us closer to nuclear disaster. They have freed workers from routine and often dangerous tasks, yet exposed us to loss of privacy. They have increased our capacity for precision, yet compounded our potential for error. Nevertheless, all de-

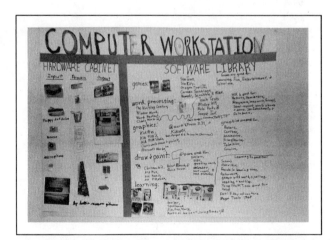

Figure 11.11. After discussing with students the roles of computers in our lives, I move on to helping them make distinctions among varieties of hardware and software. This is followed by construction of a collage, like the one shown here by third grader Hollie Russon Gilman (P.S. 6, Manhattan, Susan Renard, teacher). Reproduced with permission.

pends on the way in which computer technology is used, not on the technology itself. To be considered computer literate, students must have **reflected on these matters and formed ideas of their own**.

Students should know that unauthorized use of copyrighted software is illegal and that it is an invasion of privacy to access other people's computer files without permission. Gaining access to confidential databases (being a "cracker") is not a game; it may cause considerable damage and endanger lives.

How do you go about **teaching** computer literacy? Encourage computer use and discussion about computer technology in your classes. Present a balanced assessment of computer technology, merits and limitations. And use computers to further achievement of firm instructional objectives, not merely to satisfy popular demands for "computer literacy."[19]

Student teaching a third grade class at P.S. 6 (Manhattan) gave me an opportunity to put some of these ideas into practice. I began by developing an assessment tool that would give me some indication of prior knowledge. (See **Figure 11.12**.) Anticipating the evaluation and research potential of the tool, I asked all five third grade teachers to administer it, one section at a time, one minute for section A, five for B, and then five for C. Next, I engaged our class (cooperating teacher was Ms. Susan Renard) in small group discussions of computer functions and then had the group leaders present results to the whole class. I closed with asking students to suggest where they might obtain more information.

I assigned a computer literacy score to each student based on the number of distinct and pertinent concepts expressed on the tool. These scores, not revealed to anyone, permitted ranking for the purpose of group assignment, balanced for literacy and gender (the top six, with scores over 20, were girls). To ensure coverage of the field, and to permit specialization for completion of projects, I made up the following "Computer Club" names: Tekkies, Hackers, Database Pros, Desktop Publishers, Graphic Artists, Multimedia Moguls, Cyberspace Cadets, CAD-CAMs. We discussed these terms and each student wrote them on index cards to be placed in his or her "My Words" file. I encouraged students to think about and discuss with their parents and peers which name they would like for their group. As part of an English lesson, I assigned the writing of a short essay, "My Computer Project." These were shared among Computer Club members and compromises were made until each Club had decided upon a specialty. Soon I was being assaulted

---

Name _____

Date _____

A. How do you feel about computers? Please circle one.

    I hate them.

    I don't like them.

    I don't care.

    I like them.

    I love them.

B. For what purposes do you use computers?

    1.
    2.
    3.
    4.
    5.
    6.
    7.
    8.
    9.
    10.

C. Please write all the words you know that have to do with computers.

1.	10.	19.
2.	11.	20.
3.	12.	21.
4.	13.	22.
5.	14.	23.
6.	15.	24.
7.	16.	25.
8.	17.	26.
9.	18.	27.

Figure 11.12. This "Computer Literacy Assessment Tool" can be adapted for use with any grade level. Scoring need not be precise, just consistent across students, classes, and time (i.e., pre- and post-tests).

with requests to have one name or the other. Some friendly "coopetition" emerged as each Club had to justify its choice of specialty. Again, I asked each child to discuss project ideas with parents, siblings, and peers.

Two Macintoshes were on the way; we had just one little Apple IIe. Grand opportunity to teach basic skills. I placed a sign-up sheet by the Apple, identified and trained peer tutors (e.g., "Keyboard Kops," "RSI [repetitive strain injury] Experts," "BASIC Programmers"), and added a four finger "trekkie salute" to request access to the Apple when done with seatwork (and five fingers for access to the equally popular Reading Center). I then set seven "AppleTasks" for those who might like to be certified as an "AppleSauce Master":

- Handling diskette
- Booting up
- Keyboarding
- Adding and subtracting
- Programming in BASIC
- Finding and demonstrating software
- Teaching a peer

Consistent with constructivist thinking, I wanted project ideas to emerge in response to felt needs and interests of students. Although groups came to agreement on choice of specialty, I found that individuals within each group had expressed in their written essays quite different plans for a project. Time to present my dilemma to the class and let them decide. I gave them the options of staying with their present groups, forming new groups based on interests, or working individually, even if this meant reading and writing about computers, cutting out pictures, making a collage, or baking brownies. A chant went up, "interest groups, interest groups." Based on their essays, I formed new groups and then described once again what characterized each. Then I pulled out the plug. "You may now move to the table of your choice, or go to the Reading Center if you do not want to belong to any of these groups." When the dust settled, we had six self-selected groups in five different specialties, ownership established, eager to begin.

My biweekly lessons continued throughout the term, along with bimonthly visits to the computer lab run by Ada Korson. Each third grade class received two new multimedia Macs (LC 575 CD) and funds for software. I was hired to teach the other four third grade classes once a week. The P.S. 6 Centennial Cyberspace Station

was lifting off the launch pad. We continued through the spring term with sharing of software discovered, producing individualized letterheads and team newsletters with *The Writing Center*, and completing a second administration of the Computer Literacy Assessment Tool. I plan to have the scoring done by a disinterested colleague, and to look at results as a function of the five quite distinctive styles of the collaborating teachers, from enabling to disabling. Further refinement of the CLAT and more precise identification of treatment variables across groups will permit drawing of ever more firm implications for my teaching of "computer literacy."

Summary and Conclusions

Most problems facing CBL not only are short-term and solvable, they are dwarfed by the medium's advantages. CBL enables students to study almost any time at convenient locations. The handicapped and bedridden have ready access, slow learners can work without embarrassment, gifted students can move quickly from easy to more challenging material, and entire courses may be completed early or reviewed till performance is satisfactory.

CBL offers students familiarity with the pervasive medium of the Information Age. Many students will find that the skills they acquire in school will be of great help when applying for jobs, whether they aspire to be scientists or programmers, doctors or secretaries. Finally, computers provide multimedia, interactive instruction, practice, and testing, thereby allowing teachers more time for personal forms of diagnosis and guidance. (See **Figure 11.13**.) The next chapter highlights features of "interactive learning environments" that have been alluded to throughout this textbook, and the final chapter describes computer networks that comprise the "information superhighway."

Notes

[1]Goldstein, Herman H., *The Computer: From Pascal to von Neumann* (Princeton, NJ: Princeton University Press, 1972, 1993); Freed, Les, illustrated by Ishida, Sarah, *The History of Computers* (Emeryville, CA: Ziff-Davis, 1995).

[2]Orey, Michael A., & Nelson, Wayne A., "Development Principles for Intelligent Tutoring Systems: Integrating Cognitive Theory into the Development of Computer-Based Instruction," *Educational Technology Research and Development*, 41, 1(1993), pp. 65–66.

Figure 11.13. Following instruction and example, these students are setting up their own database files. Those having difficulty receive further guidance either from the teacher or from the computer itself by calling up a "help menu."

[3]Collis, Betty A., & Verwijs, Carla, "A Human Approach to Electronic Performance and Learning Support Systems: Hybrid EPSS," *Educational Technology*, 35 (January/February 1995), p. 12; see also, Gery, G. J., *Electronic Performance Support Systems* (Boston: Weingarten Publications, 1991); Stevens, George H., & Stevens, Emily F., *Designing Electronic Performance Support Tools: Improving Workplace Performance with Hypertext, Hypermedia, and Multimedia* (Englewood Cliffs, NJ: Educational Technology Publications, 1995).

[4]Papert, Seymour, *Mindstorms: Children, Computers, and Powerful Ideas* (New York: Basic, 1980), p. 4.

[5]Papert, Seymour, "The Next Step: LogoWriter," *Classroom Computer Learning*, 6 (April 1986), p. 39.

[6]*Ibid.*, p. 40. See also, Singh, Jagjit K., "Cognitive Effects of Programming in Logo: A Review of the Literature and Synthesis of Strategies for Research," *Journal of Research on Computing in Education*, 25 (Fall 1992), pp. 88–104. Good effects have been found on rule learning and inductive reasoning.

[7]Scott, D. F., *Programming Illustrated* (Indianapolis, IN: Que, 1994; Milheim, William D., ed., *Authoring-Systems Software for Computer-Based Training* (Englewood Cliffs, NJ: Educational Technology Publications, 1994).

[8]Kulik, James A., Bangert, Robert L., & Williams, George W., "Effects of Computer-Based Teaching on Secondary School Students," *Journal of Educational Psychology*, 75 (February 1983), pp. 19–26; Kulik, James A., Kulik, Chen-Lin C., & Cohen, Peter A., "Effectiveness of Computer-based College Teaching: A Meta-analysis of Findings," *Review of Educational Research*, 50 (Winter 1980), pp. 525–544; Kulik, James A., & Bangert-Drowns, Robert L., "Effectiveness of Technology in Precollege Mathematics and Science Teaching," *Journal of Educational Technology Systems*, 12, 2(1983–84), pp. 150–156; Farr, Marshall J., &

Psotka, Joseph, eds., *Intelligent Instruction by Computer: Theory and Practice* (New York: Taylor & Francis, 1992); Thompson, Ann, Simonson, Michael, & Hargrave, Constance, *Educational Technology: A Review of the Research* (Washington, DC: Association for Educational Communications and Technology, 1992).

[9]Levin, Henry M., & Meister, Gail, "Is CAI Cost-Effective?" *Phi Delta Kappan*, 67 (June 1986), pp. 745–749.

[10]Niemiec, Richard P., Blackwell, Madeline C., & Walberg, Herbert J., "CAI Can Be Doubly Effective," *Phi Delta Kappan*, 67 (June 1986), p. 751.

[11]Clark, Richard E., "Confounding in Educational Computing Research," *Journal of Educational Computing Research*, 1, 2(1985), pp. 139–140; "The Importance of Treatment Explication: A Reply to J. Kulik, C-L. Kulik, and R. Bangert-Drowns," *Journal of Educational Computing Research*, 1, 4(1985), p. 392; "Evidence for Confounding in Computer-Based Instruction Studies: Analyzing the Meta-Analyses," *Educational Communication and Technology Journal*, 33 (Winter 1985), pp. 251–252, 258; Clariana, Rob B., Ross, Steven M., & Morrison, Gary R., "The Effects of Different Feedback Strategies Using Computer-Administered Multiple-Choice Questions as Instruction," *Educational Technology Research and Development*, 39, 1(1991), pp. 5–17; Jones, Loretta L., & Smith, Stanley G., "Can Multimedia Instruction Meet Our Expectations?" *EDUCOM Review*, 27 (January/February 1992), pp. 39–43.

[12]Clark, "Confounding in Educational Computing Research," pp. 140–141.

[13]Clark, Richard E., "Research on Student Thought Processes During Computer-Based Instruction," *Journal of Instructional Development*, 7, 3(1984), pp. 2–5; Cennamo, Katherine S., "Students' Perceptions of the Ease of Learning from Computers and Interactive Video: An Exploratory Study," *Journal of Educational Technology Systems*, 21, 3(1992–93), pp. 251–263. There appears to be a medium × objective interaction. Instructional TV is generally perceived as best (easiest) for learning psychomotor skills and for changing attitudes. Books and computers are perceived as best (easiest) sources for acquiring verbal information and intellectual skills. The effects of perception on effort also might well be influenced by student characteristics. **Once again, no simple recipes come from research.**

[14]Hooper, Simon, "Cooperative Learning and Computer-Based Instruction," *Educational Technology Research and Development*, 40, 3(1992), pp. 21–38; Rysavy, S. Del Marie, & Sales, Gregory C., "Cooperative Learning in Computer-Based Instruction," *Educational Technology Research and Development*, 39, 2(1991), pp. 70–79.

[15]Bowers, C.A., "Teaching a Nineteenth-Century Mode of Thinking Through a Twentieth-Century Machine," *Educational Theory*, 38 (Winter 1988), p. 46.

[16]Orey, Michael A., & Nelson, Wayne A., "Development Principles for Intelligent Tutoring Systems: Integrating Cognitive Theory into the Development of Computer-Based Instruction," *Educational Technology Research and Development*, 41,

1(1993), p. 70. See also Hannafin, Robert D., & Savenye, Wilhelmina, "Technology in the Classroom: The Teacher's New Role and Resistance to It," *Educational Technology*, 33 (June 1993), pp. 26–31. A case is made for view of student use of interactive multimedia as consistent with constructivist theory of learning, and at odds with views held by teachers and society generally.

[17]Costello, Gerry, "The Systems Design Approach to Developing Computer Based Instruction," *Performance & Instruction*, 32 (May/June 1993), pp. 11–13; Duffield, Judith A., "Designing Computer Software for Problem-Solving Instruction," *Educational Technology Research and Development*, 39, 1(1991), pp. 50–62; Sorge, Dennis H., Campbell, John P., & Russell, James D., "Evaluating Interactive Video: Software and Hardware," *Tech Trends*, 38 (April/May 1993), pp. 19–26.

[18]Reiser, Robert A., & Kegelmann, Harald W., "Evaluating Instructional Software: A Review and Critique of Current Methods," *Educational Technology Research and Development*, 42, 3(1994), p. 68.

[19]Allard, Janicemarie, & Fish, Judy, "On Computer Education: Some Critical Comments," *Journal of Thought*, 21 (Winter 1986), p. 9: "Educators must gain a critical distance from the computer bandwagon in order to establish policy setting reasonable limits upon its expansion within the public school system." Larry Cuban (Stanford University) in his "Déjà Vu All Over Again?" (*Electronic Learning*, 15 [October 1995], pp. 34–37, 61) rightly explained the resistance of many teachers to electronically-mediated instruction in terms of our interest in **efficient expenditure of time and energy.** He gave us credit for setting justified priorities and for devising effective means of achieving both the mundane and highest aims of education. To be convincing, advocates of CBL need to comprehend and respect this context.

Sources

Selected **educational software titles** are listed in the Sources section at the end of this book. Discount retailers are listed at the end of Chapter **12**. Product descriptions may be obtained from:

ABC/CLIO: 1-800-422-2546
A.D.A.M. Software: 1-800-755-ADAM
Aeius Corp.: 1-408-257-0658
AfroLink Software: 1-213-731-5465
Agency for Instructional Technology: 1-800-457-4509
AIMS Media: 1-800-FOR-AIMS
Allan Communication: 1-800-325-7850
Amazing Media: 1-415-453-0686
The American Education Corp.: 1-800-222-2811
Aquarius Instructional: 1-800-338-2644
A.U. Software: 1-202-265-6443
Avtex Interactive Media: 1-800-695-GAME
Barnum Software: 1-510-465-5070

Bergwall Productions: 1-800-645-3565
BLS Tutorsystems: 1-800-545-7766
Bright Star Technology, Inc.: 1-206-451-3697
Brøderbund Software, Inc.: 1-800-521-6263
Bureau of Electronic Publishing: 1-800-828-4766
Bytes of Learning, Inc.: 1-800-465-6428
Bytes & Pieces: 1-516-751-2535
CAE Software: 1-800-354-3462
Cambium Development, Inc.: 1-800-231-1779
Cambridge Development Laboratory, Inc.: 1-800-637-0047
Cambrix Publishing: 1-800-927-7848
CD Technology, Inc.: 1-408-752-8500
Chariot Software Group: 1-800-242-7468
Claris Corp.: 1-800-3-CLARIS
Cliff Notes, Inc.: 1-800-228-4078
The College Board: 1-212-713-8165
Compact Publishing: 1-800-964-1518
Compton's New Media, Inc.: 1-800-862-2206
Compu-Teach: 1-800-44-TEACH
Computer Curriculum Corp., Simon & Schuster Educational Technology Group: 1-800-227-8324
Computer Literacy Press: 1-800-225-5413
CONDUIT: 1-800-365-9774
Contér Software: 1-800-CD-TEACH
Context Systems, Inc.: 1-215-675-5000
The Continental Press: 1-800-233-0759
Creative Learning, Inc.: 1-800-842-5360
Critical Thinking Software: 1-800-458-4849
Data Command, Inc.: 1-800-528-7390
Davidson & Associates, Inc.: 1-800-545-7677
D.C. Heath & Co.: 1-800-428-8071
Decision Development: 1-800-835-4332
DeLorme Mapping: 1-207-865-1234
Didatech Software, Ltd.: 1-800-665-0667
Discis Knowledge Research, Inc.: 1-800-567-4321
The Discovery Channel: 1-301-986-1999
EA Kids: 1-415-513-7379
Ebook, Inc.: 1-510-429-1331
EBSCO Publishing: 1-800-653-2726
Edmark Corp.: 1-800-362-2890
Educational Activities: 1-800-645-3739
Educational Resources: 1-800-624-2926
Edunetics Corp.: 1-800-969-2602
EE Multimedia Productions, Inc.: 1-801-973-0081
The Electronic Bookshelf, Inc.: 1-800-327-7323
EME Corp.: 1-800-848-2050
Encyclopaedia Britannica Educational Corporation: 1-800-554-9862
Entrex Software, Inc.: 1-800-667-0007
Excelsior Software, Inc.: 1-800-473-4572
Facts On File, Inc.: 1-800-322-8755
Follett Software Co.: 1-800-323-3397
Gamco Education Materials: 1-800-351-1404
Gessler Publishing Co., Inc.: 1-800-456-5825

Global Information Systems Technology, Inc.: 1-217-352-1165
Graphix Zone, Inc.: 1-714-833-3838
Great Wave Software: 1-800-423-1144
Greene & Associates: 1-602-730-0842
Grolier Electronic Publishing, Inc.: 1-800-285-4534
Harcourt Brace Publishers: 1-800-782-4479
Harmonic Vision, Inc.: 1-708-467-2395
Hartley Courseware: 1-800-247-1380
Houghton Mifflin: 1-800-733-2828
Humanities Software, Inc.: 1-800-245-6737
IBM Corp.: 1-800-IBM-4EDU
Ideal Learning: 1-800-441-2376
Intelligent Software, Inc.: 1-800-521-4518
Intellimation: 1-800-346-8355
IntelliTools: 1-800-899-6687
Interactive Publishing Corp.: 1-800-472-8777
International Software/Lingo Fun, Inc.: 1-800-745-8258
Interplay Productions, Inc.: 1-714-553-6655
IPS Publishing, Inc.: 1-206-944-8996
Jostens Learning Corp.: 1-800-521-8538
J. Weston Walch, Publisher: 1-800-341-6094
Kidsview Software, Inc., 1-800-542-7501
Knowledge Adventure, Inc.: 1-800-542-4240
Knowledge Engineering: 1-800-548-7947
K–12 Micromedia Publishing: 1-800-292-1997
Laser Learning: 1-800-70-LASER
Lawrence Productions: 1-800-421-4157
The Learning Co.: 1-800-852-2255; 1-510-792-2101
The Learning Co. (language): 1-800-726-5087
The Learning Improvement Co.: 1-800-759-4228
The Learning Team: 1-800-793-TEAM
Lenel Systems International, Inc.: 1-716-248-9720
Lindy Enterprises, Inc.: 1-800-937-8227
Logal Software, Inc.: 1-800-LOGAL-US
Logicus, Inc.: 1-905-939-8652
Logo Computer Systems: 1-800-321-5646
Lucerne Media: 1-201-538-1401
Macmillan New Media: 1-800-342-1338
Major Educational Resources Corp.: 1-800-989-5353
Marshall Cavendish Publishers: 1-800-821-9881
Maxis: 1-510-254-9700
McGraw-Hill Educational Resources: 1-800-722-4726
MECC: 1-800-685-MECC, ext. 549
Media Resources: 1-800-395-3333
Medio Multimedia, Inc.: 1-206-867-5500
Merit Audio Visual: 1-800-753-6488
Micrographx, Inc.: 1-800-733-3729
Micro Learningware: 1-507-674-3705
Micrograms, Inc.: 1-800-338-4726
Microsoft Corp.: 1-800-426-9400; 1-206-635-4948 (TDD)
Mindplay: 1-800-221-7911
Mindscape: 1-800-234-3088
Misty City Software: 1-800-795-0049
MPI Multimedia: 1-800-777-2223

Multicom Publishing: 1-206-622-5530
National Geographic Society: 1-800-368-2728; 1-800-548-9797 (TDD)
NCS: 1-800-447-3269
NewsBank: 1-800-762-8182
Nordic Software: 1-402-488-5086
OnLine Computer Systems: 1-800-922-9204
On/Q Corp.: 1-800-463-3425
Opcode Systems: 1-415-856-3333
Optical Data Corp.: 1-800-524-2481
Optimum Resources: 1-800-327-1473
Orange Cherry/New Media Schoolhouse Software: 1-800-672-6002
Philip Roy: 1-800-255-9085
Pierian Spring Software: 1-800-472-8578
Power Industries, Inc.: 1-617-235-7733
Pre-Engineering Software Corp.: 1-504-769-3728
Prof. Weissman's Software: 1-718-698-5219
Projac Software: 1-818-886-3234
Quality Computers: 1-800-777-3642
Quanta Press: 1-612-379-3956
Que Software: 1-800-992-0244
Rand McNally Educational Publishing: 1-800-678-7263
Redgate: 1-800-333-8760
Roth Publishing: 1-800-899-ROTH
Scholastic, Inc.: 1-800-541-5513
Science for Kids: 1-800-572-4362
Science Research Associates: 1-800-843-8855
Sierra: 1-800-757-7707
Signature Music Company: 1-800-888-7151
Skills Bank Corp.: 1-800-451-5726
SmartStuff Software: 1-800-671-3999
Social Issues Resources Series, Inc.: 1-800-232-SIRS
SoftArc, Inc.: 1-800-SOFT-ARC
Softkey International, Inc.: 1-617-494-1200, ext. 346
Software House: 1-800-541-6078
Sumeria, Inc.: 1-415-904-0800
Sunburst/Wings for Learning: 1-800-431-1934
Surfside Software, Inc.: 1-800-942-9008
Syracuse Language Systems: 1-315-478-6729
Teacher Support Software: 1-800-228-2871
Techpool Software: 1-216-382-1234
TENEX Computer Express: 1-800 PROMPT-1
Terrapin Software, Inc.: 1-800-972-8200
Tom Snyder Productions, Inc.: 1-800-342-0236
Tudor Publishing Co.: 1-800-998-4531
Ventura Educational Systems: 1-800-336-1022
Vernier Software: 1-503-297-5317
Videodiscovery: 1-800-548-3472
The Voyager Co.: 1-800-446-2001
William K. Bradford: 1-800-421-2009
Word Associates, Inc.: 1-708-291-1101
World Library, Inc.: 1-800-443-0238
WorldView Software: 1-800-34-STUDY
Worldwide Publishing, Inc.: 1-214-423-0090

Suppliers of **school administrative software** (attendance, grades, reports, etc.) identified in the *Media & Methods Buyer's Guide 1995* include:

Baker & Taylor Software: 1-800-775-4100
Bobbing Software: 1-512-295-5045
Chancery Software, Ltd.: 1-800-999-9931
Claris Corp.: 1-800-544-8554
CRS, Inc.: 1-800-433-9239
J&S Software: 1-516-944-9304
Jay Klein Productions Grade Busters: 1-719-591-9815
K–12 Micromedia Publishing: 1-800-292-1997
McGraw-Hill School Systems: 1-800-663-0544
Mountain Lake Software: 1-800-669-6574
NCS: 1-800-447-3269
Rediker Administrative Software, Inc.: 1-800-882-2994
Techbyte International, Inc.: 1-800-535-3487

Library automation software is provided by the following companies, as listed in *Media & Methods,* 31 (January/February 1995), pp. 10–12, Copyright © 1995. All rights reserved. Reprinted by permission of the publisher.

Ameritech Library Services, School Division: 1-800-288-1145
Caspr, Inc.: 1-800-852-2777
Catalog Card Co.: 1-800-328-2923
Chancery Software, Ltd.: 1-800-999-9931
COMPanion Corp.: 1-800-347-6439
Data Trek, Inc.: 1-800-876-5484
DRA/multiLIS: 1-800-753-0053
Dymaxion Research, Ltd.: 1-902-422-1973
The Follett Software Co.: 1-800-323-3397
Gateway Software Corp.: 1-800-735-3637
Gaylord Information Systems: 1-800-962-9580
Marcive, Inc.: 1-800-531-7678
McGraw-Hill School Systems: 1-800-663-0544
Nicholas Advanced Technologies, Inc.: 1-800-661-4109
SIRSI Corp.: 1-205-922-9825
Social Issues Resources Series, Inc.: 1-800-232-SIRS
Softkey International, Inc.: 1-800-843-2204
Softkey Software Products of Florida, Inc.: 1-407-367-0005
Solinet: 1-800-999-8558
Time Warner Interactive: 1-800-482-3766
T/Maker: 1-800-370-9008
Vicarious: 1-800-696-0507, ext. 2200
Walt Disney Computer Software, Inc.: 1-818-841-3326; Canada, 1-800-668-4839.
Winnebago Software Co.: 1-800-533-5430, ext. 1190

To obtain a list of companies that produce **software** compatible with the operating system of your computer, call Microsoft (1-800-555-4K12 for a copy of *Education Product Listing: A Source for Windows-based K–12 Products*), International Business Machines (1-800-342-6672 for a copy of *Directory of Products and Services for OS/2 2.X*), or Apple Computer (1-800-SOS-APPL for the Apple User Assistance Center).

If you have a **CD-ROM** drive, multimedia computer (MPC) you may test a vast variety of **applications and educational software** before purchase and be given a "key" code by phone to download it directly from the CD-ROM disk onto your hard drive (manuals and backup disks sent separately). Call:

Club Kidsoft: 1-800-354-6150
Compton's NewMedia: 1-619-929-2500
PC-SIG: 1-800-245-6717, operator 2744
Softbank: 1-408-644-7800
TestDrive: 1-800-788-8055

Commercial software generally is licensed to the buyer for use on just one machine. Additional fees usually must be paid for site and network use. Always read the copyright notices included with the software you purchase. Importing copyrighted material into multimedia presentations is subject to restrictions. For guidance, obtain ***Software Use and the Law: A Guide for Individuals, Businesses, Educational Institutions, and User Groups*** and a Self Audit Kit, both *gratis*, and related inexpensive guides, software, and videos from:

Software Publishers Association
1730 M Street, N.W., Suite 700
Washington, DC 20036
1-202-452-1600
1-800-388-7478 ("piracy hotline")

Computer basics and CBL courseware selection, production, and utilization guidelines may be found in the following. Novices are especially well-served by recent editions with their rich illustrations (tied closely to associated text, especially those by Ziff-Davis) and companion diskettes and CDs (some with hypertext links). As indicated in Chapter **6**, it truly is amazing what computer technology has done for print publication, quite in addition to non-print publication.

Alessi, Stephen M., & Trollip, Stanley R., *Computer-Based Instruction: Methods and Development*, 2nd ed. (Boston: Allyn and Bacon, 1991).

The Alliance for Technology Access, *Computer Resources for People with Disabilities: A Guide to Exploring Today's Assistive Technology* (Alameda, CA: Hunter House, 1994).

Appleman, Daniel, illustrated by Ishida, Sarah, *How Computer Programming Works* (Emeryville, CA: Ziff-Davis, 1994).

Atelsek, Jean, illustrated by Murov, Debra, *All About Computers* (Emeryville, CA: Ziff-Davis, 1993).

Azarmza, Reza, *Educational Computing: Principles and Applications* (Englewood Cliffs, NJ: Educational Technology Publications, 1991).

Bailey, Gerald D., ed., *Computer-Based Integrated Learning Systems* (Englewood Cliffs, NJ: Educational Technology Publications, 1993).

Barron, Ann E., & Orwig, Gary W., *New Technologies for Education: A Beginner's Guide* (Englewood, CO: Libraries Unlimited, 1992).

Bauersfeld, Penny, *Software by Design: Creating People Friendly Software* (New York: M&T Books, 1994).

Beekman, George, *HyperCard in a Hurry* (Belmont, CA: Wadsworth, 1990).

Beynon, John, & Mackay, Hughie, eds., *Technological Literacy and Curriculum* (New York: Falmer Press, 1992).

Beynon, John, & Mackay, Hughie, eds., *Computers into Classrooms: More Questions than Answers* (New York: Falmer Press, 1993).

Biow, Lisa, illustrated by Wattenmaker, Pamela Drury, *How to Use Your Computer* (Emeryville, CA: Ziff-Davis, 1993).

Bitter, Gary D., ed., *Macmillan Encyclopedia of Computers* (New York: Macmillan, 1992).

Bitter, Gary G., Camuse, Ruth A., & Durbin, Vicki L., *Using a Microcomputer in the Classroom*, 3rd ed. (Boston: Allyn and Bacon, 1993).

Blissmer, Robert H., *Introducing Computers: Concepts, Systems, and Applications* (New York: Wiley, 1992).

Bright, George W., *Microcomputer Applications in the Elementary Classroom: A Guide for Teachers* (Boston: Allyn and Bacon, 1987).

Brock, Patricia A., *Educational Technology in the Classroom* (Englewood Cliffs, NJ: Educational Technology Publications, 1994).

Budin, Howard, Kendall, Diane S., & Lengel, James, *Using Computers in the Social Studies* (New York: Teachers College Press, 1986).

Clements, Douglas H., *Computers in Elementary Mathematics Education* (Englewood Cliffs, NJ: Prentice-Hall, 1989).

Costanzo, William V., *Electronic Text: Learning to Write, Read, and Reason with Computers* (Englewood Cliffs, NJ: Educational Technology Publications, 1989).

Culp, George H., & Watkins, G. Morgan, *The Educator's Guide to HyperCard & HyperTalk* (Boston: Allyn and Bacon, 1993).

Doll, Carol, *Evaluating Educational Software* (Chicago: American Library Association, 1987).

Dictionary of Computing, 3rd ed. (New York: Oxford University Press, 1990).

Downing, Douglas, & Covington, Michael, *Dictionary of Computer Terms*, 3rd ed. (Hauppauge, NY: Barron's Educational Services, 1992).

Educational Software Evaluation Consortium Staff, *Educational Software Preview Guide, 1990-91* (Eugene, OR: International Society for Technology in Education, 1991).

Educational Technology Anthology Series: Volume Two, Expert Systems and Intelligent Computer-Aided Instruction (Englewood Cliffs, NJ: Educational Technology Publications, 1991).

Espinosa, Leonard J., *Microcomputer Facilities in Schools* (Englewood, CO: Libraries Unlimited, 1990).

Farmer, Lesley S.J., & Hewlett, Jean, *I Speak HyperCard* (Englewood, CO: Libraries Unlimited, 1992).

Farr, Marshall J., & Psotka, Joseph, eds., *Intelligent Instruction by Computer: Theory and Practice* (New York: Taylor & Francis, 1992).

Favaro, Peter J., *An Educator's Guide to Microcomputers and Learning* (Englewood Cliffs, NJ: Prentice-Hall, 1986).

Floyd, Steve, *IBM Multimedia Toolkit: Complete Guide to Hardware and Software Applications* (New York: Brady Computer Books, 1991).

Freed, Les, illustrated by Ishida, Sarah, *The History of Computers* (Emeryville, CA: Ziff-Davis, 1995).

Gallini, Joan K., & Gredler, Margaret E., *Instructional Design for Computers: Cognitive Applications in BASIC and Logo* (Glenview, IL: Scott, Foresman, 1989).

Gayeski, Diane M., ed., *Multimedia for Learning: Development, Application, Evaluation* (Englewood Cliffs, NJ: Educational Technology Publications, 1993).

Geisert, Paul G., & Futrell, Mynga K., *Teachers, Computers, and Curriculum: Microcomputers in the Classroom* (Boston: Allyn and Bacon, 1990).

Gibbons, Andrew, & Fairweather, Peter, *Designing Computer-Based Instruction* (Englewood Cliffs, NJ: Educational Technology Publications, 1996).

Gluck, Myke, *HyperCard, Hypertext, and Hypermedia for Libraries and Media Centers* (Englewood, CO: Libraries Unlimited, 1989).

Goldstein, Herman H., *The Computer: From Pascal to von Neumann* (Princeton, NJ: Princeton University Press, 1972, 1993).

Goodman, Danny, *The Complete HyperCard 2.0 Handbook*, 3rd ed. (New York, Bantam Books, 1990).

Gookin, Dan, & Rathbone, Andy, *PCs for Dummies*, 3rd ed. (Indianapolis, IN: IDG Books, 1995).

Grabinger, R. Scott, Wilson, Brent W., & Jonassen, David H., *Building Expert Systems in Training and Education* (New York: Praeger, 1990).

Harper, Dennis O., *Logo Theory and Practice* (Pacific Grove, CA: Brooks-Cole, 1989).

Hoskins, Jim, & Blackledge, Jack, *Exploring the PowerPC Revolution*, 2nd ed. (Gulf Breeze, FL: Maximum Press, 1995).

Iuppa, Nicholas, *The Multimedia Adventure* (White Plains, NY: Knowledge Industry, 1992).

Jamsa, Kris, *Rescued by . . . Upgrading Your PC* (Las Vegas, NV: Jamsa Press, 1994).

Jamsa, Kris, *Welcome to . . . Personal Computers*, 3rd ed. (New York: MIS:Press, 1995).

Jonassen, David H., ed., *Instructional Designs for Microcomputer Courseware* (Hillsdale, NJ: Lawrence Erlbaum Associates, 1988).

Jonassen, David H., *Hypertext/Hypermedia* (Englewood Cliffs, NJ: Educational Technology Publications, 1989).

Jonassen, David H., & Mandl, Heinz, eds., *Designing Hypermedia for Learning* (New York: Springer-Verlag, 1990).

Jones, Mark K., *Human-Computer Interaction: A Design Guide* (Englewood Cliffs, NJ: Educational Technology Publications, 1989).

Keegan, Mark, *Scenario Educational Software: Design and Development of Discovery Learning* (Englewood Cliffs, NJ: Educational Technology Publications, 1995).

Knorr, Eric, ed., *The PC Bible* (Berkeley: Peachpit Press, 1994).

Kraynak, Joe, *10 Minute Guide to PC Computing* (Indianapolis, IN: Alpha Books, 1993).

Kraynak, Joe, *Show Me PCs: A Visual Guide to the Basics* (Indianapolis, IN: Alpha Books, 1994).

Kraynak, Joe, Wang, W.E., & Flynn, J., *The First Book of Personal Computing* (Indianapolis, IN: Alpha Books, 1992).

Lajoie, Susanne P., & Derry, Sharon J., eds., *Computers as Cognitive Tools* (Hillsdale, NJ: Lawrence Erlbaum Associates, 1993).

Lamb, Annette C., *Emerging Technologies of Instruction: Hypertext, Hypermedia, and Interactive Multimedia: A Selected Bibliography* (Englewood Cliffs, NJ: Educational Technology Publications, 1991).

Lasselle, Joan, & Ramsay, Carol, *The ABCs of Your DOS PC* (San Francisco: SYBEX, 1994).

Lathrop, Ann, *Online and CD-ROM Databases in School Libraries: Readings* (Englewood, CO: Libraries Unlimited, 1989).

Lee, William W., & Mamone, Robert A., with Roadman, Kenneth H., *Computer Based Training Handbook: Assessment, Design, Development, Evaluation* (Englewood Cliffs, NJ: Educational Technology Publications, 1995).

Lewis, Rita, *Show Me the Mac: A Visual Guide to the Basics* (Indianapolis, IN: Alpha Books, 1993).

Long, Larry, & Long, Nancy, *Microcomputer: Concepts and Software*, 2nd ed. (Englewood Cliffs, NJ: Prentice-Hall, 1992).

Maddux, Cleborne D., & Johnson, Dee L., *Educational Computing: Learning with Tomorrow's Technologies* (Boston: Allyn and Bacon, 1992).

Magid, Lawrence J., illustrated by Grimes, John, edited by DiNucci, Darcy, *The Little PC Book* (Berkeley: Peachpit Press, 1993).

Mandl, Heinz, & Lesgold, Alan, eds., *Learning Issues for Intelligent Tutoring Systems* (New York: Springer-Verlag, 1988).

Mayer, Richard E., ed., *Teaching and Learning Computer Programming: Multiple Research Perspectives* (Hillsdale, NJ: Lawrence Erlbaum Associates, 1988).

McFarland, Thomas D., & Parker, O. Reese, *Expert Systems in Education and Training* (Englewood Cliffs, NJ: Educational Technology Publications, 1990).

Megarry, Jacquetta, *Inside Information: Computers, Communications, and People* (New York: Parkwest Publications, 1992).

Merrill, Paul F., Hammons, Kathy, Vincent, Bret R., Reynolds, Peter L., Christenson, Larry, & Tolman, Marvin N., *Computers in Education*, 3rd ed. (Boston: Allyn and Bacon, 1996).

Milheim, William D., *Computer-Based Simulations in Education and Training: A Selected Bibliography* (Englewood Cliffs, NJ: Educational Technology Publications, 1992).

Milheim, William D., ed., *Authoring-Systems Software for Computer-Based Training* (Englewood Cliffs, NJ: Educational Technology Publications, 1994).

Miller, Mike, *Oops! The PC Problem Solver Anybody Can Use* (Indianapolis, IN: Que, 1994).

Miller, Samuel K., *Selecting and Implementing Educational Software* (Boston: Allyn and Bacon, 1987).

Mueller, Scott, *Upgrading & Repairing Quick Reference* (Indianapolis, IN: Que, 1994).

Muffoletto, Robert, & Knupfer, Nancy Nelson, eds., *Computers in Education: Social, Political, and Historical Perspectives* (Cresskill, NJ: Hampton Press, 1993).

Myers, Linda, ed., *Approaches to Computer Writing Classrooms: Learning from Practical Experience* (Albany, NY: State University of New York Press, 1993).

Nelson, Kay Yarborough, *Voodoo Mac: Mastery Tips & Masterful Tricks*, 2nd ed. (Chapel Hill, NC: Ventana Press, 1994).

Norton, Peter, Eggebrecht, Lewis C., & Clark, Scott H. A., *Peter Norton's Inside the PC*, 6th ed. (Indianapolis, IN: Sams, 1995)

Norton, Peter, & Jourdain, Robert, *Peter Norton's PC Problem Solver*, 2nd ed. (New York: Brady Books, 1993).

O'Hara, Shelley, *The Complete Idiot's Guide to Buying & Upgrading PCs*, 2nd ed. (Indianapolis, IN: Alpha Books, 1995).

Owston, Ronald D., *Software Evaluation: A Criterion Based Approach* (Boston: Allyn and Bacon, 1987).

Pandit, Milind S., *How Computers Really Work* (Berkeley, CA: Osborne McGraw-Hill, 1993).

Papert, Seymour, *The Children's Machine: Rethinking School in the Age of the Computer* (New York: Basic Books, 1993).

Papert, Seymour, *Mindstorms: Children, Computers, and Powerful Ideas*, 2nd ed. (New York, Basic Books, 1993).

Perkins, David N., Schwartz, Judah L., West, Mary Maxwell, & Wiske, Martha Stone, eds., *Software Goes to School: Teaching for Understanding with New Technologies* (New York: Oxford University Press, 1995).

Pfaffenberger, Bryan, *Que's Computer User's Dictionary*, 4th ed. (Indianapolis, IN: Que, 1993).

Pfaffenberger, Bryan, *PCs in Plain English* (New York: MIS:Press, 1995).

Picciano, Anthony G., *Computers in the Schools: A Guide to Planning and Administration* (New York: Macmillan, 1994).

Pilgrim, Aubrey, *Upgrade or Repair Your PC* (New York: McGraw-Hill, 1995).

Pivovarnick, John, *The Complete Idiot's Guide to the Mac*, 2nd ed. (Indianapolis, IN: Alpha Books, 1994).

Pogue, David, *More Macs for Dummies* (Indianapolis, IN: IDG Books, 1994).

Poole, Bernard J., *Education for an Information Age: Teaching in the Computerized Classroom* (Madison, WI: WCB Brown & Benchmark, 1995).

Ragan, Tillman J., & Smith, Patricia L., *Programming Instructional Software: Applesoft BASIC Edition* (Englewood Cliffs, NJ: Educational Technology Publications, 1989).

Remer, Daniel, & Dunaway, Robert, *Legal Care for Your Software: A Step-by-Step Developer's Guide*, 5th ed. (San Francisco: SYBEX, 1995).

Reynolds, Angus, & Davis, Dick, *Computer-Based Learning: A Self-Teaching Guide* (New York: Wiley, 1985).

Ritchie, David, *The Computer Pioneers: The Making of the Modern Computer* (New York: Simon and Schuster, 1986).

Rizzo, John, & Clark, K. Daniel, *How Macs Work* (Emeryville, CA: Ziff-Davis, 1993).

Roberts, Nancy, Friel, Susan N., Carter, Richard C., & Miller, Margery S., *Integrating Computers into the Elementary and Middle School* (Boston: Allyn and Bacon, 1988).

Robinette, Michelle, *Macs for Teachers* (Indianapolis, IN: IDG Books, 1995).

Romiszowski, Alexander J., *New Technologies in Education and Training* (East Brunswick, NJ: Nichols Publishing, 1993).

Rooze, Gene E., & Northup, Terry, *Using Computers to Teach Social Studies* (Englewood, CO: Libraries Unlimited, 1986).

Rubin, Charles, *The Macintosh Bible: What Do I Do Now Book*, 3rd ed. (Berkeley: Peachpit Press, 1994).

Rubin, Charles, *The Little Book of Computer Wisdom: How to Make Friends with Your PC or Mac* (New York: Houghton Mifflin, 1995).

Sargent III, Murray, & Shoemaker, Richard L., *The Personal Computer from the Inside Out: The Programmer's Guide to Low-Level PC Hardware and Software* (Reading, MA: Addison-Wesley, 1995).

Schofield, Janet W., *Computers and Classroom Culture* (New York: Cambridge University Press, 1995).

Schueller, Ulrich, & Veddeler, Hans Georg, *Upgrading & Maintaining Your PC*, 3rd ed. (Grand Rapids, MI: Abacus, 1995).

Schwier, Richard A., & Misanchuk, Earl R., *Interactive Multimedia Instruction* (Englewood Cliffs, NJ: Educational Technology Publications, 1993).

Scott, D. F., *Programming Illustrated* (Indianapolis, IN: Que, 1994).

Simonson, Michael R., & Thompson, Ann, *Educational Computing Foundations*, 2nd ed. (New York: Merrill, 1994).

Simpson, Alan, *Your First Computer*, 2nd ed. (San Francisco: SYBEX, 1994).

Sloan, Douglas, ed., *The Computer in Education: A Critical Perspective* (New York: Teachers College Press, 1985).

Sloane, Howard N., Gordon, Hope M., Gunn, Carolee, & Mickelsen, Vicki G., *Evaluating Educational Software: A Guide for Teachers* (Boston: Allyn and Bacon, 1989).

Smith, Bud, revised by Gibbons, Dave, *Que's 1995 Computer Buyer's Guide* (Indianapolis, IN: Que, 1995).

Smith, Gina, & Laporte, Leo, *101 Computer Answers You Need to Know* (Emeryville, CA: Ziff-Davis, 1995).

Sobol, Mel, *Easy Macintosh*, 2nd ed. (Indianapolis, IN: Que, 1994).

Software for Schools, 1987-88: A Comprehensive Directory of Educational Software Grades Pre-K Through 12 (New York: Bowker, 1987).

Somogyi, Stephan, *The PowerPC Macintosh Book: The Inside Story on the New RISC-Based Macintosh* (Reading, MA: Addison-Wesley, 1994).

Soulier, J. Steven, *The Design and Development of Computer-Based Instruction* (Boston: Allyn and Bacon, 1988).

Stauffer, Todd, *Using Your Mac* (Indianapolis, IN: Que, 1995).

Steinberg, Esther R., *Teaching Computers to Teach*, 2nd ed. (Hillsdale, NJ: Lawrence Erlbaum Associates, 1991).

Steward, Winston, *Every Family's Guide to Computers* (Emeryville, CA: Ziff-Davis, 1995).

Sussman, Martin, & Loewenstern, Ernest, with Sann, Howard, *Total Health at the Computer: How to Be Pain Free* (Barrytown, NY: Station Hill Press, 1993).

Talab, Rosemary S., *Copyright and Instructional Technologies: A Guide to Fair Use and Permission Procedures*, 2nd ed. (Washington, DC: Association for Educational Communications and Technology, 1989).

Tessmer, Martin, Jonassen, David, & Caverly, David C., *A Non-Programmer's Guide to Designing Instruction for Microcomputers* (Englewood, CO: Libraries Unlimited, 1989).

Thompson, Ann, Simonson, Michael, & Hargrave, Constance, *Educational Technology: A Review of the Research* (Washington, DC: Association for Educational Communications and Technology, 1992).

Towne, Douglas M., *Learning and Instruction in Simulation Environments* (Englewood Cliffs, NJ: Educational Technology Publications, 1995).

Vockell, Edward L., *The Computer and Critical Thinking* (New York: Knopf, 1989).

Vockell, Edward L., et al., *The Computer in the Mathematic Curriculum* (New York: Knopf, 1988).

Vockell, Edward L., et al., *The Computer in the Reading Curriculum* (New York: McGraw-Hill, 1990.

Vockell, Edward L., & Schwartz, Eileen, *The Computer in the Classroom*, 2nd ed. (New York: McGraw-Hill, 1992).

von Neumann, John, *The Computer and the Brain* (New Haven, CT: Yale University Press, 1958, 1986).

Waggoner, Michael D., ed., *Empowering Networks: Computer Conferencing in Education* (Englewood Cliffs, NJ: Educational Technology Publications, 1992).

Wallace, James, & Erickson, Jim, *Hard Drive: Bill Gates and the Making of the Microsoft Empire* (New York: HarperCollins, 1992).

Webster's New World Dictionary of Computer Terms, 3rd ed. (Englewood Cliffs, NJ: Prentice-Hall, 1988).

White, Ron, illustrated by Downs, Timothy Edward, *How Computers Work: Includes Interactive CD-ROM* (Emeryville, CA: Ziff-Davis, 1994).

White, Ron, illustrated by Wattenmaker, Pamela Drury, *How Software Works* (Emeryville, CA: Ziff-Davis, 1993).

White, Ron, illustrated by English, Carrie, *How Anyone Can Fix and Rev Up PCs* (Emeryville, CA: Ziff-Davis, 1994).

Williams, Michael R., *A History of Computing Technology* (Englewood Cliffs, NJ: Prentice-Hall, 1985).

Willis, Jerry, *et al.*, *Computer Simulation: A Source Book to Learning in an Electronic Environment* (New York: Garland, 1987).

Wilson, Brent G., Hamilton, Roger, Teslow, James L., Cyr, Thomas A., *Technology Making a Difference: The Peakview Elementary School Study* (Syracuse, NY: ERIC Clearinghouse on Information & Technology, 1995).

Wyant, Gregg, & Hammerstrom, Tucker, illustrated by Clark, K. Daniel, *How Microprocessors Work* (Emeryville, CA: Ziff-Davis, 1994).

Wyatt, Allen, *Upgrading Your PC Illustrated* (Indianapolis, IN: Que, 1994).

Periodicals (most listed on America Online's "Teachers' Information Network") include:

Academic Computing
ACM Guide to Computing Literature
The Appleworks Educator
Bits and Bytes Review
The British Journal of Educational Technology
Byte
Children's Magic Window
Client/Server Computing
Compute
Computer Assisted English Language Learning Journal
ComputerLife
Computer Science Education
Computer Studies: Computers in Education
Computers and Education
Computers in Life Science Education
Computers in the Schools
Computerworld
Curriculum/Technology Quarterly
Desktop Publishers Journal
DOS Resource Guide
DOS World
Educational Computer Magazine
Educational Media International
Educational Software Report
Educational Software Selector
Educational Technology
Educational Technology Review
Educational & Training Technology International
Education Bulletin
Electronic Education
Electronic Learning
Family PC
Home PC
Home & School Mac
Inside Microsoft Windows
Interface: The Computer Education Quarterly
Journal of Artificial Intelligence in Education
Journal of Computer-Based Instructional Systems
Journal of Computer Science Education
Journal of Computers in Mathematics and Science Teaching
Journal of Computing in Childhood Education
Journal of Computing in Teacher Education
Journal of Educational Computing Research
Journal of Educational Technology Systems
Journal of Research on Computing in Teacher Education
Journal of Science Education & Technology
Journal of Special Education Technology
Journal of Technology Education
Journal of Technology in Mathematics
Journal of Technology and Teacher Education
Learning and Leading with Technology
Library Software Review
Logo Exchange
Mac Home Journal
Mac User
Macworld
Mathematics & Computer Education
Maximize: The Practical Guide to Windows
Media & Methods
Micro Computer Journal
Microcomputers in Education
MicroKids
National Forum of Instructional Technology Journal
National Logo Exchange
OS/2 Magazine
Parents' Guide to Highly-Rated Software
PC Computing
PC Magazine
PC Novice
PC Week
PC World
Power Windows
Science, Technology & Human Values
Shareware Magazine
Social Science Microcomputer Review
Technology and Learning

Tech Trends for Leaders in Education and Training
Windows K–12 Classroom Resource
Windows K–12 Technology Letter
Windows Magazine
Windows Sources

Information about making computer technologies **accessible to people with disabilities** may be obtained from:

Alliance for Technology Access (1-800-992-8111)
Apple Computer Worldwide Disabled Group Solutions
    (1-800-776-2333)
Closing the Gap (1-612-248-3294)
IBM Independence Series (1-800-IBM-4833 [TDD])
    (1-800-IBM-4832 [voice])

Tired of reading? Want to be **shown** how to use your computer? **Classes, videos, and instructional software** are available from:

Association for Educational Communications and Technology:
    1-202-347-7834
Chubb Advanced Training: 1-800-CHUBB-07
CompUSA: The Training Supercenter: 1-800-TRAIN 80
MacAcademy: 1-800-527-1914; 1-904-677-1918; London, 0181-445-5225
RMI Productions: 1-800-745-5480
University of Delaware: 1-302-831-8162
VideoGrafix Corp.: 1-800-842-4723; 1-918-825-6700
Video Projects, Inc.: 1-800-733-2200
Windows Academy: 1-800-527-1914; 1-904-677-1918
Ziff-Davis Publishing Co.: 1-800-688-0448; 1-510-601-2000

Students also are rich sources of information about computer functions and features. From the essay in **Figure 11.14** you can see how much one of Lorna Davis's (P.S. 6, Manhattan) fourth graders has picked up after just a few of my introductory lessons. Add to this what our students have learned from parents, peers, media, the computer lab, and from explorations on their own and we have the help we need just a plea away.

Study Items

1. Define "bits," "bytes," "RAM," and "ROM."
2. Diagram the main components of a computer system.
3. Distinguish between "hardware" and "software."
4. What are some features of hardware and software that serve to make them "user friendly?"

Figure 11.14. During my visits to elementary school classrooms, I ask students to write what they have learned, what they would change about my lessons, and what topics they would like to explore. Their responses, like the one shown here, reveal insights that guide my teaching. Reproduced with permission of P.S. 6 (Manhattan) principal Carmen Fariña, teacher Lorna Davis, Tatiana, and her parents.

5. What are some advantages of a graphics-based display (e.g., *System 7, Windows*) and "mouse" for students with disabilities?
6. Describe characteristics of early, mainframe computer-based projects (PLATO, Stanford, MECC, NDPCAL).
7. Distinguish between "tutorial" and "problem solving" CBL.
8. Distinguish between "inquiry" and "simulation" CBL.
9. Compare and contrast tutoring that may be provided by computer and that which may be provided by a teacher.
10. Describe "*LOGO*" programming.
11. Evaluate Seymour Papert's efforts to place children in control of computers rather than the other way around.

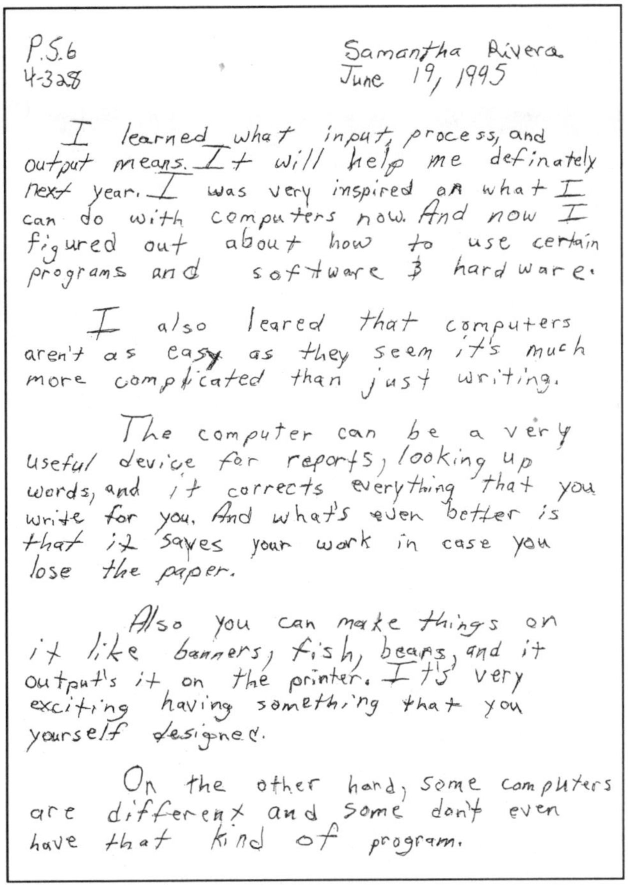

P.S.6
4-328

Samantha Rivera
June 19, 1995

I learned what input, process, and output means. It will help me definately next year. I was very inspired on what I can do with computers now. And now I figured out about how to use certain programs and software & hardware.

I also leared that computers aren't as easy as they seem it's much more complicated than just writing.

The computer can be a very useful device for reports, looking up words, and it corrects everything that you write for you. And what's even better is that it saves your work in case you lose the paper.

Also you can make things on it like banners, fish, bears, and it outputs it on the printer. It's very exciting having something that you yourself designed.

On the other hand, some computers are different and some don't even have that kind of program.

Figure 11.15. The teaching of "computer literacy" easily is integrated across the curriculum. It provides ample energized opportunities for reading, writing, discussing, sharing, and creating. And it touches every subject, from history to ethics. Here is an essay by one of Lorna Davis's fourth graders written in response to my question about what they had learned during my first few introductory lessons. Reproduced with permission.

12. Describe characteristics of any programming language (e.g., *BASIC, Pascal, C, PILOT*).

13. Speculate on merits and limitations of courseware produced commercially by specialists (former teachers, subject matter experts, computer programmers) versus that produced locally by a group of teachers.

14. How might local CBL courseware production affect a teacher's competence?

15. Assess merits of CBL when used at the preschool and elementary school levels.

16. Assess merits of CBL when used at the high school level.

17. Speculate on merits of CBL when used in special education.

Figure 11.16. Here Audrey Kaplan's fourth graders demonstrated both their knowledge and creativity, though my model (see **Figure 11.11**) tended to constrain the latter, not unlike the demands of "reality." Note, however, that the model was labeled "Computer Work**station**," and that I referred to it often as the students cut and pasted. That four of six groups substituted the more familiar term "Work**shop**" lends some credence to constructivist theory (that even what students perceive is affected as much by what they know and believe as by what a panel of rational folks would agree is before their eyes). Reproduced with permission.

18. Describe ways students might collaborate using each type of CBL, from drill-and-practice to simulation.

19. What similarities and distinctions do you see between inquiry CBL and disciplinary or interdisciplinary study?

20. In what ways does inquiry CBL ease the work of scholars in **advancing** knowledge based on information that has been codified on CD-ROM?

21. How can students emulate the work of researchers using on-line databases?

22. What are factors that might influence research comparing CBL with "conventional" teaching?

23. Assess the merits of "novelty" in achieving instructional objectives taking into account costs and student motivation.

24. List and describe criteria for selection and production of CBL courseware.

25. Define "interactivity" of CBL. Compare and contrast this with the sorts of interactions that might take place between a student and teacher.

26. Assess merits of "learner control" in CBL.

27. Distinguish between "learner control" in tutorial CBL and inquiry CBL.

28. Describe and prioritize aspects of "computer literacy."

29. Describe reservations you have about CBL in your classroom. How will you cope?

30. What activities would you sacrifice to make time to produce CBL courseware?

Suggested Activities

1. Browse through your local magazine shop to locate periodicals about personal computers. Purchase a few and decide which merit subscription.

2. Visit a computer store and ask the sales person to explain the inner workings and components of a computer.

3. Within one year I purchased three computers from three different dealers. I found defects with all three. The dealers were glad to repair or trade up, but refused or resisted strongly giving a refund. Locate a dealer with a national reputation to uphold.

4. Inventory hardware and software available in the school district where you teach.

5. Locate a local computer software dealer that permits testing of programs **before** purchase. I use Egghead Software (1-800-EGGHEAD or 1-800-949-3447 TDD for hearing impaired).

6. Assess your personal computing needs and ask three different dealers to make suitable equipment recommendations. Share findings with classmates.

7. Watch *Computer Chronicles* and write for a list of available videotapes (P.O. Box 2954, Washington, D.C. 17105). Also inquire about PC-TV programs on the Jones Computer Network—*Computers 101, @ Home, Business Computing, Users Group, MacTV.*

8. Obtain for your class and view *The Machine that Changed the World* and *The New Literacy: An Introduction to Computers* (CPB, 1-800-LEARNER).

9. Newspapers, PC magazines, and TV shows (e.g., *Computer Chronicles*, *PC-TV*) list upcoming computer exhibitions. Go to those in your area.

10. View demonstrations of each variety of CBL described in this chapter. Note if claims made match performance.

11. Search ads for courseware to find claims of having been classroom tested **and** revised. Attempt to find out if revision was based on student **achievement of specified objectives** ("learner verification") or merely on discovery of typos and bugs.

12. Locate a program that might serve in a class you teach. Evaluate it according to criteria listed in **Figure 11.09**.

13. Based on your use of **Figure 11.09**, revise the criteria and my descriptions of them.

14. Obtain descriptions of on-line databases and assess merits in relation to costs.

15. Draft a lesson plan in which you integrate a CBL program.

16. Draft a term-long strategy for imparting "computer literacy" to your students. (See **Figure 11.15**.)

17. Having students cut and paste pictures from computer catalogs serves to reinforce what has been covered in previous lessons about categories of hardware and software, and to evaluate our teaching as pictures often are pasted in imaginative places. Give it a try with your students. (See **Figure 11.16**.)

18. Locate, obtain, or share a computer that can run multimedia, CD-ROM software.

19. Let me know of errors or omissions in this chapter.

20. Share with me your responses to the above study items and your experiences with the suggested activities (Internet: hackbarths@aol.com).

Chapter 12

Interactive Learning Environments

Chapter Content and Objectives

Advances in laser and microprocessor technologies have brought to fruition what has long been envisioned—instant interactive access to text, audio, video, and human sources worldwide. CD-ROMs have provided vast data storage capacity. Ever quicker microprocessors have sped access. Software has eased orchestration of components.

Interactive learning environments long have been an ideal of pedagogy. Standards of high quality interaction have been set by great teachers from the time of Socrates. It is to these standards that we hold the so-called "interactive multimedia" programs now flooding the marketplace. Reading this chapter should enable you to:

- Characterize features of **"interactive learning environments."**

- Describe various categories of **multimedia** programs—skill builders, knowledge explorers, reference works.

- List ways in which multimedia contribute to making **knowledge more accessible**.

- Illustrate how interactive multimedia programs can make **learning more individualized**.

- **Assess pros and cons** of multimedia in the context of schooling.

- **Select and use** interactive multimedia programs.

- **Locate** current references and software.

- **Evaluate** computer software more critically in terms of the nature of "interactivity" that it provides.

Teacher/Student Interactions

The focus of educational technology long has been on getting students to learn prescribed subject matter. The specification of instructional objectives in terms of measurable behaviors permits quantitative assessments of program effectiveness. Such assessments contribute to making targeted revisions and thereby to the evolution of ever more valid, reliable, and feasible solutions to problems inherent in teaching and learning.

Nevertheless, throughout the previous chapters I have stressed the limitations of "objective" measures of learning, and of thinking only in terms of prescribed subject matter. In education, we are at least as much concerned with **how** our students learn (and how they feel about it) as with **what** they learn. This emphasis has become ever more important as the information explosion renders much of today's knowledge and many skills obsolete by the time elementary students get to college and the workplace.

Emphasis on the **process** of learning rather than merely the **products** now is evidenced in calls for changes in the way we teach. We are being encouraged (and admonished) to:

- Pay greater attention to the distinctive attributes of our students—their cultural backgrounds, experiences, interests, preferred learning styles.

- Provide students with opportunities to build creatively upon what they already know about their immediate surroundings, neighborhoods, communities.

- Think more in terms of teaching to students' strengths rather than toward remediating deficits.

- Teach across the curriculum, thinking in terms of linkages across the academic disciplines.

- Anchor subject matter in the context from which it was derived, presenting students with "real world" challenges.

- Engage small groups of students in cooperative problem-solving activities where emphasis is on the processes of working together productively and creatively rather than merely on coming up with "right" answers.

- Monitor student progress continuously with the aim of fostering learning rather than merely assigning grades.

- Align evaluation more precisely with the full range of students' classroom experiences.

- Use many alternative means of assessing processes and products—interviews, observations, check lists, demonstrations, journals, portfolios.

These developments are reflected in evolving standards across the school curriculum from mathematics and science to the language arts and social studies. The enthusiasm for reform perhaps has been expressed most ardently by advocates of the "whole language" approach to reading instruction, but has spread swiftly within the ranks of teacher organizations and college of education faculty. Indeed, Miriam Leiva, a book series editor for the National Council of Teachers of Mathematics (NCTM) proclaimed:

> Something exciting is happening in many elementary school classrooms! A vision of an innovative mathematics program is coming alive. There is a shift in emphasis in the teaching and learning of mathematics. Teachers are encouraging children to investigate, discuss, question, and verify. They are focusing on explorations and dialogues. They are using various strategies to assess students' progress. They are making mathematics accessible to all children while exposing them to the value and the beauty of mathematics.[1]

Admittedly, teachers too often have lectured to the exclusion of discussion, scribbled on the chalkboard, shown videos without adequate preparation and follow up, and assigned much solitary seat work. However, they also have asked both factual and open-ended probing questions and have responded enthusiastically to student efforts. They have engaged students in role playing,

Figure 12.01. Throughout history, teachers have provided **"interactive learning environments"** to individualize and personalize the learning experiences of their students. Here, way back when my brother was a third grade mentor teacher, we see an exemplary model of "interactivity"—intense, small group, question/answer. How might electronic media measure up?

simulation games, field trips, and group projects. From the time of Socrates through the "progressive era" led by John Dewey, classrooms always have provided **"interactive learning environments."** (See **Figure 12.01.**)

As noted in Chapter **2**, good teachers, more than any other medium, consistently display the attributes of **sensitivity**, **flexibility**, and **interactivity**. Yet, even before B.F. Skinner invented his "teaching machine," technologists had sought to automate these desirable attributes so that students everywhere could benefit equally. The best of **multimedia** programs now do respond sensitively to students' concerns, increase flexibility in approach, and permit "interaction" with sources. Furthermore, they enable our students to take **ever greater control over their own learning**.

Automating Interactivity

Psychologist Edward Thorndike early anticipated today's interactive multimedia. "If by a miracle of mechanical ingenuity," he wrote in 1912, "a book could be so arranged that only to him [or her] who had done what was directed on page one would page two become visible, and so on, much that now requires personal instruction could be managed by print."[2] In 1924, Sidney Pressey developed a device that automatically presented test items and immediately indicated if students' responses were correct. Through the 1940s, he pursued crafting of interactive media such as "punchboards" (correct answers were revealed by depth of hole beneath answer sheet) and "chemocards" (correct answers changed color when scratched).[3]

Concern about the **quality of interaction** between students and teachers, especially as this pertains to **efficient learning**, moved B.F. Skinner to automate some routine aspects of instruction. His own ground-breaking research on learning suggested that it was facilitated by frequent and prompt feedback, and he designed a "teaching machine" to incorporate these principles. If desired behaviors (selecting correct answers) are reinforced automatically by machine, wrote Skinner in 1968, students could master subject matter on their own, and the teacher, released from drill, could act, "not in lieu of a cheap machine, but through intellectual, cultural, and emotional contacts of that distinctive sort which testify to her [or his] status as a human being."[4]

Among a host of other pioneers—Patricia Callendar, Arthur Lumsdaine, Susan Markle, P. Kenneth Komoski, Robert Glaser, Thomas Gilbert, Jacquetta Megarry—one that may stand out as an **inspiration to *HyperCard* stackers** today is **Norman A. Crowder**. His *TutorText*, anticipated by Thorndike, was a "scrambled book" in which students were directed to different pages depending on their responses to a question on the current page. By 1960, Crowder had developed a computer-based *Tutor* device that could access up to 10,000 segments ("frames") of textual, audio, and visual information.[5] Imagine!

Like the **constructivists** of today, Crowder rejected behaviorists' notions of human learning. Students answer correctly, in his common sense view, because they **understand the material**, not because they have been rewarded for making certain responses. "The pressure of the program," he wrote in 1963, "should be upward, allowing the student to deal with the material on the highest level of abstraction of which he [or she] is capable, rather than downwards, forcing all students to plod through a path designed for the least able."[6] Thus, **Crowder anticipated both the mechanism and the driving theory behind modern electronic interactive multimedia**.

Another boost to the development of interactive multimedia has been enormous investment by government

"Seven—you take the cavalry back to the hill, I capture all of your artillery and advance to the edge of the moat."

Figure 12.02. Simulation gaming is a potent, highly interactive instructional **strategy** that can effectively be **mediated** by print materials alone or by teachers and computers. It typically entails active engagement, cooperative problem solving, competition against others or a standard, and ready transfer to "real" life. This cartoon captures the interplay of **rules, chance,** and **harsh reality** commonly encountered in simulation gaming. By what criteria will you judge the **educational merits** of the polished multimedia simulations available today? Source: John L. Taylor & Rex Walford, *Learning and the Simulation Game* (Beverly Hills: Sage, 1978), p. 344; copyright © 1978 by Sage Publications, Inc. Reprinted with permission of Sage Publications, Inc.

and industry. As early as 1961, for example, the U.S. military contracted with pioneer Clark Abt and his associates to design a simulation of the Cold War era. The resulting computer program, consisting of about 20,000 lines of code, played out as follows:

> . . . thirty-nine nations with conflicting interests confronted each other in economic, military, and political modes over ten-year periods broken down into weekly events. As in the real world, but as opposed to the world of traditional "war games," all sides could win long life and prosperity by practicing arms control, or could lose life and wealth in unrestrained arms races or aggression.[7] (See **Figure 12.02.**)

Could it be that Abt & Associates had more to do with peaceful resolution of the Cold War than either Democrats or Republicans?

In the late 1970s and early 80s the U.S. Defense Department conducted computerized "war games" involving thousands of participants across the nation. The Army's Janus Project pitted the forces of the two superpowers against each other. "Players" commanded tanks, aircraft, and weaponry. In brief:

> A few typed commands to a . . . minicomputer conjure up rivers, mountains and cities. Drawing on the resources of the Defense Mapping Agency, the machine can display in full topographical detail any 15-sq.-mi. slice of the earth. . . . as the action mounts, land mines explode in flashes of white, and helicopter symbols appear over enemy outposts. Artillery fire slashes across the screen like a laser sword. The flight time of the shells is preprogrammed to the millisecond; even reloading is figured in. The computer . . . takes 20 seconds to analyze the effects of a ten-kiloton blast. Towns are reduced to rubble. Forests erupt in flames. . . . Temperature, humidity and wind speed must be reckoned with; they affect the way fallout will blow and how fast the fireball will spread.[8]

Such is the ancestry of today's popular arcade combat "games" (e.g., *Mortal Kombat*) and of the home computer 3-D animated, stereo sound, fast action thrillers (e.g., *Tetris, Spectre*).

Educators were quick to adapt this powerful teaching strategy for classroom use. Harold Guetzkow's classic *Inter-Nation Simulation* (INS) has engaged countless students in the conduct of mock foreign policy making. Players representing various nations trade, negotiate, and sometimes make war. Only wise decisions ensure the well-being of all. Another simulation, *Conflict in the Middle East*, one of a series entitled *Supplementary Empirical Teaching Units in Political Science* (SETUPS), informs students about this still vital region and helps them interpret events according to different theories of international relations. Teams representing Egypt, Jordan, Israel, the Palestinians, and the superpowers prepare position papers on various issues and, by negotiating, forming alliances, or making war, strive to achieve their goals. Other games have enriched social studies (*Neighborhood, Starpower, Ghetto*), math (*Equations*), logic (*Wff'N Proof*), and science (*Elements, Circuitron*).[9]

Interactive Multimedia

The intensity of engagement in simulations and the thrill of viewing images and hearing sounds have been heightened by the merging of laser disk and computer technologies. A single 4.72 inch diameter CD-ROM can store about 300,000 pages of text, 10,000 photographic images, or over an hour of video with capacities ever increasing, thanks to data compression technologies. Microprocessors, executing millions of instructions per second, and ever more efficient CD-ROM drives quickly find desired sections, bringing together neatly integrated collages of text, images, animation, audio, and video. (See **Figure 12.03**.)

Educational diskette and CD-ROM programs (including many so much fun they qualify as "edutainment") may be divided into several interrelated categories including **skill builders** (e.g., typing, mathematical problem solving, reading, drawing, designing), **knowledge explorers** (e.g., social studies, science, fine arts, literature), and **reference works**. I provide here some exemplary titles in each category merely to serve as a launching pad in your own search for ever more suitable, more current programs. Subscriptions to such periodicals as *Electronic Learning, Multimedia World, Media & Methods*, and *MultiMedia Schools* will help us keep up to date.

Skill Builders. What *Sesame Street* is to TV, ***Allie's Playhouse*** surely is to multimedia. Targeted at preschoolers, *Allie's Playhouse*, by Opcode Interactive, boasts "16 different educational interactive activities designed to stimulate young minds." Here youngsters learn how to count, recognize letters and words, tell time, sing nursery rhymes, and apply logic. Other topics include human anatomy, the continents, the solar system, drawing, and instrumental music. Allie, a cute green alien, serves as companion, coach, and tour guide. Mario, of video arcade fame, promises preschoolers "Fun with Letters," "Fun with Numbers," and just plain "Preschool Fun" in Mindscape's (formerly The Software Toolworks) ***Mario's Early Years CD Delux***.

The Learning Company's ***Reader Rabbit***, now over 10 years on the funny trail, continues to teach elementary-level language arts—grammar, syntax, pragmatics. In ***Reader Rabbit 3***, the star hare invites children to help him write stories according to the news copy "who, what, when, where, why, how" format. They also may join the "Club Hounds" in using sentence context for clues to identify mystery characters, help "Sneaker Mole" caption cartoons, or complete sentences with "Ed Words."

The ***Living Books*** series has been running away with awards. Consistent with the "whole language" approach, titles include "quality literature" and permit learner control over pace, sequencing, and help. ***Just Grandma and***

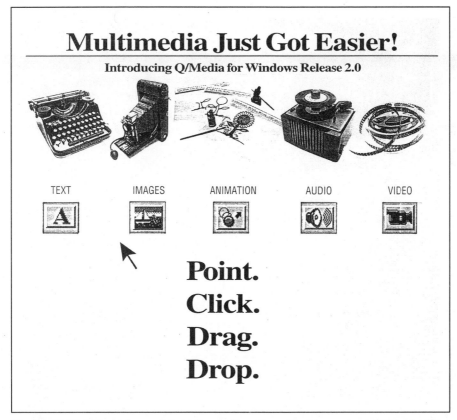

Figure 12.03. This ad for an interactive multimedia authoring program *(Q/Media)* illustrates essential features of this miraculous technology. Using a "mouse," one can point the cursor at the desired icon, double click, access wanted material, and, with "object linking and embedding" (OLE), "drag and drop" segments into place. Reproduced courtesy of Q/Media.

Me is a colorful animated adventure where clicking on words or objects elicits pronunciations (choose English, Spanish, or Japanese) and clicking on creatures brings them to life. *The Tortoise and the Hare, Arthur's Teacher Trouble,* and other titles are similarly interactive, all contributing to skills in word recognition, spelling, and comprehension sans frustration. A printed version of each book is included for convenient reference and practice. (See **Figure 12.04.**)

Learning to use the computer keyboard is made fun with Mindscape's *Mavis Beacon Teaches Typing.* Skill-building games and personalized feedback ensure growth in accuracy and speed. Video clips model ergonomic style and audio dictation adds a new dimension to practice. Word processing and composition skills are further developed in programs that guide children in the writing of stories. Using Media Vision's *Wiggins in Story-*

land, youngsters enter the world of "desktop publishing" as they type, illustrate, narrate, and then hear or print out their own tales. "Wiggins the Bookworm" also comes with a library of excerpts from such writers as Emerson and Whitman. Add a draw and paint feature and you have Brøderbund's *The Amazing Writing Machine,* Microsoft's *Fine Artist,* Davidson's *Kid Works Deluxe,* and Micrografx's *Crayola Art Studio.* (See **Figure 12.05.**)

Among the many draw and paint programs for children, Brøderbund's *Kid Pix* is the one you most likely have heard much about. Using a mouse, even preschoolers can "click and drag," mixing colors, outlining shapes, and applying "paint" with tools that make characteristic hisses and scrapes. Erasing work-in-progress might be a bit too tempting, either by firecracker or "black hole." Completed pictures can be sequenced into a "slide show"

Figure 12.04. The *Living Books* series exposes children to high quality literature in amusing and helpful ways. How might these interactive books fit into a "whole language" curriculum? Reproduced courtesy of Living Books, a Random House/Brøderbund company.

format and printed out. Text and animation may be added to create lively storybooks. Help is close at hand in English and Spanish. Older students may graduate up to **Art Explorer** (Adobe Systems) and then on to **Corel DRAW!** (by Corel), good preparation for careers in art.

Another popular basic skills builder, **Math Blaster**, has been helping children for over a decade. One distinctive feature of this program by Davidson is the way in which gaps in understanding are detected and remediated. *Math Blaster: In Search of Spot* places problem solving in the context of accomplishing a rescue mission. Six levels of complexity stretch the applicable age range of users from about six to 12.

Millie's Math House, in contrast, is targeted at preschoolers. Responsive to the NCTM's standards for teaching mathematics in the context of "meaningful" activities, this Edmark program touches on several "strands"—counting, shapes, patterns (visual and aural), spatial relationships. Basic skills are developed and applied using the "Number Machine," working in the

"Cookie Factory," and building a "Mouse House." (See **Figure 12.06.**)

Knowledge Explorers. The year 1973 marked the debut of MECC's **The Oregon Trail** for minicomputer, now adapted to CD-ROM, a simulated 1848 trip by covered wagon. Along the perilous journey, older children and youths must cope with hardships while conserving resources. During campfires, songs and tall tales of the time are heard. Historical and geographical data are just a mouse click away. Sierra's **Outpost** presents similar challenges and curricular enrichment.

Less than a decade since the first appearance of **SimCity**, this classroom staple by Maxis has evolved into the multimedia *SimCity 2000* and more recently added dramatic video clips to become Interplay Production's *SimCity Enhanced CD-ROM*. Like *SimAnt*, *SimLife*, and *SimEarth*, *SimCity* engages youths in systematic planning of dynamic communities. Upper elementary level children find *SimTown* a bit more manageable.

Figure 12.05. Youngsters enter the domain of multimedia desktop publishing using such programs as **The Amazing Writing Machine** (shown here), **Kid Works Deluxe,** and **Crayola Art Studio**. How much brainstorming, outlining, drafting, sharing, and revision would you recommend before students approach the keyboard? Reproduced courtesy of Brøderbund Software, Inc.

Figure 12.06. Only a generation enamored with Mister Rogers and Barney could love *Millie's Math House*. In spite of its goofy appearance, it does serve to introduce preschoolers to several key math "strands." What sorts of "real life" activities might easily and effectively complement those typically encountered in computer programs? Reproduced courtesy of the Edmark Corporation.

SimCity Enhanced CD-ROM generates landscapes that can be modified to afford greater challenge or charm. Then the fun begins. Specify desired characteristics for systems of transportation, utilities, government, education, and commerce. Assess taxes, pass legislation, manage finances, cope with disasters, and receive immediate feedback on effects of your decisions. And:

> Just because you do all of the above with aplomb and panache doesn't mean your city will pay its bills, generate enough jobs, attract residents, or hold down crime. Cities fail, and (at first) fail often. And that city is your baby. You have to work at it, and try again, and work some more until the darn thing is strong enough to survive on its own.[10] (See **Figure 12.07.**)

As with all simulation activities, proper introduction and follow up discussion ("debriefing") ensure effective integration into the larger curriculum. Special arrangements need be made for flexible time scheduling and enthusiastic interactions among engrossed participants. An ad for *SimCity Enhanced CD-ROM* promotes one down side of unsupervised play—"Unleash a killer quake. Meltdown a few nuclear power plants. Heck, wreak citywide havoc while you're at it. . . ."[11] Sure enough. That's precisely what I have found upper elementary students doing. Dire consequences depicted in such games may need to be highlighted with videos and news clippings of

the real thing followed by intense, reflective discussions. Also consider having your students write Interplay Productions to explain its advertising slant.

Carmen Sandiego has achieved celebrity status with her own TV series, books, a board game, and multimedia titles that take her across the planet, into outer space, and even through time. Ms. Sandiego and her VILE (Villains International League of Evil) gang have been thieving and fleeing for over a decade and still delight their adolescent pursuers. Brøderbund's *Where in the USA Is Carmen Sandiego? Deluxe CD* includes graphics, animation, voice, photos, travel guide (*Fodor's USA*), reference book, mystery, and humor. *Where in the World Is Carmen Sandiego?* adds *The World Almanac and Book of Facts* to provide clues to the thieves' whereabouts. The many titles in this award-winning series, it has been suggested, ". . . hold your children's interest by putting them in touch with real-life places and events in a way no formal geography or history lesson can match."[12] (See **Figure 12.08.**)

Topics in science lend themselves especially well to multimedia presentation. Thus we can find coverage of virtually every area from undersea life to astronomy,

Figure 12.07. *SimCity Enhanced CD-ROM* engages groups of middle and high school youths in cooperative problem solving. Video clips, like the one shown here, add dimensions of reality and urgency. Would you use *SimCity* to arouse interest in social studies, to provide practice in applying concepts, or to test knowledge and skills first learned by other means? Reproduced courtesy of Interplay Productions.

richly illustrated (3-D) and amply narrated (polyglot stereo).

An early entrant, and still on interactive videodiscs, is Optical Data Corporation's *Life Science Living Textbook* series for middle and high school students. Mindscape has since given us on CD-ROM *The San Diego Zoo Presents . . . The Animals!*, a multimedia field trip for children of all ages. Over 80 video clips, 2½ hours of audio, 1300 photos, and 2500 pages of text reveal features of over 200 different species. Their undersea title, *Oceans Below*, joined Knowledge Adventure's *Undersea Adventure* and The Learning Company's animated submarine simulation, *Operation Neptune.* With its own vast library of photos and videos, The Discovery Channel also has taken the leap into multimedia with a range that must have been inspired by a *Star Trek* movie—*In the Company of Whales* and *Beyond Planet Earth* .

Another leader in this rapidly evolving field, The National Geographic Society, has produced a *Wonders of Learning CD-ROM Library* with such titles as *Our Earth, The Human Body, Animals and How they Grow, A World of Animals, Mammals,* and *A World of Plants.* **The Human Body**, appropriate for ages four through eight, covers "Your Brain," "The Senses," "Your Bones and Mus-

cles," "Your Teeth," and "Food for your Body" with 3-D visuals and narration in English and Spanish. Clicking on page corners advances or reviews program screens, on a speaker icon starts narration, and on words produces pronunciations and definitions. A teacher's activity guide is included for each section.

Titles by **Knowledge Adventure** span the range. If I may substitute an asterisk for the word "*Adventure*," their ambitious list includes *Knowledge *, Bug *, America *, Science *, Science * II, Space *, Kid's Zoo: A Baby Animal *, Undersea *, 3-D Dinosaur *,* and *3-D Body *.* Even before the movie *Jurassic Park* and PBS's *Barney,* children were fascinated by dinosaurs. Drawings alone were sufficient to arouse such awe that terms like "tyrannosaurus rex" and "brontosaurus" were filed among "My Words" along with Dick, Jane, Spot, and Puff. Enter *3-D Dinosaur Adventure* :

> . . . two carnivores spot a second pair of dinosaurs, and the chase is on. . . . one of the predators spots the viewers and we become the prey. The clip ends with jaws snapping out of the screen as if to bite off our heads.[13]

This is just one of several dozen animated sequences that bring these beasts to life in ways students are not likely to forget.

Survivors may pursue various avenues of documentary research. An encyclopedic reference covers 15 billion years of earth history that can be accessed by clicking on maps, timelines, keywords, and index entries. Still images may be viewed in 2-D or 3-D and text may be read or heard. A "Dinosaur Museum" provides a self-guided simulated tour of exhibits and a simulation game involves players in a race to save dinosaurs from hostile creatures and an approaching comet (an objective about which I have some ambivalence). (See **Figure 12.09.**)

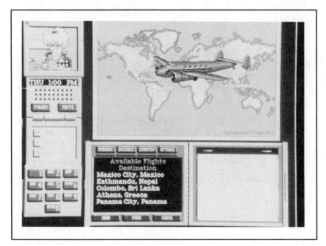

Figure 12.08. This attractive screen from **Where in the World Is Carmen Sandiego?,** filled with images, phone, notepad, and hot button access to help or information, illustrates the allure of this popular series. How will you ensure that your students aspire to become "Super Sleuths" rather than Carmen wannabes? Reproduced courtesy of Brøderbund Software, Inc.

Reference Works. In this category are included dictionaries (e.g., *The Macmillan Dictionary for Children, Merriam-Webster's Dictionary for Kids*), atlases (e.g., *U.S. Atlas, Street Atlas USA, Global Explorer, 3D Atlas*), encyclopedias (*Compton's NewMedia Interactive Encyclopedia, Encarta Multimedia Encyclopedia, The New Grolier Multimedia Encyclopedia, The Random House Kid's Encyclopedia*), trip planners (*Taxi, TripMaker*), excerpts and reviews (*Cinemania '95, The Viking Opera Guide*), almanacs, indexes to periodicals (Newsbank, Inc., for news-

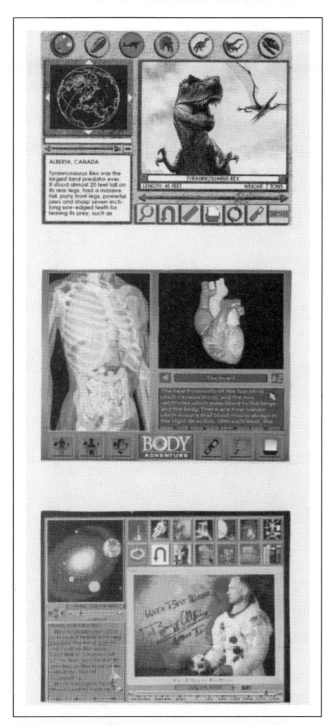

Figure 12.09. Dinosaurs, the human body, outer space, all are subjects of interactive multimedia programs like those shown above. How might these complement illustrated texts, models, and the many fine PBS videos available on related topics? Reproduced courtesy of Knowledge Adventure, Inc.

papers and EBSCO Publishing for magazines), books *(Bookshelf)*, and diverse collections of data (including "best of the Internet" titles).

Microsoft's award-winning ***Encarta Multimedia Encyclopedia*** has been one of very few educational titles to approach sales volume of popular multimedia games (e.g., *Myst, Star Wars Rebel Assault, The 7th Guest*). Its 26,000 plus articles comprise the complete text of *Funk & Wagnalls New Encyclopedia*. To these are added all the elements that define interactive multimedia—colorful visuals (9000 maps, photos, and drawings), audio (3600 clips, including samples from 60 different languages) and over 100 video clips (that our students can "paste" into their own reports), a "highly navigable" interface, and multiple "search engines" (e.g., browse, index, Boolean). A bonus is the free *Microsoft Encarta Teacher's Activity Guide* that includes "classroom tested" lesson plans. (See **Figure 12.10**.)

Microsoft's ***Bookshelf*** has set a standard for integrating top-notch reference works. Included are *The American Heritage Dictionary, Columbia Dictionary of Quotations, The Original Roget's Thesaurus, Hammond World Atlas,* the *World Almanac, The People's Chronology,* and *The Concise Columbia Encyclopedia*. Searches for desired information may be made across all seven sources at once.

As I noted in Chapter **6**, much is to be said for the Newspapers in Education sort of programs that guide teachers in helping their students make productive use of periodicals. NewsBank, Inc., has advanced this fine classroom tradition with its introduction of ***The Curriculum Resource,*** a package that includes 5 CD-ROMs updated monthly, *The Teacher Resource Guide,* and on site staff training to ensure curricular integration. The CDs contain articles from periodicals, government documents, broadcast transcripts, Spanish language news, *USA Today,* and your local newspaper—over 400,000 items from about one thousand sources, all of which easily can be searched, retrieved, and printed. The *Guide* includes lesson plans, evaluation checklists, and a glossary. This is serious stuff, costing some $30,000 for a site license and about $10,000 per year thereafter. But the ambitious goal of **"information literacy,"** knowing why and where to find it and how to use it, long has been a cornerstone of education and is well served by such integrated packages as *The Curriculum Resource*.[14] Those on a tighter budget might want to give the $24.95 ***Global NewsBase: Powerful Interactive News Service*** CD-ROM news reference library a try. It has the material—access

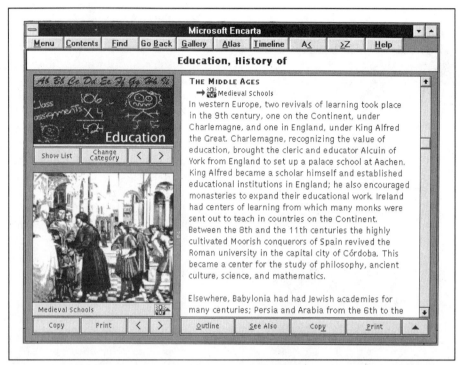

Figure 12.10. Here is a screen from Microsoft's ***Encarta*** CD-ROM encyclopedia program. Informative text interlinked with attractive visuals and navigational ease have made this a highly acclaimed and popular title. How might you incorporate its use in your classroom? Source: *Microsoft Encarta Teacher's Activity Guide* (Redmond, WA: Microsoft, 1993), cover. Reproduced courtesy of Funk & Wagnalls.

to 300,000 articles from over 1,500 newspapers, magazines, and journals from around the world—but wise usage is entirely in our hands.

Virtual Reality

Nearly every week, except when I finally decided to search for it, I encountered the same striking ad in *U.S. News & World Report*. The full-page ad was headed: ***Mind Power Breakthrough!***

The subheading read: *Plug Your Mind into the Amazing Learning Machine to Boost Mental Powers, Program Your Mind for Success & Launch Virtual Reality-Like Fantasies.*[15]

Yes, for just $299.95 plus $12 S&H you receive the Language Learning Laboratory and the *Super Phonics, Super Speed Reading, Super Memory,* and *Super Vocabulary* programs, PLUS the 3-D Mind-Sync Library and the

Inner Mind Programming Library—*Creativity Booster, Quick Energy, Stress Zapper, Mental Tune-Up, Virtual Visualization, Imagination Stimulator, Learning Accelerator, Super Intuition, Lucid Dreaming,* and *Super Zen States* (not to mention $1,000 worth of coupons for more software).

The text of the ad dilated with "being sucked into a deep, dream-like trance" as the software "links your mind directly to a multi-media computer." "The Learning Machine," it claimed boldly, "is more than virtual reality. . . . According to one college professor, 'It may be the most powerful learning tool since the invention of the book.'"

> Here's why. When you do a Learning Machine session your mind is cut off from outside distractions. Your attention becomes focused inward as the powerful sensory stimulation (light-sound matrix) bombards your imagination. Ideas and mental images float in and out of your consciousness. It feels like the best

dream you've ever had. Then while in this highly euphoric mental space, the Learning CD opens your learning centers to peak receptivity and pours in new knowledge and skills. It's the ultimate mind trip.[16]

A lot of hype, you say, for just a blindfold and a head-set that you plug into your own CD player? Welcome to virtual reality (VR) level one, the "theater of the mind" with features played locally as you read a novel or listen to an audiotape or radio program. This is powerful stuff, really, and the above ad, while perhaps misleading in terms of what will be delivered at your doorstep, does not misrepresent the capacity of our minds to be transported in wonderful ways.

Que's Computer User's Dictionary defines "virtual reality" as "a computer-generated environment that is capable of immersing the user in the illusion of a computer-generated world and of permitting the user to navigate through this world at will."[17] Donning special head and hand gear, we now can "move about" within and "interact" with computer-generated VR environments (not to be confused with holograms, which are projected images). The head-mounted display (HMD, e.g., Eyephone) provides stereoscopic images that respond to head movements in such a way that we have the sensation of scanning a stationary scene. The glove (e.g., DataGlove) tracks our hand movements and represents these within the simulated environment. Call this the cutting edge of virtual reality in the 1990s, but far from that envisioned in the movie *Total Recall*, where Arnold Schwarzenegger was given the opportunity to experience life on Mars via direct input to his brain.[18]

Somewhere in between, we have automated environments ranging from Disney's *Star Tours* (passive) to flight simulators (interactive). These combine coordinated movement, audio, and video to produce in us the sensation of being immersed in the concocted reality, a psychological state called **"telepresence."** If you have not yet experienced this, a visit to your local shopping mall's arcade will quickly bring you up to date. For a few dollars you can ride the world's fastest roller coasters, drive a race car, or fly a jet, all without leaving the mall. More elaborate demonstration exhibits permit higher levels of immersion with interactivity (e.g., snow skiing and playing basketball). (See **Figure 12.11**.)

Virtual reality technology already has found wide practical application. Architects have employed computer-aided design (CAD) techniques for years. Now they are able to "enter" their planned structures and to permit clients to conduct simulated "walkthroughs."

Figure 12.11. At Liberty Science Center (New Jersey), children don a glove that enables them to participate in "virtual reality basketball." What might they gain from such an experience? What are some more educationally promising uses of this technology?

Modifications are made based on the impressions. Firefighters may practice making their way through smoke to likely locations of survivors. Surgeons may practice techniques for which there is little margin for error. Persons with limited mobility may navigate simulated libraries, museums, airports, and city streets before embarking on actual trips. For students who find learning by conventional means especially difficult, the possibilities of virtual reality technology are enormous. Those with attention deficit (i.e., focusing) disorder, for example, may find immersion in simulated explorations of the world helpful in shutting out distracting stimuli encountered in ordinary learning environments.

A model approach to integrating virtual reality into the curriculum is the VR & Education Lab at East Carolina University, Greenville. Here, state-wide objectives have been analyzed to determine which might be achieved by employing this strategy. Areas identified range from helping children identify potential hazards in their homes to helping them comprehend management of their city's traffic patterns.[19]

Where will advances in VR lead? Students surely will be exploring not just the known universe, but imaginary ones as well. They will enter into the realms of abstract mathematics and theoretical physics. Along with classmates from across the earth connected by the Internet, they may be guided by computer-generated "virtual agents" to "boldly go where no one has gone before." Science fiction? Hilary McLellan (McLellan Wyatt Digital) has kept us abreast of exotic developments taking place at Apple Computer, the Massachusetts Institute of Technology, and elsewhere. At MIT, for example, she reported that researchers:

> are experimenting with a computer model of a human figure–a virtual actor–that can move and function in a virtual environment. If the movement of a virtual actor is slaved to the motions of a human participant in the virtual environment using cameras, instrumented clothing, or some other means of body tracking, this is a guided virtual actor. . . . It is also possible to have autonomous actors that can operate under program control with the capability of independent and adaptive behavior. These autonomous actors can interact with human participants in the virtual environment, as well as with simulated objects and events.[20]

In the feature film based on Michael Crichton's *Disclosure*, we witnessed virtual actors seeking and destroying computer files. On the Internet today, countless players are engaged in "multi-user dungeons and dragons" (MUDDs), vying for supremacy in the diverse "multi-user simulated environments" (MUSEs) of cyberspace. Science fiction is being overtaken by science fact!

Pros and Cons of Multimedia

Hypertext, hypermedia, multimedia. Which is what? The terms have been used loosely and interchangeably. Denise Tolhurst (University of New South Wales, Australia) provided much needed distinctions. In her words:

> The term *hypermedia* is used to refer to any computer-based system that allows the interactive linking, and hence nonlinear traversal, of information that is presented in multiple forms that include text, still or animated graphics, movie segments, sounds, and music . . . *hypertext* should be considered to be nonlinearly organized and accessed textual information [including] diagrams, tables, and pictures . . . *multimedia* is suggested as meaning the use of multiple media formats for the presentation of information. When presented using a computer system, multimedia may in fact overlap with the term hypermedia and hypertext, if it includes nonlinear interactive links, but multimedia does not necessarily include computer usage.[21]

Thus, multimedia is the more general term, largely encompassing the other two, text-only hypertext being excluded. (See **Figure 12.12**.)

Multimedia programs have been lauded for being **flexible, self-pacing, content-rich,** and **interactive,** and for **meeting the needs of individuals.**[22]

Flexibility pertains in part to the wide selection of titles covering every subject. Another aspect is the variety of means by which wanted information can be located—menus, icons, word-based searches. Multimedia programs also are flexible in terms of how they may be used in classrooms, by individuals or by small groups.

The **self-pacing** feature of multimedia exceeds in some respects that of paging through schoolbooks. Just as one can browse at leisure or skip to desired sections using the index of a textbook, one can stop and start exploration of a computer-mediated program at will. But when it comes to accelerating the pace, clicking on icons and typing in search words excels searching the index and flipping back and forth through pages, especially when accessing multiple resources, some of which might be in remote locations.

To assert that **content is rich** can only be an understatement. Virtually everything that can be seen or heard is finding its way onto disk. From classic literature to award winning photos, videos, musical performances, and computer software, all may be found. Rich and original resources abound and are especially accessible **to those with the savvy to locate it efficiently.**[23]

As earlier discussed in relation to music videos, TV, and films, "violence in the media" continues to haunt my observations of emerging technologies. At a time when schools increasingly are preaching peaceful conflict resolution and cooperative learning, multimedia game designers are glorifying cutthroat competition and the brutal annihilation of rivals. A full-page ad in *Multimedia World* for The Software Toolworks' (note company name change to "Mindscape.") simulation *MegaRace* featured an apparent "skinhead," eyes glaring and teeth clenched, with the challenge: "NO COPS, NO LAWS, NO WIMPS. ARE YOU A GIRLIE-MAN OR A MEGARACER? Winning is all that counts in this over-the-edge virtual driving experience." Have your students think of a creative response to counter this approach by a leading educational software developer. Address and toll-free phone number (ah!!!) are listed in Sources at end of this book. Write to the president. Set up a teleconference. Perhaps discuss with your students what impact a flood

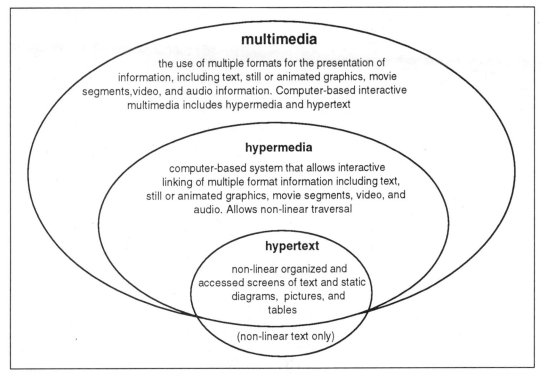

Figure 12.12. Relationships among hypertext, hypermedia, and multimedia are diagrammed and described here. "Multimedia" is an old and familiar term. Things started getting "hyper" when computers began permitting quick linkages. What does the evolution of non-linearity imply for student-centered, open-ended learning? Source: Denise Tolhurst, "Hypertext, Hypermedia, Multimedia Defined?" *Educational Technology,* 35 (March/April 1995), p. 25. Reprinted courtesy of Educational Technology Publications.

of computer-generated faxes might have on corporate operations. Then consider enlisting support from the millions of fellow teachers and parents now collaborating over the Internet. (See Chapter **13**.)

Multimedia programs are **interactive** in the sense that they are responsive to learner input. Clicking on an icon typically results in an event related to the icon—print a file, provide narration, show a video, go to another section. Entering combinations of search words may result in feedback about the number of articles that pertain. The student then may expand or restrict the search to capture a manageable number.

Nevertheless, with all varieties of "interactive learning environments" it is important to evaluate critically in what senses a program or service may be thought of as **"interactive."** The moon and stars are "interactive," as are abusive spouses, but not in any educationally constructive ways. Same with video games that merely provide points for destroying something or somebody.

"Interactivity" in the classroom implies that teachers and students **collaborate** in the learning process. They **discuss** and come to agreements about goals, aspirations, abilities, interests, activities, and evaluation. Teachers may present information from a variety of sources and ask for **contributions from students. Questions** put to students may be closed, requiring a "correct" answer, or "open," permitting creative expression. Teachers may give several seconds of **"wait time"** after asking a question to **encourage reflection** rather than quick, impulsive responding. The teacher may then pause before **requesting clarification** or elaboration. Other students may be called on. **Encouragement and guidance** are provided. Progress in **comprehension is monitored** and **adjustments in presentation made** accordingly. **Evaluation is "aligned"** with what has been taught. In these and in so many other ways, teachers interact constructively with students to enhance learning.

The "interactivity" of multimedia programs needs to be evaluated with reference to the same high standards we set for parents and teachers. And it should be no surprise that, in some respects, the electronic media excel the "merely" human.

Multimedia programs **meet the needs of individuals** in a variety of ways. For those who may have difficulty traveling to a library, they deliver storehouses of information. For slow readers, they permit audio and video access to information and print out text for later review. Gifted students may explore topics beyond their grade-level curriculum in breadth and depth. Those who view students in terms of Howard Gardner's theory of multiple intelligences will find suitable programs and related activities for each. Swift and slow students alike, whether their special talents be linguistic, logical, spatial, kinesthetic, musical, interpersonal, or intrapersonal, can benefit and then proudly share with peers what they discover.[24] (See **Figure 12.13**.)

So let us be enthusiastic in the writing of our technology plans, and get wired for the 21st century. But let us do so on solid grounds, not on the basis of being sold "silicon snake oil" (as Clifford Stoll put it). In Chapter **11**, I presented a sample of the empirical evidence in support of instructional CBL, and described caveats that need be considered in assessing that evidence. I add here reference to an October 1995 press release from

Figure 12.13. Interactive learning environments **can be made** responsive to the needs of students as well as to those of society. Some skills valued in the workplace that may be promoted in such environments are listed above. Can you name others? Source: *Phi Delta Kappan,* 75 (June 1994), p. 741. Reproduced with permission of Joel Pett.

Apple Computer, Inc., that marked the 10th anniversary of its **Apple Classrooms of Tomorrow** (ACOT) research project. This project has examined the effects of making computer access routine in several selected schools. Not surprisingly, there have been **dramatic beneficial impacts on students' attendance, grades, and test scores**. Claims are even made for revolutionizing teaching and learning (the familiar "traditional" versus "modern" straw person dichotomy).

Having heard such claims made over so many decades—for personalized systems of instruction based on print materials, for film and TV, for programmed instruction, for the "whole language" approach, for renovating the cafeteria, for the leadership of a star principal—ought to make us cautious in attributing the above noted dramatic gains to computer access alone. As noted in the previous chapter, surely there are factors at work related to the processes of massive, energized innovation above and beyond introduction of hardware and software.

Based on my recent classroom experiences, I am prepared to issue a challenge. Show me any device or procedure that keeps the inevitable two or three disruptive students occupied, and I'll show you revitalized teachers to match the Apple corps, increased attendance, and better student performance overall. Make that 10 multimedia computers (or tutors, or paraprofessionals, or parents) in each classroom (the 1 to 3 ratio of ACOT) and I'll show you dramatic transformations in the ways the newly liberated teachers teach and the carefully attended students learn.

Yes, I am a measured computer enthusiast (who also loves books and videos, etc.). After all, I've tasted the power of walking into the most chatty of elementary school classrooms and saying, "Ya wanna talk, or ya wanna play?" It doesn't matter if I've planned a half hour of process writing or research planning, all eyes are on me in eager anticipation. And this is achieved without (well, usually) having to blow a whistle, repeat "excuse me, excuse me," turn off the lights, raise two fingers, clap in unison, or scream. (Perhaps you have witnessed some more subtle techniques?) Only after having gained our students' attention (and respect!) may we play "sage on the stage" (giving instructions, modeling, etc.) in preparation for being a "guide by the side." Only then can we begin to put into practice all those wonderful techniques we learned in teacher education classes, but soon found were out of touch with the realities of classroom behavior management.

Conclusion? Let's not be mystified nor intimidated by hard core (pun, sorry) computer advocates. It is enough that our students generally want a chance to interact with these marvelous machines. It is even more wonderful that excellent programs are available, some that teach, some that provide easy access to information, some that ease organization and utilization of information. That we and our students can collaborate via the Internet on projects with peers across the globe is just one of a multitude of wondrous developments in computer-mediated communications to be discussed in the next chapter. But even at the cutting edge of CBL research, as discussed in previous chapters, no one has been able to substantiate that computers, per se, are capable of facilitating learning more effectively or efficiently than could be done by other combinations of media, including books, telephones, videos, teachers, and peers. Yet let us remain open to the possibilities.

Practical Guidelines

Selection. In the preceding chapter, I provided a generalized form to guide selection of diverse sorts of computer-based learning software. Pam Berger and Susan Kinnell provided us with an alternative that we may find more useful in evaluating interactive CD-ROM reference programs.[25]

They prefaced use of their form with the following valuable suggestions:

- Identify curriculum needs.
- Decide on your requirements.
- Identify products.
- Read reviews.
- Network with colleagues.
- Involve students.
- Get trial copies of CD-ROM discs.
- Test discs.

Our test of each CD-ROM **reference** program may be guided by attention to Berger's and Kinnell's criteria as described here.

1. **Getting Started**. Installation instructions should be easy to carry out and the process should proceed without hitches or interference with other software. Documentation should clearly ease use of the program and include a number to contact for assistance.

2. **Moving Around**. It should be quite clear from viewing the screen how to activate features or obtain guidance. Access to desired screens should be quick and easy.

3. **Searching and Results**. Look for prompts and features that facilitate either browsing or more targeted searches (e.g., by combinations of key words—Boolean "either/or, and, not" logic). Results are of most use when they can be printed out or downloaded onto a diskette.

4. **Content**. Information should be valid, current, and appropriate for your students. Text, visuals, and sound should all be of high technical quality and meaningfully interlinked.

5. **Curriculum Support and Practical Matters**. The program surely must complement other components of the curriculum, making clear contributions to achievement of educational goals. And it should be engaging.

6. **Bonus Questions**. Look for features, like quizzes and games, that involve students in practicing or applying what they have learned. Inclusion of printed handouts, suggested activities, and exam items is a plus.

For evaluation of CD-ROM *simulations,* add consideration of fidelity to phenomena simulated. For *instructional programs,* carefully assess quality of questions posed and feedback given. In every case, pay special attention to the nature of "interaction" present. Note especially how constructive—informative and motivating—are the program's reactions to student input. When selecting clip art, photography, sound effects, and video segment CD-ROMs, look for those that permit royalty-free reproduction.

To run the first generation of CD-ROM software required a "Level 1" multimedia computer (MPC)—an Intel 386 microprocessor, 2MB of RAM, and a single "speed" or "spin" (150KB/second data transfer rate) CD-ROM drive—or equivalent Macintosh configuration. Advances in computer hardware stimulated development of more sophisticated CD-ROM software to match. Thus, "Level 2" MPC standards—486SX (or Mac 68040), 25MHz cpu, 4MB RAM, 160MB hard disk, "double-spin" CD-ROM drive, 16-bit video support, 16-bit sound card—were established as a new minimum, but experts soon were recommending the next generation of 486DX (or Mac 68LC040), *Pentium,* and *PowerPC* chips running at over 60MHz and double the RAM and hard disk capacities.

The best products and vendors are rated each month in such periodicals as *PC World*, *PC Magazine*, *MacUser*, and *Macworld*. **It is imperative that you study these ratings before getting utterly taken in by a local, mail order, or online junk dealer.** There are vast differences in quality of products and service. Not surprisingly, name brands stand out—Apple, IBM, Compaq, Hewlett-Packard, AST—and Gateway comes up with great buys and high customer satisfaction ratings. Given the choice in 1994 between a fast 486DX Gateway with a double-speed CD-ROM drive for $2,300 (modem and sound card cost extra) and an IBM 486SX at 25MHz with an internal data modem for $775, I grabbed the latter. Having access to CD-ROM at New York University and anticipating dramatic developments in video quality greatly influenced my choice. And sure enough, within one year, multimedia computer prices dropped 50 percent, while hard drive capacities expanded beyond a gigabyte (1000 MB) and CD-ROM drives reached quad speed.[26]

Production. In each of the preceding survey of media chapters, I have described techniques for crafting educational programs. Criteria applying to the writing of printed text, composing of visuals, graphing of data, recording of sounds, and filming of scenes apply as well in the producing of multimedia programs. To this, add the criteria previously described about relevance of content to course objectives and demonstrated effectiveness of instructional strategies.

Of course, teachers and students alike can craft brilliant multimedia lessons and reports and should be encouraged to do so. Nevertheless, be gentle on yourselves when comparing the results with those of the experts.

Top-notch interactive multimedia production requires considerable technical expertise, subject matter mastery, and pedagogical insight. Professional multimedia software developers employ teams of experts in each area to produce prizewinning programs. Such experts typically have completed years of successful classroom teaching.

This textbook is targeted at pre-service teachers. It aims to serve as an overview of the range of strategies and media you might employ to enhance the learning of your students. It encourages you to think about the **quality** of text and visuals whether they appear in a printed handout or on a computer screen.

As you face the challenges of teaching, it is enough that you gain experience in selecting, producing, and integrating into your lesson plans simple, familiar media—books, periodicals, maps, chalkboards, audiotapes. Next will come scripting for video production. Here you can learn much from colleagues and along with your students.

Entry-level computer competence comes with gaming, word-processing, and corresponding via email. Writing interactive multimedia software is rooted in knowledge of language, form, composition, subject matter, learning, and teaching. Multimedia authoring tools (e.g., *Authorware for Windows*, *Director*, *HyperCard*, *HyperStudio*, *Icon Author*, *Digital Chisel*, *Multimedia Toolbook*, *Linkway Live!*) enable all of us to incorporate this knowledge into appealing formats. Technical expertise is best gained in collaboration with more experienced colleagues, in specialized college courses, and at professional workshops. It is my desire that this book serve both as a reference and as a springboard as you gain ever more competence in production and utilization of mediated programs. (See **Figure 12.14.**)

Utilization. Before **installing or downloading any computer software**, make backup copies of all system files. Horror stories abound about how the intricate interconnections of commands needed to run CD-ROM programs can leave performance-impairing traces, even after ordinary efforts to de-install. Michael Desmond, Assistant Editor of *PC World* put it bluntly: "Run the installation routine of a CD-ROM reference work or game, and you invite a raft of changes to your operating system and other files that could render your PC brain dead."[27] Desmond's tips (as listed below) should help *DOS* and *Windows* users, especially, cope with these challenges:

- Post messages on computer bulletin boards to learn from others about problems that might have been encountered installing a program you are considering for purchase.

- Backup the *Windows* and *Windows\System* directories and the autoexec.bat and config.sys files. (For Macs, it's the System Folder.)

- Use memory manager and CD-ROM disk cache utility software to handle high speed operating demands.

- Update your pre-1994 MSCDEX.EXE file with software available online from America Online and CompuServe, or on diskette.

Figure 12.14. Your own production of interactive multimedia courseware will best be guided in a classroom or workshop setting as shown here. Beyond creating *HyperCard* "stacks" linked by on-screen "hot buttons," successful production requires subject matter expertise, aesthetic sensibility, and pedagogical wisdom. Who in your school or district might be glad to provide a demonstration?

- Create multiple start-up configurations for desired use of RAM.
- Switch video setting to 640 by 480 resolution at 16 or 256 colors.
- Use a program like MicroHelp's *UnInstaller* to remove all traces of unwanted software.

Minimize problems by purchasing and using only the best. Avoid demonstration discs from little-known companies, keeping in mind that "All that glitters is not silver."

What is the role of evaluation in interactive learning environments? As with all classroom configurations and activities, we look at processes as well as products. Students being actively engaged, asking questions, and sharing information all give clues to what is being learned. Frequent monitoring of students' activities enables us to detect snags and to provide guidance and encouragement. Our notes permit follow up discussion with students and their parents and facilitate summative evaluation. Ask students themselves to subject mediated programs to critical analysis. Did they find the information to be current, valid, and well-organized? What about ease of use and the nature of interactions? How well did the program guide them in the search for desired information?

Products of engagement in interactive learning environments may include essays, journal entries, drawings, models, and multimedia class presentations. Portfolios of work may be judged with reference to criteria agreed upon by teachers, parents, and students. Such qualitative assessment serves to inform both students and teachers how they might improve their performance. (See **Figure 12.15.**)

Summary and Conclusions

The concept of an "interactive learning environment" is familiar. Essential elements of "interactivity" long have been held to include "individualization of instruc-

"You realize, Paul, that getting an 'A' for your time machine is contingent upon you fixing it and getting us back to Hope Valley High."

Figure 12.15. The products of engagement in interactive learning environments may be as spectacular as they are unpredictable. Criteria for assessing quality may be negotiated among students, parents, and teachers. How would **you** evaluate the student pictured here? Source: *Phi Delta Kappan,* 75 (April 1994), p. 587. Reprinted with permission of John R. Shanks.

"I'm only attending school until it becomes available on CD-ROM."

Figure 12.16. Yes, much of the school curriculum could be recorded on CD-ROM. And its presentation could be made engaging. Anything missing? Source: *Phi Delta Kappan,* 76 (September 1994), p. 11. Reprinted with permission of Martha Campbell.

tion" and "targeted feedback." Today we tend to think more in terms of students and teachers working collaboratively in mutually agreed upon ways toward both prespecified and open-ended goals.

From the time that cues, questions, and answers first appeared in textbooks, educational technologists have endeavored to automate "interactive" aspects of instruction. Computer and laser technologies have increased the quality, quantity, and accessibility of information. They also have permitted individualizing instruction and targeting feedback in ways that rival teachers. Thus, in harmony with other components of a school's larger curriculum, computer-mediated multimedia programs—skill builders, knowledge explorers, reference works—can contribute to "interactive learning environments" in the classroom, at home, and in the workplace. (See **Figure 12.16.**)

In Chapter **13** we explore the "highways" and "byways" of computer networks. As with use of multimedia programs, travels along the "information superhighway" **can be made** fun, engaging, and productive.

Notes

[1]Leiva, Miriam A., series editor in the Preface to Burton, Grace, *et al., Curriculum and Evaluation Standards for School Mathematics Addenda Series, Grades K–6: Sixth-Grade Book* (Reston, VA: The National Council of Teachers of Mathematics, 1992), p. iv.

[2]Thorndike, Edward L., *Education* (New York: Macmillan, 1912), p. 165.

[3]Pressey, Sidney L., "Development and Appraisal of Devices Providing Immediate Automatic Scoring of Objective Tests and Concomitant Self-Instruction," *Journal of Psychology,* 29 (April 1950), pp. 417–447.

[4]Skinner, Burrhus F., *The Technology of Teaching* (New York: Appleton-Century-Croft, 1968), p. 27. Keep in "mind" that although Fred Skinner used mentalistic terms, he remained a determinist behaviorist, taking up where John Brodus Watson and Edward Thorndike had left off, to the end of his life, vitally concerned about the pressing need to control the human

animal bent on nuclear holocaust. One of Skinner's star students, **Thomas F. Gilbert**, in his *Human Competence: Engineering Worthy Performance* (New York: McGraw-Hill, 1978), described the evolution of his own thought: "When I first left Skinner's laboratory and went eagerly to try my hand at engineering competent cultures, at work and at school, I was armed with what I thought were two powerful tools: the techniques of operant conditioning, and an open mind about results. These were admirable behaviors for the laboratory. But they became extinguished in those subcultures I presumed to be able to redesign, and replaced by a new set of behaviors: a technique for identifying results and their value, and an open mind about operant conditioning" (p. 105).

[5]Gilman, David A., "The Origins and Development of Intrinsic and Adaptive Programming," *AV Communication Review*, 20 (Spring 1972), pp. 64–76.

[6]Crowder, Norman A., "On the Differences Between Linear and Intrinsic Programming," *Phi Delta Kappan*, 44 (March 1963), p. 253. A "hands-on" technician, Crowder worked without reference to an explicit theory of learning. Asked later if his early efforts owed anything to Skinner, he replied, "I'm embarrassed to say that I did not know the gentleman existed." Quoted in "The Man Behind the Machine," *Times Educational Supplement*, 498 (April 5, 1963), p. 721.

[7]Abt, Clark C., *Serious Games* (New York: Viking Press, 1970), p. 46.

[8]Faflick, Philip, "Brutal Game of Survival," *Time*, 120 (August 16, 1982), p. 59.

[9]Horn, Robert E., & Cleaves, Anne, eds., *The Guide to Simulations/Games for Education and Training*, 4th ed. (Beverly Hills: Sage, 1980).

[10]Spear, Peter, "*SimCity 2000*: Multimedia Mayor," *Multimedia World*, 1 (June 1994), p. 38.

[11]*HomePC*, 1 (August 1994), p. 50.

[12]Bell, Sharon McCoy, "World Processing: The Magic of Carmen Sandiego," *HomePC*, 1 (June 1994), p. 70.

[13]Spear, Peter, Soper, Virginia, & Ladue, Ruth Ann, "*3-D Dinosaur Adventure*: Seeing All the Allosaurs," *Multimedia World*, 1 (May 1994), p. 52.

[14]Bjørner, Susanne, "*The Curriculum Resource* by NewsBank," *MultiMedia Schools*, 2 (May/June 1995), pp. 15–21.

[15]Spotts, Dane, "Mind Power Breakthrough," *U.S. News & World Report*, 117 (September 19, 1994), p. 72. Remember when ads used to be identified as such?

[16]*Ibid.*

[17]Pfaffenberger, Bryan, *Que's Computer User's Dictionary*, 4th ed. (Indianapolis, IN: Que Corporation, 1993), pp. 647–648.

[18]Franchi, Jorge, "Virtual Reality: An Overview," *Tech Trends*, 39 (January/February 1994), pp. 23–26.

[19]Thurman, Richard A., & Mattoon, Joseph S., "Virtual Reality: Toward Fundamental Improvements in Simulation-Based Training," *Educational Technology*, 34 (October 1994), pp. 56–64.

[20]McLellan, Hilary, "Virtual Reality, Interactive Stories, and Affordances for Learning," paper presented at the annual convention of the Association for Educational Communications and Technology (Anaheim, CA: February 1995). See also Pantelidis, Veronica S., "Virtual Reality in the Classroom," *Educational Technology*, 33 (April 1993), pp. 23–27.

[21]Tolhurst, Denise, "Hypertext, Hypermedia, Multimedia Defined?" *Educational Technology*, 35 (March/April 1995), p. 25.

[22]Singer, Linda A., "CD-ROM Technology: A Tool for All Students," *MultiMedia Schools*, 1 (May/June 1994), pp. 54–55. See also Burks, John, "Classroom Education and Interactive Multimedia = Formula for Revolution," *Multimedia World*, 1 (April 1994), pp. 52–69, where a market analyst is quoted as saying: "Yesterday's drill-and-practice education software is giving way to rich environments. . . . that grab a child's attention as forcefully as any video game or TV show. The vast difference in entertainment value between video games and education software—we call it the fun gap—is narrowing" (p. 61).

[23]Oliver, Ron, & Perzylo, Lesa, "Children's Information Skills: Making Effective Use of Multimedia Sources," *Educational & Training Technology International*, 31 (August 1994), pp. 219–230: "This study demonstrated that with appropriate instruction and activity, young [12-year-old] students are well able to extract descriptive and qualitative information from interactive multimedia sources [*Mammals* CD-ROM]. The findings suggest the need for teachers to be made aware of the new skills that students require for these purposes" (p. 228).

[24]Gardner, Howard, *Frames of Mind: The Theory of Multiple Intelligences*, 2nd ed. (New York: Basic Books, 1993); *Multiple Intelligences: The Theory in Practice* (New York: Basic Books, 1993).

[25]Berger, Pam, & Kinnell, Susan, "Which One Should I Buy? Evaluating CD-ROMs," *MultiMedia Schools*, 1 (May/June 1994), pp. 21–28. See also McFarland, Ronald D., "Ten Design Points for the Human Interface to Instructional Multimedia," *T.H.E. Journal*, 22 (February 1995), pp. 67–69; and Singer, Linda A., "Choosing Multimedia CD-ROM Encyclopedias, *MultiMedia Schools*, 2(September/October 1995), pp. 17–26, who reminds us to "put the integrity of the product above its dazzle."

[26]Day, Rebecca, "Your Survival Guide to PC Shopping," *HomePC*, 1 (June 1994), pp. 148–156.

[27]Desmond, Michael, "How to Avoid a Multimedia Mugging," *PC World*, 12 (July 1994), pp. 227–228.

Sources

Books pertaining primarily to **interactive multimedia** are listed below. As always, check *Books in Print* and online Internet sources by "author" and "subject" to identify more current editions and related titles. *Books in Print* is accessible via CompuServe, but costs about $2.50 for each 10 titles found ("hits"). University libraries may be reached via the Internet, but for titles hot off the press, browse the shelves of your local bookstore.

Alber, Antone F., *Interactive Computer Systems: Videotex and Multimedia* (New York: Plenum Press, 1993).

Aston, Robert, & Schwarz, Joyce, eds., *Multimedia: Gateway to the Next Millennium* (Boston: AP Professional, 1994).

Badgett, Tom, & Sandler, Corey, *Creating Multimedia on Your PC* (New York: Wiley, 1994).

Barron, Ann E., & Orwig, Gary W., illustrated by Newman, Ted, *New Technologies in Education: A Beginner's Guide* (Englewood, CO: Libraries Unlimited, 1993).

Barron, Ann E., & Orwig, Gary W., *Multimedia Technologies for Training: An Introduction* (Englewood, CO: Libraries Unlimited, 1994).

Berger, Pam, & Kinnell, Susan, *CD-ROM for Schools: A Directory and Practical Handbook for Media Specialists* (Wilton, CT: Eight Bit Books, 1994).

Bergman, Robert E., & Moore, Thomas V., *Managing Interactive Video/Multimedia Projects* (Englewood Cliffs, NJ: Educational Technology Publications, 1990).

Blossom, Jonathan, *Engines of Creation: Programming Virtual Reality on the Macintosh* (Corte Madera, CA: Waite Group Press, 1995).

Bosak, Steve, & Sloman, Jeffrey, revised by Gibbons, Dave, *The CD-ROM Book*, 2nd ed. (Indianapolis, IN: Que, 1994).

Buford, George, & Thimbleby, Harold, *Hyper Programming: Building Interactive Programs with HyperCard* (Reading, MA: Addison-Wesley, 1994).

Bunzel, Mark J., & Morris, Sandra K., *Multimedia Applications Development: Using Indeo Video and DVI Technology*, 2nd ed. (New York: McGraw-Hill, 1994).

Burger, Jeff, *The Desktop Multimedia Bible* (Reading, MA: Addison-Wesley, 1993).

Chorafas, Dimitris N., & Steinmann, Heinrich, *Virtual Reality: Practical Applications in Business and Industry* (Englewood Cliffs, NJ: PTR Prentice Hall, 1995).

Collin, Simon, *The Way MultiMedia Works* (Bothell, WA: Microsoft Press, 1994).

Cotton, Bob, & Oliver, Richard, *The Cyberspace Lexicon: An Illustrated Dictionary of Terms from Multimedia to Virtual Reality* (London: Phaidon Press Ltd., 1994).

Dempsey, John V., & Sales, Gregory C., eds., *Interactive Instruction and Feedback* (Englewood Cliffs, NJ: Educational Technology Publications, 1993).

Eddings, Joshua, illustrated by Wattenmaker, Pamela Drury, edited by Jacobson, Linda, *How Virtual Reality Works* (Emeryville, CA: Ziff-Davis, 1994).

Fawcett, Neil, *Multimedia* (Chicago: NTC Publishing Group, 1994).

Fraase, Michael, *Rapid Reference Guide to HyperCard for the Macintosh* (Homewood, IL: Business One Irwin, 1992).

Frater, Harold, & Paulissen, Dirk, *Multimedia Mania* (Grand Rapids, MI: Abacus, 1994).

Gayeski, Diane M., ed., *Multimedia for Learning: Development, Application, Evaluation* (Englewood Cliffs, NJ: Educational Technology Publications, 1993).

Goodman, Danny, *The Complete HyperCard 2.2 Handbook*, 4th ed. (New York: Random House, 1993).

Hall, Devra, *The CD-ROM Revolution* (Rocklin, CA: Prima Publishing, 1995).

Haskin, David, *The Complete Idiot's Guide to Multimedia* (Indianapolis, IN: Alpha Books, 1994).

Hellman, Mary Fallenstein, & James, W. R., *The Multimedia Casebook: 12 Real-Life Multimedia Applications* (New York: Van Nostrand Reinhold, 1995).

Henry, Paul David, *Making Multimedia with Linkway: A Practical Guide to Linkway and Linkway Live* (New York: Van Nostrand Reinhold, 1994).

Hofstetter, Fred T., *Multimedia Presentation Technology* (Florence, KY: Wadsworth, 1993).

Holsinger, Erik, *How Multimedia Works* (Emeryville, CA: Ziff-Davis, 1994).

Iuppa, Nicholas, *The Multimedia Adventure* (White Plains, NY: Knowledge Industry, 1992).

Jerram, Peter, & Gasney, Michael, *Multimedia Power Tools* (New York: Random House, 1993).

Jonassen, David H., *Hypertext/Hypermedia* (Englewood Cliffs, NJ: Educational Technology Publications, 1989).

Keyos, Jessica, ed., *The McGraw-Hill Multimedia Handbook* (New York: McGraw-Hill, 1994).

Lamb, Annette C., *Emerging Technologies and Instruction: Hypertext, Hypermedia, and Interactive Multimedia: A Selected Bibliography* (Englewood Cliffs, NJ: Educational Technology Publications, 1991).

Larijani, L. Casey, *The Virtual Reality Primer* (New York: McGraw-Hill, 1994).

Lindstrom, Robert L., *The Business Week Guide to Multimedia Presentations* (Berkeley: Osborne McGraw-Hill, 1994).

Lochte, Robert H., *Interactive Television and Instruction: A Guide to Technology, Technique, Facilities Design, and Classroom Management* (Englewood Cliffs, NJ: Educational Technology Publications, 1993).

Luther, Arch C., *Authoring Interactive Multimedia* (Boston: AP Professional, 1994).

Mash, David S., *Macintosh Multimedia Machines* (San Francisco: SYBEX, 1994).

McCormick, John A., *Create Your Own Multimedia System* (New York: Windcrest/McGraw-Hill, 1995).

McLellan, Hilary, *Virtual Reality: A Selected Bibliography* (Englewood Cliffs, NJ: Educational Technology Publications, 1992).

Mullen, Robert, *Choosing & Using Your First CD-ROM Drive* (San Francisco: SYBEX, 1994).

Multimedia Demystified: A Guide to the World of Multimedia from Apple Computer, Inc. (New York: Random House, 1994).

Multimedia & Related Technologies: A Glossary of Terms (Falls Church, VA: Future Systems, 1994).

Multimedia & Videodisc Compendium: 1994 Edition (St. Paul, MN: Emerging Technology Consultants, 1994).

Murie, Michael D., *Multimedia Starter Kit for Macintosh* (Indianapolis, IN: Hayden Books, 1994).

Nadeau, Michael, *BYTE Guide to CD-ROM*, 2nd ed. (Berkeley: Osborne McGraw-Hill, 1995).

Neuschotz, Nilson, *Welcome to . . . Macintosh Multimedia: From Mystery to Mastery* (New York: MIS:Press, 1994).

Nicholls, Paul T., *CD-ROM Buyer's Guide & Handbook: The Definitive Reference for CD-ROM Users*, 3rd ed. (Wilton, CT: Eight Bit Books, 1993).

Nix, Don, & Spiro, Rand, eds., *Cognition, Education, and Multimedia: Exploring Ideas in High Technology* (Hillsdale, NJ: Lawrence Erlbaum, 1990).

Parker, Dana, & Starrett, Bob, *New Riders' Guide to CD-ROM*, 2nd ed. (Indianapolis, IN: New Riders Publishing, 1994).

Perry, Paul, *Multimedia Developer's Guide* (Indianapolis, IN: Sams, 1994).

Philips Interactive Media Systems, *The CD-I Design Handbook* (Reading, MA: Addison-Wesley, 1992).

Pivovarnick, John, *The Complete Idiot's Guide to CD-ROM*, 2nd ed. (Indianapolis, IN: Que, 1995).

Pruitt, Stephen, *Microsoft Multimedia Viewer How-To CD: Create Exciting Multimedia with Video, Animation, Music and Speech for Windows* (Corte Madera, CA: Waite Group Press, 1994).

Purcell, Lee, *Super CD-ROM Madness* (Indianapolis, IN: Sams, 1995).

Rathbone, Andy, *Multimedia & CD-ROMs for Dummies* (San Mateo, CA: IDG Books, 1994).

Rimmer, Steve, *Multimedia Programming for Windows* (New York: Windcrest/McGraw-Hill, 1994).

Rimmer, Steve, *Advanced Multimedia Programming* (New York: Windcrest/McGraw-Hill, 1995).

Romiszowski, Alexander J., *New Technologies in Education and Training* (East Brunswick, NJ: Nichols, 1993).

Schwier, Richard A., & Misanchuk, Earl R., *Interactive Multimedia Instruction* (Englewood Cliffs, NJ: Educational Technology Publications, 1993).

Shaddock, Philip, *Multimedia Creations: Hands-On Workshop for Exploring Animation and Sound* (Corte Madera, CA: Waite Group Press, 1992).

Shelton, James H., ed., *CD-ROM Finder*, 5th ed. (Medford, NJ: Learned Information, 1993).

Sinclair, Ian R., *Multimedia on the PC: An Introduction* (Kent, United Kingdom: CIMINO Publishing Group, 1994).

Smedinghoff, Thomas J., *The Software Publishers Association Legal Guide to Multimedia* (Reading, MA: Addison-Wesley, 1994).

Stevens, George H., & Stevens, Emily F., *Designing Electronic Performance Support Tools: Improving Workplace Performance with Hypertext, Hypermedia, and Multimedia* (Englewood Cliffs, NJ: Educational Technology Publications, 1995).

Stoll, Clifford, *Silicon Snake Oil: Second Thoughts on the Information Highway* (New York: Doubleday, 1995).

Taylor, Rebecca Buffum, ed., *The Multimedia Home Companion: 400 Ratings and Reviews* (New York: Warner Books, 1994).

Towne, Douglas M., *Learning and Instruction in Simulated Environments* (Englewood Cliffs, NJ: Educational Technology Publications, 1995).

Vaughan, Tay, *Multimedia: Making It Work*, 2nd ed. (Berkeley: Osborne McGraw-Hill, 1994).

Watkins, Christopher, & Marenka, Stephen R., *Virtual Reality ExCursions: With Programs in C* (Boston: AP Professional, 1995).

Wexelblat, Alan, ed., *Virtual Reality Applications and Explorations* (Boston: AP Professional, 1993).

Wilson, Brent G., ed., *Constructivist Learning Environments: Case Studies in Instructional Design* (Englewood Cliffs, NJ: Educational Technology Publications, 1996).

Wilson, Stephen, *Multimedia Design with HyperCard* (Englewood Cliffs, NJ: Prentice-Hall, 1991).

Winkler, Dan, Kamins, Scott, & DeVoto, Jeanne, *HyperTalk 2.2: The Book*, 2nd ed. (New York: Random House, 1994).

Wodaski, Ron, *Multimedia Madness*, 2nd ed. (Indianapolis, IN: Sams Publishing, 1994).

Wolfgram, Douglas E., *Creating Multimedia Presentations* (Indianapolis, IN: Que, 1994).

Yager, Tom, *The Multimedia Production Handbook for the PC, Macintosh, and Amiga* (Boston: AP Professional, 1993).

The following **periodicals** are *in addition to* those listed in Chapter 11.

AV Video

CD-ROM

CD-ROM Librarian

CD-ROM Pocket Guide

CD-ROM Professional

CD-ROM Today

CD-ROM World

CD-ROMs in Print

Club Kidsoft

Computer Pictures

Data Communications

Digital Video Magazine

Education Technology News

Educational Media International

Electronic Entertainment

Information Searcher

Journal of Educational Multimedia and Hypermedia in Education

Medio Magazine

Multimedia Magazine

Multimedia Monitor

MultiMedia Schools

Multimedia Today

Multimedia World

NautilusCD

NewMedia Magazine
T.H.E. Journal
Virtual Reality Special Report
Virtual Reality Systems
VRWorld

Ready to buy? The following **hardware/software vendors** offer substantial discounts. Getting on their mailing lists helps keep us on top of what's "hot," just one clue to quality. It also keeps us in supply of materials for our students' cut and paste and hardware/software selection projects. Check periodicals listed above for reviews by teachers and students (see especially *MultiMedia Schools* and *Club Kidsoft*). *MultiMedia Schools'* software reviews also are available via the Internet (gopher to online.lib.uic.edu). Through America Online we can browse through *Multimedia World's* databases of software reviews, articles, and *Buyers' Guides*, and can even download from its and *PC World's* shareware libraries. CompuServe, Prodigy, eWorld, etc., also provide such services (see Chapter **13**).

Cambridge Development Laboratory (*Special Education Software for Grades K-12*): 1-800-637-0047.
CD-ROM Access: 1-800-959-5260
CD-ROM Warehouse: 1-800-237-6623
ClubMac: 1-800-ClubMac
CompuClassics: 1-800-697-2006
Comp USA: 1-800-541-7638
Computer Discount Warehouse: 1-800-865-4CDW (PC); 1-800-509-4CDW (Mac)
Computerworks!: 1-800-825-DISK
Compuwest: 1-800-663-0001 (liberal previewing policy)
Crazy Bob's: 1-800-420-2627
Dynacomp, Inc.: 1-800-828-6772
Educational Resources: 1-800-860-9005
Educorp: "Will beat any advertised price on CD-ROM."; 1-800-843-9497
Egghead Software: 1-800-344-4323; 1-800-949-3447 (TDD)
Learning Services: 1-800-877-9378
Mac Bargain$: 1-800-619-9091
MacMall: 1-800-222-2808
MacNews: 1-800-723-7744
MacWarehouse: 1-800-255-6227
MegaHaus: 1-800-786-1173 (PC); 1-800-786-1184 (Mac)
MicroWarehouse: 1-800-367-7080
Nobody Beats the Wiz: 1-800-253-0186
P.C. Connection: *PC World's* "Best Mail Order Company"; 1-800-800-0003
Software Labs: 1-800-569-7900
Software Marketing Corp.: 1-800-336-0182
Tiger Software: 1-800-888-4437 (PC); 1-800-666-2562 (Mac)

The following **videos** are available from RMI Media Productions (1-800-745-5480). Discounts are given to members of the Association for Educational Communications and Technology. Request a current AECT catalog by calling 1-202-347-7834 or Internet: aect@aect.org.

Introduction to CD-ROM
Introduction to HyperStudio
Introduction to HyperCard 2.2
Orientation to Multimedia
Hardware Introduction
Software Introduction
Accessing Data Networks
The Multimedia Design Team
Environments for Learning
Integrating Multimedia with the Instructional Process
Components of Multimedia
Elements of Design
The Multimedia Revolution—Today and Tomorrow

Study Items

1. Explain what is meant by shifting emphasis from **products** of learning to the **process** of learning.

2. What historically has characterized **interactivity** in the classroom?

3. Characterize what you believe to be the **best** senses of "interactivity" both among humans and between humans and computers.

4. Contrast contributions of B.F. Skinner and Norman Crowder to the evolution of today's interactive multimedia.

5. Describe some exemplary multimedia programs in each of three categories—skill builders, knowledge explorers, reference works.

6. Describe various means (**"search engines"**) by which students can locate desired information using CD-ROM multimedia reference works.

7. How would you integrate an intense simulation gaming activity into your curriculum, consistent with objectives, student characteristics, and time constraints?

8. Multimedia programs sometimes include unsavory characters, permit using the word pronunciation feature in nasty ways, and have options that make crashing, losing, or erasing fun. How will you cope?

9. Describe ways in which interactive multimedia educational software can make learning more individualized.

10. In what ways do multimedia reference works enhance access to information?

11. What might your students gain from immersion in virtual reality environments?

12. What sorts of technical computer skills facilitate installation and use of CD-ROM multimedia programs?

13. Assess pros and cons of interactive multimedia programs, specifically for use with your students.

14. In what ways can interactive learning environments be made responsive to **"constructivist"** themes?

15. List benefits of interactive multimedia for people having limited mobility due to illness or long-term disability.

16. Describe criteria for selection of CD-ROM reference works.

Suggested Activities

1. Conduct a survey to find out how teachers, college faculty, administrators, and educational technology specialists might differ in their characterizations of **"interactivity"** in the classroom.

2. We've seen students delight in the slaughter of buffalo while playing *Oregon Trail*, and thrill to the destruction wrought by earthquakes and plane crashes in *SimCity*. (But what a joy to see the apprehensions of a few fearful computer novices utterly dissipate as they joined in these activities.) Of course, we've also witnessed chaotic, unproductive class discussions and heated debates without resolution. Conduct a debate among your classmates assessing the pros and cons of letting students take ever greater control over their own learning, letting discussions and debates run their course rather than intervening. (See **Figure 12.17**.)

3. Obtain and play one of the classic simulation games (e.g., *Conflict in the Middle East, Starpower, Wff'N Proof*).

4. "Test drive" award-winning CD-ROM titles either at your neighborhood software store or by purchasing sampler discs. (See "Sources" above.)

5. Purchase one of the most appealing multimedia titles described in this chapter that runs on your equipment, is suitable for your students, and is consistent with your objectives (however fluid these may be), and integrate it into a lesson plan.

6. Immerse yourself wholeheartedly in an arcade simulated environment. Share with classmates the degree of telepresence you experienced.

7. Conduct a discussion among your classmates concerning how virtual reality technology might be tailored to reach students with special needs.

8. Attend a workshop on authoring interactive multimedia.

9. After examining current issues at your library and local shop, subscribe to some periodicals listed above at a fraction of list prices.

10. Install a CD-ROM program, taking precautions listed in this chapter.

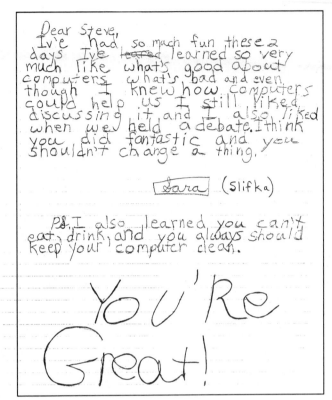

Figure 12.17. Ah. Why do we teach? As illustrated above by fourth grade Sara's note (P.S. 6, Manhattan, Suzanne Herman, teacher), the more we let students interact among themselves, providing them with rich environments and sensitive, knowledgeable guidance, the more they seem to both learn and enjoy. Reproduced with permission.

11. Obtain and view some of the above listed RMI videos.

12. Design a multifaceted (e.g., products, performances, portfolios—the "3 p's") evaluation of students' engagement in using interactive multimedia.

13. Find new editions and related titles of books listed above by checking "author" and "subject" volumes of *Books in Print*. Copies of this reference are available in libraries and bookstores and, for a fee, over CompuServe. Also try Internet sources, especially university libraries. Share results with classmates and me.

14. Please inform me of errors and omissions in this chapter via Internet: hackbarths@aol.com. Provide your email (or snail-mail) address and I'll send a text update file.

Chapter 13

The Information Superhighway

Chapter Content and Objectives

It seems inevitable that the media described in previous chapters eventually would merge. Printed words were destined to become hypertext, audio and video signals always were seeking the widest audiences, and computers have yearned to network freely.

The "global village" envisioned by the prophetic Marshall McLuhan is swiftly becoming a reality, with "virtual communities" intimately linked along the "information superhighway." Here opportunities for Internet-based learning and expression are immense! Reading this chapter should help you to:

- Describe evolution of the **Internet** and its **World Wide Web.**
- List major features of **commercial online services**.
- Suggest ways in which these computer networks contribute to making **knowledge more accessible**.
- Illustrate how computer networks can make **learning more individualized**.
- Describe several varieties of **Internet-based learning** activities.
- **Assess pros and cons** of student access to the information superhighway.
- **Make productive classroom use** of computer-mediated communications.

Evolution of Computer Networks

Just as communities have built roads connecting homes, schools, workplaces, and shopping centers, governmental, commercial, and educational agencies early began linking their computers with coaxial cables into **"local area networks"** (LANs). These LANs have permitted sharing of programs and data and transmitting of interoffice correspondence. As the largest of these LANs adopted a common language ("operating system") and began communicating across telephone lines and via satellites, we witnessed the emergence of a **public** (nobody "owns" it) **"network of networks"**—the **Internet**—and of a plethora of **commercial information access, electronic publication, and communications services** including America Online, Prodigy, CompuServe, Delphi, GEnie, The WELL ("Whole Earth 'Lectronic Link,"), AppleLink, Scholastic Network, Dow Jones, ImagiNation Network, Worldnet Direct, Lexis, Netcom, Dialog, MCI Mail, AT&T Mail, Sprintmail, eWorld, and The Microsoft Network. (See **Figure 13.01**.)

Because growth of services is explosive, the most I can do here is to provide an overview of general characteristics and invite you to contact me via email (hackbarths@aol.com) to discuss developments as they evolve.

The Internet. In 1969, the U.S. Department of Defense Advanced Research Projects Agency (ARPA, later DARPA) initiated a project to find ways to make computer networks more reliable. Linking government and university labs, "ARPAnet" soon evolved into an efficient means of exchanging information, an unanticipated bonus. Military agencies split from ARPAnet in 1983 to form MILnet, but the thread of interconnection that remained between them became known as "DARPA Internet," soon abbreviated to the "Internet."

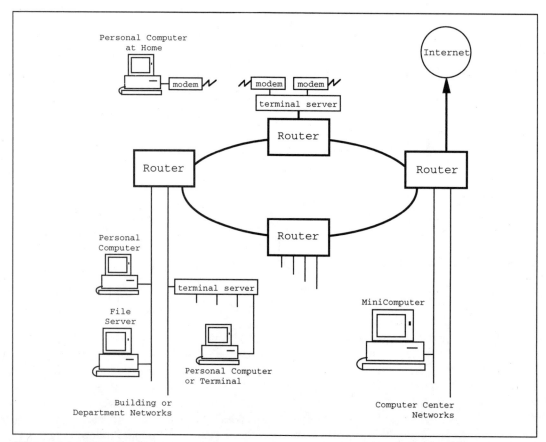

Figure 13.01. Diagramed here is a campus computer network. A high speed electronic backbone interconnects routers, forming the basic infrastructure for the network. Building and departmental local area networks, as well as dial-in modems, are attached to routers. One router also attaches the campus network to the Internet. Reproduced courtesy of the Academic Computing Facility, New York University; copyright © 1995 NYU, with thanks to ACF User Services Manager Estelle P. Hochberg and her staff.

To facilitate academic research, the National Science Foundation in 1986 tied together five supercomputer centers into "NSFnet" and then linked with ARPAnet. The key to this marriage, and to those that followed rapidly, was the *UNIX* multiuser (contrasted with *DOS*'s "just me and my PC" mentality) operating system that had been developed by AT&T Bell Laboratories and distributed widely and cheaply to educational institutions. (Macintosh LANs were using *AppleTalk* at the time, which slowed integration.)

Further impetus was provided in 1987 when Merit Network, Inc., joined with IBM and MCI in expanding NSFnet, the heir apparent to the outmoded (8-bit processor-based) ARPAnet. Jumping on the bandwagon were CSNet (computer science departments), FidoNet

(a worldwide network of personal computers), BITnet ("Because It's Time Network," primarily educational institutions), and diverse Ethernet-based (a high-speed network hardware standard) LANs also talking *UNIX*. Commercial enterprises were granted access to the Internet either via *UNIX* or across protocol translation "gateways" in the early 1990s, and today thousands of LANs, each with a "host" minicomputer (and a file "server") and individual "clients" are joined across the globe.[1]

An emergent property of this relentless evolution of computer networks has become known as **cyberspace**, from William Gibson's 1984 novel, *Neuromancer*. Within cyberspace, ever growing numbers of people are joining to form fluid, dynamic "virtual communities." Here "cybernauts" work, play, debate issues, share insights, meet soulmates, and make plans to rendezvous.

So what exactly can this sprawling electronic patchwork quilt do for us? The most promising features were put succinctly in the *Internet Primer* as follows:

- exchange of electronic mail and data files in a wide-area environment;
- on-line "real time" interaction with other network users;
- participation in electronic mailing lists and conferences;
- receipt of electronic publications;
- access to data stored on remote computers;
- access to remote scientific computing peripherals such as supercomputers, remote sensing equipment, telescopes, and graphics processors; and
- access to a wide selection of public domain and shareware software.[2]

The metaphor of an electronic "highway" or "infobahn" used to characterize the Internet has caught on quickly. Thus, we hear about various information sources being called "lanes." Our mode of "transportation" may be a PC, Mac, or Mini, each with features that make it a "sports" model (in bits per second of data transfer) or a "clunker." "On-ramps" are the services that provide access (e.g., community "Free-Nets," America Online, eWorld). You are invited to "start your engine" and, following intricate "roadmaps," go "cruising" on the "infobahn" into "cyberspace." Here, of course, you start out as a "newbie" ("cyberNOT!"), but soon earn your wings as a certified "cybernaut." (See **Figure 13.02**.)

Once aboard just about any computer built in the past decade and connected via modem and phone line to a "host" minicomputer, our key to accessing the Internet is a **TCP/IP** (Transfer Control Protocol/Internet Protocol), a *UNIX* "address." For example, while at New York University (1994–95), I could be reached at: slh4672@acfcluster.nyu.edu (username at [@] hostname [i.e., a VMS-based VAX/DEC computer], name of agency, type of agency) and also at slh4672@nyuacf.bitnet. My first use of this Internet access was to correspond via email (in a world ruled by cryptic codes, "e-mail" could not long survive) with colleagues gracious enough to critique this book. Next I "subscribed" to "listservs" (no "e")

"How are we supposed to get on the information superhighway? We can't even drive."

Figure 13.02. The information superhighway (aka "infobahn") metaphor already is jammed with other metaphors, some facilitating communication among those in the "fast lane," but leaving "newbies" "in the dust" or at "dead ends." How will you help your students to make connections and distinctions between transportation systems and computer networks? Reproduced with permission of Martha Campbell.

that supplied steady streams of messages about developments in teaching and technology and to which I could either post a message of my own or correspond directly with individuals having similar concerns.

Preparation of this chapter pushed me ever further into exploring the Internet. Thus, I learned about the thousands of "Usenet" newsgroups (aka "NetNews") that post messages on topic-specific and general-interest BBSs (bulletin board services, e.g., Exec-PC, CRS Online) and hold conferences ("forums") using IRC (Internet relay chat), "Telnet" (a *UNIX* program that effects connections to distant computers), Hytelnet (guides access to over a thousand libraries and other Telnet sites), *Gopher* (developed at the University of Minnesota [the Golden Gophers] to "ferret out" desired information from remote locations), FTP (file transfer protocol to retrieve data and software), the Wide Area Information

Server (WAIS) (which provides database searches), and more GUIs ("gooeys"–graphical user interfaces, e.g., *Mosaic, NCSA Mosaic, TurboGopher, NEXTSTEP, Win-Gopher*).

I was especially amused to discover that *Archie* (from "archives") is a program that permits search of over two million available files for FTP, whereas *"VERONICA"* (obviously, *Very Easy Rodent-Oriented Net-wide Index to Computer Archives*) works hand-in-paw with *Gopher. Jonzy's Universal Gopher Hierarchy Excavation And Display* (JUGHEAD) also does Boolean (and, or, not) word combination searches of *Gopher* menus, but one site at a time.[3]

The World Wide Web. In 1989, the European Center for Particle Physics (CERN, Geneva) developed software that permitted the linking of files among computer networks. Moving one's cursor to a highlighted term and pressing "Enter" transported users to sites that carried information related to that term. Such "hypertext" links soon evolved into "hypermedia" as the files accessed expanded to include audio, image, and video. Thus, the **World Wide Web** was spun.

What Macintosh and *Windows* did for making computer technology more easily accessible to the masses, *Mosaic* (in 1993) and its successors (e.g., *NCSA Mosaic, Enhanced Mosaic, Mosaic in a Box, InternetWorks, Lynx, Cello, MacWeb, winWeb, WebSurfer, VersaTerm, Netscape Navigator*) have done for the Internet and its World Wide Web. Now we enter a Uniform Resource Locator (URL) code (or click on an icon or on a URL from our "hot list") and our Web "browser" software downloads onto our screens illustrated "home pages" having colorful hypertext links to helpful files and other home pages. Using the simple and popular *HyperText Markup Language* (HTML) to format documents written in ASCII code, organizations and businesses are jumping on the "WebWagon," creating fresh sites to promote their products and services. Thus, the Internet itself quickly is acquiring not just a new dimension of accessibility, but a veneer of entirely new information. With Sun Microsystems' *Hot Java*, home pages have became animated, and with *Virtual Reality Markup Language* we not only visit home pages, our virtual agents "enter" them.

What is the potential of **Web-based learning**? Odvard Dyrli and Daniel Kinnaman (Faculty Co-Directors of the *Technology & Learning* Professional Development Institute) concluded their five-part series of "What Every Teacher Needs to Know About Technology" articles with the bold claim that:

The World-Wide Web and the network browsers will completely change the nature of teaching and learning. In addition to presenting topics sequentially, teachers and students can now explore topics in an infinite variety of sequences, using all sorts of multimedia and people resources wherever they are located in the world. The World-Wide Web breaks down the walls of time and geographic location, and gives every individual the ability to be a continuing and lifelong learner. Thanks to global telecommunications, the school of tomorrow will be MUCH more than a "place!"[4]

Imagine! Students across the globe communicating via email, accessing resources of the World Wide Web, and video teleconferencing via the Internet. It's happening now. The National Science Foundation *et al.* funded **Global Schoolhouse**, using PCs, phone lines, and software that included Cornell University's *CU-SeeMe*, connected during the 1993–94 school year students in 12 U.S. states and six other countries. Focus was on topics of global concern–alternative energy sources, solid waste management, space exploration, natural disasters. The Global SchoolNet Foundation (info@gsn.org; http://gsn.org) continued expanding its Global Schoolhouse (contact Yvonne Marie Andres at andresyv@cerf.net) project in 1995–96 with collaboration among students from France, Norway, Germany, Japan, the Philippines, and several other countries.[5]

Outcomes of such telecommunications projects require multidimensional process and product assessment over the long haul, in relation to sound educational aims. For example, objectives of the **School Project in Northern Norway** (SPINN) included improving the quality of education and access to it. The following recommendations, based on SPINN experiences, may readily be generalized.

It is important to get teachers engaged so that the school "owns" the project. . . . ⌊P⌋roper procedures for project development [need] be established. Evaluation is important and should be done externally. . . . [Or] self-evaluation based on plans of action should be carried out.

We recommend face-to-face contact in projects if resources are available. It is very important that students in distance education have the chance to meet each other. This will lay the foundation for better cooperation within the group.

Finally, projects should be based on real needs in education. However, experimentation with data communication often generates good ideas for use of the medium.[6]

As you join in your school's technology planning group, and begin to sign on to listservs, you will hear amidst the justified excitement concerns both about educationally relevant exploitation of the Internet and its World Wide Web, and about valid assessment of outcomes. This is as it should be, I believe, and we should take active roles.

America Online. Started in 1985 for Apple computer users, this commercial service grew from 300,000 subscribers in 1993 to over a million by the end of 1994 to more than four million by late 1995. When I signed on (1994), charges were $9.95/month for the first five hours of connect time, $3.50/hour thereafter. Their brochure read:

- Download software from our libraries of over 40,000 files.
- Participate in live conferences and message boards specializing in games, graphics, education, applications, business, and more!

- Browse the electronic pages of prominent magazines, including *TIME, OMNI, Compute, PC World,* and *Windows Magazine.*
- Communicate with other online service users through powerful electronic mail and access to the Internet!

Their software library has since grown to over 60,000 files, the hourly rate was reduced to $2.95, photos were added to text, and Internet features were expanded to include newsgroups, *Gopher,* WAIS, listservs, and the World Wide Web. A new main menu displays hot button icons for the expanded departments—Clubs & Interests, Computing, Education, Entertainment, Internet Connection, Kids Only, Marketplace, News Stand, People Connection, Personal Finance, Reference Desk, Sports, Today's News, and Travel. (See **Figure 13.03.**) These attractive features, along with aggressive distribution of free trial offer diskettes and expansion of facilities to handle the traffic, have resulted in an explosive rate of growth for AOL, surely well beyond four million in 1996.

My curiosity about America Online (AOL) was first piqued by my niece's adolescent son, who also had re-

Figure 13.03. Above is the AOL "KIDS ONLY" opening screen. Clicking on words or icons provides quick access to desired features. How will you prepare your students for such ready access? Reproduced with permission of America Online.

ceived the "10 hours free" introductory offer with purchase of a computer. My mother had noticed the busy phone line, but I assured her that James was getting a head start on his future in CAD-CAM (computer-aided design/manufacturing). Little did I know what he was up to.

The year of using only the email feature of my university account did not prepare me for having so readily at my fingertips the above AOL resources, plus fax, online computer support, help wanted ads, online homework help, member profiles (voluntary), the Internet *Gopher* and Usenet News, and fellow AOL subscribers leisurely (sometimes heatedly) "chatting" the night away. **Just think what this means to people having limited mobility—elderly, disabled, ill!** Priceless.

On the dark side, an intense debate taught me right away the value of signing on with a pseudonym and not including my surname in the membership profile. Rudeness and profanity received "warnings" from AOL monitors, but I don't know if my niece is prepared to explain to her son all the terms used. She might want to engage the block out feature.

For us educators, perhaps the most useful feature of AOL is its "Teachers Information Network." Here one not already suffering from information overload, characteristic especially of the first several years of teaching, and with money to spare, can leisurely access such departments as: "The Teachers' Forum," "The Idea Exchange," "The Newsstand," "Lesson Plan Libraries," "Educational Magazines Database," "Educational TV/Radio Database," "The Multimedia Exchange" (e.g., *HyperCard/ HyperStudio* trading post), "The Electronic School House," the "Access Excellence Network," and the "Resource Pavilion" (where one can reach the *KidsNet* database of children's audio, video, and television programming, study guides, and copyright release information). Also online are selected portions of various newspapers—*The Chicago Tribune, The New York Times, The San Jose Mercury News, USA Today.* Students enjoy exploring "Kids Only," and find the "Academic Assistance Center" a non-threatening environment in which to get help with their homework.

Navigating the full range of AOL services is simplified by a neat GUI and explicit on-screen instructions. President Steve Case has made good on his promises of providing cutting edge access to the Internet, including email, newsgroups, FTP, WAIS, *Gopher,* and NaviSoft's *InternetWorks* Web browser. You can reach me at hackbarths@aol.com.

Prodigy. This classy service provider (owned by IBM/ Sears) began in 1988 and now offers both "Core" and "Plus" features to its three million subscribers. The *Member Guide* (1993 edition) that came with my new IBM PS/1 had explicit sign up and navigational instructions. The *Guide*'s envelope listed "just some of the reasons" why we should sign up as:

- Get answers to questions about your PS/1 computer!

- You have mail waiting!

- Help your children with today's homework!

- Track your investments. Manage your money better.

- Choose this evening's family entertainment!

- Tap into a world of information, services and people . . . (See **Figure 13.04.**)

Information not included with promotional materials was amply provided during sign-on and could easily be printed out. "Core" features turned out to be access to news, sports, weather, information, and entertainment. "Plus" features include most bulletin boards, stock quotes, company news, *Eaasy Sabre* (for travel planning and reservations), and online versions of newspapers (*The Atlanta Journal/Constitution, The Milwaukee Journal/Sentinel, New York Newsday, The Los Angeles Times, The Tampa Tribune*). Charges under a "Value Plan" were $14.95 per month for unlimited use of "Core," two hours of "Plus" ($3.60/hr. thereafter). In August 1995, Prodigy matched AOL's rates of $9.95 per month for five hours (Core and Plus) usage, $2.95 per hour thereafter ("Basic Plan"). Its "Value Plan" was modified with an increase to five hours of "Plus" and a reduction to $2.95 per hour thereafter. It's new "30/30" plan provides 30 hours of access for $29.95, $2.95 per hour thereafter. My address is: rsvu05a@prodigy.com. (Lower case better discriminates letters from numbers.)

Apart from the standard news, weather, and reference features, Prodigy also offers access to like-minded people who post messages on topic-specific bulletin board services (BBSes). Topics include education, foreign languages, Internet, lifestyles, news, science and environment, singles, computers. On the "Education BB" are various subcategories such as special education and software. Here, teachers and administrators reach out to colleagues and receive advice. On the "Internet Forum BB" are posted helpful suggestions and addresses (e.g., president@whitehouse.gov). Another high-

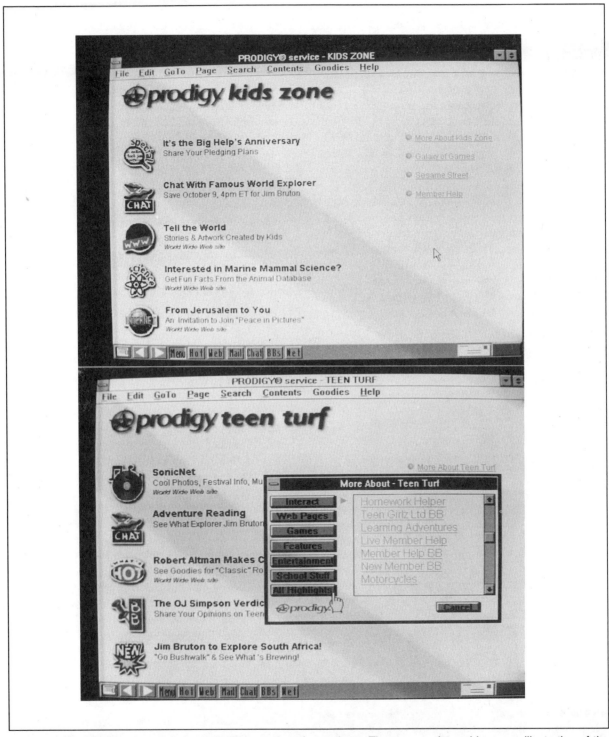

Figure 13.04. Prodigy constantly is expanding services for students. The menus pictured here are illustrative of the vast resources available to children and youths. How can we make such resources available to **all** our students and ensure that they use them wisely? Reproduced with permission of Prodigy Services Co.

light is the free "Member Exchange" BBS where I learned a great deal about features of Prodigy compared with those of various alternatives and about all those already trite email chat codes (e.g., TTYL = talk to ya later, <VBG> = "very big grin" used to soften tongue-in-cheek remarks, and the expressive faces :-) and 8< (known as "emoticons"). Access to the Internet expanded in 1995 to include email, newsgroups, *Gopher*, FTP, and a highly acclaimed Web browser. (See **Figure 13.05**.)

For youngsters, Prodigy offers versions of *Sesame Street* and *Reading Magic*. Youths can find news and reference works, explore topics in math and science, play *Where in the World Is Carmen Sandiego?* and exchange messages on preteen and teen-oriented bulletin boards. For $9.95 per month extra they can have two hours of access to "Homework Helper" (each additional hour costs $2.95). This online reference tool permits searches of about 1500 books, 500 magazines, 100 newspapers, 1500 photos, 300 maps, and countless TV and NPR radio scripts. All may easily be downloaded for pasting into reports.

"No one at the office knew that Ellen 'The Iron Maiden' Matson took part in the 'I Got it All Except my Sugar Plum' discussion group."

Figure 13.05. Any one of the major commercial online services is a convenient entry point for parents, teachers, and students desiring "computer-mediated communications" with people sharing similar interests, as shown here, and quick access to vast stores of information. Reproduced with permission of Andrew Toos.

Unlike AOL, Prodigy does not allow use of pseudonyms. To an apparently greater extent than AOL, Prodigy (1) carefully screens public notices before posting (but not legally protected private email messages sent among members), (2) discourages private chats from cluttering public bulletin boards, and (3) provides explicit guidelines for courtesy, protocol, and security. Under online safety, the Director of Member Services recommended wisely:

- Be cautious about with whom you exchange electronic messages.
- Remember the difference between the two forms of online communication. Private email generally is between two people. Public bulletin board notes can be read by millions of people.
- Think twice before disclosing personal information such as address and phone number.
- Parents should remind their kids to use the same caution here as they would going to any public place.
- Don't believe everything you read online. If it seems too good to be true, it probably is.
- Parents may want to block their children's access to certain bulletin boards.

Such explicit warnings surely qualify Prodigy as "The Family Channel" of online services. In his "A Special Note to Parents," Prodigy President Ross Glatzer wrote: "As a parent myself, I understand the dedication you feel about providing the very best environment for your children." Doesn't that sound just like Mr. Rogers?

Especially attractive to teachers is a special "commercial free" classroom version of Prodigy with "interactive language, math, science, and social studies features" plus access to the Internet and a national "Teachers' Forum." Classroom Prodigy is priced from $99 for a nine month school term (five hours of access per month) up to $449 for a 12 month school term (25 hours of access each month). The Computer Curriculum Corporation has bundled Classroom Prodigy with its *SuccessMaker Online* program. Ten hours of access per month for the nine month school year, plus a teachers manual have a price tag of $3,750.

CompuServe. Established in 1969 as a computer time-sharing service, CompuServe entered the online information service industry in 1979, and was acquired by H&R Block a year later. It has since grown to about three million subscribers worldwide and is among the most highly regarded of the full-service commercial on-liners. The *Membership Guide* (1994) touted an $8.95 per month membership fee (raised to $9.95 in 1995) that includes unlimited connect time to:

- News, sports, weather (e.g., *Associated Press Online, Accu-Weather, U.S. News & World Report, Deutsche Presse-Agentur*).
- Electronic mail (may send about 90 messages per month).
- Reference library (e.g., *American Heritage Dictionary of the English Language, Grolier's Academic American Encyclopedia, Peterson's College Database, Handicapped Users Database, HealthNet*).
- Shopping (e.g., *The Electronic Mall, Consumer Reports,* classified ads).
- Financial information (e.g., stock quotes, *FundWatch Online*).
- Travel & leisure (e.g., visa advice, *Eaasy Sabre*).
- Entertainment & games (e.g., *Roger Ebert's Movie Reviews, Science Trivia Quiz*).
- Membership support services.

Networking online in "Forums" with like-minded members was one, among other, "extended" services having a connect fee of $4.80 per hour. However, beginning in September 1995, CompuServe matched AOL with 5 hours per month of access to "virtually all" of its services for $9.95, with additional hours billed at $2.95. And it began offering a high usage option of $24.95 for 20 hours, $1.95 per hour thereafter. For "premium" services (e.g., access to *Books in Print* and *Dissertation Abstracts*), expect to pay substantial fees.

CompuServe clearly is a leading service, combining the best of features found elsewhere. Call it "The Professional Network" among commercial services. I found the graphical interface and navigational features comparable to AOL in high quality. The "Guided Tour" was helpful as was scrolling through the "Index" for a complete listing of services identified as free, "+," or "$." Instructions and practice sessions made CompuServe especially user-friendly (or as we now say, "discoverable").

CompuServe bulletin boards appear even more extensive and professionally oriented than the very good ones on Prodigy. For example, under "Education" are these "Forums": "Attention Deficit Disorder," "Computer

Training," "Education," "Educational Research," "Foreign Language," "LOGO," "Science/Math Education," and "Students." Each "Forum" has "libraries" of pertinent information. Under "Computers/Technology" were "Forums" on hardware and software as well as "Magazine/Electronic Newsstand," "Science and Technology" news, and "Softtex," where one can buy and download software.

The "Kids Students Forum" has libraries, message exchanges, and such neat places as "Homeschool World," "Let's Be Friends," "When I Grow Up," and "Computer Magic." The "Teens Students Forum" has a "Student Press Network," "What's Up TV Network," and, of course, lots of chat areas.

Also available is an "Executive News Service" ($) that scans the newswires for "clippings" according to criteria we specify and, on a continuous basis, places them in a "file" for us to read at leisure. Those who enjoy browsing can look up online versions of *Florida TODAY* and *The Detroit Free Press*, and Gannett Suburban New York daily newspapers.

Internet features include email (message charges apply), newsgroups, telnet, and FTP. Access to the Web is provided by Spry's *AirMosaic*, or by the user's own browser.

CompuServe's concern for maintaining high standards matches that found on Prodigy. The introduction to the "Consumer Electronics Forum," for example, states that it:

> STRICTLY PROHIBITS messages with PROFANE and/or OBSCENE language, PERSONAL ATTACKS against another member, Commercial Advertising, PIRACY, TRADING or COPYING of commercial computer and audio/video software. . . . ALL MESSAGES are reviewed by the SysOps [system operators] on a daily basis and if we question a message it will be taken off the main message area and placed in our section for review. . . . if it is in violation of any of the above policies, your membership privileges may be revoked. . . .

Look at this highly regarded service and share with me your impressions at 75111,1407 (or 75111.1407@ compuserve.com). (See **Figure 13.06**.)

Delphi Internet. Begun in 1992 and billing itself through 1994 as "the only major online service to offer full access to the Internet," Delphi claims over 140,000 subscribers and charges $10 per month for four hours of

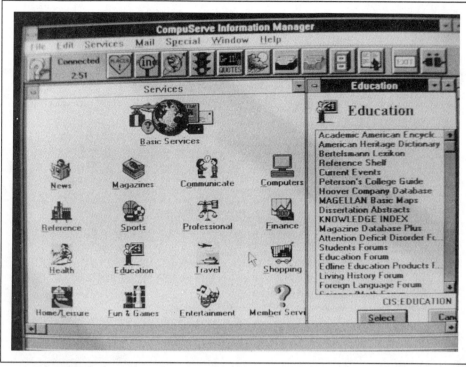

Figure 13.06. CompuServe's opening menu is as enticing as they come. Each icon is backed with a labyrinth of features. They say it's the service "you never outgrow." Reproduced with permission of CompuServe, Inc.

connect time ($4.00 per hour after that) OR $20/month for 20 hours, $1.80/hour thereafter. Internet access adds an additional $3.00 per month, and daytime use (6:00 a.m. to 6:00 p.m., M–F) over SprintNet or Tymnet adds $9.00 per hour. Benefits as listed in the membership brochure are:

- Learn about computer hardware and software from members and vendors.
- Exchange email, post messages, "chat," fax, and telex.
- Access newswires.
- Download public domain software ["freeware"] and "shareware" [pay fee on honor system if you use].
- Make travel arrangements.
- Handle investments.
- Play games online with other members.
- Create your own discussion group network.

Watch out because daytime communications and "premium" charges apply, as with other commercial pro-

viders' promotional deals, even during the "Five-Hour Free Trial."

Schools within the contiguous United States qualify for special discounted pricing. The cost for the 10 month academic year is $199 for 80 hours of usage (total, not monthly), and $4 per hour thereafter. This does not include access to "custom" (user made) forums nor to "premium" services.

Through 1995, Delphi still had a text-based screen layout, a no-WIMP [window/icon/mouse/pull-down] mentality common among hackers, but tidy menus and explicit instructions eased navigation. I had to inquire how to edit text (no delete nor backspace at first, and surely no word wrap). It was here that I found easy access to the University of California library system, the Educational Resources Information Center (ERIC), and the Library of Congress.

My first encounter via Delphi with Internet Relay Chat (IRC) was thrilling. Commands were provided up front and, following instructions, I soon found myself connected to a host computer at the Boston University. As the text scrolled by I reached for my Control-S to stop and Control-Q to continue. Wow! Over 2000 people were chatting on about 1000 different "channels." Another 2000 were "invisible" and about 100 had a "connection to the twilight zone." This was my kind of place!! I let the screen scroll past the First Amendment, and proceeded to the rules set by SysOp (system operator) Helen Rose. Rule #1: NO BOTS! ("blocks of text" that jam the screen). Rule #2: ". . . If I find you using an illegal user@host and you do not give a reason that I find acceptable, I will /kill you." [Slash!]

I ran a "list" command to find out what "channels" were available—"Welcome to Beijing," "Viva-Mexico-Lindo!!!," "Lets get together and kill Barney," "Peace and Love." With the "who" command, I got a list of people currently on each channel of interest. "/Join #Mexico" took me to a lively discussion ("*Ja, ja, ja.*") among students in Texas, Columbia, Mexico, and Massachusetts. A "*Chao me voy.*" was met with a friendly "*Ciao.*" Next I went to #Germany, *Heimat* of my distant ancestors, to practice some *Wie gehts du?* (I had been using my plastic-covered German-English dictionary for a mouse pad.) Time to compose simple questions and responses, and to look up unfamiliar terms, permitted overcoming that awkwardness that typically accompanies face-to-face efforts.

My address was hackbarths@delphi.com. Expense of daytime access and the text-based format dampened my enthusiasm, but for those who engage in extensive email, listserv, *Gopher*, and FTP activities, Delphi is a bargain.

eWorld. In contrast with their leadership in the personal computer market, Apple has lagged behind in the area of online services. Finally, in mid-1994 the first ads appeared for eWorld, but Apple apparently was too shy to include a telephone number. Several weeks after mailing in my request I received a slick brochure, diskettes, and, with a microscope, was able to locate the Assistance Center toll-free number. Of course, demand is great, and all the best services have experienced growing pains.

From **Figure 13.07** you can see that Apple's creative instincts for the user-friendly have pushed its GUI one step closer to virtual reality. By clicking on a building, one may access any one of the following:

• Learning Center (books, encyclopedias, dictionaries)

• Computer Center (news, information services)

• Business & Finance Plaza (news, investments)

• Community Center (interactive forums)

• eMail Center (Internet gateway)

• Newsstand (news services)

• Marketplace (shopping, travel arrangements)

• Arts & Leisure Pavilion (the "entertainment capital")

• Info Booth (schedule of events, directory of services)

Areas of special interest to teachers abound. In the "eWorld Educator Connection" are found lessons plans and the sharing of other resources among teachers and parents. The "RSP Funding Focus" helps locate money for study, research, and professional development. "Apple Global Education" links educators worldwide for the purpose of exchanging ideas about literature, lifestyles, teaching techniques, etc. "The Disability Connection" provides on-line periodicals, the Macintosh Disability Resources library, and information about Apple's Worldwide Disability Solutions Group.

What's the bottom line? For $8.95 you get four hours per month of connect time. Go beyond this and it's $2.95 per hour. A prepaid 12 month subscription for schools costs $199 for five hours of access each month or $1,579 for 40 hours.

The Microsoft Network. MSN was bundled in August 1995 with *Windows 95* amidst legal challenges from the competition, and investigation by the Department of Justice for possible antitrust violations. It debuted with the standard features of forums, live chat, software libraries, and Internet access. Over 50 hardware and software vendors including Dell, Gateway, and Lotus are represented. Clicking on icons takes users straight to technical support forums.

The opening screen is the simplest around, with just five hot button choices—"MSN Today," "E-Mail," "Favorite Places," "Member Assistance," "Categories." Under "Categories," the beef of the service, are: "Sports, Health, and Fitness," "Computers and Software," "Education and Reference," "Home and Family," "Science and Technology," "Business and Finance," "The Microsoft Network Beta," "Arts and Entertainment," "People and Communities," "The Internet Center," "Special Events," "The MSN Member Lobby," "Interests, Leisure, and Hobbies," and "Public Affairs."

Under the MSN "Education & Reference" area are "Colleges & Universities," "Computer Education," "Continuing Education," "Educator-to-Educator," "Field of Study," "International Students," "Primary & Secondary Education," and "Reference." Email, newsgroups, *Gopher*,

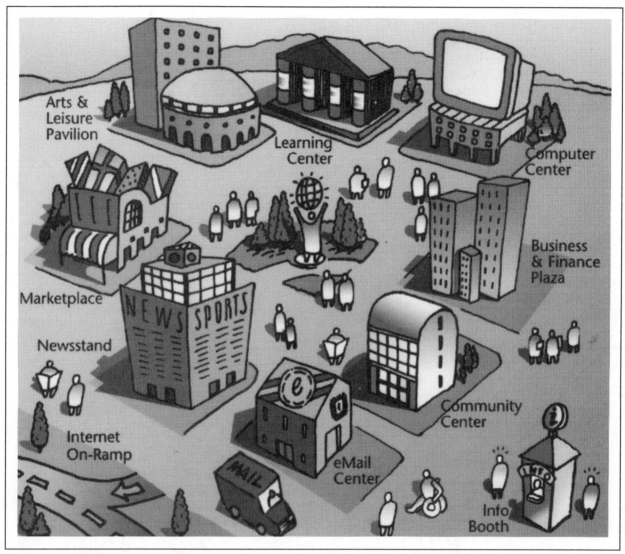

Figure 13.07. As a former Apple IIe user (one of the last holdouts to get a "SYNTAX ERROR" message) who now is an IBM PC devotee, I wish to balance my presentation by suggesting that we should never underestimate Apple Computer's devotion to innovation and service, the Steven Jobs/Wozniak legacy. First to make a GUI standard, first to include a multimedia authoring tool *(HyperCard),* Apple surely will continue to set the pace with "bilingual" laptops and user-friendly access to "eWorld" and the Internet. Reproduced with permission of Apple Computer, Inc.

FTP, and a customized version of Spyglass's *Mosaic Web* browser comprise a complete Internet package. "Basic Plan" service access fees are $4.95 a month for three hours of access ($2.50 per hour thereafter). Frequent flyers may opt for paying $19.95 a month to get 20 hours of access ($2.00 per hour thereafter).[7]

Others. Of course, there are many other commercial online services that merit consideration. Before eWorld there was **AppleLink**, the ground breaking service for school users of Apple computers. It provides tons of lessons plans, grant information, and online assistance. National Geographic's **KidsNet** is a great resource for the upper elementary grades. The **Global SchoolNet Network** (formerly *FrEd Mail*) provides school districts across the nation with email and bulletin board services. **Scholastic Network** connects students with authors, community leaders, and scientists. Access also is provided to newswires and Scholastic publications. The **AT&T Learning Network** offers courses in which groups of up to 10 classes are linked into collaborative "learning circles." Other services of AT&T include **Interchange** (hypertext links to information sources) and **PersonaLink** (email, news, shopping). Game players especially enjoy the services of **GEnie** and the **Imagi-Nation Network**.

Rapid evolution of the World Wide Web has permitted a host of new players to enter the market. Rated the best "Internet Access Provider" by *PC World*, Netcom has rapidly established a niche with its **NetCruiser Internet Service**. Understanding the magnetic appeal of exploring the Internet at leisure, Netcom offers 40 prime-time hours, and hundreds of weekend and off-peak hours, of access monthly for just $19.95! Nevertheless, competition has become fierce with challenges arising from such providers as **PSINet, iLINK, International Discount Telecommunications**, and **One World Internet**.

Watch, too, for providers such as Global Village Communication, Inc. with CE Software, Inc. ("Educate America"), Genentech, Inc. ("Access Excellence Network"), Discovery Channel Online, the Computer Curriculum Corporation (*SuccessMaker Online*), and the above listed "others" that are moving rapidly to help us integrate Internet access into our classrooms. Wondering what to do while waiting to get wired? Explore the multimedia resources listed at the end of this chapter, and perhaps simulate access with programs such as Desktop Solutions' *CyberWISE* Internet Educational Software.

To these major service providers, add scores of host computers for lease across the globe and community "Free-Nets." Schools especially should investigate access via dedicated phone lines connected to governmental, college, or community host computers. Guidebooks and videos abound, and software has made navigation transparent.

Virtues and Vices of Infobahn Access

In previous chapters, I have provided litanies of research reports purporting to tease out potent features of media. In every case, effectiveness was found to rest largely on a medium's capacity to incorporate instructional strategies (as described in Chapter **2**) that are responsive to student characteristics, especially to what they know and what they might reasonably be expected

to learn. Next came considerations of distribution and costs (e.g., in-class or distance education).

But let's face it. To evaluate mediated programs requires applying a bit of situational ("it depends") ethics. The virtues and vices of any given program, presented in any given format, depend on those concerns, long recognized by journalists as most vital—who, what, where, when, why—and then HOW.

Thus, evaluation of the information superhighway with respect to educational merits ultimately rests in our hands. Clever journalists, hyping the Internet, assure us that "There's gold in them thar hills." Increasingly we are hearing of our fellow teachers across the nation getting high on getting connected. Surely there *is* (that's Internet talk for **is**) "gold in them thar hills." But just as surely we will have to define what really is "gold" within the contexts of our largely unique situations, and then set out with our students to discover it.

Surely, nothing forces comparative analyses of mediated program alternatives as much as having to use them to achieve one's objectives. This holds true for textbooks as it does for videos and CBL. For example, as I explored features of online services according to instructions provided, I saw each at its best. But when I wanted to put the services to work for my purposes, the limitations of each became readily apparent.

Take the simple task of sending a file over the Internet. It happens that while drafting this chapter, I also was involved in testing a database retrieval program for UNICEF. The programmer, David Salant, wanted daily reports so that changes could be made and new versions tested over several cycles. How do you suppose each of the services described above held up?

David's Internet account was with the NYC, *UNIX*-based provider, Panix. Although my ultimate goal was to send reports produced using the helpful features of a word processor, I did not yet know how to do so. My NYU *VMS*-based account permitted text editing, but not word wrap and no spell check. Typing on Delphi was a nightmare at first because, until I requested from Customer Service the corrective commands, all attempts to back up or delete errors produced more ghastly errors. The Prodigy software I had downloaded for $14.95 to permit off line composition of messages that could be sent to Internet addresses did not function (credit received). The CompuServe Communications Center screens seemed (to me at the time) unnecessarily complex, one for addressing (really a neat feature), another for writing, others for sending and reading. America Online, in contrast, had one simple screen for addressing, composing, and sending messages, and each could easily be saved on diskette (but not printed out directly on my HP Laserjet). The AOL "word processor," like CompuServe's, had word wrap and editing features, but no spell check.

Given the combination of my lack of sophistication in using these services and actual feature deficiencies, I pursued the following strategy. I composed my first short report using the AOL "word processor" off line and attached the resultant ASCII ("askey," American Standard Code for Information Interchange) text file to a CompuServe message, with copy to my NYU account, to see how it would look to David at his Panix address. Worked fine. Focused on content rather than route, I then sent a few more short reports directly over the simpler, more familiar AOL.

Next, I decided to produce a report with *WordPerfect* and send it as a binary file via CompuServe, again with a copy to NYU. My goal here was merely to take advantage of the word wrap and spell check features, not to provide David with a message that he would have to manipulate to restore formatting codes. The result was not good. The first line was scrambled and hyphens had changed to the letter C.

Yikes! How to send this file without retyping? I searched the *WordPerfect* menus for converting binary documents to ASCII text. No luck. Reluctantly I scanned the *Workbook*. No luck. Only later did I discover in the *Reference* that I had overlooked the "Format" feature on the "Save As" menu. That evening, after having viewed Picasso and Dalí exhibits, I booted up *Microsoft Word*, easily found the desired feature, renamed the *WordPerfect* file (salant6.doc), imported it into *Word*, converted it to ASCII text, and sent it via CompuServe. Success. My NYU copy was clean, though letters of words at the end of lines (beyond the 80 character limit) had been pushed onto the next line. Next time I set the right margin at 1.25 (no, 1.5; no, 2.0; no, 2.1; no, 2.2) inches. Voila! Meanwhile, my NYU email account was exceeding its capacity, so I quickly learned how to "extract" the files and download them onto my home PC using *Kermit*, and then imported them into *WordPerfect* for editing and printing.

Thus we learn features of new media. Energized by pressing (excuse pun) needs, we "try and undergo," as John Dewey would say. In the context of our classrooms, given our students and their distinctive needs and preferred styles, we seek "replicable solutions to problems inherent in the challenges of teaching and learning." Published case studies and megametaanalyses of re-

search results give precious clues. Conscientious, systematic applied classroom research, undertaken daily by you and me, provides answers.

As with CD-ROMs, the information superhighway is paved with a mix of gold and litter. While recorded media are relatively dated and encyclopedic, the "live" infobahn constantly is accumulating fresh layers. Again, rich and original resources are especially accessible to those with the savvy to locate them efficiently. Sifting through the whimsical postings of "newbies," the "roadkill" (sorry) of vandals, and the opinions of "experts" to find answers to specific questions or gems of wisdom takes much time and patience. Imagine the size of the Library of Congress if everyone over the age of eight published whatever popped into his or her head—that's the information superhighway.

As I hear more and more about the World Wide Web home page rage, I see visions of Burma Shave and graffiti. Then I wonder if we have entered an Age of Neo-Scholasticism where encyclopedic rendition passes for the Classics. Yes, surely there are strands of silver and gold, but beware of cobwebs in cyberspace.

Me? For current events I suggest taking sections of yesterday's *USA Today*, *Time*, etc., and a neighborhood newspaper to share with elementary level students. Here the arts and crafts of print publication enhance raw text in a way not yet matched by MUIs (multimedia user interfaces). Let students "cut and paste" the old-fashioned way. For software reviews, I rely primarily on respected periodicals rather than the mix of insight and opinion spread across even the most illuminating bulletin boards and listservs. Want late-breaking news? Turn on the radio or CNN, not the unedited newswires.

Of course, the special needs, interests, and talents of our students often may justify seeking the more uneven electronic highways and byways. Consider, for example, the value of our students comparing local news coverage with that published abroad, or contrasting their interpretations of world events with those of students online from other parts of the world. Perhaps the "keypals" of today will negotiate the peace of the future. In every case, **the burden is on us and our students to make these journeys through cyberspace both scenic and productive.**

Along the way, we have to contend with unbridled "free speech" and "cybersex." On the Internet, anti-Semitic remarks resulted in the revocation of an account, but sexist and racist comments and foul language have become so rampant that calls have been raised for both increased regulation and stricter codes of

"netiquette." According to a *U.S. News & World Report* article: "The very strengths of the Internet—its broad accessibility, open-minded discussions and anonymity—can be used to advantage by hatemongers. Sophisticated bigots often infiltrate otherwise legitimate discussion groups on the Net that deal with history or sociology."[8] And bulletin boards abound with sexually explicit titles. These offer services ranging from looking to doing. No longer can parents and teachers be sanguine about what might be going on in the computer lab.

"Listening in" on network "party lines" has provided children with a host of delicate questions to ask about the diversity of human interactions. All this time, unable to get through the telephone line, we comforted ourselves that my niece's adolescent son was becoming a computer whiz! I think his brain has been getting fried.

Nevertheless, instant access to documentary and human resources worldwide can be an awesome boon to teachers and students alike. Owen Gaede, Professor of Computer Science at Florida State University, spoke of the information superhighway as an "electronic performance support system" (EPSS). Traditional schooling, he said, provided students with information **"just in case"** they might need it. In contrast, telecommunications provide needed information **"just in time."** That's a revolutionary shift in thinking to which we should respond affirmatively.[9] (See **Figure 13.08.**)

As we enter the 21st century, educators increasingly are moving from a conception of meeting students' needs in terms of learning prescribed subject matter to ones of **"learning to learn"** and wider **"empowerment."** Behaviorists, who early dominated the field of educational technology, emphasized achievement of prespecified objectives by reinforcing selection of "correct" answers. Cognitivists, who blossomed in the 1970s and 80s, relied on models of information processing to better control the learning process. More recently, "constructivists," rooted in the thinking of John Dewey, Jean Piaget, Paulo Friere, and Carl Rogers, have reminded us of the miraculous means by which knowledge and attitudes are appropriated by children and adults alike. This **constructivist theme** and its relation to emerging technologies was taken up in a 1994 interview with legendary educator Ralph Tyler:

> Children learn through exploration. They construct their knowledge through direct experience. We must consider how to expand their space and opportunities for learning. Dewey would muse that many teachers would simply tell children, "This is what the world is

Figure 13.08. For those who have the skills to access it, the information superhighway may serve as a vast "electronic performance support system," providing timely, current information as needed. As we immerse our students in such rich learning environments (and in those more familiar, as shown here), we become "human performance support systems," guiding our students' inquiries, responding to their questions, modeling strategies, evaluating progress, and providing encouragement. Location: The Metropolitan Museum of Art (New York City).

> like." Instead, Dewey advocated that teachers should encourage children to become actively engaged in discovering what the world is like. . . . At the present time, Americans are infatuated with the computer and telecommunications. . . . Information is what is put into the computer, but knowledge is how one uses that information. It is through the student's active use of information stored in the computer that they can solve problems and learn.[10]

Thus, as noted in previous chapters and well worth repeating, constructivists have challenged us to focus our attention on the design of:

> . . . environments which are characterized by rich contexts, authentic tasks, collaboration for the development and evaluation of multiple perspectives, an abundance of tools to enhance communication and access to real-world examples and problems, reflective thinking, modeling of problem solving by experts in the content domain, and apprenticeship mentoring relationships to guide learning.[11]

Explorations of multimedia and infobahn alike, whether guided by books, teachers, tutors, or computers, ***CAN BE MADE*** responsive to these challenges.

Jim Moody, founder in 1987 of the BBS *GlobalNet* and publisher of *PC World Online*, described in glowing terms other positive aspects of **infobahn communications**.

> Age, race, sex, and physical characteristics do not matter. You are evaluated on your thoughts, the honesty of your feelings, the clarity of your communication. Virtual communities, in contrast to the real world outside your front door, are created and maintained somewhere in the electronic matrix that is cyberspace. They are consensual realities created by the participants and limited in form, structure, and function only by the collective imagination of the participants.[12]

A self-proclaimed "cybernaut," Moody balanced his enthusiasm with widely shared concerns about ". . . who's going to be in charge of this brave new world? Will someone own it? Control it? Who? What will the social and cultural rules be? Will it be free, politically and monetarily? Who will have access?"[13]

Indeed, at least three major challenges continue to face the rapidly emerging information superhighway—**access, security,** and **utilization**.

Access to the infobahn stands out as an expressed concern, especially as the gap continues to widen between rich and poor. Driven by commercial interests, the National Information Infrastructure (NII) is evolving most rapidly in wealthy urban communities. Like the electric and telephone lines that long passed over the reservation homes of Native Americans, fiber optic cables will be slow to reach those who may not appear to be lucrative markets. Nevertheless, we are assured by the visionary Al Gore that:

> An advanced information infrastructure will bring into millions of homes information that will enrich people's economic, social and political lives. It will eliminate the constraints of geography and economic status, and give all Americans a fair opportunity to go as far as their talents and ambitions will take them. . . . It is an Administration goal that, by the year 2000, all of the classrooms, libraries, hospitals, and clinics in the United States will be connected to the NII.[14]

Surely, with government prodding, rural schools and libraries eventually will be connected to the global network. However, given the expense of computers, modems, software, and access fees, convenient home service (indoor "plumbing") will continue to be restricted to families with above-average incomes.[15] (See **Figure 13.09.**)

Since the dawn of the information age there has been ample concern about **security**, that is, unauthorized access to data. For governments, this has been a vital concern; for businesses, a matter of money. Access to state secrets may win or lose wars. Access to corporate secrets may threaten both national security and loss of competitive edge. For individuals, loss of privacy threatens loss of life and property.

As we log onto the Internet, our interests, ideas, and beliefs are added to the vast pool of data already accumulated in the memory banks of such government agencies as the Social Security Administration and such credit service bureaus as TRW. A moment's reflection on how such information could have been used by the Third Reich or during the McCarthy era, or how it could be used today to identify "liberals" or the "religious right" for persecution, or by the rising tide of radical regimes abroad for systematic extermination, should move us to join in airing legitimate concerns about security. Data encryption devices now are widely available, but the U.S. government has endorsed universal installation of the *Clipper* chip to permit its continued surveillance of suspected criminals and spies.

Yes, even after first writing these words of caution, I signed on to AOL using the up-front ID "HackbarthS." Spoiled by the professionalism of collegial Internet exchanges, I even input a "personal profile" to this service in the hopes of networking with teachers and other likeminded folks. During my first evening of interacting "live" with diverse people across the country I found myself among the few with a recognizable "handle." As the exchanges about current news events and issues heated

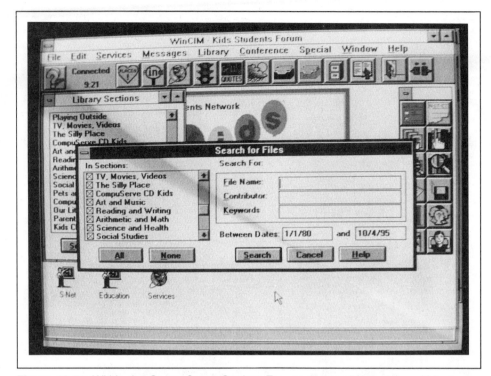

Figure 13.09. Within the CompuServe Student Forums (now split into three—kids, teens, adults) students may obtain information from vast libraries or they may post messages for peer response. What special advantages might this give those who readily can afford the hourly connect fees? Reproduced with permission of CompuServe, Inc.

up, my support for a Clinton Administration peace overture was greeted with "Let's hope so Barth." I began regretting my naivete—me, a global village idiot!

As if this were not sufficient warning, on Prodigy, where one's full name must be displayed, my sharing of ideas with the mother of a child with "attention deficit disorder" was greeted with a heated flare up ("flame") for raising feelings of guilt. I thought I had written about parental empowerment. Such potential "flame wars," I later learned, are common (often "baited") and may be avoided by qualifying text with "emoticons" (like a winking face ;-)) and with such common-coin acronyms as IMO ("in my opinion") and by never SHOUTING (i.e., avoid caps). "Newbies" also should read carefully the FAQs ("frequently asked questions") and "listen in" for a while before entering messages of their own.

Productive **utilization** of both multimedia and computer network technologies presents a challenge familiar to teachers. Long surrounded by schoolbooks, maps, study prints, audiotapes, films, videos, computers, libraries, museums, and other community resources, teachers

long have recognized that **getting students to "drink from the wellsprings of knowledge" entails more than "leading them to water."** (See **Figure 13.10.**)

Apart from the brief <g> remarks about "integrated learning" in Chapter **3**, I have managed to spare you direct reference to my doctoral studies in the philosophy of education (UCLA, 1971–1976). But recent emergence of such wide instant access to vast stores of information has given me another excuse to indulge. From reading Alfred North Whitehead, I had learned of the emptiness of "inert ideas," and from John Dewey of the role of active hypothesis creation and testing—"trying and undergoing." Pursuing these ideas in the writings of the French philosopher Maurice Merleau-Ponty, I derived a conception of learning that entailed spirited recapitulations of the actions of scholars and scientists in their quests to make sense of the "world-as-perceived" (aka the "lived world," *Lebenswelt*). "Guided inquiry," I suggested, "may be conceived as an extension of students' explorations of the universe in which they live, act, and achieve personal fulfillment."[16]

Figure 13.10. The speed and efficacy with which students travel along the information superhighway depend to a large extent on the modes of transportation and quality of roadmaps supplied by teachers. What sorts of media and methods would you recommend? Source: *Phi Delta Kappan,* 75 (June 1994), p. 761. Reprinted courtesy of James E. Hummel.

Since subject matter is derived largely from the various academic disciplines, I concluded (talk about reinventing the mule <vbg>) that students might better comprehend and appropriate such knowledge if they were engaged in the sorts of activities that characterize disciplined inquiry—mistakes, serendipity, and all. Again, from Whitehead, we may encourage our students to dally about during their romantic fascination with tidbits of data, but deeper comprehension, analysis, synthesis, evaluation, appreciation, and production require more "disciplined" study, in both senses of that term.

Of course, during the early stages of learning, students may be encouraged to wander about more or less aimlessly across the landscapes of knowledge encoded on CD-ROM and paved across lanes of the Internet. However, achieving higher order academic and affective aims of education requires, in part, that students learn to formulate and test hypotheses creatively in ways that characterize the perspectival pursuit of enlightenment in the various academic disciplines. Such disciplinary—and interdisciplinary—pursuits, I suggested, might lead to the **"integration of cognitive and affective dimensions of learning,"** the "affective" fulfillment arising from the joy of fruitful inquiry, assured, in part, by "standing on the shoulders of giants." (See **Figure 13.11.**)

Lest we get too didactic, Neil Postman has noted rightly once again that all of us, teachers, scholars, and

students alike, learn best when we have the latitude to pose our own questions, suffer consequences, and mend our ways, with guidance only as needed. He observed that: "As things stand now, teachers are apt to think of themselves as truth tellers who hope to extend the intelligence of students by revealing to them, or having them discover, incontrovertible truths and enduring ideas." Rather, he suggested that we conceive of teachers "as error-detectors who hope to extend the intelligence of students by helping them reduce the mistakes in their knowledge and skills."[17] Along with his observations that students need to learn the distinctive language of each

Figure 13.11. On any school day you will find hoards of children at museums, zoos, botanical gardens, and libraries with maps, activity guides, and notebooks. Such careful guidance of learning from community resources is a model for planning our students' encounters with the Internet and its World Wide Web. Location: The Metropolitan Museum of Art (New York City).

discipline, and that all subjects are best taught from a historical perspective to place students in the dynamic streams of the struggles (as I have tried to do in this book), Postman suggested that the on-going process of education "tell the following story":

> Because we are imperfect souls, our knowledge is imperfect. The history of learning is an adventure in overcoming our errors. There is no sin in being wrong. The sin is in our unwillingness to examine our own beliefs, and in believing that our authorities cannot be wrong.[18]

Postman concluded that:

> Far from creating cynics, such a story is likely to foster a healthy and creative skepticism, which is something quite different from cynicism. It refutes the story of the student learner as the dummy in a ventriloquism act. It holds out the hope for students to discover a sense of excitement and purpose in being part of the [Robert Maynard Hutchin's] Great Conversation.[19]

Constructive participation in the "Great Conversation" by our students requires concerted action by us in collaboration with them and with administrators, librarians, parents, and business leaders. Conditions of **security** and **orderliness** must be made to prevail, along with **high academic standards and expectations**, as called for in the American Federation of Teachers' campaign: Responsibility, Respect, Results: Lessons for Life. Albert Shanker, AFT president, reported that: "A series of recent polls and focus groups show that when it comes to public schools, the public wants exactly what we want: safety, order and academic rigor."[20] A survey by Public Agenda, a nonprofit research and public policy firm, revealed that, generally speaking:

> The American public wants learning to be fun and interesting, but . . . wants students to have a solid grounding in the basics—reading, writing and math. . . . Americans are confused about "higher order" and "critical thinking" skills and . . . wonder if schools are giving short shrift to the core academic subjects.[21]

Fortunately, reaching for the stars while justifiably assuring the public that our feet are firmly planted on the ground is a familiar challenge. But it is one that clearly we must meet more forcefully, effectively, and publicly. Harnessing computer-mediated communications in the service of sound academic goals is one of many opportune ways in which we can do so.

For those familiar with the work of Jerome Bruner (who would be first to endorse a "Web-laced spiral curriculum") and legions of curriculum specialists since, these ideas have a familiar ring. In his earlier quoted 1994 interview, Ralph Tyler reminded us one last time that "The school is composed of a body of teachers who value scholarship. The school's role is to help children—and later, adults—discover scholarly activity."[22] Devotion to the **scholarly** aims of schooling, as opposed to psychotherapeutic, also is a dominant theme in the writings of UCLA's distinguished professor emeritus George Kneller.[23] It is such devotion that promises to make **utilization** of information technologies most productive. And through such conscientious, creative, multidisciplinary utilization, **surely we can continue to contribute** to achievement of other core educational aims in the affective domain—**higher self-esteem, greater respect for human diversity, and heightened compassion for people in need.**

Practical Guidelines

Selection. "On-ramps" to the information superhighway are provided by educational institutions, government agencies, and commercial enterprises. Inquire to find one that meets your needs at minimum cost. Sample the free "get acquainted" offers of the major commercial providers found in periodicals, but watch out for communications and "premium service" charges. Also, **you must** (IMO) obtain via email (well, ask someone who **does** have an account <g>) a copy of Peter Kaminski's (kaminski@netcom.com) regularly updated ***The Public Dialup Internet Access List***: info-deli-server@netcom.com; message: Send PDial. Here you will find hourly and flat-fee, "unlimited" Internet access providers worldwide. Also see options listed in Sources at the end of this chapter.

Teachers and students can start with their own, at-home America Online, Prodigy, CompuServe, The Microsoft Network, or eWorld account. Here features are abundant and navigation is transparent.

Utilization. I'll start here with some basics to guide your first use of the Internet, and then close with suggestions for classroom use. Note that some Internet guide books assume that you are using the *UNIX* operating system.

None of my accounts were based on *UNIX* until I made a switch at NYU. Nevertheless, once you are familiar with the peculiarities of your LAN operating system, you readily can adapt the information provided. (When I think of all these diverse breeds of computers "hand-shaking" to come to agreements on protocol, I can't help thinking of dogs meeting on the street.) Bob Zen-hausern, Professor of Special Education at St. John's University, wrote explicit instructions that I have outlined below.[24]

I. Access Listservs.
  A. Find out what listservs are available at a given site.
      1. Send email to the listserv (e.g., **listserv@sjuvm.stjohns.edu**).
      2. Leave subject line blank.
      3. Type message: **lists**.
  B. Subscribe to a listserv (e.g., Altlearn [teaching approaches]).
      1. Send email to the listserv (e.g., **listserv@sjuvm.stjohns.edu**).
      2. Leave subject line blank.
      3. Message: **subscribe Altlearn yourfirstname yourlastname**.
  C. Stop subscription to a listserv (e.g., Altlearn) (esp. during vacations).
      1. See B1 above.
      2. Subject: (blank).
      3. Message: **unsubscribe Altlearn**.
II. Access Listserv Files.
  A. Get list of available files at given site.
      1. Send email to listserv (see B1 above).
      2. Subject: (blank).
      3. Message: **info**.
  B. Obtain files.
      1. Send email as in B1 above.
      2. Subject: (blank).
      3. Message: **send** filename (specify in full).
III. Download Other Files Using Anonymous FTP.
  A. Find available files.
      1. Type on command line (or select from menu) FTP followed by a space and the desired TCP/IP (e.g., **sjuvm.stjohns.edu**).
      2. For user id, type: **anonymous** (yes, that's why it's "anonymous FTP").
      3. If requested, enter your **email address** as password (never give your actual password).
      4. To see list of available files, type: **ls**.

  5. Note upper and lower case letters when writing filenames; when a system is case sensitive, no margin is given for error.
  B. Obtain Files (e.g., infoage.net [a listserv tutorial]).
      1. For text files type: get filename (e.g., **get infoage.net**).
      2. For binary files (e.g., *WordPerfect*), first enter: **type i**. (Systems vary. My NYU *VMS*-based VAX wanted: "Set file type binary" <Enter>.)
         Then type: **get** filename (specify in full). (Or follow menu instructions such as ASCII GET "remote filename" myfilename; BINARY GET . . . .)
IV. Accessing Remote Host Computers with *Gopher* and Telnet
  A. Burrowing with *Gopher*.
      1. On command line type: **gopher** (or select *Gopher* from menu), followed by a space and the desired TCP/IP (e.g., **gopher sjuvm.stjohns.edu**).
      2. From menu, select desired topic (e.g., "Education and Teaching Resources").
      3. Follow instructions to use FTP or for Telneting to other sites (e.g., NASA, The Library of Congress, your local college library).
  B. "Handshaking" (computer greetings) with Telnet.
      1. On command line type: **telnet**, followed by a space and the host's address (e.g., **telnet is.nyu.edu**). (Delphi advised me to type command /ECHO HOST prior to attempting to Telnet or IRC.)
      2. After username prompt, type: **guest** (or try visitor, newuser, anonymous, or help).
      3. After password prompt, type: your TCP/IP (not your password).

You see. No tricks. No mystery. Just feed the pets, put the kids to bed, set the morning alarm, and plug in. Let's try taking a tour of the U.S. Department of Education and ERIC as prescribed by the Council for Exceptional Children.[25]

1. At the command prompt type: **Gopher gopher.ed.gov** or select *Gopher* from the menu and then type **gopher.ed.gov**. (I could not locate

a command prompt nor *Gopher* menu item on my NYU (*VMS*/VAX) account, so I tunneled through the NYU CWIS to "Using Other Information Systems" to *VERONICA*. There I completed a successful search via NYSERNet for "OERI Publications." I later had no such problems with my Delphi account.)

2. Select: **10**. U.S. Department of Education/OERI Publications. (At first, no numbers appeared, so I backed out by typing **u** and dove back in. When access was denied, I tried various options till I got through.)

3. Press **Enter**. (Do this after each selection.)

4. Type **More**. (Or just press Enter.)

5. Select: **4**. ED/OERI Publications—Full Text. (We're on a roll now.)

6. Select: **29**. National Excellence: A Case for Developing America's Talent.

7. Press **Enter**.

8. Type **yes** (or Enter) to continue reading, or **no** to return to menu. At end (whew!), press Enter.

9. Type **BACK**. (First time through I got an "Access violation" message. After striking "control-c," "exit," and other such panic buttons, I was asked if I would like to log off. I replied "no." Back in business!)

10. Select: **2**. Index of ED/OERI Publications.

11. Select: **1**. Recent U.S. Department of Education Publications in ERIC.

12. Select **4**. Special populations.

13. Select any group of interest 1–5.

14. Press **Enter**.

15. Type **yes** (or Enter) to continue reading, **no** to quit. At end, press Enter.

16. Type **BACK** followed by pressing **Enter** (both four times).

17. Select: **6**. Educational Research, Improvement, and Statistics. . . .

18. Select: **5**. Educational Resources Information Center (ERIC).

19. Select: **2**. AskERIC. . . .

20. Select: **8**. ERIC Clearinghouses/Components.

21. Select: **2**. ERIC Clearinghouses.

22. Select: **13**. ERIC Clearinghouse on Disabilities and Gifted Education.

23. When done, type **exit**.

There are many alternative ways to search gopherspace. Such tools as *Archie*, *VERONICA*, and *JUGHEAD*

look for keywords in the menus of *Gopher* sites. WAIS (wide area information server, pronounced "wayzzz") finds keywords in the documents themselves. Let's try it.

1. Point your *Gopher* to **gopher.ub2.lu.se**. (Or follow *Gopher* menu cascade to: 6. Europe/ 43. Sweden/ 7. Lund University Electronic Library, Sweden: UB2/.)

2. Select: **6**. All WAIS databases for searching (simple version)/ **3**. Experiment with automatic classification of WAIS databases, UB2, L . ./ **2**. Subject tree (based on UDC)/. This gives you a nice classification scheme for WAIS servers.

3. Select **4**. Social sciences/ **8**. Education. Teaching. Training. Leisure/ **9**. Ask ERIC—Lesson—Plans: <?>. (Version of WAIS being used is not known.)

4. Type: **Rwandan refugees** and press **Enter**. (If wildcard endings worked here, Rwand* refuge* would have more hits, but it doesn't.

5. Press **u** and experiment with word strings [case insensitive] and Boolean connectors [in caps] for the subjects you teach.

6. Note instructions for obtaining desired lesson plans.

7. Press **u** five times to return to "All WAIS data bases for searching (simple version)."

8. Select **4**. Other subject classifications of WAIS databases/ **4**. Classification of WAIS databases (from SLU, Sweden)/.

9. Explore topics of interest.

For those having an email–only account, there are various ways to retrieve information, thanks to Fred Bremmer's **GopherMail**. The following, and much of the preceding, were covered in an online "Go-pher-it Workshop" by Thomas Copley (tcopley@arlington.com), who now offers a Web workshop. Bremmer and associates invite you to contact them if you encounter any problems or if you would like to make suggestions (gophermail-admin@mercury.forestry.umn.edu).

If you don't already know the "bookmark" (a unique set of identification codes) for a desired file, begin by addressing a blank message to a *GopherMail* server (e.g., gophermail@mercury.forestry.umn.edu; gopher@calvin. edu; gopher@solaris.ims.ac.jp; gopher@earn.net). If you know the Internet address of the *Gopher* site where the desired information is stored, put that in the subject field. Such commercial services as AOL, MCI Mail, and CompuServe may require placing something in the subject and message fields. A period will do. Shortly, you will receive a message containing a menu and, at the end, "bookmarks" that identify available files. From here, you may place an "x" immediately to the left of each numbered item (but not on the left margin) and then you return the message. Or you may address a new message to the *GopherMail* server with the *GopherMail* bookmark as the message. For example, to find out what the University of California, Irvine, has available about the Internet, send email:

To: gopher@calvin.edu
Subject: [blank, or a period if needed]
Message:
Name=Internet Assistance
Type=1
Port=7000
Path=1/gopher.welcome/peg/Internet Assistance
Host=peg.cwis.uci.edu

The message you receive will contain menu items that you can request by simply marking and then returning the entire message. Careful. No marks means that you want it all! At any point along the menu you can press the equal sign (=) to display the bookmark. (This works with *UNIX*, but you may have to explore function keys to make it work with *VMS*, *CMS*, or other operating systems. Delphi uses a SAVE command for "my favorite places.") Bookmarks also appear at the end of the menu. Note that *GopherMail* bookmarks differ somewhat from regular *Gopher* bookmarks. For example, a sample U.C., Irvine *GopherMail* bookmark format is:

Name=University of California - Irvine, PEG,
  Peripatetic, Eclectic Gopher
Numb=78
Type=1
Port=7000
Path=1/gopher.welcome/peg
Host=peg.cwis.uci.edu

If you have the option of "pointing your *Gopher*" at U.C. Irvine's PEG, you may do so by selecting menu options on your system. A much quicker route is to enter **Gopher** bookmark information, like that shown below, in a "dialog box" that appears after typing the letter "o" (with *UNIX*, or with a function key using *VMS*, or unavailable with many providers) from within the *Gopher* program.

Type=1
Name=University of California - Irvine
Path=
Host=gopher-server.cwis.uci.edu
Port=70

Obviously, bookmarks are a key to efficient use of Internet resources. As you discover sites of interest, you will learn to use the *UNIX* "a" (or "A" for just one) command (or "SAVE" on Delphi, or "point-and-click" with WIMPs, e.g., *Turbo Gopher*, *WinGopher*, *WSGopher*, *Hgopher*) to automatically save bookmarks to your personalized list. Next you will learn to organize your bookmarks into categories (e.g., Lesson Plans, Student Projects, Teaching Tips, Special Education, References, Games, Jokes, Lyrics), and caption each by entering bogus bookmarks (on *UNIX*, but WIMPs have multiple directories to ease organization). The result will be your own *Gopher* menu. Point, click, you're there!

Of course, there are other ways of accessing desired information. The major alternative to gophering is leaping across the hypermedia links of the **World Wide Web**. Here bookmark information may be typed linearly in the Uniform Resource Locator (**URL**) format: http (or gopher)//host:port/type/path, and placed after a GO command. Those with email only can use **Webmail** to access the Web just as they use *GopherMail* to access gopherspace, two routes into essentially the same domain. Try it. Send email to: webmail@curia.ucc.ie, with the message: GO http://curia.ucc.ie/info/net/webmail.html. You will receive information about guess what? *Webmail*. However, to read this "UUencoded" message requires a readily available unencoding program. Did I say Netlife was easy?

Those having SLIP (Serial Line Internet Protocol) or PPP (Point to Point Protocol) dialup IP, or direct line connections to the Internet, which permit use of such top notch browsers as *Netscape Navigator* (*gratis* from ftp.mcom.com), *InternetWorks*, and *winWeb*, will encounter within the Web a universe of "interactive multimedia." Clicking on highlighted words transports one, via URL magic carpets, to related textual, audio, and video files. One may pursue hypertext or hypermedia links across the World Wide Web and back again to the original source. Now we're in **hyperspace**!

More fun things to explore on the Internet are listed in the Sources and Suggested Activities at the end of this chapter. Note that there are many alternative routes to success, searches may take much longer than you expected, and closed doors often lead to open windows. Each journey reminds me of T.S. Eliot's: "We shall not cease from exploration, and the end of our exploring shall be to arrive where we began, and know the place for the first time." (See **Figure 13.12.**)

What about **school use of online services?** Ann Caputo, manager of Dialog's Academic Programs Group, made the following suggestions in the premiere issue of *MultiMedia Schools.*

- Use communications technology only to solve real problems, to help you to teach better and your students to learn more. Don't "jump on the electronic bandwagon just for the sake of the ride."
- For students below the fifth grade level, CD-ROM databases generally are more appropriate than online.
- Involve students and teachers in selection of services rather than imposing them from above.
- Sequence introduction of new technology so as not to overwhelm students. Start with realistic goals and expand on these as you and your students gain competence.

"It's too late! Bob's brain has been sucked into the World Wide Web."

Figure 13.12. Gophering is kinda fun, but Webbing is wholly engrossing, as shown here. Though I've crawled along the triple W with less, the recommended minimum is a multimedia computer, a 14,400 bps modem, and a flat fee high usage access option. Reproduced with permission of Andrew Toos.

- Have student mentors serve as "search buddies" to those unfamiliar with efficient strategies for productively exploring online databases.
- Impress upon students the value of carefully planning their search strategies in advance.
- Encourage students to explore beyond standard sources that could just as well be obtained in local libraries.
- Challenge students to draw upon online services to answer questions and solve problems that concern them personally.
- Foster a spirit of collaboration among teachers, librarians, students and administrators in making the best use of online services.[26]

To this I would add **notes of caution** about picking up dangerous "keypals," disclosing your password, having your computer "infected" by "viruses," encountering foul language, observing pornographic visuals, and becoming victims of "cyberscams." (See **Figure 13.13.**)

When you introduce multimedia programs or online database services, make sure that your students understand that these technologies are not **merely** toys, though fun they can be. They also are powerful tools for finding out about the world, and **changing** it! Without inhibiting playfulness and creative expression, **encourage strategic planning and purposeful inquiry.** As earlier noted, methods that characterize scholarship and research within and across the disciplines are most appropriate. Michelle Healy, in a *USA Today* article summed up the growing need for student scholarship in these terms:

> Experts say the information explosion demands a new and different set of skills, including the ability to identify a need for information, to identify appropriate resources that address the need, to evaluate the information, and to organize it sensibly, no matter what the source of information—book, computer, video or whatever.[27]

Jamieson McKenzie (Director of Technology and Media for the Bellingham [WA] School District), in a guest editorial for *MultiMedia Schools*, called for applying a set of old and well-known skills to mining the Internet. His description of a generalized **iterative research cycle** included the elements of:

- **Questioning.** Decide what information is lacking or what problem needs solving.

"Let me put it this way. I forgot to look both ways before crossing the information highway, and now all your files are roadkill."

Figure 13.13. Access to the world's computers opens up windows of opportunity along many and diverse avenues of inquiry. However, explorations in cyberspace entail risks ranging from information overload (subscribing to too many listservs, downloading unneeded software) to destruction of files on your hard disk. What precautions will you encourage your students to take? Source: *Phi Delta Kappan,* 76 (April 1995), p. 635. Reprinted with permission of Randy Glasbergen.

In a series of *The Computing Teacher* (now *Learning and Leading with Technology*) articles, Judi Harris (University of Texas at Austin) clarified distinctions among three general types of telecomputing activities—**interpersonal exchanges**, **information collections**, and **problem solving**. For each, she provided categories of activities on which teachers can base more detailed lesson plans. Within the problem solving category (broadly conceived), she described seven "telecomputing activity structures" and gave classroom-tested examples as follows.

- **Information Searches.** Students are presented with, or may pose, problems to solve and are given a variety of sources to explore, including online.

- **Electronic Process Writing.** Students post their essays and poems online and receive suggestions from others, including published authors.

- **Sequential Creations.** Here, students draft a document (perhaps multimedia) and challenge another school to elaborate. The process may be cycled around the globe.

- **Parallel Problem Solving.** Students at several sites work independently and then share their methods and findings.

- **Virtual Gatherings.** Students from around the globe engage in Internet Relay Chat (IRC), or an email arranged simultaneous gathering "in spirit," at a set time, usually to discuss a set topic.

- **Simulations.** Students collaborate online in recreating historical events, designing environments, and manipulating variables within hypothetical economic and political systems.

- **Social Action Projects.** Imagine. Global telethons to raise money for worthwhile causes. It's happening now.[29]

- **Planning.** Develop a strategy to efficiently locate valid information.

- **Gathering.** Locate the best sources, Internet and other, and collect needed information.

- **Sifting.** Select from what was found that information most pertinent to the research question.

- **Synthesizing.** Sort the information into a meaningful pattern.

- **Evaluating.** Assess progress in answering the research question, and, if needed, return to the first step in this cycle.[28]

Such basic skills long have been advocated and practiced systematically and effectively by school teachers and librarians.

Have we undervalued **creative uses** of the Internet and its World Wide Web? Not at all. "Surfing the net" without a pre-set agenda is a great way for us all to become familiar with features and sites. Even Alfred North Whitehead permitted us a "romantic stage" in our quest for knowledge. Why not infuse every stage with romance? And speaking of romance, isn't seeking contacts with like-minded folks a boon to both our professional and personal lives? Recall that our friend at Stanford,

Nel Noddings (*The Challenge to Care in Schools*), places the development of friendships at the core of her curriculum. Why shouldn't we encourage our students to have as much fun on the Net as we do? Let them cruise in a spirit of high adventure, and chat with the expectation of (supervised) meetings. And let them err, as Neil Postman has suggested (*The End of Education: Redefining the Value of School*), and err again, just like the rest of us, including the best of historians, theologians, philosophers, and scientists throughout history (as illustrated in George Kneller's *Science as a Human Endeavor*). They can haphazardly download text and graphics now; and selectively incorporate them into projects and portfolios later. Let disciplined inquiry evolve out of students' quests for meaning (as the existential psychologists used to say, and now the constructivists), or out of their needs for identity, security, and stimulation (as Robert Ardley suggested in his classic *The Territorial Imperative*). Soon enough they will be hounding us to collaborate with them in the crafting of classroom World Wide Web home pages filled with multimedia expressions of their multiple intelligences and diverse talents. (See **Figure 13.14**.)

Thus, productive classroom use of the information superhighway can be as mundane or as exotic as we *care* to make it. When I visit classrooms in my role as computer consultant, I encourage teachers to continue engaging their students in familiar forms of inquiry and problem solving, both objectives-based and open-ended. Many do not yet use computers for much beyond word processing, and feel intimidated by the loudly acclaimed advances in computer-mediated communications. By rooting effective use of these advances in areas of their better-established competencies—process writing, creative expression, documentary research, data collection/analysis, collaborative problem finding/solving, discipline-based inquiry, interdisciplinary study, information literacy, "situated learning," "anchored instruction," "cognitive apprenticeship," "authentic assessment"—I have sought to turn their deeply felt concerns into justified confidence.[30]

Summary and Conclusions

The libraries of Sumeria long have given testimony to the value of providing access to warehouses of information. Interactive learning environments have been ideals since Socrates engaged students in soul-searching dialogues. John Dewey's notions of "cooperative problem

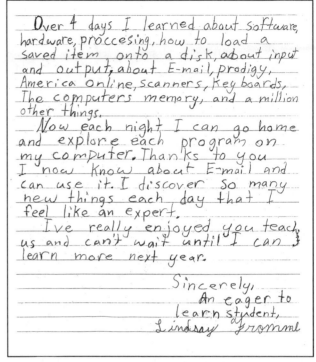

Figure 13.14. Empowering students. Isn't that a large part of our mission? Reproduced with permission of P.S. 6 (Manhattan) principal Carmen Fariña, fourth grade teacher Audrey Kaplan, Lindsay Fromme, and her parents.

solving" and of "trying and undergoing" have been revived once again by neo-constructivists vitally concerned with the integrity of each student's approach to making sense of the world.

As the challenges of the 21st century dawn upon us, it is fitting that developments in technology become ever more responsive to the highest aims of education. Rough edges aside, this is the case with interactive multimedia and the information superhighway.

These emerging technologies present as much content as teacher and text together and do so in an attractive format. Students are free to explore areas of interest at their own pace, on their own and in groups, in class and at home. In doing so, they gain both knowledge and confidence that translate into the self-discipline needed to pursue subject matter in depth.

Information technologies involve students of diverse interests and abilities on an equal footing in the quest for knowledge, bring the contents of libraries and the expertise of professionals into the classroom, save both time and money in locating and obtaining resources, foster communication and social skills, and allow for creative expression.

Just concerns remain about quality of content, equity of access, and productivity of utilization. With well over 90 percent of the financial investments being made by commercial interests, and with government regulation being insufficiently potent, we educators need to become ever more assertive on behalf of students. As teachers, we are responsible for the systematic design, development, conduct, evaluation, and revision of instruction as well as for provision of opportunities for "open-ended" learning and creative expression. Connections of mediated programs and services with the whole of the curriculum and with "real" life must be made firm and explicit, yet not restricted entirely to our preconceptions.

We are not alone in wanting the best for our students. We have allies both among these same students and their parents, among librarians and other media specialists. We can reach out to our colleagues in the lunch room and over the Internet. Community leaders, government agencies, and commercial enterprises take pride in establishing "partnerships" with schools. Gifts and grants are available.

The promises of educational technology—making instruction (broadly conceived) more enriched, valid, individualized, accessible, and economical—are being fulfilled every day in classrooms across the earth. We are partners in this challenging and noble enterprise.

Notes

[1]Fraase, Michael, *The PC Internet Tour Guide: Cruising the Internet the Easy Way* (Chapel Hill, NC: Ventana Press, 1994), pp. 9–10; Gardner, James, *A DOS User's Guide to the Internet: E-Mail, Netnews and File Transfer with UUCP* (Englewood Cliffs, NJ: PTR Prentice Hall, 1994), pp. 8–14; LaQuey, Tracy, with Ryer, Jeanne C., *The Internet Companion Plus: A Beginner's Start-Up Kit for Global Networking* (Reading, MA: Addison-Wesley, 1993), pp. 3–6. Contrast the development of the Internet with that of France's **Minitel**. *Minitel* began in 1980 as a focused government project designed to move the nation into the Information Age. Computer terminals have been distributed at no cost; users pay only for connect time. By 1990, after an investment of $2 billion, over five million terminals had been distributed (1 for each 11 citizens) and 12,000 different services were being offered. As in North America, the "pink" bulletin boards have been the biggest hit. Look for *Minitel* to link the European Economic Community.

[2]Lawley, Elizabeth Lane, & Summerhill, Craig, *Internet Primer: For Information Professionals: A Basic Guide to Internet Networking Technology* (Westport, CT: Meckler Publishing, 1993), pp. 1–2.

[3]Descy, Don E., "Tools to Ease Your Internet Adventures: Part 2," *Tech Trends,* 39 (January/February 1994), pp. 18–19; Reese, Jean, "Internet Tools of the Trade," *MultiMedia Schools,* 2 (March/April 1995), pp. 18–22.

[4]Dyrli, Odvard Egil, & Kinnaman, Daniel, "What Every Teacher Needs to Know About Technology: Part 5: Connecting Classrooms: School Is More than a Place!" *Technology & Learning,* 15 (June 1995), p. 88. For information about bringing *Technology & Learning* Professional Development Institute courses to your school, call 1-800-523-4625.

[5]Vacca, John R., "CU on the Net," *Internet World,* 6 (October 1995), pp. 80–82. See also Carmona, Jeff, "The Internet: Opening Doors for Education," *T.H.E. Journal,* 23 (August 1995), pp. 10–14; Tsikalas, Kallen, "Internet-Based Learning?" *Electronic Learning,* 14 (April 1995), pp. 14–15.

[6]Wibe, Jan, "The SPINN Project: Norway," *Learning and Leading with Technology,* 23 (September 1995), p. 49.

[7]Heim, Judy, "Best Online Services," *PC World,* 13 (June 1995), pp. 141–148. Tyre, Terian, "Commercial Online Services: Benefits to Educators," *T.H.E. Journal,* 23 (August 1995), pp. 44–45; Crawford, Leslie, "Kids in Cyberspace: A Smart, Safe Guide to Online Services," *The Computing Teacher,* 22 (March 1995), pp. 12–14; "The Win95 Road Map," *WINDOWS Magazine,* 6 (September 1995), pp. 199–206; Albinus, Philip, & Blumenfeld, Julie R., "Ride the Wave with Graphical Online Services," *WINDOWS Magazine,* 6 (September 1995), pp. 228–236; Davis, Frederic E., "*Windows 95:* The Internet's Built In," *NetGuide,* 2 (October 1995), pp. 72–80.

[8]Chesnoff, Richard Z., "Hatemongering on the Data Highway: Bigotry Carves Out a Niche in Cyberspace," *U.S. News & World Report,* 117 (August 8, 1994), p. 52.

[9]Gaede, Owen F., "The NII and Implications for Educational Leaders," audioconference at the AECT 1994 Leadership Development Conference, August 5, 1994.

[10]Hiatt, Diana, "An Interview with Ralph Tyler: No Limit to the Possibilities," *Phi Delta Kappan,* 75 (June 1994), pp. 787–788.

[11]Duffy, Thomas M., & Bednar, Anne K., "Attempting to Come to Grips with Alternative Perspectives," in Duffy, Thomas M., & Jonassen, David H., eds., *Constructivism and the Technology of Instruction: A Conversation* (Hillsdale, NJ: Lawrence Erlbaum, 1992), p. 132. See also Nix, Don, & Spiro, Rand, eds., *Cognition, Education, and Multimedia: Exploring Ideas in High Technology* (Hillsdale, NJ: Lawrence Erlbaum, 1990).

[12]Moody, Jim, "Online: Brave New World, Welcome to Cyberspace," *Multimedia World,* 1 (April 1994), p. 103.

[13]*Ibid.,* p. 104.

[14]Form letter dated May 13, 1994 (vicepresident@whitehouse.gov).

[15]Reading the laments of La Vergne Rosow ("The Working Poor and the Community College," *Phi Delta Kappan,* 75 [June

1994]: p. 801) about the California community colleges becoming "yet another public institution whose benefits are restricted to an elite," because tuition in the budget-strapped "golden" state was raised from $60 per semester up to $10 per unit, might leave one with little hope for wide access to vastly more expensive infobahn services. **Surely hope must be backed up with affirmative action!** See also Guy Kawasaki's cutting critique, "Potholes along the Information Superhighway: If This Is the Highway, I'd Rather Hitchhike Along a Country Road." *Macworld*, 11 (July 1994), p. 274; Maddux, Cleborne D., "The Internet: Educational Prospects—and Problems," *Educational Technology*, 34 (September 1994), pp. 37–42; and Glossbrenner, Alfred, "The Terrible Truth About the World-Wide Web," *Online User*, 1 (October/November 1995), p. 64: "But 'free' information is likely to be worth exactly what you pay for it." See also Stoll, Clifford, *Silicon Snake Oil: Second Thoughts on the Information Highway* (New York: Doubleday, 1995).

[16]"The Integration of Cognitive and Affective Dimensions of Learning" (unpublished doctoral dissertation, UCLA, 1976), p. 118. A summary may be found in Jelinek, John J., ed., *Philosophy of Education in Cultural Perspective* (Tempe, AZ: Far Western Philosophy of Education Society, 1977), pp. 481–496, and in a 1996 book about "confluent education" edited by Joel Brown. I am forever grateful to UCLA Visiting Professor Donald Vandenberg (now at the University of Queensland, Australia) for patiently illuminating the winding paths of phenomenology, thereby enabling my completion of this dissertation.

[17]Postman, Neil, "The Error of Our Ways," *Teacher Magazine*, 6 (August 1995), pp. 32–37; from his *The End of Education: Redefining the Value of School* (New York: Knopf, 1995).

[18]*Ibid.*, p. 37.

[19]*Ibid.*

[20]Shanker, Albert, "An Open Letter to All AFT Members," *American Teacher*, 80 (September 1995), p. 10. See also his solid "A Reflection on 12 Studies of Education Reform," *Phi Delta Kappan*, 77 (September 1995), pp. 81–83: "Some time in the past few years, curriculum reform has come to mean making curriculum interdisciplinary/multidisciplinary/cross-disciplinary, integrated, thematic, and, of course, relevant to 'real life.' (In some places, curriculum reform seems to mean just performance assessment: the tail becomes the whole dog.) This may or may not be a good thing. Most of these studies don't tell us, though most of them cite these words approvingly. And what do these words mean? Is this kind of curriculum always good? Is 'traditional' curriculum or 'nonconstructivist' pedagogy always bad or irrelevant? For whom and under what circumstances? Are we trading one rigidity for another in the name of reform?" (p. 81). Like my UCLA mentor, George Kneller, Shanker has a way of helping us maintain perspective, especially useful in these times of awesomely rapid technological change and socio/political instability.

[21]"America's Agenda: Discipline and Standards," *American Teacher*, 80 (September 1995), p. 12.

[22]Hiatt, p. 786.

[23]Kneller, George F., *Movements of Thought in Modern Education* (New York: Wiley, 1984); *Educationists and Their Vanities: One Hundred Missives to My Colleagues* (San Francisco: Caddo Press, 1994). Though a university scholar "called back to service" these past few years to inspire undergraduates at UCLA, Professor Kneller taught for many years in secondary schools where he used "magic lanterns," served during WWII in the production of educational films, and was early engaged in debates with those who sought to automate instruction toward fixed ends. At age 86, he completed the above 1994 manuscript, one "missive" per page, on a Royal typewriter, using erasable bond paper. Still unimpressed with computers, wear on the Royal, he wrote me, might compel him soon to try a word processor.

[24]Zenhausern, Bob, "Getting Up to Speed on the Information Highway," *TAM Newsletter*, 9 (June 1994), pp. 7–10. See also Monahan, Brian D., & Dharm, Matthew, "The Internet for Educators: A User's Guide," *Educational Technology*, 35 (January/February 1995), pp. 44–48.

[25]"Surf'n the Net for Gifted Education Resources," *CEC Today*, 1 (July 1994), pp. 10–11.

[26]Caputo, Anne, "Seven Secrets of Searching: How and When to Choose Online," *MultiMedia Schools*, 1 (May/June 1994), pp. 29–33.

[27]Healy, Michelle, "Kids Can Tap into a Wealth of Learning: But Figuring Out What to Do with Data Will Be Young Tech Wizards' Challenge," *USA Today* (February 9, 1995), p. 2D.

[28]McKenzie, Jamieson, "Beforenet and Afternet," *MultiMedia Schools*, 2 (May/June 1995), pp. 6–8. McKenzie also recommended checking out Columbia University's WWW Constructivist Project Design Guide (http://www.ilt.columbia.edu/LT/webcurr.html). See also Buchanan, Larry, "Tapping the World's Knowledge: Usenet," *MultiMedia Schools*, 2 (September/October 1995), pp. 54–56.

[29]Harris, Judi, "Educational Telecomputing Activities: Problem-Solving Projects," *Learning and Leading with Technology*, 22 (May 1995), pp. 59–63. See her *Way of the Ferret: Finding and Using Educational Resources on the Internet*, 2nd ed. (Eugene, OR: International Society for Technology in Education, 1995). Selected "Mining the Internet" articles and descriptions of actual projects may be found via gopher://gopher.ed.uiuc.edu, or on the WWW at http://www.ed.uiuc.edu/activity-structures. See also Dyrli, Odvard Egil, "Teacher-Initiated Telecommunications Projects," *Technology & Learning*, 15 (April 1995), pp. 20–26; Johnson, Doug, "Captured by the Web: K–12 Schools and the World-Wide Web," *MultiMedia Schools*, 2 (March/April 1995), pp. 25–30; Sherman, Thomas M., "Teaching with the Whole World Watching," *MultiMedia Schools*, 2 (September/October 1995), pp. 45–47; Sanchez, Robert, "A Wired Education," *Internet World*, 6 (October 1995), pp. 71–74; Kimeldorf, Martin,

"Teaching Online–Techniques and Methods," *Learning and Leading with Technology*, 23 (September 1995), pp. 26–31; Lamb, Annette C., & Johnson, Larry, *Crusin' the Information Highway: Internet & the K–12 Classroom* (Evansville, IN: Vision to Action, 1995); and Dyrli, Odvard Egil, "Surfing the World Wide Web to Education Hot-Spots," *Technology & Learning*, 16(October 1995), pp. 44–51.

[30]I pursue these topics in my "Exploiting Educational Features of Commercial Online Services," in Berge, Zane, & Collins, Mauri, eds., *The Online Classroom K–12* (Cresskill, NJ: Hampton Press, 1996). *Classroom Connect* (connect@ wentworth.com), *Educational Technology* (1-800-952-BOOK), *Learning and Leading with Technology* (iste@oregon.uoregon. edu), *MultiMedia Schools* (veccia@well.sf.ca.us), *Tech Trends* (aect@aect.org), *Technology & Learning* (1-800-543-4383), and RMI Media Productions (rmimedia@aol.com), just to mention a few priceless resources in addition to our **students** and **colleagues**, will continue to keep us all up to date.

News of the substantial educational benefits of **systematically and systemically integrating computer technology into schools** is reaching the mainstream in such fine articles as Means, Barbara, Olson, Kerry, & Singh, Ram, "Beyond the Classroom: Restructuring Schools with Technology," *Phi Delta Kappan*, 77 (September 1995), pp. 69–72: "Technology [Read "computers." We have a long way to go in this limiting of "technology" to its product sense, or, even worse, to computers alone.] can provide students with supports for storing and manipulating information (e.g., database and spreadsheet software), tools for writing and editing (e.g., word processing software), access to a wide array of information (e.g., through Internet searches), capabilities for communicating with content experts and other investigators (e.g., through electronic networks), and representations that give tangible form to concepts that are otherwise difficult to visualize (e.g., interactive graphic representations of such variables as acceleration)" (p. 69). Bravo! I replied to the editor with the following:

> I read with great interest and admiration the fine article by Barbara Means, Kerry Olson, and Ram Singh. The authors rightly claimed that, when systematically and systemically integrated into the core curriculum, technology can play an important role in achievement of higher order educational aims. However, throughout the article they used the term "technology" as if it were synonymous with computers, and thus were compelled to conclude that it cannot serve as a "silver bullet" for transforming education.
>
> In their *Instructional Technology: The Definition and Domains of the Field*, Barbara Seels and Rita Richey expressed the view endorsed by the Association for Educational Communications and Technology that: "Instructional technology is the theory and practice of design, development, utilization, management and evaluation of processes and resources for learning" (p. 1). In my upcoming *The Educational Technology Handbook: A Comprehensive Guide*, I define educational technology as: "a **systematic process involving application of knowledge in the**

search for replicable solutions to problems inherent in teaching and learning" (p. 11).

We agree that technology is, first and foremost, a process. Computer-based learning programs, no more nor less than textbooks, videos, and classroom management systems, at their best are **products** of this iterative process.

Thus conceived, akin to site-based research, educational technology surely can serve as a silver, if not gold (because teaching is, in large part, an exquisite art), bullet for transforming education.

Sources

Books pertaining primarily to the information superhighway are listed below. Many of these titles are annotated in "'Where to Start' for New Internet Users" by Jim Milles (millesjg@sluvca.slu.edu), which may be obtained *gratis* by sending an email message to: listserv@ubvm.cc. buffalo.edu with the message: Get newusers FAQ nettrain F=mail. The message: Get nettrain revs_1 nettrain F=mail will retrieve reviews of Internet books. Substitute 2, 3, 4, etc. for the number 1 to obtain updates.

Aboba, Bernard, *The Online User's Encyclopedia: Bulletin Boards and Beyond* (Reading, MA: Addison-Wesley, 1993).

Alspach, Ted, *Internet E-Mail Quick Tour: Sending, Receiving & Managing Your Messages Online* (Chapel Hill, NC: Ventana Press, 1995).

Angell, David, & Heslop, Brent, *The Elements of E-Mail Style: Communicate Effectively via Electronic Mail* (Reading, MA: Addison-Wesley, 1994).

Angell, David, & Heslop, Brent, *Mosaic for Dummies Windows Edition* (Indianapolis, IN: IDG Books, 1995).

Armstrong, Sara, *Telecommunications in the Classroom*, 2nd ed. (Eugene, OR: International Society for Technology in Education, 1995).

Aronson, Larry, *HTML Manual of Style* (Emeryville, CA: Ziff-Davis, 1994).

Badgett, Tom, & Sandler, Corey, *Welcome to . . . Internet: From Mystery to Mastery*, 2nd ed. (New York: MIS:Press, 1995).

Banks, Michael, *Welcome to . . . CompuServe for Windows: From Mystery to Mastery* (New York: MIS:Press, 1994).

Basch, Reva, *Secrets of the Super Searchers* (Wilton, CT: Eight Bit Books, 1993).

Benz, Christopher, illustrated by Ishida, Sarah, *How to Use America Online* (Emeryville, CA: Ziff-Davis, 1994).

Berge, Zane L., & Collins, Mauri P., eds., *Computer-Mediated Communication and the Online Classroom* (Cresskill, NJ: Hampton Press, 1995).

Berge, Zane L., & Collins, Mauri P., eds., *The Online Classroom K–12* (Cresskill, NJ: Hampton Press, 1996).

Bowen, Charles, & Peyton, David, *How to Get the Most Out of CompuServe*, 5th ed. (New York: Bantam Books, 1993).

Branwyn, Gareth, & Carton, Sean, *Mosaic Quick Tour for Windows, Special Edition: Accessing & Navigating the World Wide Web* (Chapel Hill, NC: Ventana Press, 1995).

Braun, Eric, *The Internet Directory* (New York: Fawcett Columbine, 1994).

Breivik, Patricia Senn, & Senn, J. A., *Information Literacy: Educating Children for the 21st Century* (New York: Scholastic, 1993).

Browne, Steve, *The Internet via Mosaic and World-Wide Web* (Emeryville, CA: Ziff-Davis, 1994).

Butler, Mark, illustrated by Bradshaw, Steph, *How to Use the Internet: Join the Internet Revolution Today* (Emeryville, CA: Ziff-Davis, 1994).

Cady, Glee Harrah, & McGregor, Pat, *Mastering the Internet* (San Francisco: SYBEX, 1995).

Carl-Mitchell, Smoot, & Quarterman, John S., *Practical Internetworking with TCP/IP and UNIX* (Reading, MA: Addison-Wesley, 1993).

Carton, Sean, *Internet Virtual Worlds Quick Tour: MUDs, MOOs, & MUSHes: Interactive Games, Conferences & Forums* (Chapel Hill, NC: Ventana Press, 1995).

Cedeño, Nancy, *The Internet Tool Kit* (San Francisco: SYBEX, 1995).

Clark, David, *Student's Guide to the Internet* (Indianapolis, IN: Alpha Books, 1995).

Clark, Michael, *Cultural Treasures of the Internet* (Upper Saddle River, NJ: PTR Prentice Hall, 1995).

Comer, Douglas E., *The Internet Book: Everything You Need to Know About Computer Networking and How the Internet Works* (Englewood Cliffs, NJ: Prentice-Hall, 1995).

Committee for Economic Development, *Connecting Students to a Changing World: A Technology Strategy for Improving Mathematics and Science Education* (New York: author, 1995).

Crumlish, Christian, *A Guided Tour of the Internet* (San Francisco: SYBEX, 1995).

Davis, Steve, *CompuServe Information Manager for Windows: Complete Handbook and Membership Kit* (Rocklin, CA: Prima Publishing, 1994).

December, John, & Randall, Neil, *The World Wide Web Unleased*, 2nd ed. (Indianapolis, IN: Sams.net, 1995).

Derfler Jr., Frank J., *Guide to Connectivity*, 3rd ed. (Emeryville, CA: Ziff-Davis, 1995).

Derfler Jr., Frank J., & Freed, Les, illustrated by Troller, Michael, *How Networks Work* (Emeryville, CA: Ziff-Davis, 1993).

Dern, Daniel P., *The Internet Guide for New Users* (New York, McGraw-Hill, 1994).

Diamond, Joel, Sobel, Howard, & Hilley, Valda, *Internet GIZMOS for Windows* (Indianapolis, IN: IDG Books, 1995).

Dougherty, Dale, & Koman, Richard, *The Mosaic Handbook for the Macintosh* (Sebastopol, CA: O'Reilly & Associates, 1994).

Dougherty, Dale, Koman, Richard, & Ferguson, Paula, *The Mosaic Handbook for the X Window System* (Sebastopol, CA: O'Reilly & Associates, 1994).

Duntemann, Jeff, Pronk, Ron, & Vincent, Patrick, *Web Explorer Pocket Companion* (Scottsdale, AZ: Coriolis Group Books, 1995).

Dupuy, John, *The Complete Idiot's Guide to Netscape* (Indianapolis, IN: Que, 1995).

Dvorak, John C., & Anis, Nick, *Dvorak's Guide to PC Telecommunications*, 2nd ed. (Berkeley: Osborne McGraw-Hill, 1992).

Eager, Bill, *Using the Internet* (Indianapolis, IN: Que, 1994).

Eager, Bill, & Pike, Mary Ann, *Special Edition Using the World Wide Web and Mosaic* (Indianapolis, IN: Que, 1995).

Eddings, Joshua, illustrated by Wattenmaker, Pamela Drury, *How the Internet Works* (Emeryville, CA: Ziff-Davis, 1994).

Educator's Internet Companion: Classroom Connect's Complete Guide to Educational Resources on the Internet (Lancaster, PA: Wentworth Worldwide Media, 1995).

Educator's Internet Funding Guide: Classroom Connect's Reference Guide for Technology Funding (Lancaster, PA: Wentworth Worldwide Media, 1995).

Ellsworth, Jill H., *Education on the Internet: A Hands-on Book of Ideas, Resources, Projects, and Advice* (Indianapolis, IN: Sams, 1994).

Ellsworth, Jill H., & Ellsworth, Matthew V., *The Internet Business Book* (New York: Wiley, 1994).

Ellsworth, Jill H., & Ellsworth, Matthew V., *Using CompuServe* (Indianapolis, IN: Que, 1994).

Engle, Mary, Lutz, Marilyn, Jones Jr., William W., & Engel, Genevieve, *Internet Connections: A Librarian's Guide to Dial-Up Access and Use* (Chicago: Library and Information Technology Association, 1993).

Engst, Adam C., *Internet Starter Kit for Macintosh*, 3rd ed. (Indianapolis, IN: Hayden Books, 1995).

Engst, Adam C., & Dickson, William, *Internet Explorer's Kit for Macintosh* (Indianapolis, IN: Hayden Books, 1994).

Engst, Adam C., Low, Corwin S., & Simon, Michael A., *Internet Starter Kit*, 2nd ed. (Indianapolis, IN: Hayden Books, 1995).

Ernst, Warren, *Using Netscape* (Indianapolis, IN: Que, 1995).

Estabrook, Noel, Gregory, Kate, Mann, Jim, & Parker, Tim, *Using UseNet Newsgroups* (Indianapolis, IN: Que, 1995).

Estrada, Susan, *Connecting to the Internet: A Buyer's Guide* (Sebastopol, CA: O'Reilly & Associates, 1993).

Falk, Bennett, *The Internet Roadmap* (San Francisco: SYBEX, 1994).

Fisher, Sharon, *Riding the Internet Highway* (Carmel, IN: New Riders Publishing, 1993).

Flynn, Charles E., *The Unofficial Macintosh Guide to America Online* (New York: Wiley, 1995).

Fraase, Michael, *The PC Internet Tour Guide: Cruising the Internet the Easy Way* (Chapel Hill, NC: Ventana Press, 1994).

Fraase, Michael, revised by Alspach, Ted, & Weingarten, Jan, *The Mac Internet Tour Guide: Cruising the Internet the Easy Way*, 2nd ed. (Chapel Hill, NC: Ventana Press, 1995).

Fraase, Michael, & James, Phil, *The Windows Internet Tour Guide: Cruising the Internet the Easy Way*, 2nd ed. (Chapel Hill, NC: Ventana Press, 1995).

Freed, Les, & Derfler Jr., Frank J., illustrated by Kubo, Chad, *Building the Information Highway* (Emeryville, CA: Ziff-Davis, 1994).

Gaffin, Adam, *Everybody's Guide to the Internet* (Cambridge, MA: The MIT Press, 1994).

Gaffin, Adam, & Electronic Frontier Foundation, *Big Dummy's Guide to the Internet*. Available *gratis* by FTP from: ftp.eff.org, directory /pub/Net_info/Big_Dummy, filename bigdummy.txt.

Gagnon, Eric, *What's on the Internet Summer/Fall 1995* (Berkeley, CA: Peachpit Press, 1995).

Gardner, David C., Beatty, Grace Joely, & Sauer, David, *Internet for Windows: America Online Edition* (Rocklin, CA: Prima Publishing, 1995).

Gardner, James, *A DOS User's Guide to the Internet: E-Mail, Netnews and File Transfer with UUCP* (Englewood Cliffs, NJ: PTR Prentice Hall, 1994).

Gilster, Paul, *Finding It on the Internet: The Essential Guide to Archie, Veronica, Gopher, WAIS, WWW, and Other Search Tools* (New York: Wiley, 1994).

Gilster, Paul, *The Internet Navigator: The Essential Guide to Network Exploration for the Individual Dial-Up User*, 2nd ed. (New York: Wiley, 1994).

Gilster, Paul, *The Mosaic Navigator: The Essential Guide to the Internet Interface* (New York: Wiley, 1995).

Gilster, Paul, *The SLIP/PPP Connection: The Essential Guide to Graphical Internet Access* (New York: Wiley, 1995).

Glossbrenner, Alfred, illustrated by Grimes, John, *The Little Online Book* (Berkeley, CA: Peachpit Press, 1995).

Godin, Seth, ed., *Best of the Net* (Indianapolis, IN: IDG Books, 1995).

Godin, Seth, & McBride, James S., *The 1994 Internet White Pages* (San Mateo, CA: IDG Books, 1994).

Goldman, Neal, *The Complete Idiot's Pocket Reference to the Internet* (Indianapolis, IN: Alpha Books, 1994).

Goodman, Danny, *Your Survival Guide to Life on the Information Superhighway: Living at Light Speed* (New York: Random House, 1994).

Graham, Ian S., *The HTML Sourcebook* (New York: Wiley, 1995).

Hahn, Harley, *A Student's Guide to UNIX* (New York: McGraw-Hill, 1993).

Hahn, Harley, & Stout, Rick, *The Internet Complete Reference* (Berkeley: Osborne McGraw-Hill, 1994).

Hahn, Harley, & Stout, Rick, *The Internet Yellow Pages*, 2nd ed. (Berkeley: Osborne McGraw-Hill, 1995).

Halliday, Caroline M., *The Trail Guide to Prodigy: A Rapid-Reading Reference to Using and Cruising the Prodigy Online Service* (Reading, MA: Addison-Wesley, 1995).

Harasim, Linda, Hiltz, Roxanne, Teles, Lucio, & Turoff, Murray, *Learning Networks: A Field Guide to Teaching and Learning Online* (Cambridge, MA: The MIT Press, 1995).

Hardie, Edward T. L., & Neou, Vivian, eds., *Internet: Mailing Lists* (Englewood Cliffs, NJ: PTR Prentice Hall, 1994).

Harris, Judi., *Mining the Internet for Educational Resources* (Austin: University of Texas at Austin, 1993).

Harris, Judi, *Way of the Ferret: Finding and Using Educational Resources on the Internet*, 2nd ed. (Eugene, OR: International Society for Technology in Education, 1995).

Harris, Stuart, *The irc Survival Guide: Talk to the World with Internet Relay Chat* (Reading, MA: Addison-Wesley, 1995).

Harris, Stuart, & Kidder, Gayle, *Netscape Quick Tour for Macintosh: Accessing & Navigating the Internet's World Wide Web* (Chapel Hill, NC: Ventana Press, 1995).

Harris, Stuart, & Kidder, Gayle, *Netscape Quick Tour for Windows: Accessing & Navigating the Internet's World Wide Web, Special Edition* (Chapel Hill, NC: Ventana Press, 1995).

Harrison, Mark, *The USENET Handbook: A User's Guide to Netnews* (Sebastopol, CA: O'Reilly & Associates, 1995).

Harrison, Peter John, *The Internet Direct Connect Kit* (Indianapolis, IN: IDG Books, 1994).

Hedtke, John, *Using Computer Bulletin Boards*, 3rd ed. (New York: MIS:Press, 1995).

Heslop, Brent, & Angell, David, *The Instant Internet Guide* (Reading, MA: Addison-Wesley, 1994).

Hiltz, Starr Roxanne, & Turoff, Murray, *The Network Nation: Human Communication via Computer*, revised ed. (Cambridge, MA: The MIT Press, 1993).

Hoffman, Paul E., edited by Levine, John R., *The Internet* (Indianapolis, IN: IDG Books, 1994).

Hoffman, Paul E., *50 Fun Ways to Internet* (Franklin Lakes, NJ: Career Press, 1995).

Hoffman, Paul E., *The Internet Instant Reference*, 2nd ed. (San Francisco: SYBEX, 1995).

Hoffman, Paul E., *Netscape and the World Wide Web for Dummies* (Indianapolis, IN: IDG Books, 1995).

Howard, Jim, *The Internet Voyeur: A Guide to Viewing Images on the Internet* (San Francisco: SYBEX, 1995).

How to Get Connected to the Internet: Facts and Funding: An Educator's Guide to Bringing the World into the Classroom (Lancaster, PA: Wentworth Worldwide Media, 1994).

The Internet Resource Quick Reference (Indianapolis, IN: Que, 1994).

The Internet Unleashed, 2nd ed. (Indianapolis, IN: Sams.net, 1995).

Jaffe, Lee David, & Tennant, Roy, *Introducing the Internet: A Trainer's Workshop* (Berkeley, CA: Library Solutions Press, 1994).

Johnson, Ned B., *Navigating the Internet with Prodigy* (Indianapolis, IN: Sams.net, 1995).

Jones, Steve, *CyberSociety* (Thousand Oaks, CA: Sage Publications, 1994).

Junion-Metz, Gail, *K−12 Resources on the Internet: An Instructional Guide* (Berkeley: Library Solutions Press, 1996).

Kane, Pamela, *The Hitchhiker's Guide to the Electronic Highway* (New York: MIS:Press, 1994).

Kaufeld, John, *America Online for Dummies,* 2nd ed. (Indianapolis, IN: IDG Books, 1995).

Kee, Eddie, *Networking Illustrated* (Indianapolis, IN: Que, 1994).

Kehoe, Brendan P., *Zen and the Art of the Internet: A Beginner's Guide,* 3rd ed. (Englewood Cliffs, NJ: PTR Prentice Hall, 1994).

Kent, Peter, *10 Minute Guide to the Internet* (Indianapolis, IN: Que, 1994).

Kent, Peter, *The Complete Idiot's Guide to the Internet* (Indianapolis, IN: Alpha Books, 1994).

Kent, Peter, *The Complete Idiot's Guide to the World Wide Web* (Indianapolis, IN: Alpha Books, 1995).

Kent, Peter, *PGP* [Pretty Good Privacy] *Companion for Windows: Easy Point-&-Click Encryption for Your Electronic Information* (Chapel Hill, NC: Ventana Press, 1995).

Kidder, Gayle, & Harris, Stuart, *HTML Publishing with Internet Assistant: Your Guide to Using Microsoft's HTML Add-On* (Chapel Hill, NC: Ventana Press, 1995).

Kochmer, Jonathan, & NorthWestNet, *The Internet Passport: NorthWestNet's Guide to Our World Online,* 4th ed. (Bellevue, WA: NorthWestNet, 1993).

Kraynak, Joe, *The Complete Idiot's Guide to Mosaic* (Indianapolis, IN: Alpha Books, 1995).

Krol, Ed., *The Whole Internet: User's Guide & Catalog,* 2nd ed. (Sebastopol, CA: O'Reilly & Associates, 1994).

Kurshan, Barbara L., Harrington, Marcia A., & Milbury, Peter G., *An Educator's Guide to Electronic Networking: Creating Virtual Communities* (Syracuse, NY: ERIC Clearinghouse on Information & Technology, 1994).

Lamb, Annette C., *Spin Your Own Web Site Using HTML* (Evansville, IN: Vision to Action, 1996).

Lamb, Annette C., & Johnson, Larry, *Cruisin' the Information Highway: Internet & the K−12 Classroom* (Evansville, IN: Vision to Action, 1995).

Lambert, Steve, & Howe, Walt, *Internet Basics* (New York: Random House, 1993).

LaQuey, Tracy, with Ryer, Jeanne C., *The Internet Companion: A Beginner's Start-Up Kit for Global Networking,* 2nd ed. (Reading, MA: Addison-Wesley, 1994).

Lawley, Elizabeth Lane, & Summerhill, Craig, *Internet Primer: For Information Professionals: A Basic Guide to Internet Networking Technology* (Westport, CT: Meckler Publishing, 1993).

LeJeune, Urban A., with Duntemann, Jeff, *Mosaic & Web Explorer* (Scottsdale, AZ: The Coriolis Group, 1995).

Lemay, Laura, *Teach Yourself Web Publishing with HTML* (Indianapolis, IN: Sams, 1995).

Leshin, Cynthia B., *Internet Adventures: Visiting Virtual Communities: A Step-by-Step Guide for Educators* (Phoenix, AZ: XPLORA Publishing, 1995).

Levine, John R., & Baroudi, Carol, *The Internet for Dummies* (San Mateo, CA: IDG Books Worldwide, 1993).

Levine, John R., & Baroudi, Carol, *Internet Secrets* (Indianapolis, IN: IDG Books, 1995).

Levine, John R., & Young, Margaret Levine, *More Internet for Dummies* (Indianapolis, IN: IDG Books, 1994).

Lichty, Tom, *America Online's Internet: Easy, Graphical Access−The AOL Way, Macintosh Edition* (Chapel Hill, NC: Ventana Press, 1994).

Lichty, Tom, *America Online's Internet: Easy, Graphical Access−The AOL Way, Windows Edition* (Chapel Hill, NC: Ventana Press, 1994).

Lichty, Tom, *The Official America Online for Windows Membership Kit & Tour Guide,* 2nd ed. (Chapel Hill, NC: Ventana Press, 1994).

Liu, Cricket, *et al.*, *Managing Internet Information Services* (Sebastopol, CA: O'Reilly & Associates, 1994).

Lowe, Doug, *Networking for Dummies* (Indianapolis, IN: IDG Books, 1994).

Luckman Interactive, Inc., *New Riders' Official World Wide Web Yellow Pages* (Indianapolis, IN: New Riders Publishing, 1995).

Magid, Lawrence J., *Cruising On-Line: Larry Magid's Guide to the New Digital Highways* (New York: Random House, 1994).

Marchuk, Michael, *Building Internet Applications with Visual Basic* (Indianapolis, IN: Que, 1995).

Marine, April, Kirkpatrick, Susan, Neou, Vivian, Ward, Carol, *Internet: Getting Started* (Englewood Cliffs, NJ: PTR Prentice Hall, 1994).

Martin, Jerry, *There's Gold in them thar Networks! Or Searching for Treasure in all the Wrong Places.* Available *gratis* by FTP from: nic.merit.edu, directory /introducing.the.internet, filename network.gold.

Maxwell, Bruce, *Washington Online: How to Access the Federal Government on the Internet 1995* (Washington, DC: Congressional Quarterly, 1995).

Maxwell, Christine, & Grycz, Czeslaw J., *New Riders' Official Internet Yellow Pages* (Indianapolis, IN: New Riders Publishing, 1994).

McFedries, Paul, *The Complete Idiot's Guide to Internet E-Mail* (Indianapolis, IN: Que, 1995).

Meriwether, Dan, *The Macintosh Web Browser Kit* (New York: Wiley, 1995).

Merrin, Robin, *The Mosaic Roadmap* (San Francisco: SYBEX, 1995).

Miller, Elizabeth B., *The Internet Resource Directory for K−12 Teachers and Librarians, 94/95 Edition* (Englewood, CO: Libraries Unlimited, 1994).

Miller, Michael, *Easy Internet* (Indianapolis, IN: Que, 1994).

Miller, Michael, *Using CompuServe,* 2nd ed. (Indianapolis, IN: Que, 1994).

Minatel, Jim, *Easy World Wide Web with Netscape* (Indianapolis, IN: Que, 1995).

Mizokawa, Donald T., *Everyday Computing in Academe: A Guide for Scholars, Researchers, Students, and Other Academic Users of Personal Computers* (Englewood Cliffs, NJ: Educational Technology Publications, 1994).

MKS Inc., with contributions from Gardner, James, *Internet Anywhere: All You Need to Test Drive Internet Mail and USENET News for 30 Days* (Englewood Cliffs, NJ: PTR Prentice Hall, 1995).

Moody, Glyn, *The Internet with Windows* (Newton, MA: Butterworth-Heinemann, 1995).

Morris, Mary E. S., *HTML for Fun and Profit* (Mountain View, CA: Sun Microsystems, 1995).

Morrison, Deborah, *OS/2 Warp Internet Connection: Your Key to Cruising the Internet and the World Wide Web* (Indianapolis, IN: IDG Books, 1995).

Mostafa, Newell, & Mostafa, Trenthem, *The Easy Internet Handbook* (Englewood, CO: Libraries Unlimited, 1994).

NCSA Education Group, *An Incomplete Guide to the Internet.* Available *gratis* by FTP from: ftp.ncsa.uiuc.edu, directory /Education/Education_Resources/Incomplete_Guide/Incomp.Guide.Old, filename Incomp.Guide.July.txt.

Negroponte, Nicholas, *Being Digital* (New York: Knopf, 1995).

Neou, Vivian, *Internet Mailing Lists Navigator for Windows Users* (Upper Saddle River, NJ: PTR Prentice Hall, 1995).

net.Genesis, & Hall, Devra, *Build a Web Site* (Rocklin, CA: Prima Publishing, 1995).

Nielsen, Jakob, *Multimedia and Hypertext: The Internet and Beyond* (Boston: AP Professional, 1995).

Noonan, Dana, *A Guide to Internet/Bitnet.* Available *gratis* by FTP from: vm1.nodak.edu, directory /news, filename guidev2.nnews.

NorthWestNet, *The Internet Passport: NorthWestNet's Guide to Our World Online,* 5th ed. (Englewood Cliffs, NJ: PTR Prentice Hall, 1995).

Notess, Greg R., *Internet Access Providers: An International Resource Directory* (Westport, CT: Meckler, 1993).

O'Loughlin, Luanne, *Free Stuff from America Online: Your Guide to Getting Hundreds of Valuable Goodies* (Scottsdale, AZ: Coriolis Group Books, 1995).

O'Loughlin, Luanne, *Free Stuff from CompuServe: Your Guide to Getting Hundreds of Valuable Goodies* (Scottsdale, AZ: Coriolis Group Books, 1995).

Otte, Peter, *The Information Superhighway: Beyond the Internet* (Indianapolis, IN: Que, 1994).

Peal, David, *Access the Internet* (San Francisco: SYBEX, 1994).

Person, Ron, with Laby, Lorry, & Merkel, Brady P., *Web Publishing with Word for Windows* (Indianapolis, IN: Que, 1995).

Pfaffenberger, Bryan, *The USENET Book: Finding, Using, and Surviving Newsgroups on the Internet* (Reading, MA: Addison-Wesley, 1995).

Pfaffenberger, Bryan, *World Wide Web Bible* (New York: MIS Press, 1995).

Pike, Mary Ann, & Estabrook, Noel, *Using FTP* (Indianapolis, IN: Que, 1995).

Pike, Mary Ann, & Pike, Tod G., *The Internet QuickStart* (Indianapolis, IN: Que, 1994).

Pike, Mary Ann, *et al., Using Mosaic* (Indianapolis, IN: Que, 1994).

Pivovarnick, John, *The Complete Idiot's Guide to America Online* (Indianapolis, IN: Alpha Books, 1995).

Polly, Jean Armour, *Surfing the INTERNET: An Introduction.* Available *gratis* from: nysernet.org, directory /pub/guides, filename surfing.2.0.3.txt.

Pope, Markus W., *Que's BBS Directory* (Indianapolis, IN: Que, 1994).

Powell, Bob, & Wickre, Karen, *Atlas to the World Wide Web* (Emeryville, CA: Ziff-Davis, 1995).

Price, Jonathan, *The Trail Guide to America Online: A Rapid-Reading Reference to Using and Cruising the America Online Service* (Reading, MA: Addison-Wesley, 1995).

Pyra, Marianne, *Using Internet Relay Chat* (Indianapolis, IN: Que, 1995).

Quarterman, John S., *The Matrix: Computer Networks and Conferencing Systems Worldwide* (Bedford, MA: Digital Press, 1990).

Quarterman, John S., & Carl-Mitchell, Smoot, *The E-Mail Companion: Communicate Effectively via the Internet and Other Global Networks* (Reading, MA: Addison-Wesley, 1994).

Randall, Neil, *Teach Yourself the Internet: Around the World in 21 Days* (Indianapolis, IN: Sams, 1994).

Randall, Neil, & Latulipe, Celine, *Plug-n-Play Internet for Windows* (Indianapolis, IN: Sams, 1995).

Reiss, Levi, & Radin, Joseph, *Open Computing Guide to Mosaic* (Berkeley: Osborne McGraw-Hill, 1995).

Rheingold, Howard, *The Virtual Community: Homesteading on the Electronic Frontier* (New York: HarperPerennial, 1994).

Rittner, Don, *The Whole Earth Online Almanac: Info from A–Z* (New York: Brady Publishing, 1993).

Rizzo, John, *MacUser Guide to Connectivity* (Emeryville, CA: Ziff-Davis, 1993).

Roach, J. Michael, *10 Minute Guide to Internet Assistant for Word* (Indianapolis, IN: Que, 1995).

Robison, David F. W., & Tennant, Roy, *All About Internet FTP: Learning and Teaching to Transfer Files on the Internet* (Berkeley, CA: Library Solutions Press, 1994).

Rose, Donald, *Minding Your CyberManners on the Internet* (Indianapolis, IN: Alpha Books, 1994).

Rose, Donald, *Internet Chat Quick Tour: Real-Time Conversations & Communications Online* (Chapel Hill, NC: Ventana Press, 1995).

Ross, John, *Internet Power Tools* (New York: Random House, 1995).

Rutten, Peter, Bayers III, Albert F., & Maloni, Kelly, *Netguide: Your Map to the Services, Information and Entertainment on the Electronic Highway* (New York: Random House, 1994).

Sachs, David, & Stair, Henry H., *Hands-On Internet: Beginning Guide for PC Users* (Englewood Cliffs, NJ: PTR Prentice Hall, 1994).

Sachs, David, & Stair, Henry H., *Instant Internet with WebSurfer* (Englewood Cliffs, NJ: PTR Prentice Hall, 1995).

Sadler, Will, *Special Edition Using Internet E-Mail* (Indianapolis, IN: Que, 1995).

Salkind, Neil J., *Hands-On Internet* (Danvers, MA: Boyd & Fraser, 1995).

Savetz, Kevin M., *Your Internet Consultant: The FAQs of Life Online* (Indianapolis, IN: Sams, 1994).

Savola, Tom, with Westenbrock, Alan, & Heck, Joseph, *Special Edition Using HTML* (Indianapolis, IN: Que, 1995).

Schumer, Larry, & Negus, Chris, *Using UNIX* (Indianapolis, IN: Que, 1995).

Seiter, Charles, *The Internet for Mac for Dummies Starter Kit* (Indianapolis, IN: IDG Books, 1994).

Shafran, Andy, *The Complete Idiot's Guide to CompuServe* (Indianapolis, IN: Que, 1995).

Shipley, Chris, illustrated by Bradshaw, Steph, *How to Connect* (Emeryville, CA: Ziff-Davis, 1993).

Shirky, Clay, *The Internet by E-Mail* (Emeryville, CA: Ziff-Davis, 1994).

Slick, Beth, & Gerber, Steve, *BBSs for Dummies* (Indianapolis, IN: IDG Books, 1995).

Slouka, Mark, *War of the Worlds: Cyberspace and the High-Tech Assault on Reality* (New York: Basic Books, 1995).

Smith, Richard J., Gibbs, Mark, & McFedries, Paul, *Navigating the Internet*, 3rd ed. (Indianapolis, IN: Sams.net, 1995).

Snell, Ned, *Curious About the Internet?* (Indianapolis, IN: Sams, 1995).

Stein, Lincoln D., *How to Set Up and Maintain a World Wide Web Site: The Guide for Information Providers* (Reading, MA: Addison-Wesley, 1995).

Steinberg, Gene, *Special Edition Using America Online* (Indianapolis, IN: Que, 1995).

Stoll, Clifford, *Silicon Snake Oil: Second Thoughts on the Information Highway* (New York: Doubleday, 1995).

Strangelove, M., Kovacs, D., & Okerson, Ann, eds., *Directory of Electronic Journals, Newsletters and Academic Discussion Lists*, 3rd ed. (Washington, DC: Association of Research Libraries, 1993).

Sullivan-Trainer, Michael, *Detour: The Truth About the Information Superhighway* (Indianapolis, IN: IDG Books, 1994).

Tauber, Daniel A., & Kienan, Brenda, *Mosaic Access to the Internet* (San Francisco: SYBEX, 1995).

Tauber, Daniel A., & Kienan, Brenda, *Surfing the Internet with Netscape* (San Francisco: SYBEX, 1995).

Taylor, Dave, *Creating Cool Web Pages with HTML* (Indianapolis, IN: IDG Books, 1995).

Tennant, Roy, Ober, John, & Lipgow, Anne G., *Crossing the Internet Threshold: An Instructional Handbook*, 2nd ed. (Berkeley: Library Solutions Press, 1994).

Tittel, Ed, & James, Steve, *HTML for Dummies* (Indianapolis, IN: IDG Books, 1995).

Tolhurst, William A., Pike, Mary Ann, Blanton, Keith A., & Harris, John R., *Using the Internet, Special Edition* (Indianapolis, IN: Que, 1994).

Tricks of the Internet Gurus (Indianapolis, IN: Sams, 1994).

Turlington, Shannon R., *Walking the World Wide Web: Your Personal Guide to the Best of the Web* (Chapel Hill, NC: Ventana Press, 1995).

Tyson, Herb, *Navigating the Internet with OS/2 Warp* (Indianapolis, IN: Sams, 1995).

Waggoner, Michael D., ed., *Empowering Networks: Computer Conferencing in Education* (Englewood Cliffs, NJ: Educational Technology Publications, 1992).

Wagner, Richard, *Inside CompuServe*, 3rd ed. (Indianapolis, IN: New Riders Publishing, 1995).

Warschauer, Mark, *E-Mail for English Teaching: Bringing the Internet and Computer Learning Networks into the Language Classroom* (Alexandria, VA: TESOL Publications, 1995).

Weiss, Aaron, *The Complete Idiot's Guide to Protecting Yourself on the Internet* (Indianapolis, IN: Que, 1995).

Werner, Ray, *BBS Secrets* (Indianapolis, IN: IDG Books, 1995).

Wiggins, Robert R., & Tittel, Ed, *The Trail Guide to CompuServe: A Rapid-Reading Reference to Using and Cruising the CompuServe Online Service* (Reading, MA: Addison-Wesley, 1995).

Williams, Bard, *The Internet for Teachers* (Indianapolis, IN: IDG Books, 1995).

Wyatt, Allen L., *Success with Internet* (Las Vegas, NV: Jamsa Press, 1994).

Yanoff, Scott, *Special Internet Connections* (updated frequently). Available *gratis* by FTP from: csd4.csd.uwm.edu, directory /pub, filename inet.services.txt.

Young, Margaret Levine, & Levine, John R., *The Internet for Windows for Dummies Starter Kit* (Indianapolis, IN: IDG Books, 1994).

Thomas Copley (tcopley@arlington.com), in his "Gopher-it Workshop," recommended the following source of **downloadable books**.

Regular bookmark:

Type=1
Name=Internet Information
Path=1/.Sciences/.Compsci/.Internet
Host=ucsbuxa.ucsb.edu
Port=3001

***GopherMail* bookmark:**

Name=Internet Information
Numb=9
Type=1
Port=3001
Path=1/.Sciences/.Compusci/.Internet
Host=ucsbuxa.ucsb.edu

Dr. Copley, cofounder of the Electronic University of San Francisco, now offers a "Make the Link Workshop: World Wide Web for Everyone" (http://www.crl.com/~gorgon).

The following **periodicals** are *in addition to* those listed in Chapters **11** and **12**, most of which also cover computer network services.

BBS
BBS Callers Digest
Boardwatch Magazine
Classroom Connect
CompuServe Magazine
Database
Information Searcher
InfoWorld
Interactive Publishing Alert
International Journal of Educational Telecommunications
Internet Strategies for Education Markets
Internet World
ISTE Update
I-Way
LAN: The Network Solutions Magazine
Matrix News
Multimedia Online
The Net
NetGuide
Online
Online Access
Online with Adult and Continuing Education
The Online Educator
Online Searcher
The Online User
Open Computing
SCO World
Technology Connection
Web Review (http://gnn.com/wr/)
Wired
WorldClassroom

The first Internet-based **hypermedia magazine**, the *Global Network Navigator* (also the name of the electronic publication site itself), was available *gratis* from O'Reilly and Associates (info@gnn.com) until it was purchased in mid-1995 by the "assertive" America Online for about $11 million. The September 1995 issue of *Internet World* described this and other **electronic publications**, and provided the following addresses:

The Children's Literature Web Guide
    (http://www.ucalgary.ca/~dkbrown)
Online Books Page (http://www.cs.cmu.edu/web/books.html)
Online Bookstore (http://marketplace.com/obs/obshome.html)
Ziff-Davis Publishing (http://www.ziff.com)
Global Network Navigator (http://www.gnn.com)
Yahoo (http://www.yahoo.com/Entertainment/Magazines)
Electronic Newsstand (http://www.enews.com)

NewsLink (http://www.newslink.org)
Journal of Electronic Publishing
    (http://www.press.umich.edu/jep)
Online Newspaper Services Resource Directory
    (http://www.mediainfo.com/edpub)

Find out about Internet **"on-ramps"** and features by contacting the following.

InterNIC Information Services [NSF-funded Internet information services]
General Atomics
1-800-862-0677; 1-908-668-6587
admin@ds.internic.net

To receive the electronic mail versions of their weekly Internet *Scout Report* you may: (1) send an email request to: listserv@lists.internic.net (Subject: blank. Message: subscribe scout-report), (2) send mail for *HTML* format to listserv@lists.internic.net (Message: subscribe scout-report-html). Note that 1 and 2 are not listservs, so you do not place your name in the message. Only an email address is recognized in that position, in case you want the file sent some place other than where you are originating the message. The hypertext version is at http://rs.internic.net/scout_report-index.html.

The International Internet Association (See if you quality for free access.): 1-202-387-5445
National Public Telecomputing Network (Obtain list of "Free-Nets."): 1-216-247-5800; info@nptn.org
Wentworth Worldwide Media (publisher of *Classroom Connect* and *How to Get Connected to the Internet*): 1-800-638-1639; connect@wentworth.com
America Online: (Rated best commercial online service by *Multimedia World*): 1-800-827-6364
CompuServe, Inc. (Rated best commercial online service by *PC World*; has access to selected Dialog databases.): 1-800-848-8199
DELPHI Internet Services Corp.: 1-800-695-4005
Dialog Information Services, Inc. (Provides access to an extensive database of electronic publications; has a "Classroom Instruction Program."): 1-800-3-DIALOG
eWorld Assistance Center: 1-800-775-4556; 1-408-974-1236
GEnie: 1-800-638-9636
Global Village Communications, Inc. ("Educate America"): 1-800-736-4821
International Discount Telecommunications ($15/month flat fee): 1-800-245-8000
The Microsoft Network: 1-800-386-5550
Netcom (*PC World*'s "Best Internet Provider"): 1-800-353-6600
NovaNet (CBL courseware plus Internet access): 1-800-937-6682

PSINet: 1-800-774-0852
Prodigy Services Company (1st with a WWW browser; has classroom version): 1-800-PRODIGY
The WELL: 1-415-332-4335

For detailed information about **Internet providers** outside (and within) North America see Benoit Lips' (lips@best.be) Web page (http://www.best.be/iap), or send email to iap@best.be, Subject: info.

Even those without direct access can benefit from **"Best of the Internet"** collections such as those from Full Circle (1-415-453-9989) and Microforum (1-800-465-2323; 1-416-656-6406; 1-800-268-3604 [Canada]).

Demonstration sites include: the National Demonstration Laboratory for Interactive Information Technologies, Library of Congress (1-202-707-4158); and the Technology Resources Center, U.S. Department of Education (1-202-219-1699).

Cheryl Wissick (n230149@univscvm.csd.scarolina.edu), Member of the Executive Board of the Technology and Media Division, Council for Exceptional Children, provided clear listserv instructions (see **Figure 13.15**). Prof. Wissick informed me that she now has available updated information about **listservs related primarily to special education** issues. With the "inclusion" of increasing numbers of students with disabilities in regular classrooms, these are precious resources for all of us.

Mary Tyler Knowles (Head, **English** Department, The Winsor School, Boston, MA 02215, mknowles@k12.ucs.umass.edu) recommended to me, in response to my ISED-L posting, the following: chua@uxa.cs.uiuc.edu, Subject: Course packet catalog [NCTE]; br_match@wcu.edu; Subject [blank], Message: Subscribe BR_Match Your Name [K-12 students discuss literature]; listserv@acmvm.onandaga.boces.k12.ny.us, Message: Subscribe GLBL-HS Your Name [The Global Studies High School]; iecc@stolaf.edu, Message: Request information about Intercultural Email classroom Connections Lists; for MLA and APA bibliography formats, gopher://gopher.uiuc.edu:70/11/Libraries/writers. Add to this list The Comenius Group (comenius@interport.net; http://www.comenius.com/) with its "Fluency Through Fables" pro-

---

Subscribing to a Listserv

How to subscribe to a list (using ALTLEARN as an example)

1. Send mail to address listed as the listserv address:
   Listserv @ SJUVM.BITNET
2. Leave the subject line BLANK.
3. In the body of the text indicate that you want to subscribe:
   SUBSCRIBE ALTLEARN firstname lastname
4. You will receive a message regarding your acceptance to the list and a will frequently include explanations of how to receive archived files, the etiquette for the group, etc. Take note of these items.

How to unsubscribe to a list (using ALTLEARN as an example)

1. When you are ready to leave the list you need to unsubscribe by sending mail to the listserv address:
   Listserv @ SJUVM.BITNET
2. Leave the subject line BLANK.
3. In the body of the text:
   Signoff ALTLEARN
   or
   Unsub ALTLEARN

Figure 13.15. Above are instructions for subscribing (and unsubscribing) to listservs. Source: Cheryl Wissick, "On-Ramp to the Information Highway," *TAM Newsletter*, 9 (February 1994), p. 7. Reprinted courtesy of the Council for Exceptional Children.

gram, part of **The Virtual English Language Center** that provides online resources for teachers and students of English as a second language.

The dynamic duo, Annette Lamb and Larry Johnson (The University of Southern Indiana), in their series of lively presentations, identified Internet sources by K-12 subjects. For **archaeology** try Telneting to the National Archeological Database (cast.uark.edu; login: nadb) and subscribing to MUSEUM-L@unmvma.bitnet and to ARCH-L@dgogwdg1.bitnet. Obtain data to enhance **African-American studies** by gophering to NYSER-Net/Special Col: Empire Schoolhouse/Academic Wings/

SS/Black Studies. Download lesson plans and other resources pertaining to **history** by gophering to AskERIC or to ra.msstate.edu (subdirectory: doc/history), and interact with others on NewsGroups (e.g., alt.war.civil.usa; soc.history). Gopher to ERIN to explore **environmental conservation**. Practice **foreign languages** by exchanging email over KidsSphere-request@vms.cis.pitt.edu, and by subscribing to listservs (MCLR-L@smu.bitnet, MEXICO-L@tecmtyvm.bitnet, EC@indycms.bitnet. Download **literature** by FTP from ftp mrcnext.cso.uiius.edu, subdirectory: pub/etext92. Obtain **popular music** lyrics by FTP from ftp cs.uwp.edu, subdirectory: pub/music. Study **space exploration** by Telneting to NASA Space-Link (Spacelink.msfc.nasa.gov) and to SpaceMet. phast.umass (and read *USA Today* while you're here), and by FTPing the NASA Archives (Ames.arc.nasa.gov).

Larry Johnson (ljohnson.ucs@smtp.usi.edu) emailed to me the following two sets of listservs, "one for **educators in general** and another for **media technology types** (techies)," from the book he co-authored with Annette Lamb (aclamb.ucs@smtp.usi.edu), *Cruisin' the Information Highway: Internet & the K–12 Classroom* (Evansville, IN: Vision To Action, 1995). Some I have listed elsewhere, but I want to preserve the integrity of each contributor's recommendations.

Listservs of Interest to Educators in General

Name(Topic)	Address
AATG (Amer. Assoc. of Teachers of German)	listserv@indycms.iupui.edu
ADA-LAW (Americans with Disabilities Act)	listserv@vm1.nodak.edu
AERA-C (ednl. research & learning)	listserv@asuvm.inre.asu.edu
AAHESGIT (Amer. Assoc. of Higher Ed.)	listserv@gwuvm.gwu.edu
ALTLEARN (alternative approaches to learning)	listserv@sjuvm.stjohns.edu
AMLIT-L (American literature)	listserv@mizzou1.missouri.edu
AMWEST-H (American Western history)	listserv@vm.usc.edu
BGRASS-L (Intl. Bluegrass Music Assoc.)	listserv@ukcc.uky.edu
BIOPI-L (biology, science education)	listserv@ksuvm.ksu.edu
BLUES-L (blues music)	listserv@brownvm.brown.edu
CATALYST (Journal for Community College)	listserv@vtvm1.cc.vt.edu
CFRNET-L (educ./corp./foundation partnerships)	jwmosser@mtu.edu (moderator)
CHANGE (change and leadership)	majordomo@mindspring.com
CSRNOT-L (Center for the Study of Reading)	listserv@vmd.cso.uiuc.edu
CTI-L (computers in teaching)	listserv@irlearn.ucd.ie
CYE-L (children, youths, environment)	ssi@cunyvms1.gc.cuny.edu (info)
DANCE-L (folkdances, choreography)	listserv@hearn.nic.surfnet.nl
DTS-L (Dead Teachers Society)	listserv@iubvm.ucs.indiana.edu
ECENET-L (children, birth to age 8)	ericeece@ux1.cso.uiuc.edu
EDAD-L (school administration)	listserv@wvnvm.wvnet.edu
EDLAW (law and education)	listserv@ukcc.edu
EDPOL-D (governmental policies)	EDPOL-D-request@scholastic.com
EFLIST (environmental education)	eflist-request@htbbs.com
ERL-L (educational research)	listserv@asuvm.inre.asu.edu
FLTEACH (foreign language instruction)	listserv@ubvm.cc.buffalo.edu
FUTURE-L (futures/forecasting)	listserv@bitnic.educom.edu
FROGPROF (Am. As. of Teachers of French)	listserv@bitnic.educom.edu

GIFTEDNET-L (gifted education)	listserv@listserv.cc.wm.edu
GRANTS-L (NSF grants)	listserv@jhuvm.hcf.jhu.edu
GYMN (gymnastics)	rack@athena.mit.edu (moderator)
HISTORYA (history discussion)	listserv@uwavm.u.washington.edu
IECC (teachers seeking keypals for students)	IECC-REQUEST@stolaf.edu
IMSE-L (math & science education)	listserv@uicvm.cc.uic.edu
INFED-L (computers in the classroom)	listserv@ccsun.unicamp.br
JAZZ-L (jazz music)	listserv@brownvm.brown.edu
K12ADMIN (K–12 educational admin.)	listserv@suvm.acs.syr.edu
KIDS-ACT (K–12 projects)	listserv@vm1.nodak.edu
KIDLINK (announcements)	listserv@vm1.nodak.edu
KIDSNET (global network for children)	KIDSNET-request@vms.cis.pitt.edu
KIDSPHERE (intl. communications in ed.)	KIDSphere-request@vms.cis.pitt.edu
LD-LIST (learning disabilities)	LD-List-request@east.pima.edu
LEARNING (child-centered learning)	LEARNING-request@sea.east.sun.com
L-HCAP (issues about people with disabilities)	listserv@vm1.nodak.edu
LITERACY (adult education/literacy)	listserv@nysernet.org
LRNASST (learning assistance issues)	listserv@arizvm1.ccit.arizona.edu
MIDDLE-L (middle school education)	listserv@vmd.cso.uiuc.edu
MULTIAGE (multiage schooling)	catchley@mail.coin.missouri.edu (info.)
MUSIC-ED (music education & research)	listserv@vm1.spcs.umn.edu
NEWEDU-L (new paradigms in education)	listserv@vm.usc.edu
OUTDOOR-ED (outdoor education issues)	listserv@latrobe.edu.au
ROADMAP (online class about Internet issues)	listserv@ua1vm.va.edu
SCHOOL-L (early childhood education)	listserv@irlearn.ucd.ie
SFLOVERS (science fiction literature)	SF-Lovers-request@rutvm1.rutgers.edu
SNAP (School Nature Area Project)	SNAP-request@stolaf.edu
STARnet (Students At Risk Network)	listsproc@services.dese.state.mo.us
STLHE-L (Society of Teaching & Higher Ed.)	listserv@unbvm1.csd.unb.ca
STUMPERS-L (reference questions/sharing)	mailserv@crf.cuis.edu
TEACHEFT (teaching effectiveness)	listserv@wcupa.edu
TEACH-L (classroom dynamics/teaching)	listserv@uicvm.cc.uic.edu
TEACHMAT (methods of teaching math)	listserv@uicvm.cc.uic.edu
TECHED-L (technical ed., employment)	listserv@psuvm.psu.edu
TESL-EJ (TESOL E-Journal)	listserv@cmsa.berkeley.edu
THINK-L (critical thinking)	listserv@umslvma.umsl.edu
TIMS-L (Teaching Integrated Math & Science)	listserv@uicvm.cc.uic.edu
VOCNET (vocational education)	listserv@cmsa.berkeley.edu
WRITERS (aspiring & professional)	listserv@vm1.nodak.edu

Listservs for Media Specialists

Name (Topic)	Address
AECT-L (Assoc. for Ed. Com. & Tech.)	listserv@wvnvm.wvnet.edu
AAIM-L (Assoc. for Applied Multimedia)	AAIM-L-request@citadel.edu
AMTEC (Assoc. for Media & Tech.)	listproc@camosun.bc.ca

ASAT-EVA (distance learning)	listserv@unlvm.unl.edu
AXSLIB-L (disability access to libraries)	listserv@juvm.stjohns.edu
CGE (computer graphics education)	listserv@vm.marist.edu
COLICDE (distance ed. research bulletin)	colicde-request@unixg.ubc.ca
CNI-Copyright (intellectual property)	listproc@cni.org
DEOS-L (distance education)	listserv@psuvm.psu.edu
DEOSNews (Dist. Ed. Online Symposium Jrnl.)	listserv@psuvm.psu.edu
DIGVID-L (digital video)	listserv@ucdavis.edu
DISTED (Online J. of Dist. Ed. & Commun.)	listserv@uwavm.u.washington.edu
EASI (adaptive computing issues)	listserv@sjuvm.stjohns.edu
EDNET (educational potential of the Internet)	listproc@nic.umass.edu
EDTECH (K–12 focus on educ. tech.)	listserv@msu.edu
ED2000-PILOT (instructional systems)	mailbase@mailbase.ac.uk
EDUCOM-W (tech. & ed. women's issues)	listserv@bitnic.educom.edu
EDUPAGE (Info. Tech. News Summary)	listproc@educom.edu
EDUTEL (educ. & info. technologies)	comserve@vm.its.rpi.edu
EUITLIST (ednl. uses of info. tech.)	euitlist@bitnic.educom.edu
GOPHERJEWELS (*Gopher* resources)	listproc@einet.net
HOTT (Hot Off The Tree list) Excl. your name.	listserv@ucsd.edu
INCLASS (using the Internet in class)	listproc@schoolnet.carleton.ca
INFOBITS (Inst. for Acad. Tech.'s Elist)	listserv@gibbs.oit.unc.edu
INTCOLED (intl. collab. of Internet ed.)	listserv@ist01.ferris.edu
IPCT-L (Interpersonal Cmptg. & Tech. E-Jrnl)	listserv@guvm.ccf.georgetown.edu
ITD-TOC (Info. & Tech. for Disabled Jrnl.)	listserv@sjuvm.stjohns.edu
I-TECH (instructional technology)	listproc@educom.edu
ITFORUM (instructional tech.)	listserv@uga.cc.uga.edu
ITFS-L (Instr. TV Fixed Service)	maiser@enm.uma.maine.edu
ITTE (info. tech. & teacher ed.)	listserv@deakin.oz.au
JTE-L (J. of Tech. in Ed.)	listserv@vtvm1.cc.vt.edu
LABMGR (student access to computing)	listserv@ukcc.uky.edu
LIBADMIN (library admin./management)	listserv@umab.umd.edu
LM_NET (school library media centers)	listserv@suvm.syr.edu
MCJRNL (J. of Acad. Media Librarianship)	listserv@ubvm.cc.buffalo.edu
MEDIA-L (ednl. media, instrnl. materials)	listserv@bingvmb.cc.binghamton.edu
MEDIALIB (media services in libraries)	listserv@cfrvm.cfr.usf.edu
MMEDIA-L (multimedia instruction)	listserv@itesmvf1.rzs.itesm.mx
NET-HAPPENINGS (Internet resources)	listserv@is.internic.net
PHOTO-L (photo equip. & techniques)	listserv@buacca.bu.edu
POD-L (Prof. & Orgnznl. Devel. Netwk)	listserv@lists.acs.ohio-state.edu
PUBS-IAT (Inst. for Acad. Tech. Newsl.)	listserv@gibbs.oit.unc.edu
SATEDU-L (satellite/distance educ.)	listserv@mainvm.wcupa.edu
SIGTEL-L (ISTE telecom. group)	SIGTEL-L@unmvma.unm.edu
STAFF-DEVELOPMENT (in higher ed.)	mailbase@mailbase.ac.uk
TECH-ED (technology education)	tech-ed-request@fre.fsu.und.edu
TECHNET (technical support staff)	listserv@acadvm1.uottow.ca
TIPSHEET (computer help)	listserv@wsuvm1.csc.wsu.edu
VIDEOLIB (video library collect./access)	listserv@library.berkeley.edu
VIDEOPRO (video production and oper.)	listserv@uxa.ecn.bgu.edu
VIRTU-L (virtual reality)	listserv@vmd.cso.uiuc.edu

Lamb & Johnson also have prepared a four-part series of **videos**, *Educators Guide to the Internet*, that is available from RMI Media Productions, Inc. (1-800-745-5480; rmimedia@aol.com). Titles are: *Cruisin' the Information Highway; Findin' On-Ramps and Gettin' Up to Speed; Gophers, Armadillos, and other Internet Critters: Getting Started with Internet Tools; Surfin' the Web and Beyond: Expanding your Internet Skills*. The Association for Educational Communications and Technology (1-202-347-7834; aect@aect.org) also carries such titles as *Interacting with Internet* and *Access to Data Networks*. Wentworth Worldwide Media (1-800-638-1639; connect@wentworth.com) has *The Amazing Internet, Internet Email, Searching the Internet*, and *Discovering the World Wide Web*. Master Communications Group, Inc. (1-800-862-6164; 1-612-835-6164) carries *Future Schools, Connected to the World* and *Get Ready, Get Set, Go-ONLINE*. Also consider Desktop Solutions' *CyberWISE* Internet Educational Software (1-408-354-9492; desktop-solutions@batnet.com; http://www.cyberwise.com). Its "School Pack" includes a teacher's guide, "rules and behavior standards for student Internet use," and interactive software titles ranging from *How to Get Started on the Internet* to *How to Use the World Wide Web*.

To search the **video and film catalogs** of several universities, Lamb & Johnson suggested that we *Gopher* to thorplus.lib.purdue.edu and follow path: 9. Purdue University Libraries/ 7. Media Service Items. Then take a look at each of the following options: 1. Media Availability Search Instructions; 2. Search Media availability; 6. Media Catalogs. . . ; and 10. Public Broadcasting Service (PBS) gopher.

The **Association for Educational Communications and Technology's gopher**, administered by Mike Albright (Iowa State University, mikealbr@iastate.edu), may be reached by pointing your gopher to sunbird. usd.edu 72 (or use the URL address: gopher://sunbird. usd.edu:72/1). Here you will find a gold mine of information about media and technology, including Don Descy's **listservs related to education**.

Note that all addresses are subject to change, but that trails often are left at original sites. The following (pp. 279–282) URLs worked for me in November 1995, sometimes after several attempts and at different times of day. In several cases it was necessary for me to trim the URL back to the com, org, edu, or country host extension to relocate destinations.

Don Descy (descy@vax1.mankato.msus.edu; Mankato State University) invited us to access his *Tech Trends*, **"All Aboard the Internet"** columns via his home page: http://www.lme.mankato.msus.edu/ded/don.html). He also recommended the following two, regularly updated, "cutting edge useful" **Web sites**:

Internet Resources for Educators
(http://www.lme.mankato.msus.edu/sites.html)

Developing WWW Home Pages
(http://www.lme.mankato.msus.edu/ded/int.html)

Mary Kathleen Flynn, in "Web Sites for Cybernauts," *U.S. News & World Report*, 119 (July 10, 1995), p. 50, listed the following as the **most frequently accessed World Wide Web sites** (reprinted with permission, Copyright, 1995, *U.S. News & World Report*):

Netscape (http://www.netscape.com) is the home page of the popular Web browser; it lists "What's Cool."
Yahoo! (http://www.yahoo.com) is a key word based WWW search engine.
ESPNet (http://espnet.sportszone.com) provides news, stats, and chat; updated daily.
InfoSeek (http://www.infoseek.com) is a tool for searching news wires, computer magazines, and company profiles (fees apply).
Pathfinder (http://www.pathfinder.com) provides daily news and articles from Time Warner magazines.
Playboy has photos, features, and articles.
HotWired (http://www.hotwired.com) includes cultural critiques and computer rumors.
Microsoft (http://www.microsoft.com) provides information about software and permits downloading upgrades.
Silicon Graphics (http://www.sgi.com) makes available games and graphics.
Lycos (http://www.lycos.com) is a registry of Web sites that is updated weekly.

Other **"useful and fun"** WWW sites described by Ms. Flynn include:

Virtual Tourist II (http://wings.buffalo.edu/world/vt2) has maps of major cities, and travel information, and even speaks the languages.
CyberKids (http://www.mtlake.com/cyberkids) is an online illustrated magazine written by and for children.
c:/net online (http://www.cnet.com) has computer product reviews written by John C. Dvorak, plus transcripts of the "c:/net central" TV show and downloadable shareware.

Add to these the **Web Window Shopping** sites from *PC Computing*, 8 (July 1995), p. 277.

Bibliobytes (http:/bb.com) is for book lovers.
CyberMall (http://199.171.5.200/CyberMall.html) provides links to cybermarkets.
CyberSource's Software.Net (http://software.net) is a discount source.
Internet Plaza (http://plaza.xor.com) has links to other malls.
Online Computer Market (http://www.ocm.com) has sales and consultants.

From Thomas Forbes, **"The 50 Best Web Sites,"** *Net-Guide*, 2 (September 1995), pp. 40-52, the following especially may be of interest to educators.

The Ultimate Band List (http://american.recordings.com/wwwofmusic/ubl/ubl.shtml)
FedWorld Information Network (http://www.fedworld.gov)
MIT's Media Lab (http://www.media.mit.edu)
Voyager Co. (http://www.voyagerco.com)
Kids on Campus (http://www.tc.cornell.edu/Kids.on.Campus)
Usenet FAQs (http://www.cis.ohio-state.edu/hypertext/faq/usenet)
Clearinghouse for Subject-Oriented Internet Resource Guides (http://www.lib.umich.edu/chhome.html)
BookWire (http://www.bookwire.com)
Today.Com (http://www.today.com)
Net-happenings (http://www.mid.net/NET)
Time's **Pathfinder** (http://www.pathfinder.com)

John Barnard (Arizona State University, john.barnard@asu.edu) shared with me the following annotated **WWW site URLs of special interest to educators.** I'm sure he has found more since, so tell him Steve sent ya.

Yahoo (http://www.yahoo.com/Education) is a guide to the WWW, a great place to start finding all sorts of Net resources on education.
AskEric (http://ericir.syr.edu) provides access to the ERIC databases and a great collection of lesson plans.
The Virtual Tourist (http://wings.buffalo.edu/world) is a geographic directory of WWW servers.
EdWeb (http://edweb.cnidr.org:90) enables us to hunt down online educational resources, and learn about trends in education policy and information infrastructure development.
Web 66 (http://web66.coled.umn.edu) is dedicated to helping integrate Web technology into the K–12 curriculum.

Media Literacy Project (http://interact.uoregon.edu/MediaLit/HomePage) has resources to help students develop critical thinking skills about media.
The Internet Educational Resources Guide (http://www.dcs.aber.ac.uk/~jjw0/index_ht.html) is the perfect starting point for finding useful material on the Net [assuming you can find a ~ (tilde) and a _ on your keyboard and know the difference between o and 0].
Internet Film and Video Resource Guide (http://http2.sils.umich.edu/Public/fvl/film.html) is a very useful media resource for educators. Drop the extensions after "Public" to locate a broader range of resources.
Public Broadcasting Service (PBS) Home Page (http://www.pbs.org) is a good starting point for finding PBS programs and videoconferences.
C-SPAN (Cable-Satellite Public Affairs Network) (gopher://c-span.org) has broadcast schedules and liberal copyright policy for educators.
Library of Congress (http://lcweb.loc.gov/homepage/lchp.html) has a wealth of offerings from the nation's library, including digitized historical collections (American Memory).
The White House (http://www.whitehouse.gov) lets us send messages to the President and Vice-President, as well as access publications of the executive branch of government.
THOMAS: Legislative Information on the Internet (http://thomas.loc.gov) provides the latest news from the U.S. Congress, addresses, and full text of legislation and of the *Congressional Record* (both searchable by keywords).
Le Web Louvre (http://mistral.enst.fr) takes us to France for a perfect entry point to the world's art online.
NASA (http://www.nasa.gov) is a gateway to information on U.S. space endeavors and links to a variety of science education sources.
U.S. Department of Education (http://www.ed.gov) has guides to grants and government information on education.

Rita Laws, "Finish Your Degree Online," *Online Access*, 10 (October 1995), pp. 63–66, provided descriptions of Internet sources of information about **distance education** including:

The Distance Education Clearinghouse (gopher://gopher.uwex.edu:70/11/distanceed)
Los Angeles County Office of Education (http://teams.lacoe.edu)
The Open University (http://acs-info.open.ac.uk)
Peterson's Education Center (http://www.petersons.com)

Favorite **WWW sites** of Blacksburg Middle School teachers Suzan Mauney and Donna Swenson (Thomas M. Sherman, "Teaching with the Whole World Watching," *MultiMedia Schools*, 2 [September/October 1995], p. 46) include:

Kidscom (http://www.kidscom.com) describes Internet projects for children such as finding keypals, posing questions, and posting messages.
KidsWeb (http://www.npac.syr.edu/textbook/kidsweb) is a collection of Web sites containing information of interest to K–12 students.
Montgomery County Multimedia Magazine (http://www.bev.net/schools/bms/mcmmm/MCMMMHome.html) is an ambitious project by their eighth grade students.
NASA K–12 Internet Initiative (http://quest.arc.nasa.gov) provides guidance in productive use of the Internet for learning.
WebCrawler (http://www.webcrawler.com) is a search tool that identifies sites based on topics you select.
Scholastic (http://scholastic.com) has curriculum guides, projects, and libraries.

Additional **WWW sites** of interest to K–12 educators appeared in *Internet World*, 6 (October 1995), as follows:

iWorld Web (http://www.iw.com)
The Awesome Lists
(http://www.clark.net/pub/journalism/awesome.html)
Berit's Best Sites for Children
(http://www.cochran.com/theosite/ksites.html)
Canada's SchoolNet (http://schoolnet2.carleton.ca)
KidLink (http://www.kidlink.org)
Newton's Apple (http://ericir.syr.edu/Newton/welcome.html)
Online Educator
(http://www.cris.com/~felixg/OE/OEWELCOME.html)
OSC Young Person's Guide to the Internet
(http://www.osc.on.ca/kids/kids.html)
TENET Web (http://www.tenet.edu/education/main.html)

Other sites from a variety of sources are:

The Discovery Channel (http://www.discovery.com) is billed as a "gateway to exploration and adventure."
The List of Free Computer-Related Publications
(http://www.soci.niu.edu/~huguelet/TLOFCRP)
Heartland AEA 11 Home Page
(http://www.aea11.k12.ia.us/Welcome.html)
Ontario Science Centre (http://www.osc.on.ca
Cornell Theory Center (http://www.tc.cornell.edu)
Penn State Media Database
(http://www.libraries.psu.edu/avs) is a good source of videos for rent.

ArtsEdNet (http://www.artsednet.getty.edu) caters especially to those interested in "discipline-based art education."
Top Ed Sites (http://www.pointcom.com) provides reviews of education-related Web sites.
VideoMaker (http://www.videomaker.com) gives information about video production.
WWLib (http://www.scit.wlv.ac.uk/wwlib) is a catalog of web pages at sites in the United Kingdom; indexed both by topics and keywords.

Keeping up to date with Internet developments is made easy (read *gratis* weekly on your screen) by subscribing to the above-mentioned ***Scout Report.*** Listed below are some of the **Internet (and its Web) sites** described in this weekly electronic newsletter. *(Copyright Susan Calcari, 1995. The InterNIC provides information about the Internet and the resources on the Internet to the US research and education community under a cooperative agreement with the National Science Foundation: NCR-9218742. The Government has certain rights in this material. Any opinions, findings, and conclusions or recommendations expressed in this publication are those of the author(s) and do not necessarily reflect the views of the National Science Foundation, AT&T, or Network Solutions, Inc.)*

Global Schoolhouse (http://gsn.org/gsn/ambassadors.info.html) describes the duties and benefits of becoming a Student Ambassador, one who "positively supports the concept of building the 'Global Schoolhouse.' Duties would include: discovering and describing the ways the Internet can improve the learning environment; assisting other students, teachers, parents and your local community in learning about the Internet; demonstrating positive global 'netiquette' by learning about and respecting the cultures of people around the world; demonstrating the collaboration and 'team building' potential of using technology; and sharing your experiences with the news media and the public."

WebEd K12 Curriculum Links (http://badger.state.wi.us/agencies/dpi/www/WebEd.html) connects with school sites that have been "evaluated as using structured criteria, as librarians are trained to do. The goal of the project is to serve those who are trying to apply the wonders of the . . . Web to enrich their school's curriculum. The site owner . . . aims to make the page the 'most valuable list of evaluated K–12 sites in the Universe.'"

The Roadmap Internet Training Workshop (gopher://gopher.anes.rochester.edu; or gopher to gopher.anes.rochester.edu) is a free seminar that "will teach you how to send email, join and unjoin mailing lists, perform remote logins, use the Web, FTP, Gopher and much more."

The McKinley Internet Directory (http://www.mckinley.com/about.html) is an "on-line directory of described, rated and reviewed Internet resources. [It] presents both star ratings and detailed previews of descriptions right at the first level of searching. A powerful full-text search engine allows users to further refine their searches. The subject categories are hotlinked to provide additional resource selections." Contents are screened to be suitable for children.

CNN Interactive (http://www.cnn.com) "allows users to browse hundreds of stories or to search for specific topics of interest. [It] contains today's news and a news archive stretching back . . . several years. . . . [and] has images, sounds, and video. . . ."

The National Information Infrastructure Advisory Council (http://niiac-info.org/~niiac) was brought into being by President Clinton's 1993 Executive Order. Representatives from "private industry; state and local governments; community, public interest, education, and labor groups; creators and distributors of content; privacy and security advocates; and leading experts in NII-related fields" were appointed in 1994 to serve on this advisory panel. Yes, the Information Superhighway is much larger than the Internet, its World Wide Web, and commercial online services. It includes telephone and TV cable industries, and others still on the drawing boards. Watch how these multitudes of diverse agencies interact by checking out this site.

To these, add the following **Web sites primarily of interest to educational technology and media specialists,** from Gary Ferrington (garywf@oregon.uoregon.edu), who not only surfs Webs, he spins them as well (i.e., the above-mentioned ambitious Media Literacy Project).

The CineMedia Site
(http://www.gu.edu.au/gwis/cinemedia/CineMedia.home.html) at Griffith University, Australia, provides documents and links to other sources of information about radio, film, multimedia, etc.

Job Searching on the Web
(http://interact.uoregon.edu/MediaLit/FC/WFAEEmployment) is a comprehensive gateway to job searching and position announcements.

Instructional Technology Resources
(http://interact.uoregon.edu/MediaLit/HomePage) is a gateway to instructional technology resources on the Web for use by students and others interested in the field. The Media Literacy Data Base includes **periodic updates to reference and resource sections of this book** (the one in your hands).

Please note that all addresses are subject to change. The above are suggestive of what may be found, and the sources may be relied upon for regularly updated information.

Study Items

1. Describe evolution and features of the Internet.
2. Compare and contrast features of America Online, Prodigy, CompuServe, etc.
3. In what ways do commercial online services ease access to information?
4. Describe features of the World Wide Web. Which might you find of most benefit to you and to your students?
5. What sorts of technical computer skills facilitate effective use of online services?
6. How would you prepare your students **academically** for efficient, productive research using computer-mediated communications?
7. Describe two different meanings for the phrase **"disciplined inquiry."**
8. Critically evaluate commercial online services and the Internet in the context of schooling.
9. List benefits of access to the "information superhighway" for people having limited mobility due to illness or long-term disability.
10. Elaborate on the "teenage" (*et al.*!) lament "Sometimes I feel that paper is the only thing that will listen to me." in light of computer-mediated global telecommunications.
11. How would you go about convincing your school district to invest in **computer networking of schools** and libraries with each other and with the Internet?
12. Outline the procedures for subscribing and unsubscribing to a listserv.
13. Describe some information superhighway features and resources that might complement those you currently are using in the classroom.
14. How would you evaluate your students' use of computer-mediated communications?
15. What values do you see in schools creating their own World Wide Web home pages?

Suggested Activities

1. Select at least one commercial online service, sign up, and explore its features. Beware of extra charges for "premium services" and telephonic communications, but note that my first month of local number access to three services added just $13 to my phone bill for 125 calls, many lasting from two to three hours.
2. Gain access to the Internet and begin exchanging email among friends and colleagues. Put your TCP/IP on your business card.
3. Explore options for wiring your school to the Internet.
4. Subscribe to several of the listservs listed above and share results with your class.
5. Obtain some documents using a series of messages sent via *GopherMail.*

6. Explore "cyberspace" using *Gopher* and download files with FTP.

7. Find some lesson plans using the search capabilities of *VERONICA*.

8. Use bookmarks to locate places in cyberspace related to the subject you teach.

9. Use Uniform Resource Locator codes to take you to Web sites that may be of interest to your students.

10. Arrange with a classmate for an online chat. At an agreed upon time, you type the command **talk** followed by a space and your classmate's Internet address (e.g., **talk slh4672@is2.nyu.edu**). Your classmate will receive instructions to reply using the same format (e.g., **yourid@yourhost name**). While chatting, it helps to indicate each time you end a message so the other person knows when to begin responding. End chat with a "control-c" keyboard combination.

11. Extend the above activity by locating a stranger currently online. After the **finger** command, type the address of a known host computer (e.g., **finger @is.nyu.edu**). Stop screen scrolling with control-s; resume with control-q. Write down some inviting user addresses and proceed with **talk**. Since this is intrusive, make your peaceful intentions clear from the start (e.g., I'm new to the Internet. Would you be willing to chat with me for a few minutes?).

12. Try the **finger** command with a variety of institutional addresses (e.g., nasanews@space.mit.edu; copi@oddjob. uchicago.edu).

13. Design and produce your own WWW home page.

14. Design a multifaceted (e.g., products, performances, portfolios—the "3 p's") evaluation of students' engagement in cyberspace-based learning activities.

15. Find new editions and related titles of books listed above by checking "author" and "subject" volumes of *Books in Print*. Copies of this reference are available in libraries and bookstores and, for a fee, over CompuServe. Also try the Library of Congress online catalog over the Internet. Share results with classmates and me.

16. Please inform me of errors and omissions in this chapter via hackbarths@aol.com. Provide your email (or snail-mail) address and I'll send you corrections and updates to this book.

Educational Technology

Part III. Postscript

Epilogue

The emergence of **educational technology** comes at an opportune time. The arms race among superpowers has subsided, but ethnic and ideological struggles have intensified. The economies of industrialized nations continue to grow, but the Third World is falling deeper in debt and its population is soaring. Starvation and disease, compounded by illiteracy, threaten entire nations. Countless millions of children worldwide are subjected to physical abuse and economic exploitation. The AIDS pandemic threatens to condemn more people to death than all the war casualties in history.

As earth's natural resources become increasingly scarce and spoiled, and the need to provide life rafts across the globe becomes a moral imperative, industrialized nations will not stand immune.

Within this context of increasing demands upon resources that must be diverted to food production and health care, **efficiency** and **effectiveness** become ever more compelling criteria. Focused as it is upon demonstrated achievement at reasonable costs, **educational technology** is responsive within this context.

Educational technology has drawn selectively upon arts and sciences to craft effective programs. **Fidelity** of visual and audio reproduction is fast approaching "virtual reality." **Accuracy** of content is ever more ensured by close collaboration among experts having **ready access** to information and each other. Field testing, data collection, and revision make programs more **responsive** to the groups they serve. Interactive learning environments **individualize** the pursuit of knowledge, and communications media ensure **wide distribution** at **low cost**.

Computer-based learning rivals that guided by teachers. Mass production of hardware and software brings multimedia into the reach of every classroom. Even Third World nations can adapt the best software in response to local needs, within constraints of available resources, in accord with community values. The media may change—from computers to radio scripts, print materials, and tutors—but the essential **proven integrity** of programs can be preserved.

Given the urgent need to address severe problems facing the world today, it might be considered an idle luxury to critique any approach that is making substantial contributions. We desperately need competent people to invent new sources of power, to discover cures for killer diseases, and to negotiate lasting peace. To the extent that competence is comprised of **demonstrable gains in knowledge and skill**, educational technology has much to offer.

In such troubled times, it may well be a luxury to suggest that **aims of education aspire beyond the development of competence**. Over two decades ago, in the first draft of this book, George Kneller and I did so when we proposed that:

> The moral and intellectual heritage of our civilization consists in large part of inexact knowledge, values, and works of art and thought. Such content is learned better through the active inquiry of students, guided and encouraged by teachers, than through submission exclusively to packaged programs. When students and teachers collaborate, education becomes more than the transmission and reception of information. It becomes a meeting of persons, in which teachers personalize knowledge, bringing it to life in their own ways, and students appropriate knowledge from their teachers and other sources, using it in such a way that it both reflects and contributes to growth of their personality.

To claim that progress toward achievement of lofty aims might not be subject to measure and that means toward their achievement evolves within human interaction is to claim that educational technology has **inherent** limitations. To the extent that this might be so, we need be concerned by recent intensive efforts to replace public schools with performance-based learning factories.

As you may know, government subsidies in the form of vouchers and private donations have been eagerly sought to finance establishment of private, experimental schools. Unfettered by lofty aims and teacher unions, some such schools focus primarily upon mastery of skills needed by industry to compete in the world marketplace.

On another front, public schools are caving in to pressure to document gains in memorization of subject matter above all else. Achievement test results for each school are printed in local newspapers and rankings of states make headline news. Confronted with intimidation **and** incentives, it is not surprising that teachers and administrators are prone to relinquish what remains of their roles as **educators** to multimedia and computer-managed instructional systems. School boards and legislators, too, have been quick to sell out to performance contractors that promise superior achievement at less cost. **Concern remains only for integrity of the curriculum, not of students.**

Whereas integrity of the **curriculum** relates to validity of content and efficiency of method, integrity of **students** is one of those lofty aims of education. Its essence was expressed eloquently by Henry Wotton in his 1616 poem, **"Those of Integrity."** (Source: This adapted version is from *Singing in the Living Tradition* [Boston: The Unitarian Universalist Association, 1993], p. 135.)

How happy are they, born or taught,
Who do not serve another's will;
Whose armor is their honest thought,
And simple truth their highest skill.

Whose passions not their rulers are;
Whose souls are still, and free from fear,
Not tied unto the world with care
Of public fame or private ear;

Who have their lives from rumors freed,
Whose conscience is their strong retreat,
Whose state no flattery can feed,
Nor ruin make oppressors great.

All such are freed from servile bands
Of hope to rise, or fear to fall;
They rule themselves, but not lands,
And, having nothing, yet hath all.

What, among other things, appears to be lacking in the rush to reorganize education based on models of industry is concern for means by which students may come to ascertain what is **truly** of significance—to them as individuals, and to them as members of the human community. Problems are posed **for** students, rarely **by** them. Learning "deficits" are diagnosed and remediated; distinctive talents and felt needs are overlooked. TV shows, simulation games, and multimedia draw students into passionate pursuit of answers to important questions, of solutions to problems of global consequence. In the process, students "discover" treasure stores of information.

But I wonder if, in this harried process, students are **robbed of their integrity**. Do they get wholly caught up in the games of materialism and status, or other people's causes, without having been given sufficient opportunity to reflect upon alternatives more expressive of **the higher callings of their own distinctive natures**? Do they accept subject matter "discovered" as true based on the force of intimidating media, or **have they appropriated it based on rigorous and imaginative inquiry**? Has success within a system of thoroughly "authentic," performance-based assessment taught them that being unique is a fault, digression is costly, creativity is risky, and challenging norms is fatal?

The tasks of challenging youths to join our common, high endeavors, while fostering their integrity and creativity, surely remain in the larger domain of education. As schools become ever more performance based, multiple regression analyses will serve to identify potent instructional inputs and teachers will be given admonishments and incentives to conform. It will take **courage** and **leadership** for us to reach beyond the tangible, beyond the test, beyond today. To start, I suggest that we:

- **Combat** more vigorously commercial and ideological forces bent on the **demeaning** of youth.

- **Focus on nourishment of distinctive talents**, strengths, cultural backgrounds, felt needs, and interests rather than merely on remediation of "deficiencies."

- **Think always in terms of empowering students** to ensure that they feel greater ownership of classroom activities and take ever more responsibility for their own learning.

- **Engage students** in cooperative and collaborative modes of inquiry that characterize group decision making and formulation of structured knowledge—documentary, empirical, and speculative.

- **Provide easy access** to diverse sources of information, from books and computers to museums and people.
- **Stimulate reflection** upon personal and social values, especially respect for diversity and compassion for all.
- **Enlist cooperation** of student leaders and parents representing diverse segments of the school population.
- **Invite students**, **parents**, and **community leaders** to join with us in the pursuit of **excellence** within the context of **social responsibility**.

The process of educational technology and its products have much to contribute to achievement of high personal and social aims. As parents, teachers, community leaders, and voters, you and I can act to ensure that educational technology and the schools it serves focus ever more wholeheartedly on such worthy aims.

The Educational Technology Start-up Checklist

❏ **Join two or more professional organizations.**

American Educational Research Association: 1-202-223-9485; aera@gmu.edu

Association for the Advancement of Computing in Education: 1-804-973-3987; aace@virginia.edu

Association for Supervision and Curriculum Development: 1-800-933-ASCD; 1-703-549-9110; etrc@ascd.org

Association for Educational Communications and Technology: 1-202-347-7834; aect@aect.org

The Association for Educational and Training Technology: London, 071-253-4399, ext. 3276

Council for Exceptional Children, Technology and Media Division: 1-703-620-3660 (voice/TDD); 1-800-845-6232 (voice/TDD)

International Council for Educational Media: 1-407-823-2053; cornell@pegasus.cc.ucf.edu

International Society for Technology in Education: 1-800-336-5191; 1-503-346-4414; iste@oregon.uoregon.edu

Phi Delta Kappa: 1-800-766-1156; 1-812-339-1156; sysop@pdkint.org

❏ **Subscribe to several periodicals.**

Classroom Connect: Your Practical Monthly Guide to Using the Internet and Commercial Online Services: 1-800-638-1639; connect@wentworth.com

Educational Media International: 1-407-823-2053; cornell@pegasus.cc.ucf.edu

Educational Technology: The Magazine for Managers of Change in Education: 1-800-952-BOOK; 201-871-4007

Educational Technology Review: International Forum on Educational Technology Issues and Applications: 1-804-973-3987; aace@virginia.edu

Electronic Learning: The Magazine for Technology & School Change: 1-800-544-2917

Instructor: The Whole Teacher's Handbook: 1-800-544-2917

Internet World: The Magazine for Internet Users: 1-800-573-3062; iwsubs@kable.com

Learning and Leading with Technology: The ISTE Journal of Educational Technology Practice and Policy: 1-800-336-5191; 1-503-346-4414; iste@oregon.uoregon.edu

Macworld: The Macintosh Authority: 1-800-288-6848; macworld@macworld.com

Media & Methods: Educational Products, Technologies & Programs for K−12 School Districts & Universities: 1-215-563-6005

MultiMedia Schools: A Practical Journal of Multimedia, CD-ROM, Online & Internet in K−12: 1-800-248-8466; veccia@well.sf.ca.us

Multimedia World: All Multimedia, All PC: 1-800-766-3294, ext. 205; Jennifer_Carson@pcworld.com

NetGuide: The Guide to Online Services and the Internet: 1-800-829-0421; 1-904-445-4662, ext. 420; crenta@cmp.com

Phi Delta Kappan: 1-800-766-1156; 1-812-339-1156

Teacher Magazine: 1-202-686-0800

Technology & Learning: 1-800-543-4383; 1-415-457-4333; tl2169@aol.com

Tech Trends: For Leaders in Education & Training:
1-202-347-7834; aect@aect.org

T.H.E. (Technological Horizons in Education) Journal:
1-714-730-4011

❏ Obtain lists of publications and products.

AACE: 1-804-973-3987; aace@virginia.edu

Academic Therapy Publications: 1-800-422-7249;
1-415-883-3314

AECT: 1-202-347-7834; aect@aect.org

AERA: 1-202-223-9485; aera@gmu.edu

Agency for Instructional Technology: 1-800-457-4509;
1-812-339-2203

Allyn & Bacon : 1-617-455-1273; 1-800-852-8024

American Association for the Advancement of Science:
1-202-326-6430

American Library Association: 1-800-545-2433

American Newspaper Publishers Association
Foundation: 1-703-648-1000

ASCD: 1-800-933-ASCD; 1-703-549-9110;
etrc@ascd.org

The Bookshelf: 1-800-346-1834; 1-202-686-0800

Continental Press: 1-800-233-0759

Curriculum Associates, Inc.: 1-800-225-0248;
1-508-667-8000

Dale Seymour Publications: 1-800-827-1100;
1-415-324-2800

Educational Products Information Exchange (EPIE)
Institute: 1-516-728-9100

Educational Resources: 1-800-860-9005;
1-708-888-8300

Educational Technology Publications: 1-800-952-BOOK;
201-871-4007

Educators Progress Service, Inc.: 1-414-326-3126

Educators Publishing Service, Inc.: 1-800-225-5750;
1-617-547-6706

Heinemann: 1-603-431-7894

Holt, Rinehart and Winston, Inc.: 1-800-225-5425

Houghton Mifflin Co.: 1-800-758-6762

ISTE: 1-800-336-5191; 1-503-346-4414;
iste@oregon.uoregon.edu

John Wiley & Sons, Inc.: 1-212-850-6000

KIDSNET: 1-202-291-1400

Lawrence Erlbaum Associates: 1-201-666-4110

Libraries Unlimited: 1-800-237-6124; 1-303-770-1220;
dvl@lu.com

Mecklermedia Corp.: 1-800-573-3062; 1-203-226-6967;
info@mecklermedia.com

Modern Curriculum Press: 1-800-321-3106;
1-617-455-1850

The National Audiovisual Center: 1-800-788-6282;
1-301-763-1891

National Council for the Social Studies: 1-202-966-7840,
ext. 121

National Council of Teachers of Mathematics:
1-703-620-9840

National Information Center for Educational Media:
1-800-926-8328; 1-505-265-3591;
tnaccess@technet.nm.org

Nichols Publishing: 1-908-297-2862, or Kogan Page,
U.K.

Online, Inc.: 1-800-248-8466; 1-203-761-1466

O'Reilly & Associates, Inc.: 1-800-998-9938;
1-707-829-0515

Phi Delta Kappa: 1-800-766-1156; 1-812-339-1156

Prentice Hall Computer Publishing: 1-800-428-5331

Scholastic, Inc.: 1-800-541-5513; 1-812-339-1156

Simon & Schuster: 1-800-223-2348

South-Western Educational Publishing:
1-800-824-5179

Troll Books for Schools & Libraries:
1-800-929-TROLL

Waite Group Press: 1-800-368-9369; 1-415-924-2575;
drdrax1@waite.com

Wentworth Worldwide Media: 1-800-638-1639;
1-717-393-1000; connect@wentworth.com

Ziff-Davis Publishing: 1-800-688-0448; 1-510-601-2000;
http://www.ziff.com

❏ Get on discount retailers' mailing lists.

Barnes & Noble: 1-800-242-6657

Computerworks!: 1-800-825-DISK

Compuwest: 1-800-663-0001

Educorp: 1-800-843-9497

Egghead Software: 1-800-EGGHEAD; 1-800-949-3447
(TDD)

MacMall: 1-800-222-2808

MacWarehouse: 1-800-255-6227

The Mac Zone: 1-800-248-0800

Software Marketing Corp.: 1-800-336-0182

PC Connection: 1-800-800-0003 (*PC World*'s "Best Mail
Order Co.")

❑ Connect to the information superhighway.

America Online: 1-800-827-6364 (*Multimedia World's* "Best Online Service")

CompuServe: 1-800-848-8199 (*PC World's* "Best Online Service")

Delphi Internet: 1-800-695-4005

eWorld: 1-800-775-4556; 1-408-974-1236; 1-800-833-6223 (TDD) (Mac & PC)

GEnie: 1-800-638-9636

Global Village Communication: 1-800-736-4821 ("Educate America")

The ImagiNation Network: 1-800-IMAGIN-1

International Discount Telecommunications: 1-800-245-8000 ($15/mo.)

The International Internet Association: 1-202-387-5445

InterNIC Information Services: 1-800-862-0677; 1-908-668-6587

The Microsoft Network: 1-800-386-5550; 1-206-882-8080

National Public Telecomputing Network: 1-216-247-5800; info@nptn.org ("Free-Nets")

Netcom: 1-800-353-6600 (*PC World's* "Best Internet Provider")

NovaNet: 1-800-937-6682 (CBL courseware plus Net access)

Prodigy: 1-800-PRODIGY (1st with the Web; classroom version)

The WELL: 1-415-332-4335

❑ View some videos about educational technology and its products.

AECT: 1-202-347-7834; aect@aect.org

AERA: 1-202-223-9485; aera@gmu.edu

ISTE: 1-800-336-5191; 1-503-346-4414; iste@oregon.uoregon.edu

PC-TV: 1-603-863-9322; 1-415-574-6233; 74774.13@compuserve.com

RMI Media Productions: 1-800-745-5480; rmimedia@aol.com

University of Delaware: 1-302-831-8162; podium@udel.edu

❑ Meditate

upon what it means for students systematically, yet creatively, to construct knowledge of personal and social significance within each academic discipline, and across them holistically, given the human and material resources within your reach.

❑ Please submit questions, comments, and suggestions

to hackbarths@aol.com.

The Computer Literacy
Assessment Tool

Name _____ ☐ M ☐ F

Class _____ Date _____

A. How do you feel about computers?
(Please circle one.)

I hate them.

I don't like them.

I don't care.

I like them.

I love them.

B. How skillful are you in the use of computers?
(Please circle one.)

Novice

Little skill

Moderate skill

Much skill

Expert

C. Please describe your access to computers.

I have no access to computers at home._____

I have access to the following computer(s) at home.

_____

_____

_____

_____

_____

D. For what purposes do you use computers?

1.
2.
3.
4.
5.
6.
7.
8.
9.
10.

E. Please write all the words you know that have to do with computers.

1.	14.	27.
2.	15.	28.
3.	16.	29.
4.	17.	30.
5.	18.	31.
6.	19.	32.
7.	20.	33.
8.	21.	34.
9.	22.	35.
10.	23.	36.
11.	24.	37.
12.	25.	38.
13.	26.	39.

Glossary

Acceptable Use Policy: (AUP) a written agreement among teachers, librarians, students, and parents outlining conditions of Internet use in a school.

Ada: a high-level, structured programming language named after Lady Augusta Ada Byron, a computer scientist.

aliasing: appearance of jagged edges ("jaggies") on computer-generated video images.

analog: signals that vary continuously over a range, rather than in discrete quantities.

anchored instruction: activities designed to foster learning that have direct connections with the challenges of real life outside the classroom.

anonymous ftp: a computer file transfer protocol where one accesses remote sites as an anonymous user (guest).

AppleTalk: a local area network (LAN) standard for linking Apple and Macintosh computers and peripherals.

Archie: (from "archive") a program that permits search of indexes across the Internet for files available for transfer by anonymous FTP.

artificial intelligence: simulation of human thought by computers.

ASCII file: a computer file that consist only of text and such basic formatting characters as spaces and carriage returns.

aspect ratio: ratio of image or screen height to its width.

asynchronous communication: a method of transmitting data bits one after the other, thus permitting use of phone lines (e.g., email).

authentic assessment: an approach to evaluating students' progress on the basis of direct observation of performances and products rather than relying primarily on written tests.

authoring language: a set of natural language computer codes that facilitates crafting of instructional software.

backup: a copy of computer files set aside in case of loss of original.

barcode: a printed pattern of wide and narrow black lines that represent numerical codes.

baud rate: the transmission speed of an asynchronous communications channel; technically refers to number of times per second that switching can occur.

behaviorism: a theory holding that people learn as a consequence of environmental stimuli that follow their actions.

binary number: a string of zeros and ones that represent numerical values such as 0001 for "1" and 0010 for "2."

bit: a single position within a binary number string (binary digit), the smallest unit of information held by computers.

bitmap: a black and white video image made up of dots that correspond to bits of data stored in a computer's memory ("paint format").

BITNET: "Because it's time" wide-area network of academic and research computers.

bookmark: a feature on Web browsers that permits identifying sites for quick access.

boot up: to transfer (load) a program's instructions from storage to a computer's RAM, thereby activating access to its functions.

browser: software (e.g., *Mosaic, NetScape*) that permits access to the World Wide Web.

bug: an error in a computer program's list of instructions.

bulletin board system: (BBS) an electronic database of messages that can be read and to which messages can be added.

bus: internal electronic circuitry of computer, "local" (video circuits and disk drive interfaces connected directly to extension of microprocessor) or "expansion" (leading to slots where components may be connected).

button: a simple graphic image that when addressed by pointing and clicking with a mouse, activates a computer program function (aka "hot button").

byte: a group of digits making up a binary number that represent a single number or character such as 10000001 for "a."

C: a high-level, structured programming language that is popular for its power and flexibility, and for being in the public domain. (AT&T was prohibited from getting copyright, as with its *UNIX*.)

cache memory: section of RAM set aside for frequently needed data or instructions.

CD: short for "compact disk"; plastic disk measuring about 4.75 inches (12 cm) in diameter on which information may be encoded digitally, up to 73 minutes of continuous audio.

CD-ROM: short for "compact disk, read-only memory"; a plastic disk encoded with information that can be accessed by integrated laser light and computer technologies.

CD-XA: an extension of CD-ROM architecture in which textual, audio, and graphic data are stored on a single track to be read at virtually the same time.

central processing unit: the core unit of a computer that interprets instructions, operates on data, and coordinates activities of the entire system.

cobweb site: a long neglected World Wide Web database.

cognitivism: a theory holding that people learn in accord with an "information processing" model that accounts for interactions between what they already know and how this may be interpreted and remembered.

cognitive apprenticeship: immersion of students in the methods of inquiry that characterize the academic disciplines.

collaborative learning: an approach that encourages groups of students to work together toward common ends.

computer: an electronic device capable of storing, processing, and communicating information in accordance with encoded and user-supplied instructions.

communications theory: a description of the process by which messages are transmitted from a source to a destination.

compensatory rivalry: the tendency of people to make special efforts to excel when they become aware that they are engaged in a contest.

computer literacy: knowledge of computer technology and skill in its use.

computer-managed instruction: the electronically-mediated assessment of students' abilities and learning needs, prescription of alternative means to meet these needs, presentation of lessons, and assessment of results.

constructivism: a theory holding that people draw upon what they already have come to know and believe to interpret new experiences in ways that, in some respects, are unique to each individual.

coopetitive learning: an approach that encourages teams of students to collaborate on tasks in competition with other teams.

courseware: software developed for computer-based learning, sometimes more generally applied to other media as well.

cracker: a computer hacker who illegally gains access to computers by figuring out how to circumvent system security.

crash: unintended interruption of a computer program's functioning.

cursor: a line, block, or arrow that indicates the area on a monitor where keyboard or mouse output will occur.

CU-SeeMe: video conferencing software that enables users to interact online.

cybernetics: the study of communications and control systems that incorporate a feedback loop to inform controllers of the effects on a system of their actions; a term coined by Norbert Wiener.

cyberspace: that dimension of reality created by the capabilities of computer and telecommunications circuitry.

database: a collection of related information.

debug: the process of locating errors in the sequence of instructions that comprise a computer program.

delurk: the act of posting a message on a computer BBS after having (properly) lurked about reading the messages of others to get the hang of it.

desktop publishing: use of word processing and graphics software on a microcomputer to produce printed documents, especially newsletters.

dialog box: an on-screen area that poses a question and request input from the user.

digital: representation of data as discrete binary information, thus permitting random access and compression.

dingbats: ornamental characters, like stars and flowers (see Zapf, below).

direct access: a SLIP or PPP telephone line connection to the Internet.

directory tree: a graphical representation of a hard disk drive's directories and subdirectories.

disk drive: a device that spins computer diskettes beneath a magnetic or optical head to obtain or store data.

diskette: a round, flat sheet of plastic coated with iron oxide and encased in either a 3 1/2 inch or 5 1/4 inch envelope for storage and retrieval of data by a computer.

distance education: use of radio and TV broadcast technology, supplemented by print media, to provide lessons to students in their homes or community centers.

documentation: written or online instructions for operating computer hardware or software.

DOS: short for "disk operating system"; an IBM-compatible computer software link between the user and files contained on diskettes; also called "*MS-DOS*" since it is a product of the Microsoft Corporation.

download: to obtain a file from a remote computer.

drag and drop: an editing technique in which blocks of text are moved using a mouse.

education: an inter-human enterprise concerned with preservation and enhancement of human life and culture.

educational technology: aka "instructional technology"; a systematic process involving application of knowledge in the search for replicable solutions to problems inherent in teaching and learning; products of this process.

electronic performance support system: an EPSS is a computerized database that provides interactive guidance in the solution of technical problems.

email: short for "electronic mail"; use of computer networks to transmit messages and data.

emoticon: a sideways face made out of standard ASCII characters, e.g., :-).

encryption: a process in which data are encoded in such a way that special hardware or software is needed to retrieve it.

ergonomics: the study of person/machine interactions with the goal of high productivity without strain.

ERIC: short for "Educational Resources Information Center"; a system of clearinghouses that collect, preserve, organize, and disseminate documents pertaining to education.

EtherNet: a local area computer network standard that permits high-speed sharing (10 million bits per second) of data and programs among over a thousand nodes.

expert system: a computer program that provides interactive access to information needed to solve problems within a given field.

fax: short for "facsimile"; electronic transmission of a document.

FidoNet: a set of data exchange procedures that permits connection of computer bulletin board systems over phone lines.

filter: a program designed to block access to certain sites or terminology found on the Internet.

finger: a *UNIX* command that permits locating people currently logged on to a terminal connected to the Internet.

flame: a derogatory or obscene email message, or heated response to such a message that may erupt into a "flame war."

floppy disk: a removable computer data storage medium enclosed in a plastic cover.

format: electronic preparation of a diskette for use by encoding its magnetic surface with a structure having locations that can be recognized and accessed by a computer program (aka "initialization").

ftp site: an Internet location that permits transfer of files.

gateway: a connection between two networks that have incompatible operating systems.

Gopher: a computer program developed at the University of Minnesota that facilitates searching of Internet resources.

gopher site: a computer connected to the Internet that can be accessed using *Gopher*.

graphic: a still visual that may contain pictures and text, but is distinguished by use of symbols representing the phenomena portrayed.

graphical user interface: a user-friendly computer screen layout that uses icons to represent functions.

hacker: a person who takes great pleasure in learning about and exploring new uses for computer technology.

hacker ethic: a code holding that technical information should be freely accessible to everyone, but should not be altered in such a way as to cause injury or expense to anyone.

handshaking: a process by which electronic devices coordinate the exchange of data.

hard drive: a computer disk drive that contains a stack of disks and multiple reading/recording heads encased in metal to maximize storage capacity, retrieval speed, and reliability.

high definition television: HDTV refers to video formats with resolutions ranging from 655 to 2,125 scanning lines with an aspect ratio of 3 to 5, more like a motion picture than standard television.

hit: the act of accessing a computer file.

hologram: a laser-light-generated, three-dimensional image that appears to be suspended in space.

home page: the first screen viewed when accessing a World Wide Web site.

hotlist: selected World Wide Web sites saved in a browser software file for quick access.

HyperCard: Macintosh computer software that enables user to organize and present related text, graphics, audio and animation.

hyperlearning: use of interactive CD-ROM or World Wide Web (WWW) computer technology to pursue topics of interest.

hyperlink: an electronic connection between a word or icon that appears on the screen and pertinent information stored electronically elsewhere.

hypermedia: magnetic disk and CD-ROM-based collections of textual, graphic, audio, and video information that may be accessed instantly as desired by user, usually by clicking on highlighted words or icons.

HyperTalk: the scripting language used with *HyperCard*.

hypertext: magnetic disk and CD-ROM-based collections of textual information that may be accessed one screen at a time in any desired order, usually by clicking on highlighted words.

Hypertext Markup Language: (HTML) is a set of codes placed in documents so they can be displayed on the World Wide Web.

infobot: an email address that responds automatically to requests for information.

information mapping: a technique refined by Thomas Gilbert that employs marginal notes and blocking of related text and graphics to facilitate readers' comprehension of printed material.

information superhighway: a term used to include telecommunications channels and computer networks connected by phone lines, cables, and satellites.

informative feedback: a response made to a student's performance that reveals to them if they are making progress and provides guidance in doing so.

instruction: a deliberate effort to impart information, attitudes, or skills.

instructional development: a procedural identification and analysis of problems entailed in transmission of knowledge, attitudes, and skills, and the crafting of replicable, cost-effective solutions.

instructional strategy: technique that may be used to capture attention, increase motivation or provide cues to facilitate learning.

instructional systems design: or just ID, the procedural, yet creative, aspect of the instructional development process that is informed by past experience as well as by production and field testing of prototypes.

instructional technology: see "educational technology."

integrated learning system: a term synonymous with "computer-managed instruction," but reflecting current emphasis on the teacher-as-manager of the entire schooling process and the machine-as-integrator of the diverse routine aspects of instruction.

interactive multimedia: computer software programs characterized by user-controlled access to information stored on magnetic diskettes, videodiscs, and CD-ROM.

interactivity: a characteristic of mediated programs pertaining to the extent that student engagement is elicited and, in the case of computers and teachers, the extent to which the program adjusts to student input.

Internet: called a "network of networks," the Internet is a *UNIX*-based system of connectivity among the world's local and wide-area computer networks.

Internet relay chat: real-time (synchronous) computer keyboard communication.

jaggies: term for the jagged edges that appear on computer-generated video images (aka "aliasing").

Kermit: an asynchronous communications protocol that facilitates transmission of computer files over telephone lines.

keypal: a person with whom one corresponds regularly via email.

keyword: a descriptive term used to locate related information electronically.

kilobyte: 2^{10} (1,024) bytes, about half a page of text.

kludge: a technically sloppy solution ("klooj").

learner control: a characteristic of mediated, especially video and computer, programs pertaining to empowerment of students to change pace and content of the presentation.

learner verification: the process of using student achievement to guide program revision.

learning: the process by which organisms acquire information, attitudes, and skills.

light pen: a light-sensitive stylus that permits "drawing" on a computer monitor.

LISP: a high-level programming language used in artificial intelligence research.

listserv: (originally LISTSERV, Don Descy reminds us) an automated system of receiving and sending email messages, usually on a specific topic (aka "mailing list service").

local area network: a group of interconnected microcomputers having access to programs and data on file server and host minicomputers.

local bus: a direct circuit between a computer's cpu and it's video output.

Logo: a structured programming language suitable for teaching children how to control computers rather than the other way around.

logon: to access a computer network, usually by providing a password.

lurk: to read computer bulletin board system messages without making contributions.

mailbot: an email address that responds automatically to requests for information.

mailing list: a topic-oriented email-based bulletin board.

mainframe: a computer that supports many terminals and serves the data storage and processing needs of a large organization.

media: means of transmitting messages.

media literacy: skill in analysis and creation of audiovisual programs.

megabyte: just over one million (2^{20} or 1,048,576) bytes of memory storage space.

megahertz: (MHz) one million cycles per second.

menu: a computer-generated list of options that appears on a monitor.

microcomputer: a computer designed to be self-contained for individual use on a desk top; technically, any computer with its arithmetic-logic unit and control unit on a single microprocessor.

microform: a miniature photographic copy of a printed page on a transparent roll (microfilm) or flat sheet (microfiche) of plastic.

microprocessor: a fingernail-sized chip of silicon containing the electronic circuitry of a computer's central processing unit.

MIDI: acronym for "Musical Instruments Digital Interface," a standard format for musical data that specifies duration, frequency, and tone of a wide variety of sounds.

minicomputer: a computer that can process input from several (about 4–100) terminals simultaneously.

modem: short for "modulator-demodulator"; a device that converts computer digital output into analog signals for telephonic communication and vice-versa.

Mosaic: first in a line of software programs that put a graphical interface on the Internet.

motherboard: the main circuit board of a computer.

mouse: a hand-sized input device that is moved across a surface to direct movement of a computer's cursor across a monitor.

multimedia: magnetic disk and CD-ROM-based collections of related audio and video segments that may be accessed in any order using interactive computer technology.

multiplexing: simultaneous transmission of messages over a single channel.

multitasking: execution of more that one computer program at the same time.

netiquette: informal rules for harmonious coexistence among users of computer network services, especially bulletin boards.

NetWare: a local area network operating system by Novell.

network: a group of computers that are interconnected for the purpose of sharing programs, data, and devices.

newsgroup: a computer bulletin board system devoted to a single topic.

NICEM: short for "National Information Center for Educational Materials"; one of the major producers of databases that list and describe available programs.

node: a point on a local area network that can process data, especially a workstation.

object linking and embedding: a set of standards incorporated into computer software to permit creation of links among documents, and also embedding of documents from one application into those created by another (OLE, "o-lay").

object-oriented graphic: a computer generated image composed of discrete objects that can be manipulated independently.

object-oriented programming: method in which each program element is self-contained, yet may be linked to other elements.

optical character recognition: use of a scanning device to input textual data into a computer.

Pascal: a structured programming language named after Blaise Pascal widely used in the teaching of programming and the development of applications.

Pentium: an Intel microprocessor with over three million transistors on a single chip; its primary innovative feature over the 486 series is the capacity to carry out two instructions simultaneously.

photorealism: the accurate, life-like portrayal of scenes with computer graphics.

pixel: short for "picture element" of a video image, a single dot.

plasma display: computer output in form of energized gas contained between two transparent panels.

plug-and-play: a feature of computer operating systems (e.g., *Windows 95*) that immediately recognizes newly-connected peripherals.

post: to send an email message to a bulletin board or listserv.

programmed instruction: a systematic technique for developing lesson units or written materials in a manner consistent with behavioral theories of learning (especially frequent informative feedback); products of this technique.

programming language: a set of terms, mostly character strings and symbols, that may be combined in various sequences to affect the functioning of computers.

protocol: a set of "handshaking" procedures that two computers must follow to exchange data.

public domain: software that is not copyrighted and thus may be freely used.

QuickTime: a multimedia standard developed by Apple for the integration of sound, animation, and video across all applications; also software for video compression and management of peripherals.

RAM: short for "random access memory," where instructions and data are stored during program operation for quick access by a computer's central processing unit.

raster: the horizontal pattern of lines that constitute a video image.

recontextualize: an effort to restore the multidimensional context from which subject matter has been abstracted, especially through use of multimedia.

Red Book: the first standard format for digital audio on compact discs.

ROM: short for "read-only memory," that portion of a computer's electronic configuration that contains instructions and data that can be accessed, but not modified, by users.

router: a device that handles multiple protocols among networks.

RS-232: industry standard for serial transmission devices (e.g., printers).

scanner: an input device that digitalizes print, barcode, and film images for storage in computer files.

schema: a concept in cognitive psychology used metaphorically to describe a person's mental representation of related information ("conceptual framework").

screen capture: storage on disk of a computer screen display as a text or graphics file.

screen saver: a computer program that shuts down or reduces video output after a period of inactivity.

scripting: a storyboard technique in which visual content of a planned program is described in one column and associated narration is written along with instructions in an adjacent column.

search engine: a software program that permits locating files based on keywords and their combinations.

second-person virtual reality: a computer-generated environment in which one does not become immersed, but views a screen and manipulates controls, as in a flight simulator or video game.

server: a computer devoted to sharing its files and programs with others on the network.

service provider: an organization that enables individuals to connect to telecommunication services.

set-top box: a device used to connect television sets with cable companies.

shareware: copyrighted software that you may test without charge, but if you use, you are expected to pay a fee to the author.

simulation: an abstracted representation of the elements and dynamics of a phenomenon.

smiley: a sideways face constructed out of standard ASCII characters (aka "emoticon").

snail mail: postal service as compared with email.

software: computer programs that provide instructions to operate the hardware.

storyboard: a series of sketches with associated text that trace the audio and visual content of a planned audiovisual program.

structured programming: standards for making computer code sets easier to read and more reliable, partly by avoiding the "spaghetti code" that results from overuse of GOTO statements.

study print: a still picture framed with cardboard containing printed commentary for classroom use.

surrogate travel: simulated movement within a computer-generated environment.

sysop: the system operator responsible for monitoring a computer bulletin board system.

system: a network of interconnected parts functioning under various constraints to achieve specific ends.

System 7: a version of the Apple Macintosh operating system introduced in 1991; it set the standard for graphical user interfaces.

systemic analysis: consideration of the multitude of forces that may be affecting the operation of a system.

systems engineering: a procedural approach to the analysis of problems (gaps between current situation and what is desired) and the knowledge-based synthesis of replicable solutions.

telecommunication: transmission of information between computers.

teleconference: a meeting among individuals a different locations that is mediated by video and telecommunications technologies.

telnet: a program that permits access to remote host computers over the Internet.

telepresence: the sensation of being immersed in a virtual reality environment.

timesharing: simultaneous use of a single, main computer by two or more individuals at remote terminals linked by a network.

topology: the wiring scheme of a network.

Universal Resource Locator: a World Wide Web address.

unzip program: software that expands computer files that previously have been compressed to save disk space or to facilitate transfer.

upload: to send a file to another computer on a network or the Internet.

upper memory area: in IBM compatibles running *DOS*, the RAM between the 640KB limit for conventional memory and 1MB, accessible by such programs as HIMEM.SYS, which comes with *Windows*.

USENET: one of the largest bulletin board systems with thousands of newsgroups covering diverse topics.

VERONICA: a *Gopher* program that permits locating information on the Internet using keywords.

video compression: use of algorithms to store video frames in a way that minimizes amount of disk space occupied (e.g., JPEG, MPEG, DVI, QuickTime).

videodisc: a 12-inch diameter sheet of plastic encoded with audio and visual signals that can be "read" by a laser beam.

video feedback: use of videotape recording and playback to diagnose performance.

videotext: a viewer-controlled, cable television-based information retrieval service.

virtual community: a group of like-minded people who communicate via email and by posting on computer bulletin board systems.

virtual reality: a computer-simulated environment in which a person wearing headgear and gloves and walking on a treadmill, all connected to a computer, can have the sensation of moving about and interacting with that environment.

virus: a computer program that scrambles data, fills disk space, or otherwise interrupts normal functioning of all "infected" units.

visualization: techniques that realistically portray height, depth, width.

visual literacy: skill both in analyzing and creating images.

voice mail: an office communications system that stores telephonic messages as digital files on a computer network.

Vulcan nerve pinch: an awkward combination of keystrokes needed to execute a command.

WAVE file: a Microsoft standard for storing audio data as computer files.

Webmaster: person responsible for updating information on a Web site.

Web site: a home page and links to other files on the World Wide Web.

wetware: neural tissue.

window: a box on a computer screen that provides instructions or other information.

wireless wide-area network: computers equipped with transceivers to interact via radio waves.

World Wide Web: the hypertext/hypermedia dimension of the Internet.

Xmodem: an asynchronous protocol that facilitates error-free transmission of computer files over telephone lines (also Zmodem).

Zapf Dingbats: the decorative graphics developed by the German typeface designer, Herman Zapf (e.g., ☞, ✿, ✓, ❑, ©).

References

America Online, "Computer Dictionary" (a regularly updated online source).

BABEL: A Glossary of Computer Oriented Abbreviations and Acronyms (http://www.access.digex.net/~ikind/babel95c.html, a regularly updated World Wide Web source, e.g., substitute 96a, 96b, or 96c after "babel").

Classroom Connect: Your Practical Guide to Using the Internet and Commercial Online Services (a periodical that provides definitions of terms as they arise).

Dictionary of Computer Words, revised ed. (Boston: Houghton Mifflin, 1995).

Dictionary of Computing, 3rd ed. (New York: Oxford University Press, 1990).

Downing, Douglas, Covington, Michael A., & Covington, Melody Mauldin, *Dictionary of Computer Terms*, 4th ed. (Hauppauge, NY: Barron's Educational Series, 1995).

Dyson, Peter, *The Network Press Dictionary of Networking*, 2nd ed. (San Francisco: SYBEX, 1995).

Feibel, Werner, *Novell's Complete Encyclopedia of Networking* (San Jose, CA: Novell Press, 1995).

Freedman, Alan, *The Computer Glossary: The Complete Illustrated Dictionary*, 7th ed. (New York: American Management Association, 1995).

Gibilisco, Stan, ed., *McGraw-Hill Encyclopedia of Personal Computing* (New York: McGraw-Hill, 1995).

Gookin, Dan, & Wang, Wallace, *Illustrated Computer Dictionary for Dummies*, 2nd ed. (Foster City, CA: IDG Books Worldwide, 1995).

Hansen, Douglas E., *Educational Technology Telecommunications Dictionary with Acronyms* (Englewood Cliffs, NJ: Educational Technology Publications, 1991).

Held, Gilbert, *Dictionary of Communications Technology: Terms, Definitions, and Abbreviations* (New York: Wiley, 1995).

Kelly-Bootle, Stan, *The Computer Contradictionary*, 2nd ed. (Cambridge: The MIT Press, 1995).

Latham, Roy, *The Dictionary of Computer Graphics and Virtual Reality*, 2nd ed. (New York: Springer-Verlag, 1995).

Pfaffenberger, Bryan, *Que's Computer & Internet Dictionary*, 6th ed. (Indianapolis, IN: Que, 1995).

Prodigy Services Company, "Computer Basics Glossary" & "Internet Forum Glossary" (regularly updated online sources).

Reynolds, Angus, & Anderson, Ronald H., *Selecting and Developing Media for Instruction*, 3rd ed. (New York: Van Nostrand Reinhold, 1992), pp. 239–262.

Webster's New World Dictionary of Computer Terms, 3rd ed. (Englewood Cliffs, NJ: Prentice-Hall, 1988).

Computer Hacronyms

When you read popular computing magazines, you frequently will come across such acronyms as those listed below. Many are in such common use among hackers and cybernauts that articles and ads do not spell them out. Though spelling out does not necessarily explain, I found it satisfying to have this clue to meaning. Definitions may be obtained from the references listed in the Glossary of this book and from online commercial and Internet databases. Let me know as you discover new ones.

ADB: Apple desktop bus (Mac interface standard; bus is the internal circuitry)

ADPCM: adaptive differential pulse code modulation (digital wave-form sampling)

ADSL: asynchronous digital subscriber loop (video transmission over phone lines)

AI: artificial intelligence (computer simulation of human thought)

AIFF: audio interchange file format

ALU: arithmetic-logic unit (microprocessor)

ANSI: American National Standards Institute

API: application program interface

APL: *A Programming Language*

ARCnet: Attached Resource Computer network (LAN for IBM compatibles)

ARPA: Advanced Research Projects Agency

ASCII: American Standard Code for Information Interchange ("ask-ee")

ASP: Association of Shareware Professionals

ATM: asynchronous transfer mode

A/UX: Apple *UNIX*

AV I: audio video interleaved

BASIC: *Beginners' All-Purpose Symbolic Instruction Code*

BBS: bulletin board service (or system)

BIND: Berkeley Internet Name Domain

BIOS: basic input/output system (IBM control programs stored in ROM)

BITNet: Because It's Time Network (mostly higher education institutions)

BM: bounced message (email)

BOF: birds of a feather (IRC together)

bps: bits per second (data transmission speed by modem)

CAD: computer-aided design

CADD: computer-aided design and drafting

CAI: computer-assisted instruction

CAM: computer-aided manufacturing

CAV: constant angular velocity (disk drive spin rate is constant)

CBL: computer-based learning

CBT: computer-based training (or testing)

CD-DA: compact disc-digital audio (aka Red Book audio)

CD-I: compact disc interactive

CD-IV: compact disc interactive

CD+G: compact disc plus graphics

CD-ROM: compact disc-read only memory

CD-ROM XA: CD-ROM extended architecture (for audio/video access)

CDTV: Commodore dynamic total vision

CD-XA: CD-ROM extended architecture

CERT: computer emergency response team

CGA: color graphics adaptor

CISC: complex instruction set computing (e.g. as used by Intel's *Pentium*)

CIX:	Commercial Internet Exchange	**DTP:**	desktop publishing
CLV:	constant linear velocity (at reading head of disk drives)	**DUA:**	directory user agent
		DVI:	digital video interactive
CMI:	computer-managed instruction	**EARN:**	European Academic and Research Network
CMOS:	complementary metal-oxide semiconductor (energy-saving chip)	**EBCDIC:**	Extended Binary Coded Decimal Interchange Code (for IBM mainframes)
COBOL:	*COmmon Business Oriented Language*		
cpi:	characters per inch	**EEMS:**	enhanced expanded memory specification
CP/M:	*Control Program for Microprocessors* (operating system for 8-bit PCs)	**EGA:**	enhanced graphics adaptor
CREN:	Corporation for Research and Networking	**EGP:**	exterior gateway protocol
		EISA:	Enhanced (or Extended) Industry Standard Architecture (32-bit) bus
cps:	characters per second		
CPU:	central processing unit	**EFF:**	Electronic Frontier Foundation
CRT:	cathode ray tube	**ELF:**	extremely low frequency emission (magnetic field from electrical appliances)
CSMA/CD:	carrier sense multiple access with collision detection (for LANs)		
CSU:	communications services unit	**Email:**	electronic mail
CWIS:	campus-wide information system	**EMS:**	Expanded Memory Specification (by Lotus/Intel/Microsoft, LIM EMS)
D1:	digital video format		
D2:	digital video format	**ENIAC:**	Electronic Numerical Integrator and Calculator
DA:	desk accessory (set of utility programs)		
DAP:	directory access protocol	**EOF:**	end of file
DARPA:	Defense Advanced Research Projects Agency	**EOL:**	end of line
		EPROM:	erasable programmable read-only memory (not an oxymoron)
DASD:	direct access storage device (auxiliary random access storage, "dayz-dee")		
		EPS:	electronic postal service
DAT:	digital audiotape	**ESDI:**	Enhanced System Device Interface (a standard for hard disk drives)
DBMS:	database management system		
DDE:	dynamic data exchange (for integration of programs)	**FAQ:**	frequently asked questions ("fak")
		FAT:	file allocation table (on disk)
DDN:	Defense Data Network	**FDD:**	fixed disk drive
DEK:	data encryption key	**FDDI:**	fiber distributed data interface
DES:	data encryption standard	*FORTRAN:*	*FORmula TRANslation*
DIF:	data interchange format file	**FTP:**	file transfer protocol
DIP:	document image processing	**GB:**	gigabyte (1000 MB)
DIP:	dual in-line package (plastic casing for chips; two rows of prongs)	**GIGO:**	garbage in, garbage out
		GUI:	graphical user interface ("gooey")
DISA:	Defense Information Systems Agency	**HD:**	hard (disk) drive
DMA:	direct memory access	**HDD:**	high density diskette
DMC:	dynamic motion control	**HDTV:**	high definition television
DNS:	domain name system (for identifying host computers)	**HMA:**	high memory area (the first 64 KB of RAM above 1MB)
DOS:	*Disk Operating System* by Microsoft	**HMD:**	head-mounted display (virtual reality)
dpi:	dots per inch	*HTML:*	*HyperText Markup Language* (used on the World Wide Web)
DRAM:	dynamic random-access memory		
DSA:	directory system agent	**http:**	hypertext transport protocol
DSP:	digital signal processing	**IAB:**	Internet Architecture Board
DSU:	digital services unit	**IANA:**	Internet Assigned Numbers Authority

IAV:	interactive video
IC:	integrated circuit
ICAI:	intelligent computer-assisted instruction
ICMP:	Internet control message protocol
IDE:	integrated (or "intelligent") drive electronics
IEEE:	Institute of Electrical and Electronic Engineers
IESG:	Internet Engineering Steering Group
IETF:	Internet Engineering Task Force
IGES:	initial graphics exchange specification
IGP:	interior gateway protocol
I/O:	input/output system (cpu interface)
IP:	Internet protocol
IPC:	interprocess communication (multitasking)
IPX:	internetwork packet exchange
IRC:	internet relay chat
IRQ:	interrupt request lines (or level) (how peripherals inform cpu, e.g., "ready")
IRSG:	Internet Research Steering Group
IRTF:	Internet Research Task Force
ISA:	Industry Standard (16-bit bus) Architecture
ISA:	Interactive Services Association
ISDN:	Integrated Services Digital Network
ISO:	International Standards Organization
JPEG:	Joint Photographic Experts Group (also a compression technique)
JUGHEAD:	*Jonzy's Universal Gopher Hierarchy Excavation And Display*
KB:	kilobyte (1024 bytes)
KC:	kilocharacter (thousands of characters)
LAN:	local area network
LBA:	logical block addressing
LCD:	liquid crystal display
LED:	light emitting diode (or display)
LISP:	LISt Processing
LSI:	large-scale integration (of components on a chip)
MAN:	metropolitan area network
MB:	megabyte (1,024 kilobytes; 1,048,576 bytes; 1000 MB = 1 gigabyte)
MCA:	Micro Channel Architecture (32-bit) bus
MCGA:	multicolor graphics array
MCI:	media control interface (external devices)
MDA:	monochrome display adaptor
MFM:	modified frequency modulation (double density magnetic compression)
MHz:	megahertz (one million cycles per second)
MIDI:	musical instrument digital interface
MIME:	multipurpose Internet mail extensions
MIPS:	million instructions per second
MIS:	management information system (provides info on organization's performance)
MPC:	multimedia personal computer
MPEG:	Motion Picture Experts Group
MS-DOS:	*Microsoft Disk Operating System*
MTBF:	mean time between failures
MUD:	multi-user dialog
MUDD:	multi-user dungeons and dragons
MUI:	multimedia user interface
MUSE:	multi-user simulated environment
NCSA:	National Center for Supercomputing Applications (U. of Ill., Urb.-Champ.)
NIC:	Network Information Center
NII:	National Information Infrastructure
NIST:	National Institute of Standards and Technology
NLQ:	near letter quality (dot-matrix printer)
NNTP:	network news transfer protocol
NOC:	network operations center
NOS:	network operating system
NREN:	National Research and Education Network
ns:	nanosecond (one billionth of a second)
NSF:	National Science Foundation
NTP:	network time protocol
OCLC:	online computer library catalog
OCR:	optical character recognition
OEM:	original equipment manufacturer
OLE:	object linking and embedding
OS/2:	*Operating System/2*
OSI:	open systems interconnection (reference model for LANs)
PARC:	Palo Alto Research Center (Xerox)
PC:	personal computer
PC DOS:	version of *MS-DOS* used with IBM PCs
PCI:	peripheral component interconnect (motherboard technology)
PCM:	pulse code modulation (transforms analog signals to digital)
PCMCIA:	Personal Computer Memory Card International Association

PD:	public domain software
PDA:	personal digital assistant
PDL:	page description language (for printers)
PDN:	public data network
PDU:	protocol data unit
PEM:	privacy enhanced mail
PICS:	PICT images
PICT:	picture format (Mac graphics)
PIF:	program information file (to inform *Windows* how to run non-*Windows*)
PILOT:	*Programmed Inquiry Learning Or Teaching* (early CAI authoring language)
PIM:	personal information manager
PING:	packet Internet groper (data are sent in blocks, or "packets")
PINS:	public information network services
PMMU:	paged memory management unit (to enable "virtual memory," more RAM)
POP:	point of presence (connection to Internet)
POP:	post office protocol
POV:	point of view (perspective of viewer in relation to 3D graphic)
ppm:	pages per minute (printer speed)
PPP:	point-to-point connection (to Internet)
PRAM:	parameter RAM (Mac battery-powered)
PROLOG:	*PROgramming in LOGic* (programming language used in AI)
PROM:	programmable read-only memory
PSI:	Performance Systems International
PSN:	packet switched node
PTT:	postal telegraph and telephone
QBE:	query by example (database programs)
QIC:	quarter-inch cartridge (for hard disk backup)
QWERTY:	standard keyboard layout ("kwerty")
RAM:	random-access memory
RDBMS:	relational database management system
RFI:	radio frequency interference (from electrical devices)
RGB:	red, green, blue (monitor that accepts separate inputs for each color)
RISC:	reduced instruction set computing (e.g., as used by the *PowerPC*)
RL:	real life (as opposed to "virtual" or simulated)
RLL:	run-length limited (increases hard disk storage density)

ROM:	read-only memory
r/w:	read/write (file or device can be read or changed, e.g. RAM)
RSI:	repetitive strain injury
RTF:	rich text format (encoding of formatting instructions w/o special codes)
RTT:	round trip time (send and receive)
SAA:	Systems Application Architecture (standards for IBM links)
SCO:	Santa Cruz Operation (e.g., *SCO Xenix* and *SCO Unix* operating systems)
SCSI:	small computer system interface ("scuzzy")
SIG:	special interest group
SIGACE:	Special Interest Group for the Application of CD-ROM to Education
SIMM:	single in-line memory module (plug-in RAM)
SIP:	single in-line package (plastic housing for circuit with pins along one row)
SLIP:	serial line Internet protocol connection
SMTP:	simple mail transfer protocol
SNA:	systems network architecture (IBM)
SNMP:	simple network management protocol
SNOBOL:	*String-Oriented Symbolic Language* (for text-processing applications)
SPA:	Software Publishers Association
SQL:	*Structured Query Language* (device and data independent, for networks)
SSA:	Systems Application Architecture
SVGA:	super video graphics array
SVID:	System V Interface Definition (a standard for *UNIX* operating systems)
SYSOP:	SYStem OPerator (of bulletin board, "siss-op")
TCP/IP:	transmission (or transfer) control protocol/Internet protocol
TIFF:	Tagged Image File Format (Mac and *DOS* graphics)
TIGA:	Texas Instruments Graphics Architecture (high resolution standard)
tpi:	tracks per inch (data-storage density of magnetic disks)
TSR:	terminate-and-stay-resident program (lurks in RAM)
TDD:	telephonic device used by people with hearing impairments

TTL:	time to live
TTY:	tele-typewriter
UAE:	unrecoverable application error (memory space invasion w/i *Windows*)
UART:	universal asynchronous receiver-transmitter
UMB:	upper memory block (I've had a lot of these.)
UNIX:	"yoo' nicks" (a family of operating systems written in *C*, both unacronyms)
UPS:	uninterruptible power supply (battery backup; sounds like Deity <g>)
URL:	Universal Resource Locator (Web address)
UTC:	universal time coordinated
UUCP:	*UNIX* to *UNIX* Copy (a WAN with gateways to BITNet and the Internet)
VAR:	value-added reseller (improves and repackages OEM products)
VDT:	video display terminal (monitor)
VDU:	video display unit (VDT)
VERONICA:	*Very Easy Rodent-Oriented Net-wide Index to Computerized Archives*
VESA:	Video Electronics Standards Association
VGA:	video graphics array
VLSI:	very large-scale integration (up to 100,000 components on a chip)
V*mail:	video mail
VMS:	*Virtual Memory System* (operating system)
VR:	virtual reality (a computer-generated 3-D environment)
WAIS:	wide area information servers ("ways")
WAN:	wide area network
WELL:	Whole Earth 'Lectronic Link
WIMP:	window/icon/mouse/pull-down (GUI screen layout)
WMF:	*Windows* Metafile Format (an object-oriented graphics file format)
WORM:	write-once; read-many (an optical disk drive for making CD-ROMs)
WWW:	World Wide Web
WYSIWYG:	what you see is what you get ("whiziwig")
XGA:	extended graphics adapter (or array)
XMS:	extended memory system (RAM above 1 MB)
YMCK:	yellow, magenta, cyan, black (layering of colors for printing graphics)

Below are a few **acronyms** commonly encountered in "internet relay chat" (**IRC**). You may obtain updated lists from CompuServe and other sources on the Internet. These are placed between the "greater than" and "less than" expressions to convey the writer's mood or to clarify intent. Note that using all capital letters in one's messages is considered rude, like shouting. Where **bold** lettering is not available, one emphasizes words with *asterisks*.

BBL:	I'll be back later.
BFN:	Bye for now.
BRB:	I'll be right back.
BTW:	by the way
FUBAR:	fixed up beyond all recognition
FWIW:	for what it's worth
FYI:	for your information
G:	grinning (after a tongue-in-cheek remark)
GD&H:	grinning, ducking, and hiding (got my shot in)
HSIK:	How should I know?
IAE:	in any event
IMHO:	in my humble opinion
IMO:	in my opinion
IOW:	in other words
ISO:	in search of (romance)
LOL:	laughing out loud
NBD:	no big deal
NOYB:	none of your business
OIC:	Oh, I see.
OTL:	out to lunch (someone's mind, that is)
OTOH:	on the other hand
PITA:	pain in the *
PMJI:	pardon my jumping in
PTB:	powers that be
ROTF:	rolling on the floor (laughing; follows cascade, <G>, <VBG>, <LOL>)
RSN:	real soon now
SNAFU:	situation normal, all fixed up
TANJ:	There ain't no justice.
TANSTAAFL:	There ain't no such thing as a free lunch.
TIA:	Thanks in advance.
TIC:	tongue-in-cheek
TPTB:	the powers that be
TTFN:	Ta ta for now.
TTYL:	I'll talk to you later.
VBG:	very big grin
WOA:	work of art
WTH:	what the heck

Emoticons serve to convey a writer's feelings in a "clever" way. Here are just a few of the most common. Challenge your students to explore the range of human emotions by creating more. Beware, some of these can fuel a flame war.

:-)	happy
(-:	left handed
:-D	very happy
:-o	surprised
:-(	sad
:-<	very sad

>:-(	angry
;-)	wink
|-o	yawn
8-)	wears glasses
g-)	designer glasses
:-I	hummm
:-*	smack (pickle or kiss)
=:-)	punk rocker
8:]	happy gorilla
:-\	Oh, really?
:-#	My lips are sealed.
*:o)	bozo

Sources

To save paper and thus trees, please be selective in contacting merchants, and rely on electronic communications. Toll-free numbers are primarily for placing orders, but you can use them to obtain catalogs. Fax numbers typically are provided on order forms, so have been omitted here. Telephobes like me will welcome the email addresses and Web sites. (Yes, the world is divided into synchronous and asynchronous functioning people.) Please contact me to make corrections and additions (hackbarths@aol.com), since change is the essence of existence both on *terra firma* and in cyberspace. Upon request, updates will be sent to your email address.

ACCESS ERIC (Internet-based question answering and
   referral service)
1600 Research Blvd.
Rockville, MD 20850-3172
1-800-LET-ERIC
askeric@ericir.syr.edu
http://ericir.syr.edu (AskERIC Virtual Library)

Adobe Systems, Inc. (merged with Aldus Corp.)
411 First Ave. South
Seattle, WA 98104-2871
1-800-628-2320; 1-206-622-5500
   Acrobat
   After Effects
   Gallery Effects
   Home Publisher
   Illustrator
   PageMaker
   Persuasion
   Photoshop
   Premiere
   SuperPaint

Agency for Instructional Technology
Box A, 1800 N. Stonelake Dr.
Bloomington, IN 47402-0120
1-800-457-4509; 1-812-339-2203
   AIT Catalog of Educational Materials

Following are videotape titles available with broadcasting rights:
   Applied Communication
   Arts Alive
   Econ and Me
   Exploring Technology Education
   Geography in U.S. History
   Global Geography
   The Heart of Teaching
   In Other Words
   Inside/Out
   It Figures
   Math Wise
   Math Works
   MeasureMetric
   Principles of Technology
   Solutions Unlimited
   Solve It
   ThinkAbout
   Self Incorporated
   Workplace Readiness
   Your Choice . . . Our Chance

Allyn and Bacon
Department 894
160 Gould St.
Needham Heights, MA 02194-2310
1-800-852-8024; 1-617-455-1273
   A CD-ROM Software Sampler
   Classroom Insights Videotape and Videodisc
   Classrooms at the Crossroads

Connections Videos from CNN
Innovations in Education
Snapshots Video for Special Education
Teacher Magazine Reader
Themes of the TIMES
(Call for a current catalog.)

America Online
Distribution Center, Suite 200
8619 Westwood Center Drive
Vienna, VA 22182-2285
1-800-827-6364

American Association for the Advancement of Science
1333 H St., N.W.
Washington, DC 20005
1-202-326-6430
http://www.aaas.org
  Black Churches Project
  The Children's Science Radio Project
  Earth Explorer Project
  Hispanic Outreach Program
  Science
  Science Books and Films

American Educational Research Association
1230 17th St., NW
Washington, DC 20036-3078
1-202-223-9485
aera@gmu.edu
  American Educational Research Journal
  Educational Evaluation and Policy Analysis
  Educational Researcher
  Journal of Educational Statistics
  Review of Educational Research
  Review of Research in Education

American Library Association
50 East Huron St.
Chicago, IL 60611
1-800-545-2433; 1-312-944-6780; 1-312-944-7298 (TDD)
  Best Books for Young Adults
  Book Links
  Booklist
  School Library Media Quarterly
  Selected Films for Young Adults

American Newspaper Publishers Association
Foundation
11600 Sunrise Valley Dr.
Reston, VA 22091
1-703-648-1000
  Education for Freedom Curriculum
  Educators: Try NIE
  First Amendment Rights
  Journalism Career Guide for Minorities
  The Newspaper as an Effective Teaching Tool
  Using the Newspaper in Secondary Mathematics
  Using the Newspaper in Secondary Science
  Using the Newspaper in Upper Elementary and Middle
    Grades
  Using the Newspaper to Teach About the Constitution
  Using the Newspaper to Teach Secondary Language Arts
  Using the Newspaper to Teach Secondary Social Studies

Apple Computer, Inc.
1 Infinite Loop
Cupertino, CA 95014-2080
1-408-996-1010
1-800-767-2775 (Apple User Assistance Center)
1-800-776-2333 (Apple Customer Assistance Center)
1-800-800-APPL (Education Division, k–12)
1-800-833-6223 (TDD)
http://www.info.apple.com/education
  Business Education
  Collaborative Learning Products
  Communications Bundle
  Early Childhood Connections
  Early Language Connections
  Educator Advantage Bundles
  Elementary Reference Bundle
  High School Biology Bundle
  Math Bundle: Grades 5-8
  Multimedia Learning Tools
  Network Assistant Kit
  Secondary Reference Bundle
  Spanish Language Connections
  Staff Development Workshops
  Teacher Solution Bundle
  Teaching and Learning Technology—a Planning Guide

Aris Multimedia Entertainment
4444 Via Marina, Suite 811
Marina del Rey, CA 90292
1-800-228-2747; 1-310-821-0234
  Americana
  Animal Kingdom
  MediaClips

MPC Wizard
New York, NY
WinTutor
WorldView

Arts and Sciences Teleconferencing Service
Oklahoma State University
401 Life Sciences East
Stillwater, OK 74078
1-800-452-2787; 1-405-744-7895

Arthur Mokin Productions, Inc. [videos]
P.O. Box 1866
Santa Rosa, CA 95402
1-800-238-4868; 1-707-542-4868
  A Cause for Celebration
  A Race with Destiny: African American Health
  Black College White College: A Matter of Choice
  Black Male and Successful in America
  Cede, Yield and Surrender
  Dropout: Kids in Crisis
  Mantis Science Series
  ModuMath Algebra Series
  ModuMath Arithmetic Series
  My Teacher, My Advocate
  Now Is the Future: Prenatal Care
  Parents and Schools: Success Through Partnership
  Parents Make A+ Difference
  Using Equations to Solve Problems
  Visual Literacy Series

Association for the Advancement of Computing in
  Education
P.O. Box 2966
Charlottesville, VA 22902
1-804-973-3987
aace@virginia.edu
  Educational Technology Review
  International Journal of Educational Telecommunications
  Journal of Artificial Intelligence in Education
  Journal of Computers in Math and Science Teaching
  Journal of Computing in Childhood Education
  Journal of Educational Multimedia and Hypermedia
  Journal of Technology and Teacher Education
  [Also request a list of books.]

Association for Educational Communications and
  Technology
1025 Vermont Ave., N.W., Suite 820
Washington, D.C. 20005
1-202-347-7834
aect@aect.org
  Educational Technology Research and Development
  Tech Trends
  Call for current list of publications.

The Association for Educational and Training Technology
Centre for Continuing Education
The City University, Northhampton Square
London EC1V OHB England
071-253-4399, ext. 3276
  Aspects of Educational & Training Technology
  Innovations in Education & Training International
  International Yearbook of Educational and Instructional
    Technology

Association for Media and Technology in Education in
  Canada
#3-1750 The Queensway, Suite 1318
Etobicoke, Ontario
M9C 5H5 Canada
ggallant@fac.cabot.nf.ca
  Media Message

Association for Supervision and Curriculum Development
Education & Technology Resources Center
1250 North Pitt St.
Alexandria, VA 22314-1453
1-800-933-ASCD; 1-703-549-9110
etrc@ascd.org
member@ascd.org
http://www.ascd.org
  Curriculum/Technology Quarterly
  Educational Leadership

Asymetrix Corp.
110 - 110th Ave., N.E., Suite 700
Bellevue, WA 98004-5840
1-800-448-6543; 1-206-462-0501
annb@asymetrix.com
http://www.asymetrix.com
  Compel
  Digital Video Producer
  MediaBlitz!
  Multimedia Toolbook
  3D F/X

Autodesk, Inc.
2320 Marinship Way
Sausalito, CA 94965
1-800-688-2344; 1-415-332-2344
AutoCAD LT for Windows
AutoSketch
Chaos: The Software
Multimedia Explorer
Cyberspace Developer Kit
3D Studio

Barnes & Noble
1 Pond Road
Rockleigh, NJ 07647
1-800-242-6657; 1-201-767-7079
Request catalog listing films, videos, PBS and BBC specials, CDs, cassettes.

Books on Tape, Inc.
P.O. Box 7900
Newport Beach, CA 92658
1-800-626-3333; 1-714-548-5525
Full-length readings of about 3000 best sellers.

Borland International, Inc.
100 Borland Way
Scotts Valley, CA 95066-3249
1-408-438-8400
Borland C++
Borland Pascal
dBASE IV
Delphi
Paradox

Bowker, R.R.
P.O. Box 31
New Providence, NJ 07974-9904
Books in Print
Bowker's Complete Video Dictionary
School Library Journal

Brøderbund Software, Inc. (See also Living Books.)
P.O. Box 6125
Novato, CA 94948-6125
1-800-521-6263
Algebra
The Amazing Writing Machine
The Backyard
Calculus
CNN Time Capsule
Dazzle Draw

The Electronic Whole Earth Catalog
Geometry
Kid Cuts
Kid Pix Studio
Kid Pix 2
PC Globe Maps 'n' Facts CD-ROM
Math Workshop
Myst
Physics
The Playroom
The Print Shop Deluxe
Science Toolkit
Spelunx and the Caves of Mr. Seudo
The Treehouse
Type!
VCR Companion
Where in America's Past Is Carmen Sandiego?
Where in Time Is Carmen Sandiego?
Where in the U.S.A. Is Carmen Sandiego?
Where in the World Is Carmen Sandiego?
Where in the World Is Carmen Sandiego? Junior Detective Edition

Bureau of Electronic Publishing, Inc.
141 New Road
Parsippany, NJ 07054
1-800-828-4766; 1-201-808-2700
bepmktg@aol.com
http://www.bep.com
Everything Weather
Great Authors (Like the Dickens, Much Ado About Shakespeare, Twain's World)
The Great Kat's Digital Beethoven on Cyberspeed
Great Literature Plus
Inside the White House
Monarch Notes on CD-ROM
Multimedia US History
Multimedia World Factbook
Story of the States
Teach Your Kids World History on CD-ROM
Total History
World History 1996

California Department of Education
Bureau of Publications, Sales Unit
P.O. Box 271
Sacramento, CA 95812-0271
1-800-995-4099; 1-916-445-1260
Request the *Educational Resources Catalog* for descriptions of publications such as:
The California Children's 5 A Day Campaign
A Child's Place in the Environment
English-Language Arts Framework for California Schools, K–12

English-Language Arts Model Curriculum Guide, K–8
Handbook for Planning an Effective Literature Program,
  K–12
Handbook for Planning an Effective Writing Program, K–12
History-Social Science Model Curriculum Guide
Mathematics Framework for California Schools, K–12
Mathematics Model Curriculum Guide, K–8
Read to Me: Recommended Literature for Children Ages Two
  Through Seven
Recommended Literature, Grades Nine Through Twelve
Recommended Readings in Literature, Kindergarten Through
  Grade Eight, Annotated
Recommended Readings in Spanish Literature, Kindergarten
  Through Grade Eight
Science Framework for California Schools, K–12
Secondary Textbook Review: English
Visual and Performing Arts Framework for California
  Schools, K–12

Cambium Development, Inc.
P.O. Box 296-H
Scarsdale, NY 10583-8796
1-800-231-1779; 1-914-472-6246
72650.3150@compuserve.com
  Cambium Sound Choice (music clips on CD-ROM)

CEL Communications, Inc.
CEL Educational Resources
655 Third Ave.
New York, NY 10017
1-800-235-3339; 1-212-557-3400
  Set on Freedom: The American Civil Rights Movement
  The Video Encyclopedia of the 20th Century

Centre Communications, Inc. [16mm films and
  videotapes]
1800 30th St., Suite 207
Boulder, CO 80301
1-800-886-1166; 1-303-444-1166
  Adolescent Pregnancy: A Perspective for Parents and
    Teachers
  AIDS: A Global Approach
  Black America Series
  Chicanos in Transition
  The Great English Writer's Series
  The IBM Computer Literacy Series
  Life's Little Lessons Series
  Media for Awareness Catalog
  On the Brink: An AIDS Chronicle
  On Equal Terms: Sex Equity in the Workplace
  People Matter Series
  Touch the Earth

CE Software, Inc.
1801 Industrial Circle
West Des Moines, IA 50265
1-800-523-7638; 1-515-221-1801
curtis_lee@cesoft.com
  Educate America Program

Chancery Software, Inc.
2211 Rimland Dr., #224
Bellingham, WA 98226
1-800-999-9931; 1-206-738-3211; 1-604-294-1233
  (Canada)
chancery@applelink.apple.com
  CSL ClassWorks (ILS)

Children's Television Workshop
Publishing Group
One Lincoln Plaza
New York, NY 10023
1-212-595-3456 (operator)
1-212-875-6630 (School Publishing)
magazines:
  Creative Classroom
  Kid City
  Sesame Street
  3-2-1 Contact
videos:
  Ghostwriter
  Mathnet
  Math Talk
  Square One TV
  3-2-1 Classroom Contact

Claris Corp.
5201 Patrick Henry Dr.
Box 58168
Santa Clara, CA 95052-8168
1-800-3-CLARIS
  ClarisWorks
  FileMaker II
  FileMaker Pro
  HyperCard

Cliffs Notes, Inc.
P.O. Box 80728
Lincoln, NB 68501-0728
1-800-228-4078; 1-402-423-5050
  Algebra I
  Biology
  Calculus
  CBEST

Chemistry
Economics
Enhanced ACT
GED
Geometry
GMAT
GRE
LSAT
Physics
SAT I
Statistics
Trigonometry

Compton's NewMedia, Inc.
2320 Camino Vida Roble
Carlsbad, CA 92009
1-800-261-6109; 1-619-929-2500
    CD RAMA: CD ROM SAMPLER
    Compton's Interactive Encyclopedia
    Compton's Reference Collection
    The Grammy Awards: A 34 Year Retrospective
    Imagine
    Jazz: A Multimedia History
    Mazlo's Spelling Adventure
    The Multimedia Encyclopedia of Life on Earth
    Ocean Explorers
    Rock 'N Roll Your Own
    Zak! Look It Up
    Zoo Explorers

CompuServe, Inc.
New Members Department
5000 Arlington Centre Blvd.
P.O. Box 20961
Columbus, OH 43220-9988
1-800-848-8199

Compu-Teach
16541 Redmond Way, Suite 137-C
Redmond, WA 98052-4482
1-800-44-TEACH
    CODE: EUROPE!
    Destination: Mars!
    Grade Quick!
    Joshua's reading machine
    Once Upon a Time . . .
    See the U.S.A.
    Stepping Stones
    STUDYMATE
    Test Quick!

Computer-based Education Research Laboratory
    (CERL)
252 Engineering Research Laboratory
103 South Mathews Ave.
Urbana, IL 61801
1-217-333-6210
University Communications, Inc., distributor
1-800-876-8257
    NovaNET (successor to PLATO)

Computer Curriculum Corp.
Simon & Schuster Technology Group
1287 Lawrence Station Rd.
P.O. Box 3711
Sunnyvale, CA 94089-9883
1-800-227-8324; 1-408-745-6270
cahlquis@cccpp.com
    Choosing Success
    Discover English
    English as a Second Language
    Essentials for Living & Working
    Experiences in Communication Arts
    GED Preparation
    Initial Reading
    Math Concepts and Skills [also in Spanish]
    Math Enrichment Modules
    Multimedia Reference Library
    Multimedia Science Classroom
    The New Grolier Electronic Encyclopedia
    Practical Reading Skills
    Problem Solving
    Reading Readiness
    Science Discovery
    Spelling Skills
    SuccessMaker (ILS)
    Writer's Express

Computerized Educational Resources, Ltd.
1313 5th St. S.E.
Minneapolis, MN 55414
1-612-379-3956
    The African American Experience: A History

Computerworks!
260 Main St.
Northport, NY 11768
1-800-825-DISK
    CDiscovery: A Guide to CD-ROM Products

Conexus
5252 Balboa Avenue, Suite 400
San Diego, CA 92117
1-619-268-3380
  Action Math: Rapid Addition
  Action Phonics
  Action Reading: Kenny Kite to the Rescue
  Sound It Out Land
  Sound It Out Land 2
  Sound It Out Land 3

Consumer Information Center
U.S. General Services Administration
Consumer Information Catalog
Pueblo, CO 81009
1-719-948-4000

Continental Press, Inc.
520 East Bainbridge St.
Elizabethtown, PA 17022-2299
1-800-233-0759
Source of books, tapes, and computer software including:
  AIMS: Reading Series
  Black Heritage: Data Bases on People, Places, Events
  Communities Around the World
  Computer Literacy: Introductory Course
  Critical Thinking with Literature
  Exploring English
  Focus on Problem Solving: Thinking-Skills Math
  High-Interest/Low-Level Reading
  Logo: Explore & Discover
  Map Skills Series: Practical Applications
  Mathematics: Skills, Concepts and Problem Solving
  Math Mastery Series: Straightforward Practice
  Math Mastery Series in Spanish
  Parent Handbooks: At-Home Activities for Children and Parents
  Poetry Big Books
  Puerto Rico: Its History & Culture
  Puzzle Works: Mathematics
  Reading for Comprehension
  Reading Problems in Mathematics: Real-World Math
  Ready-Set-Read
  Record & Plan Books: High-Quality Sources
  Spanish Reading Materials
  Tables and Graphs: Topical Tasks
  Teacher Resource Books: Creative Ideas and Patterns

Contér Software (a division of Jostens)
9920 Pacific Heights Blvd., Suite 100
San Diego, CA 92121-4430
1-800-801-0040
  Elementary School Bundle
  Middle School Bundle
  High School GED Bundle
  High School Math Bundle

Corel Corp.
1600 Carling Ave.
Ottawa, Ontario
Canada K1Z 8R7
1-800-772-6735; 1-613-728-8200
  Corel ArtShow
  Corel CD PowerPak
  CorelCHART
  CorelDRAW!
  CorelFlow
  Corel Gallery
  Corel Gallery 2
  CorelMOVE
  CorelPHOTO-PAINT
  Corel Professional Photos CD-ROM
  CorelSCSI
  CorelSCSI Network Manager
  CorelSHOW
  Corel Ventura
  Wildlife Babies

Corporation for Public Broadcasting
The Annenberg/CPB Multimedia Collection
P.O. Box 2345
South Burlington, VT 05407-2345
1-800-LEARNER; 1-802-862-8881
  Against All Odds: Inside Statistics
  Americas
  Art of the Western World
  The Constitution: That Delicate Balance
  Destinos: An Introduction to Spanish
  Earth Revealed
  Ethics in America
  For All Practical Purposes: Introduction to Contemporary
    Mathematics
  French in Action
  Literary Visions
  The Mechanical Universe . . . and Beyond
  The New Literacy: An Introduction to Computers
  Out of the Past
  The Pacific Century
  Perseus
  Planet Earth
  Race to Save the Planet
  The Western Tradition
  The World of Chemistry
  Voices & Visions
  War and Peace in the Nuclear Age

The Council for Exceptional Children
1920 Association Dr.
Reston, VA 22091-1589
1-800-845-6232 (voice/TDD); 1-703-620-3660
    (voice/TDD)
Request membership and publications information.

Creative Learning, Inc.
P.O. Box 829
North San Juan, CA 95960
1-800-842-5360
    Breakthrough to Language
    Breakthrough To Writing
    The Multisensory Curriculum
    Multisensory Math
    Worksheet Generator

Davidson & Associates, Inc.
19840 Pioneer Avenue
Torrance, CA 90503
1-800-545-7677; 1-310-793-0600
    Alge-Blaster 3
    Fisher-Price ABC's
    Fisher-Price Dream Doll House
    Fisher-Price Great Adventures Castle
    Fisher-Price 1-2-3's
    Fisher-Price Sing-Alongs
    Flying Colors
    Grammar Games
    Kid CAD
    Kid Keys
    Kid Phonics
    Kid Works Deluxe
    Magic Tales
    Math Blaster 1: In Search of Spot
    Math Blaster 2: Secret of the Lost City
    Math Blaster Mystery
    Math Blaster Mystery: The Great Train Robbery
    The Multimedia Workshop
    Reading Blaster
    Spell It 3
    Word Attack 3

D.C. Heath and Co.
2700 North Richardt Avenue
P.O. Box 19309
Indianapolis, IN 46219
1-800-428-8071
    Discovering French Interactive
    Interactions

DeLorme Mapping
Lower Main St.
P.O. Box 298
Freeport, ME 04032
1-800-452-5931, ext. 8180; 1-207-865-1234
    Global Explorer
    Street Atlas USA

DELPHI Internet Services Corp.
1030 Massachusetts Ave.
Cambridge, MA 02138
1-800-695-4005
info@delphi.com

Desktop Solutions
15195 El Camino Grande
Saratoga, CA 95070
1-408-354-9492
desktopsolutions@batnet.com
http://www.cyberwise.com
    CyberWISE Internet Educational Software

Dialog Information Services, Inc.
3460 Hillview Avenue
P.O. Box 10010
Palo Alto, CA 94303-0993
1-800-3-DIALOG; 1-415-858-3785
Request materials describing electronic publications and
databases.

Direct Cinema Limited
P.O. Box 10003
Santa Monica, CA 90410-1003
1-800-525-0000; 1-310-396-4774
directcinema@attmail.com
    Abortion: Desperate Choices
    Anaïs Nin Observed
    Antonia: A Portrait of the Woman
    Broken Rainbow
    Brooklyn Bridge
    Common Threads: Stories from the Quilt
    Educating Peter
    The Famine Within
    Flamenco at 5:15
    The Flight of the Gossamer Condor
    Full Circle
    He Makes Me Feel Like Dancin'
    The Man Who Planted Trees
    Marcel Proust: A Writer's Life
    Remembering Jung
    Spirit to Spirit: Nikki Giovanni
    The Statue of Liberty

The Discovery Channel
P.O. Box 4100
Crawfordsville, IN 47933-9910
1-800-457-1239; 1-317-364-7230
  Beyond Planet Earth
  In the Company of Whales
  Normandy: The Great Crusade
  Professor Iris Animal Safari
  Wings: Korea to Vietnam
  Wings Over Europe

Disney Interactive
500 So. Buena Vista St.
Burbank, CA 91521-8460
1-800-228-0988; 1-818-543-4300
sysop@disneysoft.com
  Animation Studio
  Be Our Guest
  Coaster
  Disney's Aladdin Activity Center - CD-ROM
  Disney's Animated Storybook, The Lion King - CD-ROM
  Disney's Animated Storybook, Winnie the Pooh and the
    Honey Tree - CD-ROM
  Follow the Reader
  The Lion King Print Studio
  Mickey & Crew Print Studio
  Mickey & Crew Screen Scenes
  Mickey's ABC's
  Mickey's Colors and Shapes
  Mickey's 123's
  Pocahontas Screen Scenes

Eastman Kodak Co.
Kodak Information Center
Dept. 841
R2 Riverwood
Rochester, NY 14650-0811
1-800-242-2424
http://www.kodak.com
  A Glossary of Photographic Terms
  Audiovisual Projection
  The Best of Audiovisual Notes from Kodak
  Guide to KODAK 35mm Films
  KODAK Arrange-It Photo CD Portfolio Layout Software
  KODAK Audiovisual Products Catalog
  KODAK Create-It Photo CD Presentation Software
  KODAK Digital Science Products
  KODAK Guide to 35mm Photography
  KODAK PhotoEdge Photo CD Software
  KODAK PCphotographer Software Program
  KODAK Pocket Guide to Great Picture-Taking
  KODAK Pocket Guide to 35mm Photography

  KODAK Pocket Photoguide
  KODAK Shoebox Photo CD Image Manager Software
  Slides—Planning and Producing Slide Programs
  Taking Better Pictures
  Using Your Autofocus 35mm Camera

EBSCO Publishing
83 Pine St.
Peabody, MA 01960
1-800-653-2726; 1-508-535-8500
ep@ebsco.com
  Magazine Article Summaries (on CD-ROM)

Edmark Corp.
6727 185th Ave. NE
P.O. Box 97021
Redmond, WA 98073-9721
1-800-362-2890; 1-206-556-8400
  Bailey's Book House
  Imagination Express, Destination: Ocean
  Imagination Express, Destination: Neighborhood
  Imagination Express, Destination: Rain Forest
  Imagination Express, Destination: Castle
  KidDesk
  KidDesk Plus
  Millie's Math House
  Sammy's Science House
  Thinkin' Things Collection 1
  Thinkin' Things Collection 2
  Thinkin' Things Collection 3
  Thinkin' Things School
  TouchWindow
  Trudy's Time & Place House

Educational Products Information Exchange (EPIE)
  Institute
103-3 W. Montauk Highway
Hampton Bays, NY 11946
1-516-728-9100
komoski@bnlarm.bnl.gov
  Curriculum Analysis Services for Educators
  The Educational Software Selector (TESS)
  EPIEgram: The Newsletter About Educational Materials and
    Technology
  Integrated Instructional Information Resource
  The Latest and Best of TESS
  Microcomputer PRO/FILES
  Microgram
  States Consortium for Improving Software Selection
  Textbook PRO/FILES

Educational Resources
1550 Executive Dr.
Elgin, IL 60123
1-800-624-2926; 1-708-888-8300
  Solutions Program (ILS)

Educational Technology Publications, Inc.
700 Palisade Ave.
Englewood Cliffs, NJ 07632-0564
1-800-952-BOOK; 1-201-871-4007
  Educational Technology Magazine
  Training Research Journal
Call for catalog listing current book publications.

Educators Progress Service, Inc.
214 Center St.
Randolph, WI 53956-9983
1-414-326-3126
  Educators Grade Guide to Free Teaching Aids
  Educators Guide to Free Films, Filmstrips and Slides
  Educators Guide to Free Guidance Materials
  Educators Guide to Free Health, Physical Education and
    Recreation Materials
  Educators Guide to Free Home Economics and Consumer
    Education Materials
  Educators Guide to Free Science Materials
  Educators Guide to Free Social Studies Materials
  Educators Guide to Free Videotapes
  Educators Index to Free Materials
  Elementary Teachers Guide to Free Curriculum Materials
  Guide to Free Computer Materials

EduQuest [see also IBM]
P.O. Box 2150
Atlanta, GA 30055
1-800-426-4338
  Abacus Instructional Management System
  LinkWay
  LinkWay Live!
  Picture Atlas of the World

Encyclopaedia Britannica
Britannica Centre
310 South Michigan Ave.
Chicago, IL 60604-4293
1-800-323-1229
Available in CD-ROM and online versions

ERIC Clearinghouse on Information and Technology
Syracuse University
4-194 Center for Science and Technology
Syracuse, NY 13244-4100
1-800-464-9107; 1-315-443-3640
eric@ericir.syr.edu

eWorld Assistance Center
Apple Computer, Inc.
P.O. Box 4493
Bridgeton, MO 63044-9718
1-800-775-4556; 1-408-974-1236; 1-800-833-6223 (TDD)
1-800-521-1515, ext. 165 (updated versions)
http://www.eworld.com/education/resources

Facts on File, Inc.
460 Park Avenue South
New York, NY 10016
1-800-322-8755; 1-212-683-2244
  The American Indian: A Multimedia Encyclopedia
  Landmark Documents in American History

Films for the Humanities & Sciences
P.O. Box 2053
Princeton, NJ 08543-2053
1-800-257-5126; 1-609-275-1400
  The Non-Hearing World
  People in Motion: Changing Ideas About Physical Disability
  The Psychological Development of the Child

Flame Co.
31 Marble Avenue
Pleasantville, NY 10570
1-800-5FLAMECO; 1-914-769-4132
Request catalog, *Foreign Language and American Materials for Education.*

Follett Software Co.
1391 Corporate Drive
McHenry, IL 60050-7041
1-800-323-3397; 1-815-344-8700
fscinfo@cedar.cic.net
Request catalogs describing library automation and instructional software.

Franklin Learning Resources
122 Burrs Rd.
Mt. Holly, NJ 08060
1-800-525-9673; 1-609-261-4800
Request catalog describing electronic books for learning.

Full Circle
John Boeschen & Co.
25 Valley View Avenue
San Rafael, CA 94901
1-415-453-9989
boeschen@crl.com
Order Internet documents for K–12 on CD-ROM.

Future Vision Multimedia (formerly Interactive
     Publishing Corp.)
300 Airport Executive Park
Nanuet, NY 10954
1-800-472-8777; 1-914-426-0400
     ASKABOUT Dinosaurs
     Beethoven's 5th: A Multimedia Symphony
     How Things Grow
     Interactive Storytime
     Interactivity Packs
     1000 of the World's Greatest Sound Effects
     Teddy's Big Day
     250 of the World's Greatest Music Clips

GEnie
P.O. Box 6403
Rockville, MD 20849-6403
1-800-638-9636

Genentech, Inc.
Access Excellence
460 Point San Bruno Blvd.
South San Francisco, CA 94080
1-415-225-1000
http://www.gene.com/ae

Great Plains National Instructional Television Library
Box 80669
Lincoln, NE 68501-0669
1-800-228-4630; 1-402-772-2007
     America in the Age of AIDS
     At-Risk Students: What Works?
     Child Abuse and Neglect
     Copyright
     Creating Critical TV Viewers
     Computers Across the Curriculum

Doing Chemistry Videodiscs
Dropping Out: A Long Road Taken
Drug Wise
The Earth Science Video Library
Education of the Gifted and Talented
Electing Women
ESL: Methods & Curriculum Design
Images of Indians
It Only Takes Once
Living with AIDS
Mathematics
Maths Is Fun
Minorities and the Constitution
Musical Encounter
Physics at Work Videodisc
Reading Rainbow
Teaching Reading: Strategies from Successful Classrooms
Teenage Suicide
The Tutor's Guide
3-2-1 Classroom Contact
White Man's Way
Write On!

Grolier Electronic Publishing, Inc.
Sherman Turnpike
Danbury, CT 06816
1-800-285-4534; 1-203-797-3500
     Grolier Encyclopedia Americana
     *Grolier Science Fiction: The Multimedia Encyclopedia of
          Science Fiction*
     Guinness Multimedia Disc of Records
     *How Would You Survive?: A Multimedia Adventure to the
          Worlds of the Ancient Egyptians, Vikings and Aztecs*
     The 1996 Grolier Multimedia Encyclopedia
     Prehistoria

Highlights for Children
2300 West Fifth Avenue
P.O. Box 269
Columbus, OH 43272-2002
     Activity Books
     The American Heritage Children's Dictionary
     The American Heritage First Dictionary
     Dinosaurs
     Hidden Pictures
     Highlights for Children
     Joinable Books & Tapes
     Puzzles

Humanities Software, Inc.
408 Columbia St., Suite 222
P.O. Box 950
Hood River, OR 97031
1-800-245-6737; 1-503-386-6737
human@gorge.net
    Key Words
    MediaWeaver
    Read On!
    Story Tailor
    Twain Studio
    Word Weaver
    Write On!
    Writer's Realm

IBM Independence Series
P.O. Box 1328
Boca Raton, FL 33429-1328
1-800-IBM-4832; 1-800-IBM-4833 (TDD)
    AccessDOS
    KeyGuard
    PhoneCommunicator
    Screen Magnifier/2
    Screen Reader/DOS
    Screen Reader/2
    SpeechViewer II
    THINKable/DOS
    THINKable/2
    VoiceType

IBM PC Direct
P.O. Box 12195
Bldg. 203/Dept. WN4
Research Triangle Park, NC 27709-9767
1-800-IBM-7081

Ideal Learning
8505 Freeport Parkway, Suite 360
Irving, TX 75063
1-800-999-3234; 1-214-929-4201
    Learning Expedition CD (complete K–8 ILS)

Image Smith
1313 Sepulveda Blvd.
Torrance, CA 90501
1-800-U-SNOOPY; 1-310-325-5999
imagesmith@applelink.apple.com
    Darby My Dalmatian
    The Native Americans
    Yearn 2 Learn: Flintstones Bedrock Art Gallery
    Yearn 2 Learn: Flintstones Fashion Cave
    Yearn 2 Learn: Flintstones Fun Pack

    Yearn 2 Learn: Flintstones Fossil's Photo Fixer
    Yearn 2 Learn: Flintstones Spellosaurus Quarry
    Yearn 2 Learn: Flintstones Tell-a-Tale Library
    Yearn 2 Learn: Master Snoopy's Coloring Book
    Yearn 2 Learn: Master Snoopy's Math
    Yearn 2 Learn: Master Snoopy's Spelling
    Yearn 2 Learn: Master Snoopy's World Geography
    Yearn 2 Learn: PEANUTS
    Yearn 2 Learn: Snoopy
    Yearn 2 Learn: Snoopy's Geography

Information Access Co.
362 Lakeside Dr.
Foster City, CA 94404
1-800-343-7781; 1-415-358-4621
info@cognito.com
http://www.cognito.com
    Academic ASAP
    Cognito! (a reference database on the Web)
    InfoTrac
    Magazine Index ASAP

Interactive Learning International Corp.
1223 Peoples Avenue
Troy, NY 12180
1-518-276-2098
info@ilinc.com
    LearnLink: Multimedia Distance Learning Software

International Business Machines Corp. (IBM)
Education Software Dept. 779
One Culver Road
Dayton, NJ 08810-9988
1-800-IBM-4EDU
http://www.ibm.com
http://www.infomkt.ibm.com
    Biology Series
    Classroom LAN Administration System
    Earth Science Series
    EduQuest: Software for Education Catalog
    Exploring Measurement, Time, and Money
    Get Set for Writing to Read
    Illuminated Books and Manuscripts
    Language Arts Series
    Mammals: A Multimedia Encyclopedia
    Math Concepts Series
    Mathematics Exploration Toolkit
    Math Practice Series
    Personal Science Laboratory
    Reading Comprehension Series
    Storyboard Plus
    Touch Typing for Beginners
    Writing to Read [also in Spanish]

International Discount Telecommunications (IDT)
294 State St.
Hackensack, NJ 07601
1-800-245-8000; 1-201-928-1000

The International Internet Association
2020 Pennsylvania Ave. N.W., Suite 852
Washington, DC 20006
1-202-387-5445

International Reading Association
800 Barksdale Road, P.O. Box 8139
Newark, DE 19714-8139
1-800-336-READ; 1-302-731-1600
   Journal of Reading
   Lectura y Vida
   Reading Research Quarterly
   The Reading Teacher
   Reading Today

International Society for Technology in Education
1787 Agate Street
Eugene, OR 97403-1923
1-800-336-5191; 1-503-346-4414
iste@oregon.uoregon.edu
   HyperNEXUS—Journal of Hypermedia and Multimedia
     Studies
   ISTE Update
   Journal of Computer Science Education
   Journal of Computing in Teacher Education
   Journal of Research on Computing in Education
   Learning and Leading with Technology
   Logo Exchange

InterNIC Information Services
General Atomics
P.O. Box 85608
San Diego, CA 92186-9784
1-800-862-0677
admin@ds.internic.net

Interplay Productions, Inc. (See Maxis.)
17922 Fitch Avenue
Irvine, CA 92714
1-714-553-6678
   Mario Teaches Typing
   SimCity Enhanced CD-ROM

Jostens Learning Corp.
6170 Cornerstone Court East
San Diego, CA 92121
1-800-422-4339; 1-619-587-0087; 1-602-678-7272
   Action Math
   Advanced Instructional Management System
   Middle School Language Arts
   Middle School Mathematics
   English Language Development—Primary Level
   Explorations in Science: Physical/Life/Earth
   First Connections: The Golden Book Encyclopedia
   Friends, Amigos, Companions: Bilingual Programs from
     Jostens Learning
   The Home Learning System
   Integrated Language Arts—Primary Level
   Jostens Learning Research Center with Compton's MultiMedia
     Encyclopedia
   Life and Employability Skills
   Mathematics Curriculum
   ONENET
   Reading Curriculum
   Tapestry Early Learning Programs
   TeachNet: Delivering Primary Language Arts and Bilingual
     Programs

KidsNet
6856 Eastern Ave., Suite 208
Washington, DC 20012
1-202-291-1400
kidsnet@aol.com
Request *Bulletin* describing children's radio and TV programs.

Knowledge Adventure, Inc.
1311 Grand Central Ave.
Glendale, CA 91201
1-818-246-4400
lynda_orban@adventure.com
http://www.adventure.com
   America Adventure
   Bug Adventure
   JumpStart First Grade
   JumpStart Kindergarten
   JumpStart Preschool
   Kid's Zoo: A Baby Animal Adventure
   Knowledge Adventure
   My First Encyclopedia
   Random House Kid's Encyclopedia
   Science Adventure II
   Space Adventure
   Spider-Man Cartoon Maker
   3-D Body Adventure
   3-D Dinosaur Adventure
   Undersea Adventure

Knowledge Engineering, Inc.
One Buckhead Plaza, Suite 1025
3060 Peachtree Rd., N.W.
Atlanta, GA 30305
1-800-548-7947
 The Multi Media Express: A Writing and Language
  Development Program
 The Writing Express

Knowledge Products
P.O. Box 305151
Nashville, TN 37230
1-800-876-4332; 1-615-742-3852
The Audio Classics Series includes the following categories of
tapes:
 The Giants of Philosophy
 The Giants of Political Thought
 The Great Economic Thinkers
 The United States at War
 The United States Constitution
 The World's Political Hot Spots
 Science & Discovery

The Learning Co.
6493 Kaiser Drive
Fremont, CA 94555
1-800-852-2255; 1-510-792-2101
 Ancient Empires
 The Children's Writing & Publishing Center
 Math Rabbit
 MetroGnomes' Music
 Operation Neptune
 Reader Rabbit 1
 Reader Rabbit 2
 Reader Rabbit 3
 Reader Rabbit's Interactive Reading Journey
 Reader Rabbit's Reading Development Library
 Reader Rabbit's Ready for Letters
 Read, Write & Type
 Student Writing Center
 Student Writing & Research Center
 Super Solvers Gizmos & Gadgets!
 Super Solvers Midnight Rescue!
 Super Solvers OutNumbered!
 Super Solvers Spellbound!
 Time Riders in American History
 Treasure Cove!
 Treasure MathStorm
 Treasure Mountain
 Ultimate Writing & Creativity Center
 The Writing Center

The Learning Co.
Foreign Language Division (formerly HyperGlot)
P.O. Box 10746
314 Erin Dr.
Knoxville, TN 37919
1-800-726-5087; 1-423-450-2100
rob_lindner@hyperglot.com
 Berlitz Think & Talk Spanish
 Learn to Speak French
 Learn to Speak German
 Learn to Speak Spanish

The Learning Improvement Co.
1875 So. State St.
Orem, UT 84058
1-800-759-4228
 Exam-in-a-Can Plus
 Mental Math
 Wicat Algebra I
 Wicat Algebra II
 Wicat Basic Literacy
 Wicat Basic Numeracy
 Wicat GED Social Studies
 Wicat GED Writing
 Wicat Language Arts
 Wicat Math I
 Wicat Math Toolkit
 Wicat Math II
 Wicat Reading I
 Wicat Reading II
 Wicat Science II Plus
 Wicat Spanish Math I
 Wicat Writing Plus

LearnKey, Inc.
1845 West Sunset Blvd., Room 50-5
St. George, UT 84770-9960
1-800-865-0165; 1-801-674-9733
learnkey@learnkey.com
http://www.learnkey.com
Call for a catalog listing computer applications software
training videos.

Libraries Unlimited, Inc.
P.O. Box 6633
Littleton, CO 80155-6633
1-800-237-6124; 1-303-770-1220
dvl@lu.com
 Educational Media Yearbook
 Educational Software Directory: A Subject Guide to
  Microcomputer Software
 Teacher Ideas Press (Call for current catalog.)

Lintronics Software Publishing, Inc.
1991 Mountainside Drive
Blacksburg, VA 24060
1-540-552-7204
lintronics@bev.net
Apple Pie Music: Music of American History, History of American Music
Pioneer Life in America

Living Books
160 Pacific Avenue Mall, Suite 201
San Francisco, CA 94111
1-415-352-5200
chris_jones@livingbooks.com
Arthur's Birthday
Arthur's Teacher Trouble
The Berenstain Bears Get in a Fight
Dr. Seuss's ABC
Harry and the Haunted House
Just Grandma and Me
Little Monster at School
The New Kid on the Block
Ruff's Bone
The Tortoise and the Hare

Los Angeles Times in Education Program
Times Mirror Square
Los Angeles, CA 90053
1-800-LA-TIMES ext. 74342
Curriculum guides include:
The Constitution and Bill of Rights in Our Times
Critical Thinking
English in the Present Tense
ESL
Gateways to the World (GATE)
Ideas for Your Current Events Curriculum
Life Skills
Making Social Science Current
Making the Writing Connection
Project Earth

Lotus Development Corp.
55 Cambridge Parkway
Cambridge, MA 02142
Ami Pro
Freelance Graphics
Improv
Lotus 1-2-3
LotusWorks
Smartpics
SmartSuite

Magination Press
19 Union Square West
New York, NY 10003
1-800-825-3089; 1-212-924-3344
Otto Learns About His Medication
The "Putting on the Brakes" Activity Book
Putting on the Brakes: The Interactive Newsletter for Kids with ADHD

Maxis (See Interplay Productions.)
Two Theatre Square, Suite 230
Orinda, CA 94563
1-510-253-3764
A-Train
Print Artist
SimAnt
SimCity
SimCity 2000
SimEarth
SimLife
SimTown

MECC
6160 Summit Drive North
Minneapolis, MN 55430-4003
1-800-685-MECC, ext. 549; 1-612-569-1500
info@mecc.com
http://www.mecc.com
Africa Trail
Amazing Arithmetricks
The Amazon Trail
Blue Ice: Focus on Antarctica
DinoPark Tycoon
The Geometric Golfer
MathKeys
Math Munchers DELUXE
MayaQuest
MECC Inter@ctive Explorer Series
My Own Stories
Number Munchers
Odell Down Under
Opening Night
The Oregon Trail
Oregon Trail II
Probability Lab
Science Sleuths by Videodiscovery
Storybook Weaver
Storybook Weaver DELUXE
TesselMania! DELUXE
USA GeoGraph II
World GeoGraph II
Word Munchers
The Yukon Trail

Mecklermedia Corp.
20 Ketchum St.
Westport, CT 06880
1-800-573-3062; 1-203-226-6967
info@mecklermedia.com
Request catalog of publications and list of conferences and exhibitions.

Media Vision Multimedia Publishing
47300 Bayside Parkway
Fremont, CA 94538
1-800-845-5870; 1-510-770-8600
  Wiggins in Storyland

Medio Multimedia, Inc.
P.O. Box 2949
Redmond, WA 98073-9964
1-800-788-3866
  J.F.K. Assassination: A Visual Investigation
  Vietnam: A Visual Investigation

Menninger Video Productions [also audiotapes]
Dept. C16, The Menninger Clinic
P.O. Box 829
Topeka, KS 66601-0829
1-800-345-6036
  Dyslexia: Variations in Language Development
  Effects of Learning Disabilities on Self-Esteem
  *From Theory to Reality: Practical Applications in the School
    Setting*
  *Homework and Learning Disabilities: A Common Sense
    Approach*
  Learning Disability: A Challenge for Family Members
  Learning Disability: A Family in Crisis
  Learning Disability: A Parent's Guide
  Parent-Teacher Conferences: Resolving Conflicts
  Teenage Mothers: Looking Back . . . Moving Ahead

Microforum, Inc.
1 Woodborough Avenue
Toronto, Ontario
Canada M6M 5A1
1-800-465-2323 (USA); 1-800-268-3604 (Canada); 1-416-656-6406
  Internet Edge (shareware collection on CD-ROM)

Micrografx, Inc.
1301 Arapaho Rd.
Richardson, TX 75081
1-800-733-3729; 1-214-234-1769
http://www.micrografx.com
  ABC FlowCharter 4.0
  ABC Graphic Suite
  Crayola Amazing Art Adventure
  Crayola Art & Animation Studio
  Crayola Art Studio 2
  Designer 4.1 TE
  Designer Power Pac
  Draw! 4.0
  Hallmark Connections: Card Studio
  Picture Publisher 5.0

Microsoft Corporation
One Microsoft Way
Redmond, WA 98052-6399
1-800-426-9400; 1-206-882-8080
1-206-635-4948 (TDD/TT)
  Access
  Ancient Lands
  Bookshelf
  The Case of the Blue Makva
  Cinemania
  Complete Baseball
  Dangerous Creatures
  Encarta Multimedia Encyclopedia
  Encarta Teacher's Activity Guide
  Excel
  Fine Artist
  FoxPro
  Multimedia Beethoven: The Ninth Symphony
  Multimedia Mozart: The Dissonant Quartet
  Multimedia Schubert: The Trout Quintet
  Multimedia Stravinsky: The Rite of Spring
  Multimedia Works & Bookshelf
  Musical Instruments
  Office
  PowerPoint
  Publisher
  Sound Bits
  Video for Windows
  Visual Basic
  Windows Sound System
  Windows 95
  Word
  Works

Midisoft Corp.
P.O. Box 1000
Bellevue, WA 98009-9864
1-800-776-6434; 1-206-391-3610, ext. 247
salesinfo@midisoft.com
> *Attitude for Success*
> *Braveheart*
> *Communicate*
> *Manage Stress*
> *Manage Time*
> *Multimedia Songbook*
> *MusicMagic Songbook*
> *Music Mentor*
> *Organize for Success*
> *Play Piano*
> *Presentation Partner*
> *Sound Explorer CD*
> *Studio for Windows 4.0*
> *Super Show and Tell*
> *World of Music Sampler*
> *The Writing Express*

Mind Extension University
9697 East Mineral Ave.
P.O. Box 6612
Englewood, CO 80155-6612
1-800-777-MIND; 1-303-792-3111
Request telecourse catalog.

Mindscape (formerly The Software Toolworks, Inc.)
60 Leveroni Ct.
Novato, CA 94949
1-800-234-3088
> *Guinness Disc of Records*
> *How Your Body Works*
> *Mario's Early Years CD Deluxe*
> *Mavis Beacon Teaches Typing*
> *Mavis Beacon Teaches Typing! For Kids*
> *Oceans Below*
> *Reference Library*
> *The San Diego Zoo Presents . . . The Animals!*

Multi Dimensional Communications, Inc.
New Media Schoolhouse
P.O. Box 390
69 Westchester Avenue
Pound Ridge, NY 10576
1-800-672-6002
> Call to obtain titles in their CD-ROM *Talking Storybook Series.*
> *Beauty and the Beast*

National Computer Systems, Inc.
Education Systems Division
11000 Prairie Lakes Dr.
P.O. Box 9365
Minneapolis, MN 55440
1-800-447-3269; 1-612-829-3000
> *MicroCIMS:Student Administrative Software System for Windows*
> *Performance Plus: Performance-Based Assessment Instructional Management Software*
> *Performance Plus Test Generator Software*

National Demonstration Laboratory for Interactive Information Technologies
Library of Congress
Washington, DC
1-202-707-4158

National Geographic Society
Educational Services
Washington, D.C. 20036
1-800-368-2728; 1-800-548-9797 (TDD)
> *The American People*
> *Animals and How They Grow*
> *A World of Animals*
> *A World of Plants*
> *A Geographic Perspective on American History*
> *The Human Body*
> *Kids Network*
> *Mammals: A Multimedia Encyclopedia*
> *Our Earth*
> *Picture Atlas of the World CD-ROM*
> *Planetary Manager*
> *Plants*
> *The Presidents: It All Started With George*
> *Rain Forest*
> *Solar System*
> *STV: Biodiversity*
> *Too Much Trash?*
> *Video Catalog*
> *What Are We Eating?*
> *Wonders of Learning CD-ROM Library* (a series of titles)

National Information Center for Educational Media
(NICEM)
Access Innovations, Inc.
P.O. Box 40130
Albuquerque, NM 87196
1-800-926-8328; 1-505-265-3591
tnaccess@technet.nm.org
  Audiocassette & Compact Disc Finder
  AV Marc
  AV Online
  Film & Video Finder
  Filmstrip & Slide Set Finder
  Index to AV Producers & Distributors
  Training Media Database

National Public Radio
Audience Services
635 Massachusetts Ave. NW
Washington, DC 20001
1-202-414-3232
nprlist@npr.org
  All Things Considered
  Morning Edition
  Weekend Edition

National Public Telecomputing Network (Obtain list of
"Free-Nets.")
Box 1987
Cleveland, OH 44106
1-216-247-5800
info@nptn.org

National School Products
101 East Broadway
Maryville, TN 37804-2498
1-800-627-9393; 1-615-984-3960
  Request catalogs of award winning software.

New Century Education Corp.
220 Old New Brunswick Rd.
Piscataway, NJ 08854
1-800-833-NCEC; 1-908-981-0820
  The New Century Integrated Instructional System

NewsBank, Inc.
5020 Tamiami Trail N.
Naples, FL 33940
1-800-762-8182; 1-813-263-6004

Novell Applications Group (merged with WordPerfect
Corp.)
1555 N. Technology Way
Orem, UT 84057-2399
1-800-321-3220; 1-801-225-5000; 1-800-321-3256
(TDD/TTY)
  ClipArt
  DataPerfect
  DrawPerfect
  Grammatik
  LetterPerfect
  Presentations
  Random House Webster's Electronic Dictionary and
    Thesaurus College Edition
  Random House Webster's School & Office Dictionary
  Quattro Pro
  WordPerfect
  WordPerfect for Windows Magazine
  Works

Online, Inc.
462 Danbury Road
Wilton, CT 06897-2126
1-800-248-8466; 1-203-761-1466
online@well.com
http://www.iquest.net/online/online95.html
  CD-ROM Professional
  CD-ROM for Schools
  DATABASE
  MultiMedia Schools
  ONLINE

Online Computer Systems, Inc.
20251 Century Blvd.
Germantown, MD 20874-1196
1-800-922-9204
  The New Grolier Electronic Encyclopedia
  OPTI-NET [CD-ROM LAN networking]
  POEM FINDER on Disc
  R.R. Bowker's Books in Print CD-ROM
  R.R. Bowker's Books Out of Print CD-ROM

Opcode Interactive
3950 Fabian Way
Palo Alto, CA 94303
1-800-557-2633, ext. 601
  Allie's Playhouse
  Composer Quest
  The Musical World of Professor Piccolo

Optical Data Corp.
30 Technology Drive
Warren, NJ 07059
1-800-524-2481; 1-908-668-0022
http://www.infomall.org/Showcase/opticaldata
The following videodiscs are part of the *Life Science Living
Textbook MultiMedia Library:*
    Frog Anatomy and Physiology
    The Human Body
    Mechanisms of Stability and Change
    Principles of Biology
Other videodisc titles include:
    AIDS
    Alcohol
    Drugs and Substance Abuse
    Teenage Sexuality
    Tobacco

Orange Cherry/New Media Schoolhouse Software
P.O. Box 390
Pound Ridge, NY 10576-0390
1-800-672-6002
    Basic Concepts in Science
    Basic Language Skills
    Beginning Math Concepts
    Children's Newspaper Maker
    China: Home of the Dragon
    Computer Video Reader: World of Nature
    Create-A-Story
    Drugs: Its All Right To Say No
    Educational Software Guide
    Foreign Language: Beginning French
    Foreign Language: Beginning Spanish
    Global Express Atlas
    Math Power through Mental Arithmetic
    Reading Readiness
    Solving Word Problems in Math
    Space Mission Problem Solving
    Space Shuttle Word Problems
    SuperStar Science CD
    Talking First Reader
    Talking Multiplication and Division
    Talking Schoolhouse
    Time Traveler CD: A Multimedia Chronicle of History
    Writing Fundamentals

O'Reilly & Associates, Inc. (Distributor for SPRY, Inc.)
103A Morris St.
Sebastopol, CA 95472
1-800-998-9938; 1-707-829-0515
order@ora.com
http://www.ora.com
    AIR Mosaic
    Air Series
    Global Network Navigator (acquired by America Online)
    Internet In A Box
    Mosaic Handbook for Microsoft Windows
    Mosaic Handbook for Macintosh
    WebSite (a Web server that runs on PCs)

PBS Video
475 L'Enfant Plaza, SW
Washington, DC 20024
1-800-344-3337

PC-TV
322 North Main St.
Newport, NH 03773
1-603-863-9322; 1-415-574-6233
74774.13@compuserve.com
The 300 plus *Computer Chronicles* programs available on
videotape include:
    Beginner's Guide to Computers
    CD ROM
    Computer Art
    Computer Consumer Buyer's Guide
    Computer Ergonomics
    Creativity Software
    Electronic Photography
    Electronic Publishing
    Secrets of Lotus 1-2-3
    Secrets of WordPerfect
    Self-Improvement Software
    Visual Programming Languages

Phi Delta Kappa
P.O. Box 789
Bloomington, IN 47402-0789
1-800-766-1156; 1-812-339-1156
sysop@pdkint.org
    Hypermedia: The Integrated Learning Environment
    Improving the Textbook Selection Process
    Interactive Videodisc and the Teaching-Learning Process
    Microcomputers and the Classroom Teacher
    Phi Delta Kappan
    Restructuring Education Through Technology
    Teaching and Learning in a Microelectronic Age

Technology Education Today
Technology in Rural Education
Using Captioned TV for Teaching Reading
Using Computer Technology to Create a Global Classroom
Using Electronic Mail in an Educational Setting
Using Microcomputers for Teaching Reading in the Middle School
Using Microcomputers in Teaching Science
Using Microcomputers with Gifted Students
Using Telecommunications in Middle School Reading
Ask your faculty adviser about membership.

The Pierian Press
P.O. Box 1808
Ann Arbor, MI 48106
1-800-678-2435
   Directory of National Helplines: A Guide to Toll-Free Public Service Numbers
   Media Review Digest

Pierian Spring Software
5200 S.W. Macadam Ave. Suite 570
Portland, OR 97201
1-800-472-8578; 1-503-222-2044
info@pierian.com
http://www.pierian.com
   Continent Explorer II
   The Digital Chisel
   Discovery Toolkit
   Interactive Geography

Polaroid Education Program
565 Technology Square, 3rd Floor
Cambridge, MA 02139
1-800-343-5000

Primary Source Media
12 Lunar Drive
Woodbridge, CT 06525
1-800-444-0799
http://www.psmedia.com
   Hyperlink CD-ROM titles for students, teachers, librarians, researchers

Prodigy Services Co.
500 So. Broad St.
Meriden, CT 06450
1-800-PRODIGY

Pyramid Film & Video
P.O. Box 1048
Santa Monica, CA 90406
1-800-421-2304; 1-310-828-7577
   Changing Faces on Our Land
   The Touching Tree
   Where, Why & How: A Child's Guide to Everyday Stuff, Volume 1: House

Reading Is Fundamental, Inc.
600 Maryland Ave., SW, Suite 600
Washington, DC 20024-2520
1-202-287-3220
   Children's Bookshelf
   Magazines and Family Reading
   Reading Aloud to Your Children
   The RIF Guide to Encouraging Young Readers
   Teenagers and Reading
   TV and Reading
   Upbeat and Offbeat Activities to Encourage Reading

RMI Media Productions, Inc. [videos]
1365 North Winchester St.
Olathe, KS 66061
1-800-745-5480
rmimedia@aol.com
   Accessing Data Networks
   Components of Multimedia
   Databases, Boolean Searches, and CD-ROM
   Elements of Design
   Environments for Learning
   Government Documents
   Hardware Introduction
   Indexes and Abstracts
   Information Resources
   Integrating Multimedia with the Instructional Process
   Introduction to CD-ROM
   Introduction to HyperCard 2.2
   Introduction to Hyperstudio
   The Language Construction Company
   Microfilm and Microfiche
   The Multimedia Design Team
   The Multimedia Revolution—Today and Tomorrow
   Organizing Information
   Orientation to Multimedia

Pictures, Sound, Software, and Text on a Disk
Planning an Information Search
Reference Books
Software Introduction

Scholastic, Inc.
2931 E. McCarty St.
Jefferson City, MO 65101
1-800-SCHOLASTIC; 1-314-636-5271
  Algebra Shop
  The Bank Street Prewriter
  The Bank Street Writer
  Children's Digest
  Clifford's Big Book Publisher
  College Application Essay Writer
  Electronic Learning
  Hidden Agenda
  History in Motion: Milestones of the Twentieth Century
  Instructor
  Interactive NOVA: Animal Pathfinders
  Interactive NOVA: Earth
  Interactive NOVA: The Miracle of Life
  Interactive NOVA: Race to Save the Planet
  Junior Scholastic
  The Magic School Bus
  Math Assistant
  Math Shop
  Math Tutor
  Microzine
  Operation: Frog
  Point of View 2.0: The Civil War and Reconstruction
  Point of View 2.0: Overview of U.S. History
  Point of View 2.0: State and Community History Kit
  Quations
  Reading Explorers
  The Scholastic
  Scholastic A.I.
  Scholastic Graphics and Sound Booster Packs
  Scholastic High-Tech Reports
  Scholastic Hyperscreen 2.0
  Scholastic Network
  The Scholastic Process Writer
  Scholastic Science Place
  Scholastic Slide Shop
  Scholastic Smart Books
  Scholastic SuperPrint II Graphics Packs
  Struggles for Justice
  Success with Typing
  Success with Writing
  Super Story Tree
  Talking Text Library
  Talking Text Writer

Teaching History With Point of View
Twistaplot Reading Adventures
WiggleWorks: The Scholastic Beginning Literacy Program
Writing Activity Files for the Bank Street Writer

Science for Kids
P.O. Box 519
Lewisville, NC 27023
1-800-KSCIENCE; 1-910-945-9000
  Adventures with OSLO: Save Our Planet
  Adventures with OSLO: Tools & Gadgets
  Adventures with OSLO: World of Water
  CELLebrate
  " CELL'ebration!
  Fun with FORCES
  Force & Motion
  Machines Made Simple
  Simple Machines

Sierra On-Line, Inc.
3380 146th Pl. SE
Bellevue, WA 98007
1-800-757-7707; 1-206-562-4317
  Beginning Reading
  Early Math
  EcoQuest: Lost Secret of the Rainforest
  Kid's Typing
  Outpost

Simon & Schuster
237 22nd St.
Greeley, CO 80631
1-800-910-0099
  Alistair Alien Invasion
  FIREFIGHTER
  How Many Bugs in a Box?
  I.M. Meen
  The Macmillan Dictionary for Children
  Macmillan Visual Dictionary
  Planet Earth: Explore the Worlds Within
  Star Trek Omnipedia
  Vietnam: A Multimedia Chronicle of a War that Divided America

Simulation Training Systems
Box 910
Del Mar, CA 92014
1-619-755-0272
  Bafa: A Cross Culture Simulation
  Humanus
  Rafa Rafa
  Star Power
  Talking Rocks: A Game About the Origins of Writing
  Where Do You Draw the Line?: An Ethics Game

Smartec Software
2223 Avenida de la Playa, Suite 108
La Jolla, CA 92037
1-619-456-5064
  WordSmart

Social Issues Resources Series, Inc.
P.O. Box 2348
Boca Raton, FL 33427-2348
1-800-232-SIRS; 1-407-994-0079
  Library of Congress Corner
  SIRS Information Systems
  SIRS CD-ROM Information Systems
  SIRS Custom CD-ROM Networks
  SIRS Photo Essays

SoftKey International, Inc.
One Athenaeum St.
Cambridge, MA 02142
1-800-227-5609; 1-617-494-1200
http://www.softkey.com
  The American Heritage Talking Dictionary
  America's Civil War: A Nation Divided
  AutoWorks
  Beethoven's 5th: The Multimedia Symphony
  BodyWorks
  ChemistryWorks
  CNN Newsroom Global View
  ComputerWorks
  Dinosaur Museum
  5 A Day Adventures
  Holy Bible
  Infopedia: The Ultimate Multimedia Reference Tool
  Leonardo the Inventor
  Me & My World: A Multimedia Picture Dictionary
  Mosby's Medical Encyclopedia
  MPC Wizard
  The Multimedia Encyclopedia of Knowledge
  Orbits
  PC Paintbrush ClipArt Library
  PharmAssist

  PhotoFinish
  PhotoLibrary
  Student Survival Pack
  Tchaikovsky's 1812: The Multimedia Festival Overture
  Time Almanac Reference
  Time Almanac 20th Century
  UFO CD-ROM

Software Publishers Association
1730 M St. NW, Suite 700
Washington, DC 20036
1-202-452-1600; 1-800-388-7478 (Piracy Hotline)
  Software Use and the Law
  SPAudit: A Software Management Tool

Sound Source Interactive
2985 E. Hillcrest Dr., Suite A
Westlake Village, CA 91362
1-800-877-4778; 1-805-494-9996
ssi@cris.com
http://www.cris.com/~ssi/
  AudioClips
  Interactive MovieBooks

Spry/Internet Division of CompuServe
316 Occidental Avenue South
Seattle, WA 98104
1-800-557-9614, ext. 51; 1-206-515-2995, ext. 6116
iboxinfo@spry.com
http://www.spry.com
  Internet In A Box
  Spry Mosaic

Sunburst Communications
101 Castleton St.
P.O. Box 100
Pleasantville, NY 10570-0100
1-800-321-7511
sunburst4@aol.com
  A to Zap!
  Center Stage: Romeo and Juliet
  Coral Kingdom
  A Field Trip to the Sky
  Graphers
  The Learn About Science Collection
  Life Story
  Magic Slate II
  Musical World of Professor Piccolo
  Shape Up
  Tiger's Tales
  Type to Learn

Symantec Corp.
10201 Torre Ave.
Cupertino, CA 95014-2132
1-800-441-7234
  More!
  Q&A Write
  The Norton AntiVirus
  The Norton Backup
  The Norton Disk Doctor
  The Norton Utilities
  Time Line

Systems Compatibility Corp.
401 N. Wabash, Suite 600
Chicago, IL 60611
1-312-329-0700
  The Writer's Toolkit

TeacherSoft, Inc.
903 East 18th St.
Plano, TX 75074
1-214-424-7882, ext. 201
learninglink@teachersoft.com
http://www.teachersoft.com
  InterGO (school Internet software)

Technology Resources Center
U.S. Department of Education
Washington, DC
1-202-219-1699

Technology and Information Educational Services
  (TIES)
(a consortium of school districts)
Training Center
2665 Long Lake Rd.
Roseville, MN 55113-2535
1-612-638-8780
feil@ties.k12.mn.us
  Request catalog describing on-site (MN) workshops.

TI-IN Network
1314 Hines
San Antonio, TX 78208
1-800-234-1245; 1-214-716-5426
Request telecourse information.

Timeworks
625 Academy Dr.
Northbrook, IL 60062
1-800-323-7744
  Color It!
  Data Manager
  Paint It!
  Publish It!
  SwiftCalc PC
  Word Writer PC

T/Maker Company
1390 Villa St.
Mountain View, CA 94041
1-800-986-2537
  ClickArt
  The ClickArt Design Group CD
  The ClickArt Incredible Image Pak 25,000
  VroomBooks
  World's Easiest

Tom Snyder Productions, Inc.
80 Coolidge Hill Road
Watertown, MA 02172-2817
1-800-342-0236
ask@teachtsp.com
  Anatomy of Music
  Choices, Choices: Taking Responsibility
  Classroom Newspaper Workshop
  Cultural Reporter
  Decisions, Decisions: AIDS, Relationships & Responsibility
  Decisions, Decisions: Foreign Policy
  Decisions, Decisions: Prejudice
  Decisions, Decisions: Substance Abuse, Making Smart Choices
  Decisions, Decisions: Violence in the Media
  Educational Technology Catalog
  The Environment II: Preserving What We Have Left
  Exam in a Can: Math Teacher Tools
  Geography Search
  Graph Action
  The Graph Club
  Great Teaching in the One Computer Classroom
  Great Teaching and the VCR
  Great Workshops
  Group Grammar
  GeoWorld
  InnerBodyWorks
  Mapping the World by Heart
  Math Mysteries
  Math VideoKits
  Minds-on Science Series
  MultiReadia

The One Computer Classroom Video
Pip & Zena's Science Voyage
Reading Magic Library
Saving the Earth
Snooper Troops
*Special Education: TSP's Complete Guide for Using Software
    & Video in Special Education*
Special Writer Coach
Super Scoops: Who's Mucking Up the Environment?
Timeliner
TimeShirt Radio Series
[Many titles also available in Spanish.]

TRO Learning, Inc.
4660 West 77th St.
Edina, MN 55435
1-800-44-PLATO; 1-708-781-7800
    PLATO Learning System

Troll Associates
Books for Schools & Libraries
100 Corporate Dr.
Mahwah, NJ 07430-0025
1-800-929-TROLL
Request catalog.

United Nations Publications
Room DC2-0853, Dept. 185A
New York, NY 10017
1-800-253-9646; 1-212-963-8302
Request videos and teaching guides.

Videodiscovery, Inc.
1700 Westlake Ave. N., Suite 600
Seattle, WA 98109-3012
1-800-548-3472; 1-206-285-5400
Request catalog describing instructional videodiscs.
    Science Sleuths

Virgin Sound and Vision
122 South Robertson Blvd.
Los Angeles, CA 90048
1-310-246-4666
Request catalog of CD-ROM educational titles.

Visio Corp.
520 Pike St., Suite 1800
Seattle, WA 98101-4001
1-800-248-4746; 1-206-467-6723
govisio@aol.com
    Visio 4.0 for Windows
    Visio 4.0 Technical
    Visio 3.0 Home

Waite Group Press
200 Tamal Plaza
Corte Madera, CA 94925
1-800-368-9369; 1-415-924-2575
drdrax1@waite.com
http://www.waite.com/waite

Wentworth Worldwide Media
1866 Colonial Village Lane
Lancaster, PA 17601
1-800-638-1639; 1-717-393-1000
connect@wentworth.com
http://www.wentworth.com
Request list of books and videos.
    Classroom Connect

WFF'N PROOF Learning Games Associates
1490-JW South Blvd.
Ann Arbor, MI 48104-4699
1-313-665-2269
    CONFIGURATIONS: Number Puzzles and Patterns
    EQUATIONS: The Game of Creative Mathematics
    IMP KITS: Instructional Math Play Kits
    LinguiSHTIK: A Creative Language Game
    Math Is Fun
    Math Without Tears
    ON-SETS: The Game of Set Theory
    ON-WORDS: The Game of Word Structures
    QUERIES 'N THEORIES: The Game of Science and Language
    Racism and American Education
    REDI-READ I
    REDI-READ II
    The Math Entertainer
    THE PROPAGANDA GAME
    THE REAL NUMBERS GAME
    Treasury of Negro Spirituals
    WFF'N PROOF: The Game of Modern Logic

Wisconsin Dept. of Public Instruction
Publication Sales
125 South Webster St.
Madison, WI 53707-7841
1-800-243-8782
pubsales@mail.state.wi.us
Request catalog of resource and planning guides.

World Library, Inc.
2809 Main Street
Irvine, CA 92714
1-800-443-0238; 1-714-756-9500
   Barron's Book Notes
   Classic Book Collection
   Electronic Home Library
   Greatest Books Collection
   Great Poetry Classics
   Library of the Future
   Shakespeare Study Guide

Zane Publishing
The Infomart
1950 Stemmons, Suite 4044
Dallas, TX 75207-3109
1-214-746-5555
   American Literature: A Literary History
   American Literature: Time, Life and Works
   Art and Music Series
   Biological Science Series
   British Literature: A Literary History
   British Literature: Shakespeare Collection
   The Encyclopedia of U.S. Endangered Species
   Introductory Science: Elementary Science
   Introductory Science: Junior Science
   Isaac Asimov's Library of the Universe
   U.S. Geography Series
   U.S. History Series
   World History: Charting New Territories
   World History: Times of Great Turmoil
   World Literature: European Literature
   World Literature: Myths and Legends

Ziff-Davis Publishing Co.
5903 Christie Ave.
Emeryville, CA 94608
1-800-688-0448; 1-510-601-2000
http://www.ziff.com
Request catalog of illustrated computer-related publications.

Index